PSYCHOLOGY RESEARCH PROGRESS

# METHODS AND IMPLEMENTARY STRATEGIES ON CULTIVATING STUDENTS' PSYCHOLOGICAL SUZHI

# PSYCHOLOGY RESEARCH PROGRESS

Additional books in this series can be found on Nova's website
under the Series tab.

Additional e-books in this series can be found on Nova's website
under the e-books tab.

PSYCHOLOGY RESEARCH PROGRESS

# METHODS AND IMPLEMENTARY STRATEGIES ON CULTIVATING STUDENTS' PSYCHOLOGICAL SUZHI

**DA-JUN ZHANG**
**JIN-LIANG WANG**
AND
**LIN YU**
EDITORS

*New York*

**NOTICE TO THE READER**

The Publisher has taken reasonable care in the preparation of this book, but makes no expressed or implied warranty of any kind and assumes no responsibility for any errors or omissions. No liability is assumed for incidental or consequential damages in connection with or arising out of information contained in this book. The Publisher shall not be liable for any special, consequential, or exemplary damages resulting, in whole or in part, from the readers' use of, or reliance upon, this material. Any parts of this book based on government reports are so indicated and copyright is claimed for those parts to the extent applicable to compilations of such works.

Independent verification should be sought for any data, advice or recommendations contained in this book. In addition, no responsibility is assumed by the publisher for any injury and/or damage to persons or property arising from any methods, products, instructions, ideas or otherwise contained in this publication.

This publication is designed to provide accurate and authoritative information with regard to the subject matter covered herein. It is sold with the clear understanding that the Publisher is not engaged in rendering legal or any other professional services. If legal or any other expert assistance is required, the services of a competent person should be sought. FROM A DECLARATION OF PARTICIPANTS JOINTLY ADOPTED BY A COMMITTEE OF THE AMERICAN BAR ASSOCIATION AND A COMMITTEE OF PUBLISHERS.

Additional color graphics may be available in the e-book version of this book.

**LIBRARY OF CONGRESS CATALOGING-IN-PUBLICATION DATA**

Zhang, Dajun, 1954-
Methods and implementary strategies on cultivating students' psychological
suzhi / Dajun Zhang, Jinliang Wang, Lin Yu.
p. cm.
Includes index.
ISBN: 978-1-62417-979-2 (softcover)
1. Students--China--Psychology. 2. School psychology--China. I. Wang,
Jinliang. II. Yu, Lin. III. Title.
LA1133.7.Z43 2010
371.801'9--dc22
2010033113

*Published by Nova Science Publishers, Inc. † New York*

# CONTENTS

# PREFACE

Since the proposal of the Ninth Five-Year Plan (for National Economy and Social Development), the authors have conducted the systematic research, *the Integrated Research on Adolescents` Mental Health and Psychological* Suzhi *Cultivation*, which includes four interconnected sub-research (*the Theoretical and Practice Research on Adolescents` Psychological* Suzhi *Education, Research on Adolescents` Mental Problem and Countermeasures, Research on the Cultivation Mode and Its Implementation Strategies for Adolescents` Psychological* Suzhi, *and Research on Guarantee System for Adolescents` Mental Health Education*). The book, *The Cultivation Mode and Its Implementation Strategies for Adolescents'` Psychological* Suzhi, is an important part of *the Integrated Research on Adolescents` Mental Health and Psychological* Suzhi *Cultivation,* and is also a research treatise based on the key research project of tenth five Chinese education science plan, *the Cultivation Mode and Its Strategies for Students` Psychological* Suzhi, which was established in February 2002 and was finished in December 2005. The achievement of this research project, *the Cultivation Mode and Its Strategies for Students` Psychological* Suzhi, has passed the expert check held by Chinese Education Science Plan Office. At the same time, this book is the third research achievement of the *Integrated Research on Adolescents'` Mental Health and Psychological* Suzhi *Cultivation.* The first and second research achievements, titled *Series of Books on School Mental Health Education from a New Perspective*, and *Adolescents` Mental Problem and Its Countermeasures*, were published already by Southwest Normal University Press in December 2004 and by Sichuan Education Press in February in 2010 respectively. The fourth achievement of this research project, *Research on School and Society Guarantee System for School Mental Health Education*, is also completed and is planed to be published.

As a new topic in the domain of psychology, the cultivation of students` psychological suzhi is still at its initial stage no matter with regard to its proposal, theoretical discussion, content, methods, or results analysis. Therefore, as such an exploratory research, limitations are unavoidable. The authors welcome any comments from peers and readers. The authors have three purposes to write this book. First, it is to summarize the main achievements of our research on *Cultivation Mode and Its Implementation Strategies for Students` Psychological* Suzhi through systematic generalization. Second, it is to guide the *Integrated Research on Adolescents` Mental Health and Psychological* Suzhi *Cultivation* to a higher level. Third, it is to provide some Chinese characteristic reference material and research perspective for the school mental health education and sound psychological suzhi cultivation which is increasing booming.

The accomplishment of this book was a collective work of our research team, with Dr. Da-jun Zhang as the chief editor, and Dr. Lin-Yu and Dr. Jin-liang Wang as the associate editor. Dr. Da-jun Zhang is responsible for the research project, the design of the book structure, the edition, and considerations of manuscripts. The two associate editors provided assistance on solicit contributions and edition. The authors of each chapter have been marked at the beginning of corresponding chapters.

The authors want to give their thanks to the Chinese Education Science Plan Office, the Office of Social Science Administration of Southwest University, Center for Mental Health Education of Southwest University (a Key Research Base of Chongqing Humanity Social Sciences), and Research Institute for Education Science of Southwest University. Before the publication of this book, the authors would like to give our thanks to all those who have helped us. The authors would like to give sincere thanks to the Nova Publishers for their invitation and acceptance of this book unconditionally.

The Editors
2010-7-12

# INTRODUCTION

As a Chinese-originated conception, there is no corresponding conception in the Western psychology literature for psychological sushi introduced in this book. To help readers have a better understanding on this conception, we coined the word *psychological suzhi*, in order to avoid reader's confusion. In Chinese psychology domain, this conception had also been translated as *mental quality* or *psychological quality*.

However, the word *quality* can not cover the whole meaning of suzhi, and that is the reason why we coined *psychological suzhi*.

Although psychological suzhi is originated in China, it shares common connotation with traditional conceptions in western psychology.

First, psychological suzhi focus on individual's positive and initiative psychological development and emphasize individual's adaptation towards environment, which is in consistent with the proposal of positive psychology trend in western psychology.

Second, psychological suzhi is consistent with psychological resilience in that they all attach importance to individual's adaptability.

For example, both psychological suzhi and psychological resilience are buffers and moderators between stress events and individual's mental health; they are both formed through the combination of inheritance and acquired environment effects. However, due to different research perspective, differences also exist.

For instance, psychological resilience refers more to individual's recovery capability after experiencing stress events, while psychological suzhi has a broader connotation, with it not only including individual's positive coping capabilities, but also including individual's mental qualities under normal state.

Psychological suzhi is individual's most basic, most steady, and most central part of individual's mental structure. The development of psychological suzhi is a life span process, influenced by inheritance, education, family, and individual's experience, etc.

Adolescence is a key stage for psychological suzhi development, and school plays the most important role in the development of adolescent's psychological suzhi. Based on these considerations, we publish the book on the cultivation of students` psychological suzhi, hoping that we can provide some help for the school mental health education.

The book Cultivation Mode and Its Implementation Strategies for Students` Psychological Suzhi is part of our research project, Mental Health and Sound Psychological Suzhi Cultivation for Adolescents, which we have conducted for a long time. For readers` better understanding on this book, we describe relevant information in the following part.

# 1. STUDENTS` PSYCHOLOGICAL SUZHI AND ITS STRUCTURE

The cultivation mode and its implementation strategies for students` psychological suzhi is a exploratory systematic research to develop students` psychological suzhi. As the most direct theoretical foundation of this research, the conception and structure of psychological suzhi is necessary to be introduced.

In our previous research, psychological suzhi is defined as a mental quality characterized by being steady, essential and implicit, and it has a derivative function and is closely related with individuals' adaptive, developmental and creative behaviors. Based on theoretical consideration and our empirical studies, we divided psychological suzhi into three dimensions: cognitive quality, individuality and adaptability (see Chart I).

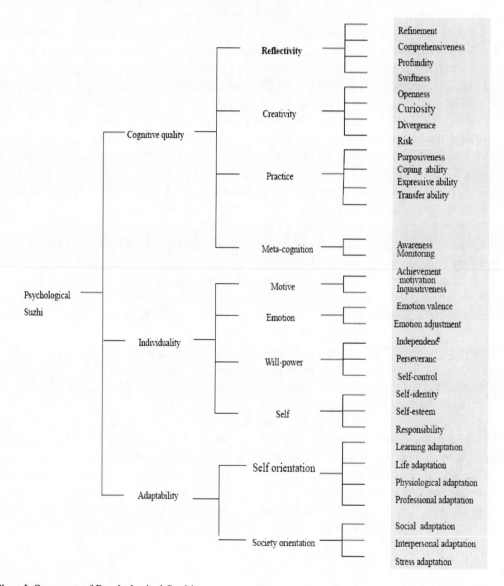

Chart I. Structure of Psychological Suzhi.

Specifically, cognitive quality can be manifested through individuals' cognitive processing and its connotation can be revealed through cognitive processing. As the most basic component of psychological suzhi, cognitive quality is involved directly in individual's cognition on objects. Individuality can be reflected through individual's actions towards objects, while it is not involved directly in individuals` cognition on objects. However, as a core part of psychological suzhi, individuality has a motivation and moderating function during cognition. Adaptability component is individuals` capabilities to arrive a consistence between themselves and the environment by changing themselves or the environment during the process of socialization. As a component which can best reflect the derivative function of psychological suzhi, the individuality component is the integrated manifestation of cognitive component and individuality component in various social environments.

## 2. THE RELATIONSHIP BETWEEN PSYCHOLOGICAL SUZHI AND MENTAL HEALTH

To understand why discuss the cultivation mode and its strategies for students` psychological suzhi development, it is necessary to comprehend the association between psychological suzhi and mental health. Psychological suzhi and mental health are two important aspects of human psychological phenomenon. Essentially, psychological suzhi is a kind of steady psychological quality, while mental health is a kind of positive and favorable psychological state. They share many aspects in common, while at the same time they are different from each other. From the perspective of the function of psychological suzhi, there is a close association between psychological suzhi and mental health. Generally, individuals with high level of psychological suzhi seldom suffer from mental problems and are often in a psychological health state. However, individuals with low level of psychological suzhi are more possibly to have mental disturbances. This means that mental health is a symbol of sound psychological suzhi. From the perspective of the measurement of psychological suzhi, the psychological suzhi scale involves many indicators for mental health, such as emotion and interpersonal relationship. At the same time, the standard for mental health also contains many components of psychological suzhi, such as sound cognition, strong will, normal personality, etc.

Psychological suzhi is a combination of both content and function aspects, while mental health only reflects the function aspect of psychological suzhi. To properly study psychological suzhi, it is necessary not only to pay attention to its personality and cognitive aspects, but also its function aspects, namely its mental health aspect. Hence, it is proper to regard individual's mental health level as an important indicator of psychological suzhi. To sum up, psychological suzhi is a multi-level self-organized system, including steady implicit psychological qualities and explicit adaptation behavior.

As the function aspect of psychological suzhi, individual's mental health is a kind of explicit behavior and psychological state. The relationship between mental health and psychological suzhi is just like that between "surface and essence". Therefore, it is an effective way to guarantee students` mental health through cultivating students` sound psychological suzhi.

## 3. METHODOLOGY CONSIDERATIONS FOR RESEARCH ON PSYCHOLOGICAL SUZHI CULTIVATION MODE AND ITS IMPLEMENTATION STRATEGIES

### 3.1. Research Purpose

The ultimate goal of conducting research on psychological suzhi cultivation mode and its implementation strategies is to promote the sound development of students` psychological suzhi and maintain their mental health. The cultivation goals of developing students` psychological suzhi can be further divided into three sub-goals, including the goal of adaptation, the goal of development and the goal of creativity. The realization of theses goals can be done through multi-perspectives, such as humanity, psychology, education, brain science, education for all-round development, etc. Under the direction of 'adaptation and development' principle, the cultivation of students` psychological suzhi should aim at students` better adaptation towards life, study and environment. To do this, we should first help students learn to adapt actively to their study, life, communication and social environment, which is the precondition of cultivating psychological suzhi. Second, on the basis of step one just mentioned, we facilitate the harmonious development of students` mentality (namely their ability, individuality, sociability, and creativity), which is the final goal of psychological suzhi cultivation.

### 3.2. The Systematic Principle

The systematic principle is the basic methodology principle that should be followed during the psychological suzhi cultivation, which can be reflected from the following aspects.

#### The Systematic Design of the Research

According to the scientific systematic viewpoint, the entire research project can be divided into four interconnected steps, including theoretical investigation, empirical investigation, mode construction, and empirical examination.

#### The Systematic Construction of the Cultivation Mode and Implementation Strategies

In this research project, we not only construct the basic mode (also called integrated mode) for the psychological suzhi cultivation, but also based on the basic mode, we create specific modes such as the specific topic training mode, the subject teaching infiltration mode, the computer-assisted mode, and the art aesthetic mode.

#### The Systematic Arrangement of Implementation Procedure

Aiming at the specific requirements and characteristics of each cultivation mode, we have made specific and systematic arrangements. For instance, in the computer-assisted cultivation mode and implementation strategies, it involves such research serials as investigation on mental problem, theoretical discussion for the mode, scripting, software development, and educational intervention, which have formed an operatable implementation system.

## 3.3. The Comprehensive Application of Multi-Methods

Psychological suzhi cultivation is a complicated system, not only involving methods of psychology science, but also relevant methods from the domain of education science, behavior science, system science, and life science. Therefore, it is necessary to comprehensively use various kinds of research methods in order to achieve research goals and guarantee the reliability of research results. In our theoretical discussion part, for example, we not only employed qualitative research methods such as literature analysis and theory construction, also we used qualitative and quantative combined methods, including investigation, interview, expert counseling, measurement and practical experience summarization, in order to understand status quo of students` psychological suzhi and mental problem. In our empirical part, we not only use empirical methods such as investigating students` mental problem, measuring their psychological suzhi, conducting interventions on psychological suzhi, and case analysis, also we applied kinds of qualitative research methods such as literature analysis, mode construction, implementation process monitoring, and student-teacher discussion. The comprehensive application of these methods have provided supplement for each other and guaranteed the reliability and validity of research conclusions.

# 4. BRIEF INTRODUCTION ON THIS BOOK

To examine the feasibility and validity of the cultivation mode and its implementation strategies for psychological suzhi, we have conducted a series of experimental studies and present them to the readers.

## 4.1. Constructing the Basic Mode and Its Implementation Strategies

On the basis of previous research on mental health education and the reality of Chinese school education, we first constructed the basic mode and implementation strategies (also called the integrated mode and implementation strategies), which is the basis of the whole research. The integrated mode should be composed of the harmonious effects of physiological elements, psychological elements, social elements, and educational elements. The integration nature of the basic mode can be reflected through the following aspects. First, it is the integration of cultivation goals, namely the integration between the goal of positive adaptation and the goal of initiative development, which are the two basic goals for the modern mental health education. Second, it is the integration of cultivation content, namely the integration of these eight aspects of content such as adapting to study, adapting to life, adapting to interpersonal communication, learning to behave, developing intelligence, developing individuality, developing sociality, and developing creativity. Third, it is the integration of cultivation steps, which includes such three steps as judgment and identification, training, and reflection. Furth, it is the integration of cultivation strategies, which includes the integration of basic cultivation strategies and specific cultivation strategies, the integration of each specific strategy, and the integration of behavior shaping strategies and the modification of cognition and emotion strategies.

The cultivation mode for student's psychological suzhi should be a system rather than a single mode. With the basic mode as its basis, the mode system also involves some background factors such as students, family, school, and society. When constructing the mode system, we take into consideration the factors such as the students' level (namely college, middle school, primary school, and kindergarten), students` individual difference (namely difference in cognition, personality, and adaptation), the cultivation situation (namely the school, the community, etc.), the cultivation goal, the means available, etc (For details, see Chapter One in this book).

## 4.2. Discussion on Specific Cultivation Mode and Its Implementation Strategies

### 4.2.1. The Mode of Specific Topic Training and Its Implementation Strategies

As the earliest and most widely used cultivation mode and implementation strategies in this research project, the application of this mode and implementation strategies can be As seen through the following two empirical studies.

### Training of Self-Monitoring on Coping with Frustration among Junior Middle School Students

Based on previous studies, this study has analyzed the theoretical connotation of self-monitoring on coping with frustration, and put forward the corresponding cultivation mode and implementation strategies according to the requirements. It was proven that the mode and implementation strategies was effective in improving self-monitoring on coping with frustration among junior middle school students (For details, see **Chapter Two**).

### Effects of Home-School-Cooperation-Based Education Mode on Self-Adaptability of Junior Middle School Students in Grade One

In this study, we first knew about the status quo of students` self-adaptability and the current situation of home-school-cooperation using relevant measurement tools, and then we applied the home-school-cooperation-based education to improve students` self-adaptability, which has been proven to be effective (For details, see **Chapter Three**).

### 4.2.2. The Subject-Infiltration Mode and Its Implementation Strategies

Cultivating psychological suzhi using subject-infiltration is a basic way to carry out psychological suzhi education at schools. According to the requirements of "specific-topic training mode and its implementation strategies", we respectively conducted studies about the effects of subject-infiltration on improving student's psychological suzhi, which has been proven to be effective.

### The Development of Learning Adaptability among Students from Junior Middle Schools in the Infiltration of PSYCHOLOGICAL SUZHI CULTIVATION in Teaching English Language

Learning adaptability is a core component of adaptability in the structure of junior middle school students` psychological suzhi. On the basis of previous research, taking the current learning adaptability problems in English learning into considerations, this study has constructed the mode of improving students` learning adaptability in English learning, and proposed corresponding teaching strategies such as "stimulating learning motivation, cultivating learning interests, teaching learning methods, and forming good learning habits". We have conducted educational experiments to examine the feasibility and validity of this mode, the results of which has shown that it can significantly improve student's English scores (For details, see **Chapter Four**).

## Experimental Research into Developing Self-Efficacy of Students in Mathematics Teaching

Learning self-efficacy, which refers to individuals` belief on their learning abilities and individuals` evaluation on the extent to which they have the abilities or skills to accomplish the learning task, is the specific application of self-efficacy theory in the domain of learning. On the basis of previous research on self-efficacy, we constructed experiment to examine the effects of the cultivation mode for improving students learning self-efficacy in Math teaching, the results of which has shown that it can not only enhance the psychological suzhi development, while at the same time can improve student's math performance (For details, see **Chapter Five**) .

## Experimental Research on Developing Students' Self-Monitoring Capabilities in Math Teaching in Primary Schools

Self-Monitoring capabilities is a core component of meta-learning abilities. On the basis of previous research, we tried to improve both students` psychological suzhi and their academic performances by enhancing students` learning self-monitoring capabilities. The educational experiment has shown that students` self-monitoring capabilities can be improved by subject- infiltration in math teaching, which in turn can lead to the improvement of student's learning capabilities and math academic performance (For details, see **Chapter Six**).

## Cultivation of Emotion Regulation Capability in the Chinese Language Teaching for Primary School Students

Emotion regulation is an important element of individuality in the structure of psychological suzhi and is an significant condition for mental health. With analyzing the current situation of emotion regulation difficulties among pupils at the beginning, we preliminarily constructed the infiltration mode in Chinese teaching to improve pupils` emotion regulation capabilities. Our educational experiment has shown that the mode and its implementation strategies can effectively improve pupils` emotion regulation capabilities, their psychological suzhi, and their Chinese academic performance (For details, see Chapter Seven).

### *4.2.3. Computer-Assisted Mode and Its Implementation Strategies*

Our previous research has found that serious problems existed in middle school students` interpersonal communication, especially for junior middle school students. Therefore, we conducted studies on computer-assisted mode and its implementation strategies from three aspects including peer relationships, teacher-student relationships, and parents-children relationships, to help students enhance their ability of interpersonal communication.

## Empirical Exploration on Improving Parent-Child Relationship by Using Psychological-Suzhi-Education Software

The parents-children relationship is an important topic in psychology research. Using the education software about parents-children relationships, we conducted the computer-assisted mode and implementation strategies to examine its effect on improving parents-children relationships, the results of which has proved its significant effects (For details, see **Chapter Eight**).

## Development of and Experimental Research intopsychological suzhi-based education Software Aiming to Improve Teacher-Student Relationship

The complicated nature of psychological suzhi cultivation has determined the fact that there are various ways to improve it. Based on investigation on teachers-students relationships at junior middle schools, we developed the relevant software and designed the computer-assisted mode to resolve the problems on teachers-students relationships. Our educational experiment has shown that this mode can effectively enhance student's psychological suzhi on teachers-students relationships. After the training, the teachers-students relationships has been significantly improved, especially on the intimacy dimension (For details, see **Chapter Nine**).

## Development of and Experimental Research on Improving Peer Relationship with Computer Assistance

According to the research ideas 'theoretical analysis-mode construction-software development-educational experiment', we explored the feasibility of using computer-assisted mode to improve peer relationships. Our results have shown that this mode and strategies can enhance students` interpersonal communication skills and improve their peer relationships (For details, see Chapter Ten).

### 4.2.4. Aesthetic Appreciation Mode and Its Implementation Strategies

With the increasing mental interruptions in modern society, it is feasible and effective to help students adjust themselves by using aesthetic appreciation.

## Impact of Music Aesthetic Appreciation on the Depressive Symptoms of College Students

On the basis of previous research, we constructed the music aesthetic appreciation mode and relevant implementation strategies and designed music aesthetic appreciation activities, in order to improve college students` depression symptoms. Our educational experiment results have shown that music aesthetic appreciation can significantly improve college students` depression symptoms, and enhance their mental health level, especially for students with low level of depression (For details, see Chapter Eleven).

**Experimental Research into Intervention in Anxiety and Depression Symptoms by Aesthetic Appreciation if Literary Works**

Based on the art aesthetic appreciation mode and its implementation strategies, we have designed the invention to explore the effects of aesthetic appreciation of literary works on college student's depression and anxiety symptoms. The results have shown that the intervention can improve subjects` depression and anxiety symptoms, and enhance their mental health level (For details, see Chapter Twelve).

*Da-Jun Zhang, Jin-Liang Wang and Lin Yu*

# PART ONE:

# BASIC MODE AND IMPLEMENTATION STRATEGIES

In: Methods and Implementary Strategies on Cultivating ...    ISBN: 978-1-62417-979-2
Editors: Da-Jun Zhang, Jin-Liang Wang, and Lin Yu    © 2013 Nova Science Publishers, Inc.

*Chapter 1*

# MODE CONSTRUCTION FOR PSYCHOLOGICAL SUZHI CULTIVATION AND THE IMPLEMENTATION STRATEGIES

## *Da-Jun Zhang*

Center for Mental Health Education in Southwest University, China

## ABSTRACT

Psychological suzhi cultivation and implementation strategies for students should not be in a single form; instead, it should be a system consisting of many modes and implementation strategies. We have, through the systematic analysis on modes for domestic and foreign mental health education and implementation strategies based on China's demands for education for all-around development and students' demands for mental health education, applied the theory to practice and then established the aforesaid system for students. This system consists of integrated (or basic) modes and implementation strategies, specific-problem-based training modes and implementation strategies, subject infiltration modes and implementation strategies, computer assisted training (CAT) modes and implementation strategies, and aesthetic-activity-based modes and implementation strategies. This chapter summarizes the major achievements in the research of psychological suzhi cultivation mode and implementation strategies, which may help readers better understand the book and pave a foundation for them to comprehend other chapters.

## INTEGRATED MODES AND IMPLEMENTATION STRATEGIES

Since integration, to a large extent, is to coordinate and combine all elements of the system so as to fully perform the function, we put forward this mode which integrates physiology, psychology, society and education for students' psychological suzhi cultivation. The key for the mode is "integration", which is not only a concept, but also a strategy. Integration, as a concept, is the basis of putting forward other modes for students' psychological suzhi cultivation, while as a strategy, it should infiltrate into other modes and implementation strategies of the aforesaid cultivation for students. Therefore, the modes and implementation strategies are the basic mode for students' psychological suzhi cultivation; other modes and implementation strategies herein are all based on this mode.

## Integration of Goals

The fundamental goal of the psychological suzhi-based education is to improve students' psychological suzhi per se. It consists of two closely connecting parts: (1) to make students actively adapt to various changes to maintain their mental health. This is to make students adapt to all changes in their study, life, communications and physiological development and enable their behaviors and thinking to fit in with such changes and developments. Whether a student is able to behave and think corresponding to changes of the study situation, task and goal, of the life experience, content, environment and requirement, of the communication environment, target and rule as well as those of the *physiological* growth and development is both the important standard to measure his/her *psychological* suzhi and the important foundation for the development of his/her psychological suzhi. Therefore, one of the goals of psychological suzhi-based education is to enable students to well deal with their study, life, interpersonal communication and the changes of themselves (mind-body coordination) in order to become a person who is able to learn new things, live a happy life and get along well with others, and who knows how to be a good man, adapts well to the changing situations and keeps mental health. This is the primary goal of psychological suzhi-based education. (2) To promote the independent psychological development and thus develop the student into a man with sound psychological suzhi. This is the advanced goal of psychological suzhi-based education. The basic requirement to achieve this goal is to realize sound and healthy development of the components and overall structure of students' psychological suzhi. Therefore, the school psychological suzhi-based education measures should not only satisfy the demands of social development and education for talents, but also be helpful to the growth and development of students at different ages. The motivation of psychological suzhi-based cultivation is to consciously and purposely improve and develop students' psychological suzhi with well-prepared plans, and this is also the final goal. Active adaptation and independent development exactly represent such two goals of psychological suzhi-based education. The two goals are put forward because: 1) Education should satisfy the requirements of modern social development. The society develops and innovates rapidly, and the mode of social production and the lifestyle is quite different from the past. Social norms are reconstructed; social competition keeps intensifying; more pressure on survival appears; the ideology and values are transmuting; the family structure and functions change significantly; the knowledge and information is updated at a higher rate and the cultural openness is improved in this age of knowledge economy etc. The changeable society with such fast pace, sharp competition and high pressure sets higher requirements for each social member's psychological suzhi, including social adaptability, personality and cognition, and gives new meanings for individuals' all-around development. Therefore, the school should satisfy the requirements of modern social development so as to raise elites for the society; 2) the education should, from the perspective of primary school and middle school students' mental health, be able to promote students' active adaptation and active development. Children and teenagers' physiological and psychological development is fast but the condition is not mature; they have much psychological contradiction but limited experiences and knowledge and poor adaptability. All of these are likely to cause mental disorder in the course of psychological development. According to the great deal of survey and research in China, approximately 10%-20% of the primary and middle school students have various mental problems of different degrees, including study weariness, playing truant, role strain and role conflict, ecocentrism, low frustration toleration, overdependence, overanxious disorder, emotional ability, aggressive behavior, interpersonal communication disturbance, loneliness and indifference etc. Such problems, caused by complicated reasons, are represented in a great variety of ways. They require educators to adopt different counseling, guiding and teaching measures for different students based on the types and causes of such problems. Our research demonstrates that students can, thanks to the adaptive education, behave and think properly based on the changes in their study, life, communications and physiological development. In addition, we should help students develop sound psychological suzhi from students' perception, personality and adaptability in order to improve their adaptability to study, life, communications and environment, relieve their psychological contradiction and pressure in the course of growth and ensure their healthy growth and development; 3) it is necessary to develop active adaptation and independent development simultaneously according to the status quo of mental health education. Presently, China's mental health education is in the ascendant, but there is still some misunderstanding during our practice: 1) improper medicalization of psychological suzhi-based education. It confines the psychological suzhi-based education targets to certain students that suffer mental disorder and just adopts the psychotherapy in the medical mode, or even deems mental disorder as mental illness and discriminates against, disregards or ignores the students with mental disorder; 2) improper simplification of psychological suzhi-based education. It deems the mental disorder caused by immature psychological suzhi and poor psychological adaptability as moral issues and just adopts didactic way or strict restraints for psychological suzhi-based education; 3) improper subject-teaching-orientation of psychological suzhi-based education. It deems the psychological suzhi-based education as the teaching of subjects and just teaches the psychology knowledge. It believes that the mental problems can be solved just by teaching the students some psychological knowledge. All the people with such misunderstanding fails comprehending the final goal of mental health education to develop sound psychological suzhi of students, ignores the fundamental functions of students' psychological suzhi for their mental health, and even misinterprets the requirements for mental health education. We believe that it marks the full performance of psychological suzhi-based education's integration functions to, via mental health education activities, actively, consciously and purposely improve and develop students' psychological suzhi and explore their psychological potential so as to develop normal intelligence and ability and healthy personality for them, improve their adaptability to the social, interpersonal, living and study environment, prevent and correct various abnormal psychology and behavior, and help them overcome the psychological and behavioral disorder.

## Integration of Content

It is to comprehensively arrange and select the psychological suzhi-based education content for a school based on the adaptation and development. Two aspects should be taken into consideration to achieve the aforesaid "comprehensive": 1) comprehensively building the psychological suzhi-based education system from an overall and specific perspective based on the staged and continuous development of students' psychological suzhi; 2) conducting cultivation and trainings focusing on the problems commonly existing in or likely to happen to students' study, life, communications and growth based on physiological and psychological development of the students in different grades, the development of their sociality, and specific psychological suzhi-based education goals. Based on the research and the aforesaid consideration, we summarize and put forward that psychological suzhi-based education consists of eight parts: 1) adapting to the study, including being accustomed to the study environment, understanding the requirements for study, reasonably arranging the duration of study, mastering learning methods, developing study habits and interest, stimulating learning motivation, skillfully using the examination skills, adjusting the examination mentality, and preventing learning fatigue and polarization; 2) adapting to the life, including being accustomed to the living environment, adjusting the life, changing the lifestyle, mastering the life skill, developing the living habit and properly coping with the pressure, conflicts and worries caused by physiological development; 3) adapting to interpersonal communication, being able to deal with various relationship, including teacher-student relationship, parent-child relationship, relationship with classmates, peer relationship and relationship with heterosexual classmates, comprehending the rules on communications with different targets, mastering the medium for communications, and developing communication skills so as to eliminate conflicts in and interpersonal communication disturbance and relieve the pressure of communications; 4) knowing how to get along well with others, including how to deal with the relation between personal interest and the collective regulations, others' demands and social morality, and how to play different social roles in different situations; 5) developing intelligence and ability by focusing on improvement of the thinking ability, mastering the basic thinking approaches and thinking strategies and enhancing individuals' ability to observe, to memorize, to imagine, and to attention; 6) developing the personality by developing students' self-cognition and self-assessment ability, self-confidence, self-respect, self-control, independence and achievement motivation so as to enable them to accept, develop and transcend themselves; 7) developing the sociality by developing students' senses of responsibility, obligation, reputation, honor, friendship, dedication, competition and cooperation; 8) developing the creativity by stimulating students' interest in and motivation and desire to create new things and enabling them to recognize their potential creativity, master the creative thinking methods and strategies and develop creative imagination so as to strengthen their sense of creation and creativity. The aforesaid eight parts are not only consistent with the final goal, but also satisfy the requirements of the two goals. In addition, they are closely linked for the same purpose, adaptation for example, or well coordinate with each other for different purposes, adaptation and development for example. This forms an organic system that helps to coordinate and integrate the education content.

## Integration of Processes

Integration of school psychological suzhi-based education processes is to integrate, at first, the formation of psychological suzhi and the psychological suzhi-based education process. The design, implementation and management assessment of psychological suzhi-based education should be based on the basic process for forming students' psychological suzhi. Education activities and process should be based on students' psychological activities and process, while the education process should be consistent with the formation process of psychological suzhi. Second, it is to integrate the three basic processes in the course of psychological suzhi-based education, i.e. judgment and evaluation, training with strategies, and reflection. Zhang and the research team on students` mental health education and psychological suzhi cultivation under his leadership [Zhang, 2000/2001] have, according to the formation of students' psychological suzhi, summarized the aforesaid three processes of psychological suzhi-based education during studying and directed the psychological suzhi-based education for primary and middle school students. Among the three processes, the first one is the beginning of the education process, the second one is the implementation of psychological suzhi-based education that enables students to master various psychological and behavioral strategies, and the third one is the key process for forming psychological suzhi that aims to internalize extrinsic stimulus. The three sectors are integral and indispensable to the psychological suzhi cultivation. Third, it is to integrate external education and self-education, and direction-based training and self-training. Students' psychological suzhi is developed by external education forces, including the family, the school, the community and the mass media, and the self-education by the students themselves. Along with students' upgrading or penetration of the psychological suzhi-based education, the effect of external education forces will be weakened and the self-education will play a more important role. Fourth, it is to integrate the social construction in the group situation the individuals' self-construction.

## Integration of Strategies

There are various strategies for school psychological suzhi-based education. Such strategies can be divided into psychological consultation (including group counseling and individual counseling), psychological counseling and education, psychotherapy, psychological training activities, and maintenance of mental health according to the different forms. They can also be divided into those on guidance and training of learning psychology, life, personality and communication psychology according to the different contents. According to the different approaches, they can also be classified into the categories of cognition, such as initiation of thinking, specific-problem-based discussion, correction of cognitions, debate and assessment methods, emotion, such as meditation, empathy, transposition and feelings in particular situation, and behavior, such as behavior training, behavior changes, role play, behavior demonstration and behavior reinforcement. Each strategy may achieve certain effect in certain situation for psychological suzhi-based education. However, how to integrate various psychological suzhi-based education strategies to fully perform the effect of the integrated strategies is the precondition for more specific and effective mental health education. We believe that the integration of psychological suzhi-based education strategies includes: 1) longitudinal integration that integrates macro and general psychological suzhi-based education strategies and micro and specific psychological suzhi-based education strategies, including integration of psychological counseling and guiding strategies, psychological suzhi-based education activity strategies, subject-infiltration psychological suzhi-based education strategies and discussion strategies, role play strategies, debate strategies, as well as integration of psychological counseling strategies and talking strategies, phone counseling strategies as well as letter counseling strategies; 2) transverse integration, including coordination and integration of strategies on specific-problem-based training and those on subject infiltration strategies, and of strategies on initiation of thinking, communication, discussion, group interaction and those on self-analysis, self-reflection, self-tempering; 3) integration of strategies on shaping external behavior and those on such psychological activities as internal cognition and emotion, including the coordination and integration of those on cognition correction trainings, empathy and role behavior reinforcement trainings. Theoretically, such integration of psychological suzhi-based education strategies should: 1) aim at the sound development of students' psychological suzhi and strive to develop, train and establish mental health of students so as to promote students' active adaptation and independent development and guide students to form healthy concepts, accumulate positive experiences, improve their adaptability and develop good habits; 2) be based on students' physiological and psychological development, the development of their sociality, their present psychological suzhi and the common or possible mental problems in respect of their study, life, interpersonal relationship and growth; 3) be made in accordance with the "agent-based principle", focus on the student, respect the student's personality, uncover, exert and develop students' potential as agent, attach importance to the student's function as agent and stimulate student's enthusiasm, initiative and creativity during their independent participation. We should, in the psychological suzhi-based education-related practice, pay attention to three aspects in respect of such integration of education strategies: 1) differences and connection between psychological suzhi-based education strategies for the students at different ages. The psychological suzhi-based education for primary school students should be simple, clear, lively and interesting as possible and focus on development of good habits; the psychological suzhi-based education for junior middle school students should be concise, clear and vivid as possible and focus on mastery of skills; the psychological suzhi-based education for senior middle school students should be concise, comprehensive and enlightening as possible and focus on internalization of experiences and all-around development. However, the psychological suzhi cultivation strategies for students at different ages should all satisfy the requirements for active adaptation and independent development; they should not only have the characteristics at specific stage, but also be consistent with the overall goal; 2) comprehensive application and integration of psychological suzhi-based education strategies with different content and of different types. Both general strategies and special strategies on specific issues are necessary for the student to learn how to well deal with their study, life and interpersonal communication and develop their intelligence, ability, personality, sociality and creativity; subject infiltration strategies and specific-problem-based training may be applied comprehensively and integrated; cognition-focused, emotion-focused and behavior-focused strategies may also be applied comprehensively and integrated. In addition, the operation methods of specific strategies should also be integrated. For example, we may, with situation creation strategy, create the problem situation, the physical situation consistent with the goal and content, the performance situation able to induce students to act, as well as the psychological situation enabling students to get psychological freedom and psychological security and triggering psychological resonance that deserve meditation or may cause students to think; 3) serialization of psychological suzhi-based education strategies for the targets at different ages, with different content and of different types. A complete set of psychological suzhi-based education strategies should include: strategies focusing on the targets of cultivation (target series strategies), strategies focusing on the characteristics at different ages (age series strategies), strategies focusing on the psychological suzhi-based education content (content series strategies), and strategies focusing on the procedures or process of forming the psychological suzhi (process series strategies). To sum up, we should integrate various education strategies for students' psychological suzhi cultivation, make full use of the advantages of all strategies and apply the comprehensive education effect of all strategies so as to provide theoretical basis and practice guidelines for developing sound psychological suzhi of students.

## Specific-Problem-Based Training Modes and Implementation Strategies

Psychological suzhi education-related Specific-problem-based training is also called psychological suzhi cultivation activity. As one of the major psychological suzhi education implementation approaches, it integrates the characteristics and advantages of curriculum mode, activity mode and training mode, and provides trainings in respect of specific problems found during the development and improvement of students' psychological suzhi. With this mode, the aim is to improve the overall structure and functions of students' psychological suzhi and promote the healthy development thereof; the training content and activity will be determined and organized based on common problems found during students' psychological development. According to the different goals, such trainings can also be divided into specific-problem-based training and systematic training. The former one is mainly targeted at the key or prominent problems, while the latter one is for systematic development of overall psychological suzhi of students at different ages. Psychological suzhi cultivation, as a kind of science-and-practice based education, is an important component of school education, but it is different from the school conventional education; it has its own features and rules. Specifically speaking, psychological suzhi cultivation is different from the teaching of curriculums; it advocates students to gain experiences independently and integrate knowledge with practice, but not to focus on knowledge and direction in class or during training activities. Psychological suzhi cultivation is also different from normative education; it emphasizes the students' sense of independence and independent experience after they cope with the intrinsic or possible mental problems, as well as their ability to improve or change corresponding psychology or behavior via specific training.

## Goals of Specific-Problem-Based Training

The fundamental goal of mental health education is to develop students' psychological suzhi. It consists of two closely connecting goals: 1) to make students actively adapt to various changes to maintain their mental health. This is to make students adapt to all changes in their study, life, communications and physiological development and enable their behavior and thinking to fit in with such changes and development. It is an important standard to measure a student's psychological suzhi and an important factor on the development of his/her psychological suzhi whether he/she is able to behave and think based on the changes in situations, tasks and goals of study, in experiences in, environment of and requirements for daily life, in environment, targets and rules of communications, as well as in physiological growth and development. Therefore, one of the goals of mental health education is to enable students to well deal with their study, life, interpersonal communication and the changes of themselves (mind-body coordination) in order to become a person who is able to learn new things, live a happy life and get along well with others, knows how to be a good man, adapts well to the changing situations and keeps mental health. This is the primary goal of mental health education; 2) to promote the independent psychological development and thus develop the student into a man with sound psychological suzhi. This is the final goal of mental health education. The basic requirement to achieve this goal is to realize sound and healthy development of the components and overall structure of students' psychological suzhi. Therefore, the school mental health education measures should not only satisfy the demands of social development and education for talents, but also be helpful to the growth and development of students at different ages. The motivation of mental health education and psychological suzhi cultivation is to consciously and purposely improve and develop students' psychological suzhi with well-prepared plans, and this is also the final goal of mental health education and psychological suzhi cultivation.

## Content of Specific-Problem-Based Training

Two aspects should be taken into consideration during the construction and selection of school psychological suzhi-based education: 1) comprehensively building the mental health education system from an overall and specific perspective based on the staged and continuous development of individual's psychological suzhi; 2) conducting trainings and determining the education requirements and content focusing on the problems commonly existing in or likely to happen to students' study, life, interpersonal communication and growth based on the physiological and psychological development of the students in different grades, the development of their sociality and specific mental health education goals. We thus, based on the research and the aforesaid consideration, summarized and put forward that psychological suzhi-based education consists of eight parts, adapting to the study, adapting to the life, adapting to interpersonal communication, knowing how to get along well with others, developing intelligence and ability, developing the personality, developing the sociality, and developing the creativity. The aforesaid eight parts are not only consistent with the final goal, but also satisfy the requirements for the two goals. In addition, they are closely linked for the same purpose, active adaptation for example, or well coordinate with each other for different purposes, active adaptation and independent development for example. This forms an organic system that helps to coordinate and integrate the education content.

The specific-problem-based training contents should focus on:

*Development.* The training focuses on cultivation, training and development of suzhi instead of counseling and solving mental problems, emphasizes the cultivation of concept, experiences, habit and ability instead of popularization of psychological knowledge.

*Interaction.* The training process emphasizes the inspiration and collision of ideas, stimulation and impact of emotions as well as excitation and restriction of behavior between students, students and teachers, parents and children, and companions. The training process should be a process of interaction.

*Basis.* The specific-problem-based training activities for improving psychological suzhi should be conducted based on students' age and characteristics, development of psychological suzhi, common mental problems among students, and actual conditions of the family, the school and the class.

## Characteristics of Specific-Problem-Based Training

*Systematic training activities.* A system of systematic psychological suzhi-based education targets should be established by setting specific-problem-based psychological suzhi-based education lessons to conduct systematic and comprehensive training on the components and overall structure of students' psychological suzhi by different levels and different categories. This may not only ensure the integrity of psychological suzhi training (PST), but also enhance the effect of psychological suzhi-based education within the unit time.

*Target-based educational content.* The content is determined based on the system of psychological suzhi-based education targets and the development of psychological suzhi of students in different grades. It aims at developing the psychological suzhi of students at different ages and solving the problems commonly existing or likely to occur among students in different grades during their psychological development. It divides psychological suzhi-based education into eight parts, including adapting to the study, adapting to the life, adapting to interpersonal communication, knowing how to get along well with others, developing intelligence and ability, developing the personality, developing the sociality, and developing the creativity, and sets several specific sub-items, under the overall framework, for the students in different grades. The educational content is highly customized since such training is conducted based on the physiological and psychological development and the sociality of the students in different grades and the students' study, life and communication, is consistent with the requirements of the final goal of psychological suzhi-based education and aims at meeting the students' future demands.

*Activity-based training.* One of the noticeable characteristics of specific-problem-based training activities is to conduct psychological suzhi-based education via the activities integrating cognition, emotion, will and action together. This expands the connotation and extension of activities and enriches the content thereof; even more important, it adopts the education modes familiar to most educators for the PST on students' adaptation-development-creation. Through the activities, educators may develop students' intelligence and ability, cultivate healthy personality for them and enhance their adaptability so as to make the activities more acceptable to students and more attractive for them, to promote students' development and fully perform the effects of such activities. Such activities are based on the deliberately organized activity and focusing on developing the psychological suzhi so as to make the operation of activity more natural and smooth and achieve the goal of psychological suzhi-based education by imperceptible influence. Any student participating in the activity should be a subject instead of an onlooker. This fully performs the student's initiative and is helpful to perform their functions as the agent. The operation of activities can meet the interest and demands of primary and middle school students, which is helpful to make them devote more to the activities and may facilitate PST.

*Development-oriented training.* Specific-problem-based training activity is focused on the development-oriented training of psychological suzhi, including training of cognition ability, change of concepts, stimulation and accumulation of emotions, and development of personality, behavior and habit. Such development-oriented training should be also conducted in accordance with the series and level. This distinguishes psychological suzhi-based education from popularization of psychological knowledge, from the psychological counseling targeted at solving mental problems, and from the comprehensive practice or general activity targeted at improving students' hands-on ability.

*Comprehensively targeted training.* The school psychological suzhi-based education is targeted at all students' development to improve all students' psychological suzhi. It is difficult to achieve this goal only by psychological counseling for a few individuals or even a certain individual; instead, this goal can be realized only by conducting specific-problem-based of psychological suzhi-based education for all students.

## Basic Goals of Specific-Problem-Based Training

We believe that the psychological suzhi-based specific-problem-based training is to:

Create or use activity-based, ecology-based and situation-based teaching means to help students understand the development of their psychological suzhi;

Teach students the fundamentals of psychological development and help them understand the causes for different psychological phenomena and the influence on their study, life, communication and growth;

Guide, via creating situations for interactive activities, students how to behave in the activity and make students master various psychological and behavioral strategies during the activity, which is the primary goal of specific-problem-based training. A necessary precondition for developing psychological suzhi is to make students master the thinking and action methods, steps, processes and strategies on solving problems;

Guide students to reflect and compare the training processes, methods and strategies and experience the feelings before and after so as to internalize the training strategy.

## Basic Requirements of Specific-Problem-Based Training

It is required that the design for psychological suzhi-based specific-problem-based training should be:

*Situation-based.* Create the problem situation that deserves meditation or may cause students to think the activity situation that may attract students to participate in activities, the physical situation that may trigger students' emotions and be consistent with the goal and content, as well as the democratic, relaxing and open psychological situation that may trigger students' innermost feelings.

*Activity-based.* Students can participate in various activities on a free, active and creative basis, including observation, behavioral operation, performance, meditation, experience, feeling, reflection, expression (via words, symbols, images etc.), debate and discussion.

*Operation-focused.* The training focuses on how the students think, act, experience and reflect; it will teach students the methods, steps and strategies.

*Role-based.* Teachers should be the designer, participant, guide and organizer in a specific-problem-based training, and the main function is to initiate, guide, regulate and control the activity. For example, they should briefly introduce the knowledge-related problem, thoroughly solve students' intrapsychic conflicts and answer their puzzles, give advice during the activity in time so as to direct students conclude, summarize and analyze in time the training effect.

## Process and Conditions for Specific-Problem-Based Training

### *1) Process of Specific-Problem-Based Training*

From the perspective of implementation process, mental health education is an educational activity in diversified forms. For example, according to the education approaches, mental health can be divided into the psychological suzhi-based specific-problem-based training, the psychological consultation and counseling and the subject infiltration; according to the educational elements, mental health education can be divided into the school, the family and the community, and these three elements can be combined to carry out mental health education; according to the targets of education activities, mental health education can be divided into the direction-based and the non-direction-based.

How to organically integrate various activities with the mental health education is very important for improving the effect of mental health education. Therefore, we should, during our guidance for colleges, middle schools and primary schools to conduct mental health educational experiments, strive to integrate the effective approaches, modes and elements of mental health education with the three basic processes, i.e. judgment and evaluation, training with strategies, and reflection.

*Judgment and Evaluation.* This process is to help students understand the status quo of their psychological suzhi via tests and whether they have sound psychological suzhi so as to arouse students' sense of identification and sense of absence, trigger the emotional resonance or shock, stimulate psychological activities and cause students to think and put forward questions. It also aims to enable students to understand the causes for certain psychological phenomenon and the significance of such psychological suzhi on their study, life, communication and growth. It mainly includes examination and judgment on the status quo of oneself, criteria of such judgment, cases of psychological performance etc. It is conducted via presentation self tests, or materialized, situation-based or dynamic-based tests; it provides a situation to enable students to make judgment amidst the daily-life-like situation; it provides cases to enable students to make conclusions and summaries; it uses small experiments to create corresponding situations for activities and make students participate in such activities.

*Training with Strategies.* This is the core process for the PST targeted at all students. The goals are to a) guide students to meditate the mental problems involved so as to improve their cognition, change their thinking modes and their point of view and establish a new concept, b) set thinking steps and action steps, c) arouse students' emotions by means of such thinking and action, and d) make students master the basic thinking process, thinking approaches and behavioral approaches according to the thinking and operational approaches and modes. The final goal of this process is to make students master corresponding behavioral strategies. Such goal may be achieved via explanation by students themselves, role play and role transposition, discussion, debate, interactive communications between students, students and teachers as well as parents and children, practical operation, visit and interview, and appropriate guide or consultation by teachers.

*Reflection.* Students will reflect their feelings, emotional experience and behavior change during the training, as well as the activity process and effect of the training in order to reflect the training process and modes; they will apply the approaches and steps mastered via the training to other similar situations; they will also summarize the training results. Reflection is arranged based on the training target and content to inspect the satisfaction of the training goal. This process may be conducted via problem-rising and comparison before and after the training, design of situations and practical operations, conclusions and summarization on cases, self-suggestion or self-reminding, determination of the direction for following thinking, experiences and action.

It should be noted that educators should have the following concepts and teaching views so that the aforesaid three processes of mental health education can successfully go on.

## 2) Requirements for Specific-Problem-Based Training

### Precondition: Active Participation by Students

Unlike the teaching of subject knowledge, development of students' recognition ability, cultivation of their sound personality and enhancement of their adaptability cannot mainly rely on the means and approaches to teaching knowledge. The mental health education should be subject to students' active participation to enable them to find problems, analyze the self, explore the causes, find out solutions, make reflection and form the psychological suzhi in respect of thinking, concept and ability during the activity. The precondition for cultivating and developing psychological suzhi is that students should participate in the activities that are rich in contents and varied in forms. a) It may drive the development of psychological suzhi and satisfy the middle school and primary school students' demands for participating in various activities. One of the primary requirements is that, if educators want to develop a student's sense and ability of independence, the student should be willing to be independent and have the demand for thinking independently, making judgment independently, making choice independently, make decision independently and behave independently; moreover, such will and demands should be stimulated and satisfied during the activity. The cultivation of students' sympathy should be first subject to their demands for sympathizing with others and such demands should also be stimulated during the activity. b) The activity may provide basis and opportunities for the performance and development of students' psychological suzhi. 3) The activity may provide contents for developing middle school and primary schools' psychological suzhi. They understand, select, judge and integrate the objective social stimuli and the information on self during the activities and then internalize, on a selective basis, the intrinsic and external stimulators into their suzhi. Therefore, it should emphasize the development of sound psychological suzhi of students during the activity. Educators should conduct, according to the different contents, requirements and the actual conditions of students, interesting activities that are rich in contents and varied in forms. Such activities should be attractive for students and easy for them to operate.

**Foundation: The Process for Developing Students' Psychological Suzhi**

We have found, via our survey of students, that students' psychological suzhi will be formed via self-cognition, theory-learning, behavioral direction with strategies, reflection and internalization, formation of psychological suzhi. Therefore, the mental health education should also be conducted in accordance with the aforesaid process. We plan to briefly introduce, with the "Flow Chart", the integration of formation process of psychological suzhi (intrinsic) and mental health education process (external).

Judgment and evaluation show the objective stimulation via materialized, situation-based or dynamic means (measuring), and they provide the judgment criteria, analyzes the causes, discusses the significance, as well as enables the students to cognize themselves via comparison and selection and to understand the truth via discussion, conclusion, performance and actual operation; training with strategies enables students to master the thinking and action approaches and steps via explanation, discussion, operation and debate etc; reflection makes students establish the concept, internalize the feelings and form the suzhi during the activities via reflecting their feelings, change of their behavior and the activity process and results.

**Feature: Creation of Interactive Situations**

Mental health education process is also a process to create interactive situations, especially to arouse or awake students' psychological activities. It can usually arouse students' sense of identification and sense of absence, stimulate emotional resonance or shock, and trigger the desire for action. Students' psychological suzhi is cultivated and developed in the psychological environment established by the interaction between students and teachers, between students, and between students and their parents. Therefore, it is the important feature of mental health education to create a harmonious interactive psychological environment. The psychological environment can be created by physical means, including playing background music and flash, arrangement of spatial position, verbal suggestion or encouragement etc., but it should rely more on psychological means, such as respecting, understanding and trusting students, achieving true equality between students and teachers and between parents and children, treating students with a tolerant and open attitude, holding the development viewpoint towards the students and deeply experiencing students' feelings and emotional responses. To sum up, the psychological suzhi-based education should be the heart-to-heart communication and exchange between students and teachers, between students and between parents and children. The psychological foundation for improving the effect of psychological suzhi-based education is to create a democratic, relaxing and open atmosphere for interaction.

# SUBJECT INFILTRATION MODES AND IMPLEMENTATION STRATEGIES

The psychological suzhi-based education for students can be divided into specific-problem-based training, psychological consultation and counseling and subject infiltration according to the different implementation approaches; correspondingly, there form three psychological suzhi-based education modes during specific implementation, training modes, consultation and counseling modes and subject infiltration modes.

However, in view of the present education, the subject-infiltration approach is at a relatively initial stage, compared with other approaches for school psychological suzhi-based education. This is because the implementation of subject infiltration modes is more complicated, it has higher requirements on teacher' quality and the theoretical research of subject-infiltration psychological suzhi-based education is inadequate during teaching of subjects.

According to the theoretical and empirical research of psychological suzhi-based education [Zhang, 2004] and the empirical research of subject infiltration [Wang, 2004; Shao, 2004; Song, 2004; Ye, 2004], we strive to conduct preliminary exploration and discussion on the theoretical issues of subject infiltration modes.

## Goals of Subject Infiltration

The goal of subject-infiltration psychological suzhi-based education is subordinate to the basic goal of school psychological suzhi-based education and its specific goal is to develop sound psychological suzhi of students while teaching the subject knowledge and skills. We believe that the goal of teaching of subjects is related and interacting with that of psychological suzhi-based education: a student's psychological suzhi is being improved when he/she is learning the knowledge, and such improvement is necessary for the mastery of knowledge; meanwhile, the improvement of a student's psychological suzhi can also effectively promote his/her mastery of the knowledge. Both of them are for the purpose of students' all-round development. The goal of subject-infiltration psychological suzhi-based education should be set based on:

### 1) Oriented to the Content of the Text Book

Teachers should, when they are setting the goal of subject-infiltration, abide by the principle that "the available educational resources related with the textbook should be those contained within the textbook" [Ye, 2004] instead of those imposed without considering the textbook. For example, *The Summer Palace*[1], *New-Type Glass*[2] and *Feet of Parthenocissus Trcuspidata*[3], expository essays in Chinese textbook for primary school students, are unsuitable for infiltration into cultivation of relevant emotional competence. We cannot blindly adopt relevant materials regardless of the content of textbooks, which fundamentally wrests the meaning of subject-infiltration and departs from the significance and value of subject infiltration for developing students' psychological suzhi.

### 2) Objective and Well Targeted

Teachers should, when they are setting the goal of subject-infiltration, pay attention to the actual conditions of the school and the clad as well as resources available. They should fully

---

[1] The Summer Palace is a text in the Chinese textbook (VII) for primary school students, published by People's Education Press.

[2] New-Type Glass is a text in the Chinese textbook (VII) for primary school students, published by People's Education Press.

[3] Feet of Parthenocissus Trcuspidata is a text in the Chinese textbook (VII) for primary school students, published by People's Education Press.

consider the psychological characteristics and development of the students in the class to set reasonable goals of psychological suzhi-based education targeted at specific problems.

In addition, they should also take into consideration the differences between individuals. For example, one of the important processes for cultivating students' study self-efficacy during the teaching of mathematics is to guide students to make positive attributions. Teachers should, if they want to guide students to conduct attribution correctly, at first investigate the attribution by different students via questionnaire survey and communications with students so as to exactly understand the characteristics of different students' attribution since the students at difference levels may have different attribution.

### 3) Imperceptible Influence

Teachers should conduct subject infiltration via imperceptible influence so as to improve the psychological suzhi via imperceptible infiltration and influence. They should "organically" integrate the goal and content of infiltration with those of the teaching of subject, and help students, when they are learning knowledge, improve their psychological suzhi by means of implicitness, implication and permeating via creating specific teaching situation, designing effective teaching strategies, exploring and dealing with relevant subject knowledge, and consciously using the psychological theories, approaches and techniques.

For example, teachers may, when they are developing students' study self-monitoring ability during the teaching of mathematics, make students estimate the test result and make comparison to determine the accuracy rate to strengthen students' sense of and feedback on self-monitoring of study.

## Selection of Content for Subject Infiltration

In respect of the subject infiltration, one of the important means for psychological suzhi-based education, educators should: select the content based on the demands for active adaptation and independent development, and comprehensively build the subject infiltration system from an overall and specific perspective according to the staged and continuous development of individuals' psychological suzhi; conduct cultivation and infiltration focusing on the problems existing in or likely to happen to students' study, life, communications and growth and determine the requirements and content of infiltration-based education for students in different grades based on physiological and psychological development of such students, the development of their sociality, and specific educational goals; fully consider the coordination between and the integrity of students' cognition, personality and adaptability based on the structure of students' psychological suzhi, and arrange and implement relevant materials according to the eight parts, i.e. Adapting to study, life and interpersonal communication, knowing how to get along well with others, developing intelligence, ability, personality, sociality, and creativity; selecting the content according to the nature of the subject, the characteristics of teaching the subject and the type of school-teaching. The resources related with subject infiltration and applicable to psychological suzhi-based education should feature:

*Comprehensiveness and diversity.* The teaching of subject involves abundant materials for psychological suzhi-based education. The infiltration during the teaching of subject covers a wide range of fields, including study, life, interpersonal communications, personality and sociality, and varies in diversified forms. A subject, or even a unit or a lesson, always involves diversified, multi-aspect and multi-dimensional content related to psychological suzhi-based education. Therefore, during the teaching of subject, teachers should understand the textbook on an overall basis, flexibly arrange the infiltration content in the course of teaching and well integrate the teaching of subject with psychological suzhi-based education.

*Dispersiveness.* The teaching of subject is arranged based on the knowledge system of the subject. It follows the logic of the subject and reflects the knowledge series. However, the formation process of students' psychological suzhi is a kind of psychological logic, and it is difficult for subject infiltration to be completely consistent with the development sequence of students' psychological suzhi, which decides the dispersiveness of subject-infiltration psychological suzhi-based education. This is one of the bottlenecks for subject-infiltration approach, and whether educators have properly solved such problems in the practice will directly influence the effect of subject infiltration.

*Potentiality.* Not all of the psychological suzhi-based education resources for the teaching of subject are explicit and direct; they are sometimes implicit and indirect. This is consistent with the imperceptible influence and integration of subject infiltration. Therefore, teachers may directly use the explicit psychological suzhi-based education resources in respect of curricula, but they should explore the implicit resources via, for example, conclusion, summarization, derivation and exploration so as to find out the connection between the teaching of subject and corresponding psychological suzhi-based education.

*Coexistence.* The psychological suzhi-based education coexists with other educational factors instead of being separated from during educational and teaching activities. In respect of subject infiltration, educators should not only use the psychological suzhi-based education resources in textbooks, but also other educational and teaching resources in classroom lessons, including teaching process and psychological environment for classroom lessons. Only by this way can the effect of subject infiltration be maximized.

## Process of Subject Infiltration

According to the aforesaid psychological suzhi-based education integrated modes and the characteristics of psychological suzhi development of students at different ages, we have, based on the research and experiment by the aforesaid research team, worked out the basic modes for infiltrating psychological suzhi-based education into the teaching of subject (please see the figure below).

The process of infiltrating psychological suzhi-based education into the teaching of subject is consistent with the basic process of psychological suzhi-based education, i.e. judgment and evaluation-training with strategies-reflection, but it also has its own characteristics. We believe that the basic process for subject-infiltration-based education includes:

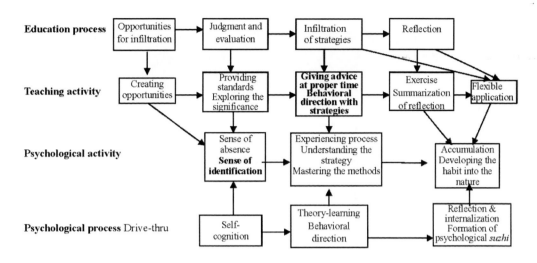

Figure 1.1. Basic Process for Infiltrating Psychological Suzhi-based Education into the Teaching of Subject.

## 1) Creating Opportunities for Infiltration

It is one of the primary steps for infiltrating psychological suzhi-based education into the teaching of subject to create opportunities for infiltration. Teachers should first create the best opportunities for infiltration, grasp the teaching goal and content on an overall basis and finally find out the best way to infiltrate psychological suzhi-based education into the teaching of subject. Then, they should, according to the characteristics of students' psychological suzhi development and the typical events in their daily life, integrate the goal and content of developing psychological suzhi with the teaching of subject as well as consider the specific teaching strategies and methods.

## 2) Judgment and Evaluation

Teachers adopt various testing methods to find the difficulties or problems during the development of students' psychological suzhi, cause students to pay attention to the development of their psychological suzhi of their one's free will, and find the causes for certain psychological phenomenon and its significance on their study, life and communication via comparison, judgment, shock, exploration so as to cause them to actively explore the causes and strategies for their mental problems as well as the significance to the development and growth of their psychological suzhi.

## 3) Infiltration with Strategies

Behavioral direction with strategies is implemented for both specific-problem-based training and subject infiltration during psychological suzhi-based education, but the implementation processes are different. The most remarkable feature of the subject infiltration mode is that such mode seeks natural and organic infiltration, and this does not allow it to conduct direct and straight specific-problem-based training on students in respect of strategies for emotional adjustment. Instead, it can only be implemented via infiltration with strategies, which is one of the most important features of subject-infiltration psychological suzhi-based education. Teachers should adopt flexible and diversified modes to infiltrate PST strategies into the teaching of subject for students and give advice at proper time so as to enable students to understand and master, during their learning of knowledge, some strategies and methods on developing psychological suzhi. This is also the core process of subject infiltration modes.

### 4) Reflection

Reflection is a process where teachers adopt various approaches to guide students to cognize, compare and reflect their psychological outcome, experiences, process, methods and behavioral changes etc. During the subject infiltration in order to promote internalization, form the psychological suzhi and even achieve transfer. We requested, during the experiment, students to experience, identify, accept, internalize the knowledge learned from psychological suzhi and corresponding strategies and methods via famous aphorism, stories of figures or practice to enable primary school students to maximally transfer them in other similar situations.

It follows that, during the teaching based on subject infiltration, "students' active participation is the precondition for successful implementation of subject infiltration, the formation process of students' psychological suzhi and the psychological process of mastering the knowledge is the psychological foundation for subject infiltration, the teaching of knowledge is the framework for subject infiltration, and the creation of interactive teaching situation is the indispensable condition to make subject infiltration more effective" [Jiang and Zhang, 2002]. Therefore, the basic process for teaching based on subject infiltration indicates:

*Students' active participation is the precondition.* The subject infiltration psychological suzhi-based education is to enable students to improve their psychological suzhi when they are learning the subject knowledge, which is in nature a process of "helping them to learn self-help". The student is the agent for developing psychological suzhi, and the psychological suzhi-based education can be effective only when it is applied to the agent. We cannot rely much on the means and approaches for teaching knowledge during the subject infiltration, as we do during the teaching of subject; instead, we should fully cognize the student's position as the agent, maximally stimulate their initiative and enthusiasm to participate in psychological suzhi-based education, and cause them to fully perform their consciousness and initiative in developing their psychological suzhi.

*The process for forming students' psychological suzhi is the foundation.* Subject infiltration content must be reasonably arranged based on the course and law of the sequential psychological change during the development and formation of students' psychological suzhi, which is the primary precondition for effective subject infiltration into students' psychological suzhi-based education. We have found, via our survey of students, that students' psychological suzhi will be formed via self-cognition, theory-learning, behavioral direction, reflection and internalization, formation of psychological suzhi [Chen and Zhang, 2002]. Therefore, subject-infiltration-based education should also be conducted in accordance with the aforesaid process.

*Teaching of knowledge is the framework.* The teaching of subject knowledge is the carrier for subject-infiltration psychological suzhi-based education, so subject-infiltration psychological suzhi-based education should be also conducted based on the teaching of subject knowledge. Specifically, we must at first fully explore relevant content on psychological suzhi contained in the teaching of subject, and properly apply it to the teaching of subject knowledge. The arrangement of subject infiltration content and the seizure of infiltration opportunities must be in accordance with the content of teaching of subject. The infiltration content should be contained in the textbook. The "rigid infiltration regardless of teaching content will not only weaken teachers' attention to the scientificity of, and the law of teaching, the subject; moreover, it makes the mistake of psychologism again" [Liu and Gu, 2004]. From this point of view, the teaching of knowledge is the basic framework for subject infiltration as well as the logic starting point for the existence of subject-infiltration psychological suzhi-based education.

*Creation of interactive teaching situation is the indispensable condition to make subject infiltration effective.* Creation of interactive teaching situation is the starting point for subject-infiltration-based teaching as well as the "pacemaker" to activate and arouse students' psychological activities. It can often stimulate students' sense of identification and sense of absence, trigger emotional resonance or shock and trigger the desire for action. Teachers should treat, understand and trust students with a tolerant and open attitude and deeply experience students' feelings and emotional responses in the interactive teaching situation to establish an equal, democratic and open relationship between students and teachers, and thus form a positive classroom atmosphere.

Only can this way enable students to be accustomed to a specific situation quickly and then to be naturally exposed to the psychological-suzhi-related resources contained in the teaching of subject; this can also make students actively pay attention to the development of their psychological suzhi and actively explore the policies and approaches on developing psychological suzhi. Therefore, the creation of interactive teaching situation is the fundamental guarantee for enhancing the effect of subject-infiltration psychological suzhi-based education.

## Strategies of Subject Infiltration

### 1) Natural Infiltration

The most intrinsic feature of subject-infiltration psychological suzhi-based education is that the infiltration is natural, integral and imperceptible; it should be naturally integrated with the curriculum system and the teaching process as a whole. Teachers should explore the reasonable infiltration point for mental health education based on the content of the teaching of subject and the available resources contained in such content; any infiltration just for infiltration is unwise. The curriculums are rich in the resources for mental health education, but it does not mean that any content is applicable for subject-infiltration psychological suzhi-based education at any time. Some teachers may force the infiltration for certain purpose, which will obviously cause more loss than gains. Subject infiltration should be natural and to the point; it should be closely and organically linked with the teaching process of the subject. It follows that the primary principle for subject-infiltration psychological suzhi-based education during the teaching of subject is to "let nature take its course" and to try the best to avoid direct and inflexible infiltration.

### 2) Moderate and Effective Infiltration

Subject infiltration and the teaching of subject are two different components of the school suzhi education and they have different starting points and goals. Any psychological suzhi-based education-oriented teaching of subject or subject-teaching-oriented, where one intends to occupy the other's position, is inadvisable. Therefore, teachers should conduct teaching based on moderate and effective subject infiltration according to the targets, modes and characteristics of subject-infiltration psychological suzhi-based education. The most important thing for the teaching based on subject infiltration is the proper duration of infiltration. Teachers should arrange the infiltration for a reasonable period, neither too long nor too short. In addition, the unique uncertainty and unpredictability of subject infiltration decides that subject infiltration should be conducted at different levels to ensure that students may accept such infiltration and such infiltration is conducted step by step [Ye, 2004]. Besides, teachers should also pay attention to the extent and scope of such infiltration to ensure the effectiveness.

### 3) Flexible and Various Strategies

Subject-infiltration psychological suzhi-based education involves both the theory and the art of education and there is no fixed approach to the teaching based on subject infiltration. The flexible use of different teaching design, infiltration modes and infiltration approaches constitutes the various strategies for infiltration. Moreover, the incidents during the teaching also request teachers to flexibly solve the problem. The aforesaid incidents may be independent of the teaching content, but teachers cannot ignore them or pass them by during subject infiltration, nor can they simply dispose such incidents by rude means or recklessly suppress them. Instead, they should flexibly deal with such incidents and use them as the "vivid examples" for psychological suzhi-based education. For example, there may be some sudden quarrel, chattering or even fight between students due to some trifle, which will disorder the class or other situations. Teachers should, at this time, flexibly take some measures in time to calm down such students and teach them, at proper time, some strategies and methods on controlling or adjusting their temper. Teachers thus cannot only properly deal with the unexpected interruptions during the teaching, but also train students at a proper time in respect of emotional regulation abilities.

### 4) Creating Interactive Situations

Creation of interactive situations is the necessary condition for the teaching of subject and the primary feature of psychological suzhi-based education [Chen and Zhang; 2002, Liu and Zhang, 2004]. From the perspective of psychological suzhi-based education, the teaching based on subject infiltration may, by creating interactive situations and stimulating students' psychological activities, cause emotional resonance between students and then increase students' demands for action so that students' psychological suzhi can be cultivated and developed in the psychological environment established by the mutual effect occurring in interpersonal communication. From the perspective of teaching of subject, the effective teaching will be achieved only by interactions in specific situations. Teachers should enable students to naturally and unconsciously absorb the knowledge and do exercise via perception, experience, practice, exploration etc. when participating in the activity, and to enjoy the course of learning when continuously absorbing the knowledge and enhancing the subject competence.

### 5) Encouraging Students to Participate in Activities

The aforesaid activities during subject infiltration means: (1) students' external behaviors and conducts, such as the specific practice in class; (2) students' internal mental operation, such as thinking, experience, feeling, reflection etc. Psychological research shows that the activity is the most important factor for the generation and development of human being's psychology and that it is the origin of psychology. Human being's advanced psychological functions are all caused by the interactions between the agent and the object, and are resulting from continuously internalizing activities and communications. The psychological suzhi-based education research shows that active participation in activities is the precondition for psychological suzhi cultivation, since students may find problems, analyze the self, explore the causes, seek solutions and make reflection during their active participation in activities to form thoughts, concepts and abilities. From the perspective of teaching of subject, students should actively participate in the teaching so that they can develop their skills and form the subject competence in the flexible and diverse learning activities. The activities include role play, onstage performance, game, team-based competition, cooperative learning etc.

### 6) Guiding Experiencing and Internalization

Experiencing and internalization is not only the key for forming psychological suzhi, but also an important process for developing students' subject competence in the teaching of subject: for the former one, experiencing is an activity that trigger emotions and generates meaning, and students may internalize, via experiencing, the external experiences and matters into their psychological suzhi, including cognition, belief, behavior and suzhi; for the latter one, students may conclude, summarize, construct and assimilate the knowledge and skill learned and then internalize them into their own cognitive structure and ability. We should guide students' experiencing and internalization in four aspects: (1) expanding the space for students' psychological freedom so as to enable students to get experience via exploration. Such exploration activities include cognition, game and behavior; (2) creating opportunities for interactive communications so that students may get experience via the learning activities in class. Interactive communications include the exchange of information on cognition, interpersonal emotions, attitude and behavior; (3) enabling students to get experience in the situation, which has been mentioned in "Creating interactive situations"; (4) enabling students to get experience via self-reflection, self-suggestion or self-reminding. This includes students' reflection on their psychology and behavior, their self-criticism and self-reminding of their faults and mistakes, their self-affirmation of their success and their control and adjustment of the self at a proper time.

## Relationships Related with Subject Infiltration Modes

Subject infiltration is not only the indispensable precondition for constructing the subject and improving the implementation strategies thereof [Chen, 2002], but also one of the effective approaches for conducting psychological suzhi-based education. However, we should, for the purpose of the subject infiltration modes, flexibly use different teaching designs, infiltration modes and infiltration methods since the subject-infiltration psychological suzhi-based education is complicated. Such designs, modes and methods constitute the different infiltration strategies. We should fully recognize the mode: it is neither a rigid mode that can be used following a prescribed order, nor an all-purpose mode applicable to all psychological suzhi-based education. Therefore, teachers should, during the implementation of such infiltration modes, be able to flexibly use the mode and make appropriate changes based on the actual situation. We believe that teachers should well deal with the following relationships in order to successfully implement the subject infiltration modes.

### 1) Subject Infiltration and Teaching of Subject

According to the feature of the subject during the teaching of subject, its infiltration is to find out the connection between teaching of subject and the development of students' psychological suzhi, apply psychological suzhi-based education approaches and strategies with clear objective and well-prepared plans, infiltrate psychological suzhi-based education content into the teaching of subject, promote students' mental health and develop sound psychological suzhi of students so as to achieve the fundamental goal of psychological suzhi-based education [Zhang, 2004]. It follows that the goals for the teaching of subject and for subject infiltration are identical; they are both for the purpose of improving all students' suzhi. From the perspective of psychological suzhi-based education, subject infiltration is helpful to find more ways for psychological suzhi-based education and enhance the functions of psychological suzhi-based education so as to realize the goal of psychological suzhi-based education and "conduct psychological suzhi-based education via teaching of subject"; from the perspective of teaching of subject, subject infiltration is helpful to increase the functions of teaching of subject so as to realize the goal of teaching of subject and "improve teaching of subject via psychological suzhi-based education"; from the perspective of suzhi education, subject infiltration may connect teaching of subject with psychological suzhi-based education and set the goal of psychological suzhi-based education in the teaching of subject, which is helpful to realize the overall objective of suzhi education. Therefore, subject infiltration is not only the extension of functions of teaching of subject, but also the extension of the approaches of psychological suzhi-based education.

### 2) Infiltration into Subjects of Different Natures

It should be recognized that the infiltration content should differ for the subjects of different natures achieve successful subject-infiltration-based education. We should, during the infiltration, pay attention to the characteristics of subjects and the difference between them and determine the best content of a certain subject for infiltration into psychological suzhi-based education. For example, in respect of the subjects on social sciences, most of the content in the textbook can be directly used for psychological suzhi-based education, while, in respect of those on natural sciences, the content for psychological suzhi-based education should be explored through the teaching process. In respect of a certain subject, Chinese features comprehensiveness, dispersiveness, potentiality and imperceptible influence, so the content about students' personality is applicable to infiltration; mathematics features unique thought, logic and other intrinsic natures, so it becomes an excellent subject to cultivate students' metacognition.

### 3) Coordination between Subject Infiltration, Specific-Problem-Based Training and Consultation and Counseling

During subject infiltration, educators will integrate the goal of psychological suzhi-based education with the teaching of subject. In this way, educators can not only achieve more than one goal, but also fully use the educational resources, which is in conformity with the principle of educational efficiency. However, such method has its own disadvantages: (1) it has higher requirements on teachers' competence. Teachers should have certain theoretical thinking and the expert knowledge on educational psychology and instructional psychology and internalize the whole infiltration concept; teacher should flexibly use the modes, change the modes into different types of lessons and properly emphasize the key points of infiltration instead of being restricted within a fixed form; teachers should own comprehensive abilities on education, not only good abilities in teaching of subject and psychological suzhi-based education, but also the ability to comprehensively use the two; (2) the content of teaching of subject is determined and arranged based on the internal logic of the subject, and the psychological suzhi-based education content contained therein is dispersive and latent. This violates the sequence of developing students' psychological suzhi, and, moreover, the intrinsic characteristics of subject infiltration makes it difficult for such infiltration to conduct well-targeted intervention according to the development of psychological suzhi; (3) subject infiltration is a system that requires coordination between the teachers of different subjects and the long-term persistence of teachers in practical teaching activities. Therefore, during the school psychological suzhi-based education, we should well coordinate subject infiltration, specific-problem-based training and consultation and counseling. The comprehensive use of the three means can further help teachers to soundly develop and improve students' psychological suzhi.

## COMPUTER ASSISTED TRAINING MODES AND IMPLEMENTATION STRATEGIES

The importance of psychological suzhi-based education for students has been increasingly recognized with the furthering of the suzhi education. The means of psychological suzhi-based education has therefore become one of the centers of focus. We propose a new mode of psychological suzhi-based education, the use of CAT. In particular, psychological suzhi-based education software will be developed based on the content of psychological suzhi-based education and be applied to the psychological suzhi-based education activities in educational institutions to improve the psychological suzhi of students.

### Necessity of CAT Modes

#### 1)Psychological Suzhi-Based Education Needs Innovation of Modes

*The Complexity of Psychological Suzhi-Based Education Requires Exploration of New Modes.* Psychological suzhi is the individual's stable, basic and derivable psychological quality and a self-organizing system that consists of four sub-systems: cognition, individual psychology, mental health and social adaptation, and the four sub-systems interact with each other and develop dynamically [Zhang, Liu and Feng, 2000]. The complexity and the diversified components of psychological suzhi require teachers to conduct cultivation and education with diversified methods. Psychological suzhi-based education is not only a brand new field for joint research of pedagogy and psychology, but also a comprehensive suzhi education activity. It needs to impose, in many ways, positive influence on all aspects of students' psychological suzhi with clear objective and well-prepared plans so as to cultivate sound psychological suzhi. Teachers should establish multi-channel, comprehensive and three-dimensional psychological suzhi-based education network, try the best to explore the approaches and systems for school psychological suzhi-based education and continuously explore new educational modes in order to effectively conduct psychological suzhi-based education.

*Innovation is urgent for existing psychological suzhi-based education.* Consultation and counseling, specific-problem-based training, subject infiltration modes are mainly applied to the school psychological suzhi-based education presently. Such modes play an important role in improving students' psychological suzhi and developing students' psychological potential, and drive the development of school psychological suzhi-based education to a certain degree. However, they also have some defects, including single educational form, inflexible educational methods, incompetent teachers and inefficient education. In addition, the development of students' psychological suzhi is a dynamic process, and it needs exploration of new education modes amidst the unceasing development. Therefore, it is the realistic need of school psychological suzhi-based education to explore new educational approaches and modes.

## 2) The Development of Multimedia Computers Provides Opportunities for Innovating Psychological Suzhi-Based Education Modes

Educational and psychological personnel strives to find out more effective psychological suzhi-based education modes that can better satisfy students' demands so as to meet the realistic need, and the development and popularization of multimedia computers exactly provide the opportunities for such exploration.

*Development of multimedia technology makes computer-assisted psychological suzhi-based education modes possible.* The computer will cause revolutionary influence on human beings, and it involves all aspects of people's life and academics. In respect of psychology, the computer has become a new research tool that is used widely. The multimedia technology can, with language, characters, sound, graphics, image, video etc., organically organize the psychological training content applicable to the students at a certain age and then displays it on the screen. Students may improve their psychological suzhi via learning. Such functions of multimedia computer make psychological suzhi-based education realizable via computers, increase the implementation approaches of psychological suzhi-based education and expand the application of computer assisted teaching to the psychology.

*The application of computers to the psychology provides references for computer assisted psychological suzhi-based education.* The rise and development of computer science provide a new way for psychological research. Computerization was found in the research on children's and teenagers' psychology during the latest ten or twenty years. The computer, as an indispensable tool for modern scientific research, has been widely used in all fields in respect of the research on children's and teenagers' psychology.

The computer provides a highly sensitive, precise and smart tool for psychological research. It can be used for designing experiments, building modes, controlling independent variables, operating experiments, recording the response, building the database, storing data, analyzing, retrieving and making statistics on the experimental results, conducting simulation experiments, verifying hypothesis, and analyzing the results got via other modern techniques and means. The successful application of computers to psychology fields provides references for computer assisted psychological suzhi-based education.

### 3) Significance of Computer Assisted Psychological Suzhi-Based Education Modes

The discussion on computer assisted psychological suzhi-based education modes can not only enrich the psychological suzhi-based education theories, but also promote the update of psychological suzhi-based education contents and forms, expand the space for psychological suzhi-based education and provides brand new approaches and modes for the furthering of school psychological suzhi-based education. From the theoretical perspective, psychological suzhi-based education can be realized in many ways. Researchers should put forward new concepts and building new modes constantly and provide theoretical guide on developing sound psychological suzhi of students in order to make the psychological suzhi-based education more effective. From the perspective of practice, computer-assisted mode is necessary for applying new technology to psychological suzhi-based education. The new multimedia technology can serve all aspects of our life, work and study, and be used for integration of computer science and psychological suzhi-based education. Development of new technology and adoption of new strategies are the realistic demands for the practice of psychological suzhi-based education as well as the requirements for using the modern teaching techniques more widely.

Psychological suzhi-based education is a systematic work. In addition to the school, psychological suzhi-based education should be applied to a wider range so that students can receive and participate in PST anywhere and at any time. This can be realized via the Internet. Via the Internet, participants will no longer be restricted by the time or the space, and they can get the PST they need for learning. This is exactly the reason why we build computer-assisted modes.

## Computer Assisted Training Modes and Implementation Strategies

### 1) Goal of CAT Modes

Whether the goal is reasonable will determine whether the school psychological suzhi-based education is effective. The goal of psychological suzhi-based education with CAT modes is consistent with that of the PST lessons and they are both following the basic goal of psychological suzhi-based education. The only difference lies in the means and forms. The basic goal of psychological suzhi-based education is to cultivate good psychological suzhi of students, and computer assisted PST is an important approach for psychological suzhi-based education. Therefore, it is also the basic goal of computer assisted psychological suzhi-based education to help students cultivate normal intelligence and ability, good personality and strong adaptability and healthily develop the components of their psychological suzhi. Meanwhile, the goal of computer assisted psychological suzhi-based education is established based on the level, the law and the characteristics of development of students' psychological suzhi. To sum up, computer assisted psychological suzhi-based education is to stimulate students' enthusiasm for interpersonal communications as well as help them overcome some difficulties in communications and improve the interpersonal relationship. It promotes students' active adaptation and active development via helping students adapt to the interpersonal communication and preventing and correcting various psychological or behavioral difficulties and obstacles in their communications caused by inadaptation.

## 2) Content of CAT Modes

The content of computer assisted psychological suzhi-based education modes should be determined based on adequate theories and firm empirical foundations. It should comply with the scientific principle. First, from the theoretical perspective, teachers should adopt traditional PST content on a selective basis, integrate it with multimedia means and arrange a series of systematic training curriculums according to students' actual situations so as to enhance students' ability to interpersonal communications and improve their interpersonal relationship. Second, the empirical research shows that the participant's psychological suzhi will be improved remarkably via the training of interpersonal communication skills with strategies on cognitive changes, behavioral guide and experience and study. Most researchers believe that the training of interpersonal communication skills can be conducted via cognitive development, emotional experience and behavioral training although the content may vary in specific trainings in previous studies.

In addition, the investigation and analysis of the status quo of interpersonal relationship also provide some realistic basis for us to prepare the training content.

According to the existing research, our computer-assisted psychological suzhi-based education modes conduct trainings mainly from the perspectives of cognition and behavior. Teachers may insert some content into such trainings to stimulate students' emotional resonance and enhance the emotional experience. The content of different themes generally starts with the situation to stimulate students' interest or resonance; then analysis will be made based on cognition; finally, directions on behavioral skills will be given.

One of the most important conditions for establishing harmonious interpersonal relationship is to correctly cognize the self, the communication target and the relationship between the two.

Only can the thorough, objective and correct cognition stimulate emotional experience and enhance the enthusiasm for action. Teachers may improve the interpersonal relationship between students via such cognitive and behavioral changes so as to improve their psychological suzhi in respect of communications.

## 3) Strategies of Computer-Assisted Training Modes

The computer assisted mode is implemented with certain psychological suzhi-based education strategies, including:

*Activity-based strategies.* This mode adopts the interactive "treasure hunt" activity, which focuses on the harmonious interaction between students and the computer. Teachers may teach students through lively activities and integrate puzzles, teaching and games together to enhance students' learning interest and thirst for knowledge. In addition, teachers should, during the teaching process, ensure the exchange and communications between students and the computer. It is neither the rigid display of computers, nor the aimless reflection of students; instead, it should be the harmonious interaction guided by the computer and dominated by students.

*Agent-focused strategies.* The implementation of computer assisted modes is actually a process where students actively participate in the training. It fully manifests the agent-focused principle that "focuses on students". This mode guides, via "simulation trainings", students to make, implement and modify the self-management plan in simulation situations so as to master correct communication skills and behavioral methods via self-control and self management.

*Situation-based strategies.* Creation of situations can make students actively pay attention to the circumstances, stimulate students' will to and interest in learning, make students more active, and enable students to get ready for the learning situations with active attitudes. We strive to create, with flash, music and images and according to the different teaching content, a series of problem situations that can make students think, activate situations that can guide students' activities and psychological situations that can trigger students' emotions in order to enrich students' perceptual materials, further students' cognitive representation and induce reproductive imagination.

### 4) Computer-Assisted Training Modes

According to the psychological suzhi formation process, i.e. "self-cognition, theory-learning, behavioral direction, reflection and internalization and development of habits into nature", proposed by Zhang et al. [Zhang and Tian, 2003], we propose the computer assisted PST modes, "import of situations, change in cognitions, behavioral guide and reflection and summarization".

*Import of situations:* The topic of a certain lesson is given by introducing experiences of the protagonist or the people around by means of flash, music, images, commentary etc. Or by telling stories as if students were personally on the scene. This can make the teaching content closer to the daily life, cause emotional resonance, trigger students' psychological activities, trigger students' curiosity and interest in the content and guide students to learn the content.

*Change in cognitions:* Students are guided, by means of questions and examinations, to make self-reflection and self-analysis via association of ideas and thinking via transposition in order to correct the original incorrect cognitions, establish correct concept and promote their self-development. If students are made to think by answering such questions as "What should the protagonist do", they are also think for themselves by giving advice to others. In addition, self-reflection is also a process of reflecting their own cognitions even though no ideas are concluded.

*Behavioral guide:* as the main component of computer-assisted training modes, it adopts the strategies of mode demonstration and role transposition, takes the content in different forms as the carrier, make students think the aforesaid question and give students various instructive advices on behavior. We should introduce each skill in accordance with the principle of "cognition first, behavior second". Teachers should first change students' cognition and then tell them what and how to do to give detailed advice on behavior.

*Reflection and summarization: teachers* end the lesson with music, songs, poems and flash and deepen the theme of the lesson with aphorisms, short poems or classical stories so that students may understand the general ideas. It is to bring out the crucial point.

Each lesson goes following the aforesaid mode generally, but the mode may also vary for specific lesson. The introduction of skills all begins from cognition and then the behavior.

According to the aforesaid computer-assisted training modes, we develop the computer-assisted software following the mode of "writing of script, development of software, evaluation of experts, modification, feedback from students, re-modification, and evaluation by experts", and take it as the research tool during following experiments to verify the effectiveness and feasibility of such computer-assisted modes.

## Effectiveness of Computer-Assisted Training Modes

The psychological suzhi-based education for students is multi-dimensional and multi-level. It should be conducted based on different psychological quality of students, which is one of the basic starting points of psychological suzhi-based education. The research proves that the parent, the teacher and the classmate are the most important factors for the psychological suzhi-based education and students' development.

Therefore, it is of crucial significance for developing corresponding psychological suzhi of students to study the interpersonal communications between students and the aforesaid three. We have designed the educational experiment in this research based on the three factors on interpersonal communication and verified the feasibility and effectiveness of computer-assisted training modes.

The theoretical analysis and experiments on computer-assisted training modes both show that the modes can be used as the new means for cultivating students' psychological suzhi.

The reasons include: a) computer-assisted modes can fully demonstrate the idea of psychological suzhi-based education on a theoretical basis, which satisfies the requirements for psychological suzhi-based education; b) the content of software is designed in accordance with the students' ages and growth demands, is close to students' daily life and features situations and simulation by means of multimedia. In addition, compared with other psychological suzhi cultivation modes and existing psychological suzhi-based education software, computer-assisted training modes also feature the following:

*More situation-based.* Compared with other psychological suzhi-based education modes frequently used at present, including psychological specific-problem-based training lessons, psychological consultation and counseling and subject infiltration, the computer-assisted modes feature vivid situations. The modes strive to, by means of the technical advantages of computers, create vivid situations for communications as much as possible with music, flash etc. in order to enable students feel the communication situation, obtain communication knowledge and skills and experiencing the pleasure of communications during watching the flash. Finally, students will form stable psychological suzhi for communications and this is difficult for other psychological suzhi-based education modes to achieve this effect.

*Systematic approaches.* Some resources for psychological suzhi-based education on the Internet presently do not run very well due to the simple content and limited functions. There still lacks a scientific and systematic psychological suzhi-based education system with complete functions. We have built up a more scientific computer-assisted mode and developed a series of psychological suzhi-based education software based on this mode to effectively cultivate and educate the students on their psychological suzhi. In respect of certain suzhi, we will train the students on a multi-aspect basis, which demonstrates a systematic approach.

*Psychology-focused.* Most of the persons responsible for researching psychological suzhi-based education software presently are computer technicians and educational professionals [Wu, 2000; Wang, 2000; Song, 2002], and they always develop software from the technical perspective. However, the most important thing for the training is the content and the thought, while the technique is just a tool for implementation. The psychological suzhi-based education software we develop based on computer-assisted modes combines the psychology-focused training content and the technical support from computer technicians. The computer is just a tool for implementation and the core of the software is still the psychological suzhi-based education content.

*Highly operational* the content of existing psychological suzhi-based education software always focuses on the introduction of psychological knowledge or assessment of psychological suzhi. It involves less psychological training and the software just simply gives some advice-based knowledge. On the contrary, the software developed based on the computer-assisted modes we build is highly operational. It focuses on the behavioral direction for students and provides practical skills for them so that students may directly apply the knowledge and skills they have learned from the software to their daily life.

## AESTHETIC-ACTIVITY-BASED MODES AND IMPLEMENTATION STRATEGIES

The mental health education mode is the connection between mental health education theories and practice. Many researchers have proposed various unique mental health education modes from different perspectives and based on different theories and educational approaches in order to enable mental health education theories to better guide the mental health education practice. We found during the exploration of aesthetic psychological process that the aesthetic activity has positive effect on mental health. Therefore, we propose the "aesthetic-activity-based modes for psychological suzhi cultivation" that integrates aesthetic activities with mental health education.

### Connotation and Characteristics of Aesthetic-Activity-Based Modes

The aesthetic activity is a unique social phenomenon of human beings. The aesthetic activity is a process where the agents obtain the spiritual enjoyment and enlightenment via the feeling and experience of their sense organs. The aesthetic-activity-based mode for psychological suzhi cultivation is a kind of mental health education practice that aims to, with the form and content of arts, help students to achieve mental health by developing students' psychological suzhi in aesthetic activities. This mode includes the target system, content system, implementation approaches and organization and management system of aesthetic-appreciation-based mental health education.

There are both connections and differences between aesthetic-appreciation-based v modes and traditional art therapy modes focusing on mental problems. The connection is that both of them conduct psychological intervention by means of arts. The difference includes: 1) the goals are different. The goal of aesthetic-appreciation-based mental health education is more comprehensive. It focuses on developing all students' psychological suzhi, aims at removing the mental disorder and, especially, strives to prevent mental disorder and to promote students' development. On the contrary, the art therapy mode is only to solve mental problems.

As Sandra Griffiths ever said, "arts in health is quite different from art therapy. The art therapy is an old traditional science and it is used to treat the patient with severe and long-term mental health problems and used for adjuvant therapy of traumas. Arts in health can be used in a much wider range than the art therapy and it is always related with the sound development and reconstruction of communities." [Griffith, 2005]. The functioning mechanism is different. The functioning mechanism of aesthetic activities focuses on aesthetic appreciation, emotional resonance and active experiencing, while that of the art therapy focuses on release and catharsis.

Compared with other mental health education modes, the aesthetic-activity-based mode features: 1) development. Aesthetic-activity-based modes aim at developing positive psychological traits and focus on developing individual's psychological suzhi and potentials; 2) amusement. Aesthetic-activity-based modes emphasize that students' active emotional experience should be triggered by aesthetic characteristics of the art so that students will feel psychological satisfaction and psychological security and then achieve active development. 3) Initiative. It attracts students to actively participate in artistic activities by the beauty of art, and make them devoted into the artistic situation so as to improve their psychological suzhi and help them to achieve mental health.


## Basis for Aesthetic-Activity-Based Modes

### 1) Theoretical Basis

### 1) Sublimation and Catharsis of Arts and the Theory of Share and Satisfaction of the School of Psychoanalysis

Freud is the founder of the school of psychoanalysis. He regards the art as the important means to sublimate and make catharsis of the Id force so as to achieve mental health. Freud believes that the personality consists of Id, ego and super-ego. Id has a huge instinctive power on a subconscious basis, most of which are sexual instincts. People's instinctive behavior is driven by happiness, which always conflicts with the reality, so it is suppressed by super-ego that represents social morality. This makes instinctive desires unrealizable and causes mental health problems or even mental illness of human beings. Freud believes that the art is a kind of "sublimation" that enables human beings to release instinctive drives. The art makes such instinctive drives released via a sublimated form acceptable to the society, which not only make instinctive drives released, but also lightens the psychological and mental burden of too depressed appreciators and creators. It is helpful for maintaining the mental health.

The school of neo-psychoanalysis also attaches great importance to the positive effect of the art on people's mental health and has expressly proposed the theory of share and satisfaction of the collective art. Fromm, an important representative of the school of neo-psychoanalysis, believes that human being's mental illness and social disease should be treated in accordance with the same principle and emphasizes the significance of collective art to human being's mental health from the perspective of social development. Fromm distinguishes the collective art from the art. He believes that "collective art" includes all kinds of artistic activities and ceremonies, and that we will, by means of senses, feel the world in a meaningful, skillful, constructive, active and shared manner. Share is extremely important in case of collective art. It may enable us to feel integrated with others in a meaningful and constructive situation. Fromm holds that collective art is not anyone's pastime in his/her "spare time", but a component of the life. It should be consistent with people's fundamental demands; if such demands cannot be satisfied, people may feel uneasy and anxious and they cannot understand the essence of the world. Fromm also emphasizes the significance of collective art to the health of the youth and the society. He said, when the youth cannot participate in meaningful and shared artistic activities, what else can they do? What can they do in addition to excessive drinking, daydreaming, committing a crime and suffering neuropathy or mental illness? If we fail to reach a consensus on human being's existence and we have no common art and ceremonies, what is the use even if there is no illiterate and the higher education is unprecedentedly popularized? [Fromm, 1989] It follows that Fromm regards collective art as the important means to help people to achieve mental health and then realize social health.

## 2) Maslow's Theory on Psychological Satisfaction of Aesthetic Appreciation and Artistic Functions of Peak Experience

Maslow, a humanistic psychologist, divides human's need into five levels, including physiological needs, safety and security needs, love and belonging needs, esteem needs and self-actualization needs. He focuses on the research of the need for self-actualization. He describes self-actualization as a person's need to be and do that which the person was "born to do". Maslow has listed the characteristics of the people who have achieved self-actualization, among which such characteristics as unceasing update of appreciation, creativeness, independence and peak experience are common in the course of artistic creation and aesthetic appreciation. Maslow also believes that human's higher level need contains the need for aesthetic appreciation. He has found that such need is even strong for someone. His early research on students proved that the environment will cause effect on students [Goble, 1987]. Maslow found human's peak experience during the research on self-actualization. The peak experience appears when humans stay in the optimum state and feel awe, a strong sense of happiness, overjoyed, perfect or gratified. The "full functioning" mentioned by Rogers during the treatment is exactly the peak experience. Maslow holds that the people reaching the peak will not only feel himself/herself better, more persistent and integrated, but also regard the world more beautiful, unified and more realistic. He can thus better understand the reality and himself/herself. Maslow believes, via the analysis, that the peak experience has the following verifiable psychological effect [Maslow, 1987]: a) it can have and indeed has some curative effect in the strict sense and can perpetually remove the mental illness; b) it can change an individual's views on himself/herself on a healthy basis; c) it can change an individual's views on others and on the relationship between him/her and others in many ways; d) it can more or less change an individual's views on the world or on some part(s) of the world; e) it can emancipate an individual to make him/her more creative, active and unique and have better expression ability; f) humans often take such experience as an important and satisfactory event, keep it in mind and strive to repeat such experience; g) an individual will be more likely to feel that the life is generally worthwhile, even if the life is boring, painful or unsatisfactory, because he/she has found the beauty, the excitation, the honesty, the frolic, the truth, the goodness and the meaning of life. He believes that the peak experience may appear during aesthetic appreciation, especially appreciation of classic music, stimulation of passion and inspiration, realization of truth, athletic contests or dancing. Maslow's theory demonstrates that aesthetic appreciation may help human to achieve self-actualization, satisfy human's aesthetic need and put humans into peak experience so as to promote humans' mental health.

### 3) Gardner's Theory of Multiple Intelligence

In view of the defects of traditional intelligence theory, Gardner proposed the theory of multiple intelligence. He viewed intelligence as "the capacity to solve problems or to fashion products that are valued in one or more cultural setting". [Gardner, 1985] The core of intelligence is the capability to solve actual problems and the creativity. In respect of the structure of intelligence, Gardner believed that human's intelligence consists of eight different intelligences independent from each other: verbal-linguistic intelligence, logical-mathematical intelligence, visual-spatial intelligence, bodily-kinesthetic intelligence, musical-rhythmic intelligence, interpersonal intelligence, self-questioning intelligence and naturalist intelligence. Gardner's theory of multiple intelligence closely connects the intelligence with artistic ability. a) Creativity is not only the core of intelligence, but also one of the two elements of art, the creativity and the skill to perform the creativity; b) Gardner believes that at least 4 of the aforesaid 8 intelligences, i.e. verbal-linguistic intelligence, musical-rhythmic intelligence, visual-spatial intelligence and bodily-kinesthetic intelligence, are directly related with the art, and are the basic elements of such arts as music, visual arts and literary and artistic creation; c) Gardner also believes that each of the aforesaid 8 intelligences may lead, during its application, to the results of artistic thinking, i.e. Creativity and expressive force, because the symbol representing each kind of the intelligences may, but not has to, be arranged on an aesthetic basis. Gardner's theory paves a theoretical foundation for promoting art education, developing human's intelligence with arts and helping humans to achieve overall development. The USA's "Arts Promotion Program" is mainly made on this theoretical basis.

### 2) Basis for Practice and Experiments

People in western countries always attach great importance to the effect of music and other arts on mental health. A large number of articles on applying music therapy to pediatric therapy have been published since the 1980s, and many documents have described the prospect of music therapy from the general sense and the therapeutic process in specific cases.

Clinicians have described how the music therapy is applied to improve the preschool-age children's motives and the development of their sociality, as well as the therapeutic process and methods for diverting one's attention to positive stimulus so as to get rid of the unfamiliar environment and the pain [Colwell, Davis and Schroeder, 2005]. Semenza explained the comprehensive functions of arts on mental health with an example [Clift, 2002]. He reported that a gathering place was built in Portland, Oregon, USA, where a huge sunflower was painted at the intersection and unique interactive arts were installed around. This stimulated residents' sense of happiness and resulted in sound social development. The World Health Organization has ever, based on extensive investigation, put forward that the quality of life consists of four dimensions, including environmental, social relationship, mental health and physiological health, each of which may be subdivided into several items. White firmly believes, based on theoretical examination and large quantity of qualitative evidence, that the participation in art-related work will influence all of the four dimensions, especially the items of the quality of mental health [White, 2004].

Colwell also found during the research that the art of painting and music can remarkably improve the teenager patients' self-concept [Colwell, Davis and Schroeder, 2005].

The potential effect of participation in artistic activities on mental health has drawn extensive attentions in recent years and the art has been used as a tool for improving the mental health. The UK thinks highly of the healthy functions of the art. It established in Manchester "the National Centre for Information on the Arts in Health Care" as early as 1988, and the British authority highly appreciated the effect of aesthetic activities on health education in the health education report for the year of 1999. The report mentioned that the Community Arts Promotion Program was progressing well and the intervention of arts enhanced human's sense of health and well-being [Semenza, 2003].

Chinese scholars have discussed a lot on the psychological effect of aesthetic education during the research on psychology of aesthetic education. Guo and other scholars believe that the aesthetic education also cause psychological effect of intellectual education, in addition to the "psychological effect of aesthetic appreciation", via the transfer of aesthetic ability structure. It may cause the effect on mental health and moral education etc. Via "transferring" effect of personality, external effect and aesthetic concept structure effect [Zhou, 2005].

The effect of aesthetic education on mental health demonstrates, from the perspective of aesthetic education, that the aesthetic appreciation can improve the mental health. Zhou and Guo have ever made experiments to study the effect of music appreciation on college students' depression symptoms. It showed that music appreciation can remarkably relieve college students' depression symptoms and other psychological symptoms. [Zhou, 2005] This also proved that it is effective to use arts to improve students' mental health.

The aforesaid experiments and exploration further showed that: the art has comprehensive functions for mental health; it can not only conduct traditional treatment, but also realize prevention and development; it is feasible to establish aesthetic-activity-based modes for mental health education and conduct aesthetic-appreciation-based mental health education so as to achieve all goals of mental health education.

### 3) The Mental Health Values of Arts Should Be Explored for the Development of Mental Health Education From an Objective Perspective

The modern school mental health education emerged in the USA and the mental health education in the USA is still well ahead of that in other countries up to now. Let's take the mental health education in the USA as an example to explain the objective need of mental health education for exploring the mental health values of arts. The school mental health services in the USA began with psychological consultation and counseling. The immigration, industrialization and urbanization from the end of the 19th century to the beginning of the 20th century caused a series of social problems for the USA, including students' puzzle on their career and the mental and behavioral problems during their study that were increasingly urgent. Psychological counseling emerged in the early 20th century to solve such problems.

The targets and goals of psychological consultation and counseling are increasing unceasingly along with the development in all aspects. Meanwhile, other mental health intervention modes, in addition to psychological consultation and counseling, have been also developed. The words "school mental health education" are applied to school education more frequently.

Compared with the past psychological consultation and counseling, the present mental health education is more focusing on the improvement of all students' psychological suzhi and the exploration of students' psychological potential.

For example, according to the "Task for Middle School Counselors" made by the American School Counselor Association, the development-oriented guide is a part of the guiding task and such guide is striving to conduct intervention on students' growth positively with well-prepared plans so as to promote students' development in the individual, social, emotional, livelihood, moral, cognitive and aesthetic aspects and integrate such development with their life style.

The school mental health education also includes many other mental health intervention modes in addition to psychological consultation and counseling. Presently, the mental health intervention measures adopted in the USA can be divided into three categories [Xiao, 2005]: (1) direct intervention for individuals. The mental health education personnel directly adopts different effective measures based on conditions of individual students to ensure their mental health.

It is generally conducted by means of classroom teaching, counseling and psychological outpatient service; (2) indirect intervention by environment (also called ecological intervention). The school mental health education personnel takes various methods, including adjusting the curricula and conducting intervention on teachers, school personnel and parents, to improve the environment surrounding the individuals and then create a positive living and study environment for them; (3) integrated intervention.

The mental health education personnel integrates various intervention together, including mental health intervention, educational assistance and social assistance, to conduct comprehensive intervention in students in many aspects. Educators are exploring new intervention means, while still using traditional intervention as the important intervention means, to improve the effect of mental health education.

The effect of psychological environment and physical environment to students' mental health will draw more and more attention, and either the ecological intervention or the integrated intervention will achieve significant development.

Such artistic means as music have been widely applied to the past psychotherapy. Along with the expansion of mental health education goals and development of intervention modes, the art will not be applied to psychotherapy only; it will be applied more and more to the psychological service for maintaining mental health and developing psychological suzhi.

Art-based intervention will become the important intervention mode for mental health education. Therefore, the objective need for the development of mental health education is to establish aesthetic-activity-based modes mental health education, perform the functions of arts in mental health education and follow the development tendency of mental health education.

## Analysis on Effect of Aesthetic Activities to Mental Health

The art improves individual's psychological suzhi mainly by stimulating positive emotional experience during aesthetic appreciation. There are different theories on the mechanisms underlie which arts stimulate emotions.

Arnheim, a Gestalt psychologist, believes according to the "heterogeneous homogeneity" theory that the art, as a field of force, can stimulate emotions and experience of relevant aesthetic appreciation [Guo and Zhao, 1998]; humanistic psychologist Maslow believes that the art may stimulate human's positive emotions via satisfying human's demands for aesthetic appreciation, self-actualization and peak experience; according to the theory on "accumulation of aesthetic psychology" of humanism, certain art may stimulate corresponding emotions by acting on the "physiological and psychological structure of aesthetic appreciation" that forms due to historic reasons and is common in the human society.

The positive emotion caused will remain during the activities of mind to provide helpful cognitive background for processing human's cognition and enhance the efficiency of cognition processing; it strengthens individuals' willpower as the component and source of the will; it can make an individual feel the world more beautiful and thus change his/her world view and outlook on life if he/she observes the circumstances with such positive emotion.

Such functions of the emotion related to cognition, will and personality will further improve individuals' mental health. The mental health of an individual in a group will also definitely improve his/her adaptability to interpersonal communications so that the whole group may achieve harmonious relationship and mental health.

In addition, aesthetic appreciation can help individuals achieve mental health either by stimulating positive emotions or by releasing the negative depressed mood. Freud, founder of the school of psychoanalysis, regards the art as a sublimation method to release the negative emotion caused when instinctive drives in Id are suppressed by super-ego. Individuals can maintain mental health by the sublimation-oriented catharsis of the art.

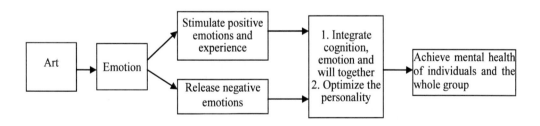

Figure 1.2. The Mechanism of Aesthetic Appreciaiton Influence Mental Health.

## Aesthetic-Activity-Based Modes and Implementation Strategies

Chinese and foreign scholars have different opinions on components of educational modes. Generally speaking, they believe that one should determine and well plan the target and goal, implementer or organizer, content, approach and method of such education to build a mode. Therefore, we preliminarily build the aesthetic-activity-based mode for mental health education that consists of four parts: the goal system, the content system, the implementation approach and the organization and management system.

## 1) Goal

The aesthetic-activity-based mode for mental health education has three goals. a) Treat mental disorder. This is targeted at a few students with remarkable mental disorder to treat their mental disorder by artistic means. The research in foreign countries has showed that approximately 20% of the students have the mental disorder to different extent. This is similar to the result of the research in China.

According to a report by the former State Education Commission of the People's Republic of China in 1989, the sample survey on the 126,000 college students across China showed that as many as 20.23% of such college students suffered mental illness [Kong and Jiang et al., 1998].

Suicide and violence often occur on campus presently and the status quo of students concerns us a lot. Students' present psychological suzhi shows that mental health education should continue the concern and treatment of students' mental disorder.

Therefore, we should take the treatment of students' mental disorder as one of the goals of aesthetic-activity-based modes. According to our survey, students' mental disorder includes anxiety, depression, phobia, apathism, mania etc. Aesthetic activities can, to certain extent, relieve or solve such mental health problems. Thus, removal of mental disorder can also be the goal of the aesthetic-activity-based modes for mental health education. b) prevent mental problems.

It is targeted at some students likely to suffer mental problems and takes the art as the important intervention means to keep them away from mental problems. The research and practice of education have proved that many students, in addition to a few students with mental disorder, are still in a sub-healthy condition.

Such students will, if this fact is ignored, be much likely to suffer mental disorder, so aesthetic-activity-based modes should attach great importance of this goal. Similarly, the art can also be helpful to achieve this prevention-oriented goal.

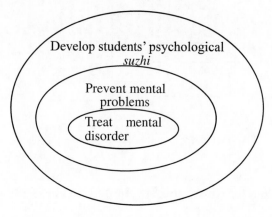

Figure 1.3. Three Goals of Aesthetic-Activity-Based Modes for mental health education.

The artistic environment can create a beautiful physical environment for students to provide students with aesthetic experience, change students' mental state and enhance students' resistance against psychological contradiction and conflicts; aesthetic activities may help students to release and overcome their inner suppression and prevent such mental problems as depression and anxiety; successful participation in aesthetic activities and the creation during aesthetic activities can improve students' self-confidence and enhance students' frustration tolerance. c) Develop students' psychological suzhi. This is to conduct aesthetic-appreciation-based mental health care on all students in order to improve all students' psychological suzhi. We should, during aesthetic activities, satisfy students' demands for aesthetic appreciation with artistic beauty, help students to realize the self-worth and achieve self-actualization, put students into peak experience with artistic beauty, develop students' creativity and explore their potential.

The indivisible three goals constitute the 3-tiered system of goals of aesthetic-appreciation-based mental health education. The first goal to treat mental disorder is targeted at a few students, but this does not mean that such students have no potential mental problem and do not need any development. Therefore, the students with mental disorder are also the target of the second and the third goals.

Similarly, some students likely to suffer mental problems are the major target of the second goal, but we should also promote their development with arts at the time of prevention. Thus the target of the second goal is also that of the third goal. The third goal should not be only targeted at the students suffering no mental problem or potential mental problem, but also at those suffering or likely to suffer mental problems.

It follows that the third goal is target at all students and is at the highest level; the second goal is next to the third goal and is in the middle of the three goals; the first goal is only targeted at a few students suffering mental disorder and is at the lowest level. Please see Figure 1-3 for the relation between the three goals.

## 2) Content

The content of aesthetic-appreciation-based mental health education can, according to the type of arts, be divided into music appreciation, fine arts appreciation, literary appreciation, dance appreciation and drama and film appreciation.

Music appreciation is to cultivate students with the melody, rhythm, harmony, polyphony, musical form and orchestration of the music to provide them with aesthetic experience. The music is an art that demonstrates human's thoughts and reflects the real life with continuous and well-structured sound, including the music performed by one or more singers and that produced by musical instruments, i.e. the vocal music and the instrumental music. The basic components of music are the melody, the rhythm, the harmony, the polyphony, the musical form and the orchestration.

Fine arts appreciation is to cultivate students with the beauty of fine arts to provide them with aesthetic experience. The fine art is an art to create, with certain materials and by means of designing and shaping, the visual matters that show certain sense of space and aesthetic value. It includes applied fine art, such as industrial art, decoration, dyeing and weaving, clothing design, architecture, landscape architecture, environment and other design-oriented arts related with the fine art, painting, such as traditional Chinese painting, engraving and oil painting, sculpture, such as free-standing sculpture and relief, as well as photography, calligraphy and seal cutting. The fine art is to create artistic images by design-oriented means. The aesthetic appreciation characteristics of the fine art are demonstrated via the formal beauty of the combination of color, lines, form and structure, light and shade and space etc. Which is consistent with the law and the goal. From the perspective of acceptance, the formal beauty of fine arts is related with the agent's physiological and psychological feelings.

Literary appreciation is to cultivate students with the figures, events and matters created by literature to provide them with aesthetic experience. The literature, including poems, novels and prose, is an art that uses linguistic symbols as the medium to create figures, express feelings and thoughts and deliver aesthetic reflection of the social life. The literature creates, with language, vivid figures originated from our life, and the reader understands such figures via imagination with the help of language.

Dance appreciation is to cultivate students with excellent rhythm, tempo and dressing in respect of the dance to provide them with aesthetic experience. Dance is an art that takes human body as the medium to express thoughts and feelings and reflect the social life via organizing regulated movements with good rhythm and tempo and well dressed dancers. The dancers' dressing and the movement may both stimulate individual's aesthetic feelings or specific emotions.

Drama and film appreciation is to cultivate students with the art of dramas and films to provide them with aesthetic experience. Either the drama or the film is the comprehensive art that integrates many artistic factors, including music, fine art, literature and dance. They tell stories, reveal the social and natural environment, portray character's personality and disclose character's psychological activities via the situation. It can enrich an individual's knowledge, cause complex emotional experience and improve his/her sentiments to appreciate dramas and films.

### 3) Implementation Approach

*Approach I:* launch artistic class. The artistic class integrates aesthetic-appreciation-based mental health education with artistic curricula to enhance students' capability of aesthetic appreciation and creativity of beauty via the teaching of artistic curricula and improve the effect of arts on students; it can stimulate students' interest in the art and make them actively participate in the artistic activities; it provides students with aesthetic experience during the teaching so as to improve their mental health.

*Approach II:* establish mental-health-oriented art club to conduct mental-health-oriented activities. Such clubs can, according to the different types of arts, be divided into mental-health-oriented painting club, mental-health-oriented calligraphy club, mental-health-oriented performance club, mental-health-oriented drama club and mental-health-oriented film club. They can also, according to the appreciation and creation of arts, be divided into mental-health-oriented art hobby and appreciation club and mental-health-oriented art hobby and creation club. Mental-health-oriented art clubs are similar to but also different from art clubs. The two both focus on art as their content and conduct artistic activities, but their goals are different. The final goal of the former one is to achieve mental health and promote psychological development, while the latter one is for the purpose of artistic appreciation and creation. For example, some colleges have established psychodrama clubs and drama clubs which are two types of clubs with different goals. Mental-health-oriented art clubs are mainly established in colleges and universities, but the qualified middle and primary schools may also established unique mental-health-oriented art clubs according to the actual conditions.

However, the mental-health-oriented art clubs in all colleges and universities do not develop very well presently, and the schools should, based on their capabilities, actively establish mental-health-oriented art clubs, such as mental-health-oriented drama clubs, mental-health-oriented film appreciation clubs and mental-health-oriented music appreciation clubs. Mental-health-oriented art clubs will launch diversified artistic activities for the purpose of mental health, which will remarkably improve students' mental health.

*Approach III:* launch large mental-health-oriented cultural and artistic activities. The mental-health-oriented cultural and artistic activity here is different from the activity conducted by mental-health-oriented art clubs: the former one is organized by a school or a department, in larger size and with broader influence. Schools and subordinate departments may either conduct mental health education activities by means of various artistic activities, or infiltrate mental health education into artistic activities.

*Approach IV:* conduct group artistic counseling. Group artistic counseling is the important means for mental health education, but general group counseling does not think highly of such artistic means. Mental health education-oriented aesthetic-activity-based modes take the art as the major content and means for group counseling. Group artistic counseling can perform its effect on mental health in two ways: a) Create a counseling environment with the sense of artistic beauty during group artistic counseling so as to enable students to have aesthetic experience when receiving other psychological counseling, imperceptibly influence the students with arts and improve the effect of group counseling in other forms; b) conduct group counseling around artistic appreciation and creation, such as the counseling on appreciation of music and paintings.

*Approach V:* make the physical environment of schools artistic. This approach is to develop the physical environment of schools for the purpose of artistic beauty and make such environment artistic. For example, architectural art and landscape art should be applied to the school development so that the buildings in and the design of the school will be beautiful in an artistic sense. Students can experience the beauty of arts and receive the cultivation of beauty at any time and in any place on an artistic campus so as to keep a happy and healthy mood.

### 4) Organization and Management

The organization and management system of aesthetic-appreciation-based mental health education can be built in two ways. a) Establish aesthetic-appreciation-based mental health education management team or assign a principal subordinate to the original mental health education management organ. For example, there are always school-level mental health education centers in colleges and universities, and a team can be set subordinate to this center to manage the aesthetic-appreciation-based mental health education. A dedicated person or team should also be assigned for the aesthetic-appreciation-based mental health education if there are mental health education management organs in the departments subordinate thereto. b) establish dedicated organs for the school and all departments to organize aesthetic-appreciation-based mental health education. Such dedicated organs may have contact with the school's mental health management organs during the work, but they are not subordinate to the latter. According to the present mental health education management, the first method is more feasible and operational.

No matter which method is adopted, there should be the principal, team or organ in each school for the school-wide aesthetic-appreciation-based mental health education. Such principal, team or organ should be responsible for planning, organizing, directing and managing the school-wide aesthetic-appreciation-based mental health education, establishing the school-wide aesthetic-appreciation-based mental health education groups, assisting all departments or all grades in establishing artistic organizations and clubs and contacting the community's artistic and cultural organizations to form a school-community integrated artistic atmosphere. Large schools or qualified schools should assign dedicated person or establish dedicated team responsible for the aesthetic-appreciation-based mental health education in subordinate departments or organs and for conducting various aesthetic-appreciation-based mental health education activities under the guided and management of superior departments.

## Advices on Implementing Aesthetic-Activity-Based Modes

### *1) Follow the Basic Rules*

Follow the basic rules of educational psychology and developmental psychology concerning students' psychological development and the effective promotion thereof. a) The highest goal of aesthetic-appreciation-based mental health education is to promote students' development, so teachers should, when implementing the mode, follow the basic rules on students' psychological development, such as understanding the characteristics and individual difference of students' psychological development at different stages, and abiding by the rules on the effect of congenital causes and acquired dispositions as well as internal and external causes on students during their psychological development. b) Because aesthetic appreciation activities are causing effect on psychology via aesthetic effect, teachers should follow the rules of educational psychology concerning psychology of aesthetic education, such as the basic law on development of aesthetic psychology and on generation of psychological effect of aesthetic appreciation.

Follow some basic rules of artistic aesthetic psychology, such as following the rules on artistic psychological dynamics to understand how to arouse students' need for arts and stimulate their motivation to participate in artistic activities; following the rules on artistic psychological elements to understand which psychological elements of students will participate in artistic activities and how they are acting; following the rules on artistic creation and appreciation to understand how to improve students' artistic creation and appreciation.

### *2) Exert Students' Initiative*

Effect of aesthetic appreciation on mental health is subject to the precondition that students should experience the beauty of arts in person, release the internal pressure during aesthetic appreciation and experience success in artistic creation. Therefore, teachers should attach great importance to the student's initiative during aesthetic-appreciation-based mental health education and make students actively participate in various aesthetic activities.

### *3) Integrate the Mode with Other Mental Health Education Intervention Modes*

The art may cause remarkable effect on some mental problems, including anxiety and depression, while it can only be used as the auxiliary means in case of other mental problems, including the puzzle on career. The art may even have no effect on certain mental health problems. It follows that it is necessary to integrate artistic intervention with other mental health education intervention measures. As the mental health education intervention modes are becoming integrated today, teachers can never achieve the goal of mental health education with the artistic means only or other certain approach.

### 4) *It is a Complex Task to Establish the Aesthetic-Activity-Based Modes and We Should Be Patient*

It has been recognized for a long time that the art can promote the mental health, but the art is applied extremely infrequently to the mental health education. The theoretical exploration and practical experiences in respect of aesthetic-appreciation-based mental health education are far from enough; it is a long-term task to establish and improve mental-health-oriented art clubs and to select and design the content and form of mental-health-oriented artistic activities; it even needs more time to build up the humanistic artistic environment and physical artistic environment on campus, and this requests the school to make its cultural environment and physical environment more artistic. All of those prove that it is a long-term task to establish the aesthetic-activity-based modes.

### 5) *We Cannot Confuse Aesthetic-Appreciation-Based Mental Health Education with Aesthetic Education or Art Therapy*

Aesthetic education and aesthetic-appreciation-based mental health education both involve some content related with the art, but the former aims to develop students' capabilities of perceiving, experiencing, appreciating and creating the beauty while the latter aims to improve students' mental health via the activities where students will perceive, experience and create the beauty. Art therapy and aesthetic-appreciation-based mental health education both use artistic means to achieve mental health, but the former is only targeted at a few students suffering mental illness to help them overcome the mental disorder, while the latter is targeted at all students to help them overcome the mental disorder and, especially, to prevent the mental disorder and promote students' development. Aesthetic-appreciation-based mental health education can never be replaced with aesthetic education or psychotherapy in practice.

## REFERENCES

Chen, J. L. (2002). *School mental health education-principle and practice*. Beijing: Educational Science Publishing House.

Chen, X., and Zhang, D. J. (2002). Exploration and discussion of integrated modes for mental health education. *Educational research*, (1), 71-75.

Clift, S. (2002). Guess editorial: The arts and health. *Health Education*, 102 (4), 153-155.

Colwell, C. M., Davis, K., and Schroeder, L. K. (2005). The effect of composition (art or music) on the self-concept of hospitalized children. *Journal of music therapy*, 42 (1), 50-51.

Colwell, C. M., Davis, K., and Schroeder, L. K. (2005). The effect of composition (art or music) on the self-concept of hospitalized children. *Journal of music therapy*, (42), 49-63.

Fromm, E. (1988). *The sane society* (Q. Ouyang, Trans.). Beijing: China Federation of Literary and Art Circles Publishing Corporation.

Gardner, H. (1985). Frames of mind: The theory of multiple intelligences. New York: Basic Books.

Goble, F. (1987). *The third force: the psychology of Abraham Maslow* (M. Chang, and H. W. Chen, Trans.). Shanghai: Shanghai Translation Publishing House.

Griffiths, S. (2005). The mental health benefits of arts and creativity for young African and Caribbean men. *The mental health review*, 10 (2), 27-28.

Guo, C., and Zhao, L. L. (1998). Aesthetic education-based psychology: to fill teaching and learning process with aesthetic feelings. Beijing: Police Officer Education Press.

Kong, Y., and Jiang, L. C. et al. (1998). *College students' mental health education*. Hefei: Anhui People's Publishing House.

Liu, H., and Zhang. D. J. (2004). On requirements of psychological suzhi education for teachers' competence. *Journal of Hebei Normal University* (educational science edition), (1), 56.

Maslow, A. (1987). *The person of self-actualization* (J. S. Xu, and F. Liu, Trans.). Beijing: Sdxjoint Publishing Company.

Semenza, J. C. (2003). The intersection of urban planning, art, and public health: The sunnyside piazza. *American journal of public health*, 93 (9), 143-145.

Shao, J. J. Research on developing students' emotional regulation capabilities during the teaching of primary school Chinese. Unpublished master's thesis, Southwest China Normal University, Chongqing, P.R.C.

Song, L. J. Experiments on students' adaptability to the study during the teaching of junior middle school English. Unpublished master's thesis, Southwest China Normal University, Chongqing, P.R.C.

Wang, C. P. Experiments on developing students' study self-efficacy during the teaching of junior middle school mathematics. Unpublished master's thesis, Southwest China Normal University, Chongqing, P.R.C.

White, M. (2004). Arts, mental health and social inclusion. *A life in the day*, 8 (1), 15-19.

Xiao, M. C. (2005). Intervention modes for mental health education in the USA. *Science of Education*, 21 (2), 60-61.

Xu, Y. G. *Experiments on infiltrating self-monitoring into the teaching of primary school mathematics*. Unpublished master's thesis, Southwest China Normal University, Chongqing, P.R.C.

Ye, Y. D. (2004). Several issues on infiltrating mental health education into the teaching of subject. *Journal of the Chinese society of education*, (3), 18-21.

Zhang, D. J. (2000). *Psychological sushi training for students from primary and middle schools* (experimental text book for primary school grade 1 to senior middle school grade 3). Chongqing: Southwest China Normal University Press.

Zhang, D. J. (2001). *Goals and functions of mental health education*. Xinhua digest, (4). Chongqing: Southwest China Normal University Press.

Zhang, D. J. (2004). *On school psychological* suzhi *education*. Chongqing: Southwest China Normal University Press.

Zhang, D. J., and Tian, L. (2003). On design and implementation strategies of psychological suzhi education. *Curriculum, teaching material and method*, (6), 66-70.

Zhang, D. J., Liu, Y. L., and Feng, Z. Z. (2000). Research on psychological suzhi and school achievements of senior middle school students. *Journal of Southwest China Normal University (natural science edition),* 25 (4), 496.

Zhou, Q. (2005). *Experiments on influence of music appreciation on college students' depression symptoms.* Unpublished master's thesis, Southwest China Normal University, Chongqing, P.R.C.

# PART TWO:

# SPECIFIC PROBLEM-BASED TRAINING MODES AND IMPLEMENTATION STRATEGIES

In: Methods and Implementary Strategies on Cultivating ...      ISBN: 978-1-62417-979-2
Editors: Da-Jun Zhang, Jin-Liang Wang, and Lin Yu      © 2013 Nova Science Publishers, Inc.

*Chapter 2*

# TRAINING OF SELF-MONITORING ON COPING WITH FRUSTRATION AMONG JUNIOR MIDDLE SCHOOL STUDENTS

## *Shou-Jun Xiang[1] and Da-Jun Zhang[2]*

[1]Chongqing Science and Technology University, China
[2]Center for Mental Health Education in Southwest University, China

## ABSTRACT

Middle school period is one of the periods with frequent occurrence of frustration, and the students have mental problems to some extent in Coping with Frustration (CWF). Solving frustration untimely may lead to mental disorders. Based on the previous research, this chapter will put forward a CWF theory of general applicability; analyze the variability of CWF and the feasibility of the training on coping skills; and put this theory into practice, i.e., developing an intervention mode based on the self-monitoring capacity to improve the capacity of junior middle school students to cope with frustration, and developing the training concerning the Self-monitoring on coping with frustration (SMOCWF) on the basis of such intervention modes. The education experiment showed that students from junior middle schools had better CWF performance, better CWF styles and higher self-monitoring level after the knowledge imparting and skill training of SMOCWF. The success of this intervention experiment mainly attributes to the all-around and reasonable training contents, accurate orientation of training focus, scientific and effective training modes, scientific training principles, etc. The successful experience may benefit mental health education researchers and educators.

## INTRODUCTION

### Why CWF?

Coping, as the mediator between stress and health, plays an important role in maintaining physical and psychological health. Pelietier put forward in the 1970s that half of human diseases nowadays were related to stress [Zimbardo, 1985]. Coping research was developed with the formation of stress psychology theories in the 1970s. Plenty of research data have been collected in these years and clinic application of coping has been available. Gentry optimistically believed that we were developing the Science of coping [Carter, Bendell et al., 1985]. However, coping research in China was just started and yet has not aroused proper attention from the psychological arena.

Frustration is common nowadays as people face more and more unpredictable and changing challenges due to fierce social competition and fast pace of life. According to Braunstein, there are four stressors [Braunstein and Toister, 1981]: 1) physical stressor, for instance, injuries; 2) psychological stressor, such as contradictions, conflicts and frustration from interpersonal relationship; 3) social stressor, for example, school failure; and 4) cultural stressor. The complicated social life results in higher requirements on people's adaptability and development. High frustration tolerance is an important psychological trait. Therefore, good CWF capacity, as a key condition for adaptability, is an important part of education for all-around development.

It has been shown that middle school students had mental problems to some extent in CWF. According to the survey to 10 key middle schools in Beijing, in "what are your weak points", 60% students thought they "lack perseverance, can not control their own emotions, can not stand frustration" [Xiao, 1997]. Six common frustration situations were designed to test the CWF capacity of junior middle school students: 1) fail an ordinary examination; 2) fail the enrollment examination; 3) be severely criticized by the teacher in front of classmates; 4) disagree with parents; 5) be laughed at by classmates; and 6) fail to realize a progressive desire. The survey showed that about 50% students had irrational reactions towards items 2), 3), 4) and 5); about 40% students had irrational reactions towards items 1) and 6). Researchers classified the said irrational reactions into five categories: inferiority, aggressiveness, anxiety, avoidance and jealousy reactions [Gao and Nie, 1997]. In general, the frustration tolerance of students from junior middle schools and primary schools was low, mainly in three aspects: 1) low frustration endurance. They were psychologically vulnerable, panic, over-anxious, easy to have bad emotions and can not get rid of them; 2) irrational aggressive behaviors, such as negative aggression, violence and over-abreaction; and 3) serious mental diseases due to frustration. A small proportion of students suffer from neurasthenia, phobia, obsessive-compulsive disease (OCD), hypochondria, depressive neurosis and other psychological disorders after serious or successive frustration.

The adolescent period is one of the periods with frequent occurrence of frustration. Middle school students are at puberty. They shoulder a lot of mental and social pressure resulting from dramatic physiological change, unstable psychological development, and heavy academic burden from school. They will have more and stronger needs with the physical and psychological development. But some of their needs can not be met through normal means because their lack of social adaptability and coping ability, as well as timely and correct external education and guidance, which then leads to psychological conflicts that are impossible to be solved.

For example, the needs resulting from sexual maturity conflict with sexual morality and sex education; the sport and entertainment needs are greatly restricted by heavy burden of family and school; their desires for independence, equality, and respect and understanding towards personality are neglected and suppressed; psychological pressure is caused by fiercer competition; psychological contradiction and conflicts in determining their values are caused by diversified social values, concepts and thoughts. To summarize, frustration is in frequent occurrence in middle school stage. Untimely coping of frustration may result in mental disorders.

Ohashi Masao's theories combine psychological development with frustration [Zhou, 1997]. He believed that an individual faces different frustration from infanthood to adulthood. An individual faces more frustration in adolescent period and adulthood. Erikson believed that corresponding problems and conflicts, including frustration, occur in every development stage of an individual.

The effects from solving or treating such problems and conflicts directly influence the development of the next stage. If they are properly solved, the development of the individual in the next stage will be promoted, otherwise, it will be obstructed. The research by Vaillant [1996] showed that significant differences in life and work were As seen among hundreds of subjects after dozens of years. It is because they adopted different coping mechanisms, namely, the individuals, by adopting mature coping mechanisms, can adapt to life and achieve development.

Therefore, the research into CWF among middle school students is significant both theoretically and practically.

## Literature

### 1) Related Concepts

### Frustration

Frustration is a feeling of tension that occurs when the efforts to reach some goals are blocked. It has three implications: a) objective and subjective factors that obstruct the realization of goals, which is the situational factor of a frustration, also called frustration situation; b) the cognition of frustration, namely, the feeling, understanding and assessment of frustration situation; c) response to frustration, which refers to the emotion and behaviors resulted from failure to meet the desires as the individual has the cognition of frustration. Among them, the cognition of frustration is the most important. Frustration situation does not directly relate to the response to frustration. The relationship between the two is determined by the cognition of frustration. The nature and degree of frustration response is mainly determined by the cognition of frustration.

### Stress and CWF

A widely used definition of coping is constantly changing cognitive and behavioral efforts to manage specific external and/or internal demands that are appraised as exceeding the capacity resources of the person [Lazarus and Folkman, 1984]. Billings et al. [1983] believed that coping is the cognitive activity and behavior that assess the significance of stressors, control or change the stress environment, and relieve the emotional reactions caused by stress [Xiao, 1992]. In contemporary scientific literature, stress has at least three distinct meanings [Rice, 2000]. First, it may refer to any event or environmental stimulus that causes a person to feel tense or aroused. In this sense, stress is something external. If stress is deemed external stimulus, it is more proper to call it stressor. Second, stress may refer to a subjective response. In this sense, stress is the internal mental state of tension or arousal. It is the interpretive, emotive, defensive, and coping processes occurring inside a person. Finally, stress may be the body's physical reaction to demand or damaging intrusions. Demand promotes a natural arousal of the body to a higher level of activity.

Either from the above meanings of stress or Braunstein's classification of stressors, it can be concluded that stress is the sub-topic of stress, thus the theories of stress are also applicable to frustration research.

Therefore, CWF can be defined as the cognitive activity and behavior that assess the significance of the sources of frustration, control or change the frustration environment, and relieve the emotional reactions caused by frustration.

Frustration tolerance

From dynamic-static psychological dimensions, we believe frustration tolerance is a type of psychological quality (or suzhi in Chinese), a stable psychological characteristics and the goal of cultivation. CWF, however, is dynamic. The development of students' capacity to tolerate frustration must be started from the specific process of CWF. Feng [1991] believed that frustration tolerance includes frustration endurance and capacity to overcome frustration. Frustration endurance is the level of an individual's ability to withstand the tension and pressure from frustration and to develop proper emotions and behaviors. The capacity to overcome frustration is the level of an individual's ability to directly adjust and transform the frustration, positively change the frustration situation and release from the state of frustration.

The differences between frustration endurance and the capacity to overcome frustration lie in that 1) frustration endurance is the passive adaptation to frustration, namely, tolerance, acceptance and accommodation. The typical characteristics is passiveness; however, the capacity to overcome frustration is the active adaptation to frustration, namely, adjustment, improvement, overcoming. It is featured by activeness. 2) Frustration endurance implies the ability to withstand frustration; the capacity to overcome frustration reflects the ability to change the frustration situation. 3) Frustration endurance implies to accept the reality and reduce the degree of emotional response; the capacity to overcome frustration is to change the current situation and strive for success.

Accordingly, there are problem-focused and emotion-focused coping strategies. Folkman and Lazarus [1980/1984] believed that people tend to use two main coping strategies: problem-focused and emotion-focused copings. Problem-focused coping is efforts to deal with the cause of the stress.

An individual using problem-focused strategy tries to change the consequence of the stress by dealing with the cause of such stress. Emotion-focused coping is efforts to change the emotional state of an individual caused by stress. People using emotion-focused strategy try to get rid of the influence of stress by changing the emotional state. Hilgard et al. also proposed similar opinions that an individual encountering frustration may employ defense or coping strategy.

Coping strategy is to change the situations causing anxiety; whereas defense strategy is to reduce the anxious emotions by using various defense mechanisms. In this sense, "defense strategy" is "emotion-focused coping" while "coping strategy" is "problem-focused coping".

## 2) Domestic and International Research

### International Research into Frustration

The international research into frustration in the recent decade is mainly to:

Probe into the factors that influence frustration and responses to frustration;

Physiologic factors, for example, different feelings of frustration between female and male and among different ages, disability and frustration, etc.; Psychological factors, for example, the influences of students' temperament, character, state and trait anxiety over frustration; different performance in coping with school frustration among genius, students with poor academic achievements and average boys, etc.; Social factors: the influence of organizations and entities' controlling points on individual's emotional and behavioral reactions in frustration; the relationship between frustration and social and economic status; the relationship between peer comparison and frustration, etc.

Probe into the factors influencing frustration endurance;

For example, the influence of physiologic factors, personality variables, environmental factors, such as noise and music on frustration endurance.

Continue to improve, supplement, verify and re-build frustration-aggression theory.

For example, they put forward some new methods to illustrate frustration-aggression theory; probed into the relationship between medicine, tranquillizer, alcohol and frustration-aggression; conducted comprehensive research and probed into the influence of age, gender, social and economic status, personality, intelligence and school achievements over the types and directions of frustration-aggression; probed into the relationship between frustration-aggression and conflicts of cultural values, cultural deprivation, etc.

### Research into Frustration in China

Research into frustration and coping among students from middle schools in China is mainly to:

Understand where the frustration of middle school students comes from;

Sun [1986] found that study, inter-person relationship, interest and desires, self-esteem, etc. are the main sources of frustration among students from junior middle schools. According to the survey, students faced more frustration in study, and the frustration frequency and number of students who encountered frustration are different from grades to grades. According to the survey and research, teenagers' stress in daily life mainly comes from study, for example, examination failure, heavy study burden and academic pressure [Liu, Yang et al., 1998].

Know how middle school students cope with frustration;

Huang et al. [2000] surveyed 1,254 students from middle schools and found that Chinese students mainly use problem-solving, help-seeking, withdrawal, abreaction and fantasy to cope with frustration and troubles; girls use more abreaction and tolerance than boys, whereas boys use more fantasy copings; students from key junior middle schools use more problem-solving copings than fantasy and withdrawal copings; there is no distinct difference in the choosing of coping styles as the students grow older.

Propose ideas and suggestions in CWF education among students from middle schools.

Many books about mental health have special chapters on frustration theories and also put forward specific methods to cope with frustration. For example, *Frustration Psychology* by Feng, *On Frustration Education* by Li and Bian deeply probe into frustration, CWF, education on frustration, etc. We read the domestic literature about psychology and pedagogy, and found that articles about the frustration education for teenagers were frequently reported in the recent decade. Those articles emphasize on the importance and urgency about CWF education and also present relevant theories. The assumption about "psychological vaccination" training [Jiang, 1998] has significant value for this experiment.

## Domestic and International CWF Research

To summarize, domestic and international CWF research has the following characteristics:

More analysis on the problem itself (the principles, contents and methods of CWF training), less on intervention training;

More introductions on specific CWF methods and less perfect theories;

The CWF research mostly focuses on general cognition rather than metacognition;

More attention paid to post-frustration coping while proactive coping is neglected (This problem was noticed by some psychologists out of China. The concept of anticipatory coping and corresponding theoretical modes were put forward and are mentioned in the theoretical basis of the experiment in this chapter);

According to the prior theoretical research, the functions and roles of self-monitoring have been noticed; however, no further theoretical research into the composition of self-monitoring is available; and

In most research into frustration, teenagers are regarded as sufferer and various factors influencing CWF of teenagers are analyzed; however, the nature of teenagers as agent in SMOCWF is neglected.

## The Problems to Be Solved in this Chapter

Based on the prior research findings, this chapter aims to: first, explore a CWF theory of general applicability. First, this chapter integrates the CWF knowledge and methods; second, it discusses the possibility for students to master the basic CWF skills within limited training time.

The goals of experimental training should be that to improve the initiative among teenagers on the basis that they have mastered certain CWF knowledge and skills, in order to improve their capacity to cope with frustration and improve the effectiveness of coping.

Second, turn the theoretical assumption into education practice, and verify and improve the theories in practice; turn the declarative knowledge such as theoretical methods into the skills of teenagers, systemize self-monitoring knowledge and skills, create self-monitoring procedures, make students skillfully master self-monitoring knowledge and realize automatic self-monitoring.

Therefore this chapter chooses training experiment as the basic means, makes better SMOCWF among students from junior middle schools as the goals of and the theoretical supports for the training, puts forward the compositions of SMOCWF skills, and tries to realize sequenced, systematic and operable CWF methods by building SMOCWF theory.

# THEORIES AND TRAINING MODES

## Theories of Self-Monitoring on Coping with Frustration

### 1) Theoretical Basis

Coping with frustration is variable and the training on coping skills is feasible in the following four aspects:

**Definition of CWF.** Coping is constantly changing cognitive and behavioral efforts to manage (including endurance, relieving, avoidance, etc) external and/or internal demands that are appraised as taxing or exceeding the adaptability of the person. This definition has two characteristics: first, it regards coping as a process. It focuses on what people think, what they do in stressful events, as well as the changes in their thinking and behavior in the course of the event. Such process-oriented opinion contrasts sharply with the trait concept. The latter focuses on how people normally behave, and emphasizes on stability rather than the course of changing. Second, coping is related to situations. How an individual assesses the importance of an event and his/her adaptability to such event influence how such individual copes with the event. In other words, coping both includes the variables of specific individual and the environment. According to the definitions of coping and coping with frustration, it is known that Coping with Frustration (CWF) is the course of "cognition and behaving", which is related to such cognitive activities as "assessment", "control" and "relief". Such cognition and behaviors are psychological processes that are unstable and variable.

**Contents of CWF.** CWF includes the skills, strategies (dynamic) and styles (stable) to cope with frustration. The CWF style is coherent with and determined by the skills and strategies. CWF skills and strategies are learned, thus they are unstable and variable.

Factors influencing CWF styles. Like any other abilities, the development of mature defense mechanism (or called "coping strategy"); the defense mechanism in psychoanalysis theory is also called "coping or adaptation mechanism" [Vaillant, 1996]) also needs two conditions: the biological preparation by the human body and properly recognized mode available psychologically [Mo, 1991]. "Rigid defenses are abandoned and replaced by more flexible means of coping" [Vaillant, 1996] via environmental influence, mode recognition, social supports, psychotherapy and other means. According to the research, factors affecting frustration endurance include physiological conditions, life experience, frequency of frustration, level of expectation, psychological preparation, cognition of frustration, ideological basis, personality traits, defense mechanism, social supports, etc. Among them, the level of expectation, cognition of frustration, defense mechanism and social supports are unstable and variable, which lead to variability and plasticity of frustration tolerance.

Research findings in stress coping. Lazarus [1993] summarized some significant findings in coping research and argued that:

Coping is complicated. People use many basic coping strategies in any stress.

Coping is determined by an individual's assessment of the nature of situations and coping resources. If an individual thinks that he/she is able to change the situation, then problem-focused coping will be dominant; otherwise, emotion-focused coping will be dominant.

In complicated stress situations, coping strategies change from stage to stage. The universal coping strategy summarized for complicated stress situations is just like the distorted image of coping process.

To summarize, CWF is dynamic. CWF styles are restricted by variable and controllable factors, including the cognition on frustration, frustration assessment, CWF skills and strategies and social supports. It is also proved that people can obtain flexible and effective means of coping via environmental influence, mode recognition, social supports, psychotherapy, etc. Therefore, CWF styles are variable and controllable to some extent. The variability and controllability of CWF are direct theoretical evidence to the feasibility of CWF training.

## The Necessity of SMOCWF

"Self-monitoring refers to individual's process of constantly, positively and initiatively planning, supervising, examining, assessing, feedback, controlling and adjusting the on-going practical activities (purposiveness is one of the characteristics of practical activities) , in order to realize their anticipated goals" [Dong, Zhou and Chen, 1996]. Sternberg's triarchic theory of intelligence emphasizes the key role of metacognition in the structure of intelligence. Metacognition control, plan, monitor and evaluate cognitive processing. Metacognition improves the initiative of behaviors and efficiency of cognition. Plenty of experiments show that in order to have effective cognitive activities and behaviors, the self-monitoring level (also called the "level of metacognition") of an individual must be improved, because "self-monitoring is the core of cognitive activities, and also the commanding center of human's psychological system" [Wo, 1996], "self-monitoring is the essential part of intelligence, which plays a dominant role in human's intelligence and controls and governs the other components of intelligence" [Dong, Zhou and Chen, 1996]. It is also found that without metacognitive strategies, the strong general cognitive ability can not play an effective role in solving problems. On the contrary, if an individual has very good metacognitive knowledge, he/she can still have good performance in solving problems even his/her general cognitive ability is high, because metacognitive knowledge makes up for poor general cognitive ability. Domestic psychologists also point out that "self-monitoring of the individual contributes to problem-solving (CWF is a kind of problem solving mode). As an implicit process, it organizes and commands the seeking, selection and implementation of problem-solving means, which not only plays an essential role in solving a specific problem, but also is very significant in improving and developing individual's problem solution capacity." The research showed that one important factor of effective coping is the control of the sources of frustration, i.e., being able to carry out corresponding measures in the course of the stress event. Four types of controls are involved in effective coping: information control (knowing what to expect), cognition control (thinking from different aspects and more constructively), decision control (making decisions based on flexible behaviors) and behavior control (taking actions to reduce the consequences of stressful events). CWF is cognitive activities and behaviors that assess the significance of the sources of frustration, control or change the frustration environment, and relieve the emotional reactions caused by frustration. CWF is essentially a series of cognitive activities (in this sense, cognition includes accessing to information, making decisions, taking actions, etc.). Cognitive activities can be influenced by various factors. Thus it leads to deviation and influences the effects of CWF. American clinical psychologist Albert Ellis created rational emotive therapy in the 1950s and ABC theory. A refers to activating event; B is an individual's understanding and beliefs of frustration, i.e., how he/she thinks, interprets and assesses the event; C is the individual's emotional response and consequences of behavior under certain situation. According to the theory, A (activating event) is only an indirect reason that leads to emotional and behavioral responses; whereas B (the beliefs, understanding and interpretation of an individual towards the activating event) directly leads to C (emotional and behavior responses).

The nature and degree of C depends on B. ABC theory focuses on the restrictions of an individual's subjective cognition on behavioral responses in the frustration. An individual can adjust his/her own emotion, minimize negative response C resulted from irrational beliefs, and eliminate the negative impact caused by distress, depression and other emotional disturbance by initiatively adjusting his/her opinion and attitude on A (activating event), trying to increase and increasing his/her rational thinking and beliefs and reducing irrational beliefs [Feng, 1993]. American psychologist Lazarus made significant contributions to stress research. He especially highlights the role of cognitive factors in the response to stress. He is involved in the research into the course of stress and is one of the most important leaders in this field [Wei et al., 1993]. Lazarus's theory especially highlights the absolute role of the course of cognition and assessment in stress and coping, which is similar to Ellis' ABC theory. Lazarus et al. also put forward cognitive-phenomenological-transactional (CPT) theory (see Figure 2.1).

Individual's cognition on stimulus is regarded as an important factor in CPT theory. According to CPT theory, thinking, experience and the significance of the event felt by an individual are the main intermediate and direct causes for stress response, i.e., whether the stress will occur and in what way it will occur depends on how an individual assesses the relationship between such individual and the environment, including preliminary assessment, re-assessment and secondary assessment.

Preliminary assessment refers to that an individual assesses the harmfulness of the event (i.e., whether the event benefits or harms his/her beliefs, values, targets, etc), the results of which might be 1) irrelevant, 2) positive, or 3) stressful. The nature of emotional response is determined by preliminary assessment, for instance, positive results lead to positive emotional response, including cheered up, relaxing, etc. Secondary assessment refers to that an individual assesses his/her coping resources and the style, strategies and capacity for coping, and considers whether new problems will be caused by his/her coping behaviors. CPT theory regards humans as higher living creature with initiatives. This theory provides a way to cope with stress in reality.

According to CPT mode, an individual can intervene or correct his/her preliminary and secondary assessments via his/her own efforts (self-help) or other's assistance (other's help); make sure where the threats he/she felt are from; design coping strategies; control the environmental pressure; timely assess the effectiveness of the coping strategies used, in order to adjust the coping behaviors and meet the needs of the environment.

According to the above two theories, it can be concluded that the effectiveness of coping depends on the cognitive activities, especially the assessment of frustration situation or frustration and coping resources. In other words, from the aspect of self-help, an individual must learn to do self-monitoring of his/her own thinking, interpretation and assessment when he/she encounters frustration and wants to reduce or eliminate emotional disturbance and improper response to frustration: whether his/her understanding and beliefs are logical or rational? Whether he/she has correct and objective assessment on frustration situation or frustration event? Whether proper coping strategies are carried out? What measures should be carried out to adjust his/her cognition, emotion, will and behaviors, if necessary? Namely, an individual, in order to effectively cope with frustration, must be active to carry out effective self-monitoring on his/her cognitive activities and behaviors.

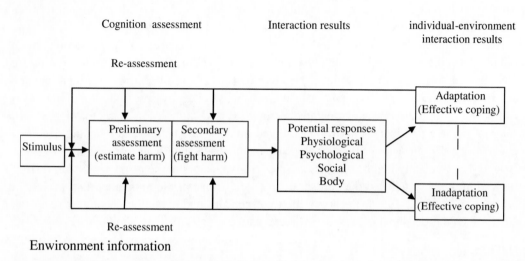

Figure 2.1. CPT Mode (Lazarus, 1966/1976/1979).

The possibility of SMOCWF

We believe that after SMOCWF training, students can carry out effective self-monitoring on their cognition and behaviors in CWF; carry out effective self-monitoring on modes and styles of coping; have correct understanding and assessment on themselves in frustration and frustration events; and choose proper modes and strategies of coping based on specific situations, thus develop adaptive and mature coping styles, and eventually improve their capacity to tolerate frustration.

## 2) Theoretical Composition

### The Connotation of SMOCWF

We believe SMOCWF, like metacognition, is also comprised of three factors: knowledge, skills and experiencing of SMOCWF.

*SMOCWF knowledge.* The knowledge includes three aspects. First, the knowledge about the agent of CWF. Namely, all characteristics of the individual (include the agent himself/herself and other people) who is the agent to cope with frustration, which can be further classified into three categories: i) the understanding about intra-individual difference. For example, to correctly understand his/her own personality, capacity; to have an objective understanding about his/her own strengths, advantages and weak points and disadvantages; how to make use of his/her own advantages and overcome weaknesses. ii) the understanding about inter-individual difference. For example, to understand the differences of values, knowledge, experience, character, etc. Such differences may lead to different effects of CWF among individuals. iii) the understanding about the universality of principal factors affecting the effects of CWF. For example, to understand that CWF capacity does not stay in static state and that the concepts and practice are important factors of effective coping. Second, the knowledge about frustration; for example, the types, severity and value of frustration. Third, the knowledge about CWF strategies. For example, what are the strategies to cope with frustration? What are the advantages and weaknesses of such strategies? Under what conditions and situations will such strategies be used? And what are CWF styles?

*SMOCWF skills.* This chapter puts forward preliminary theoretical conception about SMOCWF skills.

The SMOCWF skills include:

*Attention and Identification* refer to paying attention to and discovering potential sources of frustration, and monitoring the attention to and identification of possible internal and external clues and information of frustration. Attention should be paid to the information of potential threats when discovering potential sources of frustration. Sometimes, it also contains the interpretation of warning signals from the environment. The information about potential sources of frustration may come from the thinking of an individual. Attention and identification essentially mean answering the question of "what cause frustration" in CWF.

*Assessment* refers to that an individual monitors the assessment on his/her own coping resources and frustration situation, types of frustration (real or anticipated type) and the strategies to cope with frustration. Assessment essentially means assessing the cause of frustration in CWF.

*Plan* is the planning and arrangement of coping activities (including anticipatory coping, proactive coping and coping in the course of frustration), and choosing and adopting proper strategies and means of coping. In the early stage of coping activities, plan mainly includes knowing what are the task and targets, recalling relevant knowledge, choosing the strategies to solve the problem, determining how to solve the problems, etc. It is worth mentioning that plan not only occur in the early stage of coping activities, but also in the course of coping activities. For example, an individual plans how he/she will adjust before he/she adjusts coping activities. Plan essentially means answering the question of "what can I do with the sources of frustration" in CWF.

*Examination and summary* refer to carrying out assessment and correction on the implementation, strategies, means and results of coping as well as on the changing of the event, i.e., the feedback to the individual himself/herself in and after coping activities. In the middle stage of coping activities, "examination and summary" include knowing the progress of coping activities, examining whether any mistakes were made and whether the plan is feasible; in the later stage, "examination and summary" mean assessing the effect, efficiency and the results of coping activities, for example, whether the task is completed, whether it is efficient, what are the results, experience and lessons learned, etc. Meanwhile, proper corrective or remedy measures are carried out according to the information obtained in monitoring, including mistake correction, obstacle removal, thinking adjustment, etc. Examination and summary essentially mean answering the question of "how is the coping and what experience and lessons are learned" in CWF.

*SMOCWF experience.* It refers to the perceiving and understanding of relevant information of coping activities by an individual. In the early stage of coping activities, it refers to the experiencing of the difficulty of, familiarity with and confidence over the task; in the middle stage, it refers to the experiencing of the current progress, the obstacles and difficulties encountered; in the later stage, it refers to the experiencing of the effects, efficiency and results of the coping, and that whether the targets are realized.

## The Contents of SMOCWF

The specific-problem-based training focuses on training the self-monitoring ability students used in coping with frustration. In terms of coping mode, we also used the concepts put forward by Taylor, Folkman, Lazarus et al. to establish the theoretical framework of SMOCWF skills, namely, proactive coping (efforts and measures undertaken in advance of a potentially stressful event to prevent it or to modify its form before it occurs), anticipatory coping (efforts made in advance to prepare for a stressful event that is possible or certain to occur) and coping (efforts undertaken by an individual to master, tolerate, reduce or minimize stress or conflict) [Lisa and Shelley, 1997]. Therefore, when considering SMOCWF, we should use the mentioned theories. Proactive coping differs from coping and anticipatory coping in three aspects: first, proactive coping occurs earlier than coping and anticipatory coping. Proactive coping refers to extending coping resources and obtaining skills. Such skills are only ordinary preparation rather than specific to certain sources of frustration. Through proactive coping, imminent sources of frustration are identified and preparations are made in advance. Second, proactive coping requires different skills from coping with specific events. Because proactive coping is not used to deal with specific source of frustration, the skills of identifying potential sources of frustration before the frustration occurs play an important role in proactive coping activities. Finally, different skills and behaviors that are not successful in coping with specific frustration may be successful in proactive coping.

As shown in figure 2.2, proactive coping happens before the occurrence of specific and expected sources of frustration. During proactive coping, coping resources are stored and coping skills are obtained (resource extension). Effective proactive coping includes the accumulation of time and money, planning, skills and social supports, as well as controlling on psychological pressure as much as possible. By doing this, an individual is able to control the sources of frustration as much as possible when they are inevitably discovered. Proactive coping also includes identifying potential sources of frustration. Identification refers to being able to obtain insight into the occurrence of potential frustration events. It relies on the capacity to detect the dangers from environment and on the sensibility over internal clues. Such internal clues imply the possible occurrence of certain threats. After the sources of frustration are detected, the preliminary assessment starts. Preliminary assessment preliminarily assesses the current status ("what is it") and potential status ("what will it become") of potential sources of frustration, for example, "Should I worry about it?" and "Should I pay attention to it?" Such assessment may strengthen the attention towards sources of frustration and increase the preliminary coping efforts. Preliminary coping efforts refer to efforts undertaken to prevent or reduce the identified or guessed sources of frustration. We believe that successful proactive coping at this stage is always positive rather than evasive, which not only includes cognitive activities, such as plan, but also behavioral activities, for example obtaining information from others and taking preliminary actions. Feedback and utilization of feedback are the last stages of proactive coping. Feedback and utilizing feedback are the core. Such feedbacks are about the development and changing of a frustration event (whether it is further developed, changed in form or worse); the effects of an individual's preliminary efforts on a frustration event (whether I successfully avoid the sources of frustration) and about whether coping efforts need to be increased (what else can I do? Or do I need to stop and check whether it is a problem?) such feedback may be used to correct an individual's assessment towards potential or preliminary sources of frustration and to adjust an individual's strategies to eliminate the sources of frustration. A key factor of this mode is the feedback loop. In particular, resource accumulation, attention, assessment and adjusting the arousal of negative emotions are interrelated tasks. The assessment of a potential threat will cause the attention towards potential source of frustration to be increased, the emotions will be adjusted and the coping resources will be enriched by efforts. The preliminary assessment influences the coping efforts undertaken at the very beginning; on the contrary, the coping efforts also influence the information about the potential sources of frustration, in order to provide information for assessment process and adjusting coping efforts.

In proactive coping, the self-adjustment skills fully illustrate how an individual prepares before the occurrence of the sources of frustration, in order to prevent frustration events or minimize its impact. Matheny et al. Argued that the coping styles depend on whether the coping is combative or preventive.

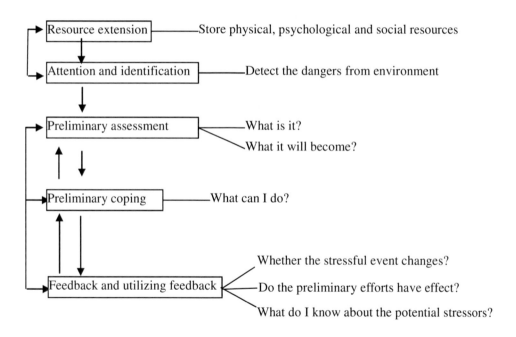

Figure 2.2.The Tasks of the Five Steps and the Feedback Loop of Proactive Coping.

Combative coping occurs when response to stressors happens, trying to reduce or combat existing stressors. Preventive coping is efforts to avoid the occurrence of stressors through the perceptive cognitive structure and continuous resistance to the consequences of stress. The increase of resources also increases the resistance to stress.

According to the mentioned coping mode, we believe that in preventive coping, SMOCWF mainly targets to monitor the implementation of tasks in every stage according to the chart of preventive coping. For example, the extension of an individual's coping resources (physical and psychological resources, social supports, etc.) especially the preparation regarding the skills to cope with frustration; whether an individual can be specially trained by himself/herself in certain aspects, such as paying attention to the information relevant to frustration, "appraisal, relaxation training, cognition restructuring, problem solving, time management, nutrition consultation, and exercise plan" [Rice, 2000]; the identification of potential sources of frustration (whether the potential signals are noticed), the evaluation on related events, the coping undertaken, such as whether corresponding adjustment are conducted according to the strategies (the level of adjustment, to avoid the sources of frustration and changing the behavioral way that causes frustration).

While coping with frustration, SMOCWF will first monitor individuals' assessment towards the frustration event, because coping style depends whether actions can be taken to change the assessment regarding the frustration situation. If an individual thinks he/she is able to change the situation, then problem-focused coping will be dominant; otherwise emotion-focused coping will be dominant. According to the role of assessment in the course of coping as mentioned above, during the course of SMOCWF, an individual should monitor whether the assessment regarding the harm resulting from frustration event and regarding his/her own coping resources are proper or accurate. An individual should try to have a clear, objective and positive assessment towards frustration and his/her coping resources. One effective means to properly cope with stress is to change the assessment towards stress and change the self-defeating cognition concerning means of stress. Thus in face with frustration situation, an individual should monitor himself/herself to seek for other plans, reconsider his/her own role, and the attribution an individual uses to interpret consequences. In addition, an individual should monitor himself/herself to re-build the cognition towards response to stress, replace self-defeating with self-motivation, and better control stressful events via changing self-talk.

Because coping style is shown after the cognitive assessment [Xiao, 1992], an individual during the self-monitoring on his or her coping style (or coping strategies, coping mechanisms) during coping course should first assess his or her performance in CWF, for example i) whether such individual adopts problem-focused coping or emotion-focused coping, or attacks or tolerates stressors, or reduces the arousals; ii) whether the coping is constructive or destructive [Zhu, 1989], negative or positive coping, adaptive coping or maladaptive coping [Carver, Scheier and Weintraud, 1989], or psychopathological, immature, neurosis and mature coping mechanisms [Vaillant, 1996]. Then an individual properly adjust the coping strategies or coping styles based on the assessment. An individual identifies, assesses and adjusts coping styles in order to adopt flexible and effective coping strategies based on frustration situation, and further to adapt to internal and external environment and maintain mental health.

In general, SMOCWF is to use SMOCWF skills to monitor the coping modes and styles. An individual, after choosing the coping modes, monitors the implementation of coping modes.

## Modes of SMOCWF Training

### 1) General Training Mode

The SMOCWF training first follows the basic mode of psychological suzhi-based education. The psychological suzhi-based education mode put forward by Zhang et al. are proved to be effective by empirical research [Zhang et al., 2000]. We believe that SMOCWF training should follow such a mode that targets basically to cultivate the students' good CWF capacity; follows the principles of adaptability and development, adopts specific-problem-based training mode; follows the five steps to improve psychological suzhi, namely self-understanding, knowledge-learning, behavioral direction, reflection and internalization, formation of psychological suzhi [Zhang et al., 2000]; highlights the learning of study and interpersonal skills, personality development and social adaptability, etc.

The training highlights practicability. According to the characteristics of psychological development and the training requirements of frustration tolerance among middle school students, the practical training is i) interesting, i.e., trying to start the training with a story, test or case illustration, which stimulates the interests of students and make them understand themselves objectively while feeling happy and interested; ii) operable, i.e., highlighting the theme of every training, designing specific training activities for joint completion by teachers and students; iii) specific-problem-based, i.e., designing training strategies for different frustration faced by students.

## 2) Specific Modes for SMOCWF

"The intermediate function of metacognition leads to that only through metacognitive experience, an individual can effectively adjust cognitive activities by using corresponding knowledge of metacognition based on the current progress of cognitive activities. Therefore, metacognitive experience is the key factor for adjustment". But then how to obtain metacognitive experience?

Zhang et al., [2000] argued that corresponding metacognitive experience can be stimulated through reflectional self-questioning. Let's take the course of problem-solving as an example, an individual, through self-questioning, can have the metacognitive experience related to the familiarity with, difficulty of and the confidence in successfully solving the problem in the early stage of a cognitive activity; the progress and obstacles of the activity in the middle stage; and the effects, efficiency and results of the activity in the later stage.

The research by Dorminowski [1990] showed that a speech activity showing the reasons facilitates problem-solving, because it results in and promotes metacognitive processing (monitoring). Such metacognitive processing (including assessment, plan, monitoring) plays an important role in problem-solving. The experiment by Atan and Hennie [1990] proved that metacognitive training can improve students' thinking skills. Alision [1991] did a research about questioning strategy in problem-solving, and found that questioning strategy among students will help to increase students' metacognitive and problem-solving capacities. Berardo-Coletta et al. [1995] did an experiment in metacognition and found that asking students the question of "why do you do that?" will promote the metacognitive processing (i.e., the thinking of the students), turn the attention from the content of information processing to the course of information processing, make the students better monitor the assessment, adjustment and correction of their cognitive activities, and eventually improve the effects of problem-solving.

Meichenbaum put forward self-instruction training [Liu, 1998] to cope with the negative emotion or affect caused by CWF. Self-instruction training, which is obviously featured by cognitive restructuring mode, was designed as inspired by Ellis' rational emotive therapy. Self-instruction training is essentially a program to treat internal dialogue in order to change an individual's thinking, cognitive structure and behavior style. Internal dialogue is the course of self-communication when an individual speaks to and listens to himself/herself. What individuals told them determines what they do. For example, the internal dialogue by self-defeated people is usually self-criticized or self-destructed.

Based on the above research findings, we use think aloud protocol (TAP) in SMOCWF training.

*What is TAP?*

TAP refers to the realization of self-monitoring on CWF activities via the adjusting function of individuals' talk to themselves. Studies in cognitive psychology, especially in the field of metacognition, has fully proved that individuals not only reflects their behaviors, emotions and other psychological activities, but also greatly influences the behaviors and psychological activities, such as plan, coordination, control, etc. On one hand, TAP is a teaching strategy by teachers. Teachers provides the examples and modes regarding study and self-monitoring for students via TAP, through which students can realize such controls as monitoring the identification, assessment, plan, examination and summary via self-narratives. On the other hand, TAP is also a study strategy by students, i.e., students undertake self-instruction via asking questions to each other, self-talk, self-questioning, etc.

*How to implement TAP?*

Generally speaking, TAP training is divided into five steps.

Firstly, explain what is TAP, including its connotation and its importance. Secondly, provide the training environment where students can "show reasons", describe the course of problem-solving, ask questions to each other, and conduct self-questioning and self-talk. Students are different and tasks they faced are of different difficulty, thus not all students need to think aloud at the same time; consequently, teachers should ask them to conduct self-talk with low volume. Thirdly, measures should be taken to avoid the negative and irrelevant thinking-aloud of students. Fourthly, specific frustration situations should be considered in TAP instruction, which includes the following:

Self-observation, i.e., students should observe their own life and study and identify the frustration situations, speak out and write the negative internal dialogue related to such frustration situation.

Seeking for positive internal dialogue, namely, students should be instructed to find the thinking style different from the previous irrational ideas, and to express the thinking with new positive internal dialogue.

Learning new skills, namely, students should practice new internal dialogue under the real situations, and be assisted to master effective coping skills, in order to better adapt to the frustration situation.

Fifthly, using TAP skills learned in life, in order to realize improved CWF of students.

# EDUCATIONAL EXPERIMENT ABOUT THE TRAINING CONCERNING SELF-MONITORING ON COPING WITH FRUSTRATION AMONG STUDENTS OF JUNIOR MIDDLE SCHOOLS

## Purpose

The CWF experiment aims to i) establish scientific and effective test tool for CWF among middle school students; ii) make students form correct frustration ideas and improve their frustration tolerance; iii) explore effective means and methods for the training of CWF skills.

## Variables

### 1) Independent Variables

Knowledge imparting and training regarding self-monitoring skills on coping with frustration among students from junior middle schools.

### 2) Dependent Variables

The performance, styles and level of SMOCWF by students from junior middle schools after the training.

### 3) Control Variables

The experimental group and control group were set. Students who were not good at CWF in one school were chosen based on certain standards, and were organized into experimental and control groups. The SMOCWF training was conducted in experimental group while no training was conducted in the control group.

During the experiment, both the experimental and control groups were informed that they would take part in an experiment, in order to avoid participants' subjective expectation effect.

## Instruments

*Semi-opened questionnaire about frustration was used to see what the main sources of frustration faced by students are, in order to highlight the focus in the training.*

*Rating scale about coping styles among middle school students.* The rating scale was designed by Huang et al.

The rating scale includes 30 questions, which classify CWF styles among middle school students into six types, namely, problem-solving, help-seeking, withdrawal, abreaction, fantasy and tolerance. The scale is rated on a 5-point Likert scale. The test-retest reliability is 0.76 ($p<0.01$). The factor analysis showed that such scale has good construct validity, which truly reflects the coping of middle school students at that time.

*CWF questionnaire.* We prepared the questionnaire by taking into consideration the dynamic-static dimensions of CWF. The CWF questionnaire captures CWF from the respect of individuals' psychological process, psychological states and psychological characteristics, and includes the frustration events generally recognized by students from junior middle schools in the open questionnaire (including frustration events in study, interpersonal relationship, personality development, adaptation to life and body development).

Nineteen items are included, which are classified into emotion, will, attribution, behavioral and efficacy dimensions. These five factors can explain 51.69% of the total variance. The internal consistency reliability is 0.81 and test-retest reliability is 0.77.

The correlation among dimensions is between 0.18 and 0.44, and the correlation between the total questionnaire and dimensions is between 0.59 and 0.75. The construct validity is good. Self-report questionnaire is adopted (options). 3-point computation methods is used, with 1 standing for "yes", 2 for "not always", and 3 for "No". In order to avoid set answers, positive and reverse scoring is used.

*SMOCWF questionnaire*. The questionnaire was designed based on self-monitoring theory and by referring to State Metacognition Inventory [O`Neil and Abedi, 1996]. Seventeen items are included, which are classified into attention and identification, assessment, plan, examination and summary dimensions. These four dimensions can explain 52.70% of the total variance.

The internal consistency reliability is 0.90 and test-retest reliability is 0.72. The correlation among dimensions is between 0.33 and 0.61, and the correlation between the total questionnaire and dimensions is between 0.63 and 0.84. The construct validity is good. Self-report questionnaire is adopted (options). 4-point computation method is used with 1 for "Rarely", 2 for "Sometimes", 3 for "Normally", and 4 for "Always".

## The Course of Experiment

The experiment took 2 months and was divided into three stages:

### Stage One: Pre-Test
Students from both the experimental and control groups participated in pre-test. The pre-test included frustration survey, anxiety inventory, and the survey concerning the performance and styles of CWF, and SMOCWF.

### Stage Two: Intervention
Self-monitoring training was carried out in the experimental group. No training was carried out in the control group. However, in order to avoid expectancy effect, researchers should also contact the students from control group but not carry out training for them.

The educational intervention for experimental group refers to that the planned, specific-problem-based and purposive intervention is carried out in various means in the education and teaching activities according to the prescribed training procedures.

In the design of teaching, the following three steps should be taken into consideration:

First, the step to obtain SMOCWF knowledge (metacognitive knowledge). Second, the step to learn CWF skills and SMOCWF skills. And last, the step to transfer and practice the skills. In the natural situations, students used skills to cope with frustration in life, or teachers established certain frustration situation which allows students to use the skills learned.

### *Teaching Strategies*

Group intervention. It used the universal methods for PST, such as discussion, play, mode demonstration, situation establishment, role-play, etc.

Individual intervention. Individual intervention and group intervention were conducted at the same time. Usually, coaching and consulting were used in individual intervention. When talking with individual student, the advisor explained to the students about the problems they encountered in study, life and interpersonal relationship, proposes specific measures to help them in problem-solving, and encourages positive coping.

The participants in the control group were not provided with the intervention.

### *Stage Three: Post-Test*

Post-test included the same contents as pre-test. Both the experimental and control groups received the post-test.

## Experimental Results and Analysis

### Table 2.1. Comparison of CWF before and after the Test for Experimental and Control Groups

| Dimensions | Groups | Pre-Test (n=20) | Post-Test (n=20) | $t$ Value |
|---|---|---|---|---|
| General | Experimental group | 37.95±3.76 | 43.20±5.93 | 3.95** |
| | Comparison group | 35.45 ±3.87 | 36.40±4.33 | 0.64 |
| | $t$ | 0.62 | 3.83** | |
| Emotion | Experimental group | 9.20±2.41 | 11.10±2.86 | 2.98* |
| | Control group | 8.27±2.54 | 8.00±1.56 | 0.46 |
| | $t$ | 0.47 | 2.79* | |
| Will | Experimental group | 8.35±1.3089 | 9.55±1.57 | 2.59* |
| | Control group | 7.52±1.6911 | 7.00±1.25 | 0.38 |
| | $t$ | 0.79 | 3.62** | |
| Attribution | Experimental group | 6.95±1.27 | 8.50±1.19 | 2.72* |
| | Control group | 6.36±1.48 | 7.30±1.42 | 1.87 |
| | $t$ | 2.26 | 2.48 | |
| Behavior | Experimental group | 7.75±1.25 | 8.70±1.49 | 2.33* |
| | Control group | 7.57±1.33 | 7.20±1.48 | 0.72 |
| | $t$ | 0.01 | 2.81** | |
| Efficacy | Experimental group | 5.70±1.53 | 7.35±1.27 | 3.54** |
| | Control group | 5.73±1.37 | 6.20±1.03 | 1.22 |
| | $t$ | 0.60 | 2.86* | |

### *1) Comparison of CWF before and after the Test for the Two Groups*

We can see from table 1 that there was no significant difference between experimental and control groups in CWF ($t=0.62$) before the experiment, including emotion, will, attribution, behavior and self-efficacy.

However, after the experiment, we can see very significant difference ($t=3.83$) in general CWF and dimensions between the two groups. After the experiment, the CWF was significantly improved for the experimental group ($t=3.95$) while no significant change were found in the control group ($t=0.64$).

*2) Comparison of CWF Styles before and after the Test for the Experimental and Control Groups*

By comparing with the CWF styles before and after the test for the two groups, it was found that:

The priority of CWF style for experimental group before the experiment is tolerance (Mean=3.03) > problem-solving (Mean=2.93) > abreaction (Mean=2.91) > withdrawal (Mean=2.91) > help seeking (Mean=2.87) > fantasy (Mean=2.28);

The priority of CWF style for experimental group after the experiment is problem-solving (Mean=3.13) > abreaction (Mean=2.97) > help seeking (Mean=2.83) > withdrawal (Mean=2.82) > tolerance (Mean=2.66) > fantasy (Mean=2.51);

The coping styles of students with bad coping capacity in the control group before the experiment: tolerance (Mean=3.05) > help seeking (Mean=2.86) > abreaction (Mean=2.82) > withdrawal (Mean=2.80) > problem-solving (Mean=2.76)>fantasy (Mean=2.46);

The coping styles of students with coping capacity in the control group after the experiment: abreaction (Mean=3.58) > withdrawal (Mean=3.24) > tolerance (Mean=3.18) > fantasy (Mean=3.00) > problem-solving (Mean=2.73) > help seeking (Mean=2.69);

From the above information, it is known that before the experiment, students from both groups mainly used negative coping or emotion-focused coping (including tolerance, withdrawal, abreaction and fantasy). After the experiment, the coping styles of experimental group were positive and problem-focused (problem-solving, help seeking), but the coping style for control group remained the same.

*3) Comparison of SMOCWF before and after the Test for the Experimental and Control Groups*

We can see from table 2.2 that there was no significant difference between experimental and control groups on SMOCWF skills ($t=1.184$) before the experiment, including dimensions of attention and identification, assessment, plan and methods, examination and summary.

However, after the experiment, we can see very significant difference ($t=2.80$) between the two groups in general SMOCWF skills and dimensions. After the experiment, the skills were significantly improved for the experimental group ($t=3.95$) and not dramatically changed for control group ($t=0.64$).

## 2.3.6. Why the Performance of Middle School Students in Coping with Frustration is Improved after the Training Concerning Self-Monitoring on Coping with Frustration

After the SMOCWF training, students' coping style changes from the previous negative coping (tolerance) to positive coping (problem-solving); and the performance of students in coping with frustration was also greatly improved, including the attribution of frustration, self-efficacy, emotional and affective responses, will and behavioral effects. According to the analysis, students' performance in coping with frustration positively correlated with the level of SMOCWF. And the level of SMOCWF was dramatically improved after the experiment, which means that the experiment is effective in improving the level of SMOCWF.

## Table 2.2. Comparison of SMOCWF Skills before and after the Test for the experimental and control Groups

| | Groups | Pre-Test (n=20) (Mean±SD) | Post-Test (n=20) (Mean±SD) | t |
|---|---|---|---|---|
| General | Experimental group | 41.05±8.73 | 44.70±8.71 | 2.81* |
| | Control group | 40.16±8.12 | 40.20±7.52 | 0.56 |
| | t | 1.18 | 2.79* | |
| Attention and identification | Experimental group | 7.75±1.71 | 9.55±2.39 | 3.34** |
| | Control group | 7.34±2.27 | 7.50±2.32 | 1.02 |
| | t | 0.41 | 2.90* | |
| Assessment | Experimental group | 10.65±2.97 | 13.05±2.14 | 3.95*** |
| | Control group | 10.04±2.74 | 10.10±1.66 | 0.45 |
| | t | 1.74 | 3.79*** | |
| Plan and strategy | Experimental group | 11.40±3.39 | 14.42±2.96 | 3.02** |
| | Control group | 10.82±2.67 | 11.40±2.80 | 0.77 |
| | t | 1.93 | 3.27** | |
| Examination and summary | Experimental group | 11.25±2.99 | 13.80±3.07 | 3.14* |
| | Control group | 11.02±3.28 | 11.20±3.55 | 1.04 |
| | t | 1.51 | 2.69* | |

The research showed that the SMOCWF experiment was successful to some extent. It enriched the skills and strategies of CWF for middle school students and improved their performance in coping with frustration. The training was successful because:

### 1) The Basic Contents of the Training (Knowledge, Skills and Strategies) are Complete and Rational

We found that students' poor performance in coping with frustration were caused by their improper, biased and incorrect understanding and concepts towards people and events involved in the frustration, limited CWF skills and lacking of knowledge in CWF strategy. In the training, we considered the possible frustration for students and first teach them declarative knowledge (also called descriptive knowledge, is knowledge to describe what, why and how is an object in order to distinguish and identify the object) of frustration; for example, what is frustration? Why do we need to properly cope with frustration? How do we dialectically treat the influence of frustration? What are the factors affecting CWF? What is problem-focused coping? And what is emotion-focused coping? Second we teach students procedural knowledge (the knowledge of what and how to perform a task) of CWF; for example, how to treat the broken relationship of parents, how to treat poor study, etc. And last, we asked students to experience and work out the strategic knowledge (the general knowledge and principles about how to cope with frustration, which are very abstract), for example, let students know when to use problem-focused coping strategy and when to use emotion-focused coping strategy, etc. The relation among these steps is not coordinating, but progressive. Declarative knowledge is the basis. Students utilized declarative knowledge in various situations and then obtained procedural knowledge, and finally acquired guiding knowledge which can be applied across various situations. Guiding knowledge, also called strategic knowledge, is the knowledge that guides an individual to adopt different coping strategies based on different situations, which is at the highest level of an individual's knowledge structure.

Imparting CWF knowledge (including specific-problem-based knowledge and metacognitive knowledge) is the basis of the training, which aims to establish rational knowledge structure relevant to people and events in frustration, in order to realize effective CWF by students. CWF skills are the focus of the training. Without such skills, students are less active and initiative and have fewer choices towards coping strategies. We not only taught students CWF skills, but also SMOCWF skills via self-dialogue, etc., such as attention and identification, assessment, plan, examination and summary. By doing this, students were able to monitor their CWF skills with such metacognitive skills, and realized more flexible and effective coping skills and strategies. CWF strategy is the soul of the training, because strategic knowledge adjusts the knowledge and skills an individual used to cope with frustration according to the characteristics of situations. Strategic knowledge enables an individual to flexibly utilize knowledge and strategies according to the real situation and specific conditions. Without strategic knowledge, even an individual masters numerous CWF skills and knowledge, he/she may not use the skills and knowledge properly, making the knowledge rigid and skills ineffective.

## 2) Accurate Focus (Self-Monitoring) of the Training

SMOCWF is the focus of CWF training. Thus we emphasized on the self-monitoring of metacognition rather than on cognition, which highlights individuals' initiative.

Recently, cognitive psychologists believed that the training of metacognitive strategies in the meantime when imparting general cognitive strategies improve students' capacity for problem-solving, because it makes people become more aware of their own cognitive processing strategies in problem-solving and more initiative to use the effective knowledge and strategies learned. Therefore, the training on metacognitive monitoring must be undertaken in order to make students master the strategies in coping with frustration and make them be able to plan, monitor and adjust the strategies learned.

Two research orientations exist in CWF realm, which are process-focused and trait-focused orientation. The former focuses on what an individual thinks and does in the course of coping, with individuals' coping process on certain life event as the key point; whereas the latter focuses on whether an individual has personality-based, relatively stable and habitual coping styles. We think these two kinds of research can be integrated. On one hand, we pay attention to what an individual thinks and does in the course of CWF in order to realize set monitoring and further to realize the individual's specific monitoring on his/her own cognition and behaviors, and eventually effective coping. On the other hand, different individuals have different personalities and other traits, thus they have personality-based, relatively stable and habitual cognitive assessment and coping styles, which restricts the styles, degree and duration of responses to frustration, as well as the degree of influences of frustration on the individuals [Chen, 1994]. And in order to adapt to the environment, individuals have to change their "cognitive assessment and coping styles" that leads to inadaptability. It is possible for them to make such changes, because psychologists have reached a common understanding that the character and personality trait, although are related to innateness to some extent, are mainly acquired by learning and are influenced by environment around individuals. Individuals must rely on self-monitoring in order to change their own traits. Therefore, SMOCWF can integrate both research orientations. It admits the relative stability and also the changing nature of CWF, and thus can maximize the initiative of individuals.

Self-monitoring is the monitoring on and adjustment of individuals' cognitive process. Research shows that frustration tolerance is affected by various factors, including students' physiological conditions, life experience, ideological level, personality, expectation, mental preparation, perception and judgment on frustration, social supports and the flexibility of thinking. It is believed that under the same or similar frustration situations, different individuals have different sense of frustration, because they have different values, achievement motivation, attribution of frustration, personality, subjective attitude to frustration, etc. Except physiological conditions, the psychological factors do not influence the coping styles and its effects without any rules; instead they are coordinated and controlled by individuals and then influence CWF. The mentioned factors are stable psychological states and characteristics, which lead to mental set over the response to the outside world and are not easily influenced by changes in outside world. In order to make individuals initiatively change with the environmental changes, the adjustment and balancing functions of self-monitoring need to be used. The self-awareness of students are fast developing in middle school period, especially in the period of junior middle school, thus these two periods are the key period to cultivate proper and positive self-awareness, including self-monitoring. Fang et al. argued that the self-regulation of middle school students is the integrated regulation of their knowledge, affect and will, which is an act controlled by individuals' will. The thinking patterns of students from junior middle schools is of "introspective" and "analyzing" characteristics, because they usually introspect and analyze their ideas as an object. Through self-monitoring, an individual is initiative and will integrate problem-focused and emotion-focused copings and adopt corresponding coping strategies according to the changing situations.

Therefore, the SMOCWF training seized the key breakthrough points for CWF training among students from junior middle schools, which enables them to improve their CWF capacity. The experimental results coincide with such theoretical assumption.

Frustration cognition is the key factor among all factors of frustration, and the cognition and judgment of frustration determine the availability, strength and endurance of individuals' response to frustration, therefore, this experiment aims to improve students' capacity for the cognition and judgment of frustration and CWF, improve their capacity for monitoring such cognition and assessment of frustration and CWF, and to realize correct cognition and assessment. Many training assumptions in previous studies pay attention to the imparting and acquiring of external knowledge but neglect the understanding and guidance of the cognition on themselves, resulting in that individuals in certain CWF activities can not correctly understand and assess themselves and frustration, and can not find corresponding strategy knowledge. Modern cognitive psychology believes that the knowledge structure of individuals plays a decisive role in problem-solving and other cognitive process and behaviors. What's more, individuals use such knowledge structure to obtain psychological-physical balance and individual-environment balance, and then to adapt to the environment and to realize development. However, if the knowledge is distorted, the concept and behavior of individuals will be misled. In the training, we strive to impart correct knowledge and concepts to students, and further to arouse students' awareness to monitor the state of their knowledge and concepts from time to time. In the training, the static knowledge concerning self-monitoring imparted to students plays a retrospective role. Such metacognitive knowledge makes students know what factors influence their cognition of and coping with frustration, how such factors work and how do they interact. The training stimulates students' subject consciousness at utmost, resulting in initiative understanding and behaviors rather than spontaneous understanding and behaviors.

According to the investigations, students' poor performance in CWF is due to insufficient training in self-monitoring skills that may lead to poor targeted coping. With insufficient training, the CWF by students is random, aimless and spontaneous, thus frustration can cause significant negative influence on them. With training, on one hand, students have better strategies and skills in coping with frustration, can correctly assess the conditions and situations to use coping strategies, and can monitor the use of such strategies. What's more, they can initiatively acquire corresponding coping strategies and skills according to the changing environment, including how to prevent frustration, how to prepare, enrich and acquire CWF experience and strategies; can flexibly adjust coping strategies based on the nature of frustration events, in order to improve the capacity to cope with frustration; and can monitor the their performance in coping with frustration by using coping strategies.

After SMOCWF training, students can skillfully use self-questioning and self-monitoring skills. They can also monitor their cognition and behaviors in CWF through attention and identification, assessment, plan, examination and summary in order to realize effective monitoring, for example reflection, feedback and assessment are undertaken, including do I really identify the nature of frustration, do I have objective assessment over the nature of frustration, do I identify their resources to cope with frustration, should I use problem-focused or emotion-focused coping strategy, whether the coping strategy is proper, is the coping style positive or negative, what else do I need to improve, etc. Meanwhile, students are required to cope with frustration from three aspects, i.e., proactive coping, anticipatory coping and CWF, in order to establish a preventive and coping system for CWF, which will then effectively strengthen the prevention of and preparation for frustration and reduce the psychological and physical harm of frustration to individuals. The experiment showed that students, in face of frustration, were able to use the strategies learned to effectively adjust their emotions, in order to reduce the emotional disturbance. The significant change in anxiety after the experiment showed that through SMOCWF training, students can consciously retrospect their performance in CWF, initiatively and effectively respond to frustration. Their capacity for coping with frustration is improved.

### 3) Effective Training Mode

Training mode reflects the concept of training and influences the effect, thus a scientific, effective and feasible training mode is important to realize the goal of experiment. We established general mode and specific-problem-based mode for SMOCWF training, according to the universal mode for psychological suzhi training and specific-problem-based mode for self-monitoring training.

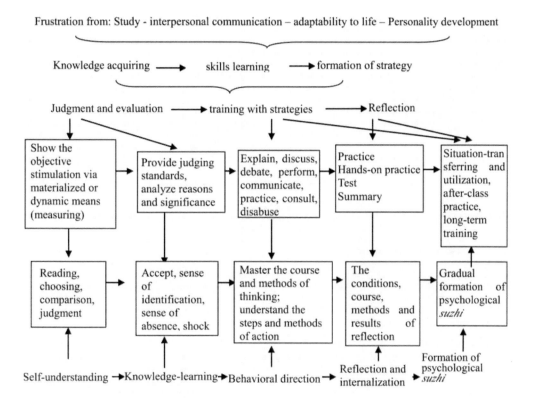

Figure 2.3. General Mode for SMOCWF Training.

According to the general mode, the training was divided into four parts (study, interpersonal communication, adaptability to life and personality development); each part is divided into three stages (knowledge acquiring, skills learning and strategy formation); each stage was further divided into three steps (judgment and evaluation, training with strategies and reflection). The training followed the five steps to realize psychological suzhi, namely, self-understanding, knowledge-learning, behavioral direction, reflection and internalization, formation of psychological suzhi. The following is the illustration of general training mode.

Since the four types of frustration have been analyzed before, we will not repeat here.

The three stages include education (knowledge acquiring), practicing coping skills (skills learning) and using coping skills to solve different sources of frustration (formation of strategy).

The education aims to make students acquire metacognitive knowledge in the course of frustration. Such knowledge base can improve their mental preparation towards frustration, can help them change the tension of feelings under dangerous situations, can help them remove the irrational cognition in their mind and make them active and initiative, and can make them adopt flexible coping strategies based on their own situation and the frustration events, in order to realize their self-efficacy in CWF.

The stage of skills learning aims to help students acquire basic skills to effectively cope with frustration. Such basic skills include re-evaluation, adjustment of emotions, stopping negative thinking, self-instruction, etc. Based on these skills, TAP such as self-questioning, self-talk and self-suggestion is used to stimulate students to undertake the training of SMOCWF skills, in order to make them master self-monitoring skills, including attention and identification, assessment, plan, examination and summary.

The last stage is to create various imagined or real frustration situations for students to practice the coping skills learned and to summarize the strategic knowledge concerning the CWF skills. For example, a student can prepare for a coming examination via imagining an ongoing examination, and then he/she is desensitized to the possible nervousness in the coming examination. So when the real examination comes, he/she can be calm down and be skillful in coping with the situations. By using these skills, students have better understanding in the conditions and scope to use strategies, and acquire conditional knowledge which will instruct them to better use such skills.

The three steps include judgment and evaluation, training with strategies and reflection.

## Judgment and Evaluation

It aims to i) make students understand the development of their SMOCWF skills; evaluate whether they have the skills or suzhi that should be available; arouse their sense of identification or absence, and emotional resonance or shocking; stimulate mental activities and their thinking of such problems; and ii) remove incorrect faith from their mind; make them understand the cause; help them establish rational knowledge structure for CWF; and understand the significance of certain CWF skills.

It includes i) the content of the test and the judgment of students' current situations (it is derived from the intention of the training, which is the detailed segmenting of certain coping skills involved in the training); ii) judging standards; iii) common CWF knowledge.

The forms of judgment and evaluation are i) test; ii) story-telling and judgment; iii) case and summary; iv) small experiment; v) creating activity situation, participation in the activities.

## Training with Strategies (The Core Part)

It aims to i) guide students to think about the problems involved in the topic, in order to improve the understanding, change the ways and angles of thinking, and establish new concept; 2) create the procedures of thinking and action; iii) arouse the emotional experiencing via thinking and action; iv) practice and master the basic course and methods of thinking and the methods of action.

It includes choosing corresponding training strategies based on the frustration faced by students. The forms include i) telling by students; ii) role-play and performance; iii) discussion; iv) debating; v) communication among students and among students and the teacher; vi) hands-on practice; vii) observation and inspiration; viii) instruction or consulting by teacher.

## Reflection

It aims to i) reflect the course and ways of training; ii) use the methods and procedures learned in the training to other similar situations; iii) summarize the results of training.

It includes checking whether the goal of training is realized by referring to the goal and content of the training.

The forms include i) problem presentation; ii) designing the situations and hands-on practice; iii) case summary; iv) comparison of students before and after the training.

The training is carried out by following the five steps to realize psychological suzhi, namely, self-understanding, knowledge-learning, behavioral direction, reflection and internalization, formation of psychological suzhi.

## 4) Scientific and Effective Principles of Training

We summarize some effective principles for successful SMOCWF training.

## 1) Knowledge Learning

Certain fundamental knowledge on coping with frustration is the basis of self-monitoring training. The course of self-monitoring is the monitoring on psychological activities of the agent, especially on the cognitive activities of the agent, thus it changes as the content of cognition changes. In particular, the knowledge on self-monitoring is the basis and precondition of self-monitoring by individuals, which instructs individuals to initiatively and effectively choose, assess, modify or abandon the tasks, targets and strategies of CWF; meanwhile, it can cause the experiencing of self-monitoring on the individuals, targets and tasks; and help individuals understand the significance of such experiencing and the influence of such experiencing on behaviors. The great significance of the knowledge on self-monitoring also lies in that it is the necessary supporting system of metacognitive activities, which provides experience for adjustment. Cognitive adjustment is essentially the rational planning, organization and adjustment to the ongoing cognitive activities. In this process, individuals' understanding of the characteristics of their own cognitive resources and the types of tasks as well as the knowledge of certain strategies play a key role in adjustment. Individuals rely on such knowledge to organize the ongoing cognitive activities. Without corresponding metacognitive knowledge, the adjustment is aimless. Therefore, the capacity to cope with frustration relies on not only the training of methods and skills, but also on how much knowledge individuals master, especially knowledge in a certain aspect.

## Mode Provided

Mode provision refers to that teachers or students with strong self-monitoring capacity present their own course of adjustment through speech, in order to serve as the self-monitoring mode for most students. Mode provision is very important because the thinking activities in coping with frustration are implicit and abstract. The content of mode provision is the same as TAP, including determination of problems, assessment, plan, choosing strategies, examination and summary. There are three types of mode, including mode provided by teachers, peers and media. The mode provided by teachers is the main means of learning by students. The mode provided by peers is also important, because it enables students to learn how peers use speech to direct themselves. In addition, mode provided by video is also effective. If students watch video for 50 minutes per week, then after two months, students will be able to use TAP similar with that provided by video, which will be internalized.

Mode provided should reflect the course and structure of CWF, which is worthy of imitation. In CWF, when individuals search from the long-term memory the mode similar to the frustration they encounter, then the problem is solved. The research showed that the difference of frustration tolerance lies in the difference of the knowledge structure of CWF. The more CWF experience and the more CWF knowledge an individual has, the stronger frustration tolerance he/she will have. It is important to help students create CWF modes in their mind, but it is more important to improve their initiative, in order to create more and better modes via observation, summary, experiencing, etc. In addition, students should compare their course of CWF with the ideal course, and obtain constructive benefits, in order to make them more initiative in learning and realize optimal coping.

### 2) Supportive Activities

Activities are the preconditions for SMOCWF training. Students can discover problems in the activities they initiatively participate in, and then analyze selfhood, explore the reasons, seek for the ways to solve the problem and undertake reflection, namely, they instruct their behaviors via using knowledge in mind, practice, self-speech, observation and reflection. First, activities drive the development of psychological suzhi and meet students' needs to participate in activities. Second, self-monitoring skills are formed and developed in activities and activities provide opportunities and basis for the existence and performance of such skills. Third, students develop their self-monitoring skills on coping with frustration in activities. They understand, select, judge and integrate the objective social stimuli and the information on self during the activities and then internalize, on a selective basis, the intrinsic and external stimulators into their psychological suzhi. Finally, students internalize social norm, values, concepts, knowledge and information into their psychological suzhi.

### 3) Sequence-Based

We divide the general training mode of self-monitoring into four parts; and for each part we have three steps, namely, knowledge acquiring, skills learning and strategy formation. From the nature of knowledge, the three steps correspond to declarative knowledge, procedural knowledge and strategic knowledge respectively. The relation among these steps is not coordinating, but progressive. Declarative knowledge is the basis. Students utilize declarative knowledge in various situations and then obtained procedural knowledge, and finally acquire guiding knowledge for situations. Guiding knowledge, also strategic knowledge, is the knowledge that guides an individual to adopt different coping strategies based on different situations, which is at the highest level of an individual's knowledge structure.

The self-monitoring skills on coping should be developed separately and then integrated. In the training, self-monitoring skills, i.e., attention and identification, assessment, plan, examination and summary, should be practiced separately until students can utilize them skillfully. And then students integrate the skills learned through participating in the situation-based activities until they can skillfully use such skills, in order to realize automatic SMOCWF skills.

## 4) Experience

In the experiment, we especially focused on experiencing by students, especially metacognitive experience. The experiencing of self-monitoring on coping with frustration is very important to the knowledge acquiring and performance of self-monitoring on coping with frustration. Through self-monitoring experience, students can supplement, delete or modify the self-monitoring knowledge he/she has acquired, i.e., acquiring self-monitoring knowledge through assimilation and adjustment mechanisms. In the real self-monitoring, self-monitoring experience helps students to re-set the target, modify or abandon the old target, and to stimulate the strategies to cope with frustration and self-monitoring strategies. Metacognitive experience is an important intermediate factor between metacognitive knowledge and cognitive adjustment, and between metacognitive activities and cognitive activities. On one hand, metacognitive experiencing is the feeling and perception of the ongoing cognitive activities. It can stimulate the corresponding metacognitive knowledge and retrieve the metacognitive knowledge from the long-term memory into individual's working memory. And individuals can use such memory to guide their adjustment. On the other hand, metacognitive experience provides necessary information for adjustment. Without experiencing the ongoing cognitive activities, metacognitive activities and cognitive activities will be disconnected. Only by clearly awareness on the changes in the ongoing cognitive activities, can the adjustment be conducted with an explicit purpose.

Creating numerous psychological situations, including story telling, music appreciation, practice, play, role-play and activities, specifically aims to arouse and strengthen students' cognitive and metacognitive experience, in order to stimulate their senses of identification and absence, emotional resonance or shock, and trigger the desire for actions.

## 5) Reflection

Reflection is an important characteristic of self-monitoring. A good training environment comprises problem-related situation, discussion and reflection, instruction and monitoring by the teacher, inspiration and assistance by peers. It takes very long time for students to change from knowing what good strategies are to cope with frustration and why they are good to being willing to practice good strategies and to developing good capacity to cope with frustration. Teachers should create problem-related situations and organize students to undertake discussion and reflection of coping with frustration. Therefore, teachers provide students with opportunities for reflection: students describe their own thought (study their own and peers' cognitive process) → classify these strategies (assess different process for the same cognition) → discuss whether there are other solutions (stimulate corresponding knowledge by purposive thinking, and further obtain metacognitive experience) → discuss what is the optimal strategy (make students discuss the advantages and weakness of different coping strategies) → ask some students to explain why they provided inferior coping strategies (study the wrong cognitive process) → share the benefits of reflection, or whether they understand or master various strategies, or estimate whether they can remember and correctly use such strategies in similar situations in the future (students further evaluate their corresponding knowledge and capacities, and treat their own and peers' cognitive course as the object of consciousness, and feel the emotions generated in the cognitive process). Therefore, students' cognitive process in coping with frustration is exposed in the situation created by teachers. Under such situations, students experience the course from unknown to known; they learn knowledge by using their own ability of thinking, which will intensify the thinking experience and develop self-monitoring skills.

According to the research, reflection diary makes students (agent) pay attention to what they think and results in better thinking. During our research, teachers asked students to write reflection diary, recording what frustration they encountered, how they coped with frustration and how the coping worked, and undertake assessment and summary based on what they learned in the training.

### 6) Feedback

One of the important self-monitoring skills on coping with frustration is to make feedback and proper evaluation about the methods, strategies and results of coping, and to adjust and optimize the future coping activities. It is one of the important SMOCWF skills and also the necessary means for SMOCWF training. Information feedback is an essential condition for self-monitoring. Without feedback skills, the effective self-monitoring activities of an individual will be greatly influenced. Consequently, the trainer should evaluate students' monitoring activities timely, accurately and properly, and instruct them to feed back and evaluate their methods, strategies and results of coping, in order to promote the development of their self-monitoring capacity. Finally the trainer should organize students to feed back the coping activities.

### 7) Situation-Transferring

The trainer uses direct explanation to make students clearly understand the conditions of using self-monitoring strategies, provides examples or their own experiences, and suggests students use self-reminding, for example, use mottoes and aphorisms to remind themselves of monitoring their own cognition and behaviors. In addition, diversified situations should be created for practicing monitoring strategies, to make students understand and experience the employment of the skills learned, in order to have a better effect in transferring situation.


## APPENDIX

## I. One Example Material for SMOCWF Training

If parents broke up

I. About the training
1. Purpose
This training is to make students be brave and strong in the face of adversity, to overcome the harm caused by such adversity and to realize progress.

2. Objectives

This training aims to 1) instruct the students to have clear understanding and correct concepts.

2) and make students to initiatively use effective strategies to cope with frustration and to continue their normal life and study.

3. Focus and difficulties

The focus of this training is to make students be able to initiatively adjust their understanding towards adversity or frustration, and to stabilize their emotion or mood by using strategies.

The difficulties of this training is to make students who have smooth life so far understand that adversity or frustration is inevitable for everyone and is the touchstone of a strong person, i.e., to stimulate such students to be vigilant in peace time.


II. Components of the Training

1. Judgment and evaluation

1) Objectives

Judgment and evaluation aims to make students experience frustration and instruct them to have a correct understanding towards frustration events.

2) Training procedures

*Step 1:* teachers start the training with a saying, "Just as the moon may be wax or wane, people have their sorrows and enjoyments, departures and reunions", to indicate that any person may encounter difficulties, obstacles or worries. And then ask students to share what worry them in life. Next, students listen to a recording about a middle school students can not accept the break up of the parents.

*Step 2:* the teacher ask students to talk about what they think about parents' breakup. And ask them what they will do suppose they were in such situation. The teacher encourages students to be practical and helps them to analyze possible problems they will encounter in terms of emotion, cognition and behaviors. The teacher can ask them to write the problems down and hand in to the teacher, if possible. And the teacher then read the problems out to students.

*Step 3:* the teacher inspired students to understand that if people can not change or prevent the occurrence of frustration, they can reduce the suffering by changing their understanding about frustration. The teacher organizes voluntary student groups, and asks them to ask and answer the questions from the book inside the group.

2. Training with strategies

1) Objectives

It aims to adjust the emotions and correct the cognition.

2) Training procedures
(1) Strategy No. 1: accept the fact.

*Step 1*: ask students to imagine in detail what will happen if parents broke up and how will they handle with the follow-up problems, for example, moving to another house, transferring to another school, gossip by others, changing of the family's economic situation, family re-composition, new interpersonal relationship, etc.

*Step 2:* choose some brave volunteers to act as the "target" for other students to "attack" in turn, i.e., other students ask the volunteers what are the problems they will face if parent broke up, and how they will overcome them. If the "attacking" students fail to ask questions within the time limit, the "attacking" students lose; and if the volunteers fail to answer the questions from the "attacking" students, the volunteers are defeated. If the volunteers win, the teacher and the students congratulate them by applauding and encourage them to make better achievements; if the volunteers are defeated, the teacher encourages them to "stand up" from their failure, because the brave smiles the last.

(2) Strategy No. 2: seeking for emotional supports

*Step 1:* the teacher and students create a short play reflecting love and friendship. The audience students, after watching the play, understand that love can reduce or cure the suffering and make people stronger in front of difficulties. It is good to sing a song about friendship or family love, for example *Friend Like Me*, if is even better to add dancing in the play.

*Step 2:* the teacher asks students to write down a true story happened to them, which is about the encouragement and supports from friends and family to them when they were in the midst of difficulties and adversity. And then the teachers collect the stories and read out to them.

*Step 3:* the teacher introduces the misfortune and suffering of one or several students, and advocates sincere encouragement from students.

(3) Strategy No. 3: turn the attention to other things.

There are many things in life people can pay attention to. The teacher explain to students "what the eye doesn't see the heart doesn't grieve for", and then ask them what they usually do to turn the attention when they face unhappy happenings, for example, travelling, writing, drawing, music, sports, etc. And also ask students to describe their feelings.

(4) Strategy No. 4: psychological defense

List of frustrations. The teacher asks students to list the frustrations they have encountered. Then the teacher present the following list of frustrations by slide, asks students to compare it with their own list and describe their feelings.

The teacher tells the students what Lincoln said after losing a senate race,

"The path was worn and slippery. My foot slipped from under me, knocking the other out of the way. But I recovered and said to myself, 'it is a slip and not a fall'".

The teacher asks the students to read this sentence loud.

The teacher asks students to use comparison method, and think what are more suffering than parents' breakup in their and others' life.

The teacher should ask students to focus on the practicing of using comparison method, because people's negative emotions are generated from distorted cognition, especially self-reproach in the mind. We need the following steps to remove the self-reproach.

1816 His family was forced out of their home. He had to work to support them.
1818 His mother died.
1831 Failed in business.
1832 Ran for state legislature — lost.
1832 Also lost his job — wanted to go to a law school but could not get in.
1833 Borrowed some money from a friend to begin a business and by the end of the year he was bankrupt. He spent the next 17 years of his life paying off this debt.
1834 Ran for state legislature again — won.
1835 Was engaged to be married, sweetheart died and his heart was broken.
1836 Had a total nervous breakdown and was in bed for six months.
1838 Sought to become speaker of the state legislature — defeated.
1840 Sought to become elector — lost.
1843 Ran for congress — lost.
1846 Ran for congress again — this time he won — went to Washington and did a good job.
1848 Ran for re-election to Congress — lost.
1849 Sought the job of land officer in his mother state — rejected.
1854 Ran for Senator of the United States — lost.
1856 Sought the Vice-Presidential nomination at his party's national convention — get less than 100 votes.
1858 Ran for U.S. Senate again — again he lost.
1860 Elected president of the United States.
And he is Abraham Lincoln who never quit.

Realize and record the self-reproach one has;

Find out what are the root causes of such wrong cognition;

Attack such wrong cognition and develop a more practical self-evaluation system. Students should follow the example as shown in the following table to correct their other wrong cognitions in mind.

| What I think (self-reproach) | The root cause of cognitive bias | Reasonable thinking |
|---|---|---|
| Parents divorced because of me. | Did not find the causes. | Parents divorced because of themselves. |
|  |  |  |
|  |  |  |

Then use one or two short play to illustrate the four strategies. Please note that the last three strategies are used to adjust emotions. On this basis, students should be calm and have right cognition, and then accept the fact.

3. Reflection

1) Objectives

It aims to make students feel the value of frustration and stimulate themselves to bravely face the frustration.

2) Training procedures

(1) The teachers show the following story through projector and ask students to talk about their feelings.

Adversity

Qingqing fell and did not cry. But two days later, she could not raise her left hand. And then her collarbone was found to be injured. It hurt and caused many inconveniences and took a long time to recover.

I felt so sorry for that, but she was happy to find out something unexpectedly, "mom, I know which side is left now!"

She is too little and could not distinguish left and right. Now she knows! The side which hurts is left!

There is a saying that "when god closes all doors, he opens a window for you". But we always cry and bang on the door, but forget that there is a window open.

(2) The teacher provides some examples. For example, when the ostrich in the desert is being chased and can not escape, it would bury its head in sand. If the danger can not be seem there is no danger. When kids break something or do something wrong, they will cover their eyes with hands. The teacher asks students to draw the cartoon about the two examples.

(3) Invite a volunteer student who has similar experience share about how he/she dealt with parents divorce and how he/she made progress.

(4) The teacher asks students to write a motto or aphorism to encourage themselves to bravely face frustration, and read it out in passionate music.

(5) Blank-filling (after all blanks are filled, ask students to read it out)

---

You can not accept the fact that your parents are divorced, emotionally you may _____. You may have some thoughts in mind. You may believe that their divorce did cause some influences on you, for example,

_____

_____. But you gradually go back to your normal life, study, interpersonal relationship through the means of _____,
so your life is full of sunshine and hopes! Besides, the frustration makes you find out that you actually have obtained some new qualities, such as _____. And you can face many things, like _____. Congratulations!
You successfully experience one of the significant tests of life. You can reward yourself with a medal for the brevity and confidence in front of frustration. Do persevere in your efforts

---

## II. List of Questions for SMOCWF Training

At the stage of attention and identification:

1. What is the problem?

What do I know about this problem? What information did I know? What can I use such information for?

At the stage of assessment:

1. Do I correctly understand the nature of frustration?

2. Do I have a comprehensive understanding towards the coping resources?

At the stage of plan:

1. What is my plan?

2. What strategies will I use?

At the stage of examination and summary:

1. Did I comply with my plan or strategies? Do I need a new plan or strategy?

2. Which strategies worked?

3. Which strategies did not work?

4. What other strategies should I use next time?

## III. List of Questions for Self-questioning for Proactive Coping

At the stage of resource extension:

Did I accumulate coping resources?

At the stage of identification:

Did I notice potential sources of frustration?

At the stage of preliminary assessment:

1. What is the potential source of frustration?

2. What will the potential source of frustration become?

3. Should I worry about that?

4. What else should I pay attention to?

At the stage of preliminary coping:

What can I do?

At the stage of stimulating and utilizing feedback:

Did the potential source of frustration change?

Is there any effect from preliminary efforts?

3. What do I know about the potential sourced of frustration?

## IV. List of Sentences for Self-talk in the Coping Process

At the stage of preparation:

I can make a plan to cope with this frustration.

I need to think about carefully about what I can do. It is much better than anxiety only.

Try to avoid negative self-talk. Try to have positive thinking.

At the stage of facing frustration:

I can handle with it, only need to follow proper sequence.

Such anxiety, as the expert said, is what I should experience. It reminds me of starting coping activities.

Relax; everything is still under my control. Breathe deeply and slowly.

At the stage of coping:

When you are scared or feel the fear, you might as well suspend.

Pay attention to the ongoing situations. What else do I have to do?

You don't need to get rid of fear completely. When you can still control, it is ok.

Among all what had happened, it is not the worst.

Think of other things.

At the stage of self-enforcement:

The coping measures worked. I can handle with the situation.

It is not as bad as I expected.

I am really happy about what I have progressed.

# REFERENCES

Alan, J. C., and Hennie, P. (1990). Training in metacognition: an application to industry. In K. J. Gilhooly, M. T. G. Keane, R. H. Logic and G. Erdos (Eds.), *Lines of thinking.* New York, NY: Wiley.

Berardi-Coletta, B., Buyer, L. S., and Dominowski, R. L. et al. (1995) Metacognition and problem-solving: A process - oriented approach. *Journal of Experimental Psychology: Learning, Memory, and Cognition, 21,* 205 - 223.

Braunstein, J. J. and Toister. R. P. (1981). *Medical applications of the behavioral sciences.* London, ENG: Year Book Medical Pub.

Carter, B. D., Bendell, R. D., et al (1985). Behavioral health: Focus on preventive child health behavior. In A. R. Zeiner, R. D. Bendell, et al. (Eds.), *Health psychology: Treatment and research issues* (pp. 8-19). New York, NY: Plenum Press.

Carver, C. S., Scheier, M. F., and Weintraud, J. K. (1989). Assessing coping strategies: A theoretically based approach. *Journal of personality and social psychology, 56,* 267-283.

Chen, E. H. (1994). Psychological stress reaction and personality traits. *Journal of Xiangtan Normal University, 4,* 69-71.

Dominowski, R. L. (1990). Problem solving and metacongnition. In K. J. Gilhooly, M. T. G. Keane, R. H. Logic and G. Erdos (Eds.), *Lines of thinking.* New York: Wiley.

Dong, Q., Zhou, Y., and Chen, H. B. (1996). *Self-monitoring and intelligence* (1st edition). Hangzhou, China: Zhejiang People's Press.

Feng, J. P. (1991). *Frustration psychology.* Taiyuan: Shanxi Education Press.

Feng, J. P. (1993). The review concerning the research into psychological frustration theory. *Journal of Hebei Normal University (social science edition), 1,* 56-60.

Folkman, S. and Lazarus, R. S. (1980). An analysis of coping in a middle-aged community sample. *Journal of health and social behavior, 21,* 219-239.

Gao, Y. B., and Nie, J. (1997). Research on the types of responses to frustration among students from junior middle schools and the educational strategies. *Science of social psychology, 4,* 34-36.

Huang, X. T., et al. (2000). A preliminary research into the coping styles of middle school students. *Psychological science, 23,* 1-5.

Jiang, Y. Q. (1998). Psychological vaccination training is an effective way to improve teenagers' frustration tolerance. *Journal of Longyan Teachers College, 2,* 21-23.

Lazarus, R. S. (1966). *Psychological stress and the coping process.* New York: McGraw-Hill.

Lazarus, R. S. (1993). From psychological stress to the emotions: A history of changing outlooks. *Annual review of psychology, 44,* 1-21.

Lazarus, R. S., and Folkman, S. (1984). *Stress, appraisal and coping.* New York, NY: Springer.

Li, H. Z., and Bian, H. P. (1995). *On frustration education.* Nanjing, JS: Jiangsu Education Press.

Liu, H. S. (1998). *School psychological counseling.* Hefei: Anhui People's Publishing House.

Liu, X. C., Yang, J., et al. (1998). Research into stressful life events and coping styles of teenagers. *Chinese mental health journal, 12,* 46-48.

Mo, W. B. (1991). A brief introduction to the cognitive phenomenology theory of stress and coping. *Journal of developments in psychology, 1,* 68-71.

O'Neil, H. F., and Abedi, J. (1996). Reliability and validity of a state metacognitive inventory: Potential for alternative assessment. *The journal of educational research, 89,* 234-245.

Rice, P. L. (2000). *Stress and health* (L. Shi, et al., Trans.). Beijing: China Light Industry Press.

Sun, Y. M. (1986). Children's problem behaviors and psychological frustration. *Journal of Nanjing Normal University (social science), 2,* 13-17.

Vaillant, G. E. (1996). *Adaptation to life* (W. W. Yan, Trans.). Shanghai: East China Normal University Press.

Wei, Y. H., et al. (1998). Several major stress theory modes and corresponding evaluation. *Psychological science, 21,* 441-444.

Wo, J. Z. (1996). *Experimental methods for intelligence research.* Hangzhou: Zhejiang People's Press.

Xiao, J. H. (1992). Coping and coping styles. *Chinese mental health journal, 6,* 181-183.

Xiao, L. H. (1997). Frustration education: An issue can not be neglected in home education. *Journal of Huizhou University, 1,* 74-78.

Zhang, D. J., et al. (2000). *Psychological* suzhi *training for students from primary and middle schools.* Chongqing: Southwest China Normal University Press.

Zhou, G. G. (1997). On frustration and frustration education. *Journal of Guizhou Education Institute (social science edition), 3,* 11-17.

Zhu, Z. X. (1989). p. 1891. In Z. X. Zhu (Ed.), *Dictionary of psychology* (pp. 1891-1891). Shanghai: Shanghai Education Publishing House.

Zimbardo, P. G. (1985). Understanding and managing stress. In P. G. Zimbardo (Ed.), *Psychology and life* (pp. 454-487). London: Froesman and Company.

*Chapter 3*

# THE DEVELOPMENT OF LEARNING ADAPTABILITY AMONG STUDENTS FROM JUNIOR MIDDLE SCHOOLS IN THE INFILTRATION OF PSYCHOLOGICAL SUZHI CULTIVATION IN TEACHING ENGLISH LANGUAGE

## *Li-Juan Song[1], Da-Jun Zhang[2], Qi Jiang[2] and Jin-Liang Wang[2]*

[1]Luzhou Medical College, Luzhou, China
[2]Center for Mental Health Education in Southwest University, China

## ABSTRACT

Learning adaptability refers to individuals' capacity to adaptively regulate psychological activities and behaviors in response to the changing learning environment and their own development requirements in order to realize better learning effects.

Learning adaptability directly influences the effects and quality of learning. It is also closely related with good personality traits and the level of individuals' mental health. Based on the literature related to learning adaptability, the present research tries to improve students' learning adaptability through the subject infiltration mode.

We used educational experiment and chose at random two homogeneous parallel classes from junior grade one as experimental group and control group respectively. We used the mode and strategies for subject infiltration (in the present research the subject refers to English language) and carried out the training of learning adaptability to the experimental group for four months.

According to the pre-test and post-test results, obvious improvements are As seen from experimental group in the adaptability, psychological suzhi, the utilization of strategies in English language learning and academic performance in English language learning, which means that the correct use of such training mode can improve the learning adaptability of students and that the modes and strategies of subject infiltration are effective in developing students' psychological suzhi.

# 4.1. INTRODUCTION

## 4.1.1. Current Research into Learning Adaptability Among Students from Junior Middle Schools

In the Western world, not many researchers probed into learning adaptability directly. And "Learning Adaptability" has not yet been developed into a term. Not many articles can be found by searching "learning adaptability" and "learning adaptation" in ProQuest Education/Psychology, Kluwer Online Journals, EBSCOhost, Cambridge University Press, etc. All the articles found are empirical research by researchers from Taiwan.

### 1) Theories about Learning Adaptability

**Definitions**

The research into learning adaptability is mainly from Chinese mainland and Taiwan. Research on topic has increased significantly since late 1990s. To summarize, the definitions of learning adaptability are as follows:

#### Table 4.1. Main Definitions of Learning Adaptability

| |
|---|
| 1. Learning adaptability, also adaptability to learning, is the tendency of an individual to overcome difficulties and obtain good learning outcomes [Zhou et al, 1991]. |
| 2. Students' psychological adaptability in learning is learning adaptability. Psychological adaptability generally refers to psychological capacity of an individual to obtain balance during the interaction between such individual and the environment by positively undertaking certain behaviors and actions to the surrounding environment [Zheng, 1994]. |
| 3. Learning adaptability refers to students' capacity to realize favorable developing conditions, i.e., the balance of internal and external learning environments, by initiatively undertaking physical and psychological adjustment according to the changes in learning conditions (learning attitude, learning methods, learning environment, etc.) in the process of learning [Tian, 2002]. |
| 4. Learning adaptability refers to the habitual tendency of an individual that is enthusiastic about learning, changes continuously learning plans and methods according to the changing learning environment and contents [Wang, 2002]. |
| 5. Learning adaptability of university students refers to the capacity characteristics of an individual to initiatively adjust learning motivation and learning activities and to improve the learning ability according to the changes of internal and external learning conditions and the needs of learning, in order to harmonize the psychology and behaviors of learning with the changing learning conditions and to realize good academic performance [Xu, 2004]. |
| 6. Learning adaptability refers to individuals' stable capacity characteristics shown in the process of self-regulation to adaptively regulate psychological activities and behaviors in response to the changing learning environment and their own development requirements, in order to realize better learning effects [Chen, 2005]. |

Despite the difference among the definitions above, there are common grounds:

> Learning adaptability is the habitual tendency of an individual developed in the process of learning activities, which has been internalized to be stable capacity characteristics and is of relatively stability.
> Learning adaptability is the process of self-regulation of an individual according to the external environment and the development requirements of such individual, which is absolutely dynamic and is of intrinsic motivation.
> Learning adaptability directly influences individuals' learning effects and quality.

Based on the definition and implication of learning adaptability in the existing literature, we define the learning adaptability of middle school students as: learning adaptability, also adaptability to learning, is individuals' capacity to adaptively regulate psychological activities and behaviors in response to the changing learning environment and their own development requirements, in order to realize better learning effects.

According to previous research, if students can not carry out positive measures for physical and psychological regulation according to the changing learning and internalizing environments which cause that the academic performance and physical and psychological health fail to meet the proper development level, then problems of learning adaptability will occur [Tian, 2002], such as unclear learning objectives, lacking of learning interest, confidence, suitable methods and good learning habits, as well as tiredness of learning, nervousness and anxiety in learning and bad relationship with peer students. Therefore, poor learning capacity is reflected by the problems of learning adaptability.

In the Western world, not many researchers probed into the problems of learning adaptability among teenagers; instead, the research focused on learning difficulty. Learning difficulty is a general word, which includes such terms as learning disorder, slow learner and learning disability. The research into learning difficulty by Chinese researchers mainly focused on bad academic performance of teenagers. According to the research, teenagers who have problems in learning adaptability and bad academic performance have normal intelligence. However, the problem of learning adaptability is broader than bad academic performance. The former includes not only the teenagers who have small problems of learning adaptability, but also teenagers who have bad academic performance resulting from poor learning adaptability. The problem of learning adaptability will inevitably cause bad academic performance. Bad academic performance also worsens the problem of learning adaptability. Therefore, these two influence each other [Bai, 1997; Nie, 2004].

2) Conceptual Structure of Learning Adaptability Among Junior Middle School Students

Learning adaptability is reflected in learning activities, thus it is related with factors affecting learning activities. So far, there are not many discussions about the conceptual structure about learning adaptability among students from junior middle schools. The typical views include:

Zhou et al. pointed out in the instructional manual of the *Academic Adaptability Test for Junior Middle School Students* that academic adaptability includes learning enthusiasm, learning with plans, methods of listening to lectures, reading and note-taking methods, memory and thinking methods, exam methods, learning environment, character, and physical and psychological health.

According to the *Learning Adaptability Scale* [Chen, Lin and Li, 1991], learning adaptability includes five aspects of learning methods, habits, attitude, environment, physical and psychological adaptability.

According to the *Learning Adaptability Test for Middle School Students* by Huarui HR Evaluation and Teaching System, learning adaptability includes motivation, expectation, methods, will, environment of learning, as well as physical and psychological health [Nie et al., 2004].

After literature review, we found that frontline teachers agree in their teaching practice that good learning adaptability of middle schools students is reflected by the way they have learning objectives, good learning attitude, suitable learning methods, and that they are interested and confident in learning, harmonious with the surrounding environment, willing to ask for help from teachers in problem-solving, able to cooperate to complete the learning task, emotionally stable, and are physically and psychologically healthy.

Therefore, we believe that there are four factors involved in learning adaptability of middle school students:

Internal learning motivation system (learning motivation, learning interest, learning attitude, etc.);

Learning method and strategy system (learning methods, learning strategies, learning habits, etc.);

Students' personality traits and physical and psychological health; and

Students' adaptation to the objective and physical environment, and interpersonal and psychological environment.

## Measurement Tools

Currently, the measurement tools for learning adaptability available are mainly for two groups: ordinary children and children who have learning difficulty. The following is a brief introduction to measurement tools of learning adaptability for ordinary children.

The *Academic Adaptability Test* (AAT) revised by Zhou et al. AAT for pupils and middle school students are both available, for which national norm is also available. AAT for middle school students includes four scales and 12 dimensions; for example, learning attitude sub-scale (the dimensions are learning interests, learning plans, methods of listening to lectures), learning technique sub-scale (the dimensions are reading and note-taking methods, learning techniques, exam methods); learning environment sub-scale (the dimensions are family environment, school environment, friend relationship); physical and psychological sub-scale (the dimensions include independence, perseverance, psychological and physical health). In this scale, learning adaptability is shown in five ratings: good, average plus, average, average minus and bad. Average minus and bad indicate poor learning adaptability. Research showed that the reliability and validity of this test are good. This test is the most popular one in Chins [Cui and Meng, 1998].

The *Learning Adaptability Scale* established by Chen, Lin, Li et al. from Taiwan. It is for students ranging from primary grade four to junior grade three. It is composed of five sub-scales: learning methods, learning habits, learning attitude, learning environment, physical and psychological adaptation. According to the confirmatory factor analysis of Sun and

Zheng [2001], the mode fitting of the total scale and sub-scales do not violate basis standard for scale development, but the construct validity of learning environment sub-scale is not good and needs to be re-structured.

The *Learning Adaptability Test for Middle School Students* from Huarui HR Evaluation and Teaching System. It divides learning adaptability into seven sub-scales, such as learning motivation, learning expectation from teachers, parents, students themselves), learning methods (plans, listening to lectures, note-taking, exam, memory, habit), learning will, school environment (peer students, teachers, schools), family environment (learning space, noise, family relationship) as well as physical and psychological health [Nie et al., 2004].

### 2) Empirical Research into Learning Adaptability

According to our analysis, empirical research into learning adaptability of middle school students mainly included investigation into the investigation on development characteristic, related research and research into utilization.

## Investigation On Development Characteristic

In general, the learning adaptability of middle school students nowadays is at normal level. The mean score on learning adaptability is slightly higher than middle level. But the learning adaptability of over 20% middle school students is still at the level of average minus or bad, indicating that they have poor learning adaptability or even difficulty in adaptation [Dai, 1997; Bai et al. 1997]. Cheng et al. surveyed 4,649 pupils and junior middle school students in Shanghai, and found that the top 10 mental problems of students are: improper learning motivation, bad learning habit, insufficient learning capacity, attention disorder, poor self-control, self-centered, low frustration tolerance, learning anxiety, inferiority complex and social withdrawal. Among them, seven are related to learning adaptability [Wu, 2001].

There are controversies over the development of learning adaptability with the upgrading of grades. Research showed that students' learning adaptability is actually decreasing as the grade upgrades [Nie et al., 2004; Wang et al., 1996; Feng, 1999]. Obviously, the learning adaptability of junior middle school students is better than senior middle school students. The proportion of students who have poor learning adaptability in senior middle schools is higher than in junior middle schools. Researchers had different opinions over the learning adaptability between female and male students [Zhang and Zhang, 2000; Dai, 1997; Wang, 1996]. But most research showed that the learning adaptability of male students is very different from female students, with female students having better learning adaptability than male students in many aspects.

Researchers had different opinions over the learning adaptability among students from different regions [Bai et al., 1997; Zhang and Zhang, 2000; Yan et al., 2000], but it was agreed that students from rural areas have remarkably better learning adaptability than city students. Significant difference in learning adaptability can be found between top students and slow learners.

The average scores of slow learners in learning adaptability are far lower than top students [Wang et al., 1998]. Obviously, students from key middle schools have better learning adaptability than students from ordinary middle schools [Nie et al., 2004].

To summarize, there are controversies in research results, which is caused by unbalanced development of learning adaptability in different regions, different places of sampling and the deviation of the representativeness of samplings.

## Related Research

Related research into learning adaptability mainly focuses on the relationship between learning adaptability and academic performance, personality traits, psychological health.

In terms of academic performance, Dai [1997] found that the learning adaptability of middle school students positively correlated with academic performance. The learning adaptability of pupils highly related to their intelligence and academic performance. The correlation between learning adaptability and academic performance was 0.331 ($p<0.001$) and was 0.367 ($p<0.001$) between intelligence and academic performance [Dai, 1997].

It reveals that learning adaptability and intelligence have great and almost the same influence over students' academic performance. Liu [2001] revealed from how learning adaptability influences students with different academic performance, and found that it had direct influence on students with average academic performance and indirect influence on those with good and bad academic performance. Therefore, good learning adaptability is an important factor to ensure good academic performance. Poor learning adaptability is an important cause for abnormal academic performance of some students, although they have normal intelligence.

Academic performance is the core indicator of learning adaptability. The level of students' learning adaptability directly influences their learning efficiency.

In terms of personality characteristics, the research by Zhang, Feng et al. showed that learning adaptability was an essential part of adaptability suzhi among middle school students, and was part of students' psychological suzhi structure. The improvement of learning adaptability naturally promoted the development of students' adaptability suzhi and even the structure and functions of psychological suzhi, and maintained a healthy personality [Zhang et al., 2000]. The results of learning adaptability tests and 16PF questionnaire showed that students with strong learning adaptability had good personality factors. They were highly stable in emotion, highly rule-conscious, highly self-reliant, highly self-disciplined, less tense, less suspicious and less worried [Song, 1999; Zha, 1993].

In terms of psychological health, learning adaptability is closely related to various psychological factors in SCL-90. Students have stronger learning adaptability are healthier psychologically, which is indicated both by general and specific indicators [Song and Yang, 1999]. Yang [2002] did a research into the relationship between anxiety and learning adaptability among students from vocational high schools and found that anxiety negatively correlated to learning adaptability. Li [1995] also found that students with poor learning adaptability had many negative emotions, such as inferiority complex, distress and disappointment.

To summarize, relevant research into learning adaptability showed that the learning adaptability of middle school students promotes academic performance, maintains good personality traits and psychological health.

## Research Into Interventional Cultivation

In recent years, experimental research aimed to improve the learning effect of middle school students as the education for all-around development progresses. Most research focused on stimulating and developing learning motivation, strengthening self-efficacy of learning, improving learning methods, mastering effective learning strategies, effectively relieving exam pressure and adjusting exam psychology. Some research was based on certain subject or independence from subjects. Such research was conducted to directly or indirectly improve students' learning adaptability. But such research only focused on a certain aspect of learning adaptability. We call such research as cultivation on part of learning adaptability.

Not many researchers did all-around research into learning adaptability. Except the all-around research by Tian [2002] into the problems of learning adaptability faced by pupils, all the rest is about subject-based research in middle school. The research in Changning District of Shanghai in East China has the largest scale and influence [Xu and Zheng, 2000]. The "learning adaptability program in five schools" has been extended to "learning adaptability program in 12 schools". In this program, the *Academic Adaptability Test* revised by Zhou is used as theoretical reference, some teachers and students from the School of Psychology and Cognitive Science of East China Normal University conducted in the general survey of learning adaptability, established guide books of learning adaptability, and organized curriculum of learning adaptability and parents' tutorial class. In addition, the research by Peng et al. from Hunan Dizhi Middle School is also influential [Peng, 1999]. They developed a three-year experimental research into students' learning adaptability when they did a psychological suzhi-based education research among middle school students.

To summarize, the experiment in the all-around development of learning adaptability among middle school students is conducted in three ways, i.e., tutorial course of learning adaptability, group counseling of learning adaptability and individual psychological counseling. All these three means have obvious effects. However, the methods used in the development are at the macro level. No specific instruction is available, for example, what psychological activities are carried out in the tutorial class of learning adaptability and what teaching strategies are undertaken to specify the different aspects of learning adaptability. This, to some extent, influences the popularization of the experiment, and is not favorable for the regulation and guidance of teaching practice.

### 3) Deficiency of the Research into Learning Adaptability

Although the existing research probed into the connotation of learning adaptability among middle school students, the characteristics and current status of learning adaptability among middle school students from China, which is significant in understanding the learning adaptability of students, there are still deficiencies:

> The theoretical discussion about the essence, structure, causes and function is not deep enough;
> Not enough experimental research in education concerning the development of learning adaptability among middle school students; and
> No empirical research into the infiltration of learning adaptability into ecological and regular classes and teaching of certain subject.

## Current Status of the Research into Infiltration of Psychological Suzhi Cultivation in Teaching of a Subject

### 1) Definition and Characteristics of Subject Infiltration

Subject infiltration refers to infiltration of psychological suzhi cultivation in teaching of a subject, which is one of the main means to undertake mental health education in schools.

## Table 4.2. Definitions of Subject Infiltration

1. It refers to that teachers consciously conduct mental health education in the teaching of a subject [Chen, 2002].
2. It refers to teachers consciously use psychological theories, methods and techniques in the normal teaching of a subject, in order to improve the psychological traits of students when they master knowledge and develop capacity [Sun and Zhang, 2003].
3. Subject infiltration is that teachers find out the connection between teaching of a subject and the development of students' psychological suzhi, applypsychological suzhi-based educationapproaches and strategies with clear objectives and well-prepared plans, and infiltratepsychological suzhi-based educationinto the teaching of a subject in order to promote students' mental, health [Jiang and Zhang, 2004

It aims to use teaching of a subject, the main means of education, to infiltrate psychological suzhi-based education when imparting knowledge and techniques. In China, both "subject infiltration" and "psychological education in teaching" are used. However, "subject infiltration" not only reflects that psychological suzhi-based education in school is an educational activity aiming to develop students' all-around psychological suzhi. It is more purposive, specific, instructional and operable and also specifies the relationship between teaching of a subject and psychological suzhi cultivation. Therefore, we use "subject infiltration".

It can be summarized from the above that subject infiltration has the following characteristics:

Teaching of a subject is the master line and psychological suzhi cultivation is the auxiliary line. The objective of teaching of a subject is the primary objective and the goal of psychological suzhi cultivation is the secondary goal.

Subject infiltration is implicit and imperceptible, which aims to develop and improve students' psychological traits by imperceptible influence.

Subject infiltration should combine psychological development with mastering knowledge, in order to realize both the objectives of teaching of a subject and psychological suzhi cultivation, and eventually to develop students' psychological suzhi in an all-around way.

### 2) Roles and Functions of Subject Infiltration

The theoretical circle does not have many discussions on the role of subject infiltration, but it is agreed that subject infiltration is an important and indivisible part of subject teaching, and it is also the basis of psychological suzhi-based education and mental health education in schools. The functions of subject infiltration are as follows:

In terms of psychological suzhi-based education, it helps to extend means of psychological suzhi-based education, strengthen the functions of psychological suzhi-based education, and finally realize psychological suzhi-based education objectives.

In terms of subject teaching, it helps to diversify the functions of subject teaching. It is the intrinsic needs of teaching activities. It promotes the realization of teaching objectives and improves the effects of teaching.

In terms of education for all-around development, it helps to solve the disconnection of subject teaching and psychological suzhi-based education, change the lacking of psychological suzhi-based education objectives in subject teaching, and to realize the general objectives of education for all-around development.

In terms of developing teachers' capacity, it helps to make teachers learn and use psychological theories and thus to enrich their theoretical knowledge and improve their capacity.

In terms of curriculum development, it promotes positively the adjustment of the curriculum structure of subjects, which promotes better strategies for curriculum implementation.

### 3) Objectives and Contents of Subject Infiltration

Chinese researchers put forward three-dimensional teaching objectives and "six learns" as well as two-dimensional objectives and "four learns and four aspects of development". For three-dimensional teaching objectives, it is proposed to set the objectives of subject infiltration from the dimensions of content, result and process [Zheng, 1999]. "Six learns" refer to making students "learn to live, learn to study, learn to create, learn to care, learn to behave themselves, learn to self-educate";

Two-dimensional teaching objectives refer to positive adaptation and self-development. In education, positive adaptation is "four learns", namely, learn to study, learn to deal with interpersonal relationship, learn to live and learn to behave themselves; self-development refers to "four aspects of development", i.e., development of intelligence, development of personality, development of sociality and development of creativeness [Zhang et al., 2000].

### 4) Means, Principles and Methods of Subject Infiltration

According to the previous research, the means of subject infiltration include making full use of the psychological resources embedded in the textbooks of the subject, and paying attention to the infiltration in the process of teaching. There are direct and indirect psychological resources embedded in the textbooks.

Such resources need to be discovered through certain methods, for example, direct utilization, exploration, extension, etc. And the connection between the normal teaching of a subject and psychological suzhi-based education needs to be found. Some researchers believed that related psychological resources can be directly used in arts curriculum; whereas, for science curriculum, the process of teaching needs to be focused [Chen, 2002]. The infiltration of psychological suzhi-based education in teaching is mainly reflected by the role of teachers, for example, teachers change the teaching concepts, improve the teaching methods, create good teacher-student relationship, establish harmonious, pleasing and loose psychological environment in class. Some researcher even pointed out that teachers are critical to the success of subject infiltration.

There are different opinions about the principles of subject infiltration. Some proposed all-around integration and hierarchical implementation [Chen and Zhang, 2002]; or advantage complementary principle, development principle, integration principle, specific-problem-based principle [Xiao, 2003]; or the principle of sustainable development of integral coordination, the principle of openness [Zheng, 1999]. Some argued that the principles should aim to realize intrinsic rules, objectiveness and purposiveness, imperceptible integration and subject specific [Chen, 2002]. Some also specifically set principles for the teaching of teachers, for example, incentive principle, agent participation principle and interest principle [Sun and Zhang, 2003].

There are also many methods to implement subject infiltration; for example, the teaching methods for ordinary subject infiltration, including experience, evaluation and discovery; and teaching methods for specific subjects, such as detailed explanation of certain word, reading aloud repeatedly, inspiring questions, practice etc. used in Chinese language class of primary schools. Ju uses in-class questions as the core methods to cultivate students' thinking capacity in Chemistry class [Chen, 2002].

### 5) Deficiencies in the Research into Subject Infiltration

We found that either the theoretical discussion or the empirical research of subject infiltration is at the beginning stage, thus deficiencies can not be avoided:

Lacking of systematic theoretical discussion into basic issues, including definitions, contents, principles, methods and evaluation.

Not many researchers did experimental research in strict accordance with the research design, which restricts scientific persuasion and the promotion in practice.

## Objectives of the Research

### 1) Probe into the Means and Methods to Cultivate Students' Learning Adaptability in Subject Teaching

Teaching students the capacity to learn is a topic that causes attention from education circles all over the world. Learn to study, learn to do, learn to live together and learn to be are the four pillars in education. The present research meets the new requirements of learning on the era of knowledge-driven economy.

Based on the existing research into learning adaptability of middle school students and infiltration of psychological suzhi-based education in teaching of a subject, this chapter focuses on the adaptive problems of English language learning faced by students from junior middle schools, and trying to find effective methods and means for developing students' learning adaptability in the teaching of a subject.

### 2) Probe into the Theoretical and Practical Problems in the Effective Integration of Psychological Suzhi Cultivation and Teaching of a Subject

Students' psychological suzhi is a multi-level and multi-dimensional self-organization system. It is influenced by many aspects of the education in school [Chen and Zhang, 2002], thus students' psychological suzhi needs to be cultivated by integrating various education modes and strategies. The present chapter takes the teaching of English language in junior middle schools as an example to discuss the theory and practice of effective integration of students' psychological suzhi cultivation and teaching of a subject through strict experimental research.

Our research focused on the learning adaptability of English language among junior middle school students, follows the rules of the experimental research in education, and tries to realize the objectives of developing students' learning adaptability while realizing the objectives of English language teaching in class.

## Research Idea and Tools of the Present Research

We, based on the research results available, collected the problems of learning adaptability in English language learning faced by junior middle school students by literature analysis and interviews.

Guided by psychological suzhi-based education integrated modes [Chen and Zhang, 2002], we theoretically discussed and developed the subject infiltration modes and teaching strategies for cultivating students' learning adaptability in teaching of a subject. In the educational experiment, we adjusted such modes and strategies, and verify the applicability and effectivity of them.

We tried to find the means and methods to improve students' adaptability in English language learning, learning adaptability, psychological suzhi and academic performance in English language learning.

The tools include:

The *Academic Adaptability Test for Junior Middle School Students* (AAT) revised by Zhou et al. The scale has good reliability and validity and is the most frequently used in China.

The *Psychological* Suzhi *Questionnaire for Middle School Students* by Zhang and Feng [1999]. It is composed of three sub-questionnaires, i.e., cognitive quality, personality traits and adaptability. The test-retest correlation of the total scale is 0.853. The test-retest correlation of factors is between 0.76 and 0.84. The internal consistency reliability of the scale is 0.839. The internal consistency reliability of the factors is between 0.72 and 0.78. The correlation of factors is between 0.25 and 0.54. Therefore, the scale has high reliability and good construct validity.

The *Strategy Evaluation Sheet for English Language Learning among Students Ranging from Grade Seven to Grade Nine*. This evaluation sheet is translated by Qin [2000] from the objectives of learning strategies for junior middle school graduates as prescribed in the *English Curriculum Standard*. It is composed of 32 items and is divided into four parts, namely, strategy for cognition, strategy for regulation, strategy for communication and strategy for resources. Five options are available after each item. It is rated on a 5-point Likert scale and positive scoring is used. (1=never use, 2=barely use, 3=sometimes use, 4=frequent use, 5=always use). The internal consistency reliability is 0.90.

Spss 11.0 for Windows 2000 software was used for data analysis.

# THEORETICAL ANALYSIS

## The Value of Developing Learning Adaptability in English Language Teaching among Students from Junior Middle Schools

### *1) The Necessity of Developing Learning Adaptability in English Language Teaching Among Students from Junior Middle Schools*

Because students from junior grade one just start their middle school life, they have problems in adapting to the learning in junior middle school, especially in English language learning. We got the information that in most areas of China, English language class in primary schools is not popular, according to our interview with some English language teachers in junior middle schools and students from junior grade one from the experimental school. Even when English language class is available, people do not pay enough attention to it because it is not the major subject and is not included in the enrollment examination. Most schools arrange fewer class hours for English language class. Therefore, in primary school, students' interest in English language is not well cultivated. Students do not have stable and effective methods to learn English language. In junior middle school, English language becomes the major subject. The difficulty in English language learning is increased in the recent curriculum reform, but the class hours are not increased. Under such circumstances, students feel difficult and painful to learn English language, which results in problems of learning adaptability. If teachers do not change their teaching concepts, or their teaching methods, we will not have optimistic results for English language learning by students. Learning adaptability is the core part of students' psychological suzhi of adaptability [Feng and Zhang, 2001]. How to guide students to strengthen their learning adaptability is the important part of mental health education and research, as well as the guidance of psychology of learning [Chen, 2004]. Therefore, it is necessary to infiltrate the education of learning adaptability in English language teaching.

### *2) The Applicability of Developing Learning Adaptability in English Language Teaching among Students from Junior Middle Schools*

It is feasible from the objectives of teaching. According to the English Language Teaching Syllabus for Nine-year Compulsory Education Full-time Junior Middle School (Trail and Revised Version)[1], "The fundamental purpose of English language teaching in junior middle school is education for all-around development; it focuses on developing

---

[1] The English Language Teaching Syllabus for Nine-year Compulsory Education Full-time Junior Middle School (Trail and Revised Version) established by the Ministry of Education of the P. R. C. Prescribes that English language course in the period of compulsory education should realize all around development of moral, intellectual, physical education; should be geared to modernization, the world and the future; and should focus on developing students innovative spirit and practical ability, in order to promote education for all-around development. Ideological and affective education should be carried out in English language course, in order to let students understand and respect the outstanding cultural traditions of other countries and ethnic groups, better understand the outstanding cultural traditions of Chinese nation. Teachers should develop students' capacity in positive and initiative thinking, extend their knowledge in culture and science, enrich their experience in cultural life, improve their ideological and moral cultivation, and make them meeting the requirements of China's development of society, economy, science and technology, as well as international communication. English language course should be available to all students, trying to create conditions for the all-around development of every student and to lay foundation for their life-long learning. This syllabus is the main basis of implementation of courses, evaluation of teaching and establishment of textbooks.

students' innovative spirit and practical ability, aiming to lay foundation for life-long learning". Life-long learning requires good learning adaptability of students. In June 2001, the English Curriculum Standard for Compulsory Education Full-time Senior Middle School[2](New English Curriculum Standard) prescribes that one of the tasks for English language course in basic education is to "stimulate and develop the interests of students in English language learning, develop the self-confidence of students, develop good learning habits and effective learning strategies" [Song and Jin, 2002]. Therefore, the objectives of English language teaching indicate that students' learning adaptability needs to be developed. It is also feasible from the contents of teaching. The critical part of subject infiltration lies in that whether resources are available in the course of the subject or the process of teaching [Ye, 2004; Chen, 2002]. The characteristics of English language subject in junior middle schools result in that there are rich psychological suzhi resources in the textbooks and the process of teaching which can be used to develop students' learning adaptability. Therefore, it is feasible to develop learning adaptability in English language teaching.

## Problems of Adaptation to English Language Leaning and Development of Learning Adaptability among Students from Junior Middle Schools

Because many factors are involved in learning adaptability, in order to ensure the pertinence of experiment intervention, we used literature analysis and interview with teachers and students to collect the problem of adaptation to English language learning faced by junior middle school students. Based on the problems collected, we carried out plans about how to develop their adaptation to English language learning.

Firstly, we searched for related literature in CNKI (Chinese National Knowledge Infrastructure) full-text databases, and several thousand articles were found. After analysis, we found that junior middle school students nowadays face eight types of problems in English language learning. Such problems are listed as follows from high to low frequency of occurrence:

*Lacking of interests and enthusiasm in learning.* Students do not have constant interests in learning. When they encounter problems, they have no learning enthusiasm. They do not actively participate in activities, and do not have desires to participate in class activities. They are weary of learning.

*Lacking of good learning habits.* They do not prepare for the lessons or review the lessons. They have the habits of waiting and relying. They are not initiative in learning and not concentrated in class. Their thinking activities are irrelevant to the contents of teaching and do not quite understand the teaching.

---

[2] The New English Curriculum Standard was issued by the Ministry of Education of the P. R. C. to solve the problems of current English language teaching in China. This standard has the following characteristics: it tries to realize advanced concepts of the curriculum standard and make it greatly operable and conforming to the times; it is the first time that the instructional documents of English language teaching for senior high school define the humanity and tool characteristics of foreign language courses; it not only reflects the integrity and basis of English language course in basic education, but also meets the individualized and diversified needs of senior middle school students; it explicitly puts forward that English language teaching in senior middle school should focus on communication based on English language, treatment of English information and thinking in English, in order to develop students' pragmatic competence.

*Lacking of scientific learning methods.* They learn English words by noting Chinese phonetics on them, memorize words by rote, tend to inquire into the root of grammar, mechanically practice the sentence pattern, write sentences by translating word-to-word from Chinese, and can not get rid of Chinese language habits.

*Weak foundation, unable to remember words and grammar.* They need to learn a lot of knowledge to catch up. They tend to forget knowledge learned very easily. They are always confused with knowledge. They have learning difficulty.

*Unclear learning objectives.* They do not know why they need to learn English. They think that English is boring. Their English language learning is aimless and blind.

*Lacking of confidence, unable to solve frustration.* They lose interests and confidence when they encounter frustration. They quit after learning of the difficulties, hardship, etc.

*Do not understand the characteristics of English language as a subject.* They do not realize that English language is a communication tool. The purpose of learning English is to acquire the ability to listen, speak, read and write in English, and to develop communication competence. They do not know numerous and repeated oral and written practice is a must in learning English language. They think English course is knowledge-based and understanding-based course. They think the target is only to understand what teachers say. They are not aware that English language learning requires accumulation, solid foundation and should be stepwise.

*Poor language skills.* They do not like speaking English. They do not usually read the text loud or follow the tapes. They do not attach importance to pronunciation and tones.

The problems listed in iv), vii) and viii) are knowledge and skill problems in English language. The other items are all about the students' psychological problems. To be specific, they are problems of learning adaptability in learning interests, learning habits and learning methods, belonging to problems of learning motivation system and learning method and strategy system. The research into educational psychology showed that the mastering of knowledge and skills is influenced by individuals' psychological activities during learning. Therefore, the problems in knowledge and skills are the external reflection of problem in students' learning adaptability. We can start with the learning interests, learning habits and learning methods to develop students' adaptability to English language learning. It exactly corresponds with the content factors of the learning adaptability of middle school students.

Before the experiment, we interviewed the English teachers for junior middle school students and students from junior grade one in the experimental school. We found that: learning adaptability is a common problem for students from this school. This school is an ordinary middle school with half students from rural areas and half from urban areas. Most parents are working in other places and have poor education. Many students live together with their grandparents or grandparents in law who are not able to tutor them. Some students live in school, and do not have high learning motivation or good learning habits. They had weak foundation in English language learning in primary school. Besides, the new curriculum is more difficult, which makes the learning adaptability in English language more serious.

Therefore, in the experiment, we focused on "stimulating motivation, developing learning interests, guiding them to develop learning methods and developing learning habits" to develop students' adaptability to English language learning.

Our experiment, i.e., to infiltrate the development of learning adaptability in English language teaching for students from junior middle school, aims to realize the psychological suzhi-based education objective of developing students' learning adaptability by "stimulating learning motivation, developing learning interests, guiding students to develop learning methods and developing learning habits". The experiment was carried out in accordance with the subject infiltration modes, teaching strategies, objectives and plans.


## Modes and Strategies to Develop Learning Adaptability in English Language Teaching among Students from Junior Middle Schools

### 1) *Optimization and Integration of Relevant Educational Resources are the Pre-conditions for Establishing the Mode*

In order to properly integrate psychological suzhi-based education with the teaching of a subject, we must find the proper connection (i.e., opportunities for infiltration) between the contents, methods of teaching a subject and its contents, methods of psychological suzhi-based education. The infiltration should be natural, proper and imperceptible, rather than farfetched. The teaching of a subject should not be turned to be a psychological suzhi-based education class.

We believe that, according to the existing research into subject infiltration and the characteristics of English language teaching in junior middle school, the modes for developing learning adaptability in English language teaching among students from junior middle school should be established by mainly optimizing and integrating the following educational resources, in addition to following the rules mentioned in chapter 1 of this book:

Firstly, rich educational resources for developing learning adaptability are embedded directly or indirectly in the textbooks.

For example, the methods to present and explain words and grammar knowledge can be combined with stimulation of learning motivation and interests; the process of understanding and memorizing words and grammar knowledge can be synchronized with the guidance of learning methods and strategies; the development of skills in listening, speaking, reading and writing requires corresponding good learning habits. Teachers can directly use the mentioned contents of teaching for developing learning adaptability. They can also summarize, derive or extend such contents of teaching and find out the connection between developing learning adaptability and teaching of a subject, to create new contents of teaching for developing learning adaptability.

Secondly, rich educational resources for developing learning adaptability are embedded in the process of teaching. English language is a subject to cultivating students' skills in listening, speaking, reading and writing, and to develop their capacity for comprehensive language application. Students need lot of practice to form language ability. But direct or mechanical practice can not stimulate students' enthusiasm in learning. Opportunities should be provided for students to practice and use English in meaningful and interesting situations. To do that, students' enthusiasm and interests in learning should be stimulated, which needs the cooperation and interaction between teachers and students, and among students. All these provide opportunities to develop learning adaptability in English language teaching.

Thirdly, the educational resources for developing learning adaptability are indirectly embedded in psychological environment in the teaching of English language. The psychological environment in teaching is composed of interpersonal relationship (teacher-student relationship, peer relationship) and psychological atmosphere of teaching [Zhang, 1997].

A good psychological environment in teaching has great influence on teaching activities. It facilitates the conveying of information in teaching, exchanging ideas, psychological compatibility and affective communication between teachers and students and among students. It helps students to overcome and reduce learning fatigue, improve learning efficiency. It helps to maintain normal teaching order and successful completion of teaching tasks. Teachers play a leading role in creating good psychological environment in teaching and even the effectivity of infiltration of psychological suzhi-based education in teaching of a subject [Zhang, 1997]. Some research even pointed out that teachers are critical to the success of subject infiltration [Zhang, 1997; Zheng, 1999]. The psychological environment in class provides opportunity for developing students' enthusiasm in learning, establishing good teacher-student relationship and peer relationship, and promoting physical and psychological health, which contribute to developing learning adaptability. Therefore, teachers should make use of such infiltration opportunities and develop learning adaptability timely, properly and neatly.

## 2) Teaching Mode for Developing Students' Learning Adaptability in English Language Teaching for Junior Middle Schools

In the present chapter, the teaching mode was created by following the laws concerning the development of students' psychological suzhi, considering the age-based characteristics of developing learning adaptability among junior middle school students. In such teaching mode, teachers play a leading role; students are the agent. The teaching mode integrates teaching program, teaching activities, students' psychological activities and their psychological experience of internalization.

### Teaching Process

Teaching process is the necessary phase for teachers to develop students' learning adaptability. It realizes the overall framework of teaching components, reflects the sequence of the teaching process. It is the basic segment of teaching and plays a leading role. The implementation of teaching is divided into three basic segments:

### Judgment And Evaluation

Judgment and evaluation include that teachers check up the latest learning adaptability of students, know the main problems from learning faced by students, make students understand the functions of learning adaptability and understand their adaptation to English language learning, and make them think whether they have good learning adaptability. Judgment and evaluation aim to arouse their sense of identification or absence, and emotional resonance or shocking; stimulate psychological activities, and develop the internal needs of improving their learning adaptability. Teaching activities for this step include: create situations, present stimulation, provide standard; stimulate passion and interests, inspire thinking, analyze the reasons. Such activities can be undertaken in the form of revision, test, situation and case demonstration, etc. The critical part of this step is that teachers find the opportunity or right connecting point to develop learning adaptability.

## Training With Strategies

In this step, teachers use various teaching strategies and methods to stimulate students' activity in participating teaching activities, trying to improve their learning adaptability. The teaching activities and methods include explanation, extension, debate and practice, situation transferring and improvement, practice and consolidation. It aims to i) guides students to think about the problems in learning adaptability, knowledge and skills in English language learning, in order to master the knowledge and skills, improve the understanding, change the ways and angles of thinking; ii) create the procedures of thinking and action; iii) arouse the emotional experiencing via thinking and action; iv) master the basic learning methods and skills in listening, speaking, reading and writing English by practicing, and further develop learning interests. Diversified activities can be carried out in this step, such as cooperation between teachers and students and among students, role-play, discussion, debate, reasonable competition among groups, self-discovery, etc. The critical part of this step is the mastering and habitual application of learning strategies by students.

## Reflection

In this step, teachers need to check up students' learning adaptability, in order that students are able to deepen their understanding, master the methods, and realize internalized manipulation and situation-transferring. Main teaching activities in this step include: the feedback and evaluation by teachers on students' learning activities; teachers together with students summarize the learning in class; establish the cognitive schema of subject knowledge and the psychological system for learning adaptability. Therefore, the main teaching strategies for this step are feedback and evaluation, summary, internalization, consolidation by practice. The critical part of this step is to guide students to ingrain learning adaptability into their nature and form internalized quality (or psychological suzhi).

## Teaching Activities

Teaching activities are the processes for teachers to develop students' learning adaptability. They are based on teaching process. Different teaching methods and activities can be carried out in different teaching process. Typical and specific methods of intervention for students' learning adaptability are provided by teachers. Teaching activities are flexible and accessible. But in each class, teachers do not need to undertake the infiltration according to all the five parts of teaching activities. They can arrange their focus according to the contents of teaching and the type of class.

Psychological activities

Psychological activities refer to the process of psychological changes in teaching activities, which correspond with teaching activities. Students' psychology is a self-organized system, which can not only undertake "independent" activities, but also select, process, control and adjust the teaching activities initiated by teachers which is reflected by needs, interests, affects, cognition, ability, character, etc. Therefore, teachers need to consider students' mental age and individual difference in subject infiltration. Besides, such psychological activities only show the general psychological pattern of students' learning adaptability. Thus not every person needs to experience all these five steps of psychological activities. Some psychological activities can be combined or ignored.

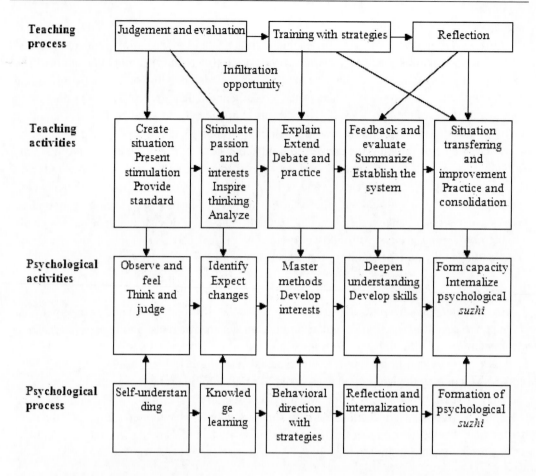

Figure 4.1. Teaching Mode for Developing Students' Learning Adaptability in English Language Teaching for Junior Middle Schools.

## Psychological Process

Psychological process is the basic process of developing psychological suzhi, which reflects the rules concerning the development of psychological suzhi. These five steps are also experienced to develop students' learning adaptability. All teaching process and teaching activities are based on the rules of these five steps. To be specific, through "self-understanding", student judges and evaluates his or her adaptation to English language learning to understand what quality needs to be improved or developed. Through "knowledge-learning", students, based on self-understanding, have the internal needs that they want to develop or improve learning adaptability, overcome difficulties and to solve the problems in English language learning. "Behavioral direction with strategies" refers to that students improve their learning adaptability by practicing in the cooperation and interaction with teachers and peers. "Reflection and internalization" refer to that students evaluate and experience the practice activities, and internalize or make them part of their psychological suzhi or quality. "Formation of psychological suzhi" refers to that students develop learning ability in English language and improve their learning adaptability through further practice and transferring.

To sum up, when establishing the mode, we try to integrate the objectives of teaching a subject and psychological suzhi-based education, and the process, the contents of teaching, the methods of developing learning adaptability with that of English language teaching; synergize the teaching objectives with students' internal needs of learning, teaching activities with students' psychological activities, and teacher-student relationship with peer relationship.

### 3) Requirements for Developing Learning Adaptability in English Language Teaching

#### Initiative Participation by Students is the Precondition for a Successful Subject Infiltration

Subject infiltration, based on teaching of a subject, uses the principles, methods and techniques of psychology in the process of teaching, to develop students' cognition, healthy personality and improve their adaptability. Psychological suzhi-based education requires students' initiative participation. Thus, as a basic means of psychological suzhi-based education, subject infiltration also requires students' initiative participation.

Firstly, it may drive the development of psychological suzhi and satisfy the demands of middle school and primary school students for participating in various activities. It meets the characteristics of teenagers' psychological age.

Secondly, the activity may provide basis and opportunities for the performance and development of students' psychological suzhi.

Thirdly, the activity may provide contents for developing students' psychological suzhi. Therefore, we designed and undertook rich, diversified interesting and high-operable teaching activities in the experiment, according to different contents of teaching and students' situations.

#### The Process of Forming Students' Psychological Suzhi is the Foundation of Subject Infiltration

Subject infiltration is one of the basic means for schools to carry out psychological suzhi-based education, which means that in our experiment, we must organize the teaching activities according to the process of forming psychological suzhi (self-understanding, knowledge-learning, behavioral direction, reflection and internalization, formation of psychological suzhi), in order to develop their learning adaptability by experiencing such psychological activities as "observation and feeling, thinking and judgment, identification, expecting changes, master methods, developing interests, deepening understanding, developing skills, forming capacity and formation of psychological suzhi".

#### Teaching of a Subject is the Framework of Subject Infiltration

The nature of subject infiltration determines that the intrinsic objectives of the knowledge, skills and capacity for teaching of a subject must be completed first in teaching. The psychological suzhi-based education objectives are only secondary and should be subordinated. Teaching of a subject is the carrier of psychological suzhi-based education. Thus subject infiltration must be supported by teaching of a subject. We advocate that "subject infiltration" should refer to that the contents suitable for developing learning adaptability are explored from the course of the subject and are integrated in the process of teaching by using certain methods.

## Creation of Interactive Teaching Situation Ensures Effective Subject Infiltration

Creation of interactive teaching situation is the characteristics of psychological suzhi-based education and ensures effective subject infiltration. It is because students' psychological activities (cognition, emotion, behavior) are stimulated or aroused in interactive teaching situation. Psychological suzhi-based education based on this can stimulate students' thinking and actions to the maximum, arouse their sense of identification or absence and result in their internal needs of changing current psychological and behavioral situations. In interactive teaching situation, it is easier for teachers to create harmonious and democratic relationship between teachers and students, create relaxing and pleasing psychological atmosphere in class, and for teachers to stay happy, enthusiastic and fresh, and to make students feel the same. Then students' psychological suzhi can be developed in the psychological environment where interaction between teachers and students, and among students are available.

## 4) Teaching Strategies for Developing Students' Learning Adaptability in English Language Teaching for Junior Middle Schools

English language as a subject especially requires students' participation in activities and practice. It requires initiative, activity-participation and cooperation of students, which corresponds with the characteristics of psychological suzhi-based education. Therefore, we propose and used the following teaching strategies:

## Creating Interactive Situations

Creation of interactive situations is the necessary condition for the teaching of a subject and the primary feature of psychological suzhi-based education [Chen and Zhang, 2002; Liu and Zhang, 2004]. The process of psychological suzhi-based education is a process to create interacting situations and stimulate students' psychological activities. It usually stimulates emotional resonance, arouses the sense of identification or shock and triggers the desire for action, and thus students' psychological suzhi is cultivated and developed in the psychological environment created through the interaction of interpersonal environment. From the perspective of English language teaching, English language is learnt in the process of using. The effective objectives of foreign language teaching must be achieved by interactions and communication in specific situations. We need to turn class into a place of communication in English and to carry out the teaching through lively activities. Teachers should enable students to naturally and unconsciously absorb the knowledge and practice via perception, experience, application, exploration etc. when participating in the activity; and to enjoy the process of learning when they are improving their basic ability in listening, speaking, reading and writing, continuously absorbing knowledge and improving their capacity for comprehensive language application. Therefore, creating interactive teaching situation is the essential condition for subject infiltration.

There are three implications in interactive teaching situation:

Create typical situations through visualized carriers, such as definite objects, pictures, action, expression and questions.

The interaction between teachers and students and among students, including behavioral interaction and psychological interactions.

Interaction between external stimuli and students' mental activities, i.e., teachers use artificially optimized environment (definite objects, pictures, action, expression and other visualized carriers, as well as good interpersonal environment and atmosphere to stimulate students' mental activities.

Therefore, we created problem-based situation in the experiment based on the conflicts between students' cognitive structure and new knowledge, in order to stimulate students' positive thinking; created activity-based situation by presentation of definite objects, language description, music atmosphere, performance and experience; created physical situation that corresponds with the objectives and contents of teaching and can stimulate students' feelings; established harmonious, tacit and cooperative teacher-student relations; and created democratic, relaxing and open psychological situation that can stimulate students' inner world.

## Encouraging Students to Participate in Activities

Activities psychologically mean

Students' external behaviors and conducts, such as the specific practice in class;
Students' internal mental activities, such as thinking, experience, feeling, reflection etc.

Psychological research showed that the activity is the most important factor for the generation and development of human being's mental activities and that it is one of the origins of psychological development.

Human being's advanced psychological functions are all caused by the interactions between the agents and the objects, and are resulted from continuously internalizing activities and communications. Research showed that active participation in activities is the precondition for Psychological suzhi-based education, since students may find problems, analyze the self, explore the causes, seek solutions and make reflection during their active participation in activities to form thoughts, concepts and abilities. From the angle of English language teaching, task-based teaching is advocated in the new textbooks, which especially highlights students' participation [Liu, 2003], in order to develop students' language skills and form capacity for comprehensive language application through diversified learning activities aiming to develop linguistic meaning.

Therefore, in the experiment, we created situations and carried out activities based on the life and learning of students, in order to make students learn, experience and comprehend what are in activities, and further to improve their learning adaptability and develop their English language competence. The activities include role play, onstage performance, game, team-based competition, team-based dialogue practice, song learning etc.

## Experiencing and Internalization under Direction

Experiencing and internalization are not only the key for forming psychological suzhi, but also an important process to develop students' capacity for language application in English language teaching: for the former one, experiencing is an activity that stimulates emotions and generates meaning, and students may internalize, via experiencing, the external experiences and matters into their suzhi, including cognition, belief, behavior and quality; for the latter one, students may conclude, summarize, construct and assimilate the knowledge and skill learned and then internalize them into their own cognitive structure and ability.

In the experiment, we guided students' experiencing and internalization mainly from four aspects:

Expanding the space for students' psychological freedom so as to enable students to get experience via exploration. Such exploration activities include cognition manipulations, games and behavior tasks;

Creating opportunities for interactive communications so that students may get experience via the learning activities in class. Interactive communications include the exchange of information on cognition, interpersonal emotions, attitude and behavior;

Enabling students to get experience in the situation, which has been mentioned in "creating interactive situations";

Enabling students to get experience via self-reflection, self-suggestion or self-reminding. This includes students' reflection on their mental activities and behaviors, their self-criticism and self-reminding of their faults and mistakes, their self-affirmation of their success and their control and adjustment of the self at a proper time.

## Making Students Experience Success

Teachers should make every type of students experience success. Students are different, for example, they may have different hobbies, learning styles, knowledge foundation, and potentials. Teachers should analyze and know the characteristics of every students and set different standards for them in objective, in-class question or feedback of learning to create opportunities of success. For example, teachers can ask students with weak foundation to answer simpler questions; encourage or guide introverted or restrained students when they have difficulty in answering questions; encourage students with lower confidence; set higher requirements for very confident students; guide students to compete with themselves and guide them to experience the success from progress.

## Guiding Students to Attribute Correctly

Psychological research showed that different attribution to success may lead to different cognitions, emotions and behavior reactions. Reasonable attribution increases self-confidence and perseverance; wrong attribution may increase inferiority complex and giving up. Therefore, it is very necessary for teachers to help students attribute correctly. In the experiment, we required that teachers should:

Timely tell students that the development of learning potential relies on self-confidence. Students should have confidence first in order to succeed. They should trust themselves no matter they fail or succeed.

Tell students that efforts are very important to success. They should be persistent in learning and should not be afraid of failure.

When students succeed, teachers should assist students to attribute their success to capacity, continuous efforts and other internal and stable reasons, in order to strengthen their expectation of success and positive emotions related to self-esteem and confidence, and to make them continue to devote to learning tasks. Teachers should teach students to attribute failures to bad mind-set or insufficient efforts, in order to maintain high expectation of success, avoid negative emotions and make students continue their learning.

Tell students that only efforts are not enough. Seeking for help and scientific learning methods are also important.

## Proper Objective Structures in Class

Psychological research showed that the objective structure of a class can be classified into three types: competitive, individual and cooperative. These three objective structures form three motivation atmospheres of competition, individualization and cooperation, stimulate the three related motivation system: egocentric motivation system, task motivation system and team motivation system. To be specific,

Competitive objective structure can easily stimulate the social comparison of students, and make students tend to attribute academic performance to capacity, which may lead to polarization of students.

Individual objective structure makes students tend to attribute academic performance to efforts. Students emphasize the task and the comparison with themselves. They believe that they can succeed with efforts and they can progress when they trust themselves.

Cooperative objective structure make students tend to attribute academic performance to helps and joint efforts. They think highly of team success, by which students with bad academic performance can be encouraged. They believe they can also succeed. Students will not attribute the team failure to themselves, thus team failure does not influence their evaluation of their own capacity.

Therefore, in the experiment, we mostly use individual objective structure and competitive – cooperative objective structure, set students' tasks at the "nearest development region", in order to make students succeed with some efforts.

# EDUCATION EXPERIMENT

## Purpose

The experiment aimed to verify the applicability and effectivity of the modes and strategies concerning the development of learning adaptability in English language teaching in junior middle schools proposed in the present research, and to provide empirical evidence for infiltration of psychological suzhi development in teaching of a subject.

## Participants

In total, 135 students from two classes of junior grade one in one middle school of Chongqing participated in the experiment. Those students were divided into an experimental group, including 34 boys and 36 girls; and a control group, including 34 boys and 31 girls.

## Measurement Tools

The Measurement tools used include the Academic Adaptability Test for Junior Middle School Students (AAT) revised by Zhou et al., the Mental Quality Questionnaire for Middle School Students (3SMQ) by Zhang and Feng, and the Strategy Evaluation Sheet for English Language Learning among Students Ranging from Grade Seven to Grade Nine by Qin. The measurement tools of academic performance are four monthly examinations in English language.

## Experimental Treatment and Procedures

In the experiment, we designed pre-test and post-test for both experimental and control groups. Please refer to Table 4.3 for experimental treatment.

According to the experimental procedures, the experiment was conducted in three phases:

### 1) Preparation Phase

Probed into domestic and international literature; established and modified experiment scheme;

Contacted the school for experiment;

Established the teaching mode for developing students' learning adaptability in English language teaching, established teaching plan for the experiment; and

Trained the teachers for the experiment, modified the teaching plan for the experiment together with the teachers for the experiment.

### 2) Implementation Phase

In the first week at the beginning of the semester, pre-test of *Mental Quality Questionnaire for Middle School Students* was conducted, and in the second week, the pre-test of academic adaptability test for junior middle school students was conducted;

Education experiment was conducted according to the teaching plan for the experiment; and

Post-Test.

### 3) Phase for Data Analysis

**Table 4.3. Experimental Treatment**

| Groups | Pre-Test | Experimental Treatment | Post-Test |
|---|---|---|---|
| Experimental Group | i) The Mental Quality Question-naire for Middle School Students ii) The Academic Adaptability Test for Junior Middle School Students | Carried out education experiment of subject infiltration, according to the modes and teaching strategies for develop-ing learning adaptability in English language teaching for junior middle schools | i) The Mental Quality Questionnaire for Middle School Students ii) The Academic Adaptability Test for Junior Middle School Students iii) The Strategy Evaluation heet for English Language Learning among Students Ranging from Grade Seven to Grade Nine. Measurement of academic performance |
| Experimental Group | i) The Mental Quality Question-naire for Middle School Students ii) The Academic Adaptability Test for Junior Middle School Students | Carried out education experiment of subject infiltration, according to the modes and teaching strategies for develop-ing learning adaptability in English language teaching for junior middle schools | i) The Mental Quality Questionnaire for Middle School Students ii) The Academic Adaptability Test for Junior Middle School Students iii) The Strategy Evaluation Sheet for English Language Learning among Students Ranging from Grade Seven to Grade Nine. Measurement of academic performance |
| Control Group | The same as the Experimental Group | Routine teaching | The same as the Experimental Group |

## Variables

*Independent variables*: mode and teaching strategies for developing students' learning adaptability in English language teaching for junior middle school.

*Dependant variables*: i) learning adaptability; ii) psychological suzhi; iii) capacity for using English language learning strategies; and iv) academic performance in English language learning.

*Control variables:* a) reasonably set the experimental and control groups. The total students and gender ratio of the two groups are almost the same. But two groups had their own teacher separately. The teachers had almost the same years of teaching experience and teaching competence (the teachers can be selected through the recommendation of the school leaders or determined by the experimenter through listening to lectures) to ensure the homogeneousness. b) controlled other factors affecting the results of the experiment. The experimenter did not change the normal teaching process, or implicitly show the purpose of the experiment to the teacher, in order to avoid expectation effect and time effect.

**Table 4.4. Comparison of General Learning Adaptability in Pre-test and Post-test between Two Groups (Person time)**

| | | Bad | Average minus | Average | Average plus | Good | $\chi^2$ |
|---|---|---|---|---|---|---|---|
| Pre-Test | Experimental Group (n=69) | 4 | 17 | 34 | 8 | 6 | 1.58 |
| | Control Group (n=65) | 2 | 15 | 30 | 9 | 9 | |
| Post-Test | Experimental Group (n=69) | 0 | 13 | 34 | 14 | 8 | 15.19 ** |
| | Control Group (n=65) | 3 | 17 | 40 | 2 | 3 | |

Note: * $p<0.05$ ** $p<0.01$

## Experimental Results and Analysis

### 1) Comparison of General Learning Adaptability in Pre-Test and Post-Test Between Two Groups

The general learning adaptability in pre-test and post-test between two groups (see Table 4.4) shows no obvious difference in learning adaptability in pre-test and significant difference after the experiment. Therefore, it is necessary to conduct an accurate significance testing of mean difference.

### 2) Comparison of Scores in Learning Adaptability in Pre-Test and Post-Test between Two Groups

The independent-sample t test (see Table 4.5) shows that there was no significant difference in total scores between two groups in the pre-test.

In terms of learning attitude and learning technique as shown in the "dimensions and related factors" column, the scores of control group were much higher than the experimental group. To be specific, for the dimension of learning attitude, the control group had higher scores on learning plan and methods of listening to lectures are obviously than the experimental group; for the dimension of learning techniques, the control group had higher scores in the learning techniques than the experimental group. For other dimensions and factors, there was no difference between two groups, except the dimension of learning environment and school environment and friend relationship factors within this dimension; the control group had higher scores on other dimensions and factors than the experimental group.

**Table 4.5. Scores in Learning Adaptability in Pre-Test and Post-Test Between Two Groups (Standard Score)**

| Dimensions and factors | Pre-Test | | | | t | Post-Test | | | | t |
|---|---|---|---|---|---|---|---|---|---|---|
| | Experimental Group(n=69) | | Control Group (n=65) | | | Experimental Group (n=69) | | Control Group(n=65) | | |
| | M | SD | M | SD | | M | SD | M | SD | |
| Learning attitude | 45.86 | 3.39 | 53.22 | 11.01 | -5.17** | 52.28 | 6.63 | 48.05 | 12.39 | 2.44* |
| Learning enthusiasm | 52.61 | 8.71 | 55.09 | 11.67 | -1.40 | 53.13 | 9.74 | 49.15 | 12.07 | 2.10* |
| Learning plan | 47.74 | 7.55 | 50.95 | 10.52 | -2.04* | 54.12 | 9.85 | 49.11 | 11.84 | 2.67** |
| Methods of listening to lectures | 52.62 | 7.90 | 55.86 | 10.18 | -2.05* | 52.36 | 8.08 | 49.45 | 11.42 | 1.71* |
| Learning techniques | 49.26 | 7.38 | 52.45 | 8.87 | -2.27* | 51.71 | 7.26 | 46.12 | 9.49 | 3.84** |
| Reading and note-taking methods | 52.62 | 7.90 | 55.86 | 10.18 | -1.54 | 52.57 | 8.74 | 48.63 | 10.04 | 2.42* |
| Learning techniques | 49.77 | 8.22 | 54.14 | 9.84 | -2.80** | 52.71 | 7.75 | 48.61 | 10.38 | 2.60* |
| Exam methods | 49.10 | 8.53 | 51.97 | 10.64 | -1.73 | 51.90 | 8.17 | 49.17 | 9.05 | 1.82 |
| Learning environment | 50.48 | 9.20 | 49.77 | 11.42 | 0.40 | 50.22 | 8.17 | 39.06 | 8.47 | 7.76*** |
| Family environment | 49.72 | 8.89 | 51.86 | 11.07 | -1.24 | 51.78 | 9.26 | 48.18 | 8.15 | 2.37 |
| School environment | 52.17 | 10.17 | 51.17 | 10.17 | 0.57 | 49.64 | 7.80 | 42.28 | 9.42 | 4.94** |
| Friend relationship | 52.89 | 10.11 | 49.49 | 11.64 | 1.80 | 53.10 | 11.98 | 40.43 | 10.33 | 6.57*** |
| Physical and psychological health | 47.83 | 8.82 | 49.54 | 11.05 | -0.99 | 50.38 | 10.16 | 38.66 | 8.90 | 7.11*** |
| Independence | 46.84 | 8.96 | 48.68 | 10.04 | -1.12 | 48.06 | 9.73 | 41.62 | 9.98 | 3.78** |
| perseverance | 53.49 | 11.71 | 55.35 | 12.69 | -0.88 | 54.62 | 12.53 | 46.26 | 10.90 | 4.11** |
| Physical and psychological health | 48.55 | 11.74 | 49.11 | 11.12 | -0.28 | 52.86 | 10.57 | 38.86 | 9.69 | 7.98*** |
| Total scale scores | 48.81 | 7.42 | 50.91 | 10.29 | -1.35 | 50.78 | 7.16 | 42.14 | 9.18 | 6.10*** |

Note: * $p<0.05$ ** $p<0.01$ *** $p<0.001$.

In the post-test, the experimental group had higher total scale score and the scores of dimensions and related factors than the control group to some extent. To be specific, the experimental group had much higher scores on the factors under learning attitude and physical and psychological health than the control group; for learning techniques, except the factor of exam methods, the experimental group had obviously higher scores on other factors than the control group; for learning environment, except the factor of family environment, the experimental group had obviously higher scores on other factors than the control group.

### 3) Comparison of Scores on Learning Adaptability Test between Two Groups

The related sample test (see Table 4.6) shows that the scores of the experimental group on total scale and dimensions of learning attitude and learning techniques and related factors in the post-test were higher or much higher than in the pre-test.

To be specific, for the dimension of learning attitude, the control group had obviously higher scores on the factors of learning plan and methods of listening to lectures than the experimental group; for the dimension of learning techniques, the scores on the factor of learning techniques in post-test were obviously higher than in the pretest.

**Table 4.6. Scores on Learning Adaptability Test between Two Groups
before and after the Experiment (Standard Score)**

| Dimensions and factors | Experimental Group (n=68) | | | | $t$ | Control Group (n=65) | | | | $t$ |
|---|---|---|---|---|---|---|---|---|---|---|
| | Pre-Test | | Post-Test | | | Pre-Test | | Post-Test | | |
| | M | SD | M | SD | | M | SD | M | SD | |
| Learning attitude | 45.84 | 3.41 | 52.34 | 6.66 | -8.43*** | 53.22 | 11.01 | 48.05 | 12.39 | 4.27*** |
| Learning enthusiasm | 52.59 | 8.78 | 53.12 | 9.82 | -0.37 | 55.09 | 11.67 | 49.15 | 12.07 | 4.73*** |
| Learning plan | 47.74 | 7.61 | 54.15 | 9.92 | -4.75*** | 50.95 | 10.52 | 49.11 | 11.84 | 1.28 |
| Methods of listening to lectures | 52.66 | 7.95 | 52.49 | 8.08 | 0.17 | 55.86 | 10.18 | 49.45 | 11.42 | 5.49*** |
| Learning techniques | 49.16 | 7.39 | 51.79 | 7.28 | -2.80*** | 52.45 | 8.87 | 46.12 | 9.49 | 5.90*** |
| Reading and note-taking methods | 51.35 | 8.14 | 52.62 | 8.80 | -1.04 | 53.86 | 9.51 | 48.63 | 10.04 | 4.35*** |
| Learning techniques | 49.66 | 8.24 | 52.90 | 7.65 | -2.96*** | 54.14 | 9.84 | 48.61 | 10.38 | 4.01*** |
| Exam methods | 49.10 | 8.59 | 51.85 | 8.22 | -2.30* | 51.97 | 10.64 | 49.17 | 9.05 | 2.34* |
| Learning environment | 50.35 | 9.21 | 50.16 | 8.21 | 0.19 | 49.77 | 11.42 | 39.06 | 8.47 | 6.85*** |
| Family environment | 49.56 | 8.85 | 51.78 | 9.33 | -1.85 | 51.86 | 11.07 | 48.18 | 8.15 | 3.08*** |
| School environment | 52.18 | 10.24 | 49.57 | 7.84 | 2.08* | 51.17 | 10.17 | 42.28 | 9.42 | 5.24*** |
| Friend relationship | 52.75 | 10.13 | 53.09 | 12.07 | -0.25 | 49.49 | 11.64 | 40.43 | 10.33 | 5.47*** |
| Physical and psychological health | 47.81 | 8.89 | 50.25 | 10.18 | -1.99 | 49.54 | 11.05 | 38.66 | 8.90 | 7.42*** |
| Independence | 46.76 | 9.00 | 48.10 | 9.80 | -1.08 | 48.68 | 10.04 | 41.62 | 9.98 | 4.98*** |
| Perseverance | 53.57 | 11.77 | 54.47 | 12.56 | -0.57 | 55.35 | 12.69 | 46.26 | 10.90 | 4.66*** |
| Physical and psychological health | 48.50 | 11.82 | 52.81 | 10.64 | -2.43* | 49.11 | 11.12 | 38.86 | 9.69 | 6.23*** |
| Total scale scores | 48.74 | 7.45 | 50.78 | 7.21 | -2.47* | 50.91 | 10.29 | 42.14 | 9.18 | 7.74*** |

Note: * $p<0.05$ ** $p<0.01$ *** $p<0.001$.

Under the dimension of physical and psychological health, the post-test scores on the factor of physical and psychological health were much higher than pre-test scores. Under the dimension of learning environment, the post-test scores on the factor of school environment were much lower than pre-test scores. The post-test scores of the control group on the total scale cores and related factors were obviously or significantly lower than pre-test scores. To be specific, for the dimension of learning attitude, except the factor of learning plan, the post-test scores on the other two factors were obviously lower than pre-test scores; for the dimensions of learning techniques, learning environment and physical and psychological health, the scores on the factor of learning techniques in post-test were obviously higher than in the pretest.

*4) Scores on Evaluating the Learning Strategies of English Language after the Experiment between Two Groups*

After the experiment, as shown in Table 4.7, the experimental group had obviously higher scores in strategy of cognition, strategy of regulation, strategy of communication and total average cores than the control group.

*5) Comparison of Pre-Test and Post-Test Scores of Psychological Suzhi between Two Groups*

In the pre-test (see Table 4.8), significant difference between two groups can only be As seen in the factor of perseverance; the experimental group had much higher scores than the control group.

In the post-test, the experimental group had much higher scores on the factors of independence, perseverance, self-confidence, creativity and self-esteem under the dimension of personality, and on the factors of learning adaptation, frustration endurance and interpersonal adaptation under the dimension of adaptability than the control group. The experimental group had much lower scores on the factor of ambition under the dimension of personality than the control group.

**Table 4.7. Scores on Evaluating the Learning Strategies of English Language after the Experiment between Two Groups**

|  | Experimental Group (n=69) | | Control Group (n=64) | | *t* |
|---|---|---|---|---|---|
|  | *M* | *SD* | *M* | *SD* | |
| Average scores of strategy for cognition | 3.66 | 0.46 | 3.24 | 0.85 | 3.52** |
| Average scores of strategy for regulation | 4.09 | 0.65 | 3.37 | 0.90 | 5.25*** |
| Average scores of strategy for communication | 3.64 | 0.83 | 3.25 | 0.77 | 2.83** |
| Average scores of strategy for resources | 3.22 | 0.83 | 3.34 | 0.85 | -0.79 |
| Total average scores | 3.66 | 0.43 | 3.31 | 0.75 | 3.31** |

Note: * $p<0.05$ ** $p<0.01$ *** $p<0.001$

## 6) Scores of Psychological Suzhi before and after the Experiment between Two Groups

For the experimental group, the post-test scores on metacognitive awareness, metacognitive planning, perseverance, learning adaptation and honesty were all much higher than pre-test scores; the post-test scores in self-control, self-confidence, sense of responsibility, self-esteem, emotional adaptation, frustration endurance and interpersonal adaptation were significantly lower than pre-test scores. For the control group, the post-test scores on metacognitive awareness and honesty were significantly higher than pre-test scores; the post-test scores on independence, self-control, self-confidence, sense of responsibility, self-esteem, physical and psychological adaptation, emotional adaptation, frustration endurance and interpersonal adaptation were all significantly lower than pre-test scores.

**Table 4.8. Pre-Test and Post-Test Scores of Psychological Suzhi between Two Groups**

| Factors | Pre-Test | | | | | t | Post-Test | | | | | t |
|---|---|---|---|---|---|---|---|---|---|---|---|---|
| | Experimental Group (n=68) | | Control Group (n=65) | | | | Experimental Group (n=69) | | Control Group (n=62) | | | |
| | M | SD | M | SD | | | M | SD | M | SD | | |
| Metacognitive awareness | 21.94 | 3.59 | 22.92 | 4.15 | | -1.46 | 25.19 | 5.36 | 25.50 | 5.84 | | -0.32 |
| Metacognitive planning | 24.35 | 4.17 | 24.89 | 4.17 | | -0.75 | 25.64 | 5.22 | 24.05 | 6.20 | | 1.59 |
| Metacognitive monitoring | 25.09 | 3.74 | 24.09 | 4.13 | | 1.46 | 24.94 | 5.46 | 25.06 | 5.71 | | -0.13 |
| Ambition | 23.47 | 4.20 | 23.60 | 4.56 | | -0.17 | 23.99 | 5.86 | 26.27 | 6.52 | | -2.12* |
| Independence | 24.44 | 3.97 | 24.06 | 4.20 | | 0.54 | 24.52 | 3.41 | 21.81 | 4.69 | | 3.75*** |
| Perseverance | 27.85 | 4.42 | 26.22 | 3.50 | | 2.38* | 31.83 | 5.36 | 25.56 | 6.91 | | 5.83*** |
| Thirst for knowledge | 26.44 | 4.54 | 26.46 | 3.96 | | -0.03 | 26.20 | 5.51 | 25.23 | 6.29 | | 0.95 |
| Self-control | 26.68 | 3.20 | 26.12 | 3.12 | | 1.01 | 19.78 | 3.96 | 18.84 | 3.51 | | 1.44 |
| Self-confidence | 25.03 | 4.60 | 25.69 | 4.54 | | -0.84 | 23.10 | 4.58 | 20.29 | 4.10 | | 3.68*** |
| Sense of responsibility | 24.91 | 3.87 | 25.69 | 3.81 | | -1.17 | 19.22 | 3.53 | 19.73 | 4.01 | | -0.77 |
| Rationality | 24.09 | 3.48 | 24.03 | 4.04 | | 0.09 | 23.68 | 4.98 | 22.58 | 5.21 | | 1.24 |
| Creativity | 24.97 | 3.36 | 24.43 | 4.56 | | 0.78 | 26.32 | 5.00 | 23.58 | 5.59 | | 2.96** |
| Self-esteem | 19.29 | 4.30 | 19.26 | 4.35 | | 0.04 | 17.81 | 3.23 | 15.69 | 3.20 | | 3.76*** |
| Physical and psychological adaptation | 25.47 | 4.64 | 25.57 | 5.61 | | -0.11 | 22.88 | 4.81 | 21.84 | 5.01 | | 1.22 |
| Learning adaptation | 29.74 | 3.97 | 30.06 | 4.29 | | -0.46 | 36.13 | 5.81 | 30.82 | 8.64 | | 4.16*** |
| Emotional adaptation | 24.47 | 3.37 | 23.54 | 4.43 | | 1.37 | 16.29 | 3.62 | 16.05 | 3.09 | | 0.41 |
| Frustration endurance | 24.35 | 3.54 | 24.31 | 3.75 | | 0.07 | 17.28 | 2.79 | 15.73 | 2.46 | | 3.36** |
| Interpersonal adaptation | 22.32 | 4.31 | 21.91 | 4.34 | | 0.56 | 14.45 | 2.73 | 12.82 | 2.78 | | 3.37** |
| Honesty | 20.03 | 4.42 | 20.68 | 4.23 | | -0.86 | 30.54 | 9.37 | 29.21 | 9.34 | | 0.81 |

Note: * p<0.05 ** p<0.01 *** p<0.001.

## 7) *Comparison of Average Scores in Four Monthly Examinations in English Language between Two Groups*

The full marks of English examination are 100. Table 4.10 shows that there was no significant difference in the four examinations between the two groups. But the standard deviations of the experimental group were higher than that of the control group.

We rated the scores of English examinations according to the rating standard of the experimental school: bad for scores lower than 65, average for scores between 65 and 85, and good for scores higher than 85. We had the statistics of the number of students at each rating. The $\chi^2$ test (see Table 4.11) shows that there was no obvious difference in the first monthly examination, and difference started to emerge from the second monthly examination (midterm examination).

**Table 4.9 Scores on Psychological Suzhi before and after the Experiment between Two Groups**

| Factors | Experimental Group (n=67) | | | | *t* | Control Group (n=62) | | | | *t* |
|---|---|---|---|---|---|---|---|---|---|---|
| | Pre-Test | | Post-Test | | | Pre-Test | | Post-Test | | |
| | *M* | *SD* | *M* | *SD* | | *M* | *SD* | *M* | *SD* | |
| Metacognitive awareness | 20.97 | 4.52 | 23.81 | 5.40 | -3.58*** | 22.58 | 3.92 | 25.50 | 5.84 | -3.10** |
| Metacognitive planning | 23.82 | 4.27 | 25.55 | 5.25 | -2.32* | 25.10 | 4.09 | 24.05 | 6.20 | 1.20 |
| Metacognitive monitoring | 25.04 | 3.57 | 24.82 | 5.45 | 0.28 | 23.90 | 4.12 | 25.06 | 5.71 | -1.30 |
| Ambition | 24.00 | 4.40 | 24.01 | 5.94 | -0.02 | 23.45 | 4.60 | 24.76 | 6.61 | -1.29 |
| Independence | 24.15 | 4.08 | 24.41 | 3.40 | -0.44 | 24.00 | 4.25 | 21.81 | 4.69 | 2.85** |
| Perseverance | 27.76 | 4.36 | 31.84 | 5.43 | -4.92*** | 26.06 | 3.42 | 25.56 | 6.91 | 0.56 |
| Thirst for knowledge | 25.94 | 4.53 | 26.01 | 5.47 | -0.08 | 26.58 | 3.96 | 25.23 | 6.29 | 1.36 |
| Self-control | 27.10 | 3.43 | 19.85 | 3.83 | 12.85*** | 25.94 | 2.99 | 18.84 | 3.51 | 12.72*** |
| Self-confidence | 24.96 | 4.35 | 23.22 | 4.56 | 2.30* | 25.90 | 4.51 | 20.29 | 4.10 | 6.92*** |
| Sense of responsibility | 24.84 | 4.14 | 19.15 | 3.50 | 8.52*** | 25.61 | 3.85 | 19.73 | 4.01 | 8.52*** |
| Rationality | 24.60 | 3.70 | 23.61 | 5.01 | 1.32 | 23.87 | 3.95 | 22.58 | 5.21 | 1.56 |
| Creativity | 24.84 | 3.41 | 26.21 | 5.03 | -1.68 | 24.45 | 4.63 | 23.58 | 5.59 | 0.99 |
| Self-esteem | 19.94 | 4.33 | 17.91 | 3.21 | 2.93** | 19.23 | 4.40 | 15.69 | 3.20 | 5.13*** |
| Physical and psychological adaptation | 24.18 | 5.05 | 22.82 | 4.86 | 1.51 | 25.55 | 5.73 | 21.84 | 5.01 | 3.49** |
| Learning adaptation | 29.64 | 4.06 | 36.13 | 5.89 | -7.34*** | 30.03 | 4.26 | 30.82 | 8.64 | -0.67 |
| Emotional adaptation | 25.07 | 3.87 | 16.31 | 3.63 | 12.39*** | 23.68 | 4.35 | 16.05 | 3.09 | 11.32*** |
| Frustration endurance | 24.39 | 3.54 | 17.32 | 2.78 | 12.41*** | 24.26 | 3.74 | 15.73 | 2.46 | 14.80*** |
| Interpersonal adaptation | 22.57 | 4.37 | 14.43 | 2.75 | 12.56*** | 22.06 | 4.36 | 12.82 | 2.78 | 13.82*** |
| Honesty | 20.36 | 4.29 | 30.37 | 9.44 | -8.33*** | 20.77 | 4.28 | 29.21 | 9.34 | -7.01*** |

Note: * $p<0.05$ ** $p<0.01$ *** $p<0.001$

**Table 4.10. Average Scores of English Language Examinations for Two Groups**

|  | The first monthly examination $M\pm SD$ | Midterm examination $M\pm SD$ | The third monthly examination $M\pm SD$ | Final examination $M\pm SD$ |
|---|---|---|---|---|
| Experimental Group (n=70) | 94.6±9.20 | 72.0±8.25 | 73.1±10.89 | 73.9±10.25 |
| Control Group (n=65) | 94.9±7.65 | 71.6±6.30 | 72.2±8.47 | 73.4±8.64 |
| *t* | -0.20 | 0.31 | 0.53 | 0.30 |

## Conclusion

### 1) Building Teaching Mode and Strategies

Research into mode is an important modern scientific methodology. Teaching mode is between teaching theory and teaching practice, which is a simplified and theoretical teaching paradigm. The teaching mode in this chapter was built to integrate the theories of psychological suzhi-based education and teaching of a subject in specific practicing aspect, represent the basic procedures for developing learning adaptability in English language teaching for junior middle school in a stable and simple way, in order to guide the infiltration of psychological suzhi-based education in teaching of a subject, test the applicability and effectivity of such mode and to provide empirical evidence for subject infiltration, a new means of psychological suzhi-based education.

The subject infiltration mode mentioned in the present research was built by making use of the available research into learning adaptability, psychological suzhi-based education, subject infiltration, teaching modeling, English language teaching for junior middle school, etc. We proposed and followed the following principles:

Learning adaptability, the objective of psychological suzhi-based education, should be organically integrated with the objectives of English language teaching. Developing students' learning adaptability can solve the problems faced by junior middle school students in adapting to learning in junior school, as it is different from primary school, and in adapting to English language learning. Our objectives of developing students' learning adaptability correspond with the teaching objectives of emotion, attitude and learning strategies prescribed in the English Curriculum Standard. It means that our objectives of developing learning adaptability can be integrated with the objectives of English language teaching; therefore, we determined the teaching objectives and contents of teaching in developing learning adaptability in English language teaching.

The process of forming students' psychological suzhi and the process of psychological suzhi-based education should be followed. The processes of forming students' psychological suzhi is "self-understanding, knowledge-learning, behavioral direction, reflection and internalization, formation of psychological suzhi", which should be followed in subject infiltration.

**Table 4.11. Number of Students at Each Rating for Two Groups
in English Examinations**

| | The first monthly examination | | Midterm examination | | The third monthly examination | | Final examination | |
|---|---|---|---|---|---|---|---|---|
| | Experimental Group (n=70) | Control Group (n=65) | Experimental Group (n=70) | Control Group (n=65) | Experimental Group (n=70) | Control Group (n=65) | Experimental Group (n=70) | Control Group (n=65) |
| Good | 43 | 37 | 20 | 8 | 18 | 5 | 19 | 8 |
| Average | 23 | 28 | 45 | 44 | 47 | 47 | 45 | 44 |
| Bad | 4 | 0 | 5 | 13 | 5 | 13 | 6 | 13 |
| $\chi^2$ | 4.77 | | 8.53* | | 10.72** | | 6.89* | |

Note: * $p<0.05$ ** $p<0.01$

The three basic teaching processes of psychological suzhi-based education class are: judgment and evaluation, training with strategies, reflection. These three processes can also be used in subject infiltration, one means of psychological suzhi-based education. We add "infiltration opportunity" sub-step to the step of "judgment and evaluation" according to the characteristics of subject infiltration, in order to seek for and create infiltration opportunities.

The process of subject infiltration should correspond with the process of English language teaching. The latest version of English language textbook is the Experimental Textbook for Compulsory Education Course Standards: English (New Target) published by Peoples Education Press. The experimental school also used the same textbook. RPDPC mode [Huang, 2003] in the teaching process: Revision – Presentation – Drill – Practice – Consolidation, and task-based language teaching methods are advocated in this textbook, in order to make students learn by participating in tasks of real life. Our teaching process for the subject infiltration mode corresponds with it. The teaching activities for the three teaching processes are: creating situation, presenting stimulation, providing standard; stimulating passion and interests; inspiration of thinking, analyzing; explanation, extension, debate and practice; feedback and evaluation, summarization, establishing the system; situation transferring and improvement, practice and consolidation. All these five parts of activities correspond with the teaching process advocated in the new textbook.

The teaching strategies meet both the characteristics of psychological suzhi-based education process and the process of English language teaching for junior middle schools. From the aspect of education process, psychological suzhi-based education emphasizes on situations, interaction, activities and reflection. Psychological suzhi-based education highlights that students generate and develop psychological suzhi in the interacting situations with teachers and peers through active participation and initiative reflection and internalization. The cooperation between students and teachers and among peers is also emphasized in the process of English language teaching; besides, knowledge is constructed and students' capacity is generated in this process. This is reflected by the teaching objectives of emotion and attitude and task-based teaching methods. Therefore, we created teaching strategies, including interacting situations, encourage participation into activities, and guiding of experience and internalization, according to the characteristics of psychological suzhi-based education process and the process of English language teaching.

The experiment showed that this subject infiltration mode and teaching strategies are reasonable and feasible, and can provide effective empirical evidence for subject infiltration, a new means of psychological suzhi-based education. Meanwhile, we noticed that this infiltration mode is not rigid. It should be flexibly used and adjusted according to different subjects, individual difference among students and age characteristics. We also noticed many theoretical and practical problems in the subject infiltration of psychological suzhi-based education that needs further research and solving, for example, the resources in curriculum, optimization, development and utilization of the resources in teaching process, the coordination among the subjects and the improvement of teachers' theoretical knowledge in education.

## 2) *Experimental Results*

### The Subject Infiltration Mode and Strategies Can Significantly Improve Students' Learning Adaptability

In the pre-test, there was no significant difference in the general learning adaptability between two groups (see Tables 4.4 and 4.5). The two groups were basically homogeneous. But there were still differences in certain dimensions and factors (see Table 4.5). That is why we selected the experimental and control groups before the pre-test. We did this because all classes available for selection are parallel ordinary classes. Students were distributed to these classes at random according to their scores in Primary School Leaving Examination; therefore, these classes are homogenous theoretically. Therefore, our standard for selecting the experimental and control groups is equal competence of English teachers. The English teachers for the two groups should not be the same person, but they should have almost equal teaching competence. The same years of teaching experience and the same gender would be preferable. We selected two English teachers through the recommendation by the school leaders and after listening to their lectures. We selected the classes of these two teachers as experimental and control groups stochastically.

After the experiment, significant differences occurred in the general learning adaptability between two groups (see Table 4.4). The experimental group had far fewer students who had average minus and bad learning adaptability than the control group, and had much more students who had average plus and good learning adaptability than the control group. The significance testing of mean difference further showed that the experimental group had much better conditions than the control group in the general learning adaptability, dimensions and factors (see Table 4.5), which indicates that our experiment is effective. In the experiment, we focused on the development of learning motivation system and learning methods and strategy system, which directly influences students' learning attitude and learning techniques.

Although no measures for learning environment and physical and psychological health were carried out in the experiment, we realized the essential role of teachers to the whole experiment. We conducted theoretical training to the teachers before the experiment. In the experiment, we listened to the lectures at random. We exchanged our opinions with teachers about teaching modes and the implementation of strategies. By doing this, teachers' teaching concepts were changed to a great extent. Teachers were cooperating in the experiment. They properly implemented the teaching strategies and methods for the experiment, and facilitated the optimization of the psychological environment in teaching, which promoted the improvement of students' learning adaptability, their sense of competence in learning, and physical and psychological health. Eventually, a virtuous circle was created and the improvement of students' learning adaptability was generally enhanced.

The pre-test and post-test scores of learning adaptability between two groups (see Table 4.6) show that the general learning adaptability of the experimental group was obviously better in the post-test than in the pre-test, especially learning attitude and learning techniques. This result perfectly corresponds with our objective, indicating that the subject infiltration mode and teaching strategies are reasonable and effective. Besides, significant decrease is As seen from the general learning adaptability, dimensions and factors of the control group in the post-test. The learning enthusiasm of the experimental group in the post-test was only at the same level as in the pre-test. These results consistent with the research results by Wang [1995], Bai [1997], Dai [1997], Nie [2004] et al, i.e., students' learning adaptability will decrease significantly with the upgrading of academic grades. Thus students' learning adaptability will decrease to a great extent without educational intervention as junior grade one students have problems in adapting to learning in junior middle schools. Therefore, improving students' learning adaptability is the responsibility of each teacher.

It is worth noting that we carried out measures to improve the psychological environment in teaching. The school environment of the experimental group in the post-test was obviously inferior to that in the pre-test; whereas the school environment of the control group in the post-test was significantly worse than in the pre-test. The experiment only slowed down the situation from getting worse. This relates with the insufficient infiltration time. It should be optimized by teachers through other means, such as team activities of the class. Special attention should be paid to the optimization of teacher-student relationship. It is because teacher-student relationship is an important component of psychological environment in teaching and the key influential factor to school environment which influences students' learning environment, and it is also the precondition and the key for students to acquire knowledge. The school should also advocate improving teachers' theoretical knowledge in teaching.

## The Subject Infiltration Mode and Strategies Can Significantly Improve Students' Learning Adaptability in English Language

The *Academic Adaptability Test for Junior Middle School Students* is not specifically for a certain subject, but our experiment was carried out in English language teaching, thus the experimental results are restricted to some extent in persuasion and pertinence. We made efforts to look for the questionnaires or tests that are able to test the learning adaptability of junior middle school students in English language, in order to compensate this defect. But we did not find any through literature research. And we decided to use *the Strategy Evaluation Sheet for English Language Learning among Students Ranging from Grade Seven to Grade*

*Nine* to test the methods, strategies and habits of English language learning, the three aspects of learning adaptability in English language learning. We believe that although learning methods, strategies and habits are different, they are closely related to each other [Guo, 2004], i.e., learning strategies can not be separated from specific learning methods because the implementation of learning strategies lies on learning methods and learning strategies are presented through learning methods. Learning methods, after being used consciously for many times, have the nature of strategies and become an indivisible part of learning strategies. Learning habits are the behavioral presentation of routine learning methods. Learning habits are developed when learning methods are presented through fixed ways of acts.

The independent-sample *t* test for the two groups after the experiment showed that (see Table 4.7) the experimental group had obviously higher scores in other dimensions than the control group, except the strategy of resources. The two groups had almost the same scores in the strategy of resources because English language in junior grade one is only ABC English, which is relatively simple. Students can smoothly complete their learning tasks through the assistance of teachers. Students do not have the consciousness to and do not learn English by using rich media resources. The obvious difference in pre-test and post-test scores of the participants from the experimental group showed that the subject infiltration mode and related teaching strategies for developing students' learning adaptability are applicable and effective.

## The Subject Infiltration Mode and Strategies Can Effectively Optimize Students' Psychological Suzhi

We tested the two groups with the *Mental Quality Questionnaire for Middle School Students* in order to find out whether the experimental intervention influenced students' psychological suzhi. The test (see Table 4.8) showed that two groups had almost the same psychological suzhi level before the test, except that the experimental group had obviously better perseverance than the control group. After the experiment, it was more obvious; what's more, the experimental group had much better personality factors such as independence, self-confidence, creativity and self-esteem, and adaptability factors such as learning adaptation, frustration endurance and interpersonal adaptation than the control group. It indicates that the subject infiltration mode and strategies have positive influence over the psychological suzhi of students in personality and adaptability. In the experiment, teachers supervised and checked the preparation and revision of lessons as well as in-time completion of homework, which promoted students to stick to personality development. We carried out many teaching strategies and methods to maintain students' interests in English language learning and to help them master the methods in English language learning; therefore, it is reasonable that the experimental group had better self-confidence and self-esteem than the control group. Then the frustration endurance also increased since students were more confident. It is also reasonable that the experimental group had better creativity and interpersonal adaptation than the control group, which is partially because of our teaching strategies and methods. The obviously better learning adaptation of the experimental group also indicates that our experiment is feasible and effective and can significantly improve students' learning adaptability.

The control group had obviously better ambition than the experimental group. The possible reason is that in the experiment, we did not guide students to set long-term targets;

instead, we emphasized on the current learning tasks and near-term targets, which should be improved in the future experiments.

The further independent-sample t test (see Table 4.9) showed that the post-test scores of the experimental group in metacognitive planning under the cognitive dimension, the perseverance under personality dimension and learning adaptation under adaptability dimension were higher than the pre-test scores. It indicates that students had accepted and used the learning method used in the experiment, i.e., developing learning adaptability by combining with the contents of teaching. Students have internalized such learning method to be a stable behavioral intention to some extent, formed a habit and have internalized it to be the stable psychological suzhi.

The post-test scores of both groups in metacognitive awareness were significantly higher than the pre-test scores, which indicates that the development of students' metacognitive awareness was not caused by the experiment but by the natural development of students' psychology. This corresponds with previous research: in junior middle school, students' physiological function continues to develop, which makes them feel like that they are adult and leads to the rapid development of self-awareness and the further development of the consciousness of self-awareness. These start to have critical influence on psychological suzhi. The research by Dong and Zhou [1995] into the capacity for self-monitoring of learning among junior middle school students also showed that the capacity of individuals for self-monitoring of learning are developing and improving, both the general capacity and capacity for other aspects, with the increase of age, and has more and more obvious influence on learning effect.

The pre-test results of two groups in personality factors, such as self-control, self-confidence, sense of responsibility and self-esteem, as well as adaptability factors such as emotional adaptation, frustration endurance and interpersonal adaptation were better than post-test results. It indicates that in the period of junior middle school, the unstable period before the mature of mentality, the development of psychological suzhi is unstable, vulnerable and complicated, making students not easy to adapt to the surrounding environment. This result correspond with the research result by Feng [1999], i.e., the personality factors and the adaptability factors of middle school students do not really improve with the increase of age, instead they are unstable and vulnerable. It also indicates that the period of junior middle school is the critical period for psychological suzhi-based education. In this period, the optimization of students' psychological suzhi should be strengthened; otherwise the psychological suzhi will be unstable and can not reach high level.

## The Subject Infiltration Mode and Strategies Can Effectively Improve Students' Academic Performance in English Language Learning

Research showed that students' learning adaptability is closely related to their academic performance. In general, the better learning adaptability they have, the better the academic performance they get. There was no significant difference between the two groups in the four English examinations (see Table 4.10), due to many reasons. First, academic performance is affected by many factors, including students' cognitive capacity, learning methods, etc. The experimental results will surely be influenced if only the learning adaptability is intervened. Second, learning adaptability is a relatively stable capacity. The internalization of educational intervention by students to be their psychological suzhi takes long time while our experiment only took four months. Within such short time, the learning adaptability can not be improved to a stable and high level. Besides, the influence of learning adaptability on academic performance was not as fast as knowledge imparting; instead it had hysteresis effect to a greater extent. Third, the difference of academic performance within the experimental group was significant, which affected the general academic performance of the group. It can be proved by that the experimental group had higher standard deviations of the academic performance. Thus we investigated the ratings of academic performance of the two groups (see Table 4.11). In the first monthly examination, a majority of students had average or good academic performance. The distribution is negative skew. It is because the test was relatively simple as the teachers considered that students just started their learning in junior middle school and they needed a period to adapt to the new environment and the new subject since a majority of students did not learn English in primary school. From the second monthly examination, the test had normal degree of difficulty, which led to a sharp drop in the number of students with average and higher academic performance, presenting the experimental results. The number of students from the experimental group with good academic performance was higher than the control group in the following three monthly examinations. The experimental group also had much fewer students with bad academic performance than the control group. It indicates that the educational intervention can effectively promote students to improve their academic performance from average to good and to slow down their academic performance getting worse from average to bad.

**Reflection of Experimental Results**

In general, experimental effects prove that the subject infiltration mode and strategies are applicable and effective, which is because we undertook efforts in two aspects:

We realized that teachers play a key role in the subject infiltration and the components of psychological environment in teaching, such as teacher-student relationship, peer relationship and psychological environment in class, influence the degree of absorption and acceptance of knowledge of a subject and psychological suzhi-based educational intervention. Thus in the experiment, we strived to establish good teacher-student relationship and peer relationship and create harmonious, relaxing and pleasing psychological environment in class, and regarded them as the means of subject infiltration.

We realized that the formation of students' learning adaptability is a mental sequence. In the process of English language teaching, both the mental development sequence and knowledge acquirement sequence exist. The intersection and overlapping of these two sequences are the process and basis of infiltration. Thus we tried to integrate the objectives of developing learning adaptability and the objectives of the teaching. We found the connection of the contents of developing learning adaptability and of teaching of a subject, found the common ground in the strategies for developing learning adaptability and English language teaching, followed the basic operating procedures and principles of subject infiltration, and carried out subject infiltration in three aspects of contents of teaching, teaching process and psychological environment in teaching.

However, the experimental results are not the best; it is because of the following three reasons:

Subject infiltration has high requirements on teachers' comprehensive competence, and it is quite difficult to change their concepts and teaching methods, which directly influence experimental results. Although teachers were cooperating in the experiment and they were very active in the experiment, they sometimes unconsciously used their old teaching mode due to their lack of basic knowledge and skills in psychology, for example, focusing on knowledge imparting, insufficient interaction between teachers and students, and stiff subject infiltration. Such situation required us to communicate with them continuously.

Psychological suzhi-based education is a long-term program. In most of the time, the realization of psychological suzhi-based education objectives in normal teaching that is hysteretic can not synchronize with knowledge imparting. Thus the effect of psychological suzhi-based education can not be As seen in teaching instantly.

Besides, psychological suzhi-based education is a systematic program. The infiltration only in one subject can not realize obvious effect. The infiltration should also be conducted in other subjects. In addition, it also needs the support of other means of psychological suzhi-based education, such as normal education, family, school and community.

Obvious improvements are seem from experimental group in the learning adaptability, psychological suzhi, the utilization of strategies in English language learning and academic performance in English language learning, which means that the mode of the present research used to develop students' learning adaptability in English language learning is effective and that the mode and strategies of subject infiltration are effective in developing students' psychological suzhi.

## Supplement 1. Academic Adaptability Test (AAT) for Middle School Students (Part)

Dear Students,

This survey is not to know whetther you have good or bad character or capacity, but to know how to fully incease your learning capacity. Thus, please answer each question honestly. If you don't, your answers will be different from your real situations, then this survey can not help you.

How to answer the questions?
There are three options (a, b, c) for each question. And on the answer sheet, there are three English letters (a, b, c) available respectively. Please use "O" to indicate your answers on the answer sheet, namely, if you choose the answer "a", please draw a circle "O" on "a" to indicate your answer; if you choose the answer "b", please draw a circle "O" on "b"; if you choose the answer "c", please draw a circle "O" on "c".

Attention:
Please answer the questions honestly as per your real thinking and actions.
You are supposed to choose one answer for each question. If there is no proper answer, please select the one which is closer to your situation.
Please do not discuss with your classmates, and do not copy from others.
If you do not understand the question or the words, please raise your hands to ask teachers.

If you need to change your answer, please use eraser to erase the answer you do not need. There is no time limit for the answering, but please do not consider for too long time. You should write down the answer which comes to your mind first.

Please take it in your mind that the question sheets will be used by others. Please keep them clean. Thus you should write down your answer on the "AAT Answer Sheet".

AAT Questions

Can you take the initiative to learn without the urging of parentsa. Yes. b. Yes, sometimes. c. No.

Do you think it is not good that you do not work hard in learning?a. Yes, always. b. Yes, sometimes. c. Yes, occassionally.

Can you start learning immediately after you sit in front of the table?a. Yes. b. Sometimes, I can atart immediately. c. No, I always can not.

When you sit in front of the table learning, do you feel boring? a. Yes, immediately. b. Yes, sometimes. c. No.

When you hate learning, do you use "headache", "stomachache" as excuses?a. Yes, sometimes. b. Always not. c. Never.

Do you think that you must work very hard in learning according to your situation?a. Yes, always. b. Yes, sometimes. c. Yes, occassionally.

Do you think that you are distractible and not persevering, thus you can not keep on learning? a. Yes, always. b. Yes, sometimes. c. No.

Do you think that learning is not interesting?a. Yes, always. b. Yes, sometimes. c. No.

Do you work harder on subjects on which you have poor performance? a. Yes . b. Yes, sometimes. c. No.

In learning, do you waste time because you are absentminded. a. Yes, always. b. Yes, sometimes. c. No.

When you study at home, do you have a plan about when you will study which subject?a. Yes . b. Yes, sometimes. c. No.


# SUPLEMENT 2. EVALUATION SHEET OF ENGLISH LANGUAGE LEARNING STRATEGIES FOR GRADE 7-9 STUDENTS

December 2004
Dear Students,

Please answer the following questions carefully. There is only one answer for each question. Please select the answer (number) which best describes your situation. Your answers are not hooked to your academic performance. The purpose of this survey is only to better understand how your English language learning is going, and further to better instruct your learning in the future. Thus, you are supposed to answer honestly.

Class _____ Name _____ Gender _____

1. You think that English language learning is _____
a. Very easy. b. Quite easy. c. Neither difficult nor easy. d. Quite difficult. E. Very difficult
2. Your academic performance in English language learning is _____
a. Very good. b. Good. c. Average. d. Bad.
(1=Never, 2=Basically not, 3=Sometimes, 4=Often, 5=Always)
Did you conduct pre-class preparation as the case may be? 1 2 3 4 5
Can you focus on English language learning? 1 2 3 4 5
Did you think initiatively in English language learning? 1 2 3 4 5
Are you good at memorizing key points in English language learning? 1 2 3 4 5
Do you use non-verbal information such as pictures to assist understanding? 1 2 3 4 5
Did you use association to learn and memorize new words? 1 2 3 4 5
Did you initiatively review, arrange and summarize what you have learned? 1 2 3 4 5
Did you pay attention to and find language rules, and use analogy in learning based on the language rules you found? 1 2 3 4 5
When using English language, can you notice mistakes and correct them? 1 2 3 4 5
Will you use Chinese knowledge to understand English language, if necessary? 1 2 3 4 5
Did you read English stories and other extra-curricular publications in English? 1 2 3 4 5
Can you use association to connect related knowledge? 1 2 3 4 5
Can you use reasoning and conclusion to analyze andsolve problems? 1 2 3 4 5
Did you have clear targets in English language learning? 1 2 3 4 5
Did you define your needs of learning? 1 2 3 4 5
Did you establish simple plans for English language learning? 1 2 3 4 5
Did you reflect your progress and shortcomings in English language learning? 1 2 3 4 5
Can you manage the key contents in English language learning? 1 2 3 4 5
Did you actively explore suitable learning methods for English language? 1 2 3 4 5
Did you have positive attitude towards English language learning? 1 2 3 4 5
Do you gradually have confidence in English language learning? 1 2 3 4 5
Did you exchange with peers and teachers learning experience? 1 2 3 4 5
Did you actively participate in curricular and extra-curricular activities concerning English language learning? 1 2 3 4 5
Did you try to communicate with others in English in curricular and extra-curricular learning activities? 1 2 3 4 5
Did you seek for and create opportunities for communicating in English? 1 2 3 4 5
In English communication, did you use gestures and facial expressions, when necessary? 1 2 3 4 5
In English language learning, did you pay attention to the difference between Chinese and foreign communication etiquettes? 1 2 3 4 5
Can you seek for help effectively when you encounter difficulties in communication? 1 2 3 4 5
Did you enrich your English language learning through tapes, discs, etc? 1 2 3 4 5
Did you search for information from simple English reference books? 1 2 3 4 5
Did you pay attention to English used in daily life and media? 1 2 3 4 5
Did you use the English language learning materials in libraries or Internet? 1 2 3 4 5

# SUPPLEMENT 3. INTERVIEW OUTLINE

For English teachers:

What requirements do the new curriculum standards have for students?
Further question: what are the difference between the new curriculum standards and the previous teaching objectives?
What are the differences between the new textbooks and the previous textbooks?
Further question: what requirements do the new textbooks have for teachers?
Where are the students mainly from?
How is the English foundation of students when they were enrolled?
How was their English language learning going when students were enrolled?
What are their problems in English language learning?
Further question: what methods did you adopt to solve these problems?

For Students of Junior Grade One:

Can you introduce your family? For example, what do your parents do?
Further question: were they involved in your learning? And how?
Do you feel any difference between the learning in the primary school and in junior middle school?
Further question: what are the differences?
Did you have English class in primary school?
If yes, how long did you study English in primary school? How many English classes do you have every week?
What were your English classes about? How do you feel about the current English language learning?
If no, how do you feel about the current English language learning?

# SUPPLEMENT 4. TEACHING DESIGN FOR DEVELOPING STUDENTS' LEARNING ADAPTABILITY IN ENGLISH LANGUAGE TEACHING

## Unit 9 Do You Want To Go To A Movie?

### Contents Of Teaching: Page 53-54 In Section A

Contents for infiltration: learning enthusiasm, methods of listening to lectures and methods of review
Targets of teaching:

To learn the vocabularies and sentence patterns;
To be able to express why one likes a type of movie;
To learn to talk about one's own interest and ask about others.

Targets of infiltration:

To be very enthusiastic in learning;

To develop good methods and habits if listening and pronunciation; and

To master and develop methods and habits of listening to lectures and note-taking.

Focus of teaching:

Vocabularies: action movie, thriller, documentary, comedy.

Learning to use key sentence patterns:

Do you want to go to a movie? Yes, I do. I want to go to …

What kind of movies do you like? I like …

Key of infiltration:

### *Maintaining Learning Enthusiasm;*

Mastering relevant methods of listening to lectures and methods of review.

### *Teaching Tools: Teaching Instruction And Tape Recording Player*

Preparation for infiltration: survey students' interests in English language; survey the situations of students in mastering and utilizing the learning methods that have been imparted

Opportunities of infiltration: i) teaching contents in Section A; the whole process of teaching

Teaching hours: 1 teaching hour

Infiltration process

### *1) Judgment And Evaluation*

### Creating Problem Situation, Presenting Stimuli

Teacher (Ask): would you like to know how to say the movie types in English? And would you like to know how to express your interests in movie and how to ask about others?

Student (answer): Yes.

Teacher: Then we will learn those today. (Present four film posters and names of movies in English through CAI, in order to arouse cognitive conflict of students and stimulate the learning motivation of students through visual and acoustic stimuli.)

### Inspiring and Thinking (Opportunity of Infiltration: Make Use of the Curiosity of Students, and Focus on the Guidance of Vocabularies and Sentence Patterns Based on the Contents of Teaching)

Teacher: there is a saying that "sharpening your axe will not delay your job of cutting wood". Before we learn new contents, let's have a look at how we learned words and sentence patterns. First of all, we will have a look at how we learned words.

Student (answer):

Summary by teacher: i) find out the pronunciation rules and spelling rules based on the letter combination; ii) whether it is open or close syllable; iii) association memory; iv) partial tone memory; v) memory based on classification

Teacher: how did we find the features of sentence patterns?

Student (answer):

Summary by teachers: i) the punctuation at the end of the sentence: full stop for declarative sentence, question mark for question sentence, exclamatory mark for interjectional sentence; ii) whether the predicate verb is verb be or action verbs; iii) whether there are interrogative at the beginning of the sentence; if yes, then it is a special interrogative sentence; iv) the answers; general interrogative sentence has answer with yes or no at the beginning.

Teacher: learning method is very important. Once we mastered them, we will achieve maximum results with little effort. A saying "a workman must first sharpen his tools if he is to do his work well" explains the same principle. It is better for you to summarize during learning.

### 2) Training with Strategies

### Explanation (Complete the Teaching Tasks in Parts 1a and 1b, CAI and Tapes Should Be Used in the Process)

Ask students to feel the characteristics of action movie, thriller, documentary and comedy; master the pronunciation and correct spelling of words; strengthen the memory methods of words. Guide students to try to explore the features of sentence patterns through varied sentence pattern; and the teacher will explain.

### Debate And Practice

Guide students to carry out pairwork activities by making use of teacher-student QandAs and communication among students, in order to complete the teaching task of oral communication in Parts 1c and 2c together.

Remind students of the methods concerning how to "listen and answer". Guide students in order to complete the teaching tasks in Parts 2a and 2b.

Teacher: it is time for listen and answer again. Who can tell me the procedures?

Student (answer):

Summary by teacher: browse the questions as fast as possible before listening, in order to be familiar with the questions. Answer the questions in your first listening; check your answers in the second listening; try to imitate the pronunciation and tones in the third listening. These procedures are very important and should not be forgotten. (When the teacher plays the tap for the third time, the teacher should pause appropriately, allowing students to imitate. At the end, the teacher announced the answers.)

### Extension (Through Creation of Situations for Activities, and Role Play)

Activity: A invites B to play basketball … (students can create their other situations). B says he would like to go to see a movie. Then A asks B what kind of movie he likes. B answers and A says he likes it too. In the end, A and B go to see a movie together.

Requirements: i) salutation should be used; use as many sentence patterns as possible. Notes: Let's play...; I want to...; what kind of movie do you like? etc.

## Feedback and Evaluation (During the Whole Teaching Activity)

The teacher encourages students to communicate and perform. The grammatical and other mistakes should only be pointed out after the performance. But the teacher should also encourage and praise students when pointing out the mistakes, in order to enhance the sense of participation and achievement, develop the habit of students to speak English.

## Inspiring and Thinking

Show the singular and plural forms of nouns through CAI; and ask students to observe and find out the rules. Ask students to answer questions (the teacher should give advice timely). The teacher summarize in the end (students are required to take notes).

Teacher: this is very important, please take notes. Think about how to take notes?

Student (answer):

Summary by teacher: i) write down the main points; ii) it is better to take notes at relevant places on the book; iii) take notes with your own habit of expression; iv) reorganize the notes timely after class; v) supplement the notes after class.

## Reflection

Practice and consolidation (creating situations, role play; encouragement, praise, feedback and evaluation by teachers)

Activity: present the photos and profile of Jay Chou, Zhao Wei, and Yao Ming (including birthday, family members, favorite colors, favorite fruits, favorite sports, etc). One student, acting as a journalist, interviewed another student acting as one of the stars (interview is based on the information of the star). Students have two minutes to prepare for the role-play. (The purpose is to develop the courage of students to show themselves; enhance the confidence of students in learning English language well through encouragement and praise by teachers; develop the verbal expression skills of students in the activity by making use of the new contents learned.)

## Summary

The teacher guides students to re-organize and review the contents learned in the class. The important points should be highlighted.

The teacher should emphasize that relevant learning methods should be used in learning, for example, when students listen to lectures, their enthusiasm, mind, eyes, mouth, ears and hands should be involved; students can try the memory-based review and the methods of note-taking.

Use quotes to prove the significance of mastering learning methods and forming learning habits.

Without correct methods, even the polymath with eyes will group blindly like the blind.

By Rene Descartes

A good learning method is like a passkey, which opens the door to knowledge for us at any time. Mastering effective learning methods is the basic condition of success.

**Transfer and Improvement**

It is realized by completion of homework by students, and the marking and comments of teachers.

# REFERENCES

Bai, J. R., Liu, G. W., and Guo, X. *M.* (1997). Research into middle school students' learning adaptability. *Journal of Developments in Psychology, 2,* 60-63.

Cha, Y. L. (1998). *Education Modeing.* Guangxi: Guangxi Education Publishing House.

Cha, Z. X. (1993). *Psychology of Supernormal Children.* Beijing: People's Education Press.

Chen, J. L. (2002). *Psychological Suzhi Education in School – Principles and Operation.* Beijing: Educational Science Publishing House.

Chen, X. (2004). *Psychological Suzhi Education in Middle School.* Chongqing: Southwest China Normal University Press.

Chen, X., and Zhang, D. J. (2002). Exploration and discussion of integrated modes for mental health education. *Educational Research, 1,* 71-75.

Chen, Y. H., Lin, Z. W., and Li, K. C. (1991). *Learning adaptability scale.* Taipei, TW: Psychological Publishing.

Cui, W. W., and Meng, Q. M. (1998). Confirmatory factor analysis of construct validity of the Academic Adaptability Test. *Psychological Science, 2,* 176-177.

Dai, Y. H. (1997). Research into the learning adaptability of middle school students. *Journal of Educational Development, 11,* 24-26.

Dong, Q., and Zhou, Y. (1995). Experimental research into students' self-monitoring of learning. *Journal of Beijing Normal University (social science education), 1,* 84-90.

Feng, Z. Z. (1999). *Research into the components of psychological* suzhi *of middle school students and its development.* Master's thesis, Southwest China Normal University, Chongqing, P.R.C.

Feng, Z. Z., Zhang, D. J. (2001). A study on the concept and elements of the middle school students' mental quality. *Journal of Southwest University (philosophy and social sciences edition).*

Guo, C. (2004). *Psychological Suzhi Education in Primary School.* Chongqing: Southwest China Normal University Press.

Huang, Z. C. (2003). *Modeing of English Language Teaching in Middle School.* Guangxi: Guangxi Education Publishing House.

Jiang Qi, Zhang, D. J. *Problems of the research into infiltration of psychological* suzhi-*based educationin teaching and countermeasures.* Unpublished materials from Research Institute of Educational Science, Southwest China Normal University, Chongqing, P.R.C.

Li, C. G. (1995). On the psychological counseling among students from vocational high school. *Vocational and Technical education, 2,* 70-71.

Liu, H., and Zhang, D. J. (2004). On the quality education and the requirements of teacher's psychological qualifications. *Journal of Hebei Normal University (Educational Science Edition), 1,* 56-60.

Liu, Q. (2003). Teaching Methods for the New English Language Curriculum of Middle School. Beijing: Kaiming Press.

Liu, Y. L. (2001). A research of the relationship between elementary school students' mental quality and their academic achievement. Master's thesis, Southwest China Normal University, Chongqing, P.R.C.

Luo, D. Q., and Qu, X. Y. (2002). Several problems concerning mental health education. *Beijing Education: Higher Education, 4,34-36.*

Nie, Y. G., Zheng, X., and Zhang, W. (2004). The study of academic adaptation condition of the senior middle school students. *Psychological Development and Education, 1,* 23-28.

Peng, Y. X. (1999). Experiment report for the Psychological Suzhi Training and Education among Middle School Students. *Modern Educational Research, 2,* 41-44.

Qin, Y. (2000). *A study on subjective learning strategies of junior English.* Master's thesis, Sichuan Normal University, Sichuan, P.R.C.

Song, G. W. (1999).A correlational study on learning adaptability, personality and mental health of senior middle school students. *Psychological Exploration, 1,* 44-47.

Song, G. W., Yang, Z. N. (1999). Comparative analysis of learning adaptability among middle school students. *Chinese Mental Health Journal, 4,* 233.

Song, G. Y., and Jin, Y. (2002). English curriculum standard for full-time compulsory education in high school: for teachers. Hubei: Central China Normal University Press.

Sun, C. H., and Zheng, R. C. (2001). Confirmatory factor analysis of study adaptation scale. *Psychological Exploration, 2,* 59-64.

Sun, Y., and Zhang, D. J. (2003). Principles of infiltratingpsychological suzhi-based educationin teaching of a subject. *Journal of Leshan Teachers College, 6,* 10-13.

Tian, L. (2002). The research on learning adaptability problem of pupils and the educational interfering. Master's thesis, Southwest China Normal University, Chongqing, P.R.C.

Wang, H. P., Li, K. X., and Shi, J. P. (1998). Research into the development of learning adaptability among junior middle school from rural areas. *Chinese Journal of Applied Psychology, 4* (1), 49-54.

Wang, P., Shi, K., and Zuo. Y. T. (1996). Developmental research into the learning mode of adaptability of middle school studnets. *Psychological Development and Education, 4,* 14-17.

Wang, T. (2002). A study on the mental quality structure and its developmental characteristics in university students. Master's thesis, Southwest Normal University, Chongqing, P.R.C.

Wu. Z. Q. (2001). *Learning psychological counseling.* Shanghai: Shanghai Education Publishing House.

Xiao, M. (2003). How to infiltrate the contents of mental health education in teaching of a subject. *Communication of Vocational Education, 7,* 56.

Xing, J. P. (2003). On the penetration of psychological education in the discipline teaching. *Journal of Anyang Normal University, 4,* 23-25.

Xu, X. J. (2004). The research of undergraduates' learning adaptability: it's structure, developmental characteristics and influential factors. Master's thesis, Southwest Normal University, Chongqing, P.R.C.

Xu, Z. N., and Zheng, M. C. (2000). About the research in "learning adaptability" in China. *Shanghai Research on Education, 5,* 51-53.

Yan, J. T., and Deng, C. Y. (1999). Report of the research into the learning adaptability of junior middle school students from rural areas. *Journal of Pingdingshan University, 1,* 39-42.

Yan, J. T., and Hu, X. C., and Wang, D. R. (2000). Research report of the academic performance of students from Qiling No. 3 middle school. *Journal of Henan Institute of Education (philosophy and social sciences), 19* (1), 21-23.

Yang, H. *F.* (2002). Research into the anxiety and learning adaptability of students from vocational high school. *Chinese Mental Health Journal, 2,* 130.

Ye, S. H. (2000). Infiltration of mental health education in teaching of a subject. *Journal of Xiamen Educational College, 1,* 58-62.

Ye, Y. T. (2004). Several problems concerning infiltrating mental health education in teaching of a subject. *Journal of the Chinese Society of Education, 3,* 18-21.

Zhang, C. *F.*, and Zhang, J. B. (2000). Survey and analysis of the learning adaptability among middle school students. *Contemporary Educational Science, 12,* 60-61.

Zhang, D. J. (1997). *Psychology in teaching.* Chongqing: Southwest China Normal University Press.

Zhang, D. J. (2003). *Strategies of Teaching and Learning.* Beijing: People's Education Press.

Zhang, D. J., Feng, Z. Z., Guo, C., et al. (2000) Problems on research of students' mental quality. *Journal of Southwest University (philosophy and social sciences edition), 3* (26), 56-62.

Zheng, H. J. (1999). The exploring of psychological education in subjects. *Educational Research, 9,* 53-57.

Zheng, R. C. (1994). *Psychological diagnosis of middle school students.* Jinan: Shandong Education Press.

Zhou, B. C., Fang, Z., et al. (1991). *Revised Academic Adaptability Test for Junior Middle School Students.* Shanghai: East China Normal University Press.

# PART THREE:

# SUBJECT INFILTRATION MODES AND IMPLEMENTATION STRATEGIES

*Chapter 4*

# EFFECTS OF HOME-SCHOOL-COOPERATION-BASED EDUCATION MODE ON SELF-ADAPTABILITY OF JUNIOR MIDDLE SCHOOL STUDENTS IN GRADE ONE

*Yuan Zang[1], Da-Jun Zhang[2], Yan-Ling Liu[2] and Jin-Liang Wang[2]*
[1]IFST University of Delaware Newark, Delaware, US
[2]Center for Mental Health Education in Southwest University, China

## ABSTRACT

This chapter is to discuss and explore the effect of home-school-cooperation-based education (HSCE) modes on cultivating students' self-adaptability via literature review, psychometrics and questionnaire. According to present situation of psychological sushi among students chosen in our research, and based on HSCE resource available, an experiment applying HSCE modes was conducted to explore the effects of HSCE mode on cultivating individuals` self-adaptability with a sample of students at grade one in junior high schools. We have found in the post-test that there was a significant difference between experimental group and control group on the total score, as well as on the dimensions including "adaptability to study", "identification of body" and "adaptability to life". In the experimental group, the score on the self-adaptability had been found significant improvement after the experiment. In the control group, no significant difference was found on the scores of self-adaptability between the pre-test and post-test. The results indicated that the HSCE modes can effectively improve junior school students' self-adaptability.

# INTRODUCTION

## Research on HSCE

### *1) Definition of HSC (Home-School Cooperation)*

No consistent agreement has been reached on the definition of home-school cooperation. In the literature, conceptions with similar meanings were also used, including "home-school partnership", "home-school collaboration" and "parent-teacher collaboration". The related terms include "parent involvement, parental involvement, parent participation", "home-school relationships", "home-school communication", "home-school liaison" etc.

Xu et al. (2003) hold that the HSC is a kind of interactive activity that aims to promote teenagers' healthy growth and it is the activity where the home and the school cooperate with, support and collaborate with each other. Ma (1999) holds that the HSC actually unites two forces, the home and the school which can cause the greatest influence on students, to educate students. The home and the school should support each other and make joint effort during the education activities. He emphasizes that the school can get the support from the home in students' education, while parents can also be guided by the school when rearing their children; the two should make a concerted effort. Such concept balances the positions and functions of the home and the school in education.

Epstein, research expert of Johns Hopkins University in the USA, et al. (1999) expand the HSC as "home-school-community partnership", emphasizing the common responsibility of the school, the home and the community for children's education and development as well as the interaction among the three in the field of children's education and development. Epstein also believes that the home and the school are equal in the HSC, and that the students themselves should also be included into the HSC. She attaches great importance to the position and functions of students as agent in the HSC.

According to the existing research, this chapter defines the HSC, from the perspective of practice, as a kind of interactive educational activity that aims to promote children's and teenagers' development with the coordination and cooperation between, and the support of, the home and the school. This definition means that:

The HSC is the interaction and coordination between the home education and school education. It is based on the mutual respect and trust of the two: parents should support the school education, while the school education should affirm the home education and provide directions for it.

The core of the HSCE is the student, the target for both of the school education and the home education. The student is, and functions as, the agent of the HSC. The final goal of HSC is to promote student's overall development.

The HSCE is for the purpose of prevention instead of remedy. Parents should join in the education since their children just enter the school instead of when there is some problem with the children at school.

The HSC is an important means for the society to involve in the school education. Parent's participation is closely connected to the society and the modern HSC will definitely involve the community and the society.

## 2) Classification of HSCE

### By The Role of Parents in HSCE

American scholar Williams found during the research that parents desire to play different roles in school education, including guiding their children, in-class support and participating in the school committee to prepare regulations and rules for the school [Ma, 1999]. Langenbrunner and Thornburg, another two scholars, have divided the parents' roles in school education into three categories [Ma, 1999]:

*Supporter and learner.* Teachers, parents and administrative personnel of the school always prefer this role for the education to children, and parents also feel relaxed and unforced during the activity. Parents may participate in the school education via parents' meeting, tabloid for parents, school for parents, counseling on home education, home-school liaison in writing, home-school liaison by phone, meeting with the parents of certain student etc. Parents will be concerned only by the progress of their own children during the aforesaid activities.

*Volunteer participant in school's activities, voluntarily providing services for the school free of any charge.* Parents may help educate students as the assistant of the head teacher, conduct individual directions for students on certain subject, deliver informal report about their experience to students, launch after-class activities for students according to their own special talent, and do some work that will not cause direct communication with students, including the work in library or parent's room or designing or sorting out the class materials and the games for learning. Such participant has infiltrated into the daily education activities at school and even the classroom teaching.

*Participant in making educational decisions for the school.* Parents will participate in making the school's educational decisions, including establishing the decisions, implementing the decisions and supervising the implementation of such decisions.

### By The Levels of Participation

Parents will desire to participate in different levels of activities in the course of HSC since their benefit, interests, needs and motivations are different. Liu [1992] has divided the aforesaid activities into three levels:

*"Formal participation"*. This is the most superficial participation and is always directed by the school. Parents will be invited to visit the school and attend the parent-teacher meeting, open days, exhibition of students' works. In addition, this also includes parent contact lists, tabloid for parents, communications on home education.

*"Interactive participation"*. This is a kind of two-way communication; parents and teachers can exchange information, ideas and advices in a friendly atmosphere. Teachers may often visit the parents of schoolchildren, while parent may participate in classroom teaching and after-class activities, help make the teaching aid and raising funds for the school.

*"Participation in management"*.

Morgan, professor of universities in Northern Ireland, et al. [1992] have also divided parents' participation in activities into low-/high-level participation and formal participation/participation in organization ( As can be As seen in Table 3.1 for details).

**By Purposes of HSC Activities**

American scholar Davies [1976] maintained that HSC activities should be divided based on their purposes. He believes that many schools request to implement the HSC to:

Solve existing problems in the present education by, for example, meeting parents by appointment and establishing the counseling committee for home education;

Cause the parents to participate in the education to their children by, for example, providing counseling on home education;

Enrich, with the community's resources for education, the content of school education by, for example, visiting the museum and building out-school educational bases;

Make parents participate in making educational decisions by, for example, establishing the parent committee, parent-teacher association etc.

**Table 3.1. Six Levels of Parents' Participation in Activities**

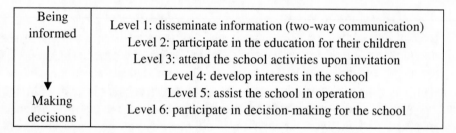

| Being informed ↓ Making decisions | Level 1: disseminate information (two-way communication)<br>Level 2: participate in the education for their children<br>Level 3: attend the school activities upon invitation<br>Level 4: develop interests in the school<br>Level 5: assist the school in operation<br>Level 6: participate in decision-making for the school |
|---|---|

*3) Influencing Factors of HSCE*

**School**

*Cognition and attitude of the school on and toward the HSC.* The president's and the teacher's cognition on the effect of HSC is an important factor that may influence the HSC. The HSC will be doomed to fail if the management personnel fail to recognize the importance of HSC and have a negative attitude toward it.

*Communications between the home and the school.* Successful exchange of information between the home and the school is the precondition for achieving effective home-school cooperation: the HSC will be effective if the school adopts two-way communication to exchange ideas with the home and actively communicates with parents on an equal basis; on the contrary, such cooperation will be definitely a failure if the school just gives orders unilaterally regardless of parents' feelings and feedback.

*Student's functions.* The student's function between the home and the school is also an important factor that possibly influences the effect of HSC: students will, if they actively transfer information between the home and the school and often encourage and request their parents to participate in the school's activities, lay a sound foundation for the HSC; or else, they will bring more difficulties for the cooperation between the home and the school.

**Home**

*Parent's conception on educational responsibility.* Parents' failure to correctly define the responsibility of the home and the school for educating children will always impact the effect of HSC; in addition, some parents do not have a mature educational conception, which is also adverse to the HSC.

*Parents' self cultivation suzhi and their way to bring up children.* The educational experience of parents can reflect, to some extent, their capability of educating the children. The parents receiving poor education will always have poor education capability. They will fear the school and the teacher and be unwilling to participate in the school's activities, which is adverse to the cooperation between the home and the school. The parents with different education suzhi will always educate their children in different ways and they will participate in different activities ordinarily, which will also influence the progress of HSC [Bonnie, 2002].

## Policy and Regulation

It will also greatly influence the establishment of HSC systems whether there are sound policies and regulations [Xu and Wu, 2003]. The policies and regulations on establishing HSC systems in China still need improvement, and the school has no tradition of cooperation. It is difficult to some extent to implement such systems.

## Personnel and Department

The HSC involves many fields and some Chinese governmental agencies, educational agencies and schools do not attach importance to it. The arrangement of personnel and departments will also influence the implementation of HSC activities.

## *4) Research on HSCE Modes in China*

## HSCE Modes Focusing on School

The HSCE modes focusing on school regard the school as the center of HSC. If we compare HSC to a wheel, the school will be the axis of the wheel and the home, the community, various HSC centers, home education supporting centers and other supporting systems will be the spokes of the wheel [Ma, 1999]. In the mode, all HSC activities are carried out around the school, and the school thus becomes the main venue of activities. Many activities are applicable to this mode, including inviting parents to visit the school, establishing home education centers, counseling provided by the school on home education, participating in students' classroom activities, participating in various activities for students, recruiting parents as volunteers, allowing parents to managing some school affairs, holding school-home discussion meetings etc. The mode is applicable to the students from kindergarten to senior middle schools and their homes; the younger the students are, the more they will participate in such activities. The activities based the mode are convenient to conduct on a concentrated basis and can attract more parents to participate in.

## HSCE Modes Focusing on Home

The HSCE mode focusing on home regards the home as the center of HSC. If we compare HSC to a wheel, the home will be the axis of the wheel and the school, the community, various HSC centers, home education supporting centers and other supporting systems will be the spokes of the wheel. The forms and levels of all activities should be determined according to the characteristics and needs of different homes [Ma, 1999]. In this mode, all HSC activities are carried out around the home, and the home thus becomes the main venue of activities. Many activities are applicable to the mode, including parent's education at homes and in communities, recruiting and training supporting staff for parent's education, establishing development centers for parents and children in communities, launching home study activities, visiting the parents of schoolchildren etc. The mode is mainly used for younger students. It may help parents further educate their children and is helpful to perform the advantages of home education. However, it requires huge input of resources.

## 5) Research on HSCE Practice in China

### Building Learning-Based Home Via HSC

Changyang Road Primary School in Qingdao, Shandong began in 2003 to build learning-based home via HSC and has achieved good effect [Cui, 2003]. The steps were: a) distributing questionnaires to understand parents' conceptions on learning-based home; b) issuing and implementing the *Standards of Changyang Road Primary School on Establishing Learning-Based Home* to define the connotation of learning-based home, and using the *Self-Evaluation Sheet of Changyang Road Primary School in Qingdao on Establishing Learning-Based Home* for psychometrics; c) fully performing the head teacher's functions as a guider during the implementation to make parents study and master the skills and to improve their capabilities of building the unique learning-based home. The activity has achieved good effect: students have made remarkable progress, and parents and teachers have improved their own capabilities.

### Launching "Harmonious Home-School Interaction"

Some middle schools and primary schools in Jinjiang District, Chengdu, Sichuan launched the educational experiment of "harmonious home-school interaction" [Wang and Zhang, 2003]. Fourteen middle schools and primary schools in the district were surveyed in respect of the status quo of HSC in the beginning, and then various activities started in these schools. Many new connotations have been supplemented to the traditional HSC methods. For example, problem-based and understanding-based home visits have been replaced with research-based, cooperation-based and heart-to-heart-talk-based home visits; the parent, the teacher and the student all become the agents of home visits. In addition, the parent, the student and the expert all attend the parents' meeting in diversified forms, deliver keynote speeches, perform in the talent show and participate in the school-wide activities. The schools also tried some new HSC activities, such as parents' salon, parent-child sports meeting and the community's cultural festival, and built up the learning-based home. They have investigated and analyzed the status quo of students' family status, held special lectures on home education, established schools for parents and the parent committee, set parents' open days and elected "excellent parents". This experiment has been commonly accepted by the home, the school and the student, and the three parties have benefited from that.

## 6) Research on HSCE Modes in Other Countries

### PTA Program In Japan

PTA, abbreviation of "Parent Teacher Association", originated in the USA from the late 19th century and was introduced into Japan after the Second World War [Nan, 2002]. PTA has, during the practice for tens of years, played a significant role in improving the communications of the school with the home and the community, and promoting the teenager's development.

The smallest PTA is a class. The parents may recommend themselves or other parents as the members and such members, together with the head teacher, compose the class-level PTA. The PTA members from each class then compose the school-level PTA. The school-level PTA is divided into different committees responsible for organizing the school's sports meeting or the competition between parents and children, organizing students to participate in various public benefit activities, launching camping, supervising the use of facilities and equipments in the school, proposing advices on the school's educational work as well as organizing and supervising children's activities in the community.

National PTA, the central institution of PTA, is responsible for guiding and coordinating all PTA activities throughout the country and launching public welfare causes in respect of HSC. Presently, the PTA organizations throughout Japan have made great progress and become an important and huge force for the education of primary schools and middle schools in Japan.

### Megaskill Program in the USA

The MegaSkill program since 1964 is a teacher training program launched by Home and School Institute. It aims to facilitate students` great achievements by improving the relationship between the school and the home [Rich, 1992]. The parents participating in the program actively help, in accordance with the direction by teacher, the student make progress in study; in addition, the parent-child relationship can also be improved and consolidated effectively via the interaction between the parents and the children. Generally speaking, parents can participate in this program free of any charge and each class may last 15-20 minutes.

### School Development Program (SDP) in the USA

SDP was launched by in 1968 in two junior middle schools in New Haven, Connecticut State [Tan, 2003]. It aims to promote students to achieve success in study via improving the relationship between the school and the home. In this program, the Board of Directors of the school is responsible for preparing plans, the school's development team is responsible for promoting the HSC on behalf of the parent, the teacher, the management personnel and the school's supporter, the parent is requested to participate actively in various activities organized by the school and the dedicated home-school coordinator is designated for better communications between the school and the community. The present SDP mainly covers the following five fields: a) counseling and training for parents, b) training for teachers, c) training for the school's management personnel, d) establishing the partnership between the school and the educational department under the State's government, e) telephone training.

## Center for the Improvement of Child Caring in the USA

The Center for the Improvement of Child Caring (CICC) was established in 1974. It has set up many regional clubs to train parents, which was significant for promoting the HSC [Tan, 2003].

CICC focuses on the relationship between parents and their children in order to help parents better educate their children, and parents study, during the activity, the skills to guide their children's behavior, such as the strategies on effective praise, oral communications, leisure and recreation with children and encouragement to children.

CICC has launched various programs to train parents' skills, held academic conferences on training guiders and provided many materials on trainings for parents and trainings on family life.

## Families and Schools Together in the USA

"Families and Schools Together" (FAST) was launched in 1988 in Madison, Wisconsin to cooperate with junior middle schools, agencies for mental health, agencies for preventing drug abuse and the home in preventing the abuse of drugs [McDonald et al., 1991]. It is to: a) make the parents prevent the children's negative behavior by improving the relationship between family members so as to improve the home's overall functions, b) help students behave well at school and prevent students from suffering excessive school failures, c) strengthen the communications between the home and the medical institutions to help children and their homes understand relevant knowledge on drugs and prevent the abuse of any narcotic, d) intensify the support for the parents of children of high risk and improve the use by the home of the facilities and resources in the community. This is a program with remarkable USA characteristics and its emergence is closely connected with the abuse of drugs.

## Teachers Involve Parents in Schoolwork

Epstein [1993] from the Johns Hopkins University (JHU) proposed in 1987 the basic concept of "Teachers Involve Parents in Schoolwork" (TIPS) for the primary education. TIPS is to: a) help parents better understand their children's schoolwork, b) make parents participate more in their children's study at home, c) make students more willing to tell parents the events occurring in school, enhance their expression capabilities and make such expression more frequent, d) make students better complete the homework on each subject.

Regular meetings are convened during the TIPS for communications between the school and the home to discuss some issues on language arts, science, health, math etc. The homework-related activities can enable parents to frequently participate in children's study. Some activities for TIPS request children to dare to, when facing other family members, express themselves, share the experience and launch explanation and discussion as well as to interact and communicate with the whole family. The teacher is responsible for designing the activities for this program and students and parents will participate in such activities once a week or once every other week.

## 7) Functions of HSCE

### Influence of HSC on Parents

Most of the research has shown that parents may benefit a lot from the HSC. The research by Liontos [1992] has shown that the parent's education efficacy can be improved in the course of HSC, the parents can become more confident and they can be clearer about their children's development and the children's characteristics at different development stages. Many parents have applied the knowledge they learned during HSC to the home education, and they can make the best use of the home environment to help their children.

### Influence of HSC on Teenagers

Large quantity of research has shown that the HSC can greatly improve students' academic performance [Clark, 1990]. Researchers have found that the successful HSC activities can help students increase their motivation, improve their academic performance, regulate their behaviors and conducts and improve their attendance. In addition, students will always hold the positive attitude toward the schoolwork and the homework. For example, the results have shown that TIPS can promote students, parents and teachers to participate in the activities and better cooperate with each other [Rioux and Berla, 1993]. Students prefer the homework assigned by TIPS, parents and students can better cooperate with each other and students hold a positive attitude toward their study. The evaluation on the effect of MegaSkill program has shown that this program can stimulate students' interest in the school, improve their attendance and academic performance, arrange the learning time more reasonably, help them make greater academic achievements, improve their scores in state-level examinations, make them perform better at school and make parents participate in activities more actively. It has been found that the SDP helps students to make great achievements in academic and social fields. For example, the students at the schools, which implement this program, have achieved remarkable improvement in reading, math, attendance and in-school performance [Tan, 2003].

### Influence of HSC on Parent-Child Relationship

Parents can improve the parent-child relationship by cooperating with the school and learning the knowledge on children's development. Siders and Sledjiski [1978] have found in the research that parents can improve the parent-child relationship by exchanging their ideas on study and life with the children since it is easier for children to accept the education from their parents and the effect is sustained. Iverson and Walberg [1982] have found in the research into 18 HSC programs that the effect of HSC is closely connected to the interaction between parents and children in respect of the children's study. Clark [1983] has found, in the research into American senior middle school students of African ancestry, that most of the American students of African ancestry with academic success come from the families where the parents communicate well with the children and attach great importance to children's study. The result of FAST has shown that this program is helpful to improve individuals' self-assessment ability, broaden the home's attention, make the relationship between family members more harmonious and promote the cooperation between the home and the school [McDonald and Bellingham, 1993].

## Influence of HSC on Schools

The school solicits the parent's opinions on education and teaching during the HSC and actively enhances its capabilities when correcting the deficiency. Lots of research has proved that the mode is of significant importance for a school's development. For example, Logan [1992] found, after his survey on 558 teachers, that 67% of those surveyed believed that the parent's opinions were extremely useful for them. Lindle [1992] investigated 385 persons among the teaching staff and got similar results.

The main achievements of HSC research include: a) it makes the home pay attention to children's study and makes students improve their academic performance; b) the parents and the teacher coordinate their expectations to the children and the targets and establish s sound monitoring system; c) it enhances the level of home education and school education; d) it helps to establish the sound home-school relationship; e) it promotes the establishment of sound parent-child relationship; f) it improves the efficacy of parent's education; g) it promotes the child's development.

## 8) Theoretical Basis of HSCE

### System-Ecological Theory

The representative figures of system-ecological theories are Hobbs and Bronfenbrenner [1917~]. Hobbs's research mainly focuses on the home's needs and he adopts the system-ecological theory to analyze the relationship between the home and the school of teenagers [Linda and Howard, 1999], while Bronfenbrenner's research focuses on preschool issues and he analyzes, with his research results, the relationship between teenagers and the environment [Tan et al., 2003].

Bronfenbrenner proposed an ecological mode to understand the social impacts, the system-ecological theory. He divided the social impacts into a series of systems and the teenager is the core thereof. The factors that can cause the most direct influence on teenagers are those in the "microsystem", i.e. the aspects in direct contact with individuals. For most teenagers, the most important microsystem is the home and the next is the friend and the school. The microsystem is changing along with the change of various social environments. The "mesosystem" is mainly the interaction against the background of the microsystem. The frequency, property and influence of such interaction can be analyzed in the mesosystem. The microsystem and the mesosystem can strengthen or weaken each other. Teenagers may, if the values in the mesosystem conflict with those in the microsystem, need to choose their values among different systems of values and feel great pressure. The "exosystem" is made of the background that can influence the teenager, but the teenager does not play an active role in it. The "macrosystem" includes the ideology, attitudes, moral ideas, customs and laws in a certain culture. Hobbs holds that the issues on children cannot be separated from their relatives, friends, schools and communities and that the teenagers' life and study are closely connected with their home while their schools and communities are just providing various services for their homes. Hobbs has validated in his program the necessity of taking the home, the community and the school into consideration.

The ecological theory, which proposes that the school, the community and the home are related to and dependent on each other, analyzes the students' problems from the perspective of the whole social environment and find out the solutions for such problems. Lewis [1997] holds that it is effective to analyze and solve the issues on teenagers and their homes and schools on a systematic basis in accordance with the ecological theory.

## Separate Responsibility

This theory was proposed by Lightfoot [1978], who believes that the mother and the teacher always bore the most responsibilities for educating the children. The female are always regarded as the major force to foster and educate children. The mother bears the major responsibilities for education before the children enter the school, while the female teacher begins to assume the responsibility after the children enter the school, especially at the first stage of compulsory education (in the primary school) when the different education given by the teacher and the parents always causes great conflicts and contradictions to children.

The mother educates her children in all aspects, but she always provides education in a private space; meanwhile, the teachers' education always focuses on the knowledge and they can lead children to a broader world.

The mother and the teacher are not natural partners in fact, although they are both responsible for educating children, so the school always believes that parents' participation in school's activities is the interference with the school and thus avoids such participation. The school and the parents have no cooperation and communications in the true sense although the parents may participate in some activities of the school. It follows that it is necessary to promote the cooperation between the home and the school.

However, the lack of communications between the home and the school may also cause positive influence. Lightfoot holds that such lack may sometimes allow more space to children to enable them to adapt to the changing world; teenagers will be less free if the ideas of the home are identical with those of the school.

## Overlapping Spheres

Gordon holds that the parents, the teacher and other adults play different roles in teenagers' development. For example, parents can be volunteers, employees, tutors, audience, decision-makers, adult learners etc. The parent-teacher collaboration modes applicable to such roles include: a) parent impact mode, b) comprehensive services mode, c) school impact mode, and d) community impact mode [Linda and Howard, 1999].

The teacher helps the home in case of the parent impact mode and teachers will teach parents some information and skill on children's development and study; the educator will satisfy the needs of children's health and social psychology with the comprehensive services mode. Parents play a negative role in such two modes and they are just the receiver of information; they are the audience. In case of the school impact mode, the parent interacts with the teacher and the parent is the decision-maker and volunteer. In case of the community impact mode, the most important thing is the relationship among the home, the community and the school, and the parent here can be any one of the aforesaid six roles.

Epstein proposed six HSC modes according to Gordon's theory. The HSC modes proposed by Epstein emphasize that the home, the community and the school should share the responsibility. The main spheres that influence the students are the home, the school and the community, each of which can cooperate with each other or function independently. The external mode of the overlapping spheres mainly indicates how each sphere is cooperating with each other and functioning independently, while the internal mode focuses on the harmonious interpersonal relationship among the home, the school and the community.

## 9) Problems in the HSCE Studies

Although previous research has launched some theoretical discussion on HSC and proposed detailed educational measures on launching activities, such research in China is far from satisfying the requirements for educational development and many theoretical and practical issues need further discussion.

## There Lacks Research on Basic Theories.

Compared with the theoretical basis and programs on HSC in foreign countries, the domestic research lacks theoretical basis and there are not many programs on HSC. In addition, the program is in simple form, it has no systematic planning and there are no systematic theories.

## Many Issues are Needed to be Resolved in Educational Practice.

Many problems on practice are to be solved although many schools and agencies have launched the activity and research on HSCE in recent years. For example:

*The activities were poorly planned.* There were no overall plans for some HSC activities and it was difficult for the school, the grade, the class and the parent to cooperate with each other. The activity cannot be conducted continuously and the effect cannot be strengthened. Moreover, such activities were not special-purposed, well prepared and organized, and just achieved very little effect.

*The activities were conducted in separate periods instead of on a continual basis.* Many schools conducted HSC activities during certain periods, such as the beginning and the end of each semester as well as the holidays. No activity was available at other time. There is no consistent HSC applicable to teenagers and children at different ages and conforming to the law of their development.

*Teachers always adopted force feeding instead of two-way communications.* Force feeding was always adopted for the communication during certain HSC activities, which was just the lecture by teachers and was less targeted and practical. In addition, teachers did not explain profound theories in simple language, so it was difficult for parents to truly accept it and internalize it into the correct ideas and conscious action so as to educate their children.

There is no fixed standard and definition for the large number of HSC approaches and it is difficult to evaluate the effect of HSC.

Most of HSC research is descriptive and there is no relevant research and experiment on the relations among various variables. Thus many conclusions are not scientific or precise. For example, experimenters did not control the variables in such research, so it was difficult to find out the relation between HSC and students' development.

The existing research focuses on the HSCE forms and there is no intensive research for cultivating students' psychological suzhi.

The key reasons why the present HSCE and relevant research achieve little progress and turn out to be a mere formality are that existing studies are not intensive enough and most of them just focus on the HSCE forms. The educational content involved is mostly the school work and the regulation, and scare studies are targeted at improving students' core suzhi, the psychological suzhi, which may restrict their academic development and their mastery of regulations. In fact, the HSCE is not only an effective cultivation approach but also the important educational resources for cultivating sound psychological suzhi for students. This is also the basic reason why this research is launched.

## Summary of the Research on Junior Middle School Students' Self-Adaptability

### *1) Theories about Self-Adaptability*

#### Adaptation and Adaptability

The word 'adaptation' derives from the Latin "adaptare". Psychological researchers always define the adaptation based on Piaget's theories. They hold that the adaptation is either a process or a state; organisms will achieve a balance between them and the environment through assimilation and adjustment. Such balance is the state of adaptation, while the dynamic change from balance to unbalance to balance is the process of adaptation. According to such theories, we can find that the core of adaptation is the process where individuals adjust themselves to make them in harmony and balanced with the changing environment [Tian, 2003].

According to the *Encyclopedia of Psychological Counseling*, the adaptability is the individual's ability to adjust his/her survival functions, development and targets to fit the changing social organizations, groups or cultural and economic factors [Che, 1991]. With the further studies on students' mental health education, some researcher regards the psychological adaptability as an important criterion of mental health and an important dimension of students' psychological suzhi. Zhang [2000] et al. hold that the adaptability is the individuals' ability to change themselves or the environment during the socialization to make themselves in harmony with the environment and that it is the reflection of cognition and personality in individuals' "adaptation-development-creation" as well as one of the necessary psychological factors for individuals' survival and development. To sum up, the adaptability is generally defined as individual's stable ability reflected in certain physiological and mental activities to make themselves in harmony with the environment.

#### Self-Adaptability

Wang [2002] holds that the adaptability is the habitual behavior tendency reflected, based on the basic capability (cognition dimension) and personality (personality dimension), by individuals during studying, responding to and defending the external social environment and controlling, understanding and adjusting the internal psychological process in the social and living background for their ages via the interaction with the social and living environment; it includes self-oriented adaptability and society-oriented adaptability. The self-adaptability is the adaptation process to control, understand and adjust the internal psychological process. In this chapter, the self-adaptability is defined as individuals' stable ability reflected during some physiological and mental activities to control and adjust the internal psychological process so as to make themselves in harmony with the environment.

## 2) Research on Junior Middle School Students' Self-Adaptability

The seventh grade is an important stage for teenagers' development as well as the turning point that connects the primary school education and the middle school education. Whether students can well adapt to the life of the seventh grade will not only influence the life in the junior middle school but also cause great influence on the future life. Some characteristics of psychological adaptation of the students in grade seven are discussed from different perspective in previous research.

According to the research of Li et al. [2004], a) the overall development of learning adaptabilities of new students in grade seven displays a "V"-shape tendency, i.e. No remarkable inadaptation occurs within the first month upon the enrollment, remarkable inadaptation appears two months upon the enrollment and such inadaptation is relieved four and a half months later; b) new students' learning adaptabilities differ significantly in different genders, different regions that students come from and different types of schools. In addition, they have indicated that the psychological problems happening to new students, within two or three months as they enter school, significantly correlate with such parents' educational styles as blind love, conformism, contradiction and inconsistency. According to the research of Yang [2000], the new students in grade seven will, due to the change of environment, always be faced with new problems that they never have in the primary school, and various psychological problems may appear when such new problems conflict with the established psychological states. For example, middle school students will study more subjects and bear greater pressure from study, and the learning demands may conflict with the motivation and targets of learning. The new student in grade seven may feel fresh and nervous about the broadened fields for study and life and it is difficult for them to adapt to such changes. Thus they may doubt whether they can well adapt to the life and study and may feel uneasy and depressed to different extents.

Lin et al. [2004] have found, via their research into middle students' stress adaptation, that the stressful events encountered by middle school students include, in order of priority, heavy academic burden, failure in examinations, study weariness, being misunderstood by others and losing face in public. According to the research of Li et al. [2003], major stressors to junior middle school students come from the stressful life events in respect of interpersonal relationship, study and social environment; the intermediate variables that may influence junior school students' response to stress are mainly the social support and some coping strategies, including "asking for help", "withdrawal", "abreaction", "tolerance" and "fantasy".

Chu [2000] has found, via the research into primary school students' and middle school students' adaptation to life, that such students' life and study, especially for the only child, greatly depends on the teacher's and the parents' arrangement since their adaptability to the life is poor.

The aforesaid research was conducted on middle school students' adaptability. It not only studied a specific aspect of the adaptability, such as the adaptation to life, the study and the stress, but also explained the problems in adaptation that students may suffer during the transition from primary school students to junior middle school students. Certain inspiration has been given on studying the adaptabilities of students in grade seven although there was no research into junior middle school students' self-adaptabilities.

## Significance of this Research

### 1) Promote Healthy Growth of Teenager Students

*The school and the home can unite together to form a joint educational force.* The home and the school may, if they form the joint force, support and cooperate with each other to strengthen the educational effect.

*HSCE may optimize the resources for education.* HSC is to make the home support the school's education in all aspects and make the school try the best to help parents solve various problems on educating their children so as to enable the home and the school to closely cooperate with each other in the course of education, make full use of their advantages and optimize the resources for home-school education.

### 2) Improve the Parent's and the Teacher's Educational Capability

The beneficiary of HSCE is more than just the student. Parents are not born to know the knowledge and ideas on educating children and must learn such knowledge and ideas if they want to be an eligible parent. HSC provides an important opportunity for parents to learn such knowledge and ideas. HSCE also creates opportunities for teachers to improve their educational capability and skills. Teachers may first obtain from parents the detailed information on students and understand students' growth experience and family background so as to comprehensively acquaint themselves with the students, well arrange and target their education and revise the educational content and improve the educational method based on the obtained information.

### 3) Enrich the Theories on HSCE and Broaden the Research on Students' Psychological Suzhi-Based Education

The HSCE does not have the abundant theoretical basis as we mentioned above and there is no specific implementation strategy and assessment standard for the practice. This chapter has, based on the investigation and research on the present HSCE, explored a series of theoretical and practical problems on HSCE through educational experiments, since the HSCE is to cultivate the self-adaptability of students in grade seven during HSC, so as to enrich the theories on HSCE and broaden the research of students' psychological suzhi-based education.

## Assumption

Assumption 1: the self-adaptability is a multi-component structure and it can be studied through various dimensions, including stress-coping strategy, identification of body, adaptation to the study, psychological adaptation during the adolescence, adaptation to life and response to stress; assumption 2: the students in grade seven are at the key stage for developing their self-adaptability, when they are faced with various changes in study and life, and their self-adaptability is important for their development in future; assumption 3: HSCE is an effective approach to promote students' development and the scientific educational experiments on HSC can improve such students' psychological suzhi, such as the self-adaptability.

## Research Method

This chapter adopts literature review, psychometrics, questionnaire and educational experiments. The literature review is to summarize previous research results via analyzing and synthesizing relevant documents so as to determine the thought of this research and logic of the empirical research; the psychometrics is mainly the pre-test and post-test on students' self-adaptability; the questionnaire is used to investigate the HSCE's status quo via interview with or questionnaire for teachers and parents of the school; the experimental intervention for HSCE is to use the HSCE modes and strategies as the experimental factor to inspect its applicability and effectivity on cultivating junior middle school students' self-adaptability.

SPSS 11.5 for Windows XP was used for data analysis in this chapter.

## DEVELOPMENT CHARACTERISTICS OF JUNIOR MIDDLE SCHOOL STUDENTS' SELF-ADAPTABILITY

### Revision of the Scale on Junior Middle School Students' Self-Adaptability

#### 1) Preparation of Preliminary Questionnaires

First, the researchers have consulted the existing scales when preparing this scale, selected some items therefrom according to their own theories, properly revised the selected items and supplemented new items. Second, the researchers investigated the junior middle school students in two middle schools in Chongqing City, China. They sampled 4 students from each grade of a school, 24 students in total, with excellent, fine or poor academic performance and the proportion of boys is approximately equal to that of girls. They tested the students (participants) in the spare time, requested students to read, within the adequate time, all items in the preliminary questionnaire one by one and mark the words and sentences they did not understand, talked with certain student on the confusing content and made proper revision.

In addition, they also talked with 8 middle school teachers, 5 masters majoring in developmental and educational psychology and 4 teachers of developmental and educational psychology in two schools. The researchers specified each item and the relevant dimension and explained the meaning of each dimension in details; they inquired the teacher's understanding of such items and discussed with them whether the item can reflect the connotations of their respective dimensions and were properly expressed; they made proper revision and adjustment on the items that may cause misunderstanding and revised the questionnaire according to such teachers' opinions.

The preliminary questionnaire thus obtained covered four dimensions, i.e. Learning adaptation, adaptation to psychology, adaptation to life and stress situations, and 46 items, each of which gave a situation applicable to the dimension and requested participants to give answers according to the actual situation. The scale was rated on a 3-point likert scale with 1 standing for "rarely" and 3 for "frequently". They investigated participants with the single forced-choice item method. Positive or reverse scoring was adopted for certain questions, and the higher the score was, the higher the individual's self-adaptability was.

## 2) Preparation of Final Questionnaires on Junior Middle School Students' Self-Adaptability

The preliminary questionnaire on junior middle school's self-adaptability was used to test 435 junior middle school students in 2 middle schools in Chongqing and 420 valid questionnaires were collected, including 290 from ordinary middle schools and 130 from key middle schools. Please see the following for analysis results.

### Analysis on Items

Discriminate validity: according to the analysis, there is only one item in the preliminary questionnaire whose $t$ value is not remarkable, indicating that the other items in the preliminary questionnaire have good discriminate validity, i.e. the items therein have good validity.

Standard deviation: generally speaking, the factors with the standard deviation lower than 0.5 should be removed from the questionnaire. The standard deviation of all factors in the questionnaire is all higher than 1.11, indicating that all items therein have excellent discriminate validity.

### Factor Analysis

Select the items for the preliminary questionnaire; then the retained items were conducted on principal components factor analysis with orthogonal rotation so as to get the final factor loading matrix. 19 items were removed and 27 items were reserved after the selection in accordance with the aforesaid procedures, which formed the final questionnaire on junior middle school students' self-adaptability. From Table 3.2 and 3.3, it can be As seen that 6 factors were obtained through factor analysis, with 27 items reserved. The 6 factors can explain 47.02% of the total variance. Factor 1 is about what learning methods is used by students to adapt to the study, therefore it is named "learning adaptation"; factor 2 is about students' stress-coping strategy to inspect whether students can adopt correct attitudes and methods for the response to stress, such as positive coping (optimistic attribution and making efforts) and negative coping (seeking support from the society excessively, being much too absorbed, denying and abreaction, coping with external control), hence it is named "coping strategy"; factor 3 is about the response to stress, i.e. Individuals' psychological reflection of their cognitions or actions to reduce the pressure or relieve the pain when they are faced with the stress situations, such as emotional experience in the response to stress (intensity, durability, primary emotions), hence it is named "response to stress"; factor 4 is to inspect students' attitude towards the life, their self-help skills in daily life and their common sense on daily life, therefore it is named "adaptation to life"; factor 5 is to inspect whether the students during growth and development can correctly identify and accept their physiological conditions, therefore it is named "identification of body"; factor 6 is to inspect whether students can correctly understand the sex from both physiological and psychological perspectives and establish correct ideas and concept on sexual issues, hence it is named "psychological adaptation during the adolescence".

### Test on Reliability of the Questionnaire

This chapter adopted the internal consistency reliability and the split-half reliability as the indicators for testing the reliability of the questionnaire on junior middle school students' self-adaptability and of the factors therein.

The internal consistency reliability of the factors in the questionnaire on junior middle school students' self-adaptability is between 0.52-0.73, and the internal consistency reliability of the scale is 0.79; the split-half reliability of all scales is between 0.51-0.72, and the split-half reliability of the scale is 0.72, indicating that this questionnaire has high reliability.

### Test on Validity of the Questionnaire

This chapter has showed via the significance testing of results that the results are closely related to each other, except the relationship of the adjustment during the adolescence with the adaptation to the study and the stress-coping strategy.

### Table 3.2. Factor Loading Matrix

| Item | Factor 1 | Factor 2 | Factor 3 | Factor 4 | Factor 5 | Factor 6 | Communality |
|------|----------|----------|----------|----------|----------|----------|-------------|
| A2 | .45 | | | | | | .36 |
| A6 | .59 | | | | | | .46 |
| A34 | .50 | | | | | | .35 |
| A36 | .49 | | | | | | .43 |
| A39 | .57 | | | | | | .42 |
| A40 | .66 | | | | | | .46 |
| A44 | .62 | | | | | | .42 |
| A22 | | .64 | | | | | .46 |
| A25 | | .68 | | | | | .48 |
| A42 | | .50 | | | | | .42 |
| A46 | | .51 | | | | | .46 |
| A1 | | | -.57 | | | | .35 |
| A5 | | | -.66 | | | | .47 |
| A9 | | | .55 | | | | .42 |
| A16 | | | .59 | | | | .40 |
| A27 | | | .42 | | | | .43 |
| A10 | | | | | | .63 | .46 |
| A15 | | | | | | .73 | .55 |
| A17 | | | | | | .53 | .43 |
| A20 | | | | | .73 | | .58 |
| A32 | | | | | .43 | | .47 |
| A26 | | | | | .78 | | .63 |
| A4 | | | | .57 | | | .47 |
| A11 | | | | .53 | | | .42 |
| A14 | | | | .48 | | | .46 |
| A21 | | | | .46 | | | .46 |
| A28 | | | | .62 | | | .47 |

**Table 3.3. Eigenvalue and Contribution of Each Factor in Questionnaire of Junior Middle School Students` Self-Adaptability**

| Factors | Eigenvalue | Contribution (%) | Accumulated Contribution (%) |
|---------|-----------|-----------------|------------------------------|
| 1 | 2.40 | 10.42 | 10.42 |
| 2 | 1.87 | 8.13 | 18.56 |
| 3 | 1.84 | 8.02 | 26.57 |
| 4 | 1.57 | 6.83 | 33.41 |
| 5 | 1.57 | 6.81 | 40.22 |
| 6 | 1.56 | 6.80 | 47.02 |

All factors highly correlate with the total score of the questionnaire, while the factors correlate lowly with each other, indicating that the questionnaire was prepared following the basic requirements and has good construct validity.

To sum up, the questionnaire on junior middle students' self-adaptability developed in this chapter has good reliability and validity and can be used as an effective measurement for junior middle school students' self-adaptability.

## Research on Characteristics of Junior Middle School Students' Self-Adaptability

Use the revised questionnaire on junior middle school students' self-adaptability to investigate 527 students (277 in grade seven, 186 in grade eight, 74 in grade nine) in three middles schools in Chongqing and Sichuan so as to find out the differences between different junior middle school students' self-adaptabilities from the perspectives of 3 socio-demographic factors, i.e. Gender, grade and nature of the school.

Then, we can further discuss the characteristics of and the problems in development of junior middle school students' self-adaptability to provide evidence for the experiment. Please see the following for analysis results.

### 1) Overall Self-Adaptability of Junior Middle School Students
Please see Table 3-4 for the overall self-adaptability of 527 junior middle school students that is obtained according to the statistics and analysis.

**Table 3.4. Average Score and Standard Deviation of Self-Adaptabilities of 527 Junior Middle School Students**

| Factors | Mean | SD |
|---------|------|-----|
| Learning adaptation | 2.35 | .47 |
| Stress-coping strategy | 2.57 | .39 |
| Response to stress | 1.96 | .27 |
| Identification of body | 2.36 | .49 |
| Psychological adaptation during the adolescence | 2.30 | .56 |
| Adaptation to life | 2.29 | .43 |
| Total average scores | 2.22 | .24 |

According to the results of descriptive statistics (Table 3.4), the average scores of all factors are moderate, which has demonstrated that the self-adaptability of junior middle school students in Chongqing is somewhat poor as a whole. In descending order of average scores, the factor shall be: stress-coping strategy > identification of body > learning adaptation > psychological adaptation during the adolescence > adaptation to life > response to stress > total average scores.

## 2) *Multifactorial Analysis of Variance on Junior Middle School Students' Self-Adaptability*

Take grade, gender and nature of the school as independent variables and take all factors of the junior middle school students' self-adaptability as dependant variables for the purpose of 3×2×2 multifactor analysis of variance.

**Table 3.5. Analysis of Variance on Students' Self-Adaptability by Grade, Gender and Nature of the School (*F* value)**

| Variables | Nature of School | Grade | Gender | Grade * Gender | School * Grade | School * Gender | School * Gender * Grade |
|---|---|---|---|---|---|---|---|
| Learning adaptation | 7.01** | 5.73** | .69 | .05 | .99 | .056 | .13 |
| Stress-coping strategy | 2.56 | 3.78* | .06 | .43 | .04 | .39 | .02 |
| Response to stress | 1.66 | 3.09* | .02 | .82 | 3.20 | 1.16 | .52 |
| Identification of body | .23 | .58 | .04 | .70 | 1.61 | .09 | .21 |
| Psychological adaptation during the adolescence | .01 | .50 | .96 | .11 | 5.73* | .13 | 1.65 |
| Adaptation to life | 11.94** | 3.80* | 3.20 | .35 | 4.72* | .02 | .63 |
| Total average scores | 10.75** | 7.89** | .85 | .18 | 5.56* | .001 | .15 |

Note: * $p < 0.05$ ** $p < 0.01$ *** $p < 0.001$.

**Table 3.6. Analysis on Simple Effect of the Grade and the School on Junior Middle School Students' Psychological Adaptation during the Adolescence**

| Source of Variance | | SS | df | MS | *F* | Post Hoc Test |
|---|---|---|---|---|---|---|
| Factor A (nature of school) | b1 (grade 7) | 2.81 | 1 | 2.81 | 9.97** | Ordinary middle schools>key middle schools |
| | b2 (grade 8) | .63 | 1 | .63 | 1.93 | |
| | b3 (grade 9) | .58 | 1 | .58 | 1.50 | |
| Factor B (grade) | a1 (key middle schools) | .69 | 1 | .69 | 2.25 | |
| | a2 (ordinary middle schools) | 2.29 | 2 | 1.15 | 3.76* | Grade 9>grade 8, Grade 9>grade 7 |

According to Table 3.5, among all the factors of the junior middle school students' self-adaptability, the nature of school and the grade have main effects on learning adaptation and adaptation to life, the nature of the school has main effect on stress-coping strategy and response to stress, while there is a grade × school interaction effect on psychological adaptation during adolescence and adaptation to life. The nature of the school and the grade has main effect on total average scores and there is a grade × school interaction effect on it.

According to the analysis of variance, there is a significant school × grade interaction effect on junior middle school students' self-adaptability, i.e. psychological adaptation during the adolescence, adaptation to life and total average scores.

Simple effect test and post hoc test should be conducted on the significant interaction effect, if any found during analysis of variance. Condition-based selection was used in this chapter for the purpose of simple effect analysis. Please see Table 3.6 for details.

According to the analysis on simple effect of nature of school, the $F$ value is significant in case of grade 7, i.e. In case of the students in grade 7, the psychological adaptation during the adolescence of the students in ordinary middle schools is much higher than that of the students in key middle schools; in respect of the grade, the $F$ value of students' psychological adaptation during the adolescence is significant in case of ordinary middle schools, and the psychological adaptation during the adolescence of students in grade 9 is much higher than that of students in grade 8 and grade 7.

According to the analysis on simple effect (Table 3.7), in respect of the nature of school, the $F$ value is significant in case of grade 9, i.e. in case of the students in grade 9, the adaptation to life of the students in key middle schools is much higher than that of the students in ordinary middle schools; in respect of the grade, the $F$ value of students' adaptation to life is significant in case of key middle schools, and the adaptation to life of students in grade 9 is much higher than that of students in grade 8 and grade 7.

According to the analysis on the simple effect of nature of school (Table 3.8), the $F$ value is significant in case of grade 9, i.e. In case of the students in grade 9, the total average scores on self-adaptability of the students in key middle schools are much higher than those of the students in ordinary middle schools; in respect of the grade, the $F$ value of total average scores on students' self-adaptability is significant in case of key middle schools, and the self-adaptability of students in grade 9 is much higher than that of students in grade 8 and grade 7.

**Table 3.7. Analysis on Simple Effect of the Grade and the School on Junior Middle School Students' Adaptation to Life**

| Source of Variance | | SS | df | MS | F | Post Hoc Test |
|---|---|---|---|---|---|---|
| Factor A (nature of school) | b1 (grade 7) | .50 | 1 | .50 | 3.16 | |
| | b2 (grade 8) | .07 | 1 | .07 | .35 | |
| | b3 (grade 9) | 1.43 | 1 | 1.43 | 12.18** | Key middle schools>ordinary middle schools |
| Factor B (grade) | a1 (key middle schools) | 1.63 | 2 | .81 | 5.60** | Grade 9>grade 8, Grade 9>grade 7 |
| | a2 (ordinary middle schools) | .56 | 2 | .28 | 1.43 | |

**Table 3.8 Analysis on Simple Effect of the Grade and the School on Total Average Scores of Junior Middle School Students' Self-Adaptability**

| Source of Variance | | SS | df | MS | *F* | Post Hoc Test |
|---|---|---|---|---|---|---|
| Factor A (nature of school) | b1 (grade 7) | .72 | 1 | .72 | 1.63 | |
| | b2 (grade 8) | .03 | 1 | .03 | .48 | |
| | b3 (grade 9) | .50 | 1 | .50 | 12.78** | Key middle schools>ordinary middle schools |
| Factor B (grade) | a1 (key middle schools) | .97 | 2 | .49 | 11.03** | Grade 9>grade 8, Grade 9>grade 7 |
| | a2 (ordinary middle schools) | .20 | 2 | .10 | 1.62 | |

## 3) Difference between Female and Male Junior Middle School Students' Self-Adaptabilities

Take junior middle school students' gender as the independent variable for the purpose of independent-sample *t* test on junior middle school students' self-adaptability. According to Table 3.9, there is no significant difference between the self-adaptabilities of female and male students as a whole. There is no significant difference between each factor in case of different genders, except for the psychological adaptation during the adolescence (male > female), which indicates that junior middle students' self-adaptability has achieved relatively balanced development despite the different genders.

## 4) Difference between Self-Adaptabilities of Junior Middle School Students in Different Types of Schools

The experiment on difference between self-adaptabilities of students in different types of schools in this chapter was to find out the gap between self-adaptabilities of students in key junior middle schools and ordinary ones.

**Table 3.9. t Test on Difference between Female and Male Junior Middle School Students' Self-Adaptabilities**

| Variables | Male (n=281) Mean±*SD* | Female (n=246) Mean±*SD* | *t* Value |
|---|---|---|---|
| Learning adaptation | 2.33±.47 | 2.36±.45 | -.59 |
| Stress-coping strategy | 2.56±.39 | 2.57±.37 | -.31 |
| Response to stress | 1.95±.28 | 1.96±.24 | -.62 |
| Identification of body | 2.36±.49 | 2.34±.49 | .35 |
| Psychological adaptation during the adolescence | 2.34±.54 | 2.24±.57 | 2.12* |
| Adaptation to life | 2.25±.44 | 2.33±.40 | -1.89 |
| Total average scores | 2.21±.25 | 2.22±.22 | -.72 |

**Table 3.10. Difference between Self-Adaptabilities of Junior Middle School Students in Different Types of Schools**

| Variables | Key Middle School (n=270) $M \pm SD$ | Ordinary Middle Schools (n=257) $M \pm SD$ | $t$ Value |
|---|---|---|---|
| Learning adaptation | 2.52±.43 | 2.38±.48 | 3.51*** |
| Stress-coping strategy | 2.61±.35 | 2.52±.40 | 2.56* |
| Response to stress | 1.95±.25 | 1.96±.27 | -.48 |
| Identification of body | 2.34±.52 | 2.36±.46 | -.59 |
| Psychological adaptation during the adolescence | 2.26±.55 | 2.32±.55 | -1.26 |
| Adaptation to life | 2.38±.38 | 2.21±.44 | 4.60*** |
| Total average scores | 2.25±.21 | 2.18±.24 | 3.33** |

According to Table 3.10, the self-adaptability of students in key junior middle schools is significantly different from that of students in ordinary junior middle schools as a whole: the former one is much higher than the latter one. The learning adaptation, stress-coping strategy and adaptation to life of students in key junior middle schools are higher than those of students in ordinary middle schools, while there is no obvious difference between their response to stress, identification of body and psychological adaptation during the adolescence.

## 5) *Difference Between Self-Adaptabilities of Junior Middle School Students in Different Grades*

Take the grade as the independent variable and the factors of self-adaptability and the total score as the dependant variables for the purpose of one-way analysis of variance.

According to Table 3.11, the self-adaptability of junior middle school students in different grades are generally significantly different, and the higher the grade is, the higher the self-adaptability is, i.e. Grade 9 > grade 8 > grade 7. The multiple comparison has proved: the learning adaptation of students in different grades is significantly different, the stress-coping strategy of the students in grade 9 is significantly different from that of the students in grade 7 and grade 8, the response to stress of the students in grade 9 is significantly different from that of the students in grade 7 and grade 8, the identification of body and psychological adaptation during the adolescence of the students in those three grades have no significant difference, and the adaptation to life of the students in grade 7 is significantly different from that of the students in grade 8 and grade 9.

# Preparation and Revision of the Questionnaire and Analysis on Characteristics

**Table 3.11. Significance Testing on Difference between Self-Adaptabilities of Junior Middle School Students in Different Grades**

| Variables | Grade 7 (n=277) M±SD | Grade 8 (n=186) M±SD | Grade 9 (n=74) M±SD | F Value | Significance | Post Multiple Comparison |
|---|---|---|---|---|---|---|
| Learning adaptation | 2.37±.47 | 2.47±.44 | 2.67±.42 | 7.91*** | .000 | Grade 9 > grade 8 > grade 7 (Significant difference lies between any two grades) |
| Stress-coping strategy | 2.56±.37 | 2.52±.42 | 2.71±.24 | 4.12* | .017 | Grade 9 > grade 7 > grade 8 (Significant difference lies between grade 9 and grades 8 and 7) |
| Response to stress | 1.94±.26 | 1.96±.27 | 2.06±.27 | 3.63* | .027 | Grade 9 > grade 8 > grade 7 (Significant difference lies between grade 9 and grades 8 and 7) |
| Identification of body | 2.34±.52 | 2.35±.46 | 2.44±.38 | .79 | .452 | |
| Psychological adaptation during the adolescence | 2.30±.53 | 2.28±.57 | 2.31±.623 | .15 | .860 | |
| Adaptation to life | 2.18±.46 | 2.33±.39 | 2.45±.38 | 10.84*** | .000 | Grade 9 > grade 8 > grade 7 (Significant difference lies between grade 7 and grades 8 and 9) |
| Total average scores | 2.17±.24 | 2.22±.22 | 2.35±.22 | 10.93*** | .000 | Grade 9 > grade 8 > grade 7 (Significant difference lies between any two grades) |

## 1) Preparation and Revision of the Questionnaire on Junior Middle School Students' Self-Adaptability

The preliminary questionnaire on junior middle school students' self-adaptability is made according to the research into various scales on adaptability and the opinions of experts, teachers and students. The final questionnaire has been made according to the large-scale questionnaire-based survey for junior middle school students as the preliminary questionnaire has been analyzed and tested with the factor analysis method and the items therein have been selected or removed. The questionnaire is made in accordance with the psychometrical principle on questionnaire revision, which fundamentally ensures that the questionnaire was made and revised following a scientific procedure. According to the analysis results, the questionnaire on junior middle school students' self-adaptability is psychometrical tool with good reliability and validity. The final questionnaire consists of 27 questions and covers 6 dimensions, i.e. Learning adaptation, stress-coping strategy, response to stress, identification of body, psychological adaptation during the adolescence and adaptation to life. Those are different from the expected dimensions: the stress adaptation is divided into stress-coping strategy and response to stress and the physiological adaptation is also divided into identification of body and psychological adaptation during the adolescence.

The questionnaire is to survey the participants' adjustment based on the external environment. Such adaptation-oriented activity is different from the social adaptation; instead, it means that individuals change their evaluation of and attitudes toward the controlled environment and such change causes behavioral change. Therefore, it is reasonable that the self-orientated stress adaptation is subdivided into the coping methods for certain situations and the psychological tolerance process during the stress. Meanwhile, the psychological adaptation during the adolescence is separated from the others, which indicates that it correlates lowly with the identification of body. Junior middle school students have not been faced with the adolescence for a long time, and they may greatly differ with each other in their cognition on typical psychological problems during adolescence and their identification of body. In respect of the former problem, many students may feel embarrassed and thus evade and suppress the problems. The scale is rated on a 3-point Likert scale and reversed scoring. The results of factor analysis have showed that the revised questionnaire has good construct validity and eigenvalue of each factor is higher than 1. The rotated six factors can explain 47.02% of the total variance. The internal consistency reliability of the factors in the questionnaire is all between 0.52 and 0.73, and the internal consistency reliability of the scale is 0.79; the split-half reliability of those factors is between 0.51 and 0.72, and the split-half reliability of the scale is 0.72. This indicates that the revised questionnaire has good reliability and validity.

## 2) Analysis on Characteristics of Junior Middle School Students' Self-Adaptability

*(1) Overall self-adaptability of junior middle school students.* The average scores of all factors on self-adaptability are moderate, which has demonstrated that the self-adaptability of junior middle school students in Chongqing is somewhat poor as a whole.

The reasons include:

The life and study in junior middle schools are quite different from those in primary schools. Some students may feel difficult to adapt to the brand new life and study, so the self-adaptability of junior middle school students is somewhat poor as a whole. For example, the study in junior middle schools covers more subjects and involves more knowledge than that in primary schools and the teaching methods are quite different. Such changes put forward new requirements for students' adaptation and require them to adopt new coping methods to adapt to the new life, which is difficult to a certain extent for some students.

Parents and teachers do not attach importance to students' adaptation and cannot help students analyze and solve the problems found during the adaptation. There are more and more problems for students, and the adaptability is increasingly poor.

Junior middles school students are managed more loosely than primary school students, and some students with poorer self-regulation may be more likely to unadapt to such difference.

*2) Difference between female and male junior middle school students' self-adaptabilities.*
The adaptability of female junior middle school students is not obviously different from that of male students as a whole. Generally speaking, the self-adaptability of male and female students has achieved balanced development.

Among the six dimensions of learning adaptation, stress-coping strategy, response to stress, identification of body, psychological adaptation during the adolescence and adaptation to life, only the psychological adaptation during the adolescence of male students is better than that of female students. This is different from the research result of Bai, Liu and Guo [1997] who have found that the learning adaptation of female junior middle school students is significantly different from that of the male students. The inconsistency might result from the differences in psychometrical tools, with different studies using different learning adaptation questionnaires.

In respect of the finding that the psychological adjustment during the adolescence of male students is better than that of female students, it may be because boys can better accept the physiological maturity and development than girls.

Boys' physiological development occurs later than girls', and boys can learn more related knowledge for better adaptation in future. In addition, girls are generally more shy and introversive than boys, and their physiological development during the adolescence is more obvious, so they may adapt to such changes more slowly. In respect of the other dimensions, there is no significant difference between female and male students, and the development is relatively balanced.

*3) Difference between self-adaptabilities of junior middle school students in different types of schools.* The self-adaptability of students in key junior middle schools is significantly different from that of students in ordinary junior middle schools as a whole: the former one is much higher than the latter one.

The learning adaptation, stress-coping strategy and adaptation to life of students in key junior middle schools are higher than those of students in ordinary middle schools, while there is no significant difference between their response to stress, identification of body and psychological adaptation during the adolescence.

The difference between learning adaptation, stress-coping strategy and adaptation to life of students in key junior middle schools and ordinary junior middle schools may be caused by the following reasons:

The suzhi of students in key middle schools is better than that of students in ordinary middle schools as a whole, which causes the difference in the aforesaid dimensions of the self-adaptability. Key/ordinary middle schools are classified according to students' academic performance and the significant difference between the students' learning adaptation is reasonable. Due to the academic success, students in key middle schools generally adopt positive coping strategies, they are more likely to take better coping attitude and methods and they can better adapt to the life;

The students in key middle schools can receive better education and the key middle schools have better teacher resources and other facilities, which causes the difference in students' self-adaptabilities. Key middle schools attach great importance to the suzhi education and will conduct comprehensive cultivation in respect of learning adaptation, academic stress and life skills;

Teachers and parents of the students in key middle schools always raise higher requirements and students are more dependent, consciously and active, so the students here have better adaptability;

The key middle schools have better atmosphere and the students here are more likely to learn from one another and make progress together.

*4) Difference between self-adaptabilities of junior middle school students in different grades.* The self-adaptability of junior middle school students in different grades are generally significantly different, and the higher the grade is, the higher the self-adaptability is, i.e. Grade 9 > grade 8 > grade 7. The multiple comparison has proved: the learning adaptation of students in different grades is significantly different, the stress-coping strategy of the students in grade 9 is significantly different from that of the students in grade 7 and grade 8, the response to stress of the students in grade 9 is significantly different from that of the students in grade 7 and grade 8, the identification of body and psychological adaptation during the adolescence of the students in those three grades have no significant difference, and the adaptation to life of the students in grade 7 is significantly different from that of the students in grade 8 and grade 9. The difference between self-adaptabilities of junior middle school students in different grades may be caused by: a) the learning adaptation of the students in different grades differs significantly, and this may be because the junior middle school students are unceasingly developing duration and adapting to the learning.

The students in grade 7 may find that the study in junior middle school is quite different from that in primary school and they must adopt different learning methods and strategies to adapt to such difference so that they may make unceasing exploration and progress. The students in grade 8 will be faced with more difficult curriculum and more major subjects, so they need make further improvement, based on their conditions in grade 7, to satisfy the brand new learning requirements. Students may have greater pressure as they are in grade 9, which further impels them to adapt to the study. Therefore, the student's learning adaptability improves significantly during this period; b) there is significant difference between the stress-coping strategy and response to stress of students in grades 9 and those of students in grades 7 and 8. The significant improvement of stress-coping strategy and response to stress of students in grade 9 may be also caused by the fact that the pressure of the senior high school entrance exams on the students in grade 9 drives them to take positive stress-coping strategies more frequently and learn how to deal with various pressure and emergency in daily life.

The adaptation to life of the students in grade 7 is significantly different from that of the students in grades 8 and 9 because the students in grade 8 or 9 are more familiar with the study and life in junior middle schools and they have greatly improved their attitudes toward the life, their self-care abilities and the common sense on daily life.

# STATUS QUO OF AND MODEING ON HSCE FOR JUNIOR MIDDLE SCHOOL STUDENTS

## Status Quo of HSCE in Junior Middle Schools

We have conducted semi-open survey on the teachers and the parents (430 parents and 145 teachers) in 3 middle schools in Chongqing in order to understand the status quo of HSCE in junior middle schools, explore the characteristics of HSCE here on a systematic basis and provide evidence for building cultivation modes and studying the educational intervention. The questionnaires designed for teachers and parents have similar structure and content so as to truly reflect the status quo of HSCE in details, but specific problems and the number of items were determined based on the conditions of teachers and parents. The two kinds of questionnaires include multiple choice items and essay questions. The items were arranged in random sequence and the answers were either in descending order or in ascending order to prevent the interference of response tendency. After we finished the initial questionnaire, we invited the teachers with many years' experience in educating middle school and primary school students for discussion to solicit their opinions; we also solicited experts' opinions and prepared the final questionnaire based on the preliminary one by comprehensively analyzing relevant opinions. Please see Table 3.12 and Table 3.13 for details.

### 1) Procedures

The survey was conducted on a concentrated basis for 25 minutes. Questionnaires were distributed by psychology teachers to teachers and parents. In addition, 10 teachers and 10 parents were also interviewed for the purpose of true survey results.

**Table 3.12. Structure, Dimensions and Number of Items of or in the HSC Questionnaire for Parents**

| Structure | Dimensions | Number of Items |
|---|---|---|
| Home education | Home education manner 1 | 3 |
| | Home education efficacy 2 | |
| Home-school liaison | Liaison frequency 2 | 4 |
| | Liaison manner 2 | |
| Home-school partnership | Content of partnership 3 | 5 |
| | Manner of partnership 2 | |
| Sense of cooperation | Will to cooperate 1 | 2 |
| | Sense of responsibility 1 | |

**Table 3.13. Structure, Dimensions and Number of Items of or in the HSC Questionnaire for Teachers**

| Structure | Dimensions | Number of Items |
|---|---|---|
| Home-school liaison | Liaison frequency 2 | 4 |
| | Liaison manner 2 | |
| Home-school partnership | Content of partnership 3 | 7 |
| | Manner of partnership 2 | |
| | Partnership efficacy 2 | |
| Sense of cooperation | Will to cooperate 1 | 2 |
| | Sense of responsibility 1 | |

*2) Survey Results and Analysis*

Home-school liaison
Liaison frequency

In respect of the frequency of home-school liaison, 4 questions were made for parents and teachers respectively and they were requested to tell how many times they have liaised with each other in half a year and how many times they thought were reasonable. Please see Table 3.14, Table 3.15, Table 3.16 and Table 3.17 for the results.

According to Table 14 and Table 15, the parents almost liaised with the school for 5 or more times per person in a semester. Most parents thought the frequency reasonable during the interview, but some parents indicated that such frequency is not high enough to meet their needs for education.

**Table 3.14. Actual Liaison Frequency (Questionnaire for parents)**

| Number of Times | N/A | 2-5 | 5 and above | Other (based on the fact) |
|---|---|---|---|---|
| Number of Parents | 21 | 156 | 252 | 10 |
| Proportion (%) | 5 | 36 | 57 | 2 |

**Table 3.15. Ideal Liaison Frequency (Questionnaire for parents)**

| Number of Times | N/A | 2-5 | 5 and above | Other (based on the fact) |
|---|---|---|---|---|
| Number of Parents | 0 | 139 | 278 | 21 |
| Proportion (%) | 0 | 32 | 63 | 5 |

According to Table 3.16, most teachers have liaised with parents for more than five times in a semester, and only a few teachers have liaised for just twice to five times. However, some of the teachers thought that it was reasonable to liaise with parents for twice to five times in a semester. During the interview with teachers, some teachers believed that it was the best to liaise with parents after the examination; if there were problem-prone students or emergencies, it would be necessary and a must to liaise with parents more frequently.

**Table 3.16. Actual Liaison Frequency (Questionnaire for teachers)**

| Number of Times | N/A | 2-5 | 5 and above | Other |
|---|---|---|---|---|
| Number of Teachers | 0 | 10 | 122 | 14 |
| Proportion (%) | 0 | 7 | 84 | 9 |

**Table 3.17. Ideal Liaison Frequency (Questionnaire for teachers)**

| Number of Times | N/A | 2-5 | 5 and above | Other |
|---|---|---|---|---|
| Number of Teachers | 0 | 31 | 92 | 24 |
| Proportion (%) | 0 | 21 | 63 | 16 |

## Liaison Manner

In respect of the liaison manner during HSC, 4 questions were made for parents and teachers respectively and they were requested to tell the frequent liaison manners during HSC and the liaison manners they wished to use. Please see following tables for the results.

According to Table 3-18, the main manner of parents for home-school liaison is actually to attend the parents' meeting, and they got the information on school and their children mainly from the student's school report card and by directly communicating with their children. They did not have many opportunities to directly communicate with the teacher. Some parents indicated during the interview that the head teacher directly liaised with them only when their children made mistakes, such as coming to school late or leaving early.

**Table 3.18. Actual Liaison Manner (Questionnaire for parents)**

| Manner | Parents' meeting | Liaison by phone | School report card and rating manual | Communication with children | Home visit | Other (school visit) |
|---|---|---|---|---|---|---|
| Number of Parents | 292 | 138 | 209 | 219 | 42 | 63 |
| Proportion (%) | 30 | 14 | 22 | 23 | 4 | 7 |

Most parents thought that the best manner was to liaise by phone, and the second best manner was to attend the parents' meeting where face-to-face communication was available. All parents indicated during the preliminary interview that they have never received the parent's guide, but the questionnaire showed that a large proportion (12%) of parents supported the distribution of parent's guide. Parents' identification of the school report card and the rating manual has proved that they were concerned by and have attached great importance to their children's study.

### Table 3.19. Ideal Liaison Manner (Questionnaire for parents)

| Manner | Parents' meeting | Liaison by phone | School report card and rating manual | Communication with children | Home visit | Report and lecture | Distributing parent's guide |
|---|---|---|---|---|---|---|---|
| Number of Parents | 334 | 386 | 188 | 21 | 42 | 73 | 136 |
| Proportion (%) | 28 | 33 | 16 | 2 | 2 | 6 | 13 |

### Table 3.20. Actual Liaison Manner (Questionnaire for teachers)

| Manner | Parents' meeting | Liaison by phone | School report card and rating manual | Communication with children | Home visit | School visit | Parent-teacher communication booklet |
|---|---|---|---|---|---|---|---|
| Number of Teachers | 146 | 142 | 80 | 68 | 17 | 3 | 7 |
| Proportion (%) | 31 | 30 | 17 | 16 | 4 | 1 | 1 |

### Table 3.21. Ideal Liaison Manner (Questionnaire for teachers)

| Manner | Parents' meeting | Liaison by Phone | School report card and rating manual | Distributing parent's guide | Home visit | Report and lecture | Parent-teacher communication booklet |
|---|---|---|---|---|---|---|---|
| Number of Teachers | 111 | 125 | 40 | 56 | 17 | 59 | 3 |
| Proportion (%) | 26 | 30 | 12 | 13 | 4 | 14 | 1 |

According to the two tables above, the parents' meeting and the liaison by phone were actually frequently used by teachers to liaise with parents. Teachers also frequently used such two manners in their practice to promote HSC. The teachers also indicated during the interview that distributing the parent's guide was a good method to promote HSC, and that the home-school manual should be printed and distributed by the school. They believed that it was improper to only rely on the subject teacher or the head teacher for such manual, which will cause much more work for them.

## HSC

*HSC Manners*

In respect of the HSC manners, 3 questions were made for parents and they were requested to tell the school's assistance they needed the most, the cooperation manner they desired the most and the things they demanded the most. Please see following tables for the results.

**Table 3.22. School's Assistance Manners that are Needed the Most (Questionnaire for parents)**

| School's Assistance | Communication | Providing Knowledge on Educating Children | Understanding Parent's Conditions | Other |
|---|---|---|---|---|
| Number of Parents | 417 | 240 | 52 | 0 |
| Proportion (%) | 59 | 34 | 7 | 0 |

**Table 3.23. Cooperation Manners that are Desired the Most (Questionnaire for parents)**

| Cooperation Manner | Educating Children at Home | Strengthening the Communication | Participating in the School's Activities | Participating in the School's Organization and Management | Other |
|---|---|---|---|---|---|
| Number of Parents | 219 | 282 | 83 | 42 | 0 |
| Proportion (%) | 35 | 45 | 13 | 7 | 0 |

**Table 3.24. The Most Needed Things for HSC (Questionnaire for parents)**

| Needed By Parents | Knowledge on Educating Children | Information on Students | Time | Cooperation of Children | Economic Support | Other |
|---|---|---|---|---|---|---|
| Number of Parents | 313 | 365 | 21 | 167 | 10 | 0 |
| Proportion (%) | 36 | 42 | 2 | 19 | 1 | 0 |

According to the three tables above on parents' choice of HSC manners, parents believed that they needed communications with the school the most and then the knowledge on educating children. Parents thought the best cooperation manner is communication, then learning how to educate children at home and participating in various activities of the school. Only 7% of the parents wished to participant in the school's organization and management.

Parents believed that, during HSC, they needed communication with the school the most, then the knowledge, and then children's cooperation. It follows that parents desire the most to understand more information on their children so that they can communicate more with teachers and reach an agreement with teachers on educating the children.

In respect of the HSC manners, 3 questions were made for teachers and they were requested to tell the school's assistance parents needed the most, the cooperation manner they desired the most and the things they demanded the most. Please see following tables for the results.

**Table 3.25. School's Assistance that are Needed the Most by Parents (Questionnaire for teachers)**

| Assistance | Communication | Providing the Knowledge on Educating Children | Understanding Parent's Conditions | Other |
|---|---|---|---|---|
| Number of Teachers | 115 | 111 | 52 | 3 |
| Proportion (%) | 40 | 40 | 19 | 1 |

**Table 3.26. Cooperation Manners that are Desired the Most (Questionnaire for teachers)**

| Cooperation Manner | Educating Children at Home | Strengthening the Communication | Participating in the School's Activities | Participating in the School's Organization and Management | Other |
|---|---|---|---|---|---|
| Number of Teachers | 45 | 139 | 52 | 0 | 0 |
| Proportion (%) | 19 | 59 | 22 | 0 | 0 |

**Table 3.27. The Most Needed Things for HSC (Questionnaire for teachers)**

| Needed by Teachers | Exchanging Experiences | Understanding the Background | Time and Energy | Cooperation of Parents | Economic Support | Other |
|---|---|---|---|---|---|---|
| Number of Teachers | 57 | 95 | 28 | 123 | 3 | 0 |
| Proportion (%) | 19 | | 9 | 40 | 1 | 0 |

The three tables above were teachers' answers on HSC manners; like the parents, teachers also believed that what the parents needed the most was to communicate with the school and then to teach children the knowledge.

In respect of the cooperation manner, the teachers, like parents, also believed that the most important manner was mutual communication, but they also believed that participating in the school's activities was also another important manner and that it was even more important than helping parents to educate children at home, which was different from parents' ideas.

Teachers held that the most important thing in HSC was the parent's coordination and then the understanding of parents' background. Some teachers have mentioned this issue during the interview. They held that many parents were busy with their work and this was an important factor that may influence the HSC.

## Content of HSC

In respect of the content of HSC, 3 questions were made for parents and parents were requested to tell the issues concerning them the most in respect of their children, the things where they wished the most to cooperate with the school and whether they know their children's conditions in school. Please see the following tables for the results.

### Table 3.28. Issues Concerning You the Most in Respect of Your Children (Questionnaire for parents)

| Issues Concerning the Parents | Academic Performance | Physiological and Psychological Development | Life Skills | Other |
|---|---|---|---|---|
| Number of Parents | 355 | 334 | 156 | 0 |
| Proportion (%) | 42 | 40 | 18 | 0 |

### Table 3.29. Things Where You Wished the Most to Cooperate with the School (Questionnaire for parents)

| Item | Academic Performance | Physiological and Psychological Development | Life Skills | Other |
|---|---|---|---|---|
| Number of Parents | 396 | 355 | 271 | 0 |
| Proportion (%) | 39 | 35 | 26 | 0 |

### Table 3.30. Do You Know Your Children's Conditions in School? (Questionnaire for parents)

| Do You Know Your Children's Conditions in School? | No | Somewhat Know | Yes | Other |
|---|---|---|---|---|
| Number of Parents | 90 | 258 | 90 | 0 |
| Proportion (%) | 21 | 58 | 21 | 0 |

The three tables above were parents' answers on the content of HSC. Among all the items, parents were most concerned about their children's academic performance, then their physiological and psychological development and then their life skills. When they were asked what activities they wished to participate in, their answers were the same as those to the previous question, and the respective proportion was closer to each other. When they were asked whether they knew their children's conditions in school, most parents selected "Somewhat Know" and the proportion of parents selecting "Yes" was the same as that of those selecting "No", both of which was 21%. This was consistent with the results of interview.

In respect of the content of HSC, 2 questions were made for teachers and parents were requested to tell the issues concerning them the most in respect of the children and the things where they wished the most to cooperate with parents. Please see the following tables for the results.

**Table 3.31. Issues Concerning You the Most in Respect of Your Children (Questionnaire for teachers)**

| Issues Concerning the Teachers | Academic Performance | Physiological and Psychological Development | Life Skills | Other (Moral Development) |
|---|---|---|---|---|
| Number of Teachers | 72 | 153 | 28 | 5 |
| Proportion (%) | 22 | 65 | 12 | 1 |

**Table 3.32. Things Where They Wished the Most to Cooperate with Parents (Questionnaire for teachers)**

| Item | Academic Performance | Physiological and Psychological Development | Life Skills | Other |
|---|---|---|---|---|
| Number of Teachers | 108 | 136 | 94 | 3 |
| Proportion (%) | 31 | 40 | 28 | 1 |

The tables above were teachers' answers on the things concerning them the most. Most teachers are most concerned by the student's physiological and psychological development, then the academic performance and then the life skills. In addition, teachers also hoped that parents can cooperate with them in such three issues; the respective proportion was close to each other. This was different from parents' idea that the student's academic performance was the most important.

**HSC Efficacy of Teachers**

In respect of teachers' HSC efficacy, 2 questions were made to inspect their cooperation efficacy and whether they knew the conditions of students' family. Please see following tables for the results.

**Table 3.33. HSC Efficacy (Questionnaire for Teachers)**

| HSC Efficacy | H | *M* | L | Other |
|---|---|---|---|---|
| Number of Teachers | 19 | 121 | 6 | 0 |
| Proportion (%) | 13 | 83 | 4 | 0 |

**Table 3.34. Do You Know the Conditions of Your Students' Family?
(Questionnaire for Teachers)**

| Do You Know the Conditions of Your Students' Family? | No | Somewhat Know | Yes | Other |
|---|---|---|---|---|
| Number of Teachers | 0 | 75 | 71 | 0 |
| Proportion (%) | 0 | 51 | 49 | 0 |

The two tables above were teachers' answers on their HSC efficacy and how much they knew about the conditions of their students' family. Most teachers selected "M" in respect of their HSC efficacy, and they were somewhat or extremely familiar with their students' family.

**Home Education**

2 questions on the methods and efficacy of home education were made in the questionnaire to inspect parents' home education. Please see following tables for the results.
Home education method

**Table 3.35. Home Education Methods (Questionnaire for Parents)**

| Method | Help Children with Their Homework | Supervising Children's Study | Communicating with Children | Other |
|---|---|---|---|---|
| Number of Parents | 115 | 354 | 292 | 0 |
| Proportion (%) | 15 | 47 | 38 | 0 |

**Home Education Efficacy**

**Table 3.36. Home Education Efficacy (Questionnaire for Parents)**

| Efficacy | H | *M* | L | Other |
|---|---|---|---|---|
| Number of Parents | 33 | 318 | 88 | 0 |
| Proportion (%) | 8 | 72 | 20 | 0 |

The two tables above were parents' answers on the manners to help their children and the home education efficacy. It was found that most parents helped their children via supervising children's study, and then via communicating with the children for enlightenment.

Only a small proportion of parents can help their children with the homework. Most parents selected "M" in respect of the home education efficacy, 20% of the parents held that it was difficult to educate children and only a small proportion of parents were confident in it.

### Sense of Cooperation

The fourth dimension in the questionnaire was to inspect teachers' and parents' sense of cooperation, including 4 questions on division of responsibilities and will to cooperate. Please see following tables for the results.

### Division of Responsibilities

**Table 3.37. Division of Responsibilities for HSC (Questionnaire for Parents)**

| Division of Responsibil ities | The School should Bear Most Responsibilitie | The School should Bear all Responsibilities . | The School and the Parent each Bear 50% of Responsibilities | The Parent should Bear Most Responsibilities. | Other |
|---|---|---|---|---|---|
| Number of Parents | 52 | 21 | 365 | 0 | 0 |
| Proportion (%) | 12 | 5 | 83 | 0 | 0 |

**Table 3.38. Division of Responsibilities for HSC (Questionnaire for teachers)**

| Division of Responsibilities | The School should Bear Most Responsi-bilities. | The School should Bear all Responsi-bilities. | The School and the Parent each Bear 50% of Responsi-bilities | The Parent should Bear Most Responsi-bilities. | Other (indivisible) |
|---|---|---|---|---|---|
| Number of Teachers | 3 | 3 | 111 | 22 | 6 |
| Proportion (%) | 2 | 2 | 76 | 15 | 5 |

Most parents and teachers agreed that the school and the parent should each bear 50% of the responsibilities for educating the children.

### Will To Cooperate

**Table 3.39. Will to Cooperate (Questionnaire for Parents)**

| What do you Think of the HSC? | Very Important | Important | It doesn't Matter | Adverse | Other |
|---|---|---|---|---|---|
| Number of Parents | 273 | 165 | 0 | 0 | 0 |
| Proportion (%) | 62 | 38 | 0 | 0 | 0 |

## Table 3.40. Will to Cooperate (Questionnaire for Teachers)

| What do you Think of the HSC? | Very Important | Important | It doesn't Matter | Adverse | Other |
|---|---|---|---|---|---|
| Number of Teachers | 132 | 14 | 0 | 0 | 0 |
| Proportion (%) | 90 | 10 | 0 | 0 | 0 |

Most teachers and parents, especially the teachers, thought the HSC very important.

### 3) Analysis on the Status Quo of HSCE

This chapter has explored the causes of the status quo of HSCE in the investigated junior middle schools through the semi-open survey on the HSCE for junior middle school students. Please see the following for details:

The home-school liaison was not frequent enough and the forms were not varied enough. This was because the HSC in each school was conducted at random and was poorly planned, and it was difficult for the school and the parents to well cooperate with each other. In addition, such cooperation was always conducted at the beginning or at the end of a semester; it was concentrated within a certain period and it was done as a mere formality.

The school and the parents lacked mutual communication and they were not familiar with each other. This was because the home-school communication had not been thoroughly conducted in the school and both the school and the parent contacted each other passively after problems occurred. There was no active communication in the true sense. There was always force feeding instead of two-way communication and there was hardly equal dialogue between the parent and the school.

Parents did not have correct educational concept and cannot provide enough support for their children. This was because the school did not attach great importance to the training for parents and failed to make best use of the family resources. The help of the school to the parents was merely the brief instruction that was not well targeted or practical. It is difficult for the parent to accept and internalize such help into the correct concept and conscious action in respect of educating their children. It follows that parents' suzhi needs further improvement.

## Building the HSCE Modes

### 1) Proposing and Meanings of HSCE Modes

Many foreign and domestic researchers have proposed some intervention modes in the course of HSC. For example, domestic researchers have proposed the HSC modes "focusing on school" that make the school the center of HSC and extend various HSC activities into other supporting systems. Meanwhile, the HSC modes "focusing on home" make the home the center of HSC to conduct various home-school activities. Japan's PTA program is a nationwide HSC program where activities are conducted on a class basis. The MegaSkill program, SDP program and TIPS program in the USA are all to improve students' academic performance, help parents learn the skills to educate and help children at home and enhance students' ability of reading, math etc. By integrating the home with the school. There is even the HSC mode for preventing abuse of drugs, the FAST program, which aims to help teenagers reduce the abuse of drugs through the cooperation between the school and the parent.

This chapter has proposed the HSCE mode based on the research into previous HSC modes, i.e. To conduct various educational activities for certain target in the aspects of home-school-home. This may promote effective integration of home education and school education and make the HSCE cause the educational effect greater than that by just combining home education and school education so as to improve students' psychological suzhi (such as the self-adaptability).

The educational modes to improve students' self-adaptability via HSC were proposed based on the level-based integration mode on psychological suzhi. Zhang [2002] held that it was an important task of suzhi education to cultivate good psychological suzhi of students. Students' psychological suzhi is the core of the suzhi structure and functions as the medium. Students' psychological suzhi should be cultivated in accordance with a systematic mode, including the factors of "student, home, school and society" and the four procedures of "physiology, psychology, society and education", and the mode should be implemented according to the characteristics of colleges, middle schools and primary schools. "Integration" is the key of such mode. Integration involves many aspects, including coordinating and integrating physiology, psychology, society and education, promoting students to integrate the targets for active adaptation and active development, promoting the integration of intelligence and ability, personality, sociality, creativity and other educational contents, and integrating such intervention manners as specific-problem-based training, counseling and consultation and subject infiltration. HSCE modes were conducted in accordance with the level-based integration mode on students' psychological suzhi. It is to explore the factors of family, school and student that influence students' psychological suzhi (self-adaptability) and fully use the four factors to coordinate the function of students' physiology, psychology, society and education so as to cultivate students' self-adaptability. During the experiment, we coordinated and improved the factors of self-adaptability according to the characteristics of cultivating junior middle school students' psychological suzhi; we also conducted, by means of various modes on cultivating psychological suzhi, various educational activities in the aspects of school, home and home-school during the implementation.

Students' psychological suzhi is cultivated in accordance with the principle of "adaptation and development" [Zhang, 2002]. We should first make students actively adapt to the study and life and then promote the overall and sound psychological development of students based on such active adaptation so as to make students' psychology and behavior adapt to the study, life and environment. HSCE modes also cultivate students' self-adaptability in accordance with this principle: a) coordinating students and the environment and properly controlling and adjust the internal psychological process; b) promoting students' overall development based on the aforesaid step.

## 2) *Implementation Strategies of HSCE Modes*

The implementation strategies of HSCE modes we established are mainly used for the educational activities in the aspects of school, home and home-school.

## School

It is based on the school, focuses on students' performance in school and requires the subject teacher, head teacher and other teachers to participate in the HSC to help students improve their self-adaptability. Meanwhile, psychological suzhi lessons on cultivating students' self-adaptability are launched in school to directly train the students, and the consultation service is provided for parents and students to improve students' self-adaptability.

*Psychological suzhi lessons for students.* We sampled the program consistent with the dimensions in scales from the Psychological Suzhi Trainings for Middles School Students, the Guide on Growth of Middle School Students, the Handbook on Psychological Counseling for Class and the Handbook on Psychological Counseling on Study and prepared the Specific-Problem-Focused Counseling on Self-Adaptability. We used the once-a-week mental health education lesson for the experimental group to conduct concentrated self-adaptability specific-problem-based training for students. The experimenter was the teacher responsible for the experimental group.

*Communications between and trainings for teachers.* We talked with the teacher of the experimental group, the head teacher and the grade chief on HSC issues to understand their cognition on HSC. We have invited them for many times to participate in HSC-related discussion, informed them of the methods of organizing HSC activities, the skills of cooperating with parents, the meanings of self-adaptability and how to cultivate the self-adaptability.

*Counseling and consultation for individuals.* We provided various consultations for the students, teachers and parents participating in the experiment: 1-2 lessons each week was/were spent in providing consultation for students in the school's mental health center and certain time was spent in providing consultation for parents. In addition, we advocated students to pour out their annoyance and problems in their psychological exercise books and the e-mail to the experimenter.

## Home-School Communications

The main task is to make the school and the teacher communicate with the parent based on the student's performance in school. Teachers and parents communicated with each other to jointly analyze the causes whenever they found problems. Teachers contacted and communicated with parents by various means to ensure that the home education was consistent with the school education and the parent and the teacher have an overall cognition of the students and can understand the student's performance on a timely basis.

*Home-school communication.* We organized the experimental group to prepare the *Home-School Communication* once a week. It included the news of the class, the news of the school, the student's excellent performance and the experiences of parents and teachers in educating children so as to inform parents of the conditions of the class and the school. Students were divided into several groups to prepare the *Home-School Communication* which was printed and distributed to parents every Monday.

*Notes.* It is also an effective communication method to let students bring home some notes with a few words therein. We encouraged and assisted the head teacher and the subject teacher to adopt this method so as to strengthen their communication with parents. Teachers recorded on the note the student's wonderful paintings, interesting words, beautiful articles and good deeds, and asked the student to bring home the note on that day.

*Home-school hot line.* We disclosed the president's phone number (office), the phone number of the school's duty room and the head teacher's office phone number and cell phone number so that parents can get through to the president or the teacher whenever they need. We set the home-school hot line to answer parents' questions on curricula, special events, student's activities, homework etc. We encouraged and urged subject teachers and head teachers to keep frequent communications with parents by phone, exchange their ideas on students' progress and academic performance, ask for information from parents and inform parents of the activities in the school or the class.

*Parent-teacher meeting.* We assisted the head teacher to hold information-based parents' meeting every month and each meeting had a certain topic, including students' general conditions, growth history, physical conditions and abilities, learning methods. We invited all parents and related teachers of the class to the meeting and left 50% of the time for the meeting to the parents for discussion and proposing new problems.

In addition, we also held the problem-based parents' meeting every month and invited some teachers, parents and students to the meeting. Those students had common problems, such as failure to abide by the regulations or finish the homework, and all those students, parents and teachers made joint efforts to find out the causes and solve the problem.

*Parent-teacher communication booklet.* We made the parent-teacher communication booklet. It was composed by booklet A, which was retained by the head teacher, and booklet B, which was retained by the parent. It was used for the communication between the teacher and the parents that lived far from the school, and were too busy with the work or were in poor physical condition to provide assistance on educating students. We encouraged teachers or parents to use the booklet to praise and advocate students' slight progress and good performance, introduce some learning methods to the students or educational experiences to the parents or solicit advice or opinions from parents on educating the student.

*School visit.* We determined a day for school visit and organized parents to visit the school. We invited parents to the school to visit students' learning environment, understand students' study and life and have a meeting with the head teacher and all subject teachers.

## Home

It is based on the school for parents to focus on improving the family environment and home education so as to cultivate students' self-adaptability. From the perspective of family environment, it is based on the family and focuses on correcting parents' educational concept and improving their educational methods so as to form the joint educational force. It strives to guide parents to establish correct concept on education and cultivation, adopt correct methods for home education and attach great importance to their communication with children. It includes distribution of guidebooks on home education, various parent-child activities, frequent communication with parents by phone and regular lecture on home education. It enriches parents' knowledge and makes them support the school's work via communication and guidance, and helps parents take advantage of the individual education at home to improve students' self-adaptability more effectively by means of feedback.

*Guide on Home Education and Necessary for Parents.* We prepared and distributed the *Guide on Home Education* once a week. The *Guide on Home Education* was distributed following the psychological suzhi lesson to help parents understand the content of the lesson. In addition, parents were made to encourage students to review the skills and strategies they learned in class and were encouraged to supervise such review so as to ensure successful implementation of strategies. Various manuals on educating children were also distributed, and many skills on educating children were taught to parents. We sometimes provided some cases of success in educating children and gave explanations so that parents can understand why those people can success and how they should educate their children.

The *Necessary for Parents* was around the self-adaptability and was composed mainly by interesting columns, including positive and negative cases on home education, aphorisms and well-known sayings, investigation report, case analysis, design of activities and questions and thinking. There were, in each topic, the discussion, speaking, writing and performance activities that needed parents' and children's participation, and parents were required to write down and deliver to the experimental teacher their impressions as they completed the task.

*Groups for parent-child activities.* We established groups for parent-child activities, such as learning math and parent-child communication, and invited parents, students and related teachers to such activities. They were required to find out the causes, understand the principle and master some skills.

*Guidance and communication by phone.* We communicated with certain number of parents every week, asked for the conditions of their children and answered their questions in educating the children. We wanted to understand parents' education methods, provide some advice on their education of children and ask for their feedback and opinions on HSC.

*Lectures on home education.* We held lectures on home education and invited some parents of unique education to introduce their experiences so as to encourage other parents. We publicized and taught parents the knowledge on education and family life to help parents better understand their children's growth, better educate their children, intensify their communication with the child and be clear about the roles of them and their children in the family and the society.

*Home visit.* We encouraged and helped the head teacher to try the best to visit each student's family during the first month upon student's enrollment so as to have a preliminary knowledge of the condition. Then they visited the family of certain problem-prone student and discussed with the parent on how to educate such student.

The implementation strategy of HSCE modes should be determined based on the four factors of students' psychological suzhi, "student, home, school and society", and the four procedures, "physiology, psychology, society and education". Students' psychological suzhi is formed through the interaction with the home, the school and the society. Teachers may, by establishing the implementation strategy based on home, school and home-school during the implementation of HSCE modes, fully use the resources for education to intervene and cultivate students on a systematic basis. All activities of the school are conducted around the home in the aspect of home (school-home-school). The home is the major base of the cooperation and its educational functions can be fully performed. With the help from the school, parents cooperate with the school in education and master various educational methods and skills. The home thus becomes an important place to improve students' self-adaptability. The school is the major force of all activities in the aspect of school (home-school-home). The school launched various activities to improve students' self-adaptability and the families of all students give their support to such activities. The school and the home make joint efforts in the aspect of school-home (home-student-school) to intensify their communication on cultivating students. The school and the home coordinate with each other in respect of their requirements and education to make them consistent and stable. To sum up, the factors of such three basic educational chains have different educational functions; they perform their own clearly defined responsibilities and duties and their unique educational functions. It can integrate the advantages of "focusing on school" and "focusing on home". Those different educational strategies for the same educational mode are practicable and effective.

### 3) Integration of Goals and Contents of HSCE Modes

The effective improvement of junior middle school students' self-adaptability with HSCE modes greatly depends on whether the goal and the activity were clearly defined in this experiment. This experiment can be successful only when the goal and the content of self-adaptability have been clearly defined. Or else, the cultivation of self-adaptability will be too generalized, less targeted and less feasible. The cultivation of students' self-adaptability with HSCE modes is mainly to promote students' active adaptation and active development and improve their intelligence and ability, adaptability and sociality by coordinating and integrating the factors of physiology, psychology, society and education. To be more specific, it is to improve all aspects of students' self-adaptability. The self-adaptability is individuals' stable ability reflected during some physiological and mental activities to control and adjust the internal psychological process so as to make themselves in harmony with the environment. It mainly includes six dimensions: learning adaptation, response to stress, stress-coping strategy, identification of body, psychological adaptation during the adolescence and adaptation to life. a) Learning adaptation is mainly to inspect whether students are able to make physiological and psychological adjustment to adapt themselves to the changes in learning conditions (such as the learning content, learning environment and learning task) and develop their abilities during the study. b) Response to stress and stress-coping strategy are the two aspects of stress adaptation and mainly focus on students' response to various pressures. The main pressure for students comes from their study. This dimension is to inspect whether students can give positive response and whether they can make positive cognition or efforts in stress situations or frustration situation to reduce the pressure and pain. c) Identification of body is to inspect whether students can correctly cognize and accept their physical conditions, including identification and acceptance of the health, physique, weight and appearance. The students in grade 7 are during the adolescence and they are in continuous physical development. Whether they can correctly identify their bodies is also a component of the school's mental health education that should be attached to great importance. d) Psychological adaptation during the adolescence is mainly to inspect whether the growing teenagers can correctly cognize the physiological and psychological development during the adolescence and make proper adjustment so as to establish healthy sexual attitudes and concepts. The six factors were cultivated on an integrated basis and in the aspects of home, school and home-school in following experiments. Such six factors were promoting each other and developing on a coordinated basis. For example, teachers may, when cultivating students' learning adaptability, help students use good learning methods to overcome the difficulties in study, and meanwhile, such activities may also help students cope with the academic pressure and improve the stress-coping capability. Teachers may, when helping students accept their own physical condition, help students understand their development during the adolescence according to the teacher's experience.

The self-adaptability is also cultivated in accordance with the principle on cultivating students' psychological suzhi, "adaptability and development": first helping students actively adapt to the study, life, stress and physical conditions, and then developing students' psychological suzhi on an overall and healthy basis after the active adaptation. The final goal of HSCE modes is to promote students to coordinate with the environment and properly control and adjust the internal psychological process and then promote students' overall development.

# EXPERIMENTAL RESEARCH IN EDUCATION

## Purpose

It is to explore the applicability and effectivity of cultivating junior middle school students' self-adaptability with HSCE modes.

## Participants

Participants were students in class 1 and class 6, grade 7 in a middle school in Chongqing. Class 6 was the experimental group composed by 50 students, while class 1 was the control group composed by another 50 students.

## Experiment Methods and Treatment

Both psychometrics and educational experiments were used in this chapter. Psychometrics is mainly to measure junior middle school students' self-adaptability and the teenager's parent-child communications, while educational experiment was to cultivate junior middle school students' self-adaptability with HSCE modes. In the experiment, we designed pre-test and post-test for both experimental and control groups. Please see Table 3.41 for details.

**Table 3.41. Experimental Treatment**

| Groups | Pre-Test | Experimental Treatment | Post-Test |
|---|---|---|---|
| Experimental Group | $O_1$ | X | $O_2$ |
| Control Group | $O_3$ | - | $O_4$ |

## Variables

Independent variable: home-school-cooperation-based education modes.

Dependent variables: a) junior middle school students' self-adaptability; b) junior middle school students' parent-child communications

Control variables: to establish the experimental group for HSC intervention and the control group for traditional home-school liaison. Note:

Establish the experimental group and the control group on a reasonable basis and make the two groups homogeneous as much as possible. That is to say, try the best to ensure that the pre-experiment self-adaptability and parent-child communication of the two groups were roughly the same;

Control other factors that may influence the experimental effect and remove the expectation effect, the difference between teachers and the time effect.

## Experimental Procedures

### 1) Stage of Preparation

a) Consult documents in Chinese to prepare or revise the experimental scheme; b) contact the school for experiment; c) study the textbook and organize materials for experiment; d) talk with the teacher and the parent about the HSC to help them understand the status quo thereof.

### 2) Implementation

a) Conduct pre-test on the self-adaptability and the parent-child communication (in the second week after the semester began); b) conduct HSC activities in the school for experiment.

### 3) Post-test

## Results and Analysis

### 1) Analysis on the Pre-Test and Post-Test Results of the Two Groups

Please see Table 3.42 for the pre-test and post-test scores of the dimensions and total scores of self-adaptabilities of the two groups.

According to Table 3.42, there was no significant difference between the self-adaptabilities of the experimental group and the control group in the pre-test; there was significant difference between the total average scores of the two groups in the post-test, but there was no significant difference between the "response to stress", "stress-coping strategy" and "psychological adaptation during the adolescence" of the two groups.

**Table 3.42. Comparison Between Mean Values and Standard Deviations of Pre-Test and Post-Test of the Two Groups**

|  | Factors | Experimental Group (N=50) $M \pm SD$ | Control Group (N=50) $M \pm SD$ | $t$ Value |
|---|---|---|---|---|
| Pre-Test | Learning adaptation | 2.32±.33 | 2.29±.31 | .75 |
|  | Stress-coping strategy | 2.41±.29 | 2.42±.34 | .22 |
|  | Response to stress | 1.96±.29 | 1.94±.27 | .9 |
|  | Identification of body | 2.24±.29 | 2.30±.36 | 1.17 |

**Table 3.42. (Continued)**

| | Factors | Experimental Group (N=50) $M\pm SD$ | Control Group (N=50) $M\pm SD$ | $t$ Value |
|---|---|---|---|---|
| | Psychological adaptation during the adolescence | 2.38±.48 | 2.32±.52 | 1.09 |
| | Adaptation to life | 2.30±.37 | 2.28±.30 | -.49 |
| | Total average scores | 2.27±.18 | 2.26±.16 | .75 |
| Post-Test | Learning adaptation | 2.48±.29 | 2.30±.34 | -3.34** |
| | Stress-coping strategy | 2.59±.40 | 2.51±.44 | -.76 |
| | Response to stress | 2.11±.34 | 2.02±.28 | -1.37 |
| | Identification of body | 2.53±.24 | 2.37±.37 | -2.12* |
| | Psychological adaptation during the adolescence | 2.47±.42 | 2.33±.51 | -1.38 |
| | Adaptation to life | 2.66±.38 | 2.33±.38 | -4.32** |
| | Total average scores | 2.47±.12 | 2.31±.23 | -3.94** |

**Table 3.43. Mean Values and Standard Deviations of Pre-Test and Post-Test of the Experiment Group**

| Factors | Pre-Test (n=42) $M\pm SD$ | Post-Test (n=42) $M\pm SD$ | $t$ Value |
|---|---|---|---|
| Learning adaptation | 2.32±.33 | 2.48±.29 | -2.13* |
| Stress-coping strategy | 2.41±.29 | 2.58±.40 | -2.16* |
| Response to stress | 1.96±.29 | 2.11±.34 | -1.81 |
| Identification of body | 2.24±.29 | 2.53±.24 | -4.56* |
| Psychological adaptation during the adolescence | 2.38±.48 | 2.47±.42 | -.84 |
| Adaptation to life | 2.30±.37 | 2.66±.38 | -4.94** |
| Total average scores | 2.27±.18 | 2.47±.12 | -5.01** |

## 2) Comparison Between the Pre-Test and Post-Test Scores of the Experimental Group

Please see Table 3.43 for comparison between the pre-test and post-test scores on self-adaptability of the experimental group.

According to Table 3.43, the self-adaptability of the experimental group during the post-test was significantly higher than that during the pre-test as a whole. Among the six dimensions in the questionnaire, the scores of "learning adaptation", "stress-coping strategy", "identification of body" and "adaptation to life" during the post-test were significantly higher than those during the pre-test.

## 3) Comparison Between the Pre-Test and Post-Test Scores of the Control Group

According to the requirements for experiment of equal group, we also need further analyze the changes in the scores of the control group's self-adaptability. Please see Table 3.44 for details.

**Table 3.44. Means Values and Standard Deviations of Pre-Test and Post-Test of the Control Group**

| Factors | Pre-Test (n=42) M±SD | Post-Test (n=42) M±SD | t Value |
|---|---|---|---|
| Learning adaptation | 2.28±.31 | 2.30±.34 | -.35 |
| Stress-coping strategy | 2.42±.34 | 2.51±.44 | -1.14 |
| Response to stress | 1.94±.27 | 2.02±.28 | -1.99 |
| Identification of body | 2.30±.36 | 2.37±.37 | -1.59 |
| Psychological adaptation during the adolescence | 2.32±.52 | 2.33±.51 | -.21 |
| Adaptation to life | 2.28±.30 | 2.33±.38 | -.77 |
| Total average scores | 2.26±.16 | 2.31±.23 | -1.60 |

According to Table 3.44, there was no significant difference between the control group's self-adaptabilities during the pre-test and the post-test, no matter whether as a whole or in each dimension.

### 4) Analysis on the Results of Developing the Two Groups' Parent-Child Communications

Students' self-adaptability was improved via HSC. Parents assisted the school at home in educating children, such as communicating more with their children, helping children with their homework at home, participating in the school's activities with the children, etc.

The activities for improving parent-child communications have been conducted for many times during the HSC activities for the experimental group in this experiment. As the experiment ended, we also tested the students' capabilities of parent-child communications to find out the relationship between junior middle school students' self-adaptability and their parent-child communication capabilities.

Please see Table 3.45 for the pre-test and post-test scores on dimensions of parent-child communications of the experimental group and the control group obtained based on statistics and analysis.

According to Table 3-45, the parent-child communication of the experimental group during the post-test was significantly better than that during the pre-test as a whole. Among the eight dimensions in the questionnaire, there was significant difference between "inclination to participate", "active listening", "flexible communication" and "open expression".

**Table 3.45. Comparison between Pre-Test and Post-Test Scores on the Experimental Group's Parent-Child Communications**

| | | Pre-Test M±SD | Post-Test M±SD | t Value |
|---|---|---|---|---|
| Experimental Group | Inclination to participate | 24.49±6.22 | 27.73±7.12 | -1.53* |
| | Emotional need | 11.61±4.08 | 11.91±4.47 | -.29 |
| | Sense of relief | 15.27±2.96 | 16.13±3.68 | -1.41 |
| | Understanding | 13.18±2.60 | 14.09±2.51 | -1.10 |
| | Active listening | 6.97±2.16 | 10.37±3.07 | -2.61** |
| | Domination demands | 10.49±2.48 | 11.09±2.65 | -.88 |
| | Flexible communication | 6.87±2.02 | 9.79±2.15 | -1.29* |
| | Open expression | 9.14±2.83 | 12.13±2.74 | -2.60* |
| | Total scores | 101.59±14.37 | 116.84±18.62 | -1.18* |

## Discussion on Experimental Results

### 1) Overall Effect

There was no significant difference between the self-adaptabilities of the experiment group and the control group in the pre-test; there was, in the post-test, significant difference between the overall condition of the experimental group and the control group, and there was also significant difference between the "learning adaptation", "identification of body" and "adaptation to life" of the two groups.

The experimental group's self-adaptability during the post-test was significantly higher than that during the pre-test as a whole, while there was no significant difference between the average scores of the control group's self-adaptability during the pre-test and the post-test as a whole.

We believed, according to the analysis on the experimental results, that the HSC can effectively improve junior middle school students' self-adaptability.

The causes for such experimental results may include:

*Implementation of this experiment.* This experiment integrated the home and the school to enhance the self-adaptability of the students in grade 7. The experimenter made the implementation strategies and plans of the experiment based on various HSC programs and the integrated modes for psychological suzhi cultivation and implemented such strategies and plans in the practice actively and strictly. Such strategies and plans have been supported and affirmed by parents and teachers during the implementation. The home and the school have made great efforts in the cooperation and well supported and cooperated with each other to coordinate their education of the students.

The experiment was conducted to improve all dimensions of the self-adaptability; different methods were adopted for different dimensions and significant effect has been achieved.

*Many methods were used to cultivate the learning adaptability.* Many researchers have made study on cultivating the learning adaptability and they found that the changes in family environment, learning methods and school environment were all helpful to improve the learning adaptability. Many methods were adopted in this chapter, including home education, small learning groups, psychological suzhi trainings and parent-teacher communication meetings, the home, the school and the student were mobilized and the functions of multi-resources for education have been fully performed. Parents learned various home education methods, cooperated with the school to help students develop good learning habits, optimize learning methods and reasonably arrange the learning time, and supervised and controlled children's performance at home. The subject teacher participated in the small learning groups to teach some students and help them improve their academic performance. Specific-problem-based trainings for learning adaptability were also conducted in the school's psychological suzhi classes. The experimental results showed that such activities were all helpful to enhance students' "learning adaptability".

*"Adaptability to life" was cultivated based on the home.* It is difficult to achieve "adaptation to life" if we solely depend on the school. Students' main activity in the school is learning and there is barely opportunity for them to develop the adaptability to life. Students' adaptability to life was cultivated in the school in this experiment, and parents were asked to assist the school to improve students' adaptability to life at home. Parents helped students apply the adaptation strategies learned in the school to the life and transform them into stable behavior. The experimental results showed that this method were helpful to effectively improve students' adaptability to life.

*Parents fully performed their functions to cultivate students'* "identification of body" and "psychological adaptation during the adolescence". Both of the two dimensions involve the problems in respect of teenager's development; they are unique and can better suit the home education. During the cultivation, we first conducted trainings in the psychological suzhi classes and then asked parents to learn specific educational methods to assist the school in cultivating the children. Parents enlightened and helped their children at home with their own stories and experiences, which was not only helpful to make the students in group trainings not bashful and achieve the expected effect, but also can enhance their capabilities of parent-child communications. The experimental results showed that this method can enhance the effect on "identification of body". However, there was no remarkable effect on "psychological adaptation during the adolescence". This may be because the physiological development of the students in grade 7 was slow and fewer activities related were conducted.

In respect of the "stress-coping strategy", students' capabilities were higher and the improvement was not so remarkable. Our psychometrics of self-adaptability showed that the scores on "stress-coping strategy" were the highest. Students were originally able to take proper strategies to cope with the academic pressure and their capabilities in this aspect were relatively high, which may be the reason for the unremarkable effect on this dimension.

The "response to stress" was a relatively stable factor. It was closely related with the personality, so the improvement was slow and the effect was not so remarkable.

It is a long term to establish and develop the self-adaptability, and the personnel, materials and funds available to the experiment were limited. In addition, only one semester was available to conduct the experiment and the time was also limited.

It was related with the suzhi of the teacher and the parent. HSC requires joint efforts of the school and the parent to drive students' development. Sometimes, the parent and the teacher cannot thoroughly comprehend the purpose and effect of the activities and certain parent did not have spare time to participate in the HSC activities. Some parents were not active. All of those have influenced the experimental results.

### 2) Influence of HSCE Modes on Parent-Child Communications

The experimental group's capabilities of parent-child communication were significantly improved after the experiment, especially in such dimensions as "inclination to participate", "active listening", "flexible communication" and "open expression".

This was mainly because HSCE modes can effectively improve the parent-child communication. Parents assisted the school at home in educating the children during the experiment. They communicated with children more frequently, helped children with their homework, participated in the school's activities with children, etc. Through such activities, parents stayed with their children for longer time, they got along with each other more harmoniously and communicated with each other better than before. This is consistent with Clark's research results and the evaluation results of the FAST program in the USA.

# SUPPLEMENT 1

## Questionnaire on Home-School-Cooperation-Based Education (for Parents)

Dear parents,

Welcome to participate in this investigation on home-school-cooperation-based education! Please spare some time to answer the following questions so as to achieve our common objective to provide good education for your children. There is no mode answer for any of such questions and you are advised to give your answer according to the fact. We will unceasingly improve our work in accordance with your opinion and advice. Thanks for your support!

Please select an option for each question and, if no option is consistent with your situation, write down your answer on the line following the question. Selection of more than one option is allowed for the questions with special description.

1. How many times did you contact the school within a semester in the past?
A. NoneB. Two to five times      C. Five times or more      D. time(s)

2. How many times do you think you should contact the school within a semester?
A. NoneB. Two to five times      C. Five times or more      D. time(s)

3. How were you informed of your children's performance at school and the information on your school?
A. Attending the parents' meetingB. Speak to the teacher on the telephone
C. Children's school report card or the performance assessment for a semester
D. Communicating with your children
E. Or

4. Which way do you prefer to contact the school? (Selection of more than one option allowed)

A. Attending the parents' meetingB. By telephone

C. Issuing the parent's guide     D. Attending the discussion and reporting meeting

E. Children's school report card or the performance assessment for a semester

F. Or


5. What do you think of the home-school-cooperation-based education for your children?

A. Very useful   B. Somewhat important   C. Negligible     D. Dislike       E. Or


6. What do you need the most if the school cooperates actively with you in educating your children? (Selection of more than one option allowed)

A. Knowledge on how to educate children       B.  Children's  performance  at  school
C. More spare time       D. Coordination from the child     E.  Economic   support
F. Others


7. What help from the school do you prefer to? (Selection of more than one option allowed)

A. Tell you more about the children's performance at school

B. Tell you how to educate the child

C. Understand more about you

D. Or


8. What concerns you the most?

A. Your child's academic performance

B. Your child's physiological and psychological development

C. Your child's self-help skills

D. Or


9. How do you educate your children at home? (Selection of more than one option allowed)

A. Guide the child to do the homework     B. Supervise the child's study

C. Communicate with the children to enlighten them       D. Or


10. How do you define your responsibilities and the school's responsibilities in educating the child?

A.  The  school  shall  bear  most  responsibilities,  while  the  parent  only  bear  slight responsibilities

B. The school shall bear all responsibilities

C. The school and the parent shall bear half responsibilities

D. The parent shall bear most responsibilities

E. Or


11. Do you know your child's performance at school?

A. No   B. Know a little  C. Yes  D. Or

12. In what aspect do you prefer to cooperate with the school? (Selection of more than one option allowed)
A. Improve students' academic performance
B. Improve students' physiological and psychological development
C. Improve students' adaptability to the life
D. Or

13. How do you think your education for your children?
A. Excellent      B. Average      C. Poor D. Or

14. What method do you prefer to cooperate with the school?
A. Assist the school in educating the child at home
B. Intensify the communication with the school
C. Participate various activities held at school
D. Participate in the school's organization and management
E. Others

At last, please write down your advice and requirements, if any, on the home-school cooperation or the school's work. Thanks a lot for your participation!

# SUPPLEMENT 2

## Questionnaire on Home-School-Cooperation-Based Education (for Teachers)

Dear teachers,

Welcome to participate in this investigation on home-school-cooperation-based education! Please spare some time to answer the following questions. There is no mode answer for any of such questions and you are advised to give your answer according to the fact. Thanks for your support!

Please select an option for each question and mark the option(s) you select. If no option is consistent with your situation, write down your answer on the line following the question. Selection of more than one option is allowed for the questions with special description.

If you are not the head teacher, please recall your past experience as a head teacher or suppose that you were a head teacher.

1. How many times did you contact the parent within a semester?
A. NoneB. Two to five times      C. Five times or more      D. Time(s)

2. How many times do you think you should contact the parent within a semester?
A. NoneB. Two to five times      C. Five times or more      D. Time(s)

3. How did you communicate with the parents on the students' performance at school?

A. Holding the parents' meeting   B. Speak to the parent on the telephone

C. Children's school report card or the performance assessment for a semester

D. Making the students communicate with their parents

E. Or

4. Which way do you prefer to contact the parent? (Selection of more than one option allowed)

A. Holding the parents' meeting   B. By telephone

C. Issuing the parent's guide       D. Attending the discussion and reporting meeting

E. Children's school report card or the performance assessment for a semester

F. Or

5. What do you think of the home-school-cooperation-based education for your children?

A. Very useful   B. Somewhat important   C. Negligible     D. Dislike       E. Or

6. What do you need the most if you cooperate with the parent in educating the student? (Selection of more than one option allowed)

A. Communicate the experiences with the parent

B. Understand the student's family background

C. More spare time and efforts

D. Coordination from the parent

E. Economic support

F. Others

7. What help from the school do you think is necessary? (Selection of more than one option allowed)

A. Tell the parent more about the student's performance at school

B. Tell the parent how to educate the student

C. Understand more about the family background

D. Or

8. What concerns you the most?

A. The student's academic performance

B. The student's physiological and psychological development

C. The student's self-help skills

D. Or

9. How do you define the parent's responsibilities and the school's responsibilities in educating the child?

A. The school shall bear most responsibilities, while the parent only bear slight responsibilities

B. The school shall bear all responsibilities

C. The school and the parent shall bear half responsibilities

D. The parent shall bear most responsibilities

E. Or

10. In what aspect do you prefer to support the parent? (Selection of more than one option allowed)
A. Improve students' academic performance
B. Improve students' physiological and psychological development
C. Improve students' adaptability to the life
D. Or

11. How do you think the home-school-cooperation-based education for the student?
A. Excellent             B. Average        C. Poor         D. Or

12. What method do you prefer to cooperate with the parent?
A. Assist the parent in educating the child at home
B. Intensify the communication with the parent
C. Organize the parents to participate in various activities held at school
D. Others

At last, please write down your advice and requirements, if any, on the home-school cooperation or the parent's education. Thanks a lot for your participation!


# SUPPLEMENT 3

## Questionnaire on Junior Middle School Students' Self-Adaptability

School:_Grade:_Test Date:

Responder's Name:_Gender:_Age:

Dear students,

Welcome to participate in this psychological test. All questions in this test are designed for obtaining information about your conditions. There is no mode answer for any of such questions. Nor is there a matter of correctness or falseness. You are advised to give your answer according to the fact. This is also a chance for you to know yourself. Please cherish it.

Attention:

Please select an option as quickly as possible after finishing reading each question, instead of wasting unnecessary time in thinking. Just respond spontaneously.
Please try to avoid selecting those "not sure" options, unless you think the other two options do not truly reflect your conditions.
Don't discuss with your classmates or copy their answers.
One option for each question.

1. I can't calm down and am always nervous when confronted with a sudden frustration.
a. Scarcely   b. Sometimes    c. Frequently

2. I constantly improve my way of learning so as to be adapted to different learning tasks.
a. Yes        b. Not sure        c. No

3. I am satisfied with my family life and seldom complain.
a. Yes        b. Not sure        c. No

4. I often feel downhearted in the case of great failure.
a. Scarcely    b. Sometimes    c. Frequently

5. When reading, I often mark those I don't understand or think important.
a. Yes        b. Not sure        c. No

6. I will be depressed for a long time in the case of frustration.
a. Yes        b. Not sure        c. No

7. I am not satisfied with my physical condition.
a. Scarcely    b. Sometimes    c. Frequently

8. I'm somehow hostile to the society as I see its dark side.
a. Yes        b. Not sure        c. No

9. Most of the time I can well arrange the daily work.
a. Frequently          b. Sometimes    c. Scarcely

10. I pay too much attention to my diet, worrying about being overweight or too thin.
a. Yes        b. Not sure        c. No

11. Most of the time, I can keep being excited in adverse situation.
a. Yes        b. Not sure        c. No

12. I often feel nervous and ashamed at my sex maturity.
a. Scarcely    b. Sometimes    c. Frequently

13. I view sex as a mysterious, embarrassed and ashamed thing.
a. Scarcely    b. Sometimes    c. Frequently

14. I like the study and life in our school and don't feel uncomfortable.
a. Yes        b. Not sure        c. No

15. I believe I can overcome all difficulties upon my constant hard work.
a. Yes        b. Not sure        c. No

16. I believe that failure teaches success and that experience is the best teacher.
a. Yes        b. Not sure        c. No

17. I think it obscene every time the other people mention sex.
a. Frequently        b. Sometimes    c. Scarcely

18. Most of the time, I try to figure out whether I can get help from the other people when confronted with frustration.
a. Scarcely   b. Sometimes    c. Frequently

19. If possible, I always want to escape from the present life.
a. Never     b. Sometimes    c. Frequently

20. I can obtain the scientific knowledge on sex through appropriate approaches (such as science and educational films, books on popular science, etc.) so as to get rid of my confusion about sex.
a. Frequently        b. Sometimes    c. Scarcely

21. I often discuss with my classmates to check what I have learned.
a. Frequently        b. Sometimes    c. Scarcely

22. Every time I successfully find a solution to a problem through great effort, I think about the feature of the method for solving such problem and consider whether this method is applicable to other questions.
a. Always   b. Sometimes    c. Never

23. Every time there are a lot of mistakes in my examination paper or homework, I carefully analyze the causes of these mistakes.
a. Yes       b. Not sure     c. No

24. Apart from the school work, I spend time in previewing or reviewing the textbooks every day.
a. Yes       b. Not sure     c. No

25. I can focus on the practice to find a solution in front of difficulties.
a. Yes       b. Not sure     c. No

26. I like the knowledge that I learnt and summed up.
a. Yes       b. Not sure     c. No

27. I am good at learning from my failures.
a. Yes       b. Not sure     c. No

# SUPPLEMENT 4

## Family Education Instructions for Parents' Meeting

| About Family Education<br>By Zang Yuan | Contents<br>☐ Creating good family environment for children<br>☐ How to help children in learning<br>☐ Skills of parent-child communication |
|---|---|
| 1.      Creating good family environment for children<br>1.1    Unconditional and positive care<br>☐    What is unconditional and positive care?<br>☐    It refers to that: we should show children that we love them, care about them and accept them. The attitude of parents to children is that: as long as you do your best in learning, No matter how the result is, we will always love you.<br>☐    Theoretical basis: Humanistic Theories of Carl Rogers | ☐    Influence on children<br>Children know that their behaviors will lead to something, and that they should make every effort to realize their targets and be responsible for their behaviors.<br>☐    Otherwise<br>They will seek for substitute love and care from the society; sometimes they will learn bad things from the bad.<br>If they are not accepted for a long time, they will be hurt psychologically and suffer from personality disorder.<br>They will have week self-value and strong self-defense, which obstruct their development and leads to less confidence.<br>They will be more dependent; will not have their own ideas and no sense of self-esteem. |
| How to express your love and care?<br>☐    Infiltrate the information of love and care and reception through speech and behaviors<br>Comfort them when they fail examinations.<br>When children do something you do not like, explain why peacefully and tell them your feelings and opinions. | 1.2    Providing a quiet learning environment for children.<br>☐    A quiet learning environment is preferably bright, far from TV with good ventilation.<br>☐    Help children to organize their desk orderly. Except those for learning, the fewer articles on the desk, the better; otherwise irrelevant articles on the desk will distract their attention. |
| Respect their opinions. Let them do the choice. | ☐    If possible, children should watch less TV, and spend more time in reading books and/or newspaper. This will not only provides a good learning environment for children, but also help children to form good learning habits, setting an example by their own action.<br>The family of Qian Zhongshu |

## Supplement 4 (Continued)

| | | | |
|---|---|---|---|
| 1.3 ☐ ☐ | Ask children to learn independently<br>Children are not tools for parents to realize self. Children should learn independently. Some parents treat children as their property. They intervene in children' learning a lot and are very strict to children. Parents always hope children to realize what they could not. Then students feel like that they learn for parents; and it is easily for children to become dependent, and have no initiative and learning motivation.<br>Thus parents must understand that students learn for their future. Children are the subject of learning; they have the right to choose the contents, time and styles of learning. Parents are only supervisors and advisors, rather than substitute and learner. | 2.<br>2.1<br>2.2<br>2.3<br>2.4<br>2.5 | How to help children in their learning<br>Help them to establish learning plan<br>Review and pre-class preparation<br>Reasonable expectation<br>Help children to attribute correctly<br>Interests in learning |

| | | |
|---|---|---|
| 2.1 | Help children to establish learning plan<br>Learning plan is critical for the effect of learning. Reasonable learning plan and implementation of learning plan help children to effectively make use of time and complete learning tasks timely.<br><br>Without learning plan, children will be dilatory; can not complete learning tasks; are not efficient; and are listless. | How to help students to establish learning plans<br>1.     Understand the learning tasks of children, the priority of tasks, time required for each task and how children complete tasks.<br>2.     The plan should be specific and implementable. Let's look at the following plan for review. |

| Content of learning | Priority | Time required | Whether completed |
|---|---|---|---|
| Memorize English words | 1 | 30 min | √ |
| Math home work | 1<br>2 | 30 min<br>20 min | √<br>√ |
| Collect biological materials | 2<br>3<br>1<br>2 | 30 min<br>15 min<br>20 min<br>40 min | <br><br><br>√ |
| Prepare for biological experiment Music appreciation Chinese homework Pre-class preparation | | | |

| | | | |
|---|---|---|---|
| Notes<br>☐ | The plan should be practical, and should not aim too high or too low. Children should be guided to | 2.2<br>☐<br><br>☐ | Review and pre-class preparation<br>What should be done the first after school?<br>Students need to attend seven to eight |

| | | | |
|---|---|---|---|
| | understand what they need to learn. The plan should be established by children. | | classes in a day in school. In schools, students do not have sufficient time to summarize and digest such knowledge; students should review what they |
| □ | Once the plan is established, | | |
| | parents should supervise students to implement it. There is no special case during the implementation. Parents should not allow giving up the plan; otherwise children will not develop good habits and the plan will not work. | | have learned the first after they go home, reorganize the knowledge and then do homework. The purpose of homework is to examine the learning of students. If students do homework without reviewing, they will make many mistakes, and then the effects of learning are not good. |
| □ | Parents should encourage and praise children when they complete the plan. | □ | Parents should remind children to form the good habit of reviewing first after they come home. |
| □ | Children should stick to establishing learning plan, making it a good habit, benefiting the whole life of children. | | |
| □ | Allow time to play for children | | |
| The importance of pre-class preparation | | 2.3 | Reasonable expectation |
| □ | It provides students with a general idea about what to learn | □ | Pygmalion Effect and Rosenthal Effect |
| □ | Children know what are the difficulties, and then they will pay more attention to the difficulties in class (which is especially important for Physics, Math and Chemistry) | □ | The expectation on students stimulates the internal learning motivation of students, which encourages students to progress and actively learn. |
| □ | It improves learning efficiency. | □ | The expectation should not be too high, and should meet the real situations of children; otherwise students will have heavy spiritual burden, which will influence the psychological and physical health of children. P5 |
| □ | It strengthens memory | | |
| □ | Parents should ask children about the class the next day, the contents to learn; and remind them to prepare. | □ | The expectation and target should be properly set. The best targets are those that can be realized by children with some efforts. |
| | For example, for English language class, learn new words, get familiar with the text, and think about what questions teacher will ask? … | | For example, a student who was ranked the 25th in the mid-term examination. Then the target of the final examination can be set at the 15th, allowing time for children to change and improve. Parents should be patient to children and provide more encouragement. |
| 2.4 | Help children to attribute correctly | □ | Many researchers have proved that The intelligence difference among students is not significant. The cause of different academic performance is different learning methods and learning habits. |
| □ | "Attribute", a psychological term. Put it in a simple way, "attribute" refers to explain the results. | | |

## Supplement 4 (Continued)

| | | | | |
|---|---|---|---|---|
| ☐ | Different attributions have different influences in the behaviors and attitude of people. For example, it students attribute poor academic performance to insufficient efforts, then they will not lose confidence in the future learning. They will spend more efforts. By doing this, they will have better performance. However, if students attribute it to insufficient capacity, they will lose confidence in future learning and fell helpless in learning. Then they will have worse and worse performance. | ☐ | Thus when students succeed or make progress, parents should help students to attribute to capacity, self-confidence and efforts. When students fail, they should help them to attribute to insufficient efforts, more difficult examination, etc. It is really a bad idea to blame that children are feebleminded and have no talent in learning; otherwise children will doubt their capacity, then they can not learn well. "Acquired helplessness" |
| | | ☐ | Anyone may have no confidence in your children, but you. | |

| 2.5 | Interests in learning | 3. | Skills of parent-child communication |
|---|---|---|---|
| ☐ | Interest is the best teacher. Curiosity is more important than knowledge itself, and interest is even more important than pure curiosity. | 3.1 | Psychological needs of children. |
| ☐ | Parents should: | ☐ | Long for understanding<br>Children long for the understanding from parents. They can share their thoughts with parents, because parents are also their friends<br>Parents should not dogmatically interrupt children. Parents should communicate more with children, understand their thoughts, and consider problem from the perspective of children. |
| | Understand the interests of children, and protect their interests. Allow children to experience happiness and success. Encourage children to what they are interested in. Support their choice. Allow children to have more practice. Develop more interests. | ☐ | Long for appreciation<br>Children long for the appreciation of parents. A smile and an encouraging sentence greatly comfort them.<br>Try to find more shining points of children. Encourage and praise them. |
| | English Disney    Computer | | |

| ☐ | Long for be respected<br>Parents should protect the self-esteem of children and should not scold and beat them. When there are problems, parents should discuss with them to find the solution; or parents can criticize them euphemistically. | 3.2 | Equality and time |
|---|---|---|---|
| | | ☐ | Equality<br>Parents should not impose their will on children. Parents should allow children to express their opinions. Parents should not always judge children with "good child" standards. Parents should respect the opinions and choice of children. |

| | Children start to have self-esteem at the age of three. Thus it is not proper to say something hurts their self-esteem, for example, "stupid". | ☐ | Time<br>Parents must spend some time every day on communicating with children and supervise the learning and homework of children, in order to help children to develop good habits, and help them solve problems in learning. For junior middle school students, parents should spend at least one hour with them per day. |
|---|---|---|---|
| ☐ | Long for relaxing<br>After studying for a day, children long for relaxing, a nap, music, beverage, etc. Parents should show their understanding. | | |

| 3.3 | School report and weekend | | |
|---|---|---|---|
| ☐ | School report<br>Parents should not judge children only | | |

| |
|---|
| through academic performance.<br>If children have poor academic performance, parents should first see whether children spent efforts and then analyzed the cause together with children to solve the problem, and encourage and support children.<br>☐   How to spend the weekend<br>Establish learning plan, complete homework.<br>Parents should allow children to do what they like, develop their interests,     Music<br>help students to review<br>and leave time for them to play. |

## SUPPLEMENT 5

## Instructions for Self-Adaptability Training Course

| Lesson 2 Time is Gold | Riddle |
|---|---|
| | ☐   What, of all things in the world, is the longest and the shortest, the swiftest and the slowest, the most divisible and the most extended, the most neglected and the most regretted?<br>☐   And why? |
| Think about it<br>☐   Writers say time is gold.<br>☐   Doctors say time is life<br>☐   Educators say time is knowledge<br>☐   Militarists says time is victory<br>☐   Aestheticians say time is the hope of life | What do you say?<br>☐   "Laziness in youth spells regret in old age"<br>☐   "a speck of time is more precious than an ounce of gold"<br>Who has more?<br>What do you say? |
| ☐   How to treat time<br>Smart person – use time<br>Stupid person – waiting<br>Workers – accumulate time<br>Lazy person – lose time<br>Determined person – win time<br>Quitter – give up time<br>Knowledge seeker – seize time<br>Gossiper – kill time<br>Hard worker – treasure time<br>Self-satisfied person – neglect time<br>Scientist – create time | Answer "Yes" or "No" to the following questions:<br>1.   Do you avoid the important points and dwell on the trivial when you treat everything?<br>2.   Do you always think that today is too short and tomorrow is long?<br>3.   Is it true that you do not like establish learning plan?<br>4.   Do you resist tasks and things?<br>5.   Are your pet praises "I will do it later", or "I will do it tomorrow"?<br>6.   Are you always absentminded in |

## Supplement 5 (Continued)

| | | |
|---|---|---|
| | Muddleheaded person – waste time<br>Which kind of person are you?<br>How do you treat time?<br>Can you give some typical examples?<br>Persons waiting for windfall? | learning?<br>7.　　　Do you always make efforts at the last moment? |
| Roles: | Perform the play "I will do it tomorrow"<br>Roles: Calendar; Xiaowei; two classmates of Xiaowei, A and B; teacher of Xiaowei (five students are needed for the play).<br><br>Xiaowei is a student who likes playing very much. He can not discipline himself after school. He will leave homework undone and play with classmates. And it results in that he did not complete his homework for the week.<br>A and B invite Xiaowei out to play in | ☐　Plot: In one week, the teacher assigns homework and how Xiaowei completes homework.<br>☐　The student holding calendar presents Monday, Tuesday …<br>☐　The teacher assigns homework before the class is dismissed. Xiaowei goes home after school. When he is about top do homework, his classmates invite him out to play, and he says yes every time.<br>☐　The calendar shows the day from Monday to Saturday. The teacher assigns |
| | turns (skating, basketball, games, internet surfacing, etc.)<br>Teacher assigns homework everyday. He checks homework the next week and finds that Xiaowei did not complete his homework.<br>Calendar and clock: students acting as the calendar are turning the calendar quickly as time elapsychological suzhi-based educations. | homework everyday. Xiaowei has more and more homework to do…<br>☐　On Monday, the teacher checks homework and criticizes Xiaowei. |
| ☐<br>☐<br>☐<br>☐<br>☐<br>☐ | What do you think after you see the play?<br>Did the same situation happen on you?<br>What are the features of people who always delay?<br>Pet phrases_____<br>Behavioral features_____<br>Excuses_____ | Why do we delay?<br>☐　We can put what we do not like aside by delay.<br>☐　By lying to ourselves, we can have peace of mind.<br>☐　By delay, we can maintain the current status, and do not need to face the risk of changes.<br>☐　We can find insufficient time as an excuse when we try to finish the work at the last moment.<br>☐　And finally, somebody else has to help you to do our work. |
| Strategy 1: make good use of every minute | | Yang Zhu (370-319 BCE), a Chinese philosopher during the Warring States period did the following calculation<br>☐　Supposed a person dies when he is 100 year-old, the childhood and elderliness almost occupy 1/3 of the whole life. Sleeping takes 1/2 of the time;<br>☐　Sickness, anger, grief and worry about personal gains and losses take 1/6;<br>☐　Then how much time do we have for learning and working? |

## Supplement 5 (Continued)

| Name | Time | Sleeping | Dining | Traveling | Learning | Entertainment | Vacancy | Others | | |
|------|------|----------|--------|-----------|----------|---------------|---------|--------|---|---|
| | 1 day | | | | | | | | | |
| | 1 week | | | | | | | | | |
| | 1 month | | | | | | | | | |
| | 1 year | | | | | | | | | |
| | Whole life | | | | | | | | | |

| Where do we lose time? |
|---|
| ☐      One student says he lose time in looking for things. The student always forgets things. Very often, he can not find his stationary during study. |

| When he is about to do his homework, he finds that he forgot his exercise book in school. It seems he loses time. |
|---|
| ☐      Which of your behaviors cause lose of time? What should we do? |

**Making use of odd moments**
- ☐ There are always odd moments, for example, the periods between classes, before and after lunch, when you are waiting for ship and vehicles, before a play, on your way to and from somewhere.
- ☐ We can use such odd moments to prepare what we need for learning, arrange the learning environment, memorize English words, read magazines and newspaper, recall the paragraphs of the text, discuss etc. If we make use of each second and moment, we will succeed.

**Howdo I spend my time?**
- ☐ In addition to go to school, I spend __ hours in learning. I study __ subjects per day.
- ☐ I spend __ hours in sleeping, to

**What can we do in 15 minutes?**
- ☐ A nap?
- ☐ Absentmindedness?
- ☐ Chatting?

**Abstractedness?**
- ☐ We can ado many things…

**Strategy 2 Establishing good learning plan**
- ☐ Establishing the list of tasks
1. How many tasks do I need to complete in the morning?
2. How many tasks do I need to complete in the afternoon?
3. What tasks do I need to complete in a day?
4. What targets do I need to realize this week?

**Learn to establish learning schedule**
- ☐ Components of learning schedules: tasks, priority of tasks, time required for each task, and whether the task is completed.

## Supplement 5 (Continued)

<table>
<tr>
<td>

to ensure sufficient sleeping.

☐    I can easily handle with _____ (name of subjects), I plan to _____.

☐    I find it difficult to handle with _____ (name of subjects), I plan to _____.

☐    I spend _____ hours on Saturday and Sunday especially for reviewing _____.

☐    When I study for quite a long time, I will take a 5-15 minutes break in between, such as a walk, _____, _____, etc.

☐    In addition to reviewing what I have learned in school, I like to _____ in my spare time, in order to relax after the intense learning activities.

</td>
<td>

☐    Notes:

When you establish the first learning schedule, do not impose very high requirements on you.

Making full use of the time in the daytime.

Do not idle away your time.

Do not waste odd moments.

Well arrange the periods of time.

Well estimate time required for each task.

Allow more time for each task.

Ensure sufficient time for sleeping.

</td>
</tr>
<tr>
<td>

Example:

| Contents of learning | Priority | Time required | Whether completed |
|---|---|---|---|
| Memorize English words | | | |
| Math home work | | | |
| Collect biological materials | 1<br>1<br>2 | 30 min<br>30 min<br>20 min | √<br>√<br>√ |
| Prepare for biological experiment | 2<br>3 | 30 min<br>15 min | |
| Music appreciation | 1<br>2 | 20 min<br>40 min | √ |
| Chinese homework | | | |
| Pre-class preparation | | | |

</td>
<td>

Strategy 3: making full use of the golden time for learning

There are four periods of golden time for learning in a day:

☐    The 1-2 hours after you get up in the morning. In this period, you have no thing influencing your learning, as you have a fresh mind.

☐    8:00-10:00 am. You are activated fully in this period. You are in the state of excitement.

☐    3:00-4:00 pm. You are refreshed after the break at noon.

☐    The 1-2 hours before sleeping in the evening. After learning, you will sleep directly, thus there will be nothing influencing what you have learned.

</td>
</tr>
<tr>
<td>

☐    You can find out the best time for you to learn. You should learn the most difficult tasks and new knowledge when you are the most energetic, happy and have peace of mind.

</td>
<td>

Homework

☐    Tell parents what happened in school today.

☐    Discuss with them what you have learned in the psychological class; and ask them to help you to establish learning plans and to supervise your implementation of the plan.

☐    Write down your feelings about the communication with parents, and how you implemented the plan.

</td>
</tr>
</table>

# REFERENCES

Austin Independent School District, (1993), Office of Research and Evaluation, Megasills. Austin, TX: Austin Independent School District.

Bai, J. R., Liu, G. W., and Guo, X. *M.* (1997). Research into middle school students' learning adaptability. *Journal of developments in psychology*, (2), 60-63.

Che, W. B. (1991). *Encyclopedia of psychological counseling.* Changchun: Jilin People's Publishing House.

Chu, C. (2000). Investigation on college and university freshmen's adaptability to the life. *Health psychology journal, 8* (5), 520-521.

Clark, R. (1983). Homework-focused parenting parenting practices that positively affect student achievement. *In N. Chavkin (ED.), Family and schools in a pluralistic society,* 85-106.

Clark, R. (1990). Why disadvantaged children succeed. *Public welfare,* (48), 17-23.

Cui, *M.* G. (2003). Building learning-based home via home-school interaction. *Administration of primary and middle schools,* (11), 41.

Davies, D. (1976). Making citizen participation word. *National elementary principal,* (55), 20-29.

Epstein, J. L. (1993). School and family partnerships. *Instructor, 103* (2), 78-76.

Ho, B. S. (2002). Application of participatory action research to family-school intervention. *School psychology review, 31* (1), 106-121.

Huang, R. S. (2001). Research into the relationship between mental health of the students in grade seven and parents' disciplining attitude. *Journal of GanZhou Teachers College (philosophy and social sciences),* (1), 107-111.

Iverson, B., and Walberg, H. (1982). Home environment and school learning: A quantitative synthesis. *Journal of experimental education, 50* (3), 144-151.

Lei, L., and Zhang, L. (2003). *Psychological development of teenagers.* Beijing: Peking University PresS.

Lewis, A. (1997). Building bridges: Eight case studies of schools and communities working together. Chicago: Cross City Campaigh for Urban School Reform.

Li, H. L., and Zhang, Q. L. (2004). A developing research on the new junior school student's learning adaption. *Studies of psychology and behavior, 2* (1), 356-359.

Li, S., and Yu, X. X. (2003). Research into junior middle school students' psychological coping and the intermediate variables. *Journal of NingBo University (educational science), 25* (3), 18-21.

Lightfoot, S. (1978). Worlds apart: Relationships between families and schools. New York: Basic Book.

Lin, J. D., Kong, Q. L., and Qin, C. F. (2004). Influence of stressful life events on the mental health of middle school student. *Jiangsu prev med, 15* (3), 26-28.

Lindle, J. (1992). Developing school based decision-making capacities in Kentucky: Communication satisfaction after the pilot year. Lexington, KY: University of Kentucky. (ERIC Document Reproduction Service No.ED378667)

Liontos, L. (1992). At-risk families and schools: Becoming partners. *Eugene, OR: ERIC Clearinhouse on Educational management.* University of Oregon (ERIC Document Reproduction Service NO. ED342055)

Liu, L. (1992). Functions and manners of parents' participation in the school education. *Educational research and experiment*, (1), 62-66.

Logan, J. (1992). *School-based decision-making: Fist year perceptions of Kentucky teachers, principals, and counselors*. Lexington, KY: University of Kentucky. (ERIC Document Reproduction Service No.ED361857)

Ma, Z. H. (1999). *Home school cooperation*. Beijing: Educational Science Publishing House.

McDonald and Bellingham (l993). *Families and schools together: Final report*. Washington, DC: U.S. Office of Human Development, Administration on Children and Families.

McDonald, L., et al. (1991). Family and schools together: An innovative substance abuse prevention program. *Social work in Education, 13* (2), 118-128.

Mega Skill Education Center of Home and School Institute, Inc., 1500 Massachusetts Avenue, NW, Washington, DC 2000. 5.

Morgan, V., Fraser, G. et al. (1992). Parental involvement in education: How do parents want to become involved? *Education studies, 18* (1), 11.

Nan, D. (2002). Exploration of effective approaches for home-school cooperation: Inspiration of Japan's PTA. *Journal of Inner Mongolia Normal University (educational science), 15* (2), 12-14.

Raffaele, L. *M*., and Knoff, H. *M*. (1999). Improving home-school collaboration with disadvantaged families: organizational principles, perspectives, and approaches. *School psychology review, 28* (3), 448-466.

Raffaele, L. *M*., and Knoff, H. *M*. (1999). Improving home-school collaboration with disadvantaged families: organizational principles, perspectives, and approaches. *School psychology review, 28* (3), 448-466.

Rich, D. (1992). *MegaSkills*. New York, NY: Houghton Mifflin.

Rioux, W., and Berla, N. (Eds) (1993). Innovations in parent and family involvement. *Princeton junction*, NJ: Eyes on Education.

Shepard, R. G., Trimberger, A. K., McClintock, P. J., and Lecklider. D., (1999). Empowering family-school partnerships: An integrated hierarchical mode. *Contemporary education, 70*, 33-37.

Siders, *M*. B., and Sledjiski, S. (1978). *How to grow a happy reader: As it relates to a child's attitudes and achievement in the acquisition of reading skills*. (Monogragh No.27). Gainsville, FL: Florida University. (ERIC Document Reproduction Service No. ED214124)

Tan, J. H. (2003). *Contact between the home and the school: How to successfully contact with parents*. (J. H. Tan, et al. Trans.) Beijing: China Light Industry Press.

Tian, L. (2002). *The Research on learning adaptability problem of pupils and the educational interfering*. Master's thesis, Southwest China Normal University, Chongqing, P.R.C.

Wang, T. (2002). A study on mental quality structure and its developmental characteristics in university students. Master's thesis, Southwest China Normal University, Chongqing, P.R.C.

Wang, Y. H., and Zhang, Z. K. (2003). Integration of educational forces: Research into "harmonious home-school interaction" launched in Jinjing, Chengdu. *Sichuan education*, (4), 11-14.

Xu, *M*. X., and W, J. C. (2003). Research into the environment that may influence the establishment of modern home-school cooperation. *Journal of Inner Mongolia Normal University (educational science)*, *16* (3), 5-7.

Yang, X. L. (2000). Analysis on mental problems and education of students in grade seven. *Journal of MianYang Teachers' College, 19* (4), 92-93.

Zhang, D. J. Materials on the program of students' psychological suzhi cultivation modes and implementation strategies. Institute of Education Science of Southwest China Normal University.

Zhang, D. J., Feng, Z. Z, Guo, C., et al. (2000). Problems on research of students' mental quality. *Journal of Southwest China Normal University (humanities and social sciences edition), 26* (3), 56-62.

In: Methods and Implementary Strategies on Cultivating …     ISBN: 978-1-62417-979-2
Editors: Da-Jun Zhang, Jin-Liang Wang, and Lin Yu     © 2013 Nova Science Publishers, Inc.

*Chapter 5*

# EXPERIMENTAL RESEARCH INTO DEVELOPING SELF-EFFICACY OF STUDENTS IN MATHEMATICS TEACHING

*Cui-Ping Wang[1], Da-Jun Zhang[2], Qi Jiang[2] and Jin-Liang Wang[2]*
[1]Xian Physical College, China
[2]Center for Mental Health Education in Southwest University, China

## ABSTRACT

Learning self-efficacy is the specific application of self-efficacy theory in learning. It influences not only the academic performance of students, but also the physical and psychological health. Therefore, developing students' self-efficacy is the basic content of psychological suzhi-based education in schools. We built the mode of developing students' self-efficacy in math learning based on overseas research into self-efficacy, the characteristics of math as a subject in middle schools, related teaching requirements and the characteristics of math learning. We also used this mode in educational intervention. The results of intervention show that the scores of participants from the experimental group in dimensions of self-efficacy and psychological suzhi were significantly improved ($p<.05$). It indicates that the mode of developing students' self-efficacy in math teaching is an effective way to improve students' learning self-efficacy.

## LITERATURE REVIEW

### Research into Theory of Self-Efficacy

#### 1) Self-efficacy Influences Human Behaviors

Bandura believed self-efficacy influences individuals' behaviors through intermediate processes, including choice of options, thinking, motivation and emotional response. First, self-efficacy influences individual's choice of behavior options. When an individual has many options of activity styles for performing the tasks they are facing, the choice of options by the individual depends on their self-efficacy of these options as different activities require different skills and knowledge. Second, self-efficacy influences individuals' thinking of goal setting and imagination of the scene of activities. Individuals with low self-efficacy tend to think more about their shortcomings. The potential difficulty in their imagination is worse than the real situation. This causes psychological pressure and makes individuals pay more attention to possible failures and negative consequences, and thus leads to lower goal setting. Individuals with high self-efficacy believe their efficacy in activities and tend to think about the scene of success. They pay attention to and concentrate their efforts on the requirements of the situation. They have more efforts stimulated by difficulty and are bold to set challenging goals. Third, self-efficacy influences motivation. Efficacy beliefs determine the level of motivation, which is reflected by the level of efforts in activities and the persistence of activities in the face of difficulty. With higher self-efficacy, individuals undertake more efforts and are more persistent. They undertake more efforts to overcome the challenges and difficulty. On the contrary, with lower self-efficacy, individuals doubt their capacity and give up efforts. Finally, self-efficacy influences emotions. Efficacy beliefs influence the pressure toleration and emotional experience of individuals in threatening situations or difficulty. Emotional responses directly or indirectly influence the behaviors of individuals through changing their thinking mode.

## 2) Means to Acquire Efficacy Information

Bandura believed that in an activity, an individual obtains and enhances self-efficacy mainly by information of four factors: success/failure experience of performance, vicarious experience, verbal persuasion, and physiological arousal. Success/failure experience of performance is the perception of an individual on the mastery achieved in practical activities. Successful performance ensures and improves the self-efficacy of an agent; whereas repeated failures (especially the failures occurred before the efficacy is enhanced) reduce self-efficacy. Vicarious experience refers to that the success of a mode with similar capacity and other personality traits can improve one's efficacy beliefs in similar activities; on the contrary, the failure can reduce one's judgment on efficacy. Verbal persuasion, the third source of self-efficacy, refers to that one believes one's efficacy after accepting the verbal encouragement from others that one is able to implement a certain task. Finally, physiological arousal refers to physical response in the face of a given task; for example, people usually judge self-efficacy before the examination, job interview and other events based on the physiological arousal such as heartbeat, blood pressure and breath. Peaceful response makes people calm and confident, while anxious responses lead to doubt about capacity.

## 3) Cognitive Processing of Self-Efficacy Information

Self-efficacy judgment, as a reasoning process, requires an individual to distinguish the capacity factors and non-capacity factors affecting the performance in actual activities and to measure the influences of such factors on performance. For example, successful completion of familiar and simple daily activities does not create new significance and value to one's experience; but the success of a difficult and challenging task presents new efficacy information to an individual and leads to sense of competence, sense of capacity and sense of achievement. The cognitive evaluation of the efforts undertaken in the activities is an important factor affecting efficacy judgment. For example, the success of challenging tasks through little efforts indicates strong capacity of the agent; whereas very hard working in the same success indicates insufficient capacity or mediocrity of the agent, making it very hard to improve one's self-efficacy.

Besides, self-efficacy is also influenced by one's preference to the self-monitoring of activities. One's preference makes one selectively pay attention to and memorize the mastery of a certain style, providing different foundation for one's efficacy judgment. If one tends to pay attention to and memorize the negative performance in an activity, such cognitive bias surely reduce one's self-efficacy. If one tends to pay attention to the success in an activity and neglect the failures, one's self-efficacy judgment tends to be exaggerated [Dowrick, 1983].

## Psychometric Tools of Self-Efficacy in Academic Field

The psychometrics and evaluation of self-efficacy is a key issue in self-efficacy research. It not only reflects the understanding of the significance and structure of self-efficacy by the researchers, but also lays foundation for further determining the relationship between self-efficacy and other related factors. There are two views on self-efficacy evaluation. Some believe that self-efficacy is for a certain field and there is no general self-efficacy, thus general self-efficacy can not be measured. The measurement of self-efficacy should be conducted in a certain field. Some argue that there is general self-efficacy which can be measured.

### Table 5.1. Psychometric Tools of Self-efficacy in Academic Field

| Developed by | Tool Name | Dimensions, Items, Tabulation Methods | Remarks |
|---|---|---|---|
| Morgan and Jinks [1999] | Morgan-Jinks Student Efficacy Scale (MJSES) | Three sub-scales: Talent (13 items); effort (4 items); context (13 items) | Research showed that the three MJSES sub-scales can provide more information about students' self-efficacy in learning. |
| Pintrich [1991] | Motivated Strategies for Learning Questionnaire (MSLQ) | Five sub-scales (nine items for self-efficacy scale); 43 items; it is rated on a 7-point Likert scale | The self-efficacy measurement in MSLQ is always regarded as the typical measurement of general self-efficacy in learning. The scale is used by many researchers as a tool to study self-efficacy, although the items of the scale are not specially designed for learning task and only 9 items are available. |
| Bandura [2001] | Children's Self-Efficacy Scale (CSES) | It includes nine tests and 57 items to assess children's self-efficacy in utilization of social resources, academic achievements, self-regulation in learning, leisure time and extracurricular activities, realization of others' expectation, seeking for supports from parents and the community, etc. | |

**Table 5.1. (Continued)**

| Developed by | Tool Name | Dimensions, Items, Tabulation Methods | Remarks |
|---|---|---|---|
| Wood and Lock [1987] | Academic Self-efficacy Questionnaire (ASEQ) | It includes 7 tests (35 items) to measure the self-efficacy in understanding, distinction of definitions, interpretation of definitions, memory, etc. | The test uses Bandura's classic 0-100 measuring methods, including the measurement of efficacy strength and efficacy range. |
| Bezt and Hackett | Mathematics Self-Efficacy Scale (MSES) | It includes three sub-scales (50 items) to measure the self-efficacy in performing every-day math tasks, persisting in math-related courses and solving math problems. It is rated on a 6-point Likert scale. | The items were collected based on the items of evaluation, including mathe-matical application, mathe-matical behaviors in daily life and academic achievements involved by different math skills. |
| Zhou and Dong [1994] | Learning Self-efficacy Questionnaire | It includes 2 dimensions (12 items). | It was developed based on the dimensions of the Teacher Efficacy Scale by Gibson and Dembo, to assess the general self-efficacy in ordinary learning activities. |
| Wang, Xin and Li [1999] | Self-Efficacy Scale | It includes two dimensions (self-efficacy in learning behaviors, self-efficacy in learning capacity); 12 items. | It was developed based on the Teacher Efficacy Scale by Gibson and Dembo. |
| Wang and Lei [2000] | Efficacy Beliefs Scale | It includes three dimensions (control belief, means-purpose belief, actor belief); 21 items | It was developed based on the theory of activity-control belief. |
| He | Mathematics Self-Efficacy Scale | It includes three sub-scales (self-efficacy in performing mathematics tasks in daily life, self-efficacy in solving math problems, and self-efficacy in completing math-related courses), 15 items. It's rated on a 5-point Likert scale. | It was developed by referring to the Mathematics Self-Efficacy Scale developed by Betz and Hackett in 1983 and revised by Bikkars and Randhawa in 1990. |

## Research into Self-Efficacy in Academic Field

### 1) International Research into Self-Efficacy in Academic Field

International research into self-efficacy in academic situation includes i) the influence of self-efficacy on choosing majors and careers by university students. Researchers [Hackett, 1985; Lent, Lopez and Beischke, 1991; Matsui, Lkeda and Ohnishi, 1989; Matsui, Mstsui and Ohnishi, 1990] found that university graduates tend to choose majors and careers they believe that they are competent for rather than those they believe they are less or not competent for. The research by Miller et al. [1995] showed that compared with mathematics scores or mathematical expectation, the self-efficacy of university students can better predict their interests in math and their choice of math-related courses and majors. ii) Gender difference in self-efficacy Eisenberg, Martin et al. argued that the gender differences in math self-efficacy is decreasing or does not exist at all. But other researchers found that gender difference of math confidence among U.S. students is common. iii) The relationship between self-efficacy and other psychological variables. Many researchers probed into the relationship between self-efficacy beliefs and goal setting [Wood and Locke, 1987], mode demonstration [Schunk, 1981/1987], problem-solving, occasional reward [Schunk, 1983], self-regulation [Zimmerman and Bandura, 1984; Zimmerman and Martinez-Pons, 1990], social comparison [Bandura and Jourden, 1991], and anxiety and self-concept [Pajares and Miller, 1994/1995]. Research showed that self-efficacy beliefs are related to the mentioned factors to some extent.

### 2) Domestic Research into Self-Efficacy in Academic Field

Domestic research into self-efficacy focuses on the development and characteristics of academic self-efficacy among students, the relationship between self-efficacy and academic performance as well as the relationship between self-efficacy and other related factors affecting academic performance. Research showed that: i) the self-efficacy of middle school students are declining, and obvious decline starts from junior grade two [Zhou, 1994]; students with learning difficulty have significantly lower self-efficacy than those with good academic performance [Zhou, 1994; Yang, 1996; Wang, 1999]. ii) Self-efficacy is closely related to academic performance, attributional styles and learning strategies. Research showed that the self-efficacy of middle school students is very significantly related to their academic performance (in Chinese language and math) [Li et al., 1998]; the level of students' self-efficacy significantly positively correlates with all aspects of self-monitoring of learning [Zhou, 1994]. iii) In terms of affecting mechanism, self-efficacy not only directly influences academic performance, but also indirectly influences academic performance by learning strategies, attributional styles and other means [Li et al., 1998; Wang, 1999]. iv) in terms of the degree of influence, self-efficacy has the most influence on academic performance, following by attributional styles and learning motivation [Wang and Liu, 2000].

## Research into Development of Self-Efficacy

In terms of styles or object of intervention, some develop the self-efficacy directly from the perspective of students; whereas some develop by training teachers to influence indirectly the self-efficacy of students.

The methods used to directly increase the self-efficacy of students mainly include: i) enhancement, i.e., increasing students' self-efficacy either by external enhancement or self-enhancement [Schunk, 1983]. ii) Attribution training. It refers to that students master the skills of attribution, remove attribution bias and develop proper attributional styles by certain procedures. For example, Guo, Lu et al. [1994] developed and increased the academic self-efficacy of pupils [Schunk, 1982/1983/1984] through different sources of efficacy information, such as success experience, mode demonstration and guiding positive attribution. Many researchers probed into improving self-efficacy by attribution training. Such development of self-efficacy was conduced under experimental situations.

Developing students' self-efficacy indirectly through training teachers is to train teachers to change their teaching process, teaching styles, in order to influence students' self-efficacy. Siegle [2003] trained teachers for their teaching strategies in three aspects (goal setting, teacher feedback and mode demonstration) by the means of 35-page training handbook (the handbook includes the basic principles of self-efficacy and the supporting research into strategies of improving students' self-efficacy) and video (the video shows how other teachers implement such strategies). The training aims to make teachers implement such strategies in teaching process, in order to increase students' self-efficacy and accordingly improve students' academic performance. Research showed that such teaching strategies as goal setting, teacher feedback and mode demonstration can improve students' self-efficacy.

## Deficiencies in the Previous Research

Most research probes into the relationship between self-efficacy and students' academic performance and other related factors, and studies the internal psychological mechanism affecting individuals' self-efficacy (for example, the different influence from female and male peers in mode demonstration). Not many researchers probed into the development of self-efficacy.

The previous research into the development of self-efficacy was conducted under experimental situations. But the development of learning self-efficacy can not be separated from specific education and teaching situations and specific subject because the experimental situations are very different from actual situations and self-efficacy essentially is the confidence of individuals in their certain behavioral competence under a certain natural situation.

The previous research into the development of self-efficacy does not build a mode specially based on the characteristics of teaching of a subject.

The object of intervention is either teacher or students. No intervention of both teacher and students are available.

## The Value and Basis of the Present Research

### 1) Value of the Present Research

### It Expands the Application Fields of Self-Efficacy, Enriches the Theory of Self-Efficacy

The theory of self-efficacy, when it was first proposed, aroused the attention of many researchers and application fields. Today international research into self-efficacy has been expanded to the fields of mental health education, psychological counseling and psychotherapy, career choice, management, learning, etc. However, most research was conducted in and most achievements were realized in the field of learning. Most of the recent research probes into the relationship between self-efficacy and variables affecting learning (such as capacity, learning strategies, learning interests, learning motivation, self-monitoring, etc.) and academic performance; the specialty and generalness of self-efficacy (for example, whether learning self-efficacy specially targets at a certain problem, a certain task, a certain subject? Does general self-efficacy exist?); the appropriateness and stability of the strength of self-efficacy (for example, is it true that the stronger the self-efficacy the better? How about the stability of learning self-efficacy?), etc. Not many researchers probed into the development of self-efficacy. Building the modes for developing students' learning self-efficacy based on the characteristics of teaching of a subject and the theory of self-efficacy is very significant in expanding the application fields of self-efficacy and enriching the theory of self-efficacy.

### It Compensates for the Deficiencies of the Research into Infiltrating Psychological Suzhi-Based Education in Teaching of a Subject, and Promotes the Further Implementation of Psychological Suzhi-Based Education.

Psychological suzhi-based education in school is a systematic program. The infiltration of psychological suzhi-based education in teaching of a subject is one of the basic means of psychological suzhi-based education in school, and also one of the sub-programs of psychological suzhi-based education program in school. Subject infiltration is to, according to the feature of the subject during the teaching, find out the connection between teaching of subject and the development of students' psychological suzhi, apply psychological suzhi-based education approaches and strategies with clear objectives and well-prepared plans, infiltrate psychological suzhi-based education content into teaching of a subject, promote students' mental health and develop sound psychological suzhi of students so as to achieve the fundamental goal of psychological suzhi-based education. From the perspective of education practice, specific-problem-based training, consultation and counseling, the two means of implementing psychological suzhi-based education in school, have been well developed in different kinds and levels of schools; however, the infiltration of psychological suzhi-based education in teaching of a subject is still weak and hysteretic. It is because infiltration of psychological suzhi-based education in teaching of a subject is relatively complicated, which requires high quality of teachers. It is also because of insufficient research into infiltration of psychological suzhi-based education in teaching of a subject. Building the mode for developing self-efficacy among middle school students based on the characteristics of teaching of a subject and the theory of self-efficacy can provide reference for infiltrating psychological suzhi-based education in teaching of a subject, in order to realize further research into this field.

### It Maintains Mental Health of Students and Promotes the Development of Students' Potentials.

Learning self-efficacy has important influence on students' learning and life. The major task of students is learning. The content of learning is new everyday. Students usually encounter difficulty and challenges in learning. Without good learning self-efficacy, the learning of students can not be supported, which will result in mental disorders such as anxiety in learning, physical and mental confusion and helplessness. Learning self-efficacy is an important variable for whether students can achieve good academic performance and whether their psychological health and health development in all their life can be ensured.

Improvement of learning efficacy can improve students' academic performance, resulting in learning and growth healthily, confidently and happily. Therefore, developing students' learning self-efficacy not only can promote the improvement of academic performance, but also is very significant in maintaining mental health and developing psychological potentials of students.

## 2) Research Basis

### Theoretical Basis:

*Research into psychological suzhi-based education theory.* Zhang et al. conducted systematic research into the basic theoretical problems of psychological suzhi-based education of students. He defined psychological suzhi and psychological suzhi-based education; analyzed the structure of students' psychological suzhi; developed psychological suzhi scale with relatively high reliability and validity for students from universities, middle schools and primary schools; probed into the objectives, principles, contents, means and implementing strategies of psychological suzhi-based education for students from middle schools and primary schools; built basic psychological suzhi-based education mode (specific-problem-based training, consultation and counseling, subject infiltration); preliminarily proposed the integrated mode of psychological suzhi-based education for students. Those research results provide solid theoretical foundation and empirical evidence for the present research.

*Research into the theory of subject infiltration.* Although the research into the theory of subject infiltration is weak and not systematic, the available theoretical research provides useful reference for the present research. For example, the implementing strategies, principles and requirements of infiltrating psychological suzhi-based education in teaching of a subject provide reference for the strategies and modes proposed in this chapter.

*Theory of self-efficacy.* The theory includes the function and connotation of self-efficacy, agent function mechanism of self-efficacy, factors affecting the formation and development of self-efficacy, and the cognitive processing mechanism of efficacy information. The connotation of self-efficacy makes the development of self-efficacy possible; the functions of self-efficacy indicate the significance of self-efficacy; factors affecting the formation and development of self-efficacy provide operating indicators for developing students' self-efficacy; the cognitive processing mechanism of efficacy information provides principles for developing self-efficacy.

### Empirical Basis:

*Teaching practice of psychological suzhi-based education and subject infiltration.* ii) Experimental research into developing self-efficacy of students. In academic field, researchers did research into self-efficacy, academic performance and other factors affecting academic performance, which provide empirical evidence for the present research.

## 5.1.7. Training of Thought and Scheme of the Present Research

### 1) Purpose and Content of Research

The present research aims to seek for effective means and strategies of developing students' learning self-efficacy in teaching of math in junior middle school through educational experiment and subject infiltration in math teaching of junior grade two; and to probe into the applicability and effectivity of the mode for infiltrating psychological suzhi-based education in teaching of a subject.

The content of research includes the following two aspects: i) building the mode for developing self-efficacy in math teaching among middle school students, in order to provide new approaches for developing self-efficacy of students, and to provide empirical evidence for how to develop students' psychological suzhi in teaching of a specific subject. ii) Implementing the mode proposed and verifying the applicability and effectivity of the mode.

### 2) Hypotheses

Hypothesis 1: developing self-efficacy in teaching of a subject can also effectively improve students' academic performance;

Hypothesis 2: developing self-efficacy in teaching of a subject (take math as an example) can maintain mental health and promote the improvement and development of students' psychological suzhi in certain aspects.

### 3) Main Tools Used in the Research

#### Self-Report Questionnaire of Self-Efficacy

This questionnaire was developed by Kou based on the *Teacher Efficacy Scale* by Gibson and Dembo [1984]. It includes 21 items. Items with positive and reverse scoring account for 50% respectively. It is rated based on a 5-point Likert scale. The test-retest reliability is 0.84. The split-half reliability is 0.77. The criterion-related validity is 0.56.

#### Questionnaire of Self-Efficacy in Math Learning for Middle School Students

This questionnaire was revised based on the *Questionnaire of Self-efficacy in Math Learning for Middle School Students* by Mao. It includes three sub-scales: curriculum sub-scale (4 items), task sub-scale (13 items), and problem sub-scale (18 items). The internal consistency reliability is 0.658 for curriculum sub-scale, 0.687 for task sub-scale; 0.724 for problem sub-scale; and 0.750 for the total scale. The validity is 0.846.

#### Attribution Questionnaire

We used the Achievement sub-scale of the *Multidimensional-Multi-attributional Causality Scale* by Lefcourt et al. [1989]. This sub-scale includes 24 items, with 12 items for success and 12 for failure. Academic achievement can be attributed to four factors, i.e., capacity and effort of internal control, luck and background of external control. It is rated on a 5-point Likert scale. The internal consistency reliability of the scale is between 0.58-0.80.

### The Mental Quality Questionnaire for Middle School Students

This questionnaire was established by Zhang, Feng et al. It includes 155 items and is composed of metacognitive sub-questionnaire, personality sub-questionnaire and adaptability sub-questionnaire. The test-retest correlation of the questionnaire is 0.853. The test-retest correlation of factors is between 0.76 and 0.84. The internal consistency reliability of the questionnaire is 0.839. The internal consistency reliability of the factors is between 0.72 and 0.78. The correlation of factors is between 0.251 and 0.541. Therefore, the scale has high reliability and good construct validity.

### The Mental Health Questionnaire for Middle School Students

This questionnaire was established by Wang in 1997 for middle school students in China with good validity and reliability. It includes 10 sub-scales and 60 items, such as compulsion, paranoia, hostility, interpersonal stress, sensitivity, depression, anxiety, learning pressure, poor adaptability, emotional imbalance, etc. It is rated on a 5-point Likert scale (no, slight, moderate, serious, very serious) to assess the total average scores and average scores of 10 factors.

The normal range of the total average scores and average scores of factors is less than 2.00; the scores between 2.00 and 2.99 indicate slight psychological problem; the scores between 3.00 and 3.99 indicate moderate psychological problem; the scores between 4.00 and 4.99 indicate serious psychological problem; and the score of 5 indicates very serious problem.

### Statistics Tools

SPSS 10.0 software for Windows 2000 was used for data analysis.

# BUILDING TEACHING MODES

## Principles and Strategies for Infiltrating Psychological Suzhi-Based Education in Teaching of a Subject

Developing students' self-efficacy in math teaching is the specific implementation of infiltrating psychological suzhi-based education in teaching of a subject; thus the principles, strategies and methods of infiltrating psychological suzhi-based education in teaching of a subject must be followed in developing students' self-efficacy in math teaching.

### 1) Principles for Infiltrating Psychological Suzhi-Based Educationin Teaching of a Subject

In addition to the general principles of psychological suzhi-based education, we believe that the following principles must be followed in infiltrating psychological suzhi-based education in teaching of a subject:

### Integration of Objectives

Infiltration of psychological suzhi-based education in teaching of a subject includes two parts, i.e., teaching of a subject and psychological suzhi-based education. The key in infiltrating psychological suzhi-based education in teaching of a subject is to handle with the relationship between the two reasonably, correctly and properly. Without correctly understanding the relationship between the two, it is easily to go two extremes, concentrating too much on psychological suzhi-based education but neglecting the teaching of a subject, and imparting the knowledge of psychological suzhi-based education but neglecting the development of psychological suzhi. The objective of teaching of a subject and psychological suzhi-based education objective are closely related to each other and influence each other. They should both be reflected in the teaching, but they are not equally important. The objective of teaching of a subject is primary, whereas psychological suzhi-based education objective is secondary. In teaching, the objective of teaching of a subject should be realized first. Even in the classroom teaching, the primary and main objective is imparting and mastering of knowledge and skills of the subject. Infiltration of psychological suzhi-based education in teaching is the secondary and auxiliary objective. However, it does not mean that psychological suzhi-based education objective is not important or it can be neglected. It is secondary only by comparing with the teaching objectives. In terms of classroom teaching, they are integrated in the teaching process.

**Intrinsic Relevance**

The content of psychological suzhi-based education must meet the intrinsic rules of teaching of a subject, namely, the content of psychological suzhi-based education is naturally derived from teaching process and the textbook, rather than beyond the teaching process or the textbook.

**Natural, Flexible and Proper Infiltration**

Natural infiltration refers to that teachers should explore the reasonable infiltration point for psychological suzhi-based education based on the available resources contained in content of the teaching; any infiltration just for infiltration is unwise. Proper infiltration is reflected by three aspects: first, proper relationship, i.e., the primary and secondary roles of the teaching of a subject and the infiltration of psychological suzhi-based education in the teaching should be properly handled with; second, proper timing, i.e., within the effective time of a class, the time for infiltrating psychological suzhi-based education should not be long; third, proper objective, i.e., the objective should not be set too high or too low, instead the objective should meet the level and characteristics of psychological development of students. Flexible infiltration is reflected by two aspects: first flexible contents, i.e., teachers determined different content of infiltration according to different situations of classes under the preconditions that teachers fully understand the psychological conditions of students and the content of infiltration meets the intrinsic rules. Second, flexible styles of infiltration, namely the styles of infiltrating psychological suzhi-based education in teaching of a subject should be flexible.

*2) Strategies for Infiltrating Psychological Suzhi-Based Educationin Teaching of a Subject*

The strategies and methods to infiltrate psychological suzhi-based education in teaching of a subject are reflected by how to reasonably determine the points of infiltration. We believe that the points of infiltration can be determined by the contents of teaching, the teaching process, teachers and the psychological environment in class.

Different subjects have different resources of psychological suzhi-based education due to their different natures. The nature of subjects can be divided into three categories: first, subjects of social sciences, such as Chinese language, history, geography, ideological and moral education, politics, etc. Rich resources of psychological suzhi-based education are directly or indirectly embedded in such subjects. Second, subjects of arts and physical education, including music, art and physical education. More psychological suzhi-based education resources can be derived from these subjects. For example, music and art classes are good carriers of psychological suzhi-based education. Thus the infiltration of psychological suzhi-based education in these two categories of subjects can be started from the contents of teaching. Third, subjects of physical science, including biology, math, physics and chemistry. The learning of such subjects requires not only cognitive activities such as observation, memory, attention, imagination and thinking, but also the supports of psychological traits. Because the content of such subjects is abstract and logic, it is very difficult to explore psychological traits as in the other two categories of subjects. Thus the infiltration in such subjects should be started from the teaching process. To develop good cognitive abilities in subjects of physical science, such as observation, memory, imagination and thinking, can be started from the content of teaching.

From the human perspective, teacher is also a point of infiltration. Teacher plays an important role in students' life. Students can not only obtain information of knowledge, but also much comprehensive psychological information of emotion, will and character. In the teaching process, students are not only the passive receiver of knowledge, but also selectively accept the information presented to them. In this communicating and experiencing environment, the psychology of students also develops. In addition, class environment is the psychological field affecting students' psychological change. Good psychological field has positive field effects, which optimizes students' psychological environment, making students feel safe and freely to express their opinions without worrying about being laughed at or criticized and thus they do not experience the anxiety and stress.

## Means and Methods to Develop Students' Self-Efficacy

### 1) Strengthening Success Experience in Learning Activities

The success/failure experience is the most basic and important means of acquiring self-efficacy and also the most reliable foundation for individuals to develop self-efficacy. The self-efficacy developed on this basis is steady and can be extended to other areas of activity [Bandura, Adams and Beyer, 1977]. The effects of self-efficacy information obtained through other resources are usually determined by the experience of success and failure in real activities. Only when an individual succeeds in activities, the information provided by vicarious experience, verbal persuasion, and physiological arousal can be accepted by the individual in the cognitive structure. Therefore, the most effective means to develop self-efficacy is to provide more opportunities of success experience for students.

## 1) Removal of the Competitive Reward Structure in Class, Building Cooperative and Individual Reward Structures

Ames [1981] did a lot research into reward structure. He classified reward structure in class into competitive, cooperative and individual reward structures. Competitive reward structure leads to comparison among individuals, and only when one's performance is better than all the rest, one can obtain reward. Cooperative reward structure requires comparison among teams, and whether an individual obtains reward depends on whether the team is successful. Individual reward structure requires comparison with oneself, and as soon as one's current performance is better than one's performance in the past, one can obtain reward.

Competition emphasizes on social comparison, which makes most students become the failure in the competition and thus harm the development of their self-efficacy. Individual reward structure requires one compares with oneself. As soon as one's current performance exceeds the past, one is successful. Generally speaking, it is not easy to exceed others' performance, but it is easier to exceed one's own performance in the past. Therefore, individual reward structure provides more success opportunities for students and thus students have confidence in their capacity and their self-efficacy is improved. Cooperative reward structure requires comparison among teams. The reward of an individual is positively related to the achievement of the team, i.e., the reward of an individual relies on team success. Under cooperative reward structure, an individual's success also helps some other people to succeed, which provides more opportunities for students with learning difficulty than the competitive reward structure, and thus students' self-efficacy is improved.

## 2) Developing Positive Expectations, Avoid Negative Expectations

Teaching is an organized social activity with plans and purposes. How teachers treat the students is always influenced by their expectation toward students. From the nature perspective, teachers' expectation towards students can be divided into positive expectations and negative expectations. Expectations of different natures make teachers treat students differently, which then influences the opportunities of students to experience success and thus influence students' self-efficacy. Positive expectation makes teachers treat students with positive attitude, thus students have more opportunities to experience success and their self-efficacy is improved. However, negative expectation makes teachers treat students with negative attitude, thus students have fewer opportunities to experience success and develop capacity, and their self-efficacy is decreased. Positive expectation is based on the actual capacity of students and the vision of development of the teachers. Research showed that if teachers have positive expectation on students rather than negative expectation, providing more opportunities for students to experience success and develop capacity, students' self-efficacy can be improved.

The key to build positive expectation and remove negative expectation is to remove the unequal teacher-student interaction mechanism and to set up equal teacher-student interaction mechanism. Self-efficacy is the self-judgment of an individual on the efficacy of activities. Such self-judgment is based on certain knowledge or information basis. In addition to individuals' direct success/failure experience and social persuasion information, vicarious success/failure experience is also an important source for an individual to develop self-efficacy. The efficacy information of vicarious success/failure experience refers to that when an individual sees another person with similar capacity succeed in an activity, the individual believes that he/she can also succeed in similar activities or situations, and then the self-efficacy of such individual is improved. In class interaction, unequal teacher-student interaction mechanism makes students with average and bad academic performance rarely have opportunity to participate in interaction. Under such situation, they rarely have chance to experience success in class, and they rarely have chance to see students with similar academic performance succeed in the teaching activities, which results in that they have less and less success experience in teaching activities, and thus the development of their self-efficacy is harmed. In addition, unequal teacher-student interaction mechanism also impacts the development of students' self-efficacy in the form of social persuasion information. Teacher is the important person in students' learning and life. Students' understanding of their own capacity can be easily influenced by teachers' speech evaluation. In the class interaction, if teachers are indifferent to the right answer of students with bad academic performance or if they criticize them for incorrect answers, these students will underestimate their capacity and thus their self-efficacy is reduced.

To build an equal teacher-student interaction mechanism, the following two aspects should be realized. First, equal interaction opportunities should be provided, for example, teachers should ask questions of proper difficulty according to the capacity of students, thus students can answer the questions with certain efforts. Second, treat all students with the same attitude, namely equal interaction. For example, if students (especially students with poor academic performance) can not answer questions or have the incorrect answer, teachers should be patient and allow enough time for thinking, or provide simple hints or ask simpler questions.

### 2) Developing Students' Positive Attributional Styles

Self-efficacy interacts with the attributional style of an individual: Students with high self-efficacy tend to attribute their success to stable internal factors (such as capacity) and attribute failure to controllable internal factors (such as insufficient efforts). Such positive attributional style strengthens their self-efficacy. On the contrary, students with low self-efficacy tend to attribute their success to external factors (such as luck, easy task) and attribute failure to uncontrollable factors (such as capacity). Such negative attributional style leads to the sense of powerless of students and dramatically reduces self-efficacy. Therefore, students' negative attributional style must be changed to positive attributional style in order to strengthen their self-efficacy. Increasing the success experience is an important means to develop positive attributional style. It is because frequent success makes individuals tend to attribute success to internal factors and attribute failure to insufficient efforts (controllable factors). In addition to increasing success experience, the following means can also be used to develop students' positive attributional style:

### Removal of Competitive Reward Structure, Building Individual Reward Structure

Reward structure is an important factor affecting the attributional styles of an individual. Under competitive reward structure, an individual often attributes failure to insufficient capacity (negative attributional style); whereas under individual reward structure, an individual tends to attribute failure to insufficient efforts (positive attributional style). It is because individual reward structure requires comparison with oneself, which makes an individual concentrate on the task and believes that effort is the means to perform task and that one will succeed with efforts. Research also proves that students under individual reward structure have more tendencies to attribute academic performance to efforts than students under competitive reward structure [Liu, 1992].

Building individual reward structure is the necessary condition for developing students' positive attributional style. The research into attribution training showed that children who received attribution training have more tendencies to attribute failure to insufficient efforts than those who did not, thus they are less influenced by failure experience. Researchers hold that the concepts of most attribution training are to help students to build their own targets of academic performance. Then students judge their academic performance based on their academic performance in the past rather than others' academic performance. Even their academic performance is worse than others', but exceeds their own academic performance in the past, then their efforts yield. Therefore, a classroom environment which helps to build students' own targets must be created, i.e., building individual reward structure, in order to develop students' positive attributional style.

### Appropriate Speech Evaluation

Teachers' verbal evaluation on students also influences students' self-attribution. Research showed that praise which is usually deemed as positive evaluation does not always work in improving students' initiative; whereas criticism which is usually deemed as negative evaluation does not always reduce students' initiative. How praise and criticism influence students' initiative depends on the difficulty of the task. The praise to students accomplishing easy tasks may lead to under-evaluation of their own capability. The criticism to students who failed easy tasks may make students attribute to insufficient efforts, and then students may feel guilty and double their efforts for success. How praise and criticism influence students' initiative depends on the difficulty of tasks, therefore the verbal evaluation of teachers on students should be based on the difficulty of tasks. Teachers should praise students who successfully accomplish difficult tasks and guide them to attribute to strong capacity and eventually to improve their self-efficacy. Teachers should properly criticize students who did not accomplish easy tasks, in order to make them make more efforts in learning. The difficulty of tasks mentioned is based on the actual capacity of certain students rather than as deemed by teachers or other students.

### Timely Help and Instruction

In teaching, teachers usually provide help and instruction for students in learning, especially for slow learners, in order to make students successfully accomplish learning tasks. But the help and instruction provided by teachers should be diversified according to different difficulty of tasks and different students. Help and instruction to students when they are smoothly accomplishing tasks do not promote independent thinking of students or improve their learning capacity, but make students attribute the help and instruction to low capacity and eventually their self-efficacy is reduced.

The last but not the least, developing students' positive attributional style does not mean students should attribute success to capacity and efforts and attribute failure to insufficient efforts at all time. If students did contribute lots of efforts but still failed, teachers should help students to attribute failure to external factors, such as difficulty of tasks and physical conditions. If students always attribute failure to insufficient efforts, they may feel powerless. It may harm their self-efficacy, or even cause depression and harm their physical health.

### 3) Instruction of Learning Methods, Strategies and Goal Setting

Research showed that students' self-efficacy, learning strategies and academic performance are significantly positively correlated to each other. Students with high self-efficacy and good academic performance usually can better utilize learning strategies; whereas students with low self-efficacy and bad academic performance usually can not utilize learning strategies well. Meanwhile, learning strategies in return influence students' self-efficacy and academic performance. If students can better utilize learning strategies, they will have better confidence and better academic performance; otherwise they will have low self-efficacy and poor academic performance. Therefore, teachers should teach students to master some basic learning strategies (for example, strategies of repeating, further processing and organization) based on specific content of teaching, and should show students how to utilize such strategies. This is also one of the important means for students to improve their self-efficacy and academic performance. In addition, proper goal setting based on the capacity of individuals can also improve their self-efficacy. Goal setting significantly influences the development of self-efficacy. Without goals set in advance as the standard for evaluating the academic performance, it is difficult for individuals to evaluate their performance and capacity. With learning goals set in advance, individuals can experience success when they realize such goals, and thus their self-efficacy is improved. In order to play the positive role of goals, teachers when instructing students to set the goals should be aware of that i) goals should be specific, i.e., what tasks should be accomplished and what level of performance should be realized; ii) goals should be challenging, because too low goals can not improve self-efficacy, whereas too high goals may result in failure although individuals contribute lots of efforts and do not promote the improvement of self-efficacy either; iii) goals should be short-term goals. It is because goals for the far-reaching future can not provide effective stimulation and instruction for the current behaviors of individuals. Short-term goals can not only tell individuals what to do at present, but also make individuals experience success when they are realized.

## Standard of Math Curriculum and New Textbooks

The *Mathematics Curriculum Standard for Full-time Compulsory Education* was issued by the Ministry of Education of the P. R. C. in July 2001. The standard, as the programmatic document for math teaching in compulsory education in the 21$^{st}$ Century, considers factors affecting math education, including the development of modern science and technology, the development of math, upgrading of educational concepts and the psychological laws of math learning among pupils and junior middle school students, and the current math teaching; systematically puts forward the basic goals and suggestions for math education in China for the next 10 years. It guides the new round of reform in math education.

### 1) Basic Concepts for the Standardization of Math Curriculum in Compulsory Education

Basic Concept One: the math curriculum in compulsory education strives to achieve that everybody can learn valuable math and obtain necessary math and different people can develop in math differently.

Basic Concept Two: effective math learning activities are reflected by independent exploration and cooperation and communication rather than copy and enhancement, i.e., the content of math teaching should promote students' math activities, such as observation, experiment, conjecture, verification, reasoning and communication; and should not be for imitation and memory.

Basic Concept Three: the evaluation of students' math learning aims to understand their math learning in all aspects, motivate their learning and improve teachers' teaching. The evaluation focuses more on vertical development of students rather than horizontal development. The evaluation should not only consider the results of learning but also the process of learning, and both the level of learning and the emotion and attitude of students in math activities, in order to help them understand themselves and build up confidence.

To sum up, the math curriculum standard, in addition to making students acquire basic knowledge and skills of math, focuses on the all-around development of students in emotion, attitude, values and ordinary capacity. Math learning methods, such as independent exploration, cooperation and communication, practice and innovation, are advocated in the math curriculum standard. The math curriculum standard emphasizes students' innovative spirits and practice capacity, and fully affirms the roles of students in the classroom teaching as the agent.

### 2) Main Characteristics of New Textbooks

First, the role of students as the agent is reflected in the new textbooks. Abundant inspiring, challenging and exploratory questions are designed in the textbooks, such as "Think", "Discussion" and "Do". Students can think in "Think" questions, practice in "Do" questions, communicate in "Discussion" questions, and discover in the "Try" questions. In the textbooks, students have the initiative in learning. Students will experience the acquiring and utilization of math knowledge through personal experience in the democratic, relaxing and pleasing classroom environment.

Second, the new textbooks provide diversified teaching environments. The textbooks have new contents and are more difficult, for example, "solid figure", "statistics and probability" etc are new for grade seven. But students are able to gradually accumulate knowledge in various experiences and feel wonderful math since the textbooks provide diversified, relaxing and pleasing environments for activities. The new textbooks especially pay attention to activity participation of students, encourage students to describe by using their own language, experience new knowledge by initiative thinking based on their own knowledge, encourage more communication with peers, motivate students to discover and innovate in practice activities, and encourage students to make breakthrough in difficult points and solve questions in the process of thinking, practice, communication and exploration.

From the mentioned analysis, we know that both the math curriculum standard and the new textbooks attach highly to the development of students' innovative spirit and practice capacity, fully affirm students' role as the agent in teaching. Thus we need to consider the new concepts of math curriculum standard and the changing of new textbooks in building the mode to develop self-efficacy.

## Building the Mode to Develop Self-Efficacy of Students in Math Teaching

We preliminarily established the "cooperation, discussion and feedback" mode (see Table 5.1) for developing students' self-efficacy in math teaching based on the theory of self-efficacy, the principles of infiltrating psychological suzhi-based education in teaching of a subject, the characteristics of math teaching in middle schools and the teaching requirements.

The following demonstrate how the mode works:

First, teachers put forward questions and learning tasks. Students independently think about the learning tasks (they can either be the trouble shooting or the preparation for the new knowledge) in order to have preliminary perceptual knowledge of the learning tasks, have their own understanding and find the difficult points (questions can be put forward at the very beginning, in the middle or at the end of the class).

Students start to communicate their understanding and experience of learning in a team. They can put forward their own opinions for discussion, evaluation and analysis in the team, listen to others' opinions, and open up thinking. Eventually, a common understanding is reached within the team. A representative is selected by turns from the team to describe the common understanding of the team. By doing this, students' initiative, participation, sense of team responsibility and sense of honor can be stimulated (team communication can be properly organized at the beginning of the class or after class, depending on how many the contents of teaching are, the progress of teaching and the difficulty of teaching). Meanwhile, teachers should guide and monitor the cooperation of each team.

The team representative (selected by turns) reports to the class about the team cooperation. The report may include the answers of the team to the learning task and the difficulties of team. The report can be in any form. Teams with different opinions can communicate with this team. Teachers can evaluate and encourage the team report. And the evaluation should not only for the representative, but also for the team.

In this process, teachers should pay attention to the following:

In order to make as many students at different levels of learning capacity experience success; teachers should set questions of different difficulty before the class or in the teaching, and ask different students the questions of different difficulty.

If students answer the questions right, teachers should positively encourage them and positively attribute their good performance. If students have difficulty in the presentation or answering the questions or their thinking is obstructed due to nervousness, anxiety and timidity, teachers should on one hand be patient and positively guide them, provide necessary hints or clues or provide more time for students to think, rather than stop or interrupt them rudely, and in no event satirize them.

On the other hand, teachers should relieve students' anxiety and nervousness through smiles, and by looking at them with encouragement and expectations.

Teachers, during the communication of students, should try to create a democratic, relaxing and harmonious atmosphere in class, in order to realize normal and orderly teaching and enthusiastic learning. Teachers should also answer the questions of the teams and the class, and find out the gap between the teaching objectives and the actual learning of students, in order to lay foundation for the teaching next time.

Extension, revealing of connotation. After learning in the mentioned processes, students may feel that they have already known the answers to the questions or have mastered the knowledge, thus they may be less concentrated and have less participative behaviors.

Therefore, teachers should put forward questions at a higher level, which can not only causes cognitive dissonance of students, stimulates students' interests, but also makes students know the relation and difference of knowledge and master the essence and principles.

Summary, highlighting the important and difficulty points, reflection and evaluation. Math as a subject is highly abstract and systematic. Besides, the abstractness of math is of different levels.

Teachers should guide students to discuss the questions at the abstract level, rather than only focusing on the question itself. Teachers should instruct students to summarize the learning and activities into systematic knowledge. Teachers should instruct students to undertake reflection and evaluation.

Through reflection, students can better connect new knowledge and old knowledge logically and firmly, in order to build new cognitive structure.

Through reflection, students can also find out the difficulty to understand knowledge in learning, evaluate the sparkles of thinking in the cognitive processing and realize thinking mathematically.

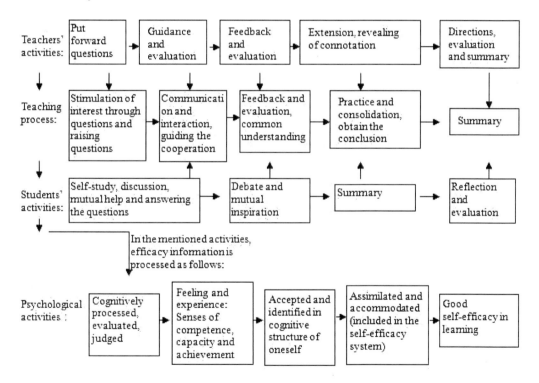

Figure 5.1. Mode to Develop Students' Learning Self-efficacy in Math Teaching.

# EXPERIMENTAL RESEARCH IN EDUCATION

## Purpose

It aims to verify whether the mode of developing students' self-efficacy in math teaching can effectively improve students' learning self-efficacy.

## Participants

Students from Class Seven and Class Eight of junior grade two from one local middle school in Chongqing participated in the experiment. Class Seven was the experimental group which consists of 79 students, including 48 boys and 31 girls. Class Eight was the control group which also consists of 79 students, including 45 boys and 34 girls.

## Design of the Experiment

In the experiment, we designed pre-test and post-test for both experimental and control groups.

### Table 5.2. Experimental Treatment

|  | Pre-Test | Discussion and Feedback Mode | Post-Test |
|---|---|---|---|
| Experimental Group | O1 | X | O2 |
| Control Group | O3 | — | O4 |

The questionnaires used in the pre-test include self-report questionnaire of self-efficacy, attribution questionnaire, mental health questionnaire for middle school students, mental quality questionnaire for middle school students, the final examination paper for junior grade one. Except the attribution questionnaire, $O_1$ is the same as $O_2$. The questionnaires used in the post-test include self-report questionnaire of self-efficacy, self-efficacy questionnaire of math learning for middle school students, mental health questionnaire for middle school students, mental quality questionnaire for middle school students, the final examination paper for the first semester of junior grade two. The psychometric tools of $O_3$ and $O_4$ are different from $O_1$.

## Variables

### Independent Variable: Mode of Developing Learning Self-Efficacy in Math Teaching

Dependent variables: level of academic self-efficacy, level of self-efficacy in math learning, academic performance of math, psychological suzhi and mental health.

## Control Variables

The experimental group and control group were reasonably determined. The academic self-efficacy, academic performance and the initial level of psychological suzhi of both experimental and control groups should be at the same level. The number of students, sex ratio of both groups should be almost the same.

Different teachers were chosen for each group respectively, in order to avoid the teacher unconsciously transfers the independent variable to the control group. However, the teachers for the groups should have the same gender, almost the same years of teaching, competence of teaching and teaching styles (teachers can be chosen through the recommendation of school leaders, teachers' resume, and information feedback by students).

Strict and unified directions should be used in the test. The scores of the test should not be recorded in the school report card. The time for the test taken by the subjects should be controlled.

## The Experiment Procedures

*Establishing cooperation teams.* First, established the cooperation team of eight students according to the math foundation, math capacity and the academic performance of math. The proportion of students with good, average and bad academic performance of math was 1:2:1. The sex ratio of the team should be reasonable. The students within a team sit together. At the beginning of the experiment, a student with strong organizing capacity, better academic performance and eager to help was appointed by the teacher or selected by team members as the team leader. The team leader functioned as a little teacher to tutor the team, and created a good atmosphere of mutual learning in the team, in order to achieve better performance for top students, progress of students with lower academic performance and overall progress of the team. Second, the team leader was trained. The training was in the form of informal discussion, focusing on the awareness to help others, team spirit and team-work. In the experiment, individual instruction can be carried out to a certain team leader according to the real situations of the team. Rotation and assignment were used for determining the team leader in the middle and late period of the experiment.

The "cooperation, discussion and feedback" teaching mode was used in every math class of the experimental group, in order to develop students' learning self-efficacy. The teaching procedure under this mode was "success experience + guiding positive attribution + mode demonstration + positive evaluation, positive expectation + learning strategies, goal setting etc → internalization as one part of the self-mental structure of students → high learning self-efficacy". The cooperative learning team was established to realize positive evaluation and expectation. Under such mode, students obtained the success experience of practice. The mode demonstration in teaching made students obtain vicarious success experience. Students were guided to attribute positively. Instructions of learning strategies were carried out in the teaching. Teachers helped students to set learning goals, learning plans and to master learning methods. The teaching of the control group was routine teaching.

## Experimental Results and Analysis

### 1) Analysis of Self-Efficacy Test Results of the Two Groups

### Results of Self-Report Questionnaire

Comparison of pre-test and post-test scores of self-efficacy between two groups.

**Table 5.3. Comparison of Pre-Test and Post-Test Scores of Self-Efficacy between Two Groups**

| Groups | Pre-Test ($M \pm SD$) | Post-Test ($M \pm SD$) | $t$ |
|---|---|---|---|
| Experimental Group (n=74) | 3.55±0.57 | 3.67±0.45 | -2.51* |
| Control Group (n=73) T | 3.53±0.51 0.29 | 3.52±0.44 2.01* | 0.04 |

Note: * p<0.05 **p<0.01 *** p<0.001.

According to Table 5.3, there was no significant difference in pre-test scores of self-efficacy between the experimental and control groups. However, the difference between two groups was significant ($p<0.05$) in the post-test. No obvious difference was found between the pre-test and post-test for the control group, while significant difference was found between the pre-test and post-test for the experimental group ($p<0.05$).

### Comparison of Students with Different Levels of Self-Efficacy between Two Groups

In order to investigate the different effects of the experiment on students with different levels of self-efficacy, we divided the students from two groups into three teams respectively according to the pre-test results of self-report questionnaire of self-efficacy (the standard for dividing the teams is the ± standard deviation of the mean value.

**Table 5.4. Comparison of Students with Different Levels of Self-Efficacy between Two Groups**

| Teams | Groups | Pre-Test ($M \pm SD$) | Post-Test ($M \pm SD$) | $t$ |
|---|---|---|---|---|
| High Self-efficacy Team | Experimental Group (n=17) | 4.26±0.15 | 4.15±0.38 | 1.49 |
| | Control Group (n=14) | 4.08±0.43 | 3.89±0.62 | 1.37 |
| Average Self-efficacy Team | Experimental Group (n=42) | 3.55±0.27 | 3.59±0.37 | 1.21* |
| | Control Group (n=44) | 3.61±0.27 | 3.42±0.36 | -0.85 |
| Low Self-efficacy Team | Experimental Group (n=15) | 2.72±0.32 | 3.56±0.44 | 2.27* |
| | Control Group (n=15) | 2.78±0.24 | 3.29±0.21 | -0.64 |

Those that were one standard deviation higher than the mean value were classified as the high self-efficacy team; those that were one standard deviation lower than the mean value were classified as the low self-efficacy team; those that were between the mentioned two teams are classified as average self-efficacy team). Then we compared the pre-test and post-test results of self-efficacy among students from three teams, as shown in Table 5-4.

According to Table 5-4, in the post-test of two groups, there was no significant difference between high self-efficacy teams. But for both the average and low level teams, the difference between the pre-test and post-test was significant, indicating that the experiment intervention was effective for students from the average self-efficacy team and low self-efficacy team.

### Comparison of Self-Efficacy among Students with Different Levels of Academic Performance from Two Groups

In order to investigate the different effects of the experiment on students with different academic performance, we classified students from two groups into top students, average students and slow learners according to the evaluation of the head teacher and the scores of the final examination of Chinese language, math and English language for junior grade one.

**Table 5.5. Comparison of Self-Efficacy Among Students with Different Levels of Academic Performance from Two Groups**

| Teams | Groups | Pre-Test ($M \pm SD$) | Post-Test ($M \pm SD$) |
|---|---|---|---|
| Top students with high self-efficacy | Experimental Group (n=8) | 4.23±0.38 | 4.02±0.33 |
| | Control Group (n=4) | 4.06±0.39 | 3.55±0.56 |
| | $t$ | 0.84 | 1.86 |
| Top students with average self-efficacy | Experimental Group (n=10) | 3.59±0.31 | 3.72±0.45 |
| | Control Group (n=11) | 3.63±0.31 | 3.45±0.35 |
| | $t$ | -0.35 | 1.59 |
| Top students with low self-efficacy | Experimental Group (n=1) | 2.90±0.24 | 3.48±0.31 |
| | Control Group (n=2) | 2.93±0.28 | 3.05±0.20 |
| | $t$ | | |
| Average students with high self-efficacy | Experimental Group (n=5) | 4.33±0.20 | 4.35±0.50 |
| | Control Group (n=8) | 4.22±0.34 | 4.14±0.48 |
| | $t$ | 0.66 | 0.75 |
| Average students with average self-efficacy | Experimental Group (n=24) | 3.61±0.25 | 3.6190±0.30 |
| | Control Group (n=26) | 3.69±0.25 | 3.4827±0.37 |
| | $t$ | -1.04 | 1.37 |
| Average students with low self-efficacy | Experimental Group (n=8) | 2.74±0.21 | 3.65±0.28 |
| | Control Group (n=7) | 2.70±0.29 | 3.29±0.23 |
| | $t$ | 0.33 | 2.65* |
| Slow learners with high self-efficacy | Experimental Group (n=3) | 4.32±0.23 | 4.27±0.33 |
| | Control Group (n=1) | 3.09±0.30 | 4.33±0.24 |
| | $t$ | | |
| Slow learners with average self-efficacy | Experimental Group (n=7) | 3.40±0.20 | 3.44±0.34 |
| | Control Group (n=7) | 3.46±0.16 | 3.31±0.24 |
| | $t$ | -0.69 | 0.82 |
| Slow learners with low self-efficacy | Experimental Group (n=6) | 2.75±0.53 | 3.50±0.65 |
| | Control Group (n=5) | 2.85±0.18 | 3.36±0.17 |
| | $t$ | -0.41 | 0.50 |

And then we compared the pre-test and post-test scores of self-efficacy (the standard to classify the teams with different levels of self-efficacy is the same as mentioned above) among students with different academic performance, as shown in Table 5.5.

Table 5.5 shows that no matter at what levels of academic performance, there was no significant difference in the post-test between the high and average self-efficacy teams. For low self-efficacy team, the post-test results of average students of both groups were significant. And only for experimental group, there was significant difference between pre-test and post-test results ($p<0.001$). The post-test scores of the top students with low self-efficacy of the experimental group were obviously higher than the pre-test scores. But there were not enough samples; we could not prove whether the improvement is significant. For the experimental group, the post-test scores of slow learners with average and low self-efficacy were higher than the pre-test scores. But the difference was not significant.

1. Results of the questionnaire of self-efficacy in math learning for middle school students
2. Comparison of scores for self-efficacy degree in math learning between two groups

We carried out research into independent sample $t$ test, in order to investigate the difference of two groups in increasing degree of self-efficacy.

### Table 5.6. Comparison of Scores for Self-Efficacy Degree in Math Learning between Two Groups

| Groups | Post-Test ($M \pm SD$) |
| --- | --- |
| Experimental Group (n=79) | 0.91±0.12 |
| Control Group (n=69) | 0.82±0.19 |
| $t$ | 3.37*** |

Table 5.6 shows that the increasing degrees for self-efficacy range in math learning between two groups were very significant.

## Comparison of Scores for Self-Efficacy Strength in Math Learning between Two Groups

### Table 5.7. Comparison of Scores for Self-Efficacy Strength in Math Learning between Two Groups

| Groups | Post-Test ($M \pm SD$) | | | |
| --- | --- | --- | --- | --- |
| | Curriculum sub-scale | Task sub-scale | Problem sub-scale | Total scale |
| Experimental Group (n=79) | 4.22±0.84 | 4.64±0.79 | 2.22±0.35 | 3.35±0.51 |
| Control Group (n=69) | 3.92±1.09 | 4.38±0.91 | 2.03±0.46 | 3.12±0.59 |
| $t$ | 1.79 | 1.848 | 2.85** | 2.54* |

Table 5.7 shows that except curriculum sub-scale and task sub-scale, there was no obvious difference between the two groups. The experimental group had obviously higher scores in problem sub-scale and the total scale than the control group.

## 2) Analysis of the Results of Mental Health Questionnaire for Two Groups

We compared the post-test and pre-test results of the experimental group and the control group in order to investigate the influence of the mode on students' mental health.

**Table 5.8. Pre-Test and Post-Test Results of Students' Mental Health Questionnaire between Two Groups (N=77 For Experimental Group; N=75 for Control Group)**

| Factors | Pre-Test ($M \pm SD$) | | Post-Test ($M \pm SD$) | $t$ |
|---|---|---|---|---|
| Interpersonal stress and sensitivity | Experimental Group | 2.55±0.77 | 2.45±0.67 | 1.12 |
| | Control Group | 2.47±0.73 | 2.56±0.82 | -1.05 |
| | $t$ | 0.63 | -0.82 | |
| Depression | Experimental Group | 2.32±0.71 | 2.21±0.66 | 1.71 |
| | Control Group | 2.34±0.75 | 2.42±0.85 | -0.99 |
| | $t$ | -0.12 | -1.69 | |
| Anxiety | Experimental Group | 2.38±0.67 | 2.38±0.68 | 0 |
| | Control Group | 2.61±0.87 | 2.51±0.80 | 1.33 |
| | $t$ | -1.76 | -1.04 | |
| Pressure from learning | Experimental Group | 2.37±0.72 | 2.27±0.66 | 1.28 |
| | Control Group | 2.55±0.90 | 2.62±0.95 | -0.59 |
| | $t$ | -1.35 | -2.59* | |
| Poor adaptability | Experimental Group | 2.28±0.62 | 2.18±0.58 | 1.39 |
| | Control Group | 2.44±0.77 | 2.52±0.76 | -0.69 |
| | $t$ | -1.45 | -3.04** | |
| Emotional imbalance | Experimental Group | 2.64±0.73 | 2.51±0.61 | 1.94 |
| | Control Group | 2.69±0.83 | 2.75±0.79 | -0.60 |
| | $t$ | -0.40 | -2.11* | |
| Factors | Pre-Test ($M \pm SD$) | | Post-Test ($M \pm SD$) | $t$ |
| Psychological imbalance | Experimental Group | 2.12±0.51 | 2.07±0.52 | 0.83 |
| | Control Group | 2.20±0.74 | 2.31±0.77 | |
| | $t$ | -0.80 | -2.21* | -1.10 |
| Psychological health | Experimental Group | 2.35±0.48 | 2.31±0.44 | 1.11 |
| | Control Group | 2.46±0.59 | 2.51±0.63 | -0.86 |
| | $t$ | -1.20 | -2.26* | |

Table 5.8 shows that before the experiment, there was no obvious difference in psychological health between two groups. Both groups had slight psychological problems. After the experiment, the level of psychological problem of the experimental group was reduced and was significantly lower than that of the control group. According to the scores of factors in Table 5.8, the psychological level of experimental group in the post-test was improved, but was not significantly better than in the pre-test. The experimental group had

significantly lower scores in pressure from learning, poor inadaptability, emotional imbalance and psychological imbalance than the control group.

### 3) Analysis of the Results of Psychological Suzhi Questionnaire of the Two Groups

We compared the post-test and pre-test results of the experimental group and the control group in order to investigate the influence of the mode on students' psychological suzhi.

**Table 5.9. Pre-Test and Post-Test Results of Students' Psychological Suzhi Questionnaire Between Two Groups (N=75 for Experimental Group; N=72 for Control Group)**

| Factors | | Pre-Test ($M \pm SD$) | Post-Test ($M \pm SD$) | $t$ |
|---|---|---|---|---|
| Ambition | Experimental Group | 1.81±0.25 | 1.83±0.27 | -0.42 |
| | Control Group | 1.78±0.25 | 1.81±0.29 | -0.01 |
| | $t$ | 0.61 | 0.42 | |
| Self-confidence | Experimental Group | 2.13±0.23 | 2.21±0.24 | -2.58* |
| | Control Group | 1.99±0.35 | 2.03±0.34 | -0.85 |
| | $t$ | 2.75** | 3.70*** | |
| Learning adaptation | Experimental Group | 1.89±0.38 | 2.07±0.32 | - |
| | Control Group | 1.93±0.35 | 1.99±0.34 | 4.84*** |
| | $t$ | -0.63 | 1.41 | -1.48 |
| Emotional adaptation | Experimental Group | 1.96±0.26 | 1.99±0.26 | -1.09 |
| | Control Group | 1.99±0.25 | 1.93±0.25 | -1.76 |
| | $t$ | -0.83 | 1.55 | |
| General quality | Experimental Group | 1.96±0.09 | 1.99±0.07 | -2.60* |
| | Control Group | 1.96±0.10 | 1.97±0.13 | 0.56 |
| | $t$ | 0.25 | 1.20 | |

Table 5.9 shows that the pre-test scores of the experimental group in the factors of ambition, self-confidence, learning adaptation, emotional adaptation and general quality were higher than the post-test scores.

The post-test scores of the experimental group in such factors were higher than that of the control group.

However, significant difference between two groups was only As seen in the factor of self-confidence. The pre-test and post-test results of the experimental group show that the difference between the pre-test and post-test scores in self-confidence, learning adaptation and general quality was very significant.

In particular, the difference between the pre-test and post-test scores in learning adaptation was very significant.

### 4) Analysis of the Results of Academic Performance of Math of the Groups

Table 5-10 shows that there was no obvious difference in the pre-test and post-test scores of academic performance of math between two groups.

**Table 5.10. Comparison of Pre-Test and Post-Test Scores of Academic Performance of Math Between Two Groups**

| Groups | Pre-Test ($M \pm SD$) | Post-Test ($M \pm SD$) |
|---|---|---|
| Experimental Group (n=72) | 94.40±25.88 | 102.38±28.61 |
| Control Group (n=77) | 95.04±25.13 | 100.76±32.17 |
| *t* | -0.15 | 0.32 |

**Table 5.11. Comparison of Pre-Test and Post-Test Scores of Academic Performance of Math Among Students with Different Levels of Self-Efficacy Between Two Groups**

| Teams | Groups | Pre-Test ($M \pm SD$) | Post-Test ($M \pm SD$) |
|---|---|---|---|
| High self-efficacy team | Experimental Group (n=16) | 98.31±29.02 | 107.50±32.17 |
| | Control Group (n=16) | 100.18±27.98 | 99.62±32.21 |
| | *t* | -0.18 | 0.69 |
| Average self-efficacy team | Experimental Group (n=39) | 95.92±23.57 | 101.33±25.68 |
| | Control Group (n=37) | 92.72±24.66 | 98.55±30.87 |
| | *t* | 0.57 | 0.44 |
| Low Self-efficacy Team | Experimental Group (n=10) | 83.90±32.15 | 96.70±36.48 |
| | Control Group (n=11) | 82.00±27.51 | 88.09±36.67 |
| | *t* | 0.15 | 0.52 |

According to the investigation of academic performance of students at different levels of self-efficacy (see Table 5.11), the average scores of math in the post-test for students with different levels of self-efficacy in the experimental group were all higher than in the pre-test. The experimental group had higher average scores of math than the control group. But the difference was not obvious.

# Conclusion

## 1) Experimental Effects of "Cooperation, Discussion and Feedback" Mode

### "Cooperation, Discussion and Feedback" Mode Obviously Improves Students' Self-Efficacy and Self-Efficacy in Math Learning

Using "cooperation, discussion and feedback" mode, without increasing the teaching hours, can improve the self-efficacy and self-efficacy in math learning of middle school students (see Table 5.3, Table 5.4). The best effects of this mode can be As seen from the students with average and low self-efficacy ($p<0.05$) (see Table 5.4). The possible reason is that students with average and low self-efficacy did not have a full understanding of and underestimated their math capacity, thus they did not undertake sufficient efforts. The experiment changes the teaching styles and teaching attitudes of teachers, classroom environment and teacher-student relationship, which to some extent stimulate the initiative, activeness and interest of students in math learning. Meanwhile, teachers' positive expectations and evaluations enhance students' confidence in math learning. Besides, the realization of goals and various success experiences also prove their capability, in particular that they are capable of learning math well; thus their self-efficacy in math is improved. In addition, the psychological game in math learning leads to that they do not negatively evaluate their math learning, they do not concentrate their energy on the failures in learning, and that they positively and objectively understand their math learning.

According to Table 5.4, the post-test scores of the high self-efficacy team of the experimental group were higher than the pre-test scores; for the control group, except the low efficacy team, the post-test scores of high and average self-efficacy teams were higher than the pre-test scores. This may be related to the development of self-efficacy. Because the self-efficacy of middle school students are declining, and obvious decline can be As seen from junior grade two [Zhou, 1994]. The experiment may improve the declining self-efficacy, but it can not change the trend of decline. The post-test of high self-efficacy teams showed no obvious difference between the experimental and control groups, which corresponds with the experimental results of Dou [1998] concerning the development and improvement of self-efficacy among pupils. The reasons may be that the self-efficacy in the pre-test was already high, it is hard to be improved greatly in the experiment, i.e., "plateau phenomenon" may appear during the development of self-efficacy. The post-test scores of the low self-efficacy team of the control group were higher than the pre-test scores. We analyzed the composition and found that the team consisted of 15 students, including three top students, six average students and six slow learners. Slow learners only took a small proportion of the number of students, which was different from the experimental group. The academic success of the top and average students together with teachers' positive evaluation thereof easily led to the improvement of their self-efficacy, therefore the post-test scores were higher than the pre-test scores.

Further observation (see Table 5.5) shows that except that the post-test scores of top students with high self-efficacy from the experimental group were lower than the pre-test scores (we could not investigate the slow learners with high self-efficacy as the number of such students is small), the post-test scores of students with different academic performance were higher than pre-test scores; and the experimental group had higher post-test scores than the control group. However, only the difference between the pre-test and post-test scores was significant for the two groups ($p<0.05$). The reason may be that this mode benefits students below average and slow learners the most, compared with previous teaching modes. Compared with slow learners, students below average was a special group, as they had relatively good foundation and they can succeed with a little bit more efforts. They can have more positive experience and positive evaluation through the positive feedback from teachers and other positive factors of the mode. However, although slow learners also had some positive experiences, the constant academic failures and negative feedback from the school and the family strengthen their cognition as slow learners and their understanding of low academic capacity. Thus it is not easy to significantly change their understanding of their academic capacity.

We tested the students with the questionnaire of self-efficacy in math learning. Such questionnaire integrates both the range and strength of self-efficacy. The results (see Tables 5-7 and 5-8) show that the scores of the experimental group in "Yes" answers were obviously higher than the scores of the control group. The experimental group had higher scores in self-efficacy strength from curriculum sub-scale, task sub-scale, problem sub-scale and the total scale than the control group. Besides the difference from the problem sub-scale was quite obvious. The difference from the total scale was obvious. The difference in curriculum and task sub-scales was not obvious. The possible reasons are that: in the period of junior middle school, the math knowledge used in related subjects (chemistry and physics) was not much; physics was a new subject for junior grade two students, thus they could not understand it well; in addition, some students had a bias towards some subjects. Therefore, the confidence in learning math well may not necessarily lead to great improvement of confidence in other subjects. The difference in task sub-scale is possibly because math itself is an abstract subject; the teaching mode can only be implemented in class, but the knowledge imparting in class was mostly abstract and was barely related to the math problems in actual life, thus there was no obvious difference in students' evaluation of math problems they encounter in daily life.

To sum up, two different questionnaires show the same conclusion. It indicates that it is applicable and effective to develop students' self-efficacy consciously through the "cooperation, discussion and feedback" mode, in order to improve the self-efficacy of junior grade two students when they are declining objectively.

### "Cooperation, Discussion and Feedback" Mode Obviously Improves Students' Mental Health and Psychological Suzhi

Tables 5.8 and 5.9 show that after the experiment, the psychological problem of the experimental group was lightened and they had better psychological suzhi. Before the experiment, there was no obvious difference in the mental health between the two groups. Both groups had slight psychological problems. After the experiment, the experimental group had lower scores in pressure from learning, poor adaptability, emotional imbalance, psychological imbalance and mental health than the control group. The difference was significant. For the experimental group, the post-test scores of mental health and other factors were lower than pre-test scores, but the difference was not significant. The possible reason is that many problems are involved in the metal health of middle school students. Such problems are not only from learning, but also from interpersonal relationship, personality, emotion, etc. Thus many factors need to be considered in order to develop and effectively improve students' mental health. Table 5.9 shows that the pre-test scores of the experimental group in the factors of ambition, self-confidence, learning adaptation, emotional adaptation and general quality were higher than the post-test scores. The post-test scores of the experimental group in such factors were higher than that of the control group. However, significant difference between the two groups was only As seen in the factor of self-confidence. The pre-test and post-test results of the experimental group show that the difference between the pre-test and post-test scores in self-confidence, learning adaptation and general quality was very significant. In particular, the difference between the pre-test and post-test scores in learning adaptation was very significant. It proves our hypotheses mentioned above to some extent.

To summarize, the "cooperation, discussion and feedback" mode is effective in improving mental health and psychological suzhi. But the effectivity is not the best. It is possibly because we only implemented this mode in math teaching, whereas the mental health and psychological suzhi of students are affected by many factors. Mental health education and psychological suzhi-based education are complicated and systematic work, which should be undertaken from many aspects. Only by infiltrating mental health education and psychological suzhi-based education in various activities and teaching of subjects, the mental health and psychological suzhi of students can be optimized.

## 2) Attribution Analysis of the Experimental Effects of "Cooperation, Discussion and Feedback" Mode

### Attribution Analysis of Improving Students' Self-Efficacy and Self-Efficacy in Math Learning

It is sure that the difference of students' self-efficacy after the experiment results from the difference between the "cooperation, discussion and feedback" mode and traditional teaching mode, since control variables were strictly controlled in the experiment. We believe that good experimental effects are due to the participation of more students in the classroom teaching, stimulation of students' interest in math learning, more positive experiences, more success experience, guiding of positive attribution, removal of unequal teacher-student interaction mechanism, building equal teacher-student interaction mechanism, as well as the positive encouragement, evaluation and expectations of teachers. First, students were divided into homogeneous teams through heterogeneous grouping. Students with different academic capacity shouldered different tasks due to the division of tasks within the team, which dramatically changed the situation resulted from traditional teaching that top students synchronize the teaching of students, average students catch some teaching of teachers and slow learners can not catch up with teaching of teachers. It also causes obvious mental changes of top and average students and slow learners. Top and average students needed to fully understand and master the content of teaching in class, because they not only needed to understand and master the content of teaching, but also shoulder the task to organize team learning, imparting learning methods within the team and ensure each team member to understand and master the content of teaching. When helping other team members, they can also experience the sense of pride and have the firm cognition of learning math well. For slow learners, learning was not "personal" any more; instead, it was related to the whole team, which prevented them from giving up, stimulated their desire and motivation to participate in classroom activities, increased their interest and initiative in math learning. Meanwhile, as part of the team, slow learners also contributed to the honor of the team. They were not useless. Their value started to be realized. In addition, the cooperative learning also made slow learners obtain more encouragement, praise and affirmation from peers and teachers. Thus the inferiority complex was removed and the senses of self-confidence, self-esteem and self-reliance were coming back. This for sure aroused more efforts of slow learners, resulting in their concentration on learning physically and mentally, and continuous success experience. From the perspective of the reward structure in class, cooperative reward structure was used in cooperative learning, which provided more opportunities to realize academic success than traditional teaching. Under such reward structure, the success of an individual also promoted the success of others (such as team members). The success experience of an individual also resulted in the success experience of team members. Second, the teachers in the experiment created questions of different difficulty according to the learning capacity of students, and helped students to set learning goals at high, intermediate and low levels according to their real situations, thus students were able to correctly answer teachers' questions within their capacity and realize their learning goals, ensuring success experience of students. When students performed well in the class (for example, actively participated in classroom teaching, correctly answered teachers' questions), the teachers in the experiment provided positive encouragement and evaluation according to the capacity of the students and the difficulty of the tasks. The positive evaluation and encouragement to students were not only reflected in the teacher-student interaction, but also in grading homework. In this sense, only red check marks and red crosses are not enough; instead, teachers should provide written or verbal evaluation on the homework and the classroom performance of the day or recently. By doing so, a certain or some students were encouraged, which functioned as mode demonstration to other students. Third, guiding students to attribute positively provides hope for students in learning math well. Guiding students to positive and correct attribution is an important means for students to correctly understand themselves. Weiner believed that the success and failure of a certain activity can be attributed to personal capacity, efforts, difficulty of the task, luck, etc. If one attributes success to unstable and controllable factors (such as efforts), one will have more expectations on future success, more self-esteem and self-confidence. On the contrary, if one attributes failure to stable and uncontrollable factors (such as capacity), one will have fewer expectation on future success, negative emotional experience. The classical attribution theory holds that students are guided to attribute success to capacity and failure to efforts. However, learning is a complicated activity, which is affected and restricted by many factors. If students always attribute failure to inadequate efforts, they may feel powerless when they see no improvement in academic performance after many efforts. It may harm their self-efficacy, cause more negative emotional experience, or even cause depression and harm their physical health. Therefore, if students did undertake efforts but no improvement in academic performance is made, students should be guided to attribute failure to the difficulty of tasks, improper learning methods, or improper learning strategies. By doing this, on one hand, students still continue their efforts; on the other hand, students will consider how to undertake efforts. According to the attribution training on children with low learning capacity by Borkowski [1998], only emphasizing on efforts is not enough, because progress will not be significant even with a lot of efforts when the children were guided by wrong cognition strategies. This will make students lose confidence in efforts. Therefore, traditional attribution training can not make students correctly attribute academic failures. In our attribution training, measures were carried out according to the characteristics of attribution of each student. To sum up, first, we made students realize that every one has the capacity to learn math well, and that some students do not learn math well due to no or insufficient efforts. Second, we made them understand that learning methods and learning strategies also contribute to math learning. We inspired them to improve their learning methods and learning strategies, and use good learning methods and techniques from peers. Fourth, we removed unequal teacher-student interaction mechanism, and built equal teacher-student interaction mechanism in class. Research showed that unequal teacher-student interaction mechanism may be caused by different academic performance, titles and genders of students. It may affect students' self-efficacy and further influence students' academic performance. Unequal teacher-student interaction mechanism is reflected by the following: i) unequal opportunities of interaction, i.e., inequality in quantity. In traditional class, the interacting opportunities with teachers for students with different academic performance are different. Compared with students with poor academic performance, students with good academic performance have more interacting opportunities provided by teachers. Teachers ask the latter questions more frequently and always respond to their answers. ii) Inequality in the process of interaction, i.e., in equality in quality. It is reflected by the response of teachers to students' answers, the time of interaction, etc. Top students, when they correctly answer the questions, are praised timely. However, slow learners are rarely praised; when they answer incorrectly, they are very likely to be criticized. When both top students and slow learners can not answer the questions, teachers tend to provide more time for top students to think and are patient to wait for the answer, or provide clues; on the contrary, for slow learners, teachers usually stop their answer immediately or ask other students to answer. Equal teacher-student interaction mechanism is reflected by that teachers treat all students equally and hold the view of development on students. They believe that every student has value as well as potential and hope to learn math well. Teachers make more students with different academic performance participate in the classroom teaching, providing them with equal interacting opportunities and interacting process. Teachers make slow learners participate in more classroom interaction, and ask them challenging questions based on their capacity. They can answer such questions through efforts. If average students or slow learners have difficulty in the presentation or answering the questions or their thinking is obstructed due to nervousness, anxiety and timidity, teachers do not stop or interrupt them rudely, or satirize them; instead, teachers are patient and positively guide them, provide necessary hints or clues or provide more time for students to think. In addition, teachers smile and encourage students, in order to relieve their anxiety and nervousness. Equal teacher-student interaction mechanism is also reflected by that teachers have positive expectations on students. Positive expectation is based on the actual capacity of students and the vision of development of the teachers. It is because students have different learning capacity. It is impossible to remove such difference by expectations. If teachers, without considering the actual capacity of students, set high standards which are impossible for students to realize, it only brings difficulty to students and harm their self-confidence in learning.

## Attribution Analysis of Improving Students' Mental Health and Psychological Suzhi

The mental health of middle school students is affected by various factors and environments. In social environment, school affects middle school students the most. School affects students psychologically and physically mainly through guiding ideology of education, teaching attitude of teachers, teacher-student relationship and peer relationship, activities organized by schools, etc. Heavy psychological burden, mental problems and negative influence to mental health of students may be caused by that schools place undue emphasis on the proportion of students entering schools of a higher level, and that students can not obtain due encouragement, support and respect from teachers, parents and peers, as well as by boring content of teaching, overburden in learning, improper teaching methods, poor interpersonal relationships, tense teacher-student relationship, sarcasm, irony and unscrupulous blame by teachers, etc. The mental health and psychological suzhi of the experimental group are improved due to equal teacher-student interaction mechanism, improvement of teacher-student relationship and peer relationship, democratic, harmonious and relaxing classroom environment, enhanced confidence in learning and maintenance of self-esteem. First, enhanced self-confidence in learning leads to improvement of self-efficacy.

Research showed that the mental problems of middle school students first lie in learning-related problems. The pressure and difficulty from learning affect the psychology of middle school students to some extent. Learning anxiety and poor adaptation to learning indicate the lack of self-confidence. Learning is their main task and activity everyday. With the upgrading of grades, they will have more subjects to learn. These subjects are more difficult and have larger gradients. Parents have new and higher requirements on the learning. In the process of learning, students inevitably face difficulty and challenges. If students have no or insufficient confidence to overcome the difficulty in learning, it is difficult for them to continue daily learning. The learning self-efficacy is reflected by every aspect of their life, which determines happy learning and life. The research by Kent et al. showed that the anxiety and distress of individuals are mainly caused by the cognition of powerless or incapability in the face of difficulty, rather than unfavorable condition or difficult task itself. The experiment, through "cooperation, discussion and feedback" mode, improves students' self-efficacy and self-efficacy in math learning, which to some extent avoids negative emotions such as anxiety and depression in the face of difficulty in learning. Thus students can experience positive emotions such as happiness and self-confidence in math learning. Second, building good psychological environment in class. School is an important setting for middle school students to grow up. A student tends to have good mental health if the student has happy, pleasant and positive experience in school. Otherwise, it is easily to cause psychological problems, including anxiety and fear. Classroom is an important place for learning and also the most frequent place of students' activities. Most learning activities are held and interpersonal communication occurs in the classroom. The improvement of students' mental health and psychological suzhi can be guaranteed by proper teaching methods, good classroom environment, equal, democratic and friendly teacher-student relationship and peer relationship, and the experience of success in learning and happiness in life in the relaxing and harmonious learning environment. Compared with the previous teaching modes, "cooperation, discussion and feedback" mode is active, flexible and vivid. It provides more opportunities for students to participate in class teaching, changes the boring teaching (i.e., teachers undertake teaching and students listen), stimulates students' interest and motivation in math learning, and makes students experience the happiness in math learning. Academic performance is always regarded as the standard, or even the only standard, by school and parents to evaluate the value and future of students as learning plays an important role in the life of middle school students. Students with poor academic performance tend to have the cognition of incapability and uselessness due to ignorance and snub of teachers, contempt of top students, complaining and criticism of parents, resulting in psychological problems such as depression and inferiority complex. "Cooperation, discussion and feedback" mode requires equal opportunities and process of teacher-student interaction, mutual help among students and sharing happiness in learning, which leads to significant respect and confidence of students with poor academic performance. Under this mode, students with poor academic performance see the possibilities and hope of success and their value. Students feel safe under such good atmosphere. They can freely express their opinions without worrying about being laughed at or criticized and thus they do not experience the anxiety and stress.

## Attribution Analysis of No Obvious Difference in Academic Performance of Math After the Experiment Between the Two Groups

The difference analysis of the academic performance of math between the two groups showed that the experimental group had better academic performance of math after the experiment. The academic performance of math after the experiment was also better than the control group. But the difference was not significant, which corresponds to the research by

Kou [1998] but was different from the research by Lu [1998] (after the experiment, the experimental group had much better academic performance of math and Chinese language than the control group). We believe that the self-efficacy of junior middle school students is closely related to academic performance. Generally speaking, students with better academic performance usually have higher self-efficacy. But high self-efficacy does not necessarily lead to good academic performance. It is because on one hand, academic performance is affected by various factors, including teaching methods, learning methods, habitual learning attitude, etc. On the other hand, it takes long time to improve self-efficacy. It is impossible to improve self-efficacy to a high level in a short period. Besides, the improved self-efficacy in a short period is not stable, the effects of which on academic performance is not the maximum. Besides, the influence of self-efficacy on academic performance may have time-delay effect, i.e., self-efficacy is gradually improved in the experiment, but the improvement of self-efficacy does not synchronize with the improvement of academic performance. In previous research and the present research, the academic performance was tested directly after the experiment. It is possible that the influence on academic performance had not emerged at that time. It is not easy to improve academic performance dramatically in a short period due to complicated influential factors and possible time-delay effect, especially for students with learning difficulty.

### 3) Notes for Developing Self-Efficacy of Students in Mathematics Teaching

Undertaking cooperative learning through building learning teams is a way to stimulate students' enthusiasm in learning and provide more success experiences for students. However, if it is not properly used, cooperative learning can turn to be a mere formality. Therefore, when organizing cooperative learning, we should pay attention to the following: first choosing the best opportunity for cooperative learning. Cooperative learning can be conducted when i) mutual inspiration is needed due to difficult tasks or questions; ii) discussion is necessary due to disagreement; and iii) many students volunteer to answer the questions put forward by teachers, but teachers can not ask all volunteer students to answer. Second, students think independently before the discussion. If students hurry to the discussion without independent thinking, on one hand, the discussion will be superficial due to insufficient independent thinking; on the other hand, students with retarded thinking and low enthusiasm in learning will only act as audience, which enhances inertia and dependency, and deprives the opportunities of independent thinking and independent learning unconsciously. Every form of learning must be based on independent thinking, thus before the discussion, teachers should ask students to think or practice independently or write down their opinions. Third, students should have equal opportunities in the discussion. Cooperative learning easily leads to that one or two top students dominate(s) the discussion, which virtually deprives the opportunities of students with poor academic performance to express their opinions and deprives their rights of learning. Teachers should pay proper attention to this situation, and strengthen monitoring and instruction, in order to make each student initiatively and positively cooperate with peers. In addition, frequent cooperative learning may bore students. Thus teachers should use diversified forms to undertake cooperative learning. Successful cooperative learning not only requires relatively good organizing capacity of team leaders, but also frequent instructions, encouragement and spur from teachers.

Teachers should regularly be informed of the cooperation of each team, in order to properly solve the problems of each team. Third, in terms of developing students' self-efficacy, only by changing the methods, strategies and attitude of teaching and by providing more efficacy information for students are not enough; students should also be guided to undertake cognitive processing of efficacy information. It is because efficacy information in various forms is not self-evident for the agent. People acting as agent need to pay attention to, know and evaluate such efficacy information. The efficacy information can be used as the standard for judging one's efficacy and determine one's self-efficacy only after cognitive processing. The "Math Learning- Game 2" was developed on this basis, aiming to guide student to pay attention and know the efficacy information from classroom teaching, and make them correctly, reasonably and objectively evaluate their math learning and capacity for math learning.

However, in order not to add burden to students and not to occupy more time of students, the implementation of cooperative learning should be controlled within four or five times. The cooperative learning should be completed under the instruction of teachers and within certain time limit. Meanwhile, students are required to master such method to evaluate their own capacity for math learning. We conducted three-month research into educational intervention concerning self-efficacy development in math teaching for junior middle schools, by using the mode of infiltrating psychological suzhi cultivation in teaching of a subject. The present research found that the scores of the subjects from the experimental group in related dimensions of self-efficacy and psychological suzhi were significantly improved ($p<.05$). It indicates that the teaching mode of developing self-efficacy in math teaching is an effective way to improve students' self-efficacy.

# APPENDIX 1: MATH LEARNING – GAME 2

## 1) More Positive Evaluation, More Confidence!

In math learning, do you sometimes feel not confident enough, worried and then doubt your capacity in math learning? Nobody was born to be a math genius. Most of the time, it is not because you are not able to learn math well, but because you pay too much attention to your bad performance and neglect your good performance. If you don't believe this, you can try to record your good performance in math learning everyday and every week. You may have a whole book of good performance one day! Well, you may not be good everyday, but we can ignore the bad performance which makes your confidence in math learning hit the rock bottom. Say goodbye to your bad performance now!

## 2) Better Self-Understanding, More Progress!

Not every student is interested in math, but every one does want to make progress in math learning! Target is the precursor of action. So find a mode who has similar performance as you but is better than you in a certain aspect and you can catch up with the mode with efforts. The mode actually is you in the future. The mode can be anyone; for instance, classmates, good friends, or yourself, as soon as you think the mode is good enough for you to make progress.

| Good performance of _____ | | Self-reward to _____ | |
|---|---|---|---|
| (Write down your good performance.)<br>For example: Realized the learning targets of the day (the content of learning of the day)<br>Realized the learning targets of the week (knowledge and content of the unit)<br>I have correctly answered ___ (number) questions in the homework;<br>I have correctly answered teacher's questions in class;<br>I was praised by the teacher;<br>I worked out one or several math problems independently;<br>I helped peers to work out one or several difficulties;<br>I am more concentrated in class and on homework;<br>I am faster in working out problems; ... | | (Write down or draw anything you desire.)<br>For example, your smile;<br>Smile of parents;<br>A reward flower;<br>One of your wishes;<br>A place where you are desiring to;<br>A book and a certain small article you are desired to buy;<br>Anyway, write down what you desire! | |
| The mode is ____ | What should I need to improve to catch up with the mode? | Efforts of ____ | Self-reward to _____ |
| (You can write down the name, or draw the portrait of the mode. In a word, you can use any method you want to describe who the mode is.) | (Sometimes you may not understand why your academic performance is not as good as the mode although you are not as bad as him/her. It is because good academic performance is determined by many factors. If you have bad performance of one certain aspect, gap is produced. So let's find out where the gap is? For example, insufficient efforts in learning;. | Draw a line to represent the gap between the mode and you. Erase part of the line to represent the progress you make until the line is gone. No matter how little the progress is, you should erase the line accordingly. As time goes by, the gap will be removed some day. | For example, I can do it as soon as I undertake efforts. As long as I want, I can do as well as him/her. I believe I can do it better! |
| The mode is ____ | What should I need to improve to catch up with the mode? | Efforts of ____ | Self-reward to _____ |
| | insufficient self-confidence;<br>not concentrated on the lecture; careless in homework; not willing to seek for help from peers; lacking of coping skills, etc. | | |

## APPENDIX 2: TEACHING PLAN OF INFILTRATION

The Characteristics of Parallelogram

Preparation before class: Give an example of parallelogram; ask each team to make a shape of parallelogram. (The teacher emphasizes that the parallelogram should not be made by one student independently but by the team together; namely, when one member makes the parallelogram, other team members should observe carefully.) (Team spirit)

### *Begin the Class by Stimulating the Interests of Students and Putting Forward the Question*

Teacher: Last time I asked each team to show some examples of parallelograms in daily life. Now I would like to check how many examples you have. I would like to ask two teams to answer my question and you will evaluate which team has the most examples through team work.

Teacher: Team x and Team y, please select one representative to democratically answer the question.

Teacher: Team x, who did you select? (The representative selected please do not say no. Team members selected you because they are confident in you) (Speech encouragement)

Student A from Team x: ? ? ? ? ? ? ? ?

Teacher: Good! You showed "a" (number) examples. Is anyone from this team has any other examples? (If students can not give any other examples, the teacher can give some.)

Teacher: Well, let's see how many examples Team y has.

Student B from Team y: ? ? ? ? ? ?

Teacher: Good! You showed "b" (number) examples.

Teacher (comments): Both teams have thought about this question carefully! Team x wins since it showed more examples than Team y (team competition). Team y should work harder now. Team y still has the opportunity to win Team x. (If there is enough time, the teacher can ask the team leader of the winning team to explain why they can show so many examples. If it is because the winning team plays the initiative of each team member and each team member is stimulated to participate in the activity. The winning team can be act as the mode)

Teacher: Does any other team have different examples?

Teacher: Good, you showed many examples of parallelograms in daily life. Can you show some examples of accurate parallelograms?

Student (answered together): ... Teacher writes down the definition of parallelograms on the blackboard.

Teacher: Just now we showed many examples of parallelograms and we knew the definition of parallelogram. Now let's look at two examples. Please distinguish which are parallelograms and which are not from the following figures. Why? Please count how many parallelograms there are. We will see which team has the correct answer the fastest.

Practice: See Figure 12.1.1.

Teacher walks around when students are thinking about the answer. Ask two students (students below average and slow learners) (the questions should be of different difficulty based on the capacity of students) from two teams to answer the question. (In order to stimulate the activeness of the class, teacher can ask students to evaluate the answer. When students correctly answer the question, other students should applaud as reward.)

Teacher: A parallelogram is a quadrilateral with two pairs of parallel sides. This is a very important characteristic of parallelogram. Just now you used this characteristic to judge parallelograms. Besides this, does parallelogram have other characteristics? Now let's see what other characteristics does parallelogram have?

### *Teamwork for Exploration*

Teacher: Now please show the parallelograms you prepared! (Teacher ask every team to show their parallelograms to ensure that every team has the parallelogram)

Then teacher described the following operating procedures:

> Put the shape of a parallelogram on a piece of paper, and draw a parallelogram according to the edge of the shape. Mark this parallelogram as ▱EFGH. Thus ▱EFGH is exactly the same as ▱ABCD, the facing sides and opposite angles should be the same.
>
> Fix the drawing pin at Point O, and then spin ▱ABCD across Point O for 180°. Observe whether spun ▱ABCD is coincident with ▱EFGH.

(In this process, teacher should walk down the platform to undertake specific instruction. The student who draws the parallelogram should be very careful. Other team members should observe very carefully.)

Teacher: finished?

Student: Yes!

Teacher: Ok, let's choose two teams to see the effect.

Questions: i) Is ▱ABCD coincident with ▱EFGH after it is spun for 180°.

ii) ▱ABCD is coincident with ▱EFGH after it is spun for 180° across Point O, which indicates that ▱ABCD is _____.

iii) What can we conclude from ▱ABCD according to the knowledge of parallelogram? AB= AD= OA= OB= ∠A= ∠B=

(Teacher can appoint students to answer questions. For the mentioned questions, teacher can ask relevant students to answer the simple ones. If they have the correct answers, teacher should positively praise them and comment that they are concentrated in this learning activity. Teacher should also express the expectation for better performance of this student. If this student can not answer the question, teacher should be patient and provide hints or ask other team members to supplement. In addition, teacher should ask students from other two or three teams to answer the question, and see whether they have the same conclusion and whether the results are the same.)

### *Further Discussion for Conclusion*

Teacher should inspire students as follows:

Let's look at ▱ABCD. We know AD and BC are sides of ▱ABCD, and they are the facing sides. The facing sides are of equal length, indicating that the quadrilateral is _____.

Meanwhile, ∠A=∠C; ∠B=∠D, which means _____.

Teacher writes on the blackboard: the characteristics of ▱: ...

Practice and consolidation

Teacher: Now let's work out two examples based on the characteristics of▱ :

Example 1 ⎫
        ⎬  Teacher explains specifically
Example 2 ⎭
Practice 1 ⎫
        ⎬  Choose two students to work out the examples by writing on the blackboard (teacher can choose Team x and Team y)
Practice 2 ⎭

Teacher: Let's give a chance to Team y. I hope Team y can catch up! (Positive expectation)

Then teacher assesses the solution on the blackboard. Teacher can use the speed of working out the problem, result, compliance, neatness, etc to assess. Teacher should encourage and praise more, but less criticism.

### *Summary*

Comments on the implementation: success experience, speech encouragement, mode demonstration, positive expectation, good class environment have been basically realized. Students have gained windfall in the discussion (one team put forward three questions worthy of considering). According to the feedback of teacher, students were very active.

### *Suggestion:*

To save time, it is not necessary to ask each team to answer the question. Teacher can ask three or four teams to answer the question by turns and ask other teams whether they agree. If there is no volunteer team, teacher can appoint teams to answer the question.

Teacher can arrange proper times of discussion according to the content and progress of teaching.

Teacher should ask different members of the team to answer the question to ensure opportunities for each team member.

During the instruction, teacher can ask about the discussion result and the problems they have.

# REFERENCES

Ames, C. (1981). Competitive versus cooperative reward structures: The influence of individual and group performance factors on achievement attributions. *American educational research journal, 18,* 273-287.

Bandura, A. (2001). The structure of children's perceived self-efficacy: A cross-national study. *European journal of psychological assessment, 17,* 87-97.

Bandura, A., and Schunk, D. H. (1981). Cultivating competence, self-efficacy, and intrinsic interest through proximal self-motivation. *Journal of personality and social psychology, 41,* 586-598.

Bandura, A., Adams, N. E., and Beyer, J. (1977). Cognitive pro-ceases mediating behavioral change. *Journal of personality and social psychology, 35,* 124-139.

Betz, N. E., and Haekett, G. (1983). The relationship of mathematics self-efficacy expectations to the selection of science based college majors. *Journal of vocational behavior, 23,* 329-345.

Bian, Y. F. (2003). *The establishment and utilization of learning self-efficacy scale.* Doctoral dissertation, East China Normal University, Shanghai, P.R.C.

Borkowski, J. G. (1988) Effects of attributional retraining on strategy-based reading comprehension in learning-disabled students. *Journal of educational psychology, 80,* 46-53.

Chen, H., and Zhou, G. T. (1999). The theoretical background and research status quo of self-efficacy and self-adjustment of attribution. *Education science, 2,* 38-40.

Chen, J. L. (0.2002). *School mental health education-principle and practice.* Beijing: Educational Science Publishing House.

Chen, X., and Zhang, D. J. (2002). A study on the integrated mode of psychological health education. *Education research, 1,* 71-75.

Dowrick, P. W. (1983). Self-modeling. In P. W. Dowrick, and S. J. Biggs (Eds.). *Using video: Psychological and Social applications* (pp. 105–124). New York: Wiley.

Feng, Z. Z., and Zhang, D. J. (2001). A study on the concept and elements of the middle school students' mental quality. *Journal of Southwest China Normal University (philosophy and social sciences edition), 27,* 56-61.

Feng, Z. Z., and Zhang, D. J. (2001). Mental quality inventory for middle school students. *Chinese journal of behavioral medical science, 3,* 223-226.

Gao, S. C. (2000). Comments on self-efficacy theory. *Psychological development and education, 1,* 60-63.

Gao, X. B., and Wang, S. Q. (2003). Research and explanation on Chinese Mathematics Curriculum Standard for Full-time Compulsory Education (trial edition). *Educational science research, 6,* 36-39.

Gibson, S., and Dembo, M. H. (1984). Teacher efficacy: A construct validation. *Journal of educational psychology, 76,* 569-582.

Hackett, G., and Betz, N. E. (1989). An exploration of the mathematics self-efficacy/mathematics performance correspondence. *Journal for research in mathematics education, 20,* 261-273.

He, D. T., et al. (2003). Research into the factors affecting the development of students' self-efficacy. *Exploring education , 1,* 162-165.

He, X. Y. (1998). Research into the relationship among self-efficacy, self-conception and academic performance in math among pupils. *Psychological development and education, 1,* 45-48.

Huang, S. R., et al. (2002). An experimental study of the influence of fencing and aerobics teaching on high middle school girls' shyness. *Psychological science, 4,* 482-483.

Huang, Z. Y. (2002). An experimental study into the training of self-efficacy sense in junior middle school students with learning disabilities. Mater's thesis, Guangxi Normal University, Guangxi, P.R.C.

Jackson, J. V. (2002). Enhancing self-efficacy and learning performance. *The journal of experimental education, 70,* 243-255.

Jiang, Q., and Zhang, D. J. Problems in the research into the infiltration ofpsychological suzhi-based educationin teaching of a subject and the countermeasures. Unpublished materials.

Jiang, Y. J. (2001). Analyzing foreign disagreements on self-efficacy to improve meta-cognition research. *Journal of Northeast Normal University (social science, 3,* 109-114.

Jinks, J., and Morgan, V. (1999). Children perceived academic self-efficacy: An inventory scale. *The clearing house, 72,* 224-330.

Kou, D. Q. (1998). The Experimental Study on the Cultivation of Pupil's Sense of Mathematics Self-efficacy. Master's thesis, Southwest China Normal University, Chongqing, P.R.C.

Kou, D. Q., Liu, D. Z., and Zeng, X. R. (2000). The experimental study on the cultivation of pupil's sense of mathematics self-efficacy. *Journal of Southwest China, 5,* 76-80.

Li, B. S., (1999). Research into the evaluation of junior middle students in their learning capacity. *Psychological development and education, 4,* 61-64.

Li, H., Xin, T., Gu, H. S., et al. (1998). Research into the relationship among self-efficacy, learning strategies and academic performance of middle school student. *Educational research and experiment, 4,* 48-52.

Li, L. H. (2000). On the psychological education in teaching of a subject. *Journal of the Chinese society, 4,* 32-33.

Li, X. D. (1999). Academic help--seeking: Its relation to self-efficacy, value, classroom context and academic achievement. *Journal of Chinese psychology, 4,* 435-441.

Lian, *M.* W. S. Self–efficacy: how confident are you that you will succeed? Interventions enhancing self- efficacy. Retrieved from http://www.positivepractices.com/Efficacy/ InterventionsEnhancingSel.html.

Liu, S. K. (1992). Influence of students' competition under classroom situation on their achievement attribution and achievements. *Acta psychological sinica, 2,* 182-189.

Lu, H. D., Liu, X. *M.*, and Guo, Z. J. (1998). Report of the experimental research into the cultivation and improvement of self-efficacy of pupils. *Modem primary and secondary education, 2,* 31-35.

Ma, *F.* (2002). Basic principles and curriculum targets of Mathematics Curriculum Standard for Full-time Compulsory Education. *Bulletin des sciences mathematics, 1,* 15-17.

Mao, L. L. (2003). Research on mathematics self-efficacy of middle school students and on correlation between mathematics self-efficacy and mathematics problem representation. Master's thesis, Nanjing Normal University, Jiangsu, P.R.C.

Matsui, T., and Ohnishi, R. (1990). Mechanisms underlying math self-efficacy learning of college students. *Journal of vocational behavior, 37,* 225-238.

Morgan, V. and Jinks, J. (1999). Children's perceived academic self-efficacy: An inventory scale. *The clearing house, 72,* 224-230.

Pajares, F., and Miller, M. D. (1995). Mathematics Self-Efficacy and Mathematics Outcomes: The need for specificity of assessment. *Journal of counseling psychology, 42,* 190-198.

Pajares. F. (1997). Current directions in self-efficacy research. In *M.* Maehr, and P. R. Pintrich (Eds.) *Advances in motivation and achievement* (pp. 1-49). Greenwich, CT: JAI Press.

Pintrich, P. R. (1991). A manual for the use of the motivated strategies for learning questionnaire (MSLQ). The University of Michigan, Ann Arbor, MI.

Schunk, D. H. (1984). Enhancing self-efficacy and achievement through rewards and goals: Motivational and informational effects. *Journal of educational research, 78,* 29-34.

Shi, S. J. (2001). Research into the infiltration of moral education under the aesthetic teaching mode of chemistry in junior middle school. Master's thesis, Southwest China Normal University, Chongqing, P.R.C.

Siegle, D. (2003). *Influencing student mathematics self-efficacy through teacher training.* Paper presented at the Annual Meeting of the American Association, Chicago.

Wang, J. P. (2004). Trail textbook based on the curriculum standard for full-time compulsory education. Shanghai: East China Normal University Press.

Wang, K. R., Xin, T., and Li, Q. (1999). Research into the relationship among self-efficacy, attribution and academic performance of middle school students. *Psychological development and education, 4,* 22-25.

Wang, L., and Lei, L. (2000) Efficacy beliefs processing style and failure-coping strategy: Characteristics of self-regulated learning and the relationships among its components. Psychological development and education, 3, 30-35.

Wang, Y. Q. (2000). Infiltration of mental health education in teaching of a subject. *China, 3,* 43.

Wang, Z. H. (1999). Research into the relationship between academic self-efficacy and academic achievements among middle school students. *Psychological development and education, 1,* 39-43.

Wang, Z. H., and Liu, P. (2000). The influence of motivational factors, learning strategy, and the level of intelligence on the academic achievement of students. *Journal of Chinese psychology, 1,* 65-68.

Wood. and Locke. (1987). The relation of self-efficacy and grade goals to academic performance. *Educational and psychological measurement, 47,* 1013-1024.

Yang, X. D., (1996). Research into the self-efficacy of students with learning difficulty. *Psychological science, 3,* 185-187.

Yao, B. X., (2000). The negative tendency and developmental trend of the current mental health education in school. *Journal of the Chinese society, 4,* 26-29.

Zhang, D. J., and Guo, C. (2000). Exploring the principles of instructional psychology, conducting the research on education of mental quality. *Journal of Southwest China Normal University (humanities and social science edition), 6,* 104-111.

Zhang, D. J., and Tian, L. (2003). On the design and implementation strategy of mental quality education. *Curriculum, teaching material and method, 6,* 66-70.

Zhou, G. T., Liu, X. *M.,* Li, L. P., and Wang, J. (1994). Research into the learning capacity of junior middle school students. *Educational theory and research, 5,* 49-51.

Zhou, G. T., Zhang, P., Li, L. P., and Liu, Q. H. (1997). A study of the relationships among perceived competence, learning strategies and achievement in junior middle school students' equation learning. *Psychological science, 4,* 324-328.

Zhou, Y., and Dong, Q. (1994). Research into the relationship among learning motivation, attribution, self-efficacy and self-monitored learning of students. *Psychological development and education, 3,* 30-33.

Zimmerman, B. J., and Martinez-Pons, *M.* (1990). Student Difference in Self-Regulated Learning: Relating grade, sex and giftedness to self-efficacy and strategy use. *Journal of education psychology, 82,* 51-59.

In: Methods and Implementary Strategies on Cultivating …        ISBN: 978-1-62417-979-2
Editors: Da-Jun Zhang, Jin-Liang Wang, and Lin Yu      © 2013 Nova Science Publishers, Inc.

*Chapter 6*

# EXPERIMENTAL RESEARCH ON DEVELOPING STUDENTS' SELF-MONITORING CAPABILITIES IN MATH TEACHING IN PRIMARY SCHOOLS

## *Yan-Gang Xu[1] and Da-Jun Zhang[2]*
[1]Sichuan Normal University, China
[2]Center for Mental Health Education in Southwest University, China

## ABSTRACT

The capacity for self-monitoring of learning is one of the core components of students' meta-learning capability. This chapter is to, in the teaching of math, improve students' academic performance and develop students' related psychological suzhi by improving their self-monitoring based on the previous research achievements the research results have showed that cultivating students' capacity for self-monitoring of learning in math teaching is an effective method to improve students' awareness and planning of self-monitoring.

The experimental effects on students of different genders were different: in respect of male students, there was significant improvement in their methods, planning and awareness of self-monitoring, while in respect of female students, there was significant improvement only in their awareness of self-monitoring. The experimental effects on students from different families were also different: such intervention strategies were more helpful to improve urban students' planning and awareness of self-monitoring, while they were more effective in improving rural students' planning and methods of self-monitoring.

# LITERATURE REVIEW

## Definitions

### 1) Self-Monitoring

The self-monitoring, also called metacognitive monitoring or self-supervision, was first proposed by Snyder [1972]. Cognitive psychology and educational psychology always regard it as a special cognitive capability (metacognition); personality and social psychologists regard the self-monitoring as a special capacity of social cognition and interpersonal communication and take it as one of the dimensions of personality.

Researchers differ from each other in the comprehension of self-monitoring. Snyder [1972] held that the self-monitoring was an individual's psychological structure in respect of the self-performance and his/her capacity of self-observation, self-control and self-adjustment guided by situations of social adaptability.

Lennox [1984] held that the self-monitoring was an individual's sensitivity to others' expressive behavior and his/her capacity of adjusting the self-performance. Sanz [1996] *et al.* held that the self-monitoring was the degree to which individuals observed, adjusted and controlled their performance during the social communication. Robbins [1998] held that the self-monitoring was the individuals' capacity of adjusting their own behavior based on the external situations.

From the perspective of the process, Dong [1996] divided the self-monitoring process into self-supervision, self-guidance and self-intensification. To sum up, according to this chapter, the self-monitoring is an intelligent monitoring. It is a dynamic process where the agent conducts continuous self-supervision, self-control and self-adjustment on his/her practice so as to achieve the predetermined goal.

### 2) Students' Self-Monitoring of Learning

The representative of students' self-monitoring of learning is Zimmerman. He held, according to the WHWW structure for self-monitoring he proposed in 1994, that the self-monitoring of learning was a structure of thought composed by motivation, methods, results and environment and the research on it was to improve students' self-monitoring of learning by cognizing, analyzing and intervening in students' self-monitoring of learning so as to better perform students' functions as the agent and their initiatives. Dong [1994] *et al.* held that students' self-monitoring of learning was the student's capacity of continuously conducting active and conscious planning, supervision, inspection, evaluation, feedback, control and adjustment on his/her learning activities in progress, as the object of consciousness, throughout the whole learning activities so as to ensure successful study, improve the learning effect and achieve the learning goals.

Students' self-monitoring of learning is not the planning, supervision, evaluation, feedback and adjustment on/of certain learning activity during a short period, but the conscious planning, supervision, evaluation, feedback and adjustment of all aspects of their learning activities and systems throughout a long period.

It will not only include planning, supervising, adjusting and controlling such individual's cognitive processes as preparation of learning plans, determination of learning methods and strategies, use of learning materials and inspection and correction of learning results, but also such non-cognitive factors as their learning interest, learning attitudes, attention paid, level of motivation and emotional state.

According to the aforesaid analysis, the student's self-monitoring of learning in this chapter is defined as the dynamic process where students, as the agent, continuously and actively plan, supervise, evaluate, feedback, control and adjust the cognitive and non-cognitive factors of the learning activities in progress (pre-learning, while-learning and post-learning) so as to achieve the predetermined learning goals (long-term or short-term).

## Measurements for Self-Monitoring

Questionnaires are the major tool for the measurement of self-monitoring. Foreign countries were researching into self-monitoring scales as they were probing into the self-monitoring structure, especially probing into the preparation of self-monitoring scales from the single-factorial and multifactorial perspectives.

From the single-factorial perspective, Snyder held that the self-monitoring was a unidimensional structure. The self-monitoring scale he prepared was composed by 25 descriptive yes-no questions initially, and then it was revised into 18 questions in five aspects, including a) concerns about the social adaptability of self-performance, b) concerns about the social comparison information and taking it as the proper clue for self-expression, c) capacity of controlling and correcting their self-performance and expressive behaviors, d) ability to use the aforesaid capacity in special situations, e) degree of inter-situational consistency or variability between expressive behaviors and behavioral performance. Tang (1993) has, based on Snyder's self-monitoring scales (25questions) and Wolfe' and Lennox's ideas [1984], developed a scale to examine the relationship between middle school students' self-monitoring and prosocial behavior (including 55 questions, 5 of which are for lie-detection). The scale was rated on a 6-point Likert scale. The test-retest reliability was 0.84, while the split-half reliability was 0.68. The head teacher was taken as the criterion (r=0.43). According to the research, the self-monitoring is an intermediate variable between value orientation and prosocial behavior that can adjust the prosocial behavior. Weng (1993) used and revised this scale and obtained a new scale composed by 28 questions. Four dimensions similar to Lennox's and Wolfe's ideas [1984] were obtained via factor analysis, which can explain 40% of the total variance. The internal consistency reliability was 0.83, while the split-half reliability was 0.81. According to the concept on self-monitoring in a broad sense, Li (2001) held that, in addition to those mentioned above, there are another two kinds of individuals: a) individuals that incline to make self-monitoring but lack the capacity of adjustment, b) individuals that have the capacity of self-monitoring but do not incline to do so. He has, after revising the self-monitoring scales according to the Chinese college students, obtained the subscale composed of 23 items: subscale on self-monitoring inclination and subscale on self-monitoring. Ju and Cheng （2002） have, based on previous research, made a set of questionnaires for self-evaluation of self-monitoring. They used it for the school's leading group for the first time to explore the relationships between the leaders' self-monitoring, their organizational commitment and their satisfaction with the work. They attempted to introduce the self-monitoring, a personality trait, into the study on leaders' psychology. Dong and Zhou et al. （1996） have, from the perspective of students' self-monitoring of their learning, divided students' self-monitoring of learning into three stages, pre-learning, while-learning and post-learning, and eight aspects. They have prepared the "scale on self-monitoring of learning" composed of 70 six-point self-descriptive items to measure students' self-monitoring in eight aspects, i.e. planning, preparation, awareness, method, implementation, feedback, remedy and summarization. The internal consistency reliability of this scale was 0.975 and the split-half reliability of the total scale was 0.973.

The representatives of multifactorial analysis are Briggs, Wolfe, Cheek et al. Briggs *et al.* (1996) held, according to the factor analysis, that the self-monitoring scale includes three item groups: expressive self-control, performance in the society and other-directedness factor. Therefore, they held that the self-monitoring was never a simple unidimensional structure, but a three dimensional structure. The self-monitoring scale should include three sub-scales such as extraversion factor, other directedness and performance. Lennox and Wolfe have revised Snyder's SMS. They held that a self-monitoring scale should be composed of two components: a) to measure individuals' sensitivity to others' expressive behavior and their capacity to regulate the self-performance, and b) to measure individuals' concerns about the acting factor and the social comparison confidence. According to the research of Briggs and Cheek, the revised SMS composed of 18 questions actually included two parts: public performance and other directedness. John, Cheek and Klohnen (1996) used the Q classification method to analyze and study the structure of self-monitoring and the results have proved the aforesaid idea. They held that the revised scale composed of 18 questions was not as helpful as the original scale composed by 25 questions to measure the individuals' inclination to self-monitoring.

To sum up, among the great number of scales to test self-monitoring, only the scale prepared by Tang *et al.* on research into the relationships between middle school students' self-monitoring and prosocial behavior and the "scale on self-monitoring of learning" prepared by Dong *et al.* were directly targeted at students and applicable to measure and test junior middle school and primary school students' self-monitoring of learning.

## Research into Self-Monitoring

### 1) Factors Influencing Self-Monitoring

### Age

Students' self-monitoring of learning is unceasingly improving as a whole as they are growing up [Zimmerman and Martinez-paris, 1988; Dong and Zhou, 1995]. From the perspective of development, students' feedback on their study develops from vague understanding to precise understanding since the teaching methods develop from detailed methods that are easy to understand complicated and highly integrated ones [Fu et al., 2002; Zhou, 1994]. From the perspective of specific monitoring effect, all aspects of students' self-monitoring of learning also tend to develop as they grow up. In addition, such development differs in the speed and the characteristics and it is unbalanced [Chen, 1991; Wo and Lin, 2000].

## Environment

The environment plays an important role in developing children's self-monitoring. Among the environment factors that may influence the development of individuals' self-monitoring, the home and the school, two environment variables, can cause comprehensive, profound and direct influence on the development of individuals' self-monitoring [Wang, 2002]; there is no significant difference between the capacity of self-monitoring of learning of the students from different regions and different ethnic groups [Fu *et al.*, 2002]. Different methods to control and influence experiments can significantly influence students' capacity of monitoring their memory [Kelemen, 2000; Roebers, 2002].

## Individual Factors

There is significant correlation among students' age, intelligence and non-intelligence factors and capacity of self-monitoring of learning. Students' cognitive style can cause certain influence on the capacity of self-monitoring of learning, and the degree of influence and the dimensions influenced will be different due to the different grades [Fu *et al.*, 2002]. Students' learning motivation, attribution and self-efficacy are all the important internal factors that can influence the self-monitoring of learning. There is significant negative correlation between the surface learning motivation and the self-monitoring of learning, there is significant positive correlation between the deep learning motivation and the self-monitoring of learning, while there is no significant correlation between the motivation of achievement-oriented learning and the self-monitoring of learning; the score on internal control of attribution of success is in direct proportion to the self-monitoring of learning, while there is no significant correlation between the attribution of failure and the self-monitoring of learning; there is positive correlation between the self-efficacy and the self-monitoring of learning [Dong and Zhou, 1995]. Students of different genders have different capacity of self-monitoring of learning: female students' capacity is higher than male students' [Fu *et al.*, 2002]. The learning-based objective is helpful to establish successful manners for self-monitoring of learning, while the academic-performance-based objective will definitely cause unsuccessful ones [Wo et al., 2001]. There is high positive correlation between the learning self-monitoring of students with medium academic performance and such personality straits as stable emotion, rule-consciousness and self-discipline, while there is negative correlation between the aforesaid learning self-monitoring and such personality traits as anxiety and tension [Lian and Meng, 2003]. High-task-oriented college students incline to more frequently use the self-monitoring strategy and are more motivated to avoid negative evaluation [Riverro et al., 2001]. There is significant difference between the learning self-monitoring of slightly mentally handicapped students and that of normal students at the same age [Zhao and Zuo, 2002].

## 2) Relationships between Self-Monitoring and Academic Performance

Students' self-monitoring is closely related to their academic performance [Yi, 2002]. Students' self-monitoring of learning indirectly influences their academic performance through the self conception and learning strategies [Li and Yu, 2002]. The difference between remedial and summative self-monitoring is an important cause for the different academic performance of math of students with medium academic performance and those with excellent performance; there is no significant correlation between the self-monitoring of students with medium academic performance and their academic performance of Chinese and English, while there is significant positive correlation between the self-monitoring of students with excellent academic performance and their academic performance of English, especially their awareness, methods, feedback etc.; in addition, there is also significant positive correlation between some components of their self-monitoring, i.e. awareness and methods, and their academic performance of Chinese [Luo and Lian, 2002]. Students' academic performance and special skills on the following subjects can be improved by cultivating students' self-monitoring during the teaching of specific subject: Chinese (mainly concentrated in the cultivation on and research into reading and writing) [Xie, 2000], math [Luo and Lian, 2002] and physical education (PE) [Song and Peng, 2002].

The math is an active area for the research into students' self-monitoring of learning, and the previous research was mainly concentrated on the relationships with math, the importance, characteristics of development, influential factors, detailed cultivation measures etc. Luo and Lian [2002] indicated the close relationships between students' self-monitoring and their academic performance of math via analyzing and comparing the academic performance of math of students with medium and excellent academic performance. Zhang [1998] has, according to the characteristics of math, deepening of math-based cognitive activities, effective cultivation of students' academic performance of math and improvement of all middle school students' academic performance of math, described the importance of the research into self-monitoring of math learning, proposed the program of researching into math-learning self-monitoring and emphasized the thoughts, ideas and issues that great importance or attention should be attached to. According to Ning's [2001] research, the effective monitoring and adjustment on cognitive activities can establish substantive connections between the new and old knowledge and remarkably improve the transfer of mathematic skills; students' self-monitoring and adjustment capacity should be improved to transfer the skills for solving unconventional problems, and this cannot be achieved only by large quantity of exercise. Wu and Zhang [2002] explained the meaning and functions of evaluation on math self-monitoring and proposed that evaluation on middle school students' math self-monitoring was the key and basis for the reform of math education. Li [1992] held that the development of primary school students' self-monitoring of math learning was composed of three stages: a) grade 2 - grade 3 to understand and cognize the monitoring skills, b) grade 3 - grade 4 to practice and master the preliminary monitoring skills, and c) grade 4 - grade 5 to use skills proficiently and begin to fall into the habit of self-monitoring. According to the research of Li [1997], the motivation, attribution, self-confidence and will traits of math learning can all significantly influence the self-monitoring of students' math learning. In respect of the degree of influence, the will traits cause the greatest influence, then the self-confidence and then the attribution; the motivation causes the smallest influence. Ni [2002] proposed the modes of cultivating self-monitoring during the process of solving word problems. Ni held that the process of solving the word problem can be divided into six steps: representation of problems, determining the concept to solve the problem, formulating for calculation, examining results, remedy and summarization.

### 3) Cultivation of Students' Self-Monitoring

Wang [2000] held that the guide of methods was important for the cultivation of students' self-monitoring and proposed the teaching procedures for reading under self-monitoring consistent with students' cognition laws. Rubman et al. [2000] held that primary school students' self-monitoring can be enhanced remarkably with storyboard so as to improve their academic performance in reading. Xie [2000] indicated that teachers should consciously teach students the knowledge on self-monitoring, set a good example (such as think aloud) to enable students to understand the positive functions of self-monitoring in reading comprehension, and adopt such methods as QandA or role transposition in the teaching process to strengthen students' awareness of self-monitoring. Zhang *et al.* [2002] used the self-monitoring theory to improve college students' writing ability, holding that the self-monitoring training played a significant role at the stages of designing the writing, expressing the thoughts and revising and improving the writing and that the guide and training of self-monitoring should be persistent to ensure the long-term effect. Luo and Gao [1999] proposed the basic methods and strategies to cultivate students' self-monitoring during the teaching of PE. Zhong *et al.* [2000] held that the self-monitoring enabled students to be more goal-focused, more plan-based and more initiative and conscious via the experimental research into the teaching of PE, that it was precondition for cultivating the self-monitoring to focus on the information-based strategy and that it was the essence of cultivating the self-monitoring to integrate practice and thinking. You [1997] used the Chinese and math textbooks and optional textbooks to, via the intensive training and daily teaching for the students in grade 3 and grade 5, explored the effective approach to enhance their awareness of strategy and self-monitoring of thinking. Zhang and Xiang [2002] have, from the perspective of psychological suzhi-based education, discussed the knowledge on self-monitoring of coping with frustration, trained the skills on self-monitoring of coping with frustration, strengthened the experience in self-monitoring of coping with frustration, etc.

## Deficiencies of the Previous Research

### *1) From the Perspective of Research Tools, the Testing Tool is not Directly Targeted at Certain Students*

The testing tools of students' self-monitoring of learning in China are mostly made based on the research into and the revision of scales introduced from western countries, and the well targeted tool is only the "scale on self-monitoring of learning" by Dong *et al.* This scale, although it is applicable to testing middle school and primary school students' learning self-monitoring, is neither directly targeted at the primary school students, nor at the math teaching for primary school students. From the perspective of time and testing target, this scale is not well targeted either in view of its content and the expression.

### *2) From the Perspective of Research Field, Only a Little Research Amidst the Great Deal of Research Is Directly Targeted at the Self-Monitoring of Learning in the Math Class*

In respect of the research target, many researchers held that primary school students were at the beginning stage of development according to the development characteristics of students' self-monitoring of learning and that most research should focus on college students and middle school students. Therefore, there is little research into primary school students' self-monitoring of their learning.

In respect of the research content: a) the existing research mainly focused on the empirical research into the relationships between the theoretical discussion on students' self-monitoring of their learning and the development characteristics, influential factors and academic performance, and b) the research mainly involved reading comprehension and writing of Chinese and other subjects, including math and physical education. Among such research, there was little empirical research into the relationships between students' self-monitoring of their learning in the math class and the development of all aspects.

### 3) From the Perspective of Research Methods the Empirical Research was Too Simplified

Although the research into students' self-monitoring of their learning was increasingly furthered and sub-defined in recent years and the empirical research tended to be better, the research methods were not comprehensive and systematic.

The investigation and research focused on the horizontal or vertical comparison of development characteristics of students' self-monitoring of their learning; the experimental research focused on the changes in students' academic performance or learning capacity (traits); there were also some problems in cultivation and research: the specific-problem-based training was conducted in simple manner, all subjects were not closely connected with each other, there were no systematic methods and attentions were paid to the one-dimensional and short-term effect of good academic performance. There was scarcely research with comprehensive manners, multiple targets and systematic methods.

## Significance of the Research

### 1) It Can Not Only Enrich China's Research into the Self-Monitoring of Learning, but Also Be Helpful to Explore New Modes for School's Psychological Suzhi Education

The theory on self-monitoring of learning is a theory about students' learning that emerged in western countries in the 1970s. According to this theory, learning is a motivation-driven, metacognition-based and behavioral self-monitoring process. It emphasizes human's value and potential and attaches great importance to students' initiative of learning. Since the 1990s, many Chinese experts and scholars have, based on the research of foreign countries, made the empirical research into the self-monitoring of learning. From the perspective of scope, such research concentrated on the development of and comparative study on students' self-monitoring of learning; from the perspective of targets, such research were mainly targeted at college students and middle school students; from the perspective of content, such research focused on its development characteristics, influential factors and the relationships with academic performance etc.

In respect of the psychological suzhi-based education, this chapter, based on the teaching of math, took the primary school students in grade 5 as the research target, discussed the characteristics of their self-monitoring of learning, explored the approaches and methods to connect the cultivation of their self-monitoring of learning to the teaching of math, and indicated the relationships between students' self-monitoring of learning and their psychological suzhi and academic performance via cultivating psychological suzhi by "subject infiltration" in order to enhance primary school students' self-monitoring of learning, perfect their psychological suzhi and improve their academic performance. It can be used not only to explore the modes for infiltrating the psychological suzhi-based education into the school's classroom teaching, but also to enrich the study on and research into students' self-monitoring of learning.

### 2) It ss Not Only Helpful to Achieve the Objective for Subject Teaching, But Also Can Increase the Approaches for Psychological Suzhi-Based Education

The psychological suzhi-based education is to develop students' cognitive capacity and healthy personality and cultivate good social adaptability for them with scientific educational means in accordance with the principle of students' psychological adaptation and development. The basic psychological suzhi-based education approaches include specific-problem-based training, subject infiltration and consultation and counseling. The "research team on students' mental health education and PST" led by professor Zhang has conducted systematic research on the "specific-problem-based training" and "consultation and counseling" ofpsychological suzhi-based educationin recent years, while the research into "subject infiltration" was at starting stage.

The cultivation mode of "subject infiltration" requires to find out the connection between teaching of a subject and the development of students' psychological suzhi, apply psychological suzhi-based education strategies with clear objectives and well-prepared plans and infiltrate psychological suzhi-based education into the teaching of a subject in order to effectively realize the objective for the teaching of a subject and help students develop sound psychological suzhi. This chapter organically integrated the study on textbooks with the analysis on students' psychological traits based on the math textbook for primary school students in grade 5 and according to the development characteristics of primary school students' self-monitoring of learning and the characteristics of math teaching. It focused on the teaching of a subject and increased its functions so as to realize the integrated educational functions of "conductingpsychological suzhi-based educationvia teaching of a subject" and "improving teaching of a subject via psychological suzhi-based education".

### 3) It Can Promote the Development of Primary School Students' Intelligence and Ability and Enhance Their Academic Performance

The development of students' self-monitoring of learning can cause direct influence on the development of their intelligence; it can also demonstrate students' thinking capacity and intelligence. Students' self-monitoring of learning becomes the key factor for their academic performance if they have acquired certain basic knowledge.

Good self-monitoring of learning can help students analyze the learning task, make feasible learning plans and select appropriate learning methods according to the different learning contents and their own learning characteristics; it can direct students to apply the selected methods during the learning and supervise the learning progress to make it consistent with the schedule; it can promote students to reflect, summarize or evaluate the effect achieved to learn from the experience and prepare for the following learning.

Senior primary school students are exactly at the stage to develop their cognitive capability, learning capacity and habits. Therefore, improving students' self-monitoring of learning plays an extremely important role in developing students' intelligence, helping students perform their initiative and consciousness, reducing students' burden in learning, improving their learning efficiency, cultivating the learning capability, etc. In addition, it can also help students develop some good living and learning habits and well solve their problems, such as "how to learn", "study weariness and truancy" and "carelessness and arbitrariness", so as to lay a foundation for improving the learning efficiency.

### 4) It is Not Only Helpful to Solve Students' Psychological Problems in Learning, But Also Can Promote the Sound Development of Primary School Students' Psychological Suzhi.

According to the survey of Bian and Zheng [1997] in respect of the mental health of primary school students in Hangzhou, China, Chinese primary school students' problems in their study, emotion and behavior are more and more prominent due to the increasingly sharp competitions during social development and the mistakes in home education and school education.

Great importance should be attached to the issues on students' psychological suzhi. Primary school students are in the fundamental stage for the development of individual's suzhi.

Thanks to the unique and great openness and plasticity of primary school students' psychological development, such students are in a good period for individuals to form good psychological suzhi and behavioral habits. In addition, senior primary students are faced with an important transition during the student life: the content of learning and life is richer and more complicated. Only when their psychological suzhi is developed on a healthy basis, can they better adapt to the current life and study and pave the way for better development of future life and study.

Students' self-monitoring of learning is the core component of the cognition dimension of students' psychological suzhi structure. It plays a primary and crucial role in students' learning activities and meanwhile restricts the formation and development of other psychological traits. Good self-monitoring of learning can stimulate and maintain attentions, good emotions and motivations of students and help students transform from "someone makes me learn" into "I want to learn"; it can improve students' personality and help students actively adapt to the life, the study and the society; it is helpful for the overall, harmonious and healthy development of students' suzhi.

## Contents and Hypotheses of the Research

### 1) Main Contents

First, make and revise the questionnaire on primary school students' self-monitoring of learning and prepare the tools for pre-test and post-test of the experimental research. Second, survey and analyze the characteristics of learning self-monitoring of primary school students in grades four, five and six with the aforesaid questionnaire, and well prepare for the selection and arrangement of experimental contents. Third, well prepare for the experimental research in the aspect of methods and theories by theoretically analyzing the necessity and feasibility of infiltration cultivation as well as its mode and implementation strategies. Fourth, implement the experimental plan and verify the hypotheses according to the results of preparation and revision of questionnaires, characteristic analysis and theory construction.

### 2) Basic Hypotheses

*Hypothesis 1:* students' self-monitoring of learning is a diachronic process as well as a synchronic structure. The individual traits of primary school students' self-monitoring of learning have the uncertainty of differentiation.

*Hypothesis 2:* students' self-monitoring of learning is not only the psychological precondition for enhancing students' learning capacity, but also the effective indicator to forecast students' academic performance.

*Hypothesis 3:* students' self-monitoring of learning can be cultivated via subject infiltration. The systematic infiltration-based cultivation during the classroom teaching of math is feasible and effective to enhance students' self-monitoring of learning. Hypothesis 4: the modes of systematically infiltrating the cultivation of students' self-monitoring of learning into the classroom teaching of math can promote the development of their psychological suzhi.

## REVISION AND CHARACTERISTIC ANALYSIS OF QUESTIONNAIRE ON PRIMARY SCHOOL STUDENTS' SELF-MONITORING OF LEARNING

In order to provide the pre-test and post-test tools with good reliability and validity for the experimental research on infiltrating cultivation of students' self-monitoring of learning into the classroom teaching of math for primary school students in grade 5, this chapter first revised the "Questionnaire on Primary School Students' Self-Monitoring of Learning", then used this questionnaire to analyze the development characteristics of the learning self-monitoring of primary school students in grades four, five and six. This has, from the perspective of content, provided some basis and reference for the implementation of the experiment.

## Revision of the Questionnaire on Primary School Students' Self-Monitoring of Learning

### 1) Basis for Revising Items in the Questionnaire

This questionnaire was revised in accordance with such principles as the components should match with the item and the psychological characteristics should be consistent with the primary school students' age. The self-descriptive scale method was used for the research into students' self-monitoring of learning.

The items in the questionnaire were determined in accordance with the following basis:

The dimension structure was made according to the dimension structure on students' self-monitoring of learning in the "scale on self-monitoring of learning" by Dong *et al.* This structure divided students' self-monitoring of learning into three aspects: a) planning and arranging the learning activities in advance; b) supervising, evaluating and giving feedback on the actual learning activities; c) adjusting, correcting and controlling the learning activities based on the aforesaid two steps.

To be specific: a) pre-learning self-monitoring: planning, students' plan and arrangement of learning activities in advance. For example, students may make plans before the learning, which will determine what the learning content is and how, when and how long they will learn. Preparation: students' specific preparation for the learning activities in advance.

For example, students may prepare the learning tools, create a good learning environment and adjust and maintain the good emotion and energy. b) self-monitoring during learning: awareness, students' awareness of the learning objectives, targets and tasks during the learning activities, such as understanding why the teacher teaches the certain content in class. Methods: students' emphasis on strategies during such learning activities as preparing for class, learning in class, doing homework and reviewing after class, and their selection and adoption of appropriate learning methods.

For example, students may, when they are preparing for class, mark the knowledge that they cannot understand, comprehend the teacher's thoughts in class by means of comprehension-based memory. Implementation, students' control of their implementation of learning plans during the learning activities and removal of relevant interference to ensure the learning effect.

For example, students may insist in starting other things after completing the learning task. c) Post-learning self-monitoring: feedback, students' inspection, feedback and evaluation on the learning status and effect after their learning activities. Remedy: the remedial measures that students adopted against the learning effect after their learning activities according to the feedback.

For example, they may, if they find that they fail to master a certain part of the content, spend more time or take more measures so as to achieve good learning effect. Summarization: students' reflection and summarization of their learning experiences after the learning activities.

For example, students may summarize or use for reference their own or other's good learning methods and experiences or those mentioned in books to distill and improve their own learning approaches and methods.

In respect of the source of such items: a) we used the 70 items in the "scale on self-monitoring of learning" for reference and improved the expression manner to make them more suitable for primary school students and the classroom teaching of math; b) we determined the representative daily behavior and psychological description based on the actual teaching experience and the inquiry for primary school students.

## 2) Procedures for Revising the Questionnaire

Determine the structure of the questionnaire: to improve and determine the eight dimensions according to the framework of the "scale on self-monitoring of learning" by Dong *et al.*

Prepare the pilot questionnaire: to finish the initial questionnaire (65 questions) according to the specific structure of the questionnaire and the basis for determining the items therein.

Determine the participant: to determine the participant according to the objective and needs of the research. The selected participants were almost the representative primary school students in grades four, five and six in Sichuan and Chongqing due to the objective conditions.

Conduct group test: to conduct formal group tests on the selected participants and 653 effective participants were obtained, where 195 were in grade 4, 271 were in grade 5 and 187 were in grade 6.

Analyze the forecast questionnaire: to make statistics and analysis on the recovered effective questionnaires to mainly inspect the difficulty, discrimination, reliability and validity of the questionnaire. Use SPSS10.0 and AMOS4.0 for analysis and processing.

Complete the final questionnaire: adjust the factors and items according to the pilot study results, revise and adjust the questionnaire and then complete the final questionnaire for the purpose of further analysis and experimental research.

### 3) Analysis and Verification of the Results of Revising the Questionnaire

**Analysis of Items**

The discrimination was used in this chapter to evaluate the quality of items and to select items. According to the analysis of the correlation between all items and the total score of the questionnaire (table omitted), 46 items in the questionnaire have good discrimination (the discriminability index is above 0.4), accounting for 70.8% of the total number of 65 items; 19 items in the questionnaire have ordinary level of discrimination (the discriminability index is between 0.2 and 0.4), accounting for 29.2% of the total number; no item in the questionnaire has poor discrimination (the discriminability index is below 0.2). Use the independent sample $t$ test to test the difference between the high score team (accounting for 27% of the total participants) and the low score team (accounting for 27% of the total participants) in respect of each item. The $t$ values of the 65 questions in the questionnaire were significantly different, indicating that each item of the initial questionnaire had good discriminate validity.

**Exploratory Factor Analysis**

*First-order factor analysis*

Conduct principal component analysis and factor analysis with orthogonal rotation on the questionnaire items. It is reasonable to extract 8 factors, which can explain 42.260% of the total variance. Remove 23 items from the aforesaid questionnaire and reserve 42 items. Conduct factor analysis again and 8 factors were obtained, which can explain 48.369% of the total variance (please see Table 6.1 and Table 6.2).

According to the principle of naming a factor (i.e. observing which dimension of the theoretical conception is the major source of the items of the factor, and using for reference the items with high loading value): most items of factor 1 came from the "remedy" factor of the theoretical conception, and some coming from the factors of "methods" and "awareness" still aimed to describe the content in respect of "remedy", so it was named "remedy"; most items of factor 2 came from the original "feedback" factor, so it was named "feedback"; most items of factor 3 came from the original "preparation" factor, so it was named "preparation"; most items of factor 4 came from the original "summarization" factor, so it was named "summarization"; most items of factor 5 came from the original "methods" factor, so it was named "methods"; most items of factor 6 came from the original "planning" factor, so it was named "planning"; most items of factor 7 came from the original "implementation" factor, so it was named "implementation"; most items of factor 8 came from the original "awareness" factor, so it was named "awareness".

*Second-order factor analysis*

Take the eight factors obtained via the first-order factor analysis as new variables and conduct a second order factor analysis. It's proper to extract three factors, which can explain 71.848% of the total variance (please see Table 6.3 and Table 6.4).

**Table 6.1. First-Order Factor Analysis on Factor Loading of the Questionnaire of Primary School Students' Self-Monitoring of Learning**

| Items | Factor 1 | Factor 2 | Factor 3 | Factor 4 | Factor 5 | Factor 6 | Factor 7 | Factor 8 | Communality |
|---|---|---|---|---|---|---|---|---|---|
| $N_{15}$ | | | | | | | | | .582 |
| $N_{23}$ | | | | | | | | | .483 |
| $N_{56}$ | | | | | | | | | .465 |
| $N_{11}$ | | | | | | | | | .549 |
| $N_7$ | | | | | | | | | .478 |
| $N_{62}$ | | | | | | | | | .484 |
| $N_{61}$ | | | | | | | | | .445 |
| $N_{31}$ | | | | | | | | | .486 |
| $N_{63}$ | | | | | | | | | .467 |
| $N_{43}$ | | | | | | | | | .399 |
| $N_{51}$ | | | | | | | | | .421 |
| $N_{30}$ | | | | | | | | | .533 |
| $N_{38}$ | | | | | | | | | .455 |
| $N_{36}$ | | | | | | | | | .350 |
| $N_{44}$ | | | | | | | | | .472 |
| $N_{41}$ | .633 | | | | | | | | .424 |
| $N_{28}$ | .612 | | | | | | | | .380 |
| $N_{33}$ | .605 | | | | | | | | .492 |
| $N_{34}$ | .598 | | | | | | | | .576 |
| $N_{42}$ | .581 | | | | | | | | .546 |
| $N_{39}$ | .576 | | | | | | | | .502 |
| $N_{26}$ | .570 | | | | | | | | .470 |
| $N_{18}$ | .517 | | | | | | | | .482 |
| $N_6$ | .506 | .699 | | | | | | | .595 |
| $N_{14}$ | .499 | .548 | | | | | | | .672 |
| $N_8$ | .415 | .496 | | | | | | | .574 |
| $N_{16}$ | | .491 | | | | | | | .534 |
| $N_{50}$ | | .471 | .730 | | | | | | .496 |
| $N_{64}$ | | .469 | .584 | | | | | | .491 |
| $N_{58}$ | | .444 | .561 | | | | | | .497 |
| $N_{35}$ | | | .443 | .692 | | | | | .499 |
| $N_{65}$ | | | .433 | .669 | | | | | .456 |
| $N_9$ | | | | .647 | .606 | | | | .616 |
| $N_1$ | | | | .502 | .601 | | | | .480 |
| $N_5$ | | | | | .574 | | | | .424 |
| $N_{59}$ | | | | | .439 | | | | .437 |
| $N_{49}$ | | | | | .430 | .697 | | | .413 |
| $N_{48}$ | | | | | | .631 | .625 | | .448 |
| $N_{55}$ | | | | | | .568 | .582 | | .456 |
| $N_{22}$ | | | | | | | .503 | .570 | .438 |
| $N_{20}$ | | | | | | | .410 | .523 | .478 |
| $N_{46}$ | | | | | | | | .503 | .424 |

**Table 6.2. First-Order Factor Analysis on the Eigenvalue and Contribution of Each Factor of Primary School Students' Self-Monitoring of Learning**

| Factors | Eigenvalue | Contribution (%) | Factors | Eigenvalue | Contribution (%) |
|---|---|---|---|---|---|
| 1 | 4.437 | 10.565 | 5 | 2.256 | 5.371 |
| 2 | 2.891 | 6.883 | 6 | 2.064 | 4.915 |
| 3 | 2.547 | 6.063 | 7 | 1.893 | 4.507 |
| 4 | 2.387 | 5.683 | 8 | 1.841 | 4.382 |
| Total | | | | | 48.369 |

**Table 6.3. Second-Order Factor Analysis on Factor Loading of the Questionnaire on Primary School Students' Self-Monitoring of Learning**

| Variables | Factor 1 | Factor 2 | Factor 3 |
|---|---|---|---|
| Remedy | .847 | | |
| Methods | .825 | | |
| Summarization | .783 | | |
| Implementation | | .819 | |
| Preparation | | .802 | |
| Feedback | | .664 | |
| Planning | | | .862 |
| Awareness | | | .612 |

**Table 6.4. Second-Order Factor Analysis on the Eigenvalue and Contribution of Each Factor of Primary School Students' Self-Monitoring of Learning**

| Factors | Eigenvalue | Contribution (%) | Accumulated Contribution (%) |
|---|---|---|---|
| 1 | 2.164 | 27.051 | 27.051 |
| 2 | 2.155 | 26.935 | 53.986 |
| 3 | 1.429 | 17.862 | 71.848 |

Factor 1 includes remedy, methods and summarization. They mainly came from the "post-learning" dimension of the theoretical conception and were mainly to describe students' mastery of while-learning strategies and their active adjustment of post-learning strategies. Therefore, factor 1 is named as "optimization of learning". Factor 2 includes implementation, preparation and feedback.

They mainly came from the "while-learning" dimension of the theoretical conception and were mainly to describe students' operation and implementation of pre-learning, while-learning and post-learning activities. Therefore, factor 2 is named as "implementation of learning". Factor 3 includes planning and awareness.

They mainly came from the "pre-learning" dimension of the theoretical conception and were mainly to describe students' awareness and planning of the whole learning process. Therefore, factor 3 is named as "planning of learning". According to the results of second-order factor analysis, we can conclude the empirical mode on primary school students' self-monitoring of learning (please see Figure 6.1).

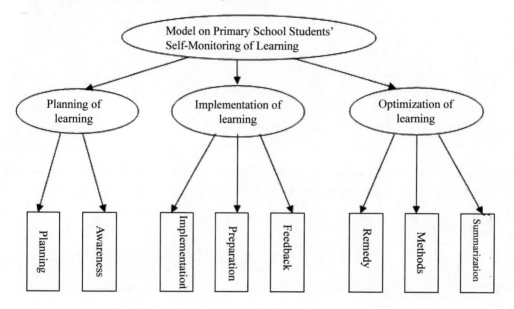

Figure 6.1. Empirical Mode of Primary School Students' Self-Monitoring of Learning.

## Test Of Reliability

We mainly aim to test the internal consistency reliability and the split-half reliability of the questionnaire. According to the analysis (table omitted), the internal consistency reliability of all sub-scales is between 0.536 and 0.846, while that of the total scale is 0.909; the split-half reliability of all sub-scales is between 0.468 and 0.831, while that of the total scale is 0.885. This indicates that the questionnaire has good reliability.

## Test Of Validity

The construct validity of the questionnaire was estimated based on the correlation between factors, between each factor and the total score of the questionnaire, between sub-scales and between each sub-scale and the total score of the questionnaire.

The results (table omitted) have shown that the correlation between factors is between 0.132 and 0.613, a moderate correlation, and that the correlation between sub-scales is between 0.289 and 0.636, also a moderate correlation. This indicates that the questionnaire has good construct validity.

## Confirmatory Factor Analysis

Generally speaking, a mode with high degree of fit should have low value respect of $\chi^2$, RMSEA and RMR and $\chi^2/df{\leq}5$ and RMSEA${\leq}0.05$. It is held that RMSEA${\leq}0.08$ and RMR${\leq}0.10$ are also acceptable; the closer GFI, AGFI, NFI, NNFI, CFI and IFI are to 1, the better the mode is. Anderson [1984], Cole [1987] et al. have proposed that GFI${\geq}0.85$ and AGFI${\geq}0.80$ are also acceptable.

We assumed the following modes during the analysis:

SS1: first-order eight-factor mode, with the eight factors including remedy, feedback, preparation, summarization, methods, planning, implementation and awareness.

SS2: second-order one-factor and first-order eight-factor mode and eight-factor homogeneous test mode, with the second-order factor named "planning of learning".

SS3: second-order two-factor and first-order eight-factor mode, with the second-order factor named "planning of learning" and "implementation of learning".

SS4: second-order three-factor and first-order eight-factor mode, with the second-order factor named "planning of learning", "implementation of learning" and "optimization of learning".

SS5: third-order one-factor, second-order three-factor and first-order eight-factor mode, with the second-order factor named "planning of learning", "implementation of learning" and "optimization of learning".

The results are demonstrated in Table 6.5. Among the five modes, SS1 mode has been rejected obviously and the indicators following modes improve one by one, where SS4 mode and SS5 mode are better than the previous modes and SS5 mode is the most ideal one. (Please see Figure 6.2).

### 4) Conclusion of the Revised Questionnaire on Primary School Students' Self-Monitoring of Learning

#### 1) Scientificity

The revised *Questionnaire on Primary School Students' Self-Monitoring of Learning* in this chapter has consulted, from the theoretical perspective, the structure of students' self-monitoring of learning in the "scale on self-monitoring of learning" by Dong *et al.*; it was revised in accordance with such principle as the component should match with the item and the psychological characteristics should be consistent with the primary school students' age; it was revised following the procedure of determining the structure of questionnaire-preparing the initial questionnaire-determining the test targets-conducting group test-analyzing the initial questionnaire-completing the final questionnaire; it selected the students in grades four, five and six in representative schools and regions as the test targets; the test was standard and strict; in case of questionnaire processing, the final questionnaire and the theoretical mode were established and validated following the steps of item discrimination analysis, exploratory factor analysis and confirmatory factor analysis. The analysis and validation have shown that the questionnaire has good reliability and effectiveness and can be used as the effective tool for the characteristic analysis and experimental research of self-monitoring of learning of primary school students in grades four, five and six.

#### 2) Results of Analysis on the Questionnaire's Structure

The results of exploratory factor analysis and confirmatory factor analysis have shown that the third-order one-factor, second-order three-factor and first-order eight-factor mode is the most ideal one. It is consistent with our theoretical hypotheses, except for the naming of second-order factors. The second-order factors of students' self-monitoring of learning were named as pre-learning, while-learning and post-learning in the "scale on self-monitoring of learning" by Dong *et al.*

**Table 6.5. CFA Indicators of the Five Hypothesis Modes on Primary School Students' Self-Monitoring of Learning**

| Mode | $\chi^2$ | df | $\chi^2/df$ | p | RMSEA | GFI | AGFI | RMR | NFI | IFI | CFI | TLI |
|------|--------|-----|-------|-----|-------|-------|-------|-------|-------|-------|-------|-------|
| SS1 | 3278.4 | 819 | 4.003 | 0.0 | 0.068 | 0.764 | 0.740 | 0.286 | 0.579 | 0.855 | 0.645 | 0.627 |
| SS2 | 1813.4 | 811 | 2.236 | 0.0 | 0.044 | 0.881 | 0.867 | 0.108 | 0.767 | 0.647 | 0.856 | 0.846 |
| SS3 | 1711.1 | 810 | 2.112 | 0.0 | 0.041 | 0.884 | 0.870 | 0.109 | 0.780 | 0.871 | 0.870 | 0.860 |
| SS4 | 1384.7 | 808 | 1.714 | 0.0 | 0.033 | 0.905 | 0.894 | 0.067 | 0.822 | 0.917 | 0.917 | 0.911 |
| SS5 | 62.008 | 17 | 3.648 | 0.0 | 0.032 | 0.977 | 0.951 | 0.025 | 0.967 | 0.976 | 0.976 | 0.960 |

**Table 6.6. Mean Values and Standard Deviations of all Factors of Primary School Students' Self-Monitoring of Learning**

| Variables | M / SD |
|-----------|--------|
| Remedy | 3.936 / .729 |
| Feedback | 3.419 / .845 |
| Preparation | 3.913 / .946 |
| Summarization | 3.641 / .874 |
| Methods | 3.703 / .779 |
| Planning | 3.492 / .947 |
| Implementation | 3.442 / .921 |
| Awareness | 3.262 / .998 |
| Optimization of Learning | 3.760 / .666 |
| Implementation of learning | 3.592 / .762 |
| Planning of learning | 3.377 / .816 |
| Total average scores | 3.665 / .585 |

Such names were determined based on the time when students completed a learning task and it is definitely helpful to understand the sequence of teaching and learning. However, such inflexible division as self-monitoring of pre-learning, while-learning and post-learning activities is inconsistent with the actual self-monitoring of learning.

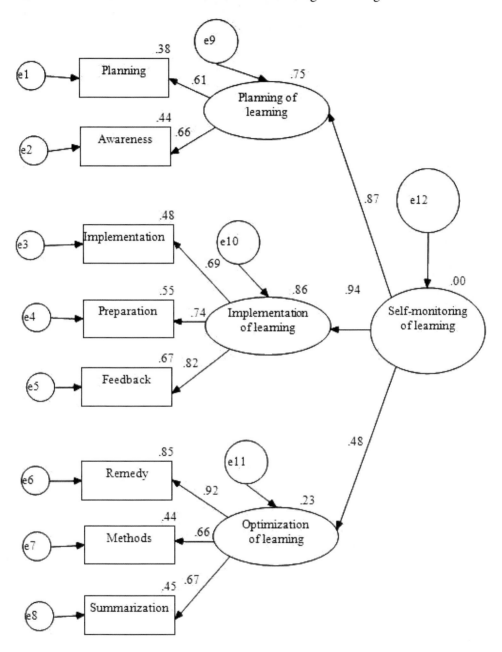

Figure 6.2. Third-Order One-Factor, Second-Order Three-Factor and First-Order Eight-Factor Mode on Primary School Students' Self-Monitoring of Learning.

It has been found through the analysis that: students' self-monitoring of learning is not only a diachronic process, but also a synchronic structure, and the individual traits of primary school students' self-monitoring of learning have the uncertainty of differentiation; awareness is involved in all factors of pre-learning, while-learning and post-learning activities and is linked with planning more closely; methods may be involved in planning, implementation and remedy; there is interaction between methods and summarization, feedback and remedy, as well as preparation and awareness. Therefore, according to this chapter, it can better accord with the actual condition to name the factors based on the self-monitoring stages that students have experienced during a learning task (planning of learning, implementation of learning and optimization of learning) since it can better demonstrate students' psychological development and changes and can make the teaching and learning better targeted.

## Characteristics of Primary School Students' Self-Monitoring of Learning

Inspect the obtained effective participants when using the revised "Questionnaire on Primary School Students' Self-Monitoring of Learning" for the test on participants, discuss the general characteristics of and the specific difference between the self-monitoring of learning of primary school students in different grades, of different genders, from different families and in different types of schools so as to provide necessary evidence for further experimental research.

### 1) General Characteristics of Primary School Students' Self-Monitoring of Learning

According to the results of descriptive statistics (please see Table 6.6), the average scores of all factors are within a moderate range, from 3.262 to 3.936. The first-order factors, in descending order of average scores, are: remedy > preparation > methods > summarization > planning > implementation > feedback > awareness. The second-order factors, in descending order of average scores, are: optimization of learning > implementation of learning > planning of learning.

### 2) Analysis of Variance of Primary School Students' Self-Monitoring of Learning

A 2×3×2×2 multifactorial analysis of variance was made in this chapter on the difference between all factors of self-monitoring in different types of schools, in different grades, of different genders and from different family locations (please see Table 6.7).

The results have shown that there is no significant difference between the main effects of the gender, grade and type of school on learning self-monitoring, but there is significant difference in case of the factor of family background; there is no significant difference between the second-order interaction of primary students' learning self-monitoring as a whole, while there is significant difference in the interaction between certain factors of the self-monitoring and type of school × class, type of school × gender, type of school × location of family, class × location of family etc.

**Table 6.7. Analysis of Variance of Self-Monitoring of Students in Different Schools and Grades, of Different Genders and from Different Families (F value)**

| Factors | Type of School | Grade | Gender | Location of Family | Type of School × Class | Type of School × Gender | Type of School × Location of Family | Class × Location of Family |
|---|---|---|---|---|---|---|---|---|
| Remedy | 3.175 | .115 | .119 | 2.213 | 3.212* | 1.706 | .837 | 1.302 |
| Feedback | .810 | .384 | 2.020 | 15.455*** | 1.085 | .677 | 9.643** | 2.736 |
| Preparation | .111 | .756 | 2.678 | 9.886** | .984 | .131 | 8.471** | 3.705* |
| Summarization | .029 | .150 | .368 | 3.624 | 4.310* | .000 | 2.637 | .383 |
| Methods | 1.324 | .431 | .087 | .944 | 2.969 | .963 | .657 | .298 |
| Planning | .026 | 4.769** | .869 | 10.248** | 2.255 | 5.273* | 5.267* | 6.563** |
| Implementation | 1.132 | 2.493 | .614 | 11.608** | 1.570 | .827 | 4.175* | 2.638 |
| Awareness | .910 | .855 | 1.670 | 13.715*** | .019 | .749 | 4.640* | .542 |
| Optimization of Learning | 1.044 | .193 | .259 | 3.114 | 4.516* | .728 | 1.874 | .474 |
| Implementation of learning | .409 | 1.363 | 2.348 | 17.475*** | 1.677 | .046 | 10.308** | 4.181* |
| Planning of learning | .474 | 2.087 | .066 | 17.472*** | .837 | .652 | 7.209** | 3.802* |
| Total average scores | .085 | 1.039 | 1.201 | 15.132*** | 3.798* | .581 | 8.299** | 3.088* |

Note: * $p < 0.05$, ** $p < 0.01$, *** $p < 0.001$.

### 3) Analysis Of Difference Between Primary School Students' Self-Monitoring Of Learning

1) Difference between self-monitoring of learning of female and male primary school students

Table 6.8 has shown that female students' self-monitoring of learning is better than male students' and there is significant difference between the two as a whole. In respect of the factors, female students' development is better than male students' and there is significant difference between the factors of remedy, preparation and implementation.

2) Difference between self-monitoring of learning of primary school students from different types of schools

This chapter is to investigate the difference between the learning self-monitoring of students from ordinary and key primary schools. Table 6.9 has shown that there is significant difference as a whole between the self-monitoring of learning of students in different types of schools. The self-monitoring of learning of students in key primary schools is much better than that of students in ordinary primary schools.

To be specific, the students in key primary schools perform obviously better than those in ordinary ones in case of the remedy, the feedback, the preparation, the planning and the awareness, and perform significantly better than them in case of the summarization, the methods and the implementation.

**Table 6.8. Analysis on Difference between Self-Monitoring of Learning of Female and Male Primary School Students**

| Variables | Male (n=325) $M \pm SD$ | Female (n=328) $M \pm SD$ | t Value |
|---|---|---|---|
| Remedy | 3.8492±.7607 | 4.0225±.6868 | -3.055[**] |
| Feedback | 3.3675±.8336 | 3.4708±.8548 | -1.564 |
| Preparation | 3.7920±.9400 | 4.0335±.9378 | -3.287[**] |
| Summarization | 3.5869±.9071 | 3.6936±.8379 | -1.561 |
| Methods | 3.6548±.7783 | 3.7506±.7770 | -1.575 |
| Planning | 3.4605±.9216 | 3.5224±.9727 | -.834 |
| Implementation | 3.3362±.9229 | 3.5473±.9089 | -2.945[**] |
| Awareness | 3.2338±.9055 | 3.2907±.9904 | -.727 |
| Optimization of Learning | 3.6970±.6824 | 3.8222±.6444 | -2.411[*] |
| Implementation of learning | 3.4985±.7634 | 3.6839±.7495 | -3.130[**] |
| Planning of learning | 3.3472±.8088 | 3.4065±.8223 | -.929 |
| Total average scores | 3.5934±.5884 | 3.7349±.5737 | -3.111[**] |

Note: * $p < 0.05$, ** $p < 0.01$, *** $p < 0.001$.

**Table 6.9. Analysis on Difference between Self-Monitoring of Learning of Primary School Students from Different Types of Schools**

| Variables | Ordinary Primary School (n=364) $M \pm SD$ | Key Primary School (n=289) $M \pm SD$ | t Value |
|---|---|---|---|
| Remedy | 3.7980±.7218 | 4.1104±.7017 | 5.562[***] |
| Feedback | 3.2900±.8035 | 3.5823±.8695 | 4.452[***] |
| Preparation | 3.7203±.9523 | 4.1564±.8811 | 6.007[***] |
| Summarization | 3.5563±.8391 | 3.7465±.9064 | 2.777[**] |
| Methods | 3.6104±.7351 | 3.8194±.8164 | 3.434[**] |
| Planning | 3.3452±.9172 | 3.6759±.9542 | 4.495[***] |
| Implementation | 3.3771±.8663 | 3.5242±.9815 | 2.032[*] |
| Awareness | 3.1392±.9510 | 3.4175±.9642 | 3.573[***] |
| Optimization of Learning | 3.6549±.6359 | 3.8921±.6805 | 4.589[***] |
| Awareness | 3.1392±.9510 | 3.4175±.9642 | 3.573[***] |
| Optimization of Learning | 3.6549±.6359 | 3.8921±.6805 | 4.589[***] |
| Implementation of learning | 3.1625±.7240 | 3.7543±.7780 | 4.950[***] |
| Planning of learning | 3.2422±.7675 | 3.5467±.8435 | 4.819[***] |
| Total average scores | 3.5392±.5447 | 3.8222±.5965 | 6.321[***] |

Note: * $p < 0.05$, ** $p < 0.01$, *** $p < 0.001$.

3) Difference between self-monitoring of learning of primary school students from different family locations

Table 6.10 has shown that the self-monitoring of learning of urban students is significantly better than that of rural students as a whole. To be specific, urban students perform significantly better than rural students in case of the feedback, the preparation, the planning, the awareness, the remedy and the implementation, and perform extremely better than them in case of the feedback, the preparation, the planning and the awareness.

**Table 6.10. Analysis on Difference between Self-Monitoring of Learning of Primary School Students from Different Families**

| Variables | Rural Student (n=178) $M \pm SD$ | Urban Student (n=475) $M \pm SD$ | $t$ Value |
|---|---|---|---|
| Remedy | 3.7993±.6788 | 3.9876±.7413 | 2.956[**] |
| Feedback | 3.1966±.7603 | 3.5029±.8610 | 4.174[***] |
| Preparation | 3.6461±.9686 | 4.0135±.9184 | 4.484[***] |
| Summarization | 3.5632±.8407 | 3.6695±.8853 | 1.385 |
| Methods | 3.6146±.6918 | 3.7360±.8068 | 1.777 |
| Planning | 3.2360±.9337 | 3.5874±.9356 | 4.276[***] |
| Implementation | 3.2388±.8849 | 3.5184±.9240 | 3.483[**] |
| Awareness | 2.9757±.9534 | 3.3698±.9935 | 4.564[***] |
| Optimization of Learning | 3.6590±.6118 | 3.7977±.6820 | 2.377[*] |
| Implementation of learning | 3.3605±.7194 | 3.6783±.7598 | 4.827[***] |
| Planning of learning | 3.1058±.7530 | 3.4786±.8156 | 5.309[***] |
| Total average scores | 3.4837±.5190 | 3.7322±.5943 | 4.921[***] |

Note: * $p < 0.05$, ** $p < 0.01$, *** $p < 0.001$.

4) Difference between self-monitoring of learning of primary school students in different grades

Table 6.11 has shown that the self-monitoring of learning of primary school students in grade 4, 5 and 6 improves as the grade is higher: grade 6 > grade 5 > grade 4. However, such difference is not significant. Multiple comparisons have shown that there is significant difference between primary school students' self-monitoring of learning in case of the preparation and the awareness: grade 6 > grade 4.

5) Analysis of characteristics of primary school students' self-monitoring of learning

Chinese primary school students in grade 4, grade 5 and grade 6 do not have good self-monitoring of learning as a whole. They perform well in the remedy and the preparation, but poorly in the feedback and the awareness. The relatively better preparation may be caused by primary school teachers' intensified education or authoritative management on students' regulated learning; the relatively better remedy may be caused by the way that primary school students do their homework (do homework-correct mistakes-do homework) and teachers read and remark the homework (read and remark-reject-read and remark) as well as the inflexible teaching methods of teachers; the relatively weaker awareness and feedback may be caused not only by the slow development of students' psychological suzhi, but also by the undemocratic and non-heuristic teaching methods, which makes students think in an inactive, dependent and suppressed manner.

**Table 6.11. Analysis of Difference between Self-Monitoring of Learning of Primary School Students in Different Grades**

| Variables | Grade 4 (n=195) $M\pm SD$ | Grade 5 (n=271) $M\pm SD$ | Grade 6 (n=187) $M\pm SD$ | $F$ Value | Sig. |
|---|---|---|---|---|---|
| Remedy | 3.8732±.8004 | 3.9165±.7054 | 4.0306±.6780 | 2.406 | .091 |
| Feedback | 3.3971±.8680 | 3.3943±.8356 | 3.4790±.8367 | .652 | .522 |
| Preparation | 3.7918±.9606[1] | 3.9048±.9559 | 4.0524±.9014 | 3.672[*] | .026 |
| Summarization | 3.6090±.9385 | 3.6448±.8566 | 3.6671±.8319 | .216 | .806 |
| Methods | 3.7467±.8772 | 3.7299±.7453 | 3.6182±.7108 | 1.581 | .207 |
| Planning | 3.4342±.9426 | 3.5055±.9510 | 3.5312±.9495 | .550 | .577 |
| Implementation | 3.4359±.9084 | 3.4502±.8844 | 3.4372±.9894 | .017 | .983 |
| Awareness | 3.1214±1.0235 | 3.2903±.9700 | 3.3690±.9982[2] | 3.143[*] | .044 |
| Optimization of Learning | 3.7429±.7510 | 3.7637±.6425 | 3.7720±.6058 | .098 | .907 |
| Implementation of learning | 3.5416±.7653 | 3.5831±.7523 | 3.6562±.7711 | 1.110 | .330 |
| Planning of learning | 3.2778±.7924 | 3.3979±.8074 | 3.4501±.8450 | 2.292 | .102 |
| Total average scores | 3.6172±.5995 | 3.6615±.5470 | 3.7181±.5838 | 1.428 | .241 |

Notes: 1. There is significant difference between the self-monitoring of learning of primary school students in grade 4 and grade 6. 2. There is significant difference between the self-monitoring of learning of primary school students in grade 4 and grade 6.

Female students perform better than male students in self-monitoring of learning and there is significant difference between them, which is consistent with the conclusion of Fu [2002], Li *et al* [2001] that the self-monitoring of learning of female students is better than that of male students and there is quite significant difference. This is because the female's brain is mature earlier, they are more careful and introspect more often and they make more subjective efforts.

In respect of types of schools, the self-monitoring of learning of students in key schools is significantly better than that of those in ordinary schools. This is consistent with the research result of Li [2001], but the research targets are quite different: Li's research is targeted at the junior middle school student. This may be because the key schools provide better educational environment, enroll better or more students, pose greater learning expectation and create more competition pressure than ordinary schools.

In respect of location of families, the self-monitoring of learning of students from urban families is significantly better than that of those from rural families. This conclusion, together with the difference between students from different types of schools, further proves Wang's [2002] research: the environment can make significant influence on the development of children's self-monitoring; among all of the environment factors that may influence the development of individual's self-monitoring, the family and school environment can cause overall and profound direct influence on the development of individual's self-monitoring. This may be because the parents of urban families and the family members have received higher education and their devotion into and competition during their work as well as the independence and hardship in their life have caused earlier development of urban students' independent personality; the relatively better environment of urban families and the higher requirements and expectations of parents and family members to their children require that urban students should withstand lots of seducement, which makes them establish the awareness of self-monitoring earlier.

In respect of the grade, the self-monitoring of learning of primary school students in grade 4, 5 and 6 improves as the grade is higher: grade 6 > grade 5 > grade 4. This conclusion is consistent with the research of Dong *et al.* [1995] (students' self-monitoring of learning continues to improve as they grow older as a whole; from the perspective of specific monitoring traits, all aspects of students' self-monitoring of learning also continues to improve as they grow older) and Fu *et al.* [2002] (students' self-monitoring of learning improves as the grade is higher). This is because the functions of primary school student's brains are improving steadily, the school is conducting long-term and consistent regulated education and the students' learning tasks are increasing and deepening.

Different from the previous research, it has been found through further analysis that there is no significant difference between the students in such three grades as a whole. Multiple comparisons have shown that there is significant difference between the self-monitoring of learning of primary school students in grade 6 and grade 4 in the aspect of preparation and awareness.

It follows that educators should, during the education and cultivation of students' self-monitoring of learning, carefully select the school which the experimental group and the control group come from (mainly the ordinary primary school or the quasi-key primary school), select the grade which the experimental group and the control group are in (mainly grade 5), fully consider the location of family of the experimental group and the control group and the ratio of male students to female students (generally equal), and further analyze and process the data on the students of different genders and from the families in different locations when processing the experimental data.

# BUILDING OF TEACHING MODES AND RESEARCH INTO EDUCATIONAL EXPERIMENT

## Theoretical Analysis of Cultivating Students' Self-Monitoring of Learning in Mathematic Teaching in Primary Schools

### *1) Feasibility of Cultivating Students' Self-Monitoring of Learning During Math Teaching in Primary Schools*

#### Reasonable Research Methods

Subject infiltration is one of the three basic methods for psychological suzhi education as well as the important research approach for application of theories, natural education and diversification of teaching. To be specific, the subject-infiltration-based cultivation in this chapter takes the teaching of a subject as the main task and follows the educational and teaching rules. It aims to organically integrate education and teaching, textbooks and formation of students' psychological traits through the study of textbooks and analysis of students' psychological traits so as to establish a set of systematic infiltration-based cultivation modes, respect and influence the student during the "natural" classroom teaching and achieve the effect of "imperceptible influence". The diversified and natural form is easy to be accepted during the actual teaching.

## Proper Research Focus

The research in this chapter, based on summarization and analysis on the previous research, is different from other research in two aspects. a) Other research only focuses on the direct change or effect of relevant capacity or traits, but this chapter focuses more on the change and perfection of students' overall psychological suzhi in addition to inspecting the change of students' self-monitoring of learning and its relationships with the academic performance so as to seek the long-term educational benefit. b) The research in this chapter focuses more on the systematic research into infiltration. It established the teaching modes of "cultivating students' self-monitoring of learning during math teaching in primary schools" based on the solid theoretical foundation and many years' research achievements of "psychological suzhi education". It takes the teacher and the student, the two agents, as the main participants and establishes, based on teachers' infiltration-based teaching and formation of students' traits, the education process and teaching activity system, where the teacher is the agent, and the psychological activity and psychological process system, where the student is the agent.

## Appropriate Subject Nature

Math is the major subject for primary school students to learn and, thanks to its own intrinsic nature, such as the unique thinking and logic, becomes an excellent subject for cultivating students' self-monitoring of learning. Luo's and Lian's (2003) research has shown that the self-monitoring has the closest relationship with the math. We can understand the relationships between the two in this way: from the perspective of resources for education, it can undoubtedly save the resources for education to find out the connections between the subject and psychological traits; from the perspective of students' psychological development, the close relationship between the teaching content and the development of students' psychological suzhi provides conditions for the timely and effective development of students' psychological suzhi; from the perspective of the infiltration-based cultivation itself, they are highly linked with each other in the aspects of the form and the content and have created many breakthrough points and opportunities for infiltration-based cultivation. In addition, since the math subject has the aforesaid characteristics, the traditional teaching features single task, monotonous form and only objective. However, the infiltration-based cultivation has unique dual or multiple task objectives, diversified infiltration as well as proper and moderate inspiration and guidance and can, to a great extent, overcome the existing disadvantages of teaching, fully perform students' activeness, interests and activity during their learning and develop students' functions as an agent, their initiative and the effectiveness during and of the learning based on abiding by the concept of suzhi education and new curriculum reform.

### *2) Building Modes for Cultivating Students' Self-Monitoring of Learning during Math Teaching in Primary Schools*

## Objective for Building Modes

It is to establish a bridge between the theory and practice of psychological suzhi education and lay the foundation for the following experimental research by defining a set of scientific and systematic teaching procedures for cultivating students' self-monitoring of learning during math teaching in primary schools.

## Basis of Building the Modes

### *Theoretical Basis*

First, "psychological suzhi-based education" theories and the conception on infiltratingpsychological suzhi-based educationduring the teaching of a subject; second, theories on "educational mode construction" and the different perspectives to build educational modes are the theoretical basis.

### *Practical Basis*

"Psychological suzhi-based education" team has obtained achievements in the research into psychological suzhi trainings, other researchers' achievements in the research into different psychological suzhi trainings of students, psychological health education integrated modes and many cases of educational modes.

### *Principle Of Building The Modes*

Typical modes: the mode to be built should be not only in accordance with certain kind or certain quantity of theories, but also come from the reality. It should be the abstract and generation of the reality as well as a simple and economic expression form.

Well-targeted modes: the mode to be built should focus on infiltration-based cultivation and consider students' age characteristics, interests and hobbies for the purpose of the teaching of math for primary school students, primary school students' self-monitoring of learning and its development characteristics, and the change in traditional or dogmatic educational methods and the single teaching objective.

## Chart on Building Modes

The "mode for cultivating students' self-monitoring of learning during math teaching in primary schools" (please see Figure 6.3) in this chapter is consistent with the psychological health education integrated mode. It takes the teacher and the student, the two agents, as the main participants, and establishes the education process and teaching activity system, where the teacher is the agent, and the psychological activity and psychological process system, where the student is the agent, from the macro teaching procedures to subtle psychological change.

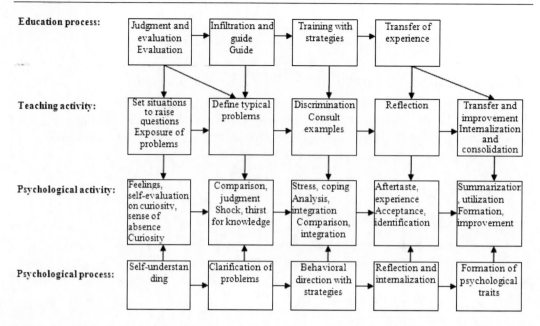

Figure 6.3. Mode for Cultivating Students' Self-Monitoring of Learning during Math Teaching in Primary Schools.

## Systematic Modes

### Integral Process Of Education

The complete educational process is the system that the teacher needs to master and internalize before cultivating primary school students' self-monitoring. It aims to integrate diversified education and teaching activities so that the infiltration content and form will not be scattered disorderly. This system is mainly composed by four stages, judgment and evaluation, infiltration directedness, training with strategies and transfer of experience. It establishes the strict system to cultivate students' self-monitoring of learning via "testing-guidance-training-examination". To be specific, judgment and evaluation is to test the current self-monitoring of learning of students, infiltration directedness is to guide students to pay attention to their self-monitoring of learning, training with strategies is to train students' self-monitoring of learning, and transfer of experience is to examine the formation of students' self-monitoring of learning. This system is compatible with and overlaps the subject education process in many aspects, and is consistent with basic process of students' knowledge leaning, so it plays a leading role and is feasible.

### Whole Process Of Teaching Activities

The whole process of teaching activities is the system that the teacher needs to select and apply when cultivating primary school students' self-monitoring during the teaching. It aims to provide teachers with typical operational procedures and methods of specific infiltration teaching, and it forms a system since it features the whole process during teachers' infiltration teaching activities. This system includes five procedures: setting situations to raise questions and exposing problems; defining typical problems; discriminating and consulting examples; reflection; transfer and improvement, internalization and consolidation. To be specific: the first procedure is at the judgment and evaluation stage of the educational process and is the precondition diagnosis stage of target teaching; it exposes the problems or deficiency in infiltrating students' self-monitoring of learning via demonstrating relevant problems or making such problems materialized, situation-based or dynamic problem. The second one is at the stage of judgment and evaluation and infiltration directedness of education process and is the target demonstration stage of target teaching; it guides and specifies the key infiltration content for students via judging, analyzing and concluding students' answers and response to the infiltration-related question. The third one is at the stage of training with strategies of the educational process and is at the reaching-standard teaching stage of target teaching; it enables students to operate and practice the infiltration content in activities and provides them with reference and criteria via analysis, comparison, explanation and playing roles. The fourth one is at the transfer-of-reflection stage of the educational process and is the reaching-standard examination stage of target teaching; it promotes students' internalization and formation of infiltration traits via comparison, conclusion and summarization, implication or warning, discussion on experience or gains or by studying, comparing or reflecting some aphorisms or incorrect ideas related with the infiltration content. The fifth one is at the reflection stage of the educational process and is the target correction stage of target teaching; it promotes students to internalize and improve their infiltration traits via flexible and diversified tests or by solving practice-related word problems. In view of the particularity of infiltration, this system is open and flexible. That is to say, not all lessons should be infiltrated following such five procedures; different lessons can focus on different aspects according to the different contents and forms.

*Sequence Of Psychological Activities*

The sequence of psychological activities is the process of primary school students' psychological change throughout the process of infiltrating self-monitoring of learning into teaching activities. It aims to disclose the change of students' psychological activities during the interactive teaching activities between teachers and students and forms a system since it features the sequence of learning infiltration traits. This system is composed of five psychological procedures: feeling, curiosity, self-assessment and absence; comparison, judgment, shock and thirst for knowledge; stress, coping, analysis and integration; recall, experience, acceptance and identification; summarization, application, formation and perfection. To be specific: the aforesaid five psychological procedures are the typical psychological activities that the teacher will make students experience in five infiltration teaching activities as well as the main course of psychological changes that the student voluntarily reveal and actively experience during the teacher's interactive infiltration teaching. Similarly, this system can only demonstrate the general sequence of students' learning infiltration traits. Not all students should experience al the psychological activities in such five psychological procedures and they may even suffer alternation and skip-over.

*Step-By-Step Improvement Of Psychological Process*

The step-by-step improvement of psychological process is the formation of primary school students' infiltration traits throughout the process of infiltrating self-monitoring of learning into teaching activities. It aims to demonstrate the process to form students' self-monitoring suzhi of learning and forms a system since it features the step-by-step improvement and integrality of the formation process of infiltration traits. This system may appear in all procedures of psychological activities. Like the educational process system and the teaching activity system, it also serves the psychological activity system of students' internalization and infiltration of favorable traits through learning. This system includes five stages: self-cognition, identification of problems, behavioral direction with strategies, reflection and internalization, and formation of psychological suzhi. To be specific: self-cognition is that students achieve self-understanding and judgment on absence of traits and deficiencies through the judgment and testing of problems on infiltration traits or problem situations; identification of problems is that students define and identify the degree of the absence of traits and deficiencies; behavioral direction with strategies is that students operate and have a try in practical manners under the teachers' guide; reflection and internalization is that students evaluate and reflect their operation and try as well as compare and identify the self-change in infiltration traits; formation of psychological suzhi is that students ingrain the infiltration traits into their nature through further practice and exercise.

## 1) Implementation Strategies on Cultivating Students' Self-Monitoring of Learning in Math Teaching in Primary Schools

### Scientific Design of Infiltration Cultivation

a) Comprehensive and reasonable infiltration objectives

The infiltration cultivation of students' self-monitoring of learning is no longer targeted at the single objective like before, but focuses more on comprehensive educational objectives. That is to say, the objectives of infiltration cultivation shall include cognitive objectives (i.e. self-cognition and cognition on strategies), emotion, will and attitude related objectives (i.e. Feelings and experience, adjustment and control etc.) And behavior and habit related objectives (i.e. Reflection and inspection, correction and improvement etc.). Educators cannot target the education only at a certain aspect and ignore or neglect other aspects; instead, they should prepare the infiltration plans based on multi-aspect and multi-level comprehensive educational objectives.

Subject infiltration requires teachers to, based on the characteristics of a subject, find out the connection between teaching of the subject and the development of students' psychological suzhi, applypsychological suzhi-based educationapproaches and strategies with clear objectives and well-prepared plans, infiltratepsychological suzhi-based educationinto the teaching of the subject and finally cultivate sound psychological suzhi for students. In view of the difference between it and the specific-problem-based training, the objectives shall be designed in proper quantity and to proper extent. First, educators shall well control the quantity of infiltration: the teaching of math is the main task. Generally speaking, the infiltration for 3-5 minutes is enough in one lesson and such 3-5 minute infiltration cannot concentrate in a certain period of time; or else, it should be the psychological suzhi training. Second, educators shall try their best to consider various students' needs and design the infiltration with proper level and validity based on the difficulty of the teaching content, the acceptability of primary school students, students' actual conditions and their response in class.

### Stage-Based and Life-Based Infiltration Content

The primary school stage consists of three parts, junior, intermediate and senior periods, each of which is composed of different grades and requires and focuses on different infiltration contents. Along with the upgrading, educators shall pay attention to the transformation from simple traits that are easy to understand to abstract and comprehensive traits as well as the reasonable arrangement thereof. Since students' self-monitoring awareness of learning is vague and uncertain in the junior and intermediate primary school period, it is improper to cultivate, based on infiltration, the traits of students' self-monitoring of learning (i.e. planning, methods, implementation, summarization) in the junior and intermediate primary school period; instead, they should, in the senior primary school period, cultivate students' self-monitoring of learning on a selective basis in some certain aspects. Such infiltration should also be conducted based on the plans at different stages.

Primary school students are more interested in and can more easily accept the life-based infiltration content. Teachers should select the ,focal and difficult problems close to students' infiltration traits, thoroughly understand students' self-monitoring of learning in actual life, or make the infiltration content realistic, vivid and interesting by investigating the teachers, the parents and the students or consulting or collecting relevant documents and materials; they shall arouse strong learning desire, the sense of identification and absence of students through the design and demonstration of a series of typical contents so as to enable students to experience, reflect and deepen them in typical problems, typical situations and typical activities.

## Diversified and Specific Infiltration Methods

The indirect subject infiltration and the relatively dull math require diversified and specific infiltration methods. Generally speaking, educators shall, according to students' characteristics and infiltration content, flexibly use the infiltration modes and reasonably apply the techniques and methods related with specific-problem-based training (role play method, practical operation method etc.) and consultation and counseling (cognitive method, behavioral change method) to create a lively interactive teaching situation. To be specific, situation-setting and question-raising method, academic performance calculation method, self-judgment method etc. can be applied at the judgment and evaluation stage of the mode; typical problem method, persona hypothesis method, comparison and judgment method etc. can be applied at the infiltration directedness stage of the mode; debates, example consulting method, discussion and analysis method, experience exchange method, playing games, tests and role play method can be applied at the training-with-strategies stage of the mode; reflection method, feeling exchange method, self-analysis method, mutual disclosure method etc. can be applied at the transfer-of-experience stage of the mode.

## Diversified and Multi-Level Infiltration Opportunities

Cultivating students' self-monitoring of learning during math teaching in primary schools is neither to simply combine the content relevant to psychological suzhi with the math lesson and thus reduce the content of math teaching, nor to find out corresponding traits from math textbooks for training and thus overshadow the leading role of math teaching. Instead, it is to organically integrate the study on textbooks with the analysis on students' psychological traits to find out proper opportunities for infiltration teaching. It focuses on the teaching of a subject and broadens the functions of the teaching of a subject so as to achieve the effect of "conductingpsychological suzhi-based educationvia teaching of a subject" and "improving teaching of a subject via psychological suzhi-based education".

*Natural opportunities in textbooks.* The math lesson for primary school students is rich inpsychological suzhi-based educationresources and this is the first-level study on infiltration opportunities. Primary school teachers should be good at seizing and using such resources. For example, the abstract conception, principle and theorem in math textbooks and the use of such conception, principle and theorem to solve problems are all the natural sources for cultivating students' self-monitoring of learning in the math teaching. Teachers should find out one or more infiltration points in those resources and make proper arrangement and ingenious design so as to well prepare for the infiltration.

*Accidental opportunities in the teaching process.* Since the actual teaching process is a dynamic and changeable process, so the study and preparation on psychological resources in textbooks is necessary but inadequate. That is to say: i) we should forecast the answering and problem demonstration manners of students that are likely to happen during the classroom teaching (including teaching of knowledge and infiltration points); especially, we should make second-level study on the infiltration content in respect of the primary school student's "lots of questions" and "strange ideas" so as to find out the correlations and relationships between such problems, performance, phenomena and the infiltration traits and well prepare for the infiltration teaching; ii) teachers should have the psychological preparation for and capacity of managing the classroom teaching flexibly, follow the infiltration teaching plans but not confined by the rigid plans and be able to grasp the dynamic, accidental and valuable infiltration points or opportunities, which may appear in the classroom teaching at any time, for timely, proper and thorough infiltration cultivation.

*Created opportunities for infiltration content.* The natural resources for infiltration and the accidental infiltration resources in the teaching process are both limited. Now that the infiltration is a long-term task, we should not conduct infiltration intermittently or lack the perseverance. Therefore, the teacher should, in addition to the study on and the grasp of static and dynamic infiltration points, study and prepare for creating infiltration opportunities, i.e. The third-level study on the infiltration opportunities. Such creative study is not made out of the void or at random; it must be correlated with the procedures of infiltration teaching, the infiltration content should be linked with the teaching contents and the infiltration manner should be natural and reasonable. For example, the teacher may disclose students' problems in a certain aspect of their self-monitoring of learning through timely raising question to students on infiltration traits, make students understand, feel and realize something through proper problem direction and evaluation of infiltration traits, guide students to evaluation, feel and reflect the matters through creation of small situations and cases for infiltration and make them learn and achieve improvement in practical operation and comparison, and make students internalize and sublimate the corresponding psychological suzhi through ingenious use of and analysis on words of wisdom.

## Objective and Process-Based Evaluation on Infiltration

Infiltration cultivation focuses more on the long-term effect and overall development of students' psychological suzhi, which requires the objective and process-based evaluation on infiltration. "Objective" means that the evaluator should abandon the original impression of the targets and make evaluation in accordance with the scientific procedures and indicators. Only in this way can the evaluator have a sensitive cognition on the changes in the target's infiltration traits so as to find out the effectiveness of the infiltration cultivation more objectively. "Process-based" means that the evaluation should be made based on students' development, focus on the design of discrimination and detection on each infiltration point, well record the evaluation on infiltration for each student, communicate with students and put forward the hope at proper time, properly evaluate certain students face to face and put forward detailed and changeable measures. To be specific, the difference between the pre-experiment and post-experiment scores of students' infiltration traits can be compared via questionnaire evaluation method in case of qualitative evaluation; the development of students' infiltration traits can be evaluated with the activity analysis method; teaching evaluation questionnaires can also be designed so that students may evaluate the teaching effect. The qualitative evaluation focuses on students' understanding, feelings, requirements and advice of and on the infiltration lessons and makes overall inspection on students' performance in other classes, after class and at home so as to have an objective and overall evaluation on the actual effect.

## 2) Teaching Strategies of Infiltration Cultivation

## General Strategies of Infiltration Teaching

### To Be Targeted At All Students And Focus On Special Individuals

The infiltration targets include all primary students. The infiltration teaching should be targeted at every student instead of being targeted at certain student or discriminating against any student due to any special reasons; teachers cannot show unequal or extreme teaching behavior during the implementation of infiltration, and they shall patiently answer the infiltration-related questions raised by each student and reasonably evaluate the infiltration performance of each student; teachers should have acute discernment, pay attention to individuals' special performance and response at any time, actively show solicitude for the infiltration-trait-related problem-prone children and provide corresponding advice and improvement measures in time.

### To Make It More Interesting and Inspire Students' Thirst for Knowledge

The infiltration teaching cannot be inflexible and dull for the purpose of convenience since primary school students are of high plasticity, are lively and active and can remember quickly but forget quickly either. Teachers should pay attention to the status and performance of students' cognition, emotion and behavior, create a democratic and active atmosphere for infiltration teaching and adopt some methods, including exposing problems, role play, discuss and analysis, playing games, tests, reflection, mutual disclosure etc., during the implementation of infiltration so as to actively inspire students' curiosity and thirst for knowledge.

### To Perceive and Grasp the Opportunity

Infiltration teaching is a special teaching activity. Like the teaching in other grades and of different subjects, the math teaching in primary schools has its own inherent knowledge structure and unique educational and teaching methods. The infiltration teaching of students' self-monitoring of learning requires that teachers should integrate the traits with their normal teaching content and integrate the cultivation and education tangibly or intangibly. Therefore, the teacher's infiltration teaching should be well reasoned, smooth, natural and flexible;

teachers should have acute observation and discernment in class and grasp, thoroughly study and flexibly use the dynamic infiltration points; teachers should internalize the infiltration content, infiltration strategies, properly demonstrate the infiltration content, reasonably select the infiltration methods and wisely solve various problems of students' during infiltration so as to achieve circumstances-based and perfect infiltration teaching.

### To Promote Experience and Internalize Traits

Experiencing and internalization have played a key and qualitative role in the formation of students' infiltration traits. Teachers should, during the infiltration teaching, intensify students' reflection, experience, digestion and application of the infiltration content, strategies and methods, make students experience the infiltration positively, actively and truly and prevent students from negative, passive and false experiencing; teachers may understand the direction of students' feelings, experiences and reflection by assigning proper quantity of external operational tasks or raising proper questions so as to promote and deepen their internal experience by means of external activities and help students internalize and form the infiltration traits.

## Specific Strategies of Infiltration Teaching

### Strategies on Exposing Problems

It means that the teacher demonstrates relevant problems via such methods as setting situations to raise questions, self-judgment, academic performance calculation etc., discloses the problems or deficiencies in students' self-monitoring of learning and make students have such psychological activities as feelings, curiosity, self-evaluation and sense of absence so as to achieve clear self-cognition. To be specific, teachers should, at the judgment and evaluation stage of infiltration teaching, either create an interesting, lively, real or inspiring situation to raise infiltration-related problems in the situation, or inquire students' self-feeling and judgment on relevant behavior and habit, or make students evaluate their train of thought and academic performance via the thinking or solution of math questions.

### Strategies of Defining Typical Problems

It means that the teacher adopts such methods as typical problem, persona hypothesis and comparison and judgment at the judging and evaluating stage and the infiltration directedness stage so as to direct and define the key infiltration content for students, make students have such psychological activities as comparison, judgment, shock, thirst for knowledge etc. and preliminarily analyze the problem. To be specific, teachers should define the key points with brief and clear words: they may design the question closely connected to the infiltration traits to define the key points, put students into the status of the role by means of hypothesis, or achieve positive judgment for knowledge and improvement through comparison.

### Strategies of Consulting Examples

It means that the teacher adopts such methods as debates, discussion and analysis, tests, experience exchange, playing games, role play etc. at the training-with-strategies stage of educational process to conduct operational trainings for students so that students can operate and practice the infiltration content during the activities. In addition, teachers should provide standards for reference at proper time to achieve behavioral direction and enable students to experience the psychological process of stress, coping, analysis and integration. To be specific, students' discrimination and analysis, discussion and analysis between students, tests and analysis on questions and answers of teachers and students and experience exchange, games and role play between students should all demonstrate the reference standards at proper time during the operation or practice for students' comparison and integration. It should be noted that this standard is made based on the large quantity of data collected by teachers and is for the reference and comparison of primary school students; it is not the standard answer.

*Strategies of Reflection*

It means that the teacher causes students to evaluate and reflect their operation and practice and compare and internalize the self-changes in infiltration traits via the cognition and dissection as well as comparison and analysis of aphorisms and well-known sayings or typical ideas (both correct and incorrect) so as to make students have such psychological activities as aftertaste, experience, acceptance, identification etc. For example: teachers may, at the stage of reflecting the importance of infiltration pre-class preparation, quote "Sharpening your axe will not delay your job of cutting wood", "To work without plans is like to launch a war that may fail"; they may also, at the stage of reflecting the methods of infiltration pre-class preparation, quote students' common but incorrect ideas, such that "I have prepared for this lesson, but it seems useless", "Pre-class preparation is to look through the examples to be taught" etc.

*Strategies of Internalization and Consolidation*

It means that the teacher may adopt such methods as feeling exchange, self-analysis and mutual disclosure to make students discuss their experiences, gains, progress, deficiencies and hope and further reflect the learning of infiltration traits. Teachers may also promote students to internalize and intensify the infiltration traits via flexible tests or solution and assignment of practice-related word problems so as to achieve transfer and improvement of infiltration traits. It aims to enable students to experience such psychological activities as summarization, application, formation, improvement etc. so as to ingrain the infiltration traits into their nature.

### 3) Discussion on Modes for Cultivating Students' Self-Monitoring of Learning during Math Teaching in Primary Schools

The subject infiltration mode for primary school students' self-monitoring of learning is based on the mental health education integrated mode and it is a bridge that connectspsychological suzhi-based educationtheories and the educational and teaching practice. The experimental results have shown that effective implementation of this mode may improve the traits relevant to primary school students' self-monitoring of learning, enhance their learning capacity and better their academic performance in the aspect of math and is helpful for them to improve the development of their psychological suzhi. Therefore, we held that thepsychological suzhi-based education"subject infiltration" mode is one of the effective ways to implement the psychological suzhi-based education.

In view of the complexity of psychological suzhi-based education, particularity of the "subject infiltration" mode and the long-term effect of infiltration education, there are high requirements for teachers to operate this mode: a) teachers should acquire a better understanding of students' objective reality, respect, be concerned about and accept students' performance and behavior and establish democratic, equal and harmonious relationships with students; they should have rich knowledge of the subject, be able to flexibly use the textbook as a whole, can grasp and find out thepsychological suzhi-based educationresources contained in the textbook, understand knowledge on developmental psychology, educational psychology, instructional psychology etc. And understand the age characteristics of primary school students' psychological development; b) teachers should acquire certain theoretical thinking to internalize the whole train of thought on infiltration; they should deeply study the infiltration points to overall arrange the teaching points and flexibly show the infiltration concept; they should flexibly use the mode for different types of lessons, instead of sticking to fixed pattern, and reasonably stress the key points of infiltration; c) teachers should have relatively high comprehensive capacity of education. The subject infiltration mode has two objectives, intelligence education and psychological education. Teachers should not only have high capacity of teaching of the subject and psychological suzhi education, but also be able to comprehensively apply the capacities to achieve such two objectives. In addition, the effective implementation of this mode also needs the school leader's attentions, optimized arrangement of teaching environment, coordination and cooperation with other subjects etc.

## Experiments on Cultivating Students' Self-Monitoring of Learning in Math Teaching in Primary Schools

### 1) Purpose

It is to improve students' learning capacity and academic performance and thus improve the traits relevant to their psychological suzhi by cultivating students' self-monitoring of learning during math teaching in primary schools. That is to say, teachers may discuss the effectiveness and feasibility of the infiltration cultivation systems and methods to disclose the relationships between primary school students' self-monitoring of learning and their psychological suzhi and academic performance, provide theoretical basis for popularizing experimental research and provide empirical basis for cultivating the self-monitoring of learning of senior primary school students in China.

### 2) Participants and Methods

The participants were two classes (2 and 3) in grade 5 of a whole-day primary school in Chongqing. Please see Table 6.12 for details.

Psychometrics, measurement of academic performance and educational experiments were used in this chapter. Psychometrics included the *Questionnaire on Primary School Students' Self-Monitoring of Learning* developed by ourselves targeted at primary school students' self-monitoring of learning and the *Questionnaire on Primary School Students' Psychological Suzhi* developed by Zhang et al. to examine students' psychological suzhi. The measurement of academic performance is mainly to measure the scores of final examination of math.

**Table 6.12. Components of Experimental Group and Control Group**

| Group | Male (person) | Female (person) | Total |
|---|---|---|---|
| Experimental Group (5.2) | 33 | 19 | 52 |
| Control Group (5.3) | 27 | 24 | 51 |

### 3) Experimental Variables

### Independent Variables

Modes and strategies for cultivating students' self-monitoring of learning during math teaching in primary schools

### Dependent Variables

Primary school students' self-monitoring of learning; b) primary school students' psychological suzhi; c) primary school students' academic performance in math

### Control Variables

*Reasonably determined the experimental group and control group.* The academic performance, psychological suzhi and the initial level of the self-monitoring of learning of both experimental and control groups should be at the same level. The number of students and sex ratio of both groups should be almost the same.

*Control other factors affecting the results of the experiment.* Experimenters should not intenionally publicize the purpose of the experiment to the teachers and students of the experimental group. They should not create a competitive atmosphere between experimental group and control group before or after the experiment so as to ensure the stable emotion of students during the experiment. The experimental teacher should take it easy instead of having a too high expectation on the experimental results.

### Experimental Treatment

In the experiment, we designed pre-test and post-test for both experimental and control groups (please see Table 6.13).

**Table 6.13. Design of Experimental Treatment**

| Group | Pre-Test | Experimental Treatment | Post-Test |
|---|---|---|---|
| Experimental Group | Testing self-monitoring of learning Measuring middle school students' psychological suzhi Measuring academic performance | Cultivating students' self-monitoring of learning during the teaching of math | The same as pre-test |
| Control Group | Testing self-monitoring of learning Measuring middle school students' psychological suzhi Measuring academic performance | N/A | The same as pre-test |

## Course Of Experiment

*Preparation*

Consult domestic and international literature, establish and modify experiment scheme;

Revise and prepare the Questionnaire on Primary School Students' Self-Monitoring of Learning and determine the psychometric tools;

Contact the school for this experiment and determine the class for experiment;

Draw the figure of "Mode for Cultivating Students' Self-monitoring of Learning during Math Teaching in Primary Schools"

Prepare the *Cultivating Students' Self-monitoring of Learning during Math Teaching for Primary School Students' in Grade Five*, collection of teaching plans, according to the math textbook for autumn semester 2004 of primary school students in grade 5, the *Textbook on Primary School Students' Psychological* Suzhi developed by Zhang *et al.*, the research of Dong et al. into the development characteristics and structural components of primary school students' self-monitoring of learning, the revision and preparation of questionnaires and the questionnaire analysis results at the initial stage of the research as well as the established "Mode for Cultivating Students' Self-monitoring of Learning during Math Teaching in Primary Schools";

Train the experimental teachers;

Conduct pre-test on academic performance.

*Implementation*

Conduct pre-test (in the second week as the term begins) on experimental group and control group in respect of their self-monitoring of learning and psychological suzhi;

Cultivating the self-monitoring of learning of the experimental group in two or three math lessons every week according to the prepared collection of teaching plans named *Cultivating Students' Self-monitoring of Learning during Math Teaching for Primary School Students' in Grade Five*;

Conduct post-test on experimental group and control group in respect of their self-monitoring of learning, psychological suzhi and academic performance.

Processing

Make statistics, analysis and processing on the pre-test and post-test data to prepare the thesis.

*Results And Analysis*

As shown in Table 6.14, the average scores of the two groups in respect of all dimensions were almost the same in the pre-test and there was no difference; in respect of the second-order factors and the total average scores, the experimental group had slightly higher scores than the control group, but there was no significant difference. The average scores of the experimental group were higher than the control group in respect of all dimensions in the post-test; however, there was no significant difference between the two in five dimensions: remedy, feedback, preparation, summarization and implementation; there was significant difference between the two in two dimensions: planning and awareness, and the average scores of the experimental group were significantly higher than the control group; in addition, there was no significant difference between the two groups in the aspect of methods, but the average scores of the experimental group were significantly higher than the control group, indicating that the experimental group has improved a lot in the aspect of methods; there was significant difference between the two groups in respect of a second-order factor named planning of learning.

1) Comparison between pre-test and post-test scores on the self-monitoring of learning of experimental group and control group:

**Table 6.14. Comparison between Pre-Test and Post-Test Scores on the Self-Monitoring of Learning of Experimental Group and Control Group**

|  | Variables | Experimental Group (n=52) $M \pm SD$ | Control Group (n=51) $M \pm SD$ | $t$ Value |
|---|---|---|---|---|
| Pre-Test | Remedy | 3.79±.57 | 3.79±.59 | .004 |
| | Feedback | 3.17±.79 | 3.14±.80 | .156 |
| | Preparation | 3.62±.92 | 3.58±.99 | .184 |
| | Summarization | 3.70±.83 | 3.69±.82 | .036 |
| | Methods | 3.64±.71 | 3.60±.71 | .301 |
| | Planning | 3.19±.96 | 3.14±.91 | .298 |
| | Implementation | 3.15±.99 | 3.13±.96 | .112 |
| | Awareness | 2.78±.94 | 2.76±.88 | .132 |
| | Optimization of Learning | 3.73±.53 | 3.72±.55 | .113 |
| | Implementation of learning | 3.31±.73 | 3.28±.75 | .185 |
| | Planning of learning | 2.99±.83 | 2.95±.76 | .251 |
| | Total average scores | 3.47±.46 | 3.44±.45 | .240 |
| Post-Test | Remedy | 3.88±.61 | -3.85±.61 | 211 |
| | Feedback | 3.22±.82 | 3.19±.84 | .145 |
| | Preparation | 3.67±.99 | 3.64±1.02 | .113 |
| | Summarization | 3.78±.82 | 3.74±.84 | .235 |
| | Methods | 3.85±.71 | 3.65±.73 | 1.430 |
| | Planning | 3.61±.95 | 3.18±.95 | 2.267[*] |
| | Implementation | 3.17±.99 | 3.16±.98 | .033 |
| | Awareness | 3.35±.80 | 2.79±.89 | 3.333[**] |
| | Optimization of learning | 3.86±.54 | 3.78±.55 | .668 |
| | Implementation of learning | 3.35±.75 | 3.23±.76 | .126 |
| | Planning of learning | 3.48±.73 | 2.98±.79 | 3.276[**] |
| | Total average scores | 3.61±.45 | 3.49±.46 | 1.241 |

2) Comparison between pre-test and post-test scores on the self-monitoring of learning of students in experimental group with high, intermediate and low self-monitoring of learning

We divided the experimental group into high-score team (27% of the group with the highest scores), intermediate score team (46% of the group with intermediate scores) and low score team (27% of the group with the lowest scores) based on the pre-test scores on their self-monitoring of learning to find out the difference between the intervention effect of this experiment on the self-monitoring of learning of students with different levels of self-monitoring. Then we compare the significant difference between pre-test and post-test scores (please see Table 6.15).

**Table 6.15. Comparison between Pre-Test and Post-Test Scores on the Self-Monitoring of Learning of Students in Experimental Group with High, Intermediate and Low Self-monitoring of Learning**

| | Variables | Pre-Test M ± SD | Post-Test M ± SD | t Value |
|---|---|---|---|---|
| High Score Team (n=16) | Remedy | 3.7898±.6313 | 4.1193±.4247 | 1.652 |
| | Feedback | 3.6500±.8532 | 3.9500±.7394 | 1.131 |
| | Preparation | 3.3750±.8062 | 3.5833±.6939 | .825 |
| | Summarization | 3.8594±.7581 | 4.1250±.5701 | .913 |
| | Methods | 3.3393±.9212 | 3.8929±.4222 | 2.306[*] |
| | Planning | 2.9844±1.0664 | 4.0303±.8209 | 2.735[*] |
| | Implementation | 3.4583±.9418 | 3.7083±1.039 | .972 |
| | Awareness | 3.5500±1.0770 | 4.4375±.5277 | 2.062[*] |
| | Optimization of learning | 3.7688±.6058 | 4.0781±.3371 | 1.606 |
| | Implementation of learning | 3.4167±.7503 | 3.6458±.7979 | 1.055 |
| | Planning of learning | 3.3164±.8054 | 4.0977±.3722 | 3.358[**] |
| | Total average scores | 3.5461±.4325 | 4.0238±.2678 | 4.123[**] |
| Intermediate score Team (n=22) | Remedy | 3.8099±.4907 | 3.8388±.5951 | .194 |
| | Feedback | 3.0195±.6723 | 3.0909±.7653 | .296 |
| | Preparation | 3.6182±.6964 | 3.6273±.7682 | .036 |
| | Summarization | 3.5568±.8179 | 3.5795±.9028 | .081 |
| | Methods | 3.5818±.6645 | 3.9818±.5981 | 2.139[*] |
| | Planning | 3.3485±.7799 | 3.5455±.9059 | .760 |
| | Implementation | 2.7614±.7379 | 3.0682±.8632 | 1.227 |
| | Awareness | 2.5909±.8845 | 3.3182±.7452 | 2.460[*] |
| | Optimization of learning | 3.7068±.4302 | 3.8182±.4745 | .870 |
| | Implementation of learning | 3.1761±.4251 | 3.2188±.5802 | .259 |
| | Planning of learning | 2.9697±.6375 | 3.4318±.6508 | 2.240[*] |
| | Total average scores | 3.3994±.1736 | 3.5346±.3771 | 1.455 |
| Low Score Team (n=14) | Remedy | 3.7590±.5407 | 3.7688±.5853 | .203 |
| | Feedback | 3.0089±.6532 | 3.0897±.7734 | .284 |
| | Preparation | 3.5937±.6894 | 3.6148±.7547 | .048 |
| | Summarization | 3.5466±.8238 | 3.5798±.9130 | .087 |
| | Methods | 3.5723±.6446 | 3.6818±.6918 | .837 |
| | Planning | 3.3357±.7989 | 3.5595±.9250 | .734 |
| | Implementation | 2.7594±.7496 | 2.9862±.8339 | .977 |
| | Awareness | 2.5587±.8685 | 2.8182±.8058 | 1.443 |
| | Optimization of learning | 3.6869±.4364 | 3.7182±.4943 | .856 |
| | Implementation of learning | 3.1463±.4436 | 3.2087±.5894 | .247 |
| | Planning of learning | 2.9504±.6457 | 3.2307±.5549 | 1.240 |
| | Total average scores | 3.3824±.1806 | 3.5283±.3781 | 1.402 |

Table 6.15 showed that this experiment has improved the self-monitoring of learning of the aforesaid three teams to different degrees; the post-test scores of the high score team were significantly higher than their pre-test scores in the aspects of methods, planning and

awareness, and the post-test level of the high score team, as a whole, was also significantly higher than their pre-test level; the post-test scores of the intermediate score team were significantly higher than their pre-test scores in the aspects of methods and awareness, and there was no significantly difference between the pre-test and post-test level as a whole; the post-test scores of the low score team on each dimension has been improved to different extents although there was no significant difference between the pre-test and post-test level of each dimension and the overall level.

(3) Comparison between pre-test and post-test scores on the self-monitoring of learning of experimental group students of different genders

Table 6.16 has shown that, for the experimental group, there was no significant difference between the pre-test and post-test scores of female and male students as a whole; for both female and male students, their scores on the dimensions of methods, planning and awareness in the post-test had significantly improved, compared with the scores in the pre-test.; there was no significant difference between male students' pre-test and post-test scores of the three dimensions; female students' post-test scores were significantly higher than their pre-test scores only in the dimensions of awareness.

### Table 6.16. Comparison between Pre-Test and Post-Test Scores on the Self-Monitoring of Learning of Experimental Group Students of Different Genders

| | Variables | Pre-Test $M \pm SD$ | Post-Test $M \pm SD$ | $t$ Value |
|---|---|---|---|---|
| Male (n=33) | Remedy | 3.76±.65 | 3.80±.70 | .197 |
| | Feedback | 3.38±.80 | 3.40±.84 | .064 |
| | Preparation | 3.69±.92 | 3.70±1.04 | .045 |
| | Summarization | 3.67±.80 | 3.71±.83 | .146 |
| | Methods | 3.65±.80 | 3.83±.73 | .958 |
| | Planning | 3.36±.86 | 3.72±.88 | 1.481 |
| | Implementation | 3.08±1.11 | 3.16±1.06 | .255 |
| | Awareness | 2.86±1.00 | 3.41±.78 | 1.9669 |
| | Optimization of learning | 3.71±.61 | 3.79±.61 | .425 |
| | Implementation of learning | 3.40±.75 | 3.43±.78 | .135 |
| | Planning of learning | 3.11±.85 | 3.57±.71 | 1.966 |
| | Total average scores | 3.51±.51 | 3.62±.51 | .701 |
| Female (n=19) | Remedy | 3.83±.47 | 3.98±.49 | 1.114 |
| | Feedback | 2.92±.72 | 3.01±.75 | .404 |
| | Preparation | 3.54±.93 | 3.61±.93 | .326 |
| | Summarization | 3.72±.89 | 3.85±.83 | .453 |
| | Methods | 3.63±.61 | 3.87±.69 | 1.277 |
| | Planning | 3.00±1.04 | 3.47±1.02 | 1.632 |
| | Implementation | 3.22±.83 | 3.17±.91 | -.205 |
| | Awareness | 2.69±.86 | 3.26±.82 | 2.240[*] |
| | Optimization of learning | 3.76±.43 | 3.92±.44 | 1.252 |
| | Implementation of learning | 3.19±.69 | 3.24±.71 | .253 |
| | Planning of learning | 2.84±.78 | 3.36±.73 | 2.449[*] |
| | Total average scores | 3.41±.39 | 3.58±.37 | 1.648 |

4) Comparison between pre-test and post-test scores on the self-monitoring of learning of experimental group students from different family locations

Table 6.17 has shown that there was no significant difference between the pre-test and post-test scores of urban students and rural students as a whole; for urban students, their scores on the dimensions of planning, implementation and awareness in the post-test had significantly improved, compared with the scores in the pre-test, but their post-test scores were significantly higher than their pre-test scores only in the dimensions of awareness; for rural students, their scores on the dimensions of methods, planning and awareness in the post-test had significantly improved, compared with the scores in the pre-test, but their post-test scores were significantly higher than their pre-test scores only in the dimensions of methods.

### Table 6.17. Comparison between Pre-Test and Post-Test Scores on the Self-Monitoring of Learning of Experimental Group Students from Different Families

| | Variables | Pre-Test $M \pm SD$ | Post-Test $M \pm SD$ | $t$ Value |
|---|---|---|---|---|
| Urban Family (n=16) | Remedy | 3.87±.44 | 3.67±.72 | -1.013 |
| | Feedback | 3.12±.61 | 3.30±.81 | .736 |
| | Preparation | 3.41±.92 | 3.71±1.02 | .829 |
| | Summarization | 3.82±.60 | 3.59±.91 | -.832 |
| | Methods | 3.60±.75 | 3.51±.77 | -.345 |
| | Planning | 2.93±.79 | 3.58±.97 | 1.902 |
| | Implementation | 2.68±1.01 | 3.32±.61 | 1.924 |
| | Awareness | 2.58±.89 | 3.41±.68 | 2.554* |
| | Optimization of learning | 3.79±.46 | 3.62±.64 | -.946 |
| | Implementation of learning | 3.10±.63 | 3.44±.65 | 1.400 |
| | Planning of learning | 2.76±.69 | 3.50±.64 | 2.850* |
| | Total average scores | 3.38±.32 | 3.53±.43 | .996 |
| Rural Family (n=36) | Remedy | 3.76±.62 | 3.98±.54 | 1.484 |
| | Feedback | 3.19±.87 | 3.18±.82 | -.038 |
| | Preparation | 3.71±.92 | 3.64±.98 | -.298 |
| | Summarization | 3.64±.92 | 3.86±.78 | .941 |
| | Methods | 3.66±.70 | 4.01±.63 | 2.207* |
| | Planning | 3.31±1.01 | 3.62±.95 | 1.384 |
| | Implementation | 3.36±.92 | 3.10±1.11 | 1.052 |
| | Awareness | 2.87±.95 | 3.31±.85 | 1.889 |
| | Optimization of learning | 3.71±.56 | 3.96±.45 | 1.866 |
| | Implementation of learning | 3.39±.75 | 3.30±.79 | -.471 |
| | Planning of learning | 3.09±.87 | 3.46±.77 | 1.910 |
| | Total average scores | 3.50±.51 | 3.64±.45 | 1.082 |

5) Comparison between pre-test and post-test scores of academic performance of math for experimental group and control group

Table 6.18 has shown that: the average pre-test scores of the two groups' academic performance of math were close to each other; the average post-test scores of the two groups' academic performance of math were lower than the pre-test scores; the average scores of the experimental group were 2.65 points higher than the control group although there was no significant difference between the average post-test scores of the two groups' academic performance of math.

**Table 6.18. Comparison between Pre-Test and Post-Test Scores of Academic Performance of Math for Experimental Group and Control Group**

|  | Pre-Test $M \pm SD$ | Post-Test $M \pm SD$ |
|---|---|---|
| Experimental Group | 81.18±10.56 | 77.51±11.88 |
| Control Group | 81.13±8.64 | 74.87±13.12 |
| *t* Value | .024 | -1.764 |
| Significance | .981 | .081 |

6) Comparison between the pre-test and post-test scores of math academic performance of students in experimental group with high, intermediate and low self-monitoring of learning

We divided the experimental group into high score team, intermediate score team and low score team according to the pre-test scores of students' self-monitoring of learning (the detailed methods of division were the same as the aforesaid ones) to find out the effect of this experiment on the pre-test and post-test scores of the math academic performance of students with different levels of self-monitoring of learning (please see Table 6.19).

**Table 6.19. Comparison Between the Pre-Test and Post-Test Scores of Math Academic Performance of Students in Experimental Group with High, Intermediate and Low Self-Monitoring of Learning**

| Variables | High Score Team (n=16) $M \pm SD$ | Intermediate Score Team (n=22) $M \pm SD$ | Low Score Team (n=14) $M \pm SD$ | $F$ | Significance |
|---|---|---|---|---|---|
| Math Academic Performance | -3.18±9.84 | -3.15±7.99 | -3.61±7.44 | .014 | .986 |

Table 6.19 has shown that there was no significant increase in the math academic performance of the high score team, intermediate score team and low score team divided based on their self-monitoring of learning.

7) Comparison between pre-test and post-test scores on psychological suzhi of experimental group and control group

Table 6.20 has shown that: the average scores of the two groups in respect of all dimensions of psychological suzhi were almost the same in the pre-test and there was no difference; in respect of the second-order factors and the total average scores, the experimental group had slightly higher scores than the control group, but there was no significant difference. In the post-test, the experimental group's scores on the five dimensions of the first-order factor, i.e.

**Table 6.20. Comparison between Pre-Test and Post-Test Scores on Psychological Suzhi of Experimental Group and Control Group**

| | Variables | Experimental Group (n=52) $M \pm SD$ | Control Group (n=51) $M \pm SD$ | $t$ Value |
|---|---|---|---|---|
| Pre-Test | Awareness | 2.15±.30 | 2.13±.33 | .388 |
| | Planning | 2.22±.37 | 2.19±.37 | .417 |
| | Monitoring | 2.25±.35 | 2.21±.34 | .550 |
| | Ambition | 2.55±.28 | 2.52±.30 | .550 |
| | Independence | 2.36±.32 | 2.33±.31 | .570 |
| | Perseverance | 2.27±.37 | 2.26±.39 | .134 |
| | Thirst for knowledge | 2.30±.39 | 2.26±.36 | .548 |
| | Self-control | 2.33±.35 | 2.32±.38 | .124 |
| | Self-confidence | 2.38±.41 | 2.35±.42 | .334 |
| | Sense of responsibility | 2.50±.39 | 2.48±.39 | .325 |
| | Rationality | 2.03±.30 | 2.00±.30 | .439 |
| | Creativity | 2.22±.25 | 2.19±.25 | .533 |
| | Mind-body coordination | 2.18±.39 | 2.17±.39 | .056 |
| | Emotional adaptation | 2.20±.29 | 2.18±.29 | .437 |
| | Learning adaptation | 2.19±.37 | 2.16±.38 | .396 |
| | Interpersonal adaptation | 2.47±.38 | 2.44±.41 | .330 |
| | Frustration endurance | 2.26±.43 | 2.23±.46 | .428 |
| | Metacognition | 2.21±.23 | 2.18±.26 | .638 |
| | Personality | 2.32±.18 | 2.29±.18 | .717 |
| | Adaptation | 2.24±.27 | 2.22±.28 | .467 |
| | Total average scores | 2.27±.20 | 2.25±.20 | .656 |
| Post-Test | Awareness | 2.40±.32 | 2.17±.32 | 3.623*** |
| | Planning | 2.45±.38 | 2.22±.38 | 3.022** |
| | Monitoring | 2.38±.34 | 2.26±.34 | 1.691 |
| | Ambition | 2.66±.28 | 2.55±.29 | 1.900 |
| | Independence | 2.38±.33 | 2.37±.33 | .181 |
| | Perseverance | 2.30±.43 | 2.29±.39 | .071 |
| | Thirst for knowledge | 2.46±.43 | 2.29±.38 | 2.067* |
| | Self-control | 2.36±.39 | 2.36±.39 | .059 |
| | Self-confidence | 2.40±.46 | 2.38±.44 | .174 |
| | Sense of responsibility | 2.53±.41 | 2.52±.40 | .209 |
| | Rationality | 2.03±.3153 | 2.03±.30 | -.137 |
| | Creativity | 2.24±.2704 | 2.22±.26 | .319 |
| | Mind-body coordination | 2.29±.4163 | 2.20±.40 | -.047 |
| | Emotional adaptation | 2.22±.3089 | 2.21±.30 | .251 |
| | Learning adaptation | 2.29±.3842 | 2.20±.39 | 1.207 |
| | Interpersonal adaptation | 2.52±.4001 | 2.50±.40 | .316 |
| | Frustration endurance | 2.28±.4657 | 2.27±.45 | .026 |
| | Metacognition | 2.41±.2686 | 2.22±.24 | 3.766*** |
| | Personality | 2.36±.2173 | 2.32±.19 | .872 |
| | Adaptation | 2.29±.2897 | 2.25±.28 | .598 |
| | Total average scores | 2.34±.2308 | 2.28±.21 | 1.330 |

Awareness, planning, monitoring, ambition and thirst for knowledge, and on the cognition dimension of the second-order factor were obviously higher than the control group; there was extremely significant difference between the pre-test and post-test scores of the awareness dimension and significant difference between the pre-test and post-test scores of such dimensions as planning and thirst for knowledge, but there was no significant difference between pre-test and post-test scores of such two dimensions of monitoring and ambition; the post-test scores of the experimental group in respect of the metacognition dimension of the second-order factor were extremely significantly higher than that of the control group; there was no significant difference between the total average scores of the two groups.

8) Effect of the experiment on cultivating students' self-monitoring of learning during math teaching in primary schools

This experiment has fully considered the types of schools for experiment (secondary schools); students in the experimental group from urban families were almost in the same number as those from rural families, and the male students in the group were almost in the same number as the female students; experimenters discussed with the experimental teacher in advance, carefully designed the infiltration objective, infiltration content, infiltration methods, infiltration opportunities and infiltration evaluation, determined the operable infiltration teaching plan and discussed and analyzed the feasibility of the infiltration teaching plans in accordance with the plan and the subject infiltration mode; then they implemented the infiltration teaching plan in two or three math classes every week, analyzed and evaluated the infiltration effect after class and adjusted and improved the following infiltration teaching plans. This experiment has continued for a semester and achieved satisfactory effect.

*The Awareness And Planning Of The Experimental Group's Self-Monitoring Of Learning Was Significantly Higher Than The Control Group; Their Methods Were Much Better Than The Control Group, But There Was No Great Change In Other Traits.*

The main causes of such results included the limited time and energy. This experiment was mainly for the infiltration cultivation of students' awareness, planning and methods during pre-class preparation, problem settlement and after-class review instead of the overall cultivation.

*This Experiment Was More Helpful For The High Score Team, Compared With The Intermediate Score Team And The Low Score Team, To Improve The Relevant Traits Of Their Self-Monitoring Of Learning. There Was No Significant Difference Between The Improvement In The Math Academic Performance Of The Three Teams.*

This experiment improved the relevant traits of self-monitoring of learning of the high, intermediate and low score teams to different extents and, relatively, it significantly improved the infiltration traits of high score team's self-monitoring of learning. Further analysis showed that the high score team generally had better academic performance. That is to say, such students had better intelligence and learning methods and habits than the intermediate and low score students. This may be because such students were more sensitive to the infiltration traits and can accept such traits more easily.

There was no significant difference between the improvements on math academic performance of the three teams. This may be because students' self-monitoring of learning was almost consistent with their math academic performance. That is to say, the students with high self-monitoring of learning would not, although their relevant traits of self-monitoring were improved greatly, achieve great improvement in their math academic performance because their academic performance was excellent from the beginning; the students with poor self-monitoring of learning had poor intelligence and bad learning methods and habits and they were not sensitive to the infiltration traits, so their slight improvement in self-monitoring traits reduced the improvement in their math academic performance; similarly, it was understandable that the students with intermediate self-monitoring of learning failed to significantly improve their math academic performance.

*Both Female And Male Students Have Improved Their Self-Monitoring Of Learning In The Three Dimensions Of Methods, Planning And Awareness, And There Was Significant Difference Between The Pre-Test And Post-Test Scores Of The Female Students' Awareness.*

This experiment has greatly improved relevant traits of female and male students' self-monitoring of learning; compared with male students, there is significant difference between the pre-test and post-test scores of female students' awareness of self-monitoring of learning. This may be because the female students were more careful, introspected more frequently and made more efforts subjectively. There was no significant difference between male and female students on an overall basis, and we cannot determine whether it was easier to cultivate male students' self-monitoring of learning or female students' self-monitoring of learning just because there was significant difference in one dimension.

*Both Urban Students' And Rural Students' Planning And Awareness Have Been Greatly Improved. There Was Significant Difference Between The Pre-Test And Post-Test Scores Of Urban Students' Awareness And Between Those Of Rural Students' Methods.*

This experiment improved the relevant traits of urban students' and rural students' self-monitoring of learning, but there was also some difference since their family background was different. The significant difference between the pre-test and post-test scores of urban students' awareness may be caused by their excellent learning and living conditions and the varied living environment; students in such environment were likely to become indolent and self-conceited and to accept the new concept and ideas, and the original poor self-monitoring awareness was greatly improved. The significant difference between the pre-test and post-test scores of rural students' methods may be caused by their poor learning and living conditions and the simple living environment; such environment make students have more housework, consider adopting proper methods to save the time and always study hard for their high expectation and strong desire for success.

*The Average Pre-Test Scores Of The Two Groups' Math Academic Performance Were Close To Each Other; The Average Post-Test Scores Of The Two Groups' Math Academic Performance Were Lower Than The Average Pre-Test Scores; The Average Post-Test Scores Of The Experimental Group's Math Academic Performance Were 2.65 Higher Than Those Of The Control Group; There Was No Significant Difference.*

The average pre-test scores of the two groups' math academic performance were close to each other, which indicated that the two groups were almost the same at the beginning; the average post-test scores of the two groups' math academic performance were lower than the average pre-test scores, which may be caused by the difficult final examination or the strict marking standard; the average post-test scores of the experimental group's math academic performance were 2.65 higher than those of the control group, which indicated that the infiltration cultivation of students' self-monitoring of learning greatly improved students' math academic performance; there was no significant difference between the pre-test and post-test scores of the experimental group's math academic performance, which may be because: a) the improvement of students' math academic performance were influenced by many factors, including individual's intelligence, achievement motivation, willpower, attributional styles, teachers' teaching methods, teaching effect, learning atmosphere, regular education of the school etc.; b) the subject infiltration mode applied in this experiment was used to develop students' self-monitoring of learning only for a short term or the use of this mode was restricted within the limited time in class; c) the natural infiltration resources for students' self-monitoring of learning directly connected with the math subject were relatively limited. That is to say, the teaching content of math was selected and arranged based on the intrinsic logic of math, and the content on students' self-monitoring of learning contained therein featured dispersiveness, potentiality and incontinuousness.

*The Experimental Group's Planning And Awareness Of Metacognition Of Psychological Suzhi Were Significantly Higher Than The Control Group, Its Monitoring Dimension On The Meta-Cognition Subscale And The Ambition Dimension On The Individuality Subscale Have Been Greatly Improved, And The Experimental Group's Thirst For Knowledge On The Personality Dimension Was Significantly Higher Than The Control Group.*

This conclusion was consistent with the research conclusion of You [1997] (primary school students had great potential in developing their metacognition and the education and training has made significant progress). The results obtained by the *"Questionnaire on Primary School Students' Psychological Suzhi"* and the *"Questionnaire on Primary School Students' Self-Monitoring of Learning"* in this chapter were almost the same. This was mainly caused by the close relationships between students' self-monitoring of learning and their psychological suzhi; that is to say, students' self-monitoring of learning was an important component of the metacognition dimension of students' psychological suzhi. The results proved the sound realibility and validity of the *"Questionnaire on Primary School Students' Self-Monitoring of Learning"* and showed that the infiltration cultivation method in this chapter can effectively help the sound and healthy development of students' psychological suzhi. It forecasted the favorable prospect of the subject infiltration mode forpsychological suzhi-based educationin enhancing students' learning capacity, developing students' personality, improving students' learning adaptability and perfecting students' psychological suzhi.

# CONCLUSION

Cultivating students' self-monitoring of learning in math teaching is an effective way to improve students' awareness and planning of self-monitoring.

Cultivating students' self-monitoring of learning in math teaching may have different effects on students of different genders: the improvement of male students' methods, planning and awareness was significant, while only the improvement of female students' awareness was significant.

Cultivating students' self-monitoring of learning during math teaching may have different effects on students from different families: this intervention strategy was more helpful for urban students to increase the scores of their awareness and planning, while it was more helpful for rural students to increase the scores of their planning and methods.

## APPENDIX: TEACHING PLAN OF INFILTRATION (EXCERPT)

### Plan I

I. Teaching content: decimal multiplies integral number, example 1 on page 1 of the textbook and "Do", items 1-4 in Exercise I.

Infiltration content: awareness-the importance of pre-class preparation (including planning and preparation)

II. Teaching objective:

1. To understand the meaning of multiplying decimal by integral number;
2. To master the algorithm of multiplying decimal by integral number;
3. To correctly apply the algorithm to multiply decimal by integral number;
4. To cultivate students' transferring and analogizing capacity;
5. To inspire students' curiosity and thirst for knowledge of math.

Infiltration objective: to make students understand the importance of pre-class preparation and preview of the content to be learned.

III. Teaching focus: 1. Meaning of multiplying decimal by integral number; 2. The algorithm on multiplying decimal by integral number.

Infiltration focus: significance of pre-class preparation

IV. Preparation of teaching tools: a picture where a mother is buying the cloth

Infiltration preparation: blackboard-writing on significance of pre-class preparation

V. Main teaching opportunity: 1. Tteaching of example 1; 2. Comments and appraisal on the exercise.

Main infiltration opportunity: 1. The creation situations after reviewing the guidance items; 2. The teaching situation of teachers' analysis and summarization on "after teaching example 1".

VI. Infiltration process:

## 1. Judgment and Evaluation

★ Disclosure of problems (teachers raised questions based on students' performance after reviewing the guidance items so as to disclose the problems in students' awareness of pre-class preparation)

Teachers' questions and relevant standards:

Do you know why we should do the aforesaid exercise (reviewing the guidance items)?

(1) To examine your mastery of the knowledge taught in the past.

(2) To prepare for learning new knowledge.

Do you know why some students perform better than other students?

(1) Some students can better master the knowledge learned in the past than other students.

(2) Some students have prepared for the knowledge to be learned, while other students did not.

(3) Some students prepared carefully, while other students did not.

*Conclusion of teachers*: the main problems in students' pre-class preparation: 1) they were unwilling to make pre-class preparation; 2) they deemed the pre-class preparation unimportant.

## 2. Infiltration Directedness

★ Defining typical problems (find out the core problem based on students' typical performance of poor awareness of pre-class preparation and make key-problem-based guidance)

Typical performance:

I often review my lesson as the teacher requires me to do so.

The pre-class preparation is a waste of time since the teacher will explain the knowledge in class.

Guide on key problems:

Pre-class preparation is very important.

Pre-class preparation is effective.

## 3. Training with Strategies

★ **Consulting examples** (teachers make students analyze and discuss the problem via operable activities in the teaching situation of analysis and summarization on "after teaching example 1" and provide standards for reference to enable students to understand the importance of pre-class preparation)

Activity: How will a battle be if there is no plan? (for discussion and analysis)

Reference answer:

1) In a mess; 2) passive; 3) confused; 4) failed.

Teacher's conclusion: to learn without pre-class preparation is like to combat without plans.

Students cannot answer even a simple question if we don't know what to learn;

Students think slowly and have to follow the teacher passively;

Students do not know which knowledge is important;

Students feel difficult to follow the teacher in class since they fail to thoroughly understand the knowledge.

### 4. Transfer of Experience

★ Reflection (teachers make students know the advantages of pre-class preparation by means of aphorisms and well-known sayings)

Example: sharpening your axe will not delay your job of cutting wood! (Distribute cards with the words on and require students to keep such cards)

Advantages:

Students know what to learn and what the key content is;

Students can find out the knowledge difficult to understand and take it as the learning focus in class;

It can help students find out the deficiencies and catch the teacher's meaning in class more easily;

It can help students improve their thinking capacity and further understand the knowledge;

It can help students cultivate their self-study capacity.

★ Internalization and consolidation (students further understand the importance of pre-class preparation via training of transfer)

Give your advice: Wang Gang said, "the pre-class preparation reduces the time for playing, which is not worthwhile".

Your opinion:

## Plan II

I. Teaching content: multiplication and multiplication, multiplication and addition, multiplication and subtraction, example 6 on page 9 of the textbook and "Do", items 1-3 in Exercise III (pre-class preparation is required)

Infiltration content: methods-methods for pre-class preparation (including awareness, preparation and implementation)

II. Teaching objective: 1. To master the computation sequence and the algorithm on multiplication and multiplication, multiplication and addition, multiplication and subtraction;

2. To cultivate students' transferring and analogizing capacity.

Infiltration objective: 1. To make students master some methods for pre-class preparation;

2) To make students further understand the significance of careful pre-class preparation or good methods for such preparation.

III. Teaching focus: 1. The computation sequence of multiplication and multiplication, multiplication and addition, multiplication and subtraction; 2. The algorithm on multiplication and multiplication, multiplication and addition, multiplication and subtraction.

Infiltration focus: making students master some methods for pre-class preparation.

IV. Preparation of teaching tools: video on examples and some exercise

Infiltration preparation: blackboard-writing or video on specific methods for pre-class preparation

V. Main teaching opportunity: 1. Teaching of example 6; 2. Comments and appraisal on the exercise.

Main infiltration opportunity: 1. The creation situations during inspection of pre-class preparation; 2. The teaching situation of teachers' analysis and summarization on "after teaching example 6".

VI. Infiltration process:

## 1. Judgment and Evaluation

★ Disclosure of problems (teachers inspect the pre-class preparation by raising questions and disclose students' problems in the methods for such preparation)

Teachers' questions:

Have you prepared for this lesson, my class?

How do you prepare for it?

*Conclusion of teachers*: there are mainly two problems in students' pre-class preparation: 1) they do not carefully prepare for the lesson; 2) they fail to adopt good methods for the pre-class preparation.

## 2. Infiltration Directedness

★ Defining typical problems (find out the core problem based on students' typical performance of improper methods for pre-class preparation and make key-problem-based guidance)

Typical performance:

I just browse the content to be taught during pre-class preparation;

I just mark the important words during pre-class preparation;

I just do the exercise above and below during pre-class preparation.

Guide on key problems:

Students should carefully prepare for the lesson.

Students should adopt proper methods for pre-class preparation.

### 3. Training with Strategies

★ Consulting examples (teachers make students understand some focuses of the pre-class preparation and master some methods for such preparation in "after teaching example 6" by raising questions for conclusion and then provide some reference)


Questions for reference:

What do you think is the key point of this section?
What is the knowledge related with the aforesaid key point?
Is there any important written explanation or conclusion on this section in the textbook?
Is there anything you cannot understand before this class?
Have you considered the aforesaid problems during the pre-class preparation?
Have you considered the solutions for the aforesaid problems during the pre-class
    preparation?

Reference answer: (give explanations based on the aforesaid problems)
Read: read the title and the content.
Find: find out the issues on important knowledge to be solved.
Consult: review and consult the important knowledge directly related with this lesson.
Think: try the best to think independently and raise some problems you cannot solve.
Mark: mark the important or difficult points in the textbook.

### 4. Transfer of Experience

★ Reflection (teachers make students realize the advantages of making pre-class preparation carefully and using proper methods by analyzing the common ideas)
Idea: I have prepared for it, but it seems useless.
Reasons:

He/she do not carefully prepare for the lesson at all.
He/she fails to adopt proper methods for pre-class preparation.
He/she just makes preparation as a mere formality.

Advantages: (carefully preparing for the class and adopting proper methods)

Students can master the key content.
Students can further understand the content.
Students' knowledge can be more logic.
Students will dare to raise their hands to answer questions.
Students can think more flexibly.
Students can better understand their mastery of the knowledge to be learned.
Students can develop better learning habits.

★ Internalization and consolidation (students can further understand and consolidate the knowledge they have learned by doing the homework assigned by teachers)
Practice: how will you prepare for the next class?

# REFERENCES

Bian, Y. *F.*, and Zheng, Y. Q. (1997). Report on mental health of primary school students in Hangzhou. *Journal of Hangzhou University (philosophy and social sciences)*, (6), 138-142.

Briggs, S. R., and Cheek, J. *M.* (1986). The role of the factor analysis in the development and evaluation of personality scales. *Journal of personality*, (54), 106-148.

Chen, H. B. (1991). Research into middle school students' strategies on arranging their time of academic learning. *Psychological development and education*, (2), 60-64.

Chen, H. B., and Shen, J. L. (1993). Development of middle school and primary school students' sense of academic responsibility. *Psychology science*, (2), 113-115,

Chen, X., and Zhang, D. J. (2002). A study on the integrated mode of psychological health education. *Education research*, (1), 71-75.

Dong, Q., and Zhou, Y. (1994). On students' self-monitoring of learning. *Journal of Beijing Normal University (social science edition)*, (1), 8-14.

Dong, Q., and Zhou, Y. (1995). Experimental research into students' self-monitoring of learning. *Journal of Beijing Normal University (social science education)*, (1), 84-90.

Dong, Q., and Zhou, Y. (1995). Research into the component, development and functions of the self-monitoring capacity of learning of 10-16-year-old children. *Psychology science, 18* (2), 75-79.

Dong, Q., Zhou, Y., and Chen, H. B. (1996). *Self-monitoring and intellect.* Hangzhou, China: Zhejiang People's Press.

Feng, Z. Z., and Zhang, D. J. (2001). A study on the concept and elements of the middle school students' mental quality. *Journal of Southwest China Normal University (humanities and social sciences edition), 27* (6), 56-61.

Feng, Z. Z., Zhang, D. J., and Wu, *M.* X. (2002). On the articulation between EQO education and psychological education in schools. *Journal of the Chinese Society of Education*, (3), 48-51.

Fu, J. Z., Fu, *M.* H, Yang, Y. Y. et al. (2002).The development of the self-monitoring learning ability of the primary and high school students. *Journal of Yunan Normal University (philosophy and social sciences edition), 34* (2), 100-106.

Hu, Z. J., and Xu, S. Y. (2001). An experimental study on situational factor influencing the self-monitoring ability of undergraduates. *Exploration of psychology*, (4), 35-39.

John, O. P., Cheek, J. *M.*, and Klohnen, E. C. (1996). On the nature of self-monitoring construct explication with q-sort ratings. *Journal of personality and social psychology, 71* (4), 763-776.

Kelemen, W. L. (2000). Metamemory cues and monitoring accuracy: Judging what you know and what you will know. *American journal of educational psychology, 92* (4), 800-810.

Lennox, R. D., and Wolfe, R. N. (1984). Revision of the self-monitoring scale. *Journal of personality and social psychology, 46* (6), 1349-1364.

Li, H. R. (1992). Relations between the development of primary school students' metacognition on math and their self-efficacy on math. Beijing Normal University.

Li, *M. Z.* (1997). Research into relationships between students' motivation, attribution, self-confidence, will straits of math learning and their self-monitoring of math learning. *Journal of mathematics education, 6* (2), 46-47.

Li, S., Yu, X. X. (2002). Effects of self-conscious and self-disciplined behaviors and strategy in study upon junior school student's achievements. *Journal of Ningbo University (educational science edition), 24* (3), 18-22.

Li, Z, Y. (2001). An investigation on the characteristics of the adaptability levels of junior grade one students. *Journal of Zhuzhou Teachers College*, (6), 26-29.

Lian, R., and Meng, Y. *F.* (2003). The investigation of the relations between the self-supervised study abilities and the personality characteristics for the average-achieving students. *Journal of Fujian Normal University (philosophy and social science edition), 3* (120), 128-131.

Lin, C. D., and Wo, J. Z. (2000). A research on the development of the self-monitoring ability in adolescents. *Psychology science, 23* (1), 10-15.

Luo, B. Q., and Gao, R. (1999). Discussion about self-management strategies in physical education learning. *Journal of Beijing Teacher College of Physical Education, 11* (3), 34-38.

Luo, L. *F.*, and Lian, R. (2002). Relation between self-regulation and performance in Chinese, mathematics, and English for average-achieving and high-achieving students. *Journal of Fujian Teachers University*, (1), 141-144.

Ni, J. J. (2002). Study on strategies of compound word problems: Cultivation of self-monitoring capacity during solution of word problems. *Modern primary and secondary education*, (8), 31-34.

Ning, L. H. (2001). Experimental research into the function of self-monitoring regulation strategies upon transferring math skills. *Bulletin des sciences mathematics*, (12), 10-12.

Perry, N. E. (1998). Young children's self-regulated learning and contexts that support it. *Journal of educational psychology, 90*, 715-729.

Roeber, C. *M.* (2002). Confidence judgments in children's and adults' event recall and suggestibility. *Developmental psychology, 38* (6), 1052-1067.

Rubman, C. N., and Waters, H. S. A .B. (2000). Seeing: The role of constructive processes in children's comprehension monitoring. *American journal of educational psychology, 92* (3), 503-514.

Snyder, *M.* (1974). Self-monitoring of expressive behavior. *Journal of personality and social psychology*, (30), 526-537.

Song, Q. Z., Wo, J. Z., and Lin, C. D. (2002). The study of construct students' self-monitoring learning abilities on physics problem-solving in high school. *Psychology development and education*, (2), 79-84.

Song, Y. Q., and Peng, J. Z. (2002). Experimental study of cultivating students in technique teaching of physical education. *Journal of Beijing University of Physical Education, 25* (4), 534-535.

Suarez, Riveiro J *M.*, Cabanach R G, Arias A V. (2001). Multiple-goal pursuit and its relation to cognitive, self-regulatory, and motivational strategies. *British journal of educational psychology, 71*, 561-572.

Sun, J. *M.* (2000). A review of the self-regulated learning theory and its theoretical modes. *Journal of the northwest normal university (social sciences), 37* (3), 21-24.

Tang, Z. Q. (1993). Research into relations among middle school students' value orientation, self-monitoring and prosocial behavior. *Research into social psychology, 15* (3), 1-10.

Wang, J. Y. (2002). The influence of environment on children's ability to self-control. *Journal of Xinyang Teachers College, 22* (5), 46-48.

Wang, L., and Hu, C. B. (2002). Pedagogy base of mental quality education. Journal of Southwest China Normal University (humanities and social sciences edition), 28 (6), 92-95.

Wang, T. Y. (2000). Cultivating middle school students' self-monitoring capacity during the teaching of reading. *Inner Mongolia education*, (4), 34-35.

Weng, X. D. (1993). Relations between psychological resistance and control points, and between self-monitoring and situation pressures. *Research into social psychology*, (2).

Winne, P. H. (1997). Experimenting to bootstrap self-regulated learning. *Journal of educational psychology, 89*, 397-410.

Wo, J. Z., and Lin, C. D. (2001). Impacts of processing speed and self-monitoring on cognitive performance. *Psychology science*, (5), 537-540.

Wolters, C. A. (1998). Self-regulated learning and college students' regulated of motivation. *Journal of educational psychology, 90*, 224-235.

Wu, X. H., and Zhang, G. Z. (2002). Evaluation on middle school students' self-monitoring capacity of math. *Modern primary and secondary education*, (8), 35-37.

Xie, Q. (2000). Self-controlling in Chinese reading comprehension. *Journal of Luoyang Teachers College, 19* (4), 82-85.

Yi, X. *M*. (2002). The relation between self-supervision and academic performance of college students. *Chinese journal of clinical psychology, 10* (2), 116-117.

You, J. P., Leng, Z. B. (1997). Experimental research into implementing metacognition education for primary school students. *Journal of Sichuan Teachers College (philosophy and social sciences)*, (2), 1-8.

Zhang, D. J. (2002). Strengthen mental health education in schools and foster students' psychological quality. *Journal of Hebei Normal University (educational science)*, (1), 17-23.

Zhang, D. J. (2004). *On school psychological* suzhi *education*. Chongqing: Southwest China Normal University Press.

Zhang, D. J. et al. (2000). Problems on research of students' mental quality. *Journal of Southwest China Normal University (humanities and social science edition)*, (3), 56-62.

Zhang, D. J., and Guo, C. (2000). Exploring the principles of instructional psychology, conducting the research on education of mental quality. *Journal of Southwest China Normal University (humanities and social science edition)*, (6), 104-111.

Zhang, D. J., and Tian, L. (2003). On the design and implementation strategy of mental quality education. *Curriculum, teaching material and method*, (6), 66-70.

Zhang, D. J., and Wang, L. (2001). Upon mental health and creativity. *Journal of Ningbo University (educational science edition), 23* (6), 1-4.

Zhang, D. J., and Xiang, S. J. (2002). An initial study of self-monitoring of frustration coping. *Journal of Southwest China Normal University (natural science), 27* (6), 981-986.

Zhang, J. Y. (1998). Research into self-monitoring capacity of math subject. *Psychology development and education*, (4), 50-55.

Zhang, J. Y., and Lin, C. D. (2000). On developing the ability of self-monitoring in studying mathematical subjects among secondary school students. *Journal of the Chinese Society of Education*, (4), 46-49.

Zhang, X. J., Tian, H. W., and Zhao, X. F. (2002). The role of self-regulation theory in cultivating university students' writing ability. *Journal of Luoyang Agricultural College, 22* (2), 152-153.

Zhao, Q. *M.*, Zuo, Y.F. (2002). Survey on and research into the obstacles of mildly mentally handicapped students' intelligence, self-monitoring capacity and learning adaptation. *Journal of Lvliang Higher College, 17* (4), 34-37.

Zhong, Y., Liu, X. *M.*, Lin, J., et al. (2000). Developing the self-monitoring ability of students and the experimental research for optimizing teaching in swimming skill instruction. *Journal of Xi'an Institute of Physical Education, 17* (4), 67-69.

Zhou, D. J. (1999). On cultivating the self-monitoring during the teaching of solving math problems. *Journal of Suzhou College of Education*, (3), 78-80.

Zhou, Y. (1994). Research into the structure, development and influential factors of middle school and primary school students' self-monitoring capacity of learning. Beijing Normal University.

Zimmerman, B. J. and Martinez-paris, *M.* (1988). Construct validation of a strategy mode of student self-regulated learning. *Journal of educational psychology, 80*, 284-290.

Zimmerman, B. J., and Schunk, D. H. (1989). *Self-regulated learning and achievement.* New York: Spingerverlay.

In: Methods and Implementary Strategies on Cultivating …      ISBN: 978-1-62417-979-2
Editors: Da-Jun Zhang, Jin-Liang Wang, and Lin Yu      © 2013 Nova Science Publishers, Inc.

*Chapter 7*

# CULTIVATION OF EMOTION REGULATION CAPABILITY IN THE CHINESE LANGUAGE TEACHING FOR PRIMARY SCHOOL STUDENTS

## *Jing-Jin Shao[1], Da-Jun Zhang[2] and Jin-Liang Wang[2]*

[1] Beijing Normal University, China
[2] Center for Mental Health Education in Southwest University, China

## ABSTRACT

Emotion regulation is one of the necessary processes for individual adaptation and social development, as well as one of the important components of personal characteristics in psychological *sushi* structure. For a long time, people just pay attention to the development of students' cognitive competence, and the emotion factor has not been fully integrated into the target system of school education and resulted in increasingly serious and negative effects on students, such as poor learning efficiency, serious study weariness and school dropout, lopsided personality development, etc. For that reason, we tried to construct the intervention program of the cultivation of emotion regulation competence in the Chinese language teaching for students and conducted the education experiment in this chapter. Data analysis showed that the level of difficulty in emotion regulation among students in experimental group was not significantly different from that of the control group during the pre-test. After the experiment intervention, the overall effect of the experimental group and the control group did not vary significantly, but the result showed that both levels of difficulty in coping strategies and difficulty in understanding emotion of the experimental group were improved better than those of the control group. Based on the analysis of comparison result between the pre-test and the post-test respectively for the experimental group and the control group, for the control group, average scores of the difficulty in emotion regulation during the post-test were a little lower than those during the pre-test, but it did not vary significantly from the pre-test to the post-test; for the experimental group, average scores of the difficulty in emotion regulation during the post-test were much lower than those during the pre-test, and both levels of difficulty in coping strategies and difficulty in understanding emotion varied significantly from the pre-test to the post-test, and the level of impulse behavior control during the post-test was also improved significantly. Based on the comprehensive analysis of experimental results, we thought that the PSE infiltration mode in Chinese language class of primary schools could effectively improve the level of difficulty in emotion regulation and promote the emotion regulation competence of students from primary schools.

## LITERATURE REVIEW

### Definitions

*Emotion regulation.* Emotion regulation is a rather vague concept, including two kinds of regulation phenomena: regulating emotion and regulated emotion. They belong to different research scopes: the former refers to the change of aroused emotion (e.g. Regulation of emotion on cognition or behavior); the latter refers to the arousal of emotion change (e.g. Regulation of cognition or behavior on emotion). Essential difference between them is which emotion is first aroused in the case of separately defining regulation. Gross indicates that the former is mainly similar to the concept of emotion because the main function of emotion is to coordinate with various response systems. This chapter is understood in accordance with the meaning of the latter, and in this sense emotion regulation is still a concept with meaningful connotation. Qiao et al. (2000) thought that defining methods of emotion regulation connotation were divided into three categories: 1. Adaptability, emphasizing that emotion regulation is emotional and behavioral responses for the purpose of adapting to the social reality (Cole, Michel and Teti, 1994); 2. Efficacy, emphasizing that emotion regulation aims at serving the personal purposes (Masters, 1991); 3. Characteristic, making definition based on a certain characteristic or feature of emotion regulation (Dodge, 1989; Cicchetti, Ackerman and Izard, 1995; Huang and Guo, 2000; Chen, 2002).

In a sense, these three defining methods are interrelated to help us understand the nature of emotion regulation from different perspectives and aspects. We think that the emotion regulation is a psychological process that individuals manage and regulate their emotional responses and others by the use of certain strategies and methods purposefully in a planned way to make individuals' emotional responses flexible, adaptive and effective in overall function. Huang et al. thought that emotion regulation process mainly had the following characteristics:

Emotion regulation includes all positive and negative emotions, a process which maintains balance between positive emotion and negative emotion ( Cole and Michael, 1994; Walden and Smith, 1997);

Emotion regulation not only consists of strong feelings and excessively physiological arousal emotions, but also includes low-intensity emotions which need to be enhanced (Dodge, 1989; Cole, 1994; Cicchetti et al, 1995);

During the emotion regulation, regulation contains a wide range of main components: physiological responses, subjective experience, body expression and behavioral expression (Thompson, 1990; Eisenberg and Fabes, 1992; Gross and Levenson, 1993, 1997);

Emotion regulation has certain purpose or goal orientation (Thompson, 1994; Cole, 1994; Cicchetti et al, 1995;

Emotion regulation is a psychological process that individuals manage and regulate emotions by the use of certain strategies consciously and flexibly in a planned way (Underwood, 1997).

*Distinction Between Emotion And Emotion Regulation.* Emotion regulation is one of the important components in the field of emotion research, as well as the natural extension and development of the emotion. There is undoubtedly a close relationship between emotion concept and emotion regulation concept. Kagan (1994), Stansbury and Gunnar (1994) even thought that it was difficult to distinguish the two concepts and that regulation was regarded as an intrinsic attribute of emotion. However, most emotion psychologists regard emotion and emotion regulation as two concepts with different connotions: emotion is an integrated psychological process that objectively interacts with the needs of people to cause subjective experience, physiological arousal, expressions and behaviors while emotion regulation refers to a process that individuals affect themselves what emotions they have, when these emotions arise and how to experience and express these emotions (Gross, 1998).In this sense, we can think that specific aroused emotion and emotion regulation are two independent psychological processes.

*Emotion Regulation Competence.* Emotion regulation is a psychological process that individuals coordinate and regulate subjective experience, physiological arousal and behavioral response. From the perspective of individual development, emotion regulation can form stable psychological characteristics to develop a specific competence, i.e. Emotion regulation competence. It mainly means that individuals regulate emotions of themselves and others to improve the competence of task-oriented behavior (Huang, 2001).Many researchers (Salovey and Mayer, 1990, 1997; Wang, 2000; Buckley, Storino and Saarni, 2003; Xu, 2004) define emotion regulation from the perspective of competence and think that emotion regulation competence is one of the main components for emotional intelligence. However, other people have different definitions on the connotation and category of emotion regulation competence. For example, Chinese scholar, Meng, thought that emotion regulation was the super ordinate concept of emotional intelligence and that emotional intelligence reflects the problems of emotion regulation or the problems of emotion regulation competence. Essentially, emotion competence reflects the problems of emotion regulation or the problems of emotion regulation competence. Kim L.Gratz and Lizabeth Roemer also proposed a similar viewpoint that there was a lot in common between the emotion regulation competence and the emotional competence. We think emotion regulation competence is the capability that individuals cope with, regulate and manage various emotional events and disturbances independently, flexibly and effectively in accordance with external situations and is the relatively stable psychological trait caused by immersion and accumulation of emotion regulation psychological process in personality structure.

## Current Status of Emotion Regulation Research

Emotion regulation is an important part of the early childhood social development and one of the fields concerned by psychologists all the time. Since 1980s, emotion regulation has become a relatively independent research subject in developmental and educational psychology. At present, emotion regulation concept is already widely applied to relevant psychology literatures and closely related to many disciplines including physiological psychology, cognitive psychology, personality psychology, developmental psychology and social psychology, involving children, adults, clinical, health, education and other fields, and emotion regulation is becoming the frontier and hotspot issue of emotion research.

*Consensual Process Mode Of Emotion Regulation From Gross.* Gross (1998) proposed the Consensual Process Mode of Emotion Regulation and thought that emotion reflected mutual relationship between individual response and environment and that individuals generated emotions due to important stimuli. According to the emotion regulation process mode, emotion regulation occurs at any time in the process of the subjective assessment for emotion clues (including the process of emotion generation and emotion response tendency).In other words, emotion regulation can occur during the assessment of emotion source process and the experience, expressions, behaviors and physiological response tendencies of emotion response process. These response tendencies may be adjusted so as to determine the final form of emotion response. During the emotion regulation, basic types of emotion regulation mainly include reason regulation (i.e. Directly adjusting the emotion tendency presentation process which has been aroused; main strategies of emotion regulation contain situation selection, situation correction, attention allocation and cognitive change) and response regulation (increasing or decreasing the emotion which has been aroused, such as response adjustment).

## Functions of Emotion Regulation

Emotion regulation and adaptation function. Saarni and Campos (1998), Brenner and Salove (1997) et al. Thought that good emotion regulation helps to promote the health of individuals, keep the feeling of emotional balance, maintain the self-efficacy and the communication feeling with others, properly evaluate environment (including social environment) and adopt constructive problem-solving strategies.Many clinical theories emphasized catharsis and adjustment of impulsive emotions and indicated that excessive suppression of emotion was regarded as the major reason of many psychological disorders. Dodge and Garder (1991) and Keenan (2000) made the research and found that the failure of emotion regulation made individuals become weak and helpless and was one of the most dangerous factors causing children psychopathology, which was harmful to their development of social behaviors. Eisenberg and Losoya (1997), Saarni, Mumme and Campos (1998) et al. Thought that low level of emotion regulation was one of the main characteristics for children with explicit and implicit behavior problems. According to the research, Richard and Dodge (1982) indicated that the children with social withdrawal and the children with the aggressive behavior in grades 2-5 of a primary school rarely used positive emotion regulation strategies in pressure situations and that there was no difference in the statistic and in the age between the former and the latter. According to the research, Caspi, Bem and Elder (1989) indicated that children with lack of control had poor capabilities of emotion expression and control. Those factors properly predicted assessments of parents and teachers towards 9, 11 and 13 year-old children: inattention, hyperactivity and antisocial behaviors. Chinese research on teenagers' emotion regulation also had similar conclusion; Qiao (1999) and Yu (1999) et al. made the research and thought that teenagers had low development level of emotion regulation competence and did not know effective methods of emotion regulation and control.

Emotion regulation and cognition promotion function. Emotion regulation, the medium between emotion and cognition system, can make people maintain task-oriented behaviors and have systematic influence on the relationship among information processing components and the approach to adopt strategies. We think that emotion regulation is very significant for emotion arousal level, as well as being related to the efficacy of emotion. For example, emotion regulation can affect the efficacy of cognition operation. According to the Yerkes-Dodson Law, middle level of emotion arousal can effectively exert the function of emotion regulation towards intelligence operation process. Some researchers thought that good state of mind could improve persistence, and make people more endured, and self-confident (Salovey and Birnbaum, 1989). Siner and Salovey et al. found that information which is consistent with the state of mind shares common status of emotion so that it is more likely to be accepted and learned. However, research indicated that it was not necessarily easier for mood depression to recall the unpleasant memories and that it may be attributed to the result that people make regulation of negative emotions. Gumora et al (2002) conducted helpful research on the relationship between emotion regulation and academic performance; the research result showed that emotion regulation of students had quite significant impact on their academic performance and played an important role in other cognition processes. It is also thought that emotion disturbance would result in the deficiency of learning capability in the future. According to the research, Zhou and Cha (1997) and Wang (1998) found that the degree of children's emotion stability directly affected their learning capability. Therefore, the fact that emotion and its regulation are available for thinking process can generate more flexible plans and more creative thoughts, promote task orientation behaviors and cognitive activities, enhance academic performance, make people achieve the best state of cognitive function.

### *Research on Influencing Factors of Childrens Emotion Regulation*

Emotion regulation and temperament factor. Emotion regulation development in early childhood is closely related to their temperament characteristics; the frequency and strength of negative emotions are usually regarded as important basis of temperament measurement. Eisenberg et al. (1992) thought that the assessment on two important temperament dimensions (the emotion strength parameter and the stable individual difference during the regulation) could be carried out to predict emotion regulation strategies adopted in early childhood, such as attention shift and concentration, behavioral initiation or inhibition. According to the research, Davies and Cummings (1995) found that children whose positive emotions had been initiated had less bad mood and more positive cognition when they felt angry. According to the research, Wang and Chen (1998) showed that behavioral inhibition type children would mostly seek comfort from adults in strange situations while non-inhibition type children would mostly adopt positive activities and distraction strategies. In addition, emotion strength and regulation degree are main factors which cause children individual difference of emotion regulation. Middle regulation level and emotion strength may be the best for children who have emotion expression capability, planning capability, problem-based coping capability and other capabilities that they flexibly use various strategies of emotion regulation.

Emotion regulation and PCR. PCR plays an important role in the development of emotion regulation competence for children. Fabes, R. A., et al. (1994) thought that parents would have positive influence on emotion regulation of children and their strategy development if parents could respond to emotions of children in the way which meets socialization practices of children's emotions. Many foreign studies indicated that, if children grew up in families where more emotional topics were talked about, these families not only helped them better understand emotions and feelings of other people as well as develop social communication skills, but also caused that preschool-age or school-age children show good moral emotions. Halberstadt (1991) showed that the response of parents or supporters to children's emotional behaviors or the emotional interaction between parents or supporters (such as conflicts between parents) had a significant influence on the development of children's emotion regulation competence and peer communication capability. With children growing up, their dependence on parents'support gradually reduce, but parents continue to play an important role in emotion development of early school-age children. Researchers presumed that parents paid attention to emotional response of children in primary schools and found that most children still showed real emotional expression such as anger, anxiety, sadness and pain. In particular, early school-age children regarded mothers as the best object of anger expression and expressed willingness to accept help when they lacked regulation skills (Saarni, 1988; Zeman and Shipman, 1996).

Emotion regulation and peer relationship. Peer relationship is a symmetrical interaction process that the parties have equal social status and behavioral rights, and it requires children to have certain level of social initiative and self-regulating capability (Eisenberg and Fabes, 1992). Peer relationship exerts an extensive and far-reaching influence on the development of children's emotion and regulation competence. First, group or friendship formed among peers can inhibit or enhance their emotional experience and expression to some extent so that the development of children's emotion and emotion regulation competence shows certain uniqueness or age characteristics. In many cases, peer groups tend to inhibit emotional expression. Peers usually reject children who do not obey the rule of emotional expression. For example, those children who always explode in anger or gloated over failure of other children will be rejected by peers (Volling, B. Et al, 1993), and envy of others' success is also related to the rejection of peers. Secondly, if peers have many similarities, they will be more likely to understand each other's emotional development and play the role of coordinator between each other. Children gradually learn to regulate their emotions through appropriate strategies so as to form relatively mature emotion regulation competence (Eisenberg, Fabes and Losoya, 1997; Eisenberg, et al, 1996; Eisenberg, et al, 1995). According to his research on emotion regulation strategies for primary-school students, Von Salisch $M$ (2001) showed that older children adopted the method of Silent Treatment more than younger children, transferring attentions and keeping away from peers who enraged them; there was no difference of age in the case of seeking social support from peers. According to their research, Underwood et al. (1999) found that it was easier for children in grade 6 than children in grade 2 to make silent response to provocations of peers whom these children did not know, show neutral facial expression as well as the shrug. According to their research, Murphy and Eisenberg (1996) indicated that more and more older children would avoid direct confrontation and know how to transfer attentions to alleviate painful experience when peers aroused their anger.

Emotion regulation and specific situation. Emotion regulation occurs in specific situations for social communication and is related to situation requirements and cognitive assessment of individuals on these requirements. These situations include characteristics of stimuli which directly trigger emotions and of environmental background such as family and school, as well as characteristics of social relationship type among people during the generation of emotions. According to the research, Diener found that children adopted more strategies of emotion regulation in situations of frustration than in the situations of fear.

According to their research, Lempers and Clark-lempers (1992) indicated that children at the age of 11-17 had fewer conflicts among friends than younger children  and seemed to have good emotion regulation among friends. However, Gottnan and Mettetal (1986) doubted the research result and thought that individuals in childhood and early adolescence required more skills to deal with negative emotions and maintain friendship. In addition, relevant manner of acceptable children emotion expression and its development track vary with gender because influences of social culture and subculture are different. It has been found that boys chosen angry response more than girls; they had less restriction on the selection of anger expression manner and considered how to make themselves feel better more than girls. According to the research, Denhanm and Barrett also proved that regulation competence of negative emotions for girls was affected by socialization of their parents more significantly than that for boys; additionally, different cultural backgrounds have different influences on the rule of children's emotion expression (Joshi and Maclean, 1994).

### *Research Tendency of Emotion Regulation*

Emotion regulation development of children mainly has close relationship with the development of cognitive capability, social cognition and social skills (Campos et al, 1989; Gunnar et al, 1989). With the growth of age, representation capability, information processing capability and social cognitive capability of children are improved rapidly; emotion regulation of children is gradually transformed from dependence to independence, with more abundant regulation strategies and more flexible means, so as to make their emotion regulation competence enhanced continuously and more mature.

Emotion regulation and cognitive capability. In a sense, individual's cognitive capability development, cognitive explanation and its expectation determine his or her emotion responses towards events. Lazarus (1966) thought that different individuals would provide different explanations of the same emotion arousal, while cognition of people with regard to event sense would affect generation of emotional responses. According to their research, Harter and Buddin et al. Showed that improvement of children's representation capability and information processing capability enhanced the understanding capability of emotions and the coping capability of adaptability to develop emotion regulation competence of children. Pulkkinen (1986) thought that children could regulate aggressive emotions through cognitive assessment and cognitive coping strategies, and cognitive capability of emotion control would be enhanced with the increase of age. According to their research, Altshuler and Ruble found that preschool children sought social support and adult's help as solutions of emotion regulation while older children adopted direct problem solutions and cognitive strategies. Li made comparative assessment on emotion experience of primary-school students at different levels of adaptability and the mal-adaptive pupils were sensitive to negative meanings but held back the expression. According to their research, Luo and Guo et al. indicated that there was difference in the capability that higher-grade students at primary schools distinguishing dominance of different emotion expression and triggering emotions of recipients; there was difference in which lower-grade students understood subsequent behaviors of recipients.

Emotion regulation and social cognitive capability. From its relationship with social development, emotion regulation is a sociality process which is not only processed internally by individuals but also occurs in situations of social relationship and social interaction. Thomposon (1994) found that emotion regulation competence of children is related to their social cognition of stimulators and their understanding or predictive capability of emotional responses from themselves and others. Research showed that children gradually enhanced their control and regulation capabilities of emotions and learned to decrease angry expression so as to coordinate with conflicting opinions of peers or regenerate new opinions. (Gottman and Parker, 1986; Cumming, 1987; Fabes and Eisenberg, 1994; Murphy and Eisenberg, 1996; Underwood et al, 1999; Parkinson et al, 1999) Compared with younger children, older children tend to utilize an approach which is beneficial to achieving the goal but not damaging interpersonal relationship and they try to cope with emotional conflicts among people through a constructive approach that points to others. According to the research on social cognition of school-age children, Saami (1997) found that it was regard as the best strategy for the protagonist to keep away from peers who damaged him or her while it was regarded as the best method when the protagonist was humiliated by peers. Altshuler and Ruble (1989), Strayer (1989) and Vinden et al (1999) thought that younger children could not effectively regulate their emotions because of low development level of their social cognitive capability ,and children under the age of five were difficult to understand negative emotion experience of others so that it was difficult for them to determine the manner and scope of emotion regulation. Many psychologists thought that formation of children's prosocial behavior should take the development of certain cognitive capability and other emotional resonance response (empathy) as premises. According to the research, Feshbach et al. (1968) and Eisenberg et al. (1998) showed that empathy level of sad emotions is closely related to prosocial behavior. According to the research, Eisenberg et al. (1995, 1997) found that those children who flexibly used regulation strategies and effectively regulated emotions had better development of social behavior.

### *Research Methods of Emotion Regulation*

Based on respective theory perspectives and different research emphases, emotional psychologists generally discussed one or several components of children's emotion regulation competence so that their research methods were different. At present, main methods for emotion regulation research include: 1. Physiological measurement method that some psychologists combine certain physiological changing index of children with research, such as calculating variability of heart rate and skin resistance; 2. Experiment method that psychologists design specific experiment situations for triggering emotions, such as delay of gratification, separation of parents or generation of disappointment, to observe specific status of children's emotion regulation; 3. Naturalistic observation method that psychologists observe emotion regulation behavior of children in natural situations; 4. Self-report method that children report how they make assessment of own emotions; 5. Assessment method that psychologists prepare some questionnaires and require parents, teachers or children to make assessment of emotion regulation competence in accordance with actual experience.

At present, assessment method is one of the common methods for emotion regulation measurement and relevant psychometric tools mainly contain: 1. Emotion Regulation Checklist (ERC, Shields, A. M., and Cicchetti, D, 1995); 2. Emotion Regulation Q Classification Scale (Ann Shields and Dante Cicchetti, 1997); 3. Difficulties in Emotion Regulation Scale (DERS, Kim L.Gratz and Lizabeth Roemer, 2004); 4. Emotion Regulation Questionnaire (ERQ, James J. Gross and Oliver P John, 2003); 5. Emotion Regulation Scale Measurement Scale (Shields et al, 1994). However, most rating scales are evaluated by psychotherapists, parents or teachers, and corresponding revisions have not been found in China. In China, rating scales for emotion regulation are rarely found; relevant rating scales mainly include: 1. Emotion Regulation Scale of Students in Junior Middle Schools (Hu and Zheng, 2003); 2. Emotion Regulation Scale of Students in Middle Schools (Wo, 2003); 3. Emotional Quality Questionnaire of Students in Middle Schools (Qiao, 1999); 4. Emotional Regulation Questionnaire (Huang, 2001); 5. Negative Emotion Scale of Students in Primary Schools (Wo, 2003). Thus, it can be As seen that there is currently lack of psychometric tools with good reliability and validity, which are suitable for normal emotion regulation of students in primary schools.

### *Relevant Research on Cultivation of Emotion Regulation Competence*

In the past 20 years, emotion regulation is an emerging research subject in the field of emotion research; foreign researchers mostly focus on the development of emotion regulation and factors related to it, but rarely study the intervention of emotion regulation competence; most research is limited to clinical skill training and psychotherapy of patients in mental hospitals or other hospitals, including intervention of emotional disorders such as depression, anger, sadness, loneliness, fear, inferiority, anxiety and hostility. Relevant researchers (Axline, 1969; Gardner, 1993; Sandler, Kennedy and Tyson, 1980) thought that emotional experience in dialogues and participation in children activities could help them regulate emotions and promote emotional health and adaptability. Slade (1994) thought that therapy included common construction between children and therapists, releasing conflicts and chronic experience of children. Lazarus and Folkman et al. are interested in emotional focus and coping strategies. In addition, RET of A. Ellis has great influence on the research.

Compared with their research, research on emotion regulation in China has just started, which is sparse and scattered. Existing research mainly contains development research of emotion regulation and factors related to it (Huang, 1986; Qiao, 1999; Wo andCao, 2003; Wo and Liu, 2003; Wang, 2001; Huang and Guo, 2001; Chen, 2002; Lu, 2004; Jia et al, 2004), and there are very few studies on intervention of emotion regulation competence. At present, in addition to Shen et al. who made research of non-intelligence factors and cultivation, Hu and Zheng et al. (2003) made experiment intervention in emotion regulation competence of students in junior middle schools in the manner of cognitive training and then found that cultivation of cognitive capability in education situations could enhance emotion regulation competence of students in junior middle schools; according to the experiment research, Wang (2004) indicated that it was applicable and effective to carry out self-emotion education of students in junior middle schools through research-based learning approach in order to cultivate emotion regulation competence of students in junior middle schools. In addition, Huang (1989) from Taiwan indicated that emotional education experiment was closely related to cultivation of emotion regulation competence to a large extent. The experiment was carried out in the group–oriented way, i.e. The catalysis-oriented or the experience-oriented, by use of feeling and emotion education experience curricula to make experimental research on attitude and academic performance of children in grade 4 of primary schools. The result showed that emotional education improved the attitude of children to themselves, others and schools, as well as promoted academic performance of Chinese language.

## Deficiencies in the Research Available

*Lack Of Research On Basic Theories.* Compared with foreign research, Chinese research on emotion regulation is relatively lacking and backward, still at the stage of translation and introduction about relevant foreign research. Existing research is mostly limited to experience description of importance or local issue; research of basic theories is relatively lacking, e.g. Some pending issues of definition and structure about emotion regulation have yet to be clarified so as to restrict further research of emotion regulation in China.

*Confined research field.* First, in terms of the objects of research, research field of emotion regulation is mainly for infants, discussing characteristics and laws of generation and development for emotion and emotion regulation in early life. However, under the influence of lifespan development perspective, research object of emotion regulation tend to be extended gradually from infants and pre-school children to school-age population, such as carrying out some research of emotion and emotion regulation for middle-school and university students, but there is little research of school-age children in the critical period of emotion regulation development so that it is difficult to reveal age characteristics, psychological mechanism and regulation strategies of emotion regulation development for primary-school students. Second, research of emotion regulation is mostly single field of research, mainly including discussing emotion awareness, understanding and emotion regulation strategies, or just coping with emotional disorders such as anxiety, depression, aggression, capriciousness, inferiority and hostility. Third, there is few intervention research on emotion regulation competence which is not closely related to the teaching of subjects. Existing research mostly focuses on the function of emotion and emotion regulation, i.e. Mainly studying interrelation between the emotion and emotion regulation and the cognitive process and behavior characteristics from the perspective of teaching skills and strategies. The only intervention research is mostly the Medical Mode implemented clinically towards problem children,which is still limited to the research pattern such as emphasizing remedy and adjustment, ignoring development and potential development; and intervention research on how to enhance emotion regulation competence of children is rarely discussed, especially cultivation of emotion regulation competence for most normal children has not caused full attention.

*Single research method.* Relevant research of emotion regulation is mostly to adopt experiment method, physiological measurement method, naturalistic observation method and others to study status and development characteristics of emotion regulation competence. However, in the process of further understanding individual emotion regulation activities, various methods also showed some limitations because single research method is difficult to make full understanding of children's emotion regulation. Emotional psychologists also tend to think that research of emotion regulation needs comprehensive utilization of many research methods, especially for primary-school students. Nevertheless, based on existing literature, most research is carried out by use of daily observation, experience conclusion or relevant rating scales of specific emotion as reference index of emotion regulation measurement and assessment, and currently there is no psychometric tool for emotion regulation with good reliability and validity, which are suitable for primary-school students in China.

## Significance of the Research

*Objective need of mental health development for students.* With the further development of social transformation, the increase of social competition and the lack of certain functions in school education, many students have different types and degrees of psychological and behavioral problems, such as study weariness, anxiety, depression, aggression, capriciousness and inferiority. Many researchers found that mental health problems of primary-school students were increasingly prominent; many mental problems had the age-lowering tendency; children and teenagers already had a large number of mental disorders, but mental health problems of primary-school students had not caused full attention. According to their research, Tang et al. Thought that total detectable rate of various behavioral problems for primary-school student in China was 12.93±2.19% and that poor emotion regulation competence was one of the important characteristics in psychological and behavioral problems of primary-school students. According to their survey, Bian et al. showed that students with obvious mental health problems were about 9.5%, among which anxiety of academic performance is the main problem of primary-school students. Chen thought that mental health problems of primary-school students were mainly learning, behavior and emotion which accounted for 10-20%. Detectable rate of emotional disturbance and mental problems is becoming higher and higher, and emotional disturbance or difficulty in emotion regulation already becomes one of the important reasons which cause mental disorders of children. Therefore, cultivation of emotion regulation competence for primary-school students has important significance in the improvement of their mental health development, and good emotion regulation is one of the main indexes to measure mental health.

*Need of psychological sushi development for students.* Psychological *sushi* is that individuals internalize the experience and influence externally gained into stable, basis and derivative psychological traits that are closely related with human's social adaptation and creating behaviors, based on physiological conditions. Emotion regulation is one of the important components in personality characteristics of individual psychological sushi structure, mainly referring to control degree of individual emotion and flexibility of emotion regulation. With the increase of age and the development of cognition, self-awareness and self-control capability for primary school students, primary school students begin to conscientiously select targets, actively regulate and manage their psychology and behaviors, gradually to decrease emotional explicitness and impulsiveness; their emotion regulation competence is further promoted accordingly. According to their research, Cole and Kaslow (1988) showed that emotion regulation mode began to develop and became more stable in the middle childhood. According to the research, Chen thought that pre-school children made significant development of capability for controlling and regulating their emotion after the training of organized school life and group activities; students in middle and higher grades of primary schools gradually learned to control and inhibit their impulse, continuously to reduce emotional impulsiveness. Yang and Ma et al. found that level of negative emotion for children in grades 3 and 4 of primary schools reduced significantly, and the decrease showed that primary-school students enhanced their emotion regulation competence. Thus, middle and senior grades of primary schools are the key development period of emotion regulation competence; the research of emotion regulation competence for children helps researchers understand the formation, development mechanism and process of children's emotion regulation competence, which is necessary for sound development of psychological *suzhi*.

*Extension of PSE approaches of and enrichment of teaching psychology theories.* At present, specific problem-based training, consultation and counseling among implementing approaches of PSE have been developed quite a bit in all kinds of schools at all levels, but the infiltration of PSE in teaching of subjects is still weak and hysteretic. It is largely related to high requirement of teachers' quality, as well as hysteretic research of subject-infiltration PSE which undoubtedly becomes main "bottleneck" restricting further continuous development in this field. The long-term separation between PSE and subject teaching causes that PSE have not really and effectively become mainstream of school education yet. According to characteristics of a subject during the teaching of the subject,subject infiltration is to find out the connection between subject teaching and the development of students' psychological *suzhi*, apply PSE approaches and strategies with clear objective and well-prepared plans, infiltrate PSE content into the subject teaching, promote students' mental health and develop sound psychological *sushi* of students so as to achieve the fundamental goal of PSE. Subject infiltration is not only the function extension of subject teaching, but also the extension of PSE research domain. In addition, the teaching of each subject directly or indirectly contains many resources for MHE which can be utilized and in conformity with the principle of educational efficiency. Therefore, from the perspective of subject teaching, this chapter extends functions of subject teaching and accelerates the realization of subject teaching goals, as well as extends research scope of instructional psychology; from the perspective of PSE, cultivation of students' emotion regulation competence during the teaching of Chinese language in primary schools can provide reference for the teachers infiltrating PSE into the teaching of a subject and improving scientific and effective implementation of PSE in the mainstream of school education.

## Research Design

### 1) Objectives

Based on the content of Chinese language teaching in grade 4 of a primary school,this chapter is planned to use education experiment method in the means of subject infiltration to discuss effective approaches, strategies and effects for cultivating students' emotion regulation competence in the Chinese language teaching of a primary school. Basic flow (see Figure 7.1):

### 2) Hypothesis

Hypothesis 1: Difficulty in emotion regulation consists of many components which can be studied through comprehensive survey on observable and typical external reflection of primary school students;

Hypothesis 2: Grades 4 and 5 of primary schools are the key development period of emotion regulation competence, which can promote emotion regulation capability and sound development of psychological *sushi* for primary school students;

Hypothesis 2: Emotion regulation competence can be improved through education training; target-based infiltration education intervention in the Chinese language teaching of primary schools is an effective approach to enhance emotion regulation competence of students;

Hypothesis 4: Improvement of emotion regulation competence can effectively enhance students' emotions of academic performance and promote effects of cognitive operation so as to improve the academic performance of students.

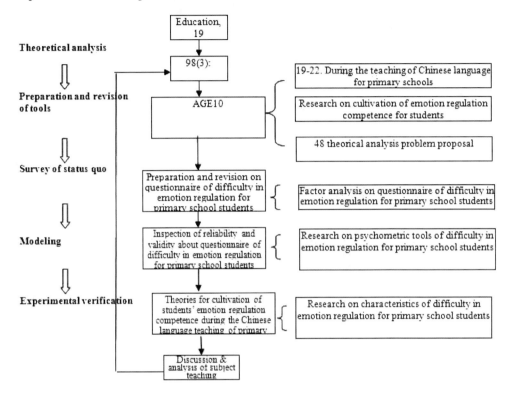

Figure 7.1. Flow Chart for Cultivation of Emotion Regulation Capability in the Chinese Language Teaching for Primary School Students.

### 3) Participants

Full-time primary school students.

### 4) Methods

This chapter adopts comprehensive methods, mainly including literature review, questionnaire, academic performance tests and educational experiments. Literature review aims at concluding the past research achievement and determining the research thought flow and logic starting point of empirical research through analysis and synthesis of relevant literature; questionnaire mainly refers to measurement of students' emotion regulation competence and psychological *sushi* development level; academic performance test refers to measurement of relevant learned Chinese language knowledge and skills; educational experiment is to fully explore corresponding educational resources based on the teaching content of Chinese language and investigate the applicability and effectiveness for cultivating emotion regulation competence of students during the teaching of Chinese language for primary schools.

## 5) *Statistics tool*

This chapter adopted SPSS 12.0 for Windows 2000 to make statistics of data.

# DEVELOPMENT CHARACTERISTICS OF DIFFICULTY IN EMOTION REGULATION FOR PRIMARY SCHOOL STUDENTS

We aim at finding out the different difficulties in emotion regulation for primary school students in terms of socio-demographic factors, i.e. Gender, grade, nature of schools and location of family, discussing problems and characteristics in the development of emotion regulation competence for primary school students, and providing necessary basis for further experiment research. At first, we prepared and revised the questionnaire of difficulty in emotion regulation for primary school students.

## Preparation and Revision on Questionnaire of Difficulty in Emotion Regulation for Primary School Students

### 1) *Preparation and Translation of Preliminary Questionnaire*

In this chapter, based on the *Difficulties in Emotion Regulation Scale* (DERS) by Kim L. Gratz and Lizabeth Roemer and the theoretical conception, we selected relevant items of subscale on empathy capability from the BarOn Emotional Quotient Inventory of Middle School Students (Version for young teenagers) revised by Yang, Xu and Zhang et al. During the preparation and translation of this questionnaire, we mainly adopted the method of mutual-translation between Chinese and English. At first, we invited five master students majoring in developmental and educational psychology to respectively translate items of original questionnaire from English to Chinese and then compared these five questionnaire versions to determine a Chinese translation draft; second, we invited two English professionals to translate the Chinese translation draft into an English version, compared the English version with the original questionnaire and then revised the English version to make it faithfully follow the original questionnaire; third, two doctors majoring in developmental and educational psychology discussed and analyzed application of topics and then made comprehensive consideration of the previous suggestions to form the first draft of questionnaire. After the first draft of questionnaire was determined, we invited 12 primary school teachers to revise the draft; we specified each item and corresponding dimension and explained the meaning of each factor in details. We inquired each teacher's understanding of the items and discussed with them whether the items can reflect the connotations of respective dimensions and the understandings of item description for primary school students. These teachers made marks on the items which they have different understandings and then made corresponding revisions according to their understandings. Then, we made comprehensive consideration of opinions from these teachers and revised the first draft to form the second draft. At last, we tested the students (participants) in the spare time. We investigated two groups of students respectively in a key primary school and a common primary school of Chongqing. They sampled 6 students from each grade from grade 4 to grade 6 in each school, 36 students in total, with excellent, fine or poor academic performance and the proportion of boys is approximately equal to that of girls. We requested students to read all items one by one in the second draft questionnaire, and markwords and sentences which they did not understand, then we talked with some students about the confusing content and made proper revisions to the preliminary questionnaire.

## 2) Formation of Formal Questionnaire

We adopted the preliminary questionnaire of difficulty in emotion regulation for primary school students, sampled some students from 3 primary schools in Chongqing as measuring objects (551 participants in total, including 192 in grade 4, 263 in grade 5 and 96 in grade 6), verified the theoretical conception of difficulty in emotion regulation for primary school students and made revisions based on the survey to prepare the suitable formal questionnaire of difficulty in emotion regulation for primary school students in China. The preliminary questionnaire consists of seven factors: 1. Non-acceptance of Emotional Responses/ NONACCEPTANCE; 2. Difficulties Engaging in Goal-Directed Behavior/GOALS; 3. Impulse Control Difficulties/IMPULSE; 4.Lack of Emotional Awareness/AWARENESS; 5. Limited Access to Emotion Regulation Strategies/STRATEGIES; 6. Lack of Emotional Clarity/ CLARITY; 7. Lack of Empathy/EMPATHY. The questionnaire contains 49 items (including 5 for lie-detection). It was rated on a 5-point Likert scale and the five candidate answers ranged from "scarcely" to "frequently".

They investigated participants with the single forced-choice item method. It showed that participants with higher scores had more serious difficulty in emotion regulation and lower development level of emotion regulation competence. Please see the following analysis results.

## Analysis on Items

Discrimination validity. We used independent sample test to verify the difference between high-score group (27%) and low-score group (27%) in terms of each item. The analysis showed that the value of each item was significant and the discrimination validity of each item is better in the preliminary questionnaire.

Standard Deviation. In general, factors with the standard deviation lower than 0.5 should be removed from the questionnaire. The standard deviation of all factors in the questionnaire was 0.77-0.91, indicating that all items therein have excellent discrimination validity.

## Factor Analysis

Principal component factor analysis and orthogonal rotation analysis are carried out for the questionnaire, 22 items are eliminated and 22 effective items are reserved, and 6 factors can explain 56.154% of the total variance. (See Table 7.1. and Table 7.2.)

In Table 7.1. and Table 7.2, factor 1 means that individuals cannot concentrate on tasks effectively when they experience negative emotion, called "Difficulties of Engaging in Goal-Directed Behavior"; factor 2 means that individuals cannot effectively maintain the control of their impulsive behaviors when they experience negative emotion, called "Impulse Control Difficulties"; factor 3 means that individuals cannot perceive and understand others' emotion effectively and timely, called "Lack of Empathy"; factor 4 means that individuals cannot pay attention to emotional response or lack awareness of emotional response, called "Lack of Emotional Awareness"; factor 5 means that individuals cannot adopt effective strategies to make corresponding regulation of experienced negative emotion when they encounter emotional disturbance; called "Limited Access to Emotion Regulation Strategies"; factor 6 means that individuals cannot accurately know and understand the experienced emotion, i.e. they cannot accurately clarify the experienced emotion, called "Lack of Emotional Clarity".

**Table 7.1. Factor Loading Matrix of Difficulty in Emotion Regulation for Primary School Students**

| Item | Factor 1 | Factor 2 | Factor 3 | Factor 4 | Factor 5 | Factor 6 | Communality |
|------|----------|----------|----------|----------|----------|----------|-------------|
| $A_{30}$ | .77 | | | | | | .60 |
| $A_{27}$ | .76 | | | | | | .58 |
| $A_{19}$ | .75 | | | | | | .59 |
| $A_{40}$ | .63 | | | | | | .42 |
| $A_{21}$ | | .76 | | | | | .71 |
| $A_{44}$ | | .73 | | | | | .66 |
| $A_{29}$ | | .59 | | | | | .68 |
| $A_5$ | | .51 | | | | | .49 |
| $A_{41}$ | | .47 | | | | | .61 |
| $A_{11}$ | | | .79 | | | | .61 |
| $A_2$ | | | .74 | | | | .61 |
| $A_{28}$ | | | .72 | | | | .56 |
| $A_{46}$ | | | .59 | | | | .50 |
| $A_9$ | | | | .82 | | | .67 |
| $A_{12}$ | | | | .81 | | | .53 |
| $A_3$ | | | | .74 | | | .59 |
| $A_{49}$ | | | | | .79 | | .59 |
| $A_{48}$ | | | | | .69 | | .36 |
| Item | Factor 1 | Factor 2 | Factor 3 | Factor 4 | Factor 5 | Factor 6 | Communality |
| $A_{34}$ | | | | | .64 | | .65 |
| $A_6$ | | | | | | .75 | .42 |
| $A_{13}$ | | | | | | .67 | .27 |
| $A_7$ | | | | | | .61 | .56 |

**Table 7.2. Eigenvalue and Contribution of Each Factor in Questionnaire of Difficulty in Emotion Regulation for Primary School Students**

| Factors | Eigenvalue | Contribution | Accumulated Contribution (%) |
|---------|-----------|--------------|------------------------------|
| 1 | 2.40 | 10.91 | 10.91 |
| 2 | 2.32 | 10.55 | 21.47 |
| 3 | 2.26 | 10.30 | 31.77 |
| 4 | 1.96 | 8.92 | 40.70 |
| 5 | 1.74 | 7.91 | 48.61 |
| 6 | 1.65 | 7.53 | 56.15 |

### 3) Test on Reliability

This chapter adopted the internal consistency reliability and the split-half reliability as the indicators for testing the reliability of the questionnaire for primary school students' difficulty in emotion regulation and factors therein.

The internal consistency reliability of these factors in the questionnaire for primary school students' difficulty in emotion regulation is between 0.52-0.77, and the internal consistency reliability of the questionnaire is 0.79; the split-half reliability of all sub-questionnaires is between 0.52-0.80, and the split-half reliability of the questionnaire is 0.73, indicating that this questionnaire has high reliability.

### 4) Test on Validity

In this chapter, based on the correlation between factors and the total score of the questionnaire, the construct validity of the questionnaire was estimated . The analysis showed that, except for that correlation between GOALS, AWARENESS is not obvious, the correlation between other factors is middle or low; the correlation between each factor and the total score of the questionnaire is relatively high, within 0.28-0.70. This indicates that the questionnaire conforms to requirements of psychometrics with good construct validity.

### 5) Discussion of Revision on Questionnaire

In this chapter, we made comprehensive consideration of opinions from experts, teachers and students, including preparation, revision and survey of the questionnaire, and revised the *Difficulties in Emotion Regulation Scale* by Kim L.Gratz and Lizabeth Roemer, then formed the preliminary questionnaire of difficulty in emotion regulation for primary school students. The final questionnaire was made according to the large-scale questionnaire based on the survey for primary school students after the preliminary questionnaire had been analyzed and tested with the factor analysis method and the items therein had been selected or removed. The questionnaire was made in accordance with the psychometrical principle, which fundamentally ensured that the questionnaire was made and revised following a scientific procedure. The result showed that the revised questionnaire of difficulty in emotion regulation for primary school students, has good reliability and validity index, and it could be regarded as the psychometric tool to evaluate difficulty in emotion regulation for primary students. However, there were still some defects in the questionnaire. For example, the questionnaire was just tested in three primary schools of Chongqing, therefore it has insufficient representative samples; and internal consistency reliability and the split-half reliability of the questionnaire were relatively low. These defects are to be improved further in the future research.

In addition, Non-acceptance of Emotional Responses in the original DERS referred to that individuals had negative secondary emotional responses to their negative emotion or did not accept their negative emotional responses. Nevertheless, the analysis result of items and factors in the revised questionnaire showed that 6 items reflected individuals' non-acceptance of emotional responses were removed due to low contribution of discriminability and factor analysis result. The reason may be that the factor of Non-acceptance of Emotional Responses is mainly related to individuals' negative secondary emotional responses to their own negative emotion in order to substantially survey self-assessment capability of individuals on emotions which they had perceived or experienced. In other words, individuals with mature emotion regulation competence can properly evaluate, respect and accept their emotions, feelings and performance, as well as experienced happiness.

For primary school students, especially those in senior grade, their self-assessment capability of emotions is enhanced gradually; their assessment standard is also changed gradually from the other standard that students depend on parents and teachers to the self-standard. However, the level of development for primary school students is relatively high in comparison with that of pre-school children. In general, primary school students have relatively low overall development level of emotion regulation competence and rapidly change their emotions according to external situations or stimuli, and they have unstable or even capricious emotions. They have sincere and natural feelings and experience on objective stimuli and on whether their needs to be satisfied; they can generally accept their feelings and rarely inhibit, deny or reject their real emotional experience of negative emotion events, e.g. Primary school students often become angry due to others' invasion, cry due to poor academic performance, or feel unhappy due to teachers' criticism.......

## Analysis on Characteristics of Difficulty in Emotion Regulation for Primary School Students

We adopted the revised questionnaire of difficulty in emotion regulation for primary school students to survey the development of difficulty in emotion regulation for primary school students (participants as before). Please see the following analysis results.

### 1) Overall Level of Difficulty in Emotion Regulation for Primary School Students

Referring to Table 7.3. The overall level of difficulty in emotion regulation for 551 primary school students is obtained according to the statistics and analysis.

In general, total average score of difficulty in emotion regulation for primary school students is 2.63. It is close to the middle level (3), basically reflecting the overall status and level of difficulty in emotion regulation for primary school students and showing that the overall level of difficulty in emotion regulation for primary school students in China is close to the middle level.

Development of each factor in difficulty of emotion regulation is not balanced; the overall characteristics include that cognition capability in the development of emotion regulation competence is better than explicit behavior and the scores of Difficulties Engaging in Goal-Directed Behavior and Impulse Control Difficulties are relatively high; this coincides with current situation of difficulty in emotion regulation for primary school students.

### 2) Multifactorial Analysis of Variance of Difficulty in Emotion Regulation for Primary School Students

We took grade, gender, nature of the school and location of family as independent variables and took all factors of difficulty in emotion regulation as dependant variables for the purpose of 3×2×2×2 multifactorial analysis of variance.

In Table 7.4, for the factor of Impulse Control Difficulties among all factors of difficulty in emotion regulation for primary school students, nature of a school and gender have main effects; grade, gender and location of family have significant interaction.

**Table 7.3. Average Score and Standard Deviation of Difficulty in Emotion Regulation for Primary School Students**

| Variables | Difficul-ties Engaging in Goal-Directed Behavior | Impulse Control Difficul-ties | Lack of Empathy | Lack of Emotional Awareness | Limited Access to Emotion Regula-tion Strategies | Lack of Emo-tional Clarity | Total average scores |
|---|---|---|---|---|---|---|---|
| M | 2.79 | 2.87 | 2.45 | 2.35 | 2.46 | 2.69 | 2.63 |
| SD | 1.19 | 0.96 | 0.92 | 1.02 | 1.07 | 1.09 | 0.61 |

**Table 7.4. Analysis of Variance on Difficulty in Emotion Regulation by Grade, Gender, Nature of School and Location of Family (F value)**

| Variables | Nature of School | Grade | Gender | Location of Family | Grade * Gender | School * Grade | School * Family | Grade * Family | Gender * Family | School * Gender |
|---|---|---|---|---|---|---|---|---|---|---|
| MB | 0.49 | 0.13 | 0.70 | 1.80 | 1.29 | 1.40 | 0.15 | 0.45 | 2.09 | 0.05 |
| XW | 6.75** | 2.40 | 4.45* | 0.23 | 4.75** | 3.76 | 1.07 | 4.77** | 6.07 | 1.79 |
| YQ | 0.02 | 6.61*** | 3.55 | 5.35* | 3.99* | 0.02 | 0.58 | 1.47 | 0.01 | 0.26 |
| JZ | 0.11 | 0.05 | 0.24 | 2.97 | 1.73 | 1.67 | 0.25 | 0.42 | 0.13 | 0.07 |
| CL | 1.81 | 0.25 | 0.38 | 0.81 | 3.77* | 0.001 | 0.62 | 1.06 | 0.27 | 0.10 |
| LJ | 1.82 | 0.43 | 0.09 | 3.11 | 0.69 | 0.21 | 0.88 | 0.43 | 0.90 | 0.02 |
| ZJ | 4.02* | 0.47 | 0.15 | 5.61* | 6.94*** | 1.01 | 0.01 | 1.46 | 3.52 | 0.07 |

Note: MB refers to Difficulties of Engaging in Goal-Directed Behavior; XW refers to Impulse Control Difficulties; YQ refers to Lack of Empathy; JZ refers to Lack of Emotional Awareness; CL refers to Limited Access to Emotion Regulation Strategies; LJ refers to Lack of Emotional Clarity; ZJ refers to total average score.

For the factor of Lack of Empathy, grade and location of family have main effects; grade and gender have significant interaction.

For the factor of Limited Access to Emotion Regulation Strategies, grade and gender have significant interaction.

According to the analysis of variance, gender and grade have significant interaction effect on difficulties in emotion regulation for primary school students as a whole. Simple effect test and post hoc test should be conducted on the significant interaction effect, if there are any findings during the analysis of variance. Condition-based selection was used in this chapter for the purpose of simple effect analysis. Please see Table 7.5. for details.

**Table 7.5. Analysis on Simple Effect of Grade and Gender for Primary School Students' Difficulty in Emotion Regulation**

| Source of Variance | | SS | Df | MS | $F$ | Post Hoc Test |
|---|---|---|---|---|---|---|
| Factor A (gender of students) | $b_1$ (grade 4) | 2.378 | 1 | 2.378 | 6.859** | Male > Female |
| | $b_2$ (grade 5) | 2.7899 | 1 | 2.7899 | 7.922** | Male > Female |
| | $b_2$ (grade 6) | 0.359 | 1 | 0.359 | 0.784 | |
| Factor B (grade) | $a_1$ (boys) | 10.391 | 2 | 5.195 | 15.194*** | 4>6; 5>6 |
| | $a_2$ (girls) | 1.410 | 2 | 0.705 | 1.938 | |

Note: *P<0.05; ** P<0.01; *** P<0.001.

According to the result of analysis on simple effect, $F$ refers to values of gender factor in grade 4 ($F=6.859$, P<0.01) and grade 5 ($F=7.922$, P<0.01) are significantly high. Among students in grade 4 and grade 5, boys have significantly higher level of difficulty in emotion regulation than girls; values of grade factor are significantly different for boys in different grades, e.g. Boys in grade 4 and grade 5 both have significantly higher levels of difficulty in emotion regulation than boys in grade 6.

**Table 7.6. Difference in Gender for Difficulty in Emotion Regulation for Primary School Students**

| Variables | Male (n=279) | Female (n=272) | $t$ Value |
|---|---|---|---|
| | $M\pm SD$ | $M\pm SD$ | |
| Difficulties Engaging in Goal-Directed Behavior | 2.84±1.15 | 2.73±1.22 | 1.036 |
| Impulse Control Difficulties | 2.91±0.96 | 2.82±0.94 | 1.083 |
| Lack of Empathy | 2.60±0.96 | 2.29±0.84 | 4.079*** |
| Lack of Emotional Awareness | 2.41±1.04 | 2.95±0.98 | 1.391 |
| Limited Access to Emotion Regulation Strategies | 2.60±1.09 | 2.31±1.01 | 3.188** |
| Lack of Emotional Clarity | 2.69±1.07 | 2.68±1.10 | 0.136 |
| Total average scores | 2.70±0.61 | 2.55±0.60 | 3.023** |

### 3) Difference in Gender for Difficulty in Emotion Regulation for Primary School Students

In Table 7.6., from the overall level of difficulty in emotion regulation, there is significant difference in gender, i.e. Boys have significantly higher level of difficulty in emotion regulation than girls. For each factor, scores of boys are all higher than those of girls; for the factor of Lack of Empathy, there is significant difference in gender; for the factor of Limited Access to Emotion Regulation Strategies, there is significant difference.

### 4) Difference in Location of Family for Difficulty in Emotion Regulation for Primary School Students

In Table 7.7, there is significant difference between urban students and rural students in overall level of difficulty in emotion regulation for primary school students; urban students have significantly lower level of difficulty in emotion regulation than rural students. For the factor of Difficulties of Engaging in Goal-Directed Behavior, urban students have lower level than rural students; for other factors such as Lack of Emotional Awareness, Lack of Emotional Clarity and Lack of Empathy, urban students have significantly lower level than rural students.

**Table 7.7. Difference on Location of Family for Difficulty in Emotion Regulation for Primary School Students**

| Variables | Urban Family (n=457) | Rural Family (n=94) | $t$ Value |
|---|---|---|---|
| | $M \pm SD$ | $M \pm SD$ | |
| Difficulties Engaging in Goal-Directed Behavior | 2.73±1.19 | 3.07±1.11 | -2.536[*] |
| Impulse Control Difficulties | 2.85±0.97 | 2.95±0.87 | -0.882 |
| Lack of Empathy | 2.34±0.90 | 2.95±0.86 | -5.946[***] |
| Lack of Emotional Awareness | 2.29±1.01 | 2.64±1.02 | -3.046[**] |
| Limited Access to Emotion Regulation Strategies | 2.43±1.08 | 2.60±0.95 | -1.460 |
| Lack of Emotional Clarity | 2.63±1.11 | 2.96±0.95 | -2.702[**] |
| Total average scores | 2.57±0.62 | 2.88±0.50 | -4.536[***] |

### 5) Difference in Nature of School for Difficulty in Emotion Regulation for Primary School Students

This chapter is to investigate the difference between ordinary primary schools and key primary schools. In Table 7.8, there is significant differences between students in key primary schools and students in ordinary schools on difficulty in emotion regulation, i.e. Students in key primary schools have lower level than those in ordinary primary schools; for the factor of Limited Access to Emotion Regulation Strategies, students in key primary schools have lower level than those in ordinary primary schools; for other factors such as Difficulties Engaging in Goal-Directed Behavior, Impulse Control Difficulties, Lack of Empathy and Lack of Emotional Clarity, students in ordinary primary students have higher level than those in key primary schools.

**Table 7.8. Difference on Nature of School for Difficulty in Emotion Regulation for Primary School Students**

| Variables | Key Primary School (n=289) | Ordinary Primary School (n=262) | t Value |
|---|---|---|---|
| | $M\pm SD$ | $M\pm SD$ | |
| Difficulties Engaging in Goal-Directed Behavior | 2.61±1.22 | 2.98±1.12 | -3.672[***] |
| Impulse Control Difficulties | 2.70±1.03 | 3.05±0.82 | -4.355[***] |
| Lack of Empathy | 2.24±0.89 | 2.68±0.89 | -5.805[***] |
| Lack of Emotional Awareness | 2.31±1.02 | 2.38±1.01 | -0.804 |
| Limited Access to Emotion Regulation Strategies | 2.36±1.11 | 2.56±1.01 | -2.253[*] |
| Lack of Emotional Clarity | 2.46±1.11 | 2.94±1.00 | -5.271[***] |
| Total average scores | 2.47±0.65 | 2.80±0.52 | -6.532[***] |

**Table 7.9. Difference in Grade for Difficulty in Emotion Regulation for Primary School Students**

| Variables | Grade 4 (n=192) | Grade 5 (n=263) | Grade 6 (n=96) | F Value | Significance |
|---|---|---|---|---|---|
| Difficulties Engaging in Goal-Directed Behavior | 2.80 (1.17) | 2.87 (1.16) | 2.53 (1.26) | 2.915 | 0.055 |
| Impulse Control Difficulties | 2.88 (0.91) | 2.96 (0.91) | 2.59 (1.09) | 5.396[**] | 0.005 |
| Lack of Empathy | 2.62 (0.89) | 2.52 (0.91) | 1.89 (0.79) | 24.046[***] | 0.000 |
| Lack of Emotional Awareness | 2.44 (1.03) | 2.32 (0.97) | 2.23 (1.10) | 1.595 | 0.204 |
| Limited Access to Emotion Regulation Strategies | 2.50 (1.10) | 2.51 (1.01) | 2.23 (1.11) | 2.679 | 0.070 |
| Lack of Emotional Clarity | 2.75 (1.09) | 2.73 (1.07) | 2.46 (1.10) | 2.637 | 0.072 |
| Total average scores | 2.69 (0.59) | 2.69 (0.57) | 2.34 (0.67) | 13.593[***] | 0.000 |

Notes: 1. Significant difference between students in grade 5 and students in grade 6; 2. Significant difference between students in grade 4/5 and students in grade 6; 3. Very significant difference between students in grade 4/5 and students in grade 6.

### 6) Difference in Grade for Difficulty in Emotion Regulation for Primary School Students

In Table 7.9, levels of difficulty in emotion regulation for primary school students in different grades are generally significantly different; the lower the grade is, the higher the level of difficulty is, i.e. Grade 4 > grade 5 > grade 6. Multiple comparisons have shown that there is significant difference between primary school students in grade 4 or 5 and those in grade 6, which indicates that grade 4 and grade 5 of primary schools are the key development period of emotion regulation competence for primary school students; for two factors of Impulse Control Difficulties and Lack of Empathy, there is significant difference in different grades.

For the factor of Impulse Control Difficulties, it shows that grade 5 > grade 4 > grade 6. Multiple comparisons have shown that there is significant difference between primary school students in grade 5 and those in grade 6, which indicates that grade 5 is the key grade for development of impulse control.

For the factor of Lack of Empathy, it shows that grade 4 > grade 5 > grade 6. Multiple comparisons have shown that there is significant difference between primary school students in grade 4 or 5 and students in grade 6.

### 7) Reason Analysis on Characteristics of Difficulty in Emotion Regulation for Primary School Students

Overall level of difficulty in emotion regulation for primary school students. In Table 7-3, overall level of difficulty in emotion regulation for primary school students is close to the middle level, which indicates that overall development of emotion regulation competence for primary school students in China is in the middle-low level. It basically coincides with the research conclusion of Huang, Chen and Zhang et al. In addition, development of all factors in emotion regulation for primary school students is not balanced; in which the Difficulties of Engaging in Goal-Directed Behavior, the Impulse Control Difficulties, the Lack of Emotional Clarity and the Limited Access to Emotion Regulation Strategies have high scores while the Lack of Emotional Awareness and the Lack of Empathy have relatively low scores; it also indicates that issues of difficulty in emotion regulation for primary school students in China mainly focus on emotional understanding, behavioral control and regulation and coping strategies of negative emotion. It can be proved to certain extent by the research of Li, Yu and Qiao et al. on characteristics of teenagers' emotional development. The phenomenon may be caused by many reasons, but we think that main reasons are as follows: first, influence of current educational system. Under the influence of traditional examination-oriented educational system, elementary Education of primary schools in China has the feature of the utilitarian, which pays much attention to the development of cognitive capability and knowledge, but does not bring the emotional development fully into the target system of school education and does not take emotional problems seriously. As a result, it largely ignores the students' emotional education in primary school. A lot of primary school students lack strategies and methods to get rid of emotional disturbance and they can't effectively control and regulate their impulsive behaviors so as to get out of troubles. Secondly, the influence of backward educational concepts from parents and teachers. Since primary school students have unstable or capricious emotions, many parents and teachers think that it is normal for children to be capricious, cry and get angry. The idea causes that parents and teachers of primary school students are rarely aware of the significance of emotion and personality development of children. When children encounter emotional disturbance, parents and teachers generally adopt simple methods, such as comfort or even ignore them. As a result, some students cannot accurately understand their own emotional status and are not good at regulating their emotions. For example, they may be sad or angry due to some unimportant things or feel depressed due to a certain examination... Thirdly, characteristics for development of emotion regulation competence for primary school students. Under the influence of school education, awareness and capability of emotion regulation for primary school students are developed so that students can inhibit some their own thoughts and desires to certain extent, overcome difficulties to accomplish their tasks, improve the stability and balance of emotions and gradually decrease the impulsiveness and changeability. The level of development for primary school students is relatively high just in comparison with that for pre-school children. Nevertheless, for overall level, primary school students have impulsive and unstable emotions, as well as immature capability for controlling and regulating their own emotions and behaviors.

Difference in Gender for Difficulty in Emotion Regulation for Primary School Students. There is significant difference in gender for overall level of difficulty in emotion regulation for primary school students. Level of difficulty in emotion regulation for boys is much higher than that for girls. It can be proved to certain extent by the research of Shen and Wo et al. For two factors of Lack of Empathy and Limited Access to Emotion Regulation Strategies, scores of primary school boys are significantly higher than those of girls. Possible reasons are as follows: first, from the perspective of developmental psychology, compared with boys, girls have earlier and more mature psychological and psychological development, obtain better self-education and self-control capability, and develop higher level of the awareness and understanding of others' emotions and the coping strategies. Therefore, they have fewer difficulties in emotion regulation; Due to abundant and fine emotional experience, girls may pay more attention to own emotions and adopt more strategies and methods to cope with emotional disturbance and problems effectively. Secondly, it is related to education of gender roles for children. Since the birth, people have begun to make education of different gender roles for boys and girls. Yang thought that gender difference is mainly caused by different social evaluation and treatment towards the male and the female. In this sense, it seems to be more reasonable that difference in gender for difficulty in emotion regulation for primary school students attributes to the socialization of early childhood and the different gender roles and education manners therein. In particular, under the influence of Chinese traditional culture, people always expect that boys become brave, independent and ambitious and girls are tender, considerate and obedient. At present, there are similar expectations of male and female roles in school education. Therefore, primary school girls are often good at understanding others' emotions and feelings and pay more attentions to controlling and regulating of their emotions. It coincides with the fact that teachers prefer girls in primary schools.

Difference in the location of family for difficulty in emotion regulation for primary school students. There is significant difference in locations of family for overall level of difficulty in emotion regulation for primary school students. For the factor of Difficulties of Engaging in Goal-Directed Behavior, urban students have lower level than rural students; for other factors such as Lack of Emotional Awareness, Lack of Emotional Clarity and Lack of Empathy, urban students have significantly lower level than rural students in primary schools.

This situation may be mainly caused by the difference of family educational resources and cultivation manners. Urban students have more abundant family educational resources than rural students and obtain more opportunities of emotional education and counseling. In addition, urban parents have received higher education and adopted more democratic and equal family cultivation manners, and they pay more attentions to emotional and personality development of their children. They may discuss more topics about emotions and feelings with their children, teach their children how to deal with emotional events, tell their children their assessments on emotional events and reasonable manners of emotional expressions, and help children accurately clarify emotional experience. Therefore, urban children have better target orientation capability. Compared with urban parents, rural parents pay more attentions to physical needs and requirements rather than emotional needs and development. We think that the difference between locations of families in terms of difficulty in emotion regulation for primary schools may be mostly related to the attention of parents to their development of emotions and feelings.

Difference in the nature of school for difficulty in emotion regulation for primary school students. There is significant difference in nature of school for difficulty in emotion regulation for primary school students. The overall level of difficulty in emotion regulation for students in key primary schools is significantly lower than that of students in ordinary primary schools. In terms of Difficulties of Engaging in Goal-Directed Behavior, Impulse Control Difficulties, Emotional Clarity, Lack of Empathy and Limited Access to Emotion Regulation Strategies, levels of students in key primary schools are significantly lower than that of students in ordinary primary schools. Possible reasons are as follows: firstly, key primary schools have relatively abundant educational resources, better educational environment and more teacher resources, and pay more attentions to standard education and cultivation of primary school students. In addition, students in senior grades of primary schools are in the key period of emotion regulation development, with high convertibility, and their development largely depends on educational environment and influence of teachers' quality. Therefore, fewer students in key primary schools encounter emotional disturbance; Second, students in key primary schools have more excellent learning capability and stronger achievement motivation. In order to obtain better academic performance, they can put more energy into the study consciously and actively. They may be better at mastering their own emotional status, effectively relieve emotional disturbance and control impulsive behaviors to make themselves be fully devoted to learning targets and rarely interfered by external environment. It can be proved by the research of Chinese researchers. Zhang found that scores in terms of self-control for students with excellent academic performance were much higher than those for students with poor academic performance. According to the research, Qian indicated that students with excellent academic performance had better emotional stability and self-control than those with poor academic performance. Liu also indicated that psychological *sushi* (including emotional adaptability, self-control and frustration endurance) in the student group of excellent academic performance was significantly better than that in the student groups of ordinary and poor academic performances. Thus, it is easy to understand why the level of difficulty in emotion regulation for students in key primary school is lower than that of students in ordinary primary schools

Difference in grade for difficulty in emotion regulation for primary school students. Levels of difficulty in emotion regulation for primary school students in different grades are generally significantly different; the lower the grade is, the higher the level of difficulty is, especifically grade 4 > grade 5 > grade 6. Significant difference mainly occurs between grade 4/5 and grade 6 in primary schools. In other words, grade 4 and grade 5 are the key development period of emotion regulation competence; it is easy to obtain good effects if corresponding cultivation and education are carried out for students in grade 4 and grade 5. The result coincides with research conclusions of Cole and Kaslow, Chen, Yang and Ma et all; level of development is not balanced in terms of each factor, and there are significant differences between different grades mainly in terms of Impulse Control Difficulties and Lack of Empathy. In terms of Impulse Control Difficulties, scores of students in grade 5 of a primary school are higher than those in grade 4/6, and there is significant differences between students in grade 5 and students in grade 6, which indicates that grade 5 is the key grade for development of impulse control capability; in terms of Lack of Empathy, scores of primary school students decrease with the increase of grades, i.e. Empathy capability of primary school students is improved with the increase of grades so that grade 4 and grade 5 in primary schools are the key period for development of empathy capability. The result is different from the research conclusion of Shi and Wang et al. We think that main reasons are as follows: first, it is related to gradual improvement of brain functions. With the increase of age for primary school students, their development of physiological functions gradually becomes mature. For example, inhibition and coordination functions of primary school students' brains are improved gradually from involuntary behaviors to voluntary behaviors, which lay the physiological foundation to effectively inhibit and regulate emotional behaviors. Secondly, it is related to characteristics for development of psychological *sushi* for primary school students. With the increase of grade for primary school students, both quantity and quality of educational content increase, they have achieved a giant leap for development level of psychological *suzhi*, such as development of cognitive capability, enhancement of self-awareness and extension of social communication scope, which all provide necessary conditions for their development of emotion regulation competence. Thirdly, it is related to school education. Main activities of primary school students are gradually changed from the preschool game-based activities to the learning-based activities; organized learning and group activities become one of the most important parts in their daily life. Primary schools pay much attention to education and cultivation of students in terms of learning goals, learning habits and behavioral habits, especially behavioral restriction and standardization of daily principles and rules; students gradually learn to inhibit and regulate their own emotions and behaviors to reduce impulsive behaviors. It plays an important role in the development of emotion regulation competence for primary school students. In addition, during the school life, mainly including communications with teachers and peers, primary school students will encounter a variety of emotional events or disturbances. They can learn connotations of some emotional words from the school life, accurately understand subjective experience of themselves or others, master effective strategies and methods to cope with various emotional disturbances, these help primary school students improve their emotion regulation competence.

# BUILDING TEACHING AND CULTIVATING MODES

## Necessity of Cultivation of Emotion Regulation Capability in the Chinese Language Teaching for Primary School Students

With the increase of social competition and the lack of some functions in school and family education, primary school students are also facing an increasing number of emotional problems which became one of the most important factors affecting the development of their mental health. According to our investigation results, the overall condition of the emotion regulation difficulty of primary school students in China is not good, because the emotion regulation capability is developed at a low level. In this sense, it is of great urgency to research the cultivation of emotion regulation capability of primary school students to promote a harmonious development of children's mental health. However, the emotion regulation and education, even the implementation of the overall PSE is currently carried out through two ways, i.e. Specific-problem-based training and psychological consultationand counseling, while the research which fully finds out relevant resources contained in the subject teaching to cultivate emotion regulation capability is only made in aspect of theoretical discussion and experience summarization. As far as the modern educational concept is concerned, the complete education theory should be focused on not only the cognitive achievement but also the growth and development of children's emotion. Therefore, emotion regulation and self-control should be a major education program. We think that, the initial research on "psychologization of curriculum" of subjects should focus on integrated development of people by subjects and then to the subject-infiltration PSE, which are active construction of the curriculum and also the improvement and upgrading of curriculum implementation strategy. Because of the shortage of PSE professionals and the already shaped curricula of primary school in China, it is necessary to carry out subject-infiltration PSE in order to avoid the curricula tendency caused by special PSE class and shortcomings of simply teaching the psychological knowledge. In short, it is necessary for us to conduct research on the infiltration mode of emotion regulation capability in the Chinese language teaching for primary school students, which is of critical importance for expansion of subject teaching functions and discussion on the way to implement the PSE.

## Feasibility of Cultivation of Emotion Regulation Capability in Chinese Language Teaching for Primary School Students

The key for implementing the experiment on the cultivation of emotion regulation capability in the Chinese language teaching for primary school students is "if there are resources available in the curricula during the teaching process". In terms of curricula content, there are a plenty of resources about emotion regulation to be utilized, which existes in Chinese language class of primary school. Most of the texts are selected from the life of primary school students, which are close to their real life. For example, happiness, angriness, sadness and joy of writing are contained everywhere in the people gallery, fables and fairy tales and historical quotations which provide a colorful space for primary school students and a platform for infiltration of emotion regulation capability. For example, in the text Great Wall Bricks, we can use this fable to conduct education on awareness, understanding and corresponding emotion regulation strategy on inferiority for primary school students and they are able to learn relevant strategies and methods about regulating inferiority emotion. This will improve their emotion regulation capability to a large extent. In addition, abundant teaching and education resources are also contained in the teaching process of the interaction between teachers and students or among students. In short, the theoretical concept of experiment on cultivation of emotion regulation capability in the Chinese language teaching for primary school students is reasonable and feasible.

## Building Infiltration Modes of Cultivation of Emotion Regulation Capability in Chinese Language Teaching for Primary School Students

Based on the theoretical modes about PSE and emotion regulation made by our predecessors and following the basic concept of integrated PSE mode, we built the infiltration modes of cultivating emotion regulation capability in Chinese teaching for primary school students during the cultivation of emotion regulation capability in Chinese teaching for primary school students, which include guide specifications of the objective, content, principle and methods of subject infiltration.

### 1) Setting Teaching Goal of Cultivation of Emotion Regulation Capability in Chinese Language Teaching for Primary School Students

Principles for setting teaching goal of cultivation of emotion regulation capability in the Chinese language teaching for primary school students.

*Oriented to the content of the text book.* The so-called oriented to the content of the text book means that when teachers creates emotion regulation capability content in the textbooks, a full consideration should be made as "relevant educational resources available in the textbook should be contained therein" instead of imposing relevant emotion regulation content not contained in the textbook. For example, in the text the Summer Palace, New Type of Glass and Feet of Boston Ivy, it is difficult to make infiltration about emotion regulation. We can not put content relating to emotion regulation capability into the text without considering the content system of the textbook and even integrate them mechanically which fundamentally misinterprets the meaning of subject-infiltrated PSE and is away from the significance and value of development of psychological *sushi* of students. Secondly, in every class, the infiltration of emotion regulation capability should be contained in the textbook itself, i.e. Iinfiltration is not carried out consistently in every class from every text. In short, the infiltration of emotion regulation capability in Chinese language teaching should be based on the infiltration opportunity contained in the text so as to find out the best point for integration infiltration.

*Objective.* Teachers should pay attention to the actual conditions of the school and the class as well as resources available, when they are setting the goal of subject-infiltration PSE. They should fully consider the psychological characteristics and development of the students in the class to set reasonable goals of PSE targeted at specific problems. In addition, they should also take into consideration the differences between individuals without applying one mode for all students. In order to be more objective and well targeted, we should consider: (a) specific conditions of experimental school. In our experiment, the experimental school is a remote village school with poor conditions. Most of the students are peasants' children. Their parents are less educated and most of them are very busy in making a living and have little time to pay attention to their children's education. In addition, there are a lot of migrant workers' children, school transferring is frequent. The formative education for primary school students is to be further enhanced. A lot of students are facing various emotional problems. (b) Characteristic of current condition of emotion regulation difficulty of primary school students. Based on the investigation on the condition of emotion regulation difficulty of primary school students, we conducted the infiltrated cultivation targeting at emotional understanding, impulse behaviors control and emotion regulation strategy. (c) Typical emotional events of primary school students. Teachers should learn to take an active interest in changes in mood of students, get to know the typical events in their lives and organically integrate them with subject teaching. By doing so, our experiment can be well targeted and make their emotional disturbance mitigated in order to improve the emotion regulation capability of primary school students.

*Imperceptible influence.* The so-called imperceptible influence means that the PSE shall be carried out by focusing on the influence made imperceptibly to achieve the goal of optimizing psychological *sushi* during natural infiltration. The experiment of emotion regulation capability in Chinese language teaching for primary school students pays special attention to "organically" integrating the goal and content of infiltration with those of the teaching of a subject, and helping students. When they are learning knowledge, teachers should improve their emotion regulation capability by means of implicitness, implication and permeating via creating specific teaching situation, designing effective teaching strategies, exploring and dealing with relevant subject knowledge, and consciously using the psychological theories, approaches and techniques. It is just like "the wind sneaked into the night, moisten things silently" instead of imposing the filtration content artificially, intentionally, directly and explicitly. In short, the setting of subject infiltration goal should avoid excessive "linearization" as much as possible; instead, it shall organically integrate the emotion regulation with the subject teaching to make the primary school students improve their emotion regulation capability imperceptibly.

Teaching goals of cultivation of emotion regulation capability in Chinese language teaching for primary school students. The effective implementation of subject infiltration PSE largely depends on whether there is clear definition between the goal of PSE itself to be infiltrated and activities. The basic objective of subject-infiltrated emotion regulation capability in Chinese language teaching for primary school students is to cultivate a good emotion regulation capability of students. However, we still need to make a further clear definition to the specific goal of emotion regulation capability. In this way, the implementation of experiment can be guaranteed. Specifically speaking, the specific goal of our experiment is focusing on improving the capability of primary school students in understanding emotion, control of impulse behaviors and emotion regulating strategies, targeting the characteristic and current status of the emotion regulation difficulty of primary school students. Only in this way can the implementation of experiment of emotion regulation capability of primary school students be well targeted and operable and avoid ambiguity and extensiveness to a large extent.

## 2) *Design of Teaching Content of Cultivation of Emotion Regulation Capability in Chinese Language Teaching for Primary School Students*

Based on the Questionnaire of Difficulty in Emotion Regulation for Primary School Students prepared and revised by our research institute, combined with the investigation and analysis on the difficulty characteristic of emotion regulation of primary school students, the teaching content of emotion regulation capability for primary school students mainly consists of the following four items. 1. Goal-orientation capability; 2. Capability in controlling impulse behavior; 3. Empathy capability; 4. Emotional awareness capability; 5. Coping with strategies of emotion regulation; 6. Capability in understanding emotion. Therefore, we thought the experiment of subject-infiltrated emotion regulation capability in Chinese language teaching for primary school students shall focus on the above-mentioned six aspects. Based on the specific infiltration objective set by our research institute, we conducted the infiltrated cultivation by focusing on particularly the capability in understanding emotion, controlling impulse behaviors and coping with the strategy of emotion regulation.

## 3) *Implementation Methods of Cultivation of Emotion Regulation Capability in Chinese Language Teaching for Primary School Students*

Chinese language teaching of primary school contains a plenty of resources relating to emotion regulation, but the infiltrated PSE in Chinese language teaching is featured as extensiveness, dispersiveness, potentiality and imperceptibility. Thus we should fully find out the corresponding educational resources relating to emotion regulation in Chinese textbook to achieve the final goal of improving the emotion regulation capability of primary school students. In addition, we should actively search the lively, vivid and operable implementation methods. Otherwise, the subject-infiltrated emotion regulation capability will become the realm of fancy and cannot be put into practice. Based on the previous research results and combined the experience of Chinese language teaching in China, our experiment was implemented through the following ways.

### Word Infiltration

The so-called word infiltration method means that Chinese language teachers "grasp the key words in the text, then make students understand the meaning of word and be influenced psychologically". One of the major methods during our experiment implementation was to learn the new words in the texts and explain the key words to conduct the education on emotion regulation capability. Taking the text Racing against Time for example, students are asked to look up the new words such as "sad", "grief" and "sorrowful" in the dictionary by themselves before class and use these new words to make sentences. At the beginning of the new lesson, students were checked for the performance on new words learning to see the preparation performance of students. In addition, students were asked to find out the sentences describing the mood of author and explain the meanings of these words when learning the first and second paragraph, then students are checked to see whether they understand the cause of author's sufferings and if there is any similar experience in their own lives.

## Situation Creation

Situation creation is to create the interactive situations during PSE, which activates or arouses the psychological activities of students, and induces the willingness to act in order to make the psychological *sushi* of students cultivated and practiced in the psychological environment formed by interaction between students and teachers, and among students. The psychological environment can be created by physical means, such as music, animation, spatial location, verbal suggestion or motivation. For example, in the case of learning text Huang Jiguang and Precious Textbook, we can play some videos about wars for students to make them know the background of the text in an intuitive, lively, vivid and real way and naturally understand the mood of the people in the text. However, the objective conditions of the experimental school are limited and there is less application of creating situations by physical means. The psychological means is to create corresponding problem situations by languages regarding the text. This method better conforms to our real condition of the experimental school and it is also one of the extensively applied ways to create situations during our experiment implementation. The problem situations can stimulate the students' interest in learning and guide them to feel the emotions of the people in the text. Moreover, the students are likely to link their real life and typical events to the situation in the text, thus, their own emotions are aroused and they get real emotional experience.

## Reading

Reading is a common, but the most important basic skill for primary school students. The teaching syllabus of Chinese in primary school specifies that teachers should "try to read more and explain less, reading instead of explaining and spend more time reading aloud the text with emotion……the key is to guide the students experience the situation of the text and sense the thoughts and emotions of the text through reading." Reading aloud can fully make all sense organs of students receive information and activate their imaginations, thus, they get influenced deep in their hearts. For example, when learning Ms. Lin Qingxuan's prose Racing against Time, at the beginning of the text, the protagonist lost his/her grandma and was very sad. The tone of reading shall be made melancholy and sadly; In the case of protagonist's feelings the time lapses, the reading tone should be slowly and lowered with a slight sorrow; in the second half the text, when protagonist experienced the happiness from racing against time, the tone should be higher and speed faster. From the free reading of the text, students can experience the characteristic of the emotional changes of the protagonist in the text and their own emotion will be changed accordingly. By doing so, while learning the lesion, the students improve their awareness, understanding and empathy for their emotions.

## Inspiration-induced

The so-called inspiration-induced means that teachers can use the educational resources contained in Chinese language teaching during the teaching to set problems elaborately, which are linked together step by step to make students actively experience the author's intention gradually and thus get inspired psychologically. When teaching the third paragraph of Sanwei Study, teachers can ask questions gradually: a) Mr. Lu Xun was late for school due to some objective reasons, but he was severely criticized by his teacher. What did he feel at that time? b) What did he do? What's the meaning of the word "silently" and "inscribe" in the text? c) Mr. Lu Xun felt misunderstood, but why he did not explain it? What should we learn from Mr. Lu Xun? d) In our real life, think about if we have similar experience, for example, we were criticized or misunderstood by our teachers, parents and classmates? What were you feeling then and what did you do? When students think about these questions step by step, they get the education on emotion regulation imperceptibly. In other words, students can learn to be aware and understand their emotions by learning this text in an immersive way and learn from Mr. Lu Xun to restrain and regulate their own emotions.

## Discussion

The so-called discussion means that the extensive and deep opinion exchanges between teachers and students, and among students, will guide students to think actively step by step, to improve their awareness and thus grasp the scientific action steps. There are several types of discussions such as class discussion, debate, group discussion, brainstorming, matching conversation and discussion on action plan. In this experiment, group discussion of four students is mostly applied and effective. For example, when learning the text Great Wall Bricks, we can organize students to discuss if they have felt they were not as good as others, then ask them to discuss in four-people group how to get rid of such feelings of inferiority and designate some groups to share their discussion results with the rest of the students. In this way, the whole class can quickly learn the strategies and methods of regulating the inferiority and can mitigate such feelings quickly if they run into similar emotional disturbances in their future life and study.

## Role playing

The primary school students are very good at imitation and imagination. Moreover, they are very willing to take part in role playing activities. Playing roles in the text can make the students feel as the people in the text do and get influenced psychologically imperceptibly. When learning the text Pot and Tin, we asked the students to make a play under the guidance of teacher by targeting the characteristic of the text. We created the specific situations according to the text and let students play the roles they would like to play and encouraged them to image freely with exaggerate expressions and motions. The role-play made students not only understand the text better, but also experience the psychology and action of the roles they played in person.

## Operation and Practice

Operation and practice method is one of the indispensable methods in subject-infiltrated PSE in Chinese language teaching. We implemented this method mostly through the homework of students, for example, we made proper design for their homework which not only made them understand what they have learned better, but also one of the major methods of PSE. During the experiment implementation, we paid much attention to the infiltration and education on emotion regulation through the practice of homework.

For example, when teaching the text Precious Textbook, we asked students to write a composition titled as When I came back to the Classroom......, making imaginations, expressing "my" feeling and reaction at that time, the astonishment of classmates upon the sight of blooded textbook and grief upon getting to know the instructor sacrificed for protecting books. Doing these homework helped students improve their emotion understanding naturally.

## Internalized Experience

Internalized experience means that students were asked to actively attend activities, which emphasizes their reflection on the content and strategies based on the fact that they have understood and grasped the infiltration content. Writing weekly journal is one of the most common ways for internalized experience and also one of the most important methods applied in our experiment on subject-infiltrated emotion regulation capability in Chinese language teaching. Weekly journal reflects the students' psychological traces and history. It is "real-time, casual but also real and practical.

It will not only improve students' writing skills, but also help students release troubles, anxiety and restlessness to keep mental health." As the emotional disturbances increasing, the negative emotions of primary school students should be mitigated through proper ways. Weekly journal provides a platform for paying attention to their emotions and releasing, shifting and distilling their negative emotions generated in case of getting frustrated. In this way, students can change the disordered psychological activities into words and thus help them improve the emotion regulation capability.

### *4) Basic Teaching Process of Cultivation of Emotion Regulation Capability in Chinese Language Teaching for Primary School Students*

### Basic Procedure of Teaching Implementation of Cultivation of Emotion Regulation Capability in Chinese Language Teaching for Primary School Students

According to the integrated mode of PSE put forward by Chen and Zhang et al, combing with the age characteristic of the development of emotion regulation capability of primary school students,and based on the specific implementation of experiment, we put forward the infiltration modes of cultivation of emotion regulation capability in Chinese language teaching for primary school students, i.e. it is a theoretical and clear expression of our experiment implementation process (shown as Figure 7.2.).

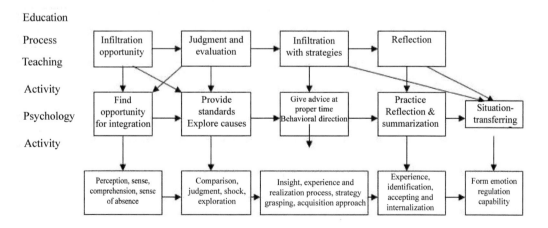

Figure 7.2. Basic process figure of cultivation of emotion regulation capability in Chinese language teaching for primary school students.

## Basic Process of Teaching Implementation of Cultivation of Emotion Regulation Capability in Chinese Language Teaching for Primary School Students

From the perspective of implementation process, the implementation of teaching of cultivation of emotion regulation capability in Chinese language teaching for primary school students still follow the three basic processes in the course of PSE, i.e. Judgment and evaluation, training with strategies, and reflection. However, the implementation of subject infiltration experiment has its own characteristics. We think that the basic process of subject infiltration experiment mainly contains the following steps.

### Infiltration Opportunity

It is one of the primary steps for infiltrating PSE into the teaching of a subject to create opportunities for infiltration. Teachers should find out the best opportunities first for infiltration, grasp the teaching goal and content on an overall basis and finally find out the best way to infiltrate emotion regulation capability into the teaching of a subject. Then, they should integrate the goal and content of developing emotion regulation capability with the teaching of a subject as well as consider the specific teaching strategies and methods, according to the characteristics of students' emotion regulation capability development and the typical events in their daily life.

### Judgment and Evaluation

Adopting various methods to find the difficulties or problems during the development of students' emotions, teachers arouse students attention to the development of their emotion regulation capability, and find their emotional status and emotional disturbances via comparison, judgment, shock, exploration so as to cause them to actively explore the causes and strategies for their emotional disturbances as well as the significance of the development and growth of their emotions. For example, teachers show typical emotional events to students in manner of homework. Then, students make proper choices based on actual conditions. In this way, teachers can grasp the development of emotion regulation capability of primary school students based on their teaching experience, and understand their emotional disturbance and current development status. Thus, teachers can make the subject infiltration more typical and well targeted.

### Infiltration with Strategies

Behavioral direction with strategies is implemented for both SPT and subject infiltration during PSE, but the implementation processes are different. The most remarkable feature of the subject infiltration mode is that such mode seeks natural and organic infiltration, and this does not allow it to conduct direct and straight SPT on students in respect of strategies for emotional adjustment. Instead, it can only be implemented via infiltration with strategies, which is one of the most important features of subject-infiltration PSE. Teachers should adopt flexible and diversified modes to infiltrate emotion regulation strategies into the teaching of a subject for students and give advice at proper time so as to enable students to understand and master. During their learning of Chinese language, some strategies and methods on developing emotion regulation should be used. This is also the core process of subject infiltration modes.

**Reflection**

Reflection is a process where teachers adopt various approaches to guide students to cognize, compare and reflect their psychological outcome, experiences, process, methods and behavioral changes etc. During the subject infiltration, in order to promote internalization, form the psychological *sushi* and even achieve transfer, during the experiment, we requested students to experience, identify, accept, and internalize the knowledge they learned on emotion regulation and corresponding strategies and methods via famous aphorism, stories of figures, and requested them to practice to maximally in order to transfer them into other similar situations.

## Basic Concept of Teaching Implementation of Cultivation of Emotion Regulation Capability in Chinese Language Teaching for Primary School Students

It follows that, during the teaching based on subject infiltration, "students' active participation is the precondition for successful implementation of subject infiltration, and the formation process of students' psychological *sushi* and the psychological process of mastering the knowledge is the psychological foundation for subject infiltration.

The teaching of knowledge is the framework for subject infiltration, and the creation of interactive teaching situation is the indispensable condition to make subject infiltration more effective". Therefore, the basic process for teaching based on subject infiltration indicates:

*Students' active participation is the precondition.* The subject infiltration PSE is to enable students to improve their psychological *sushi* when they are learning the subject knowledge, which is in nature a process of "helping them to learn self-help". The student is the agent for developing psychological *suzhi*, and the PSE can be effective only when it is applied to the agent. We cannot rely much on the means and approaches for teaching knowledge during the subject infiltration, as we do during the teaching of a subject; instead, we should fully cognize the student's position as the agent, maximally stimulate their initiative and enthusiasm to participate in emotion regulation education, and cause them to fully perform their consciousness and initiative in developing their emotion regulation.

*The developing process of emotion regulation capability of primary school students is the basis of psychology.* The experiment of subject-infiltrated emotion regulation capability should be implemented based on the procedures and principles of psychological sequence changes formed by the emotion regulation capability of primary school students to prepare relevant content properly. Wherein, every specific quality such as the forming of capability of goal orientation, impulse behavior control, emotion awareness and emotion understanding shall follow the perception, sense, comprehension, sense of absence, comparison, judgment, shock, exploration, insight, experience and realization process, strategy grasping, acquisition approach, experience, identification, accepting and internalization to form the basic sequence of emotion regulation capability. Only in this way, the implementation of subject infiltration experiment can effectively promote the improvement of emotion regulation capability of primary school students.

*Teaching of knowledge is the framework.* Subject teaching is the carrier of subject-infiltration-based PSE. The implementation of experiment of cultivation of emotion regulation capability in Chinese language teaching for primary school students should also base on the subject teaching. Specifically speaking, we should fully find out the content of emotion regulation capability contained in the subject teaching and integrate them organically into the subject teaching. The subject infiltration content and infiltration opportunity should be based on the specific content of subject teaching and should be contained in the textbook. The "inflexible infiltration regardless of teaching content make teachers ignore the science and education principles of subjects and repeat mistakes on psychology in history." In this sense, knowledge teaching is the framework for subject infiltration and the logical starting point for subject-infiltration-based PSE.

*Creation of interactive teaching situation is the indispensable condition to make subject infiltration effective.* Creation of interactive teaching situation is the starting point for subject-infiltration-based teaching as well as the "pacemaker" to activate and arouse students' psychological activities. It can often stimulate students' sense of identification and sense of absence, trigger emotional resonance or shock and trigger the desire for action. Teachers should treat, understand and trust students with a tolerant and open attitude, and deeply experience students' feelings and emotional responses in the interactive teaching situation, which is helpful to establish an equal, democratic and open relationship between students and teachers and form a positive classroom atmosphere. In this way, students can be soon exposed to the specific situation to experience the emotions of the people in the text naturally, and students will be also aroused to pay attention to their own emotions so that they actively explore strategies and methods of emotion regulation. Therefore, the creation of interactive teaching situation is the fundamental guarantee for enhancing the effectivity of subject-infiltration PSE.

## Basic Strategy of Teaching Implementation of Cultivation of Emotion Regulation Capability in the Chinese Language Teaching for Primary School Students

Subject infiltration, SPT on psychological sushi and psychological consultation and counseling are three major approaches of implementation of psychological sushi education in schools. Therefore, the teaching implementation of infiltration modes of cultivation of emotion regulation capability in Chinese language teaching for primary school students should follow four basic strategies, i.e. Harmonious interaction, behavior change, experience internalization and teaching monitoring. In addition, the following strategies can be considered based on the basic characteristics of subject-infiltrated teaching.

### Natural Infiltration

During experiment implementation, teachers should fully utilize the specific content and available resources contained in the content to find out the best point to integrate infiltration of emotion regulation capability. How to integrate the infiltration into the teaching of Chinese language subject naturally is one of the big challenges faced by the experiment. The experiment implementation of infiltration modes of cultivation of emotion regulation capability in Chinese language teaching for primary school students should fully find out the education resources contained in the texts and seek the best opportunity and methods to be adopted for infiltrating the content into the subject teaching. The most intrinsic feature of subject-infiltration PSE is that the infiltration is natural, integral and imperceptible; it should be naturally integrated with the curriculum system and the teaching process as a whole. For this reason, teachers are very likely to have misunderstandings during the practice of subject-infiltration-based education. For example, some teachers think that subject infiltration is just to teach something about PSE more in the class and explain in a wrong way by making random links and applying mechanically regardless of the content of textbook. Many of the content are irrelevant, or they take the "fill patch" approach and teach the PSE in last minutes of class by feeding students some psychological knowledge  in an improvisational style, regarding the subject infiltration just as the something trivial for the teaching in class. What they did not only does not conform to the principle of natural integration of subject infiltration, adding to much "artificial traces", but result in the weakening and absence of the integral function of subject infiltration and thus deepen the misunderstanding to subject-infiltration-based PSE.

## Moderate and Effective Infiltration

Subject infiltration and the teaching of a subject are two different components of the school *sushi* education and they have different starting points and goals. Any PSE-oriented teaching of a subject or subject-teaching-oriented PSE, where one intends to prevail the other, is inadvisable. Therefore, we should conduct teaching based on moderate and effective subject infiltration according to the targets, modes and characteristics of subject-infiltration PSE. The most important thing for the teaching considering subject infiltration is the proper duration of infiltration. Teachers should arrange the infiltration for a reasonable period for each text and even each class, neither too long nor too short. If the subject infiltration takes too much time in the class, it will make the subject teaching tend to PSE, i.e. The subject teaching becomes the PST class, which fundamentally affects the subject knowledge acquisition. However, subject infiltration time should not be too short, otherwise, the subject-infiltrated psychological *suzhi* is not guaranteed in terms of sufficient time and it is difficult to improve the psychological *suzhi* of students. Subject infiltration generally takes 3 - 5 minutes a class. Teachers can arrange the time required according to the content and method of the infiltration. The subjection infiltration of emotion regulation capability in Chinese language teaching for primary school students is of the unique uncertainty and unpredictability nature, which decides that the during implementation of subject infiltration, attention should be paid to followings. 1. The filtration gradient. The tool nature of the Chinese textbook determines the characteristic of dispersiveness of subject infiltration and makes the emotion regulation resources contained therein inconsistent with the development of the overall emotion regulation capability and different in extent. This requires teachers to grasp the educational resources relating to emotion regulation contained in the textbook as a whole and the age characteristic of emotion regulation capability development of primary school students to ensure "students can accept and infiltration can be made step by step". 2. Degree and scope of infiltration. Teachers should grasp the content and scope of infiltration in each paragraph, text and class, and present the infiltration content in the Chinese textbook to a proper degree according to the task of emotion regulation capability development of primary school students, so as to make it "integrate with the text naturally and make students influenced imperceptibly to a proper degree". 3. Validity of infiltration. Teachers should often collect relevant dynamic information about students, find out the best opportunity for infiltration and adjust strategies of infiltration of emotion regulation at proper time, which ensures the subject infiltration of cultivation of emotion regulation capability can be well implemented.

## Flexible and Various Strategies

Subject-infiltration-based PSE is a science of education and a kind of art educating people without fixed way to follow for the implementation. The flexible use of different teaching design, infiltration modes and infiltration approaches constitutes the various strategies for infiltration. In our experiment, we made emphasis on the combination between all factors of emotion regulation capability and specific subject. The goal orientation, impulse behavior control, emotion awareness and emotion understanding are implemented in different ways. In addition, teachers are required to take flexible measures to solve some incidents in a smart way during the teaching. The aforesaid incidents may be independent of the teaching content, but teachers cannot ignore them or pass them by during subject infiltration of emotion regulation capability in Chinese language teaching for primary school students, nor can they simply dispose such incidents by rude means or recklessly suppress them. Instead, they should flexibly deal with such incidents and use them as the "vivid examples" for emotion regulation. For example, there may be some sudden quarrels, chattering or even fights between primary school students due to some trifles, which will disorder the class or other situations. Teachers should, at this time, flexibly take some measures in time to calm down such students and teach them, at proper time, by using some strategies and methods on controlling or adjusting their temper in specific occasions. Thus Teachers cannot only properly deal with the unexpected interruptions during the teaching, but also train students at a proper time in respect of emotional regulation abilities.

# EXPERIMENTAL RESEARCH INTO THE TEACHING

## Purpose

This research aimed at discussing the feasibility and effectiveness of infiltration mode for cultivating emotion regulation competence during the teaching of Chinese language in primary schools, showing relationships between emotion regulation competence of primary school students and their psychological *suzhi* between emotion regulation competence and academic performance, as well as providing empirical basis for cultivating emotion regulation competence of primary school students in China.

## Participants

Students from Class 2 and Class 3 in grade 4 of one primary school in Chongqing participated in the experiment. Class 3 is the experimental group which consists of 42 students, including 25 boys and 17 girls. Class 2 is the control group which consists of 35 students, including 21 boys and 14 girls.

## Methods

Psychometrics, measurement of academic performance and educational experiment were used in this chapter. Psychometrics mainly refers to the measurement of difficulty in emotion regulation and the measurement of psychological *sushi* development level for primary school students. Measurement of academic performance mainly refers to the measurement of Chinese language knowledge. Educational experiment is carried out in the way of filtration of emotion regulation competence in Chinese language teaching for primary school students.

## Tools

*Questionnaire of Difficulty in Emotion Regulation for Primary School Students.* The questionnaire was revised based on *Difficulties in Emotion Regulation Scale* (DERS) by Kim L. Gratz and Lizabeth Roemer, including 22 items and 6 factors such as Difficulties Engaging in Goal-Directed Behavior, Impulse Control Difficulties, Lack of Empathy, Lack of Emotional Awareness, Limited Access to Emotion Regulation Strategies and Lack of Emotional Clarity. The internal consistency reliability of each factor in the questionnaire is all between 0.518 and 0.773, and the internal consistency reliability of the questionnaire is 0.795; the split-half reliability of each factor is between 0.524 and 0.804, and the split-half reliability of the questionnaire is 0.731.

*Psychological sushi Questionnaire for Primary School Students.* This questionnaire was developed by Zhang et al in the Southwest China Normal University. It includes 108 items and is composed of metacognitive sub-questionnaire, personality sub-questionnaire and adaptability sub-questionnaire. The internal consistency reliability of the questionnaire is 0.572-0.786, and the split-half reliability of the questionnaire is 0.557-0.732; the correlation (0.407-0.512) between each item and its sub-questionnaire is higher than that (0.102-0.317) between the item and any other sub-questionnaires, with good split-half reliability and internal consistency reliability. Middle correlation between all factors (max. of 0.484 and min. of 0.215) shows good construct validity.

Academic Performance. Academic performance of Chinese language in final examinations of the second semester in grade 3 and of the first semester in grade 4 of a primary school are regarded as the measurement index to respectively carry out the pre-test and the post-test for the experimental group and the control group.

This experiment adopts SPSS 12.0 for Windows 2000 to make statistics of data.

## Experimental Procedures

### 1) Experimental Treatment

In the experiment, we designed pre-test and post-test for both experimental and control groups. Please see Table 7.10. for details.

## Table 7.10. Experimental Treatment

| Groups | Pre-test | Experimental Treatment | Post-Test |
|---|---|---|---|
| Experimental Group | $O_1$ | X | $O_2$ |
| Control Group | $O_3$ | - | $O_4$ |

### 2) Experimental Variables

*Independent variables*: Infiltration education mode for cultivation of emotion regulation competence in Chinese language teaching for primary school students.

*Dependent variables*: Emotion regulation competence for primary school students; development level of psychological *sushi* for primary school students; academic performance of Chinese language for primary school students.

*Control of irrelevant variables*: Establish experimental and control groups to make educational intervention on the experimental group rather than the control group. Notes:

Establish the experimental group and the control group on a reasonable basis and make the two groups homogeneous as more as possible. That is to say, try the best to ensure that the pre-experiment levels of emotion regulation competence, psychological *sushi* and academic performance for the two groups were roughly the same;

Control other factors that may influence the experimental effect and remove the expectation effect, the difference between teachers and the time effect.

### 3) Experimental Procedures

The experiment included three stages:

a) Preparation
    Review relevant literatures, establish and modify experiment scheme;
    Contact with the school for experiment;
    Research textbooks and prepare experimental materials;
    Coach and train the experimental teachers;
    Conduct the pre-test on academic performance of Chinese language.
b) Implementation
    Make the pretest with the Questionnaire of Difficulty in Emotion Regulation for Primary School Students and the Psychological sushi Questionnaire for Primary School Students (in the second week of school);
    Stay in the experimental school, discuss with experimental teachers about the best opportunity for combining the subject teaching with the emotion regulation content and the strategies and methods for teaching, collect materials, prepare plans for lessons together with experimental teachers.
    Attend lessons of experimental teachers everyday, make feedback, communicate and discuss with these teachers to improve the teaching quality;

Learn about development trends and characteristics of students' emotion regulation and master typical emotional events of students to enhance pertinence and collect materials.

Post-test

## Experimental Results and Analysis

### 1) Analysis on the Results of Difficulty in Emotion Regulation for Students in Experimental and Control Groups

Comparison on pre-test and post-test scores of each factor and total average scores of difficulty in emotion regulation for students in experimental and control groups. Comparison on pre-test and post-test scores of each factor and total average scores of difficulty in emotion regulation for students in experimental and control groups (see Table 7.11.).

In Table 7.11. During the pre-test, there is no significant difference ($p>0.05$) of difficulty in emotion regulation between students in experimental group and students in control group; during the post-test, total average scores for students in experimental group is lower than those of students in control group, but the difference is not significant ($p>0.05$).

**Table 7.11. Comparison on Pre-test and Post-test Sores of Difficulty in Emotion Regulation for Students in Experimental Group and Control Group**

| | Factors | Experimental Group (n=42) | Control Group (n=35) | t value |
|---|---|---|---|---|
| | | $M\pm SD$ | $M\pm SD$ | |
| Pre-test | Difficulties Engaging in Goal-Directed Behavior | 2.43±0.86 | 2.75±0.92 | -1.541 |
| | Impulse Control Difficulties | 2.85±0.69 | 2.93±0.97 | -.432 |
| | Lack of Empathy | 2.88±0.85 | 2.97±0.92 | -.415 |
| | Lack of Emotional Awareness | 2.71±0.82 | 2.37±1.18 | 1.487 |
| | Limited Access to Emotion Regulation Strategies | 2.58±0.65 | 2.57±0.91 | .046 |
| | Lack of Emotional Clarity | 3.10±0.90 | 2.92±1.14 | .770 |
| | Total average scores | 2.76±0.33 | 2.75±0.40 | .091 |
| Post-Test | Difficulties Engaging in Goal-Directed Behavior | 2.32±0.96 | 2.56±0.94 | -1.114 |
| | Impulse Control Difficulties | 2.60±0.82 | 2.69±1.04 | -.455 |
| | Lack of Empathy | 3.02±0.92 | 2.79±0.81 | 1.185 |
| | Lack of Emotional Awareness | 2.85±0.85 | 2.42±1.06 | 1.952 |
| | Limited Access to Emotion Regulation Strategies | 2.02±0.71 | 2.58±0.79 | -3.254[**] |
| | Lack of Emotional Clarity | 2.34±0.87 | 2.97±0.99 | -2.916[**] |
| | Total average scores | 2.53±0.40 | 2.67±0.55 | -1.313 |

Among all factors, in terms of the Limited Access to Emotion Regulation Strategies and the Lack of Emotional Clarity, scores for experimental group are significantly lower (p<0.01) than those for control group.

Comparison on pre-test and post-test sores of difficulty in emotion regulation for students in experimental group. Comparison on pre-test and post-test sores of difficulty in emotion regulation for primary school students in experimental group (see Table 7.12.).

According to Table 7.12, level of difficulty in emotion regulation for the experimental group students during the post-test is significantly lower ($p<0.01$) than that during the pre-test as a whole. Among six factors of the questionnaire, scores of the Limited Access to Emotion Regulation Strategies and the Lack of Emotional Clarity both decrease very significantly ($p<0.001$), and score of Impulse Control Difficulties decreases relatively significantly ($p<0.01$).

**Table 7.12. Comparison on Pre-test and Post-test Sores of Difficulty in Emotion Regulation for Students in Experimental Group**

| Factors | Pre-Test (n=42) | Post-Test (n=42) | $t$ value |
|---|---|---|---|
| | $M \pm SD$ | $M \pm SD$ | |
| Difficulties Engaging in Goal-Directed Behavior | 2.4345±0.8644 | 2.3214±0.9616 | -.546 |
| Impulse Control Difficulties | 2.8524±0.6929 | 2.6000±0.8276 | -2.138[*] |
| Lack of Empathy | 2.8869±0.8575 | 3.0298±0.9226 | .827 |
| Lack of Emotional Awareness | 2.7143±0.8283 | 2.8571±0.8590 | .755 |
| Factors | Pre-Test (n=42) | Post-Test (n=42) | $t$ value |
| | $M \pm SD$ | $M \pm SD$ | |
| Limited Access to Emotion Regulation Strategies | 2.5857±0.6576 | 2.0238±0.7115 | -3.848[***] |
| Lack of Emotional Clarity | 3.1032±0.9031 | 2.3492±0.8741 | -4.853[***] |
| Total average scores | 2.7628±0.3326 | 2.5302±0.4018 | -3.309[**] |

Comparison on pre-test and post-test sores of difficulty in emotion regulation for students in control group. According to the requirements for experiment of equal group, we also need to further analyze the changes of scores for difficulty in emotion regulation in the control group. Please see Table 7.13. for details.

According to Table 7.13, there is no significant difference ($p>0.05$) between the pre-test and the post-test for scores of difficulty in emotion regulation for students in control group, no matter whether as a whole or in each factor.

Comparison on pre-test and post-test scores of difficulty in emotion regulation for students in experimental group with high, middle and low levels. In order to investigate the difference of intervention effects for students with different levels of difficulty in emotion regulation, we divided students in the experiment group into three teams according to the pre-test scores of difficulty in emotion regulation: high score team of 27% students with highest scores, low score team of 27% students with lowest scores and middle score team of the rest students. Comparison on pre-test and post-test sores of difficulty in emotion regulation for primary school students in experimental group with high, middle and low levels (see Table 7.14.).

**Table 7.13. Comparison on Pre-test and Post-test Sores of Difficulty in Emotion Regulation for Students in Control Group**

| Factors | Pre-Test (n=35) | Post-Test (n=35) | $t$ value |
|---|---|---|---|
| | $M \pm SD$ | $M \pm SD$ | |
| Difficulties Engaging in Goal-Directed Behavior | 2.7500±0.9295 | 2.5643±0.9420 | -.861 |
| Impulse Control Difficulties | 2.9371±0.9747 | 2.6971±1.0453 | -1.155 |
| Lack of Empathy | 2.9714±0.9271 | 2.7929±0.8101 | -.908 |
| Lack of Emotional Awareness | 2.3714±1.1875 | 2.4286±1.0682 | .209 |
| Limited Access to Emotion Regulation Strategies | 2.5771±0.9150 | 2.5843±0.7994 | .083 |
| Lack of Emotional Clarity | 2.9238±1.1407 | 2.9714±0.9979 | .181 |
| Total average scores | 2.7552±0.4067 | 2.6731±0.5510 | -.857 |

According to Table 7.14, there are different degrees of improvement about the status of difficulty in emotion regulation for students in high, middle and low score teams in this experiment: For low score team, the Impulse Control Difficulties, the Limited Access to Emotion Regulation Strategies and the Lack of Emotional Clarity are improved after the experiment, but the difference between pre-test and post-test is not significant ($p>0.05$); for middle score group, total scores of difficulty in emotion regulation during the post-test are significantly lower ($p<0.05$) than those during the pre-test, and there is very significant difference ($p<0.001$) between pre-test and post-test in terms of the Limited Access to Emotion Regulation Strategies and the Lack of Emotional Clarity; for high score team, total scores of difficulty in emotion regulation during the post-test are very significantly lower ($p<0.001$) than those during the pre-test, and sores in terms of all factors of the questionnaire during the post-test are significantly lower than those during the pre-test, especially in terms of the Difficulties Engaging in Goal-Directed Behavior and the Limited Access to Emotion Regulation Strategies.

## 2) Analysis of the Results of Psychological Sushi Development for Experimental and Control Groups

In order to investigate the relationship between emotion regulation competence and psychological *sushi* development, we selected seven factors related to emotion regulation competence from the *Psychological sushi Questionnaire for Primary School Students* as index, including perseverance, self-control, physical and psychological adaptability, emotional adaptability, learning adaptability, interpersonal adaptability and frustration endurance. According to the statistics and analysis, we made comparisons between pre-test and post-test scores on seven factors of psychological *sushi* for experimental group and control group (see Table 7.15.).

**Table 7.14. Comparison on Pre-test and Post-test Scores of Difficulty in Emotion Regulation for Students in Experimental Group with High, Middle and Low Levels**

| | Factors | Pre-test $M \pm SD$ | Post-Test $M \pm SD$ | $t$ value |
|---|---|---|---|---|
| High Score Team (n=12) | Difficulties Engaging in Goal-Directed Behavior | 2.7292±0.5883 | 2.2083±0.8246 | -2.253[*] |
| | Impulse Control Difficulties | 3.0167±0.6793 | 2.7167±0.7158 | -1.092 |
| | Lack of Empathy | 3.5833±0.6513 | 3.2292±1.0737 | -1.267 |
| | Lack of Emotional Awareness | 3.3611±0.4597 | 2.8889±0.7956 | -1.653 |
| | Limited Access to Emotion Regulation Strategies | 3.0000±0.4264 | 2.1944±0.9996 | -2.465[*] |
| | Lack of Emotional Clarity | 3.0556±0.8267 | 2.4722±0.9996 | -2.508[*] |
| | Total average scores | 3.1243±0.1473 | 2.6183±0.3757 | -4.903[***] |
| Middle Score Team (n=18) | Difficulties Engaging in Goal-Directed Behavior | 2.5972±0.9241 | 2.4583±0.8713 | -.407 |
| | Impulse Control Difficulties | 2.8667±0.6894 | 2.7000±0.7889 | -1.073 |
| | Lack of Empathy | 2.5694±0.9188 | 3.0556±0.9798 | 1.591 |
| | Lack of Emotional Awareness | 2.6481±0.7625 | 2.7593±0.8387 | .432 |
| | Limited Access to Emotion Regulation Strategies | 2.6444±0.5299 | 2.0185±0.5298 | -4.414[***] |
| | Lack of Emotional Clarity | 3.4259±0.8229 | 2.2407±0.7213 | -4.630[***] |
| | Total average scores | 2.7920±8.943E-02 | 2.5387±0.3899 | -2.708[*] |
| Low Score Team (n=12) | Difficulties Engaging in Goal-Directed Behavior | 1.8958±0.8150 | 2.2292±1.2407 | .740 |
| | Impulse Control Difficulties | 2.6667±0.7253 | 2.3333±0.9847 | -1.511 |
| | Factors | Pre-test $M \pm SD$ | Post-Test $M \pm SD$ | $t$ value |
| | Lack of Empathy | 2.6667±0.5149 | 2.7917±0.6557 | .527 |
| | Lack of Emotional Awareness | 2.1667±0.8103 | 2.9722±0.9996 | 2.031 |
| | Limited Access to Emotion Regulation Strategies | 2.0833±0.7265 | 1.8611±0.6270 | -.675 |
| | Lack of Emotional Clarity | 2.6667±0.9640 | 2.3889±1.0034 | -1.131 |
| | Total average scores | 2.3576±0.2348 | 2.4294±0.4539 | .531 |

According to Table 7.15, there is significant difference ($p<0.05$) of scores in terms of perseverance in the psychological *sushi* questionnaire for experimental and control groups during the pre-test, but there is no significant difference ($p<0.05$) in terms of other factors during the pre-test; scores for control group during the post-test do not achieve significant level ($p>0.05$), and scores in terms of seven factors in the psychological *sushi* questionnaire for experimental group during the post-test are higher than those for control group, but there is significant difference ($p<0.05$) only in terms of emotional adaptability among the seven factors; pre-test and post-test scores in terms of the seven factors for experimental group are improved, but only scores in terms of physical and psychological adaptability and interpersonal adaptability achieve significant level ($p<0.05$), and there is relatively significant difference ($p<0.01$) between pre-test and post-test in terms of emotional adaptability.

**Table 7.15. Analysis of Results of Psychological *sushi* Development for Experimental and Control Groups**

| Factors | Groups | Pre-test M±SD | Post-Test M±SD | t value |
|---|---|---|---|---|
| Perseverance | Experimental Group | 3.7429±0.6466 | 3.7905±0.8310 | -.351 |
| | Control Group | 3.3657±0.8196 | 3.5143±0.8869 | -.965 |
| | t value | 2.257[*] | 1.408 | |
| Self-control | Experimental Group | 3.7524±0.8575 | 3.8190±0.7442 | -.477 |
| | Control Group | 3.5943±0.7538 | 3.5600±0.7337 | .210 |
| | t value | 0.851 | 1.533 | |
| Physical and psychological adaptability | Experimental Group | 3.1524±0.7376 | 3.4667±0.8516 | -2.258[*] |
| | Control Group | 3.2629±0.5735 | 3.2514±0.7582 | .073 |
| | t value | -.739 | 1.160 | |
| Emotional adaptability | Experimental Group | 3.3429±0.4925 | 3.6048±0.5273 | -2.860[**] |
| | Control Group | 3.2286±0.5660 | 3.3457±0.6055 | -1.153 |
| | t value | 0.947 | 2.006[*] | |
| Learning adaptability | Experimental Group | 3.4857±0.5537 | 3.6571±0.7222 | -1.369 |
| | Control Group | 3.3143±0.7550 | 3.5257±0.6546 | -1.420 |
| | t value | 1.116 | 0.829 | |
| Interpersonal adaptability | Experimental Group | 3.8048±0.6499 | 4.0571±0.7843 | -2.185[*] |
| | Control Group | 3.6171±0.6866 | 3.7543±0.7374 | -1.009 |
| | t value | 1.229 | 1.743 | |
| Frustration endurance | Experimental Group | 3.3524±0.8887 | 3.6095±0.7914 | -1.682 |
| | Control Group | 3.2514±0.8518 | 3.2743±0.9593 | -.122 |
| | t value | 0.506 | 1.681 | |

## 3) Analysis on Results of the Pre-Test and Post-Test Academic Performances for Experimental and Control Groups

Comparison between pre-test and post-test on academic performances for experimental group and control group . In order to investigate the relationship between emotion regulation competence and academic performance of primary school students, we first tested homogeneity of academic performance for participants in experimental and control groups; With consideration of large difference in difficulties between the final examination of second semester in grade 3 and the midterm examination of first semester in grade 4 of a primary school, we made statistics and analysis of the score increase, i.e. The difference between the post-test score and the pre-test score for each participant, then calculated the average of differences respectively for the two groups and finally made significance test of the average differences for two groups. Please see Table 7.16. And Table 7.17. For details. According to Table 7.16, no matter in the pre-test or in the post-test, no significant difference was found between the two groups. However, for both the control group and the experimental group, the differences between pre-test and post-test were significant ($p<0.001$). It may be mainly related to different examination difficulties and grading standards during the pre-test and the post-test. According to the further analysis (see Table 7.17.), we find that academic performance of Chinese language for experimental group is higher than that of control group, but the difference between two groups is not significant ($p>0.05$) based on the statistics and analysis.

Comparison on pre-test and post-test scores of academic performance for students in experimental group with high, middle and low levels of difficulty in emotion regulation .In order to investigate the difference between pre-test and post-test scores of academic performance for students with different levels of difficulty in emotion regulation, we divided the students in experimental group into three teams (in the same way above): high score team, middle score team and low score team. Comparison on pre-test and post-test sores of difficulty in emotion regulation for primary school students in experimental group with high, middle and low levels (see Table 7.18.). Good internal consistency reliability for the item 1-1801; Difficulties, Limited Access to Emotion Regulation Strategies; According to Table 7.18, the increased amplitude of academic performance in terms of difficulty in emotion regulation for middle and low score teams is higher than that for high score team, but there is no significant difference between them based on the analysis.

**Table 7.16. Comparison between Pre-test and Post-test Academic Performances of Chinese Language for Experimental Group and Control Group**

| Groups | Pre-test | Post-Test | t value |
|---|---|---|---|
| | $M\pm SD$ | $M\pm SD$ | |
| Experimental Group (n=42) | 63.95±8.97 | 82.07±9.38 | -17.725[***] |
| Control Group (n=35) | 61.67±7.87 | 78.28±8.72 | -15.417[***] |
| t value | 1.173 | 1.819 | |

**Table 7.17. Comparison on Score Increase of Academic Performance for Experimental Group and Control Group**

| Variables | Experimental Group (n=42) | Control Group (n=35) | t value |
|---|---|---|---|
| | M±SD | M±SD | |
| Increase | 18.11±6.62 | 16.61±6.37 | 1.009 |

**Table 7.18. Comparison on pre-test and post-test scores of academic performance for students in experimental group with high, middle and low levels of difficulty in emotion regulation**

| Variables | High Score Team (n=12) | Middle Score Team (n=18) | Low Score Team (n=12) | F Value | Significance |
|---|---|---|---|---|---|
| | $M\pm SD$ | $M\pm SD$ | $M\pm SD$ | | |
| Academic Performance | 16.37±5.63 | 18.80±8.39 | 18.83±4.28 | 0.570 | 0.570 |

## Discussion on Experimental Results of Cultivation of Emotion Regulation Capability in Chinese Language Teaching for Primary School Students

Infiltration modes about cultivation of emotion regulation capability in Chinese language teaching for primary school students the experimental research of cultivation of emotion regulation capability in Chinese language teaching for primary school students is an intervention research on emotion regulation capability. Moreover it is a useful attempt to explore the way to implement psychological sushi of subject infiltration to increase the approaches for PSE. This research primarily developed the infiltration modes of cultivation of emotion regulation capability in Chinese language teaching for primary school students and analyzed theoretically the objectives, content, methods as well as strategies and operation procedures of infiltration of emotion regulation capability in Chinese language teaching for primary school students based on the exploration of difficulties characteristic of emotion regulation capability of primary school students and Chinese language teaching for primary school students and by referring to the integrated mode of MHE to find out the abundant educational resources on emotion regulation contained therein. Then, it discussed the feasibility and effectiveness of subject infiltrated emotion regulation capability by providing empirical evidences. The research results show that the subject infiltration modes can effectively improve the difficulties in emotion regulation of children, promote the development of emotion regulation capability and sound development of psychological sushi of primary school students as well as the academic performance of Chinese. Therefore, we think that subject infiltration is one of the effective approaches to implement PSE. However, we also noticed that there are still a lot of theoretical and operational issues to be resolved in the field of subject-infiltration PSE due to its complexity, such as arrangement of school environment, coordination of different subjects, improvement of teachers' quality, relationship between the subject teaching and psychological sushi as well as resources development and utilization during teaching process and others which are to be continuously improved and completed in further research. We should fully recognize the mode: it is neither a rigid mode that can be used following a prescribed order, nor an all-purpose mode applicable to all PSC. Therefore, teachers should, during the implementation of such infiltration modes, be able to flexibly use the mode and make appropriate changes based on the actual situation. It is necessary to take account of not only the characteristics of infiltrated psychological suzhi, age characteristics of children and individual difference, but also subject nature, characteristics of the subject teaching and different type of school teaching. By doing so, a sound development of children's psychological sushi can be effectively promoted.

### *Experimental Results Of Cultivation Of Emotion Regulation Capability In Chinese Language Teaching For Primary School Students*

### (1) Overall Experimental Results About Emotion Regulation Capability of Primary School Students

Table 7.11, 7.12. and 7.13. show the result analysis of cultivation of emotion regulation capability in Chinese language teaching for primary school students, which indicates that the infiltration modes of Chinese language teaching improved the difficult situation of emotion regulation capability of primary school students and thus promote the development of emotion regulation capability. The level of difficulty in emotion regulation for experimental group was not significantly different from that for the control group during the pre-test. After the experiment intervention, overall effect between the experimental group and the control group did not vary significantly, but the statistical result showed that both levels of difficulty in coping with strategy and difficulty in understanding emotion for the experimental group were improved more than those for the control group. Based on the analysis of comparison results between the pre-test and the post-test respectively for the experimental group and the control group, for the control group, average scores of the difficulty in emotion regulation during the post-test were a little lower than those during the pre-test, but it did not vary significantly from the pre-test to the post-test; for the experimental group, average scores of the difficulty in emotion regulation during the post-test were much lower than those during the pre-test, and both levels of difficulty in coping strategy and difficulty in understanding emotion varied significantly from the pre-test to the post-test, and the level of impulse behavior control during the post-test was also improved significantly. We think, through a comprehensive analysis on the experiment results, that the infiltration mode of Chinese language teaching can improve the difficult situation of emotion regulation capability of primary school students effectively. The causes for such experimental results may include:

*Implementation of this experiment.* The intervention manners of experiment of emotion regulation capability infiltrated in Chinese language teaching for primary school students can fully utilize the emotion regulation content contained in the Chinese textbook which conforms to not only the basic target of education of primary schools but also principles of educational efficiency. However, the Chinese subject infiltration has its own insurmountable weakness. The teaching content was selected and arranged based on its intrinsic logic, and the content on emotion regulation contained therein featured dispersiveness and potentiality, which are inconsistent with the sequence of development of emotion regulation capability of primary school students and moreover the characteristics of the subject infiltration makes it difficult to make targeted intervention in strict accordance with the difficult situation of the emotion of primary school students. Considering the teaching content of the Chinese subject and characteristic of development of emotion regulation capability of students in primary school, we made infiltrations in respect of emotion understating of the primary school students, coping with strategy and impulse behavior control during our test.

*Characteristic of development of emotion regulation capability.* Emotion regulation capability is part of the psychological *sushi* of primary school students, which takes a long time to form and develop instead of a short duration of time. Considering the characteristic of subject infiltration and limit of personnel, material and financial resources, we only have one semester available to conduct the experiment, which is not enough compared with the total time of infiltration implementation of formation and development of emotion regulation capability of primary school students.

*Teachers' quality.* Teachers' quality is one of the main "bottlenecks" in the application of the subject infiltrated psychological *suzhi*. The subject infiltration requires teachers to be good at penetrating into the real life of students and respect, care and accept their performance and behaviors. The democratic, equal and harmonious TSR is a prerequisite to conduct subject-infiltration-based education effectively. In addition, it requires teachers to have rich knowledge of the subject, be able to flexibly use the textbook as a whole, can grasp and find out the PSE resources contained in the textbook, understand knowledge on developmental psychology, educational psychology, instructional psychology etc. And understand the age characteristics of primary school students' psychological development in order to make targeted infiltration. Moreover, teachers should be able to use the PSE resources during the subject teaching, "The influence of the hidden resources is even greater than that of the content resources of curriculum itself." Because of the limitations of objective conditions, the experiment is mostly focused on the infiltration of the teaching content of Chinese subject without giving consideration to the emotion regulation resources contained in the process of teaching.

*Formative education of primary school students.* As far as our experiment is concerned, the fourth grade of primary school is the key for implementing the formative education. Schools carry out formative education on disciplines, norms and habits to students through different ways during the morning meeting, class meeting and flag raising ceremony, wherein many aspects are closely related with emotion regulation. These will greatly improve the emotion regulation capability of students in the control group and thus "pollute" the post-test data of the control group, which somewhat interfere the evaluation on our experiment results. In addition, the Chinese subject infiltration is a systematic work requiring cooperation of teachers of all subjects. Taking the perspectives above into consideration, our experiment results are reasonable.

## (2) Experiment Results of Students with Different Levels of Difficulty in Emotion Regulation

Table 7.13. Showed that the implementation of subject infiltration modes will improve the students with high, middle and low emotion regulation capability to different extent; this experiment did not make a significant achievement in improving the emotion regulation capability of low score students but high score and middle level students.

The middle level students made significant improvement in difficulty in coping with strategy and difficulty in understanding emotion while high score students in difficulty in coping with strategy, understanding emotion and goal orientation. This supports the research conclusions of Wu to a certain extent. We think that the difficulty of emotion regulation of primary school students is a developmental problem.

As long as the method is appropriate and reasonable, the emotion regulation capability of students with different levels of difficulty will be improved to a certain extent, but the infiltration mode of emotion regulation is most effective for improving emotion regulation difficulty of high and middle level students. This might be because that the emotion regulation capability of low score students develops well and they can make effective regulation for their own emotions and then reduce emotional distresses.

By comparison, few of high score and middle level students can grasp their emotional experience accurately and they have difficulty explaining their own emotional state, do not know the cause and harm of negative emotions and have no common methods necessary for emotion regulation and control. Therefore, it is difficult for them to effectively inhibit emotional impulses when running into emotional distress or problems or they are arbitrary and thus have difficulty in maintaining an effective goal orientation behavior.

Therefore, the cultivation of emotion regulation is of critical significance for high score and middle level students with difficulty in emotion regulation, which is proved by the research on teenagers' emotional *sushi* made by Qiao to a certain degree.

## (3) Effect of Filtration Modes on Psychological Sushi Development of Emotion Regulation of Primary School Students

Table 7.15. showed that students of experimental group and control group do not have significant difference in the pre-test scores except that in perseverance factor in the psychological *sushi* questionnaire. The post-test scores of students of control group did not show a significant improvement compared with the pre-test scores, while the post-test scores of students of experimental group on seven factors of psychological *sushi* questionnaire are higher than that of control group, but the significant difference is only in emotional adaptability factor through the test. The scores of pre-test and post-test of seven factors of psychological *sushi* questionnaire of experimental group students are somewhat improved, but the significant level is only achieved in psychological adaptability and interpersonal adaptability. The difference of scores of pre-test and post-test is significant in emotional adaptability factor. This result is probably related to the close relationship between emotion regulation capability and psychological *suzhi*. Psychological *sushi* is a complicated self-organization system, including cognition, personality and adaptability and emotion regulation capability is one of the key compositions of emotional adaptability factor of the psychological *sushi* structure, which is proved by the research of Liu Yanling. Therefore, it is not difficult for us to understand that the improvement of emotion regulation capability will improve the level of individual emotional adaptability and thus promote a sound development of psychological *suzhi*; on the other hand, as the key of psychological straits, the psychological *suzhi* has a relative stability once formed and is unlikely to change. In addition, the development of individual psychological *sushi* is influenced by many factors, such as the existing knowledge and experience, social, family and community environment. As a result, we think that emotion regulation capability is one of the key compositions of psychological *sushi* of students and infiltration modes of psychological *sushi* can effectively improve the development of psychological *sushi* accordingly.

## (4) The Impact of Infiltration Modes of Emotion Regulation of Primary School Students on their Academic Performance

The statistics in Table 7.16. and 7.17. Show that no significant difference both in the pre-test and post-test was obtained between the scores of the control group and the experimental group. However, significant difference was observed between the scores in the pre-test and post-test, both for the control group and the experimental group. This might be due to the big difference of the difficulties between the final examination of second semester of grade 3 and midterm examination of first semester of grade 4 and difference ingrading standards. Our research conclusion was also proved by what shown in Table 17 that comparison of difference between the experimental group and control group showed that the academic performance of Chinese of control group was somewhat improved and there is not significant difference between them through statistical analysis. Compared with the study results on emotion education made by Pierson, Walker and Tibanan, 1983, Zhou Tianci (1988) and Huang Yuexia (1989), our experiment on subject infiltrated emotion regulation capability also improved the academic performance of students, but the improvement of Chinese academic performance did not reach the level as significant as that of above-mentioned experiments. Similar results are acquired in the investigation on the academic performance of students with different levels of difficulties in emotion regulation. We think such result is probably caused by:

The improvement of academic performance is influenced by many factors, such as individual's intelligence, achievement motivation and teaching, having a great impact on improvement of academic performance.

Extensiveness of scope of emotional education. The emotional education is mainly composed of four aspects (Brown, 1971): subject-related emotion, school-related emotion, self-concept of students and mental health. Zhou (1988) et al. Thought that there is a causality relationship between the level of emotion of the students to a subject and success/failure experience of the subject, especially the attitude and learning motivation of students which usually impact the achievement of the subject. However, our experiment on subject infiltrated emotion regulation capability of students did not make special discussion on the emotion to the subject but mainly focused on whether the development and completeness of emotion regulation capability impact on the variation of the academic performance.

In terms of the way of special training or counseling to the students' emotion, the subject infiltration has a relatively short intervention time for the development of students' emotion regulation capability which might caused that the difference of academic performance of the primary school students did not reach a significant level. In short, we think that the improvement of emotion regulation capability of primary school students can effectively promote the improvement of their Chinese academic performance.


## Conclusions

The adoption of subject-infiltrated PSE in Chinese education of primary school will make better the difficult situation of children's emotional regulation, promote the development of emotion regulation capability of primary students and the Chinese academic performance and is a key approach for cultivating a sound psychological *suzhi* of students.

The experiment results showed: a) the experimental group improved more significantly than the control group in "difficulty in coping with strategy" and "difficulty in understanding emotion"; b) middle level group made significant achievements in the factor of "difficulty in coping with strategy" and "difficulty in understanding emotion"; students of high score group made significant achievements in the factor of "difficulty in coping with strategy" and "difficulty in understanding emotion" and "difficulties engaging in goal-directed behavior"; c) the scores of pre-test and post-test in all factors were improved, wherein significant level was achieved in factor of "psychological adaptability" and "interpersonal adaptability" and difference between the pre-test and post-test in "psychological adaptability" is relatively significant; d) the comparison on the difference between the experimental group and control group showed that the Chinese academic performance of the experimental group improved more than that of the control group but not reaching a significant level analyzed in the statistics.

# APPENDIX 1

Questionnaire of Difficulty in Emotion Regulation for Primary School Students

School: Class: Age:

Student No.: Gender: Male□ Female□

Location of Family: Urban □ Rural □

Dear students,

I am glad that you participate in the psychological test. We use the questionnaire to know participants, but every participant is different, so there are not standard answers of these questions. Please answer these questions carefully according to your actual situations. We hope that you can know yourself through the questionnaire. Thanks for your participation and support!

Notes:

      Please answer questions honestly. Answer questions according to your actual situation.

      Please answer questions carefully. Do not omit any question.

      There is no time limit, but it is unnecessary to spend much time to consider answers for each question. Please choose the answer which is most suitable for your actual situation based on the first impression.

      Please choose single answer for each question with the mark of √ in the place of letter that the answer is most suitable for your situation.

Thank you very much!

## Institute of Education Science of Southwest China Normal University

$A_6$. I do not know that I am happy or unhappy now.

a. Scarcely; b. Less scarcely; c. Normally; d. Less frequently; e. Frequently

$A_3$. I pay attention to my feelings.

a. Scarcely; b. Less scarcely; c. Normally; d. Less frequently; e. Frequently

$A_{34}$. I can find a way to make my mood getting better when I am upset.

a. Scarcely; b. Less scarcely; c. Normally; d. Less frequently; e. Frequently

$A_2$. I can understand feelings of others.

a. Scarcely; b. Less scarcely; c. Normally; d. Less frequently; e. Frequently

$A_5$. I cannot control my mood.

a. Scarcely; b. Less scarcely; c. Normally; d. Less frequently; e. Frequently

$A_{19}$. I cannot finish homework on time when I am upset.
a. Scarcely; b. Less scarcely; c. Normally; d. Less frequently; e. Frequently

$A_7$. I cannot make clear what I feel in my mind.

a. Scarcely; b. Less scarcely; c. Normally; d. Less frequently; e. Frequently

$A_3$. I care about my feelings.

a. Scarcely; b. Less scarcely; c. Normally; d. Less frequently; e. Frequently

$A_{48}$. I know how to deal with unhappy situations.

a. Scarcely; b. Less scarcely; c. Normally; d. Less frequently; e. Frequently
$A_{28}$. I can know feelings of others.

a. Scarcely; b. Less scarcely; c. Normally; d. Less frequently; e. Frequently

$A_{41}$. I make many troubles.

a. Scarcely; b. Less scarcely; c. Normally; d. Less frequently; e. Frequently

$A_{40}$. I cannot concentrate on a thing when I feel upset.

a. Scarcely; b. Less scarcely; c. Normally; d. Less frequently; e. Frequently

$A_{13}$. I do not know whether my mood is good or not.

a. Scarcely; b. Less scarcely; c. Normally; d. Less frequently; e. Frequently

$A_{12}$. I care about my feelings very much.

a. Scarcely; b. Less scarcely; c. Normally; d. Less frequently; e. Frequently

$A_{49}$. I know how to live happily.

a. Scarcely; b. Less scarcely; c. Normally; d. Less frequently; e. Frequently

$A_{11}$. I can understand feelings of others easily.

a. Scarcely; b. Less scarcely; c. Normally; d. Less frequently; e. Frequently

$A_{29}$. I cannot control myself when I feel upset.

a. Scarcely; b. Less scarcely; c. Normally; d. Less frequently; e. Frequently

$A_{30}$. I can still finish homework when I am upset.

a. Scarcely; b. Less scarcely; c. Normally; d. Less frequently; e. Frequently

$A_{21}$. I am easily impulsive.

a. Scarcely; b. Less scarcely; c. Normally; d. Less frequently; e. Frequently

$A_{46}$. If my friend feels unhappy,I can perceive .

a. Scarcely; b. Less scarcely; c. Normally; d. Less frequently; e. Frequently

$A_{27}$. I cannot concentrate on homework when I feel upset.

a. Scarcely; b. Less scarcely; c. Normally; d. Less frequently; e. Frequently

$A_{44}$. I always feel angry because of bad mood.

a. Scarcely; b. Less scarcely; c. Normally; d. Less frequently; e. Frequently

# APPENDIX 2

## Lesson 146 Crested Ibis Fly Back

### --Design of Teaching Plan of Emotion Regulation Infiltration

1. Content: In the case of experiencing certain emotion, keep the capability to finish tasks by controlling impulsive behaviors.
2. Goals:
Experience emotional status by learning feeling and emotional words and sentences;
Cultivate the perseverance and self-control that students make efforts to achieve goals and bravely overcome difficulties to solve problems;
Grasp strategies and methods of emotional control to finish learning tasks.
3. Materials: videos and pictures of crested ibis, strategy chart and others.
4. Procedures:

Infiltration opportunities: paragraphs 6-9 and 11-13 of the text.

### *Judgment and Evaluation:*
Tell the truth

I am always anxious so as to get poor examination performance. ( )
I am often distracted in class when I am upset. ( )
I will make many unnecessary mistakes in my homework if parents chatter endlessly. ( )
After the class begins, I still keep in mind the interesting thing during the break. ( )
I cannot concentrate on a thing after I am criticized by a teacher. ( )
I am always angry so that I cannot pay attention to what the teacher says in the class. ( )
I forget to finish homework because of playing games sometimes. ( )
I always do not know what the teacher mentioned in the text if I am unhappy. ( )
I often cannot finish homework on time because of upsetting mood. ( )
I want to do nothing in a rage many times. ( )

Creation of situation. Students, please look at these numbers:1=1; 1=8760; 1=? (board writing). "1=1" means that one kind of living thing dies out per hour; "1=8760" means that 8760 kinds of living things disappear in this beautiful planet each year; "1=?" do you know the price of a panda? Please guess. (free talking of students) The panda is priceless. There is a kind of birds in Qinling of Shanxi Province, China. They are fewer than the quantity of panda so that they are much rare. Do you know what are them? (Show pictures)

This text describes the story that scientists overcome hardships in the help of children to find and protect crested ibis and make them reproducing. How significant it is! When you read the text, you need to carefully experience the emotional change in the process of finding crested ibis and the behaviors of scientists and children. What touches your heart? What is worthy of learning for you?

Guide with strategies:

Filteration of words: What is meaning of Shy? (students' answer) Then, please make sentences or provide examples according to your life.

Load reading of text:The teacher asks students to read aloud paragraphs 6-9 of the text, express naive, lovely and enthusiastic attitudes of Xiaoguang and Xiaopangzi and experience their expressions, behaviors and words. Which sentence in the text can represent their happy mood? (students' answer)

Group discussion: Please carefully read these sentences in the paragraph 11 of the text, "It is very hot. They are troubled by the continuous bite of insects, but they bear it and reduce activities as more as possible to avoid interference of observation."

What do you learn from these sentences? (hardship in the process of finding crested ibis)

Which word or sentence do you know it through? (It is very hot, bite of insects, wait and gently)

What do they behave and express in the painful situation? (bear, control)

Why do they behave like this? (in order to avoid interference of observation)

Heuristics: (students read aloud paragraph 12 and the teacher asks questions)

The text adopts some words, such as innumerable trials and hardships, to describe the process of searching crested ibis. Do you think what do they (scientists, Xiaoguang and Xiaopangzi) feel after finding out crested ibis? (very exciting)

What is the response of scientists? (inhibit, carefully, quietly, nervously) How about Xiaoguang and Xiaopangzi? (exciting but control own emotion) The teacher guides students: Please look at yourselves in comparison with scientists and children. Are you easily distracted from class or homework when you are excited or upset? For example, you do not know what the teacher said in the text when you feel intoxicated; you cannot concentrate on homework when you feel upset or depressed. (Students answer: yes) Please ask some students to answer questions in the portion of "Tell the truth" above. Then, ask students how to control own emotions to be better devoted into the learning activity. (Free talking of students) By use of guide and explanation, the teacher helps students understand own problems and importance of self control, appropriately provide students with strategies and methods for self control of emotion regulation.

### Infiltration with Strategies

Enhance the control to be the master of emotion (strategies of emotion regulation)

If you are depressed or excited, you first need to adjust own emotional status. I already tell you relevant strategies and methods of emotion regulation. Please think about which strategies can be used!

### Improve Self-Control

Self-instruction: Write instructions on a paper and paste the paper on the desk, such as Do not look around! Pay attention to what the teacher says!

Marking: When you find yourself abstracted, you can write a marking on a paper to remind yourself.

Use of pencil during the reading. While you are reading, you can mark important parts with a pencil or write comments.

### Reflection (After Class):

Examples of famous persons:

In order to know living habits of ants, French entomologist Fabre ever crawled on wet and dirty ground for four hours, and used a magnifying glass to observe the activity that the ants moved a dead fly. When Archimedes at the age of 75 years old, the great mathematician in ancient Greece, was drawing a geometric figure on the ground in his room, roman soldiers suddenly intruded into his room, but he was unaware of it. Until a roman soldier used a sword to point at him, he just knew what happened. But he calmly said, "Please wait a minute. You can kill me after I finish the geometric theory, or else I leave a theory which has not been demonstrated!"

### Practice

During the learning, we may experience some happy things to show excitement in facial expressions or encounter some unhappy things to be depressed or cry at any time. They are normal phenomena which everyone may encounter everyday. Nevertheless, the key point is how we can become the master of emotion when we encounter these things: try our best to control emotion rather than being intervened by emotion to finish tasks on time, such as examination, attendance in class, homework. Pleas think about which things you encountered and what you felt at that moment. Happy, joyous, angry, depressed or pessimistic? Which measures did you adopt to successfully finish tasks at last?

**Feeling Diary**

| Activities | Events | Feelings | Measures |
|---|---|---|---|
| Examination | | | |
| Class | | | |
| Homework | | | |
| Read | | | |

## REFERENCES

Altshuler, J. L., and Ruble, D. N. (1989). Developmental changes in children's awareness of strategies for coping with uncontrollable stress. *Child Development, 60,* 1337-1349.

Axline, V. (1969). *Play therapy: The inner dynamics of childhood.* Boston: Houghton Mifflin.

Bai, J. S. (2000). *Moral Education Language Arts.* Beijing: China Forestry Publishing House.

Ban, H. (1994). *Psycho-educational theory.* Hefei: Anhui Education Publishing House.

Bian, Y. *F.,* and Zheng Y. Q. (1997). The mental health survey report of Hangzhou primary. *Journal of Hangzhou University,* (4), 138-142.

Bower, G. H., Gillian, S. G., and Monteriro, K. P. (1981). Selectivity of Learning Caused by Emotional States, *Journal of Experimental Psychology*: General, *110,* 451-473.

Brenner, E., and Salovey, P. (1997). Emotion regulation during childhood: Developmental interpersonal and individual considerations. In P. Salovey and D. Sluyter (Eds.), *Emotional literacy and emotional development* (pp. 168–192). New York: Basic Books.

Brenner, E., and Salovey, P. (1997). Emotion regulation during childhood: Developmental

Buckley, *M.,* Storino, *M.,* and Saarni, C. (2003). Promoting emotional competence in children and adolescents: Implications for school psychologists. *School Psychology Quarterly, 18,* 177-191.

Buckley, *M.,* Storino, *M.,* and Saarni, C. (2003). Promoting Emotional Competence in Children and Adolescents: Implications for School Psychologists. *School Psychology Quarterly, 18,* 177-190.

Cai, X. L. (2001). *Emotion Regulation.* Hefei: Anhui People's Publishing House.

Campos, J. J., Campos, R.G., andBarrett, K. C. (1989). Emergent themes in the study of emotional development and emotion regulation. *Developmental Psychology, 25,* 394-402.

Caspi, A., Bem, D., and Elder, G. (1989). Continuities and consequences of interactional styles across the life course.*Journal of Personality, 57,* 375-406.

Chen, J. L. (2002). *School Mental Health Education-Theory and Operation.* Beijing: Science Education Publishing Company.

Chen, Y. L. (2002). *The study of teacher's classroom emotion regulation.* Master's thesis, Capital Normal University, P.R.C.

Chen, Y. S. (1994). *Primary mental health.* Jinan: Shandong Education Press.

Cicchetti, D., Ackerman, B. P., and Izard, C. E. (1995). Emotions and emotion regulation in developmental psychopathology. *Development and Psychopathology, 7* (1), 1-10.

Clyve, S. P., and Zeman, J. (2002). Initial Validation of the Emotion Expression Scale for Children (EESC). *Journal of Clinical Child and Adolescent Psychology, 31,* 540-547.

Cole, P. M., Martin, S. E and Dennis, T. A. (2004). *Emotion Regulation as a Scientific Construct: Methodological Challenges and Directions for Child Development Research. Child Development, 75,* 317-333.

Cole, P. M., Michel, M. K., and O'Donnell-Teti, L. (1994). The development of emotion regulation and dysregulation: a clinical perspective. *Monographs of the Society for Research in Child Development, 59* (73–100), 250-283.

Cole. P. M. and Kaslow. N. (1988). Interactional and cognitive strategies for affect regulation: Developmental perspective on childhood depression. In L Alloy (Ed), *Cognitive processes in depression* (PP. 310-343). New York: Guilford.

Cumming, A. (1987). Writing expertise and second language proficiency in ESL writing performance. Unpublished doctoral dissertation. University of Toronto, Toronto.

Davies, P.T., and Cummings, E.*M.* (1995). Children's emotions as organizers of their reactions to interadult anger: A functionalist perspective. *Developmental Psychology, 31,* 677-684.

Denham, S. A., Mitchell-Copeland, J., Strandberg, K., Auerbach, S. and Blair, K. (1997). Parental Contributions to Preschoolers' Emotional Competence: Direct and Indirect Effects. *Motivation and Emotion, 21,* 65-86.

Diener, E. (1984). Subjective well-being. *Psychological Bulletin, 95,* 542-575.

Dodge, K. A. (1989) Coordinating responses to aversive stimuli: Introduction to a special section on the development of emotion regulation. *Developmental Psychology, 25* (3), 339-342.

Dodge, K. A., and Garber, J. (1991). Domains of emotion regulation. In K. A. Dodge and J. Garber (Eds.), *The development of emotion regulation and dysregulation.* (pp. 3-14). UK: Cambridge University Press.

Eisenberg ,N., Fabes R. A. et al (1997). Emotional Responding: Regulation, Social, Correlations, and Socialization. In Salovey. P, Sluyter. D. Jeds. *Emotional Development and Emotional Intelligence Educational Implication* (pp.129-163). Basic Books Inc.

Eisenberg, N. and Moore, B. S. (1997). Emotional Regulation and Development, *Motivation and Emotion, 21,* 1-6.

Eisenberg, N., and Fabes, R. A. (1992). Emotion, regulation, and the development of social competence. In *M.*S. Clark (Ed.), *Emotion and social behavior* (Vol. 14, pp. 119-150). Newbury Park, CA: Sage.

Eisenberg, N., Cumberland, A., and Spinrad, T.L. (1998).Parental socialization of emotion. *Psychological Inquiry*, *9*, 241-273. [PubMed: 16865170]

Eisenberg, N., Fabes R. A. et al. (1995). The Role of Emotionality and Regulation in Children's Social Functioning: A Longitudinal Study. *Child Development*, *66*, 1360-1384.

Eisenberg, N., Losoya, S., and Guthrie, I.K. (1997) Social Cognition and Prosocial Development. *The Development of Social Cognition*, 329-364. Psychology Press.

Fabes, R. A., Eisenberg. N., Karbon., et al ., (1994). Socialization of Children's Vicarious Emotional Responding and Prosocial Behavior: Relations with mother's Perceptions of Reactivity, *Developmental Psychology*, *30*, 44-45.

Feshbach, N., and Roe, K. (1968). Empathy in six- and seven-year olds. *Child Development*, *34*, 133-145.

Fox, N. A., and Calkins, S. D. (2003). The Development of Self-control of Emotion: Intrinsic and Extrinsic Influences. *Motivation and Emotion*, *27*, 7-26.

Gardner, H. (1993). Multiple intelligences: The theory in practice. New York: Basic Books.

Gottman, J. *M*, and Parker, J. (1986). *Conversations of friends: Speculations on affective development*. New York: Cambridge University Press.

Gross, J. J., and Levenson, R. W. (1997). Hiding feelings: the acute effects of inhibiting negative and positive emotion. *Journal of Abnormal Psychology*, *106*, 95–103.

Gross, J.J., Levenson, and Robert W. (1993). Emotional suppression: Physiology, self-report, and expressive behavior. *Journal of Personality and Social Psychology*. *64* (6), 970-986.

Gumora, Gail and Aresnio, William, F. (2002). Emotionality, Emotion Regulation, and School Performance in Middle Schhool Children. *Journal of School Psychology*, *40*, 395-413.

Guo, H. J., and Song, N. (2002). *The training of primary psychological suzhi*. Shanghai: Shanghai Education Publishing House.

H. H. Goldsmith and Richard J. Davidson. (2004). Disambiguating the Components of Emotion Regulation, *Child Development*, *75*, 361-365.

Halberstadt, A. (1991). The ecology of expressiveness: Family expressiveness in particular and a mode! In general. In R. S. Feldman andB. Rime (Eds.), *Fundamentals in nonverbal behavior* (pp. 106-162). Cambridge, England: Cambridge University Press.

Harter, S. and Buddin, B. J. (1983). *Children's understanding of the simultaneity of two emotions: a developmental acquisition sequence*. Paper presented at the Biennial Meeting of the Society for Research in Child Development.

Hu, K. Z., Zheng, H. J., and Zhang, T. (2003). Experiment for Training Junior High School Students' Ability of Emotion-Regulation by Cognitive-Training. *Journal of Educational Science of Hunan Normal University*, (1), 83-88.

Huang, M. E. (2001). *Processes of emotion regulation and individuality*. Doctoral Dissertation, Capital Normal University, P. R. C.

Huang, *M*. E., and Guo, D. J. (2000). The essence of emotion regulation. *Psychological Science*, (1), 109-110.

Huang, Y. X. (1989). *Emotional education and developmental guidance* (pp.197-279). Taibei, 5 Southern Book Publishing Company press. .

Huang, Y. X. (1989). *Emotional education and developmental guidance.* Taibei: 5 Southern Book Publishing Company press.

James J. Gross. (1998). Antecedent- and Response-Focused Emotion Regulation: Divergent Consequences for Experience, Expression, and Physiology. *Journal of Personality and Social Psychology*, 74, 224-237.

James J. Gross. (1998). The Emerging Field of Emotion Regulation: An Integrative Review. *Review of General Psychology, 2*, 271-299.

James J. Gross. (1999). Emotion regulation: Past, Present, Future. *Cognition and Emotion*, *13*, 551-573.

James J. Gross. and John, O.P. (2003). Individual differences in two emotion regulation processes: Implications for affect, relationships, and well-belling. *Journal of Personality and Social Psychology*, 85, 348-362.

Jiang, Q., and Zhang, D. J. *Problems and strategies in the research of subject infiltration PSE.* Research Center of Mental Health Education, Southwest University.

Jiang, Q., and Zhang, D. J. Problems and strategies in the research of subject infiltration PSE. Internal data.

Kagan, J. (1994). *The Nature of the Child.* New York: Basic Books press.

Kate Keenan. Emotion Dysregulation As a Risk Factor for Child Psychopathology. *Clinical Psychology: Science and Practice, 7*, 418-434.

Kim, L . Gratz and Lizabeth Roemer (2004). Multifactorial Assessment of Emotion Regulation and Dysregulation: Development, Factor Structure, and Initial Validation of the Difficulties in Emotion Regulation Scale. *Journal of Psychopathology and Behavioral Assessment*, *26*, 41-54.

Laura E. Berk (author), Wu, Y. et al. (translator) (2002). *Development of Children*. Nanjing: Jiangsu Education Press.

Lazarus, R. S., and Opton, E.*M.*, Jr. (1966). The study of psychological stress: a summary of theoretical formulations and experimental findings. In: C. D. Spielberger (Ed.), *Anxiety and behavior* (pp.225-262). New York: Academic Press.

Lempers, J. D. and Clark-Lempers, D. C. (1992). Young, Middle and Late Adolescents Comparisons of the Functional Importance of Five Significant Relationships. *Journal of Youth and Adolescence*, *21*, 53-96.

Li, X. W. (2002). Comparing different adaptive pupils' feelings: A research on the mechanism of self-regulation. *Psychological Science*, (6), 683-686.

Li, Z. K. (2000). *MHE guide of primary school students (for teachers)*. Changsha: Hunan Education Press.

Li, Z. S. (2002). Research on the Mental Health and Learning Adaptability of Pupils. *Journal of Chongqing Teachers College (Natural Science Edition)*, (9), 68-71.

Lisa, *M.* Diamond and Lisa, G. Aspinwall. (2003). Emotion Regulation across the life Span: An Integrative Perspective Emphasizing Self-Regulation, Positive Affect, and Dyadic Processes. *Motivation and Emotion, 27*, 125-156.

Liu, G. X., and Fang *F.* X. (2003). Review on Children's Moral Emotion Judgment. *Journal of Developments in Psychology*, (1), 55-60.

Liu, G. X., Fang *F.* X., and Yang, X. D. (2003). Advances of Studies on Children's Emotional Development. *Journal of Nanjing Normal University (Social Science Edition)*, (6), 98-104.

Liu, X. *M.*, and Zhang, B. L. (1999). *Mental health and psychological consultation of primary school students.* Changchun: Northeast Normal University Press

Liu, X. P., and Gu, Q. (2004). Study on the Role Ambiguity of Chinese School Psychologists: Reasons and Solutions. *Teacher Education Research,* (4), 61-65.

Liu, Y. L. (2001). A Research of the Relationship Between Elementary School Students' Psychological suzhi and Their Academic Achievement. Master's thesis, Southwest Normal University, Chongqing, P. R. C.

Liu, Y. L. (2001). Research on relationship between psychological suzhi and academic performance of primary school students. Chongqing: Master's thesis of the Southwest China Normal University.

Lu, F. (2004). The study about the development of preschool children's emotion regulation strategies. Shanghai: Master's thesis of East China Normal University, P. R. C.

Lu, F., and Chen, G. P. (2003). Development of children's emotional regulation. *Psychological Science,* (5), 928-929.

Lu, J. *M.* (2002). *Optimize teaching with emotion--Theoretical and Empirical Study,* 17. Shanghai: Shanghai Education Publishing House.

Luo, Y. (1989). *Theories and methods of emotion control.* Beijing: Guangming Daily Press.

Luo, Z., Guo, D. J., and Fang, P. (2002). Elementary School Students' Understanding of the Social-regulatory Functions of Emotion. *Psychological Development and Education,* (3), 34-39.

Mayer, J. D., and Salovey, P. (1997). What is emotional intelligence? In P.Salovey and D.J. Sluyter (Eds.), *Emotional development and emotional intelligence: Educational implications.* New York, NY: Basic Books, Inc.

Meng, Z. L. (1989). *Emotion of human beings.* Shanghai: Shanghai People's Press.

Meng, Z. L. (2000). Psychology in Contemporary China: Emotion psychology started at Peking University. Beijing, People's Education Press. 215-219.

Murphy, B C., and Eisenberg, N. (1996) Provoked by a peer: Children's anger related responses and their relation to social functioning. Merrill Palmer Quarterly, 42 (1), 103-124.

Park, R. D. (1994). Progress, paradims, and unresolved problems: A commentary of recent advances in our understanding of children's emotions. *Merrill-Palmerly, 40,* 157-169.

Parkinson, J. A., Robbins, T.W., and Everitt, B.J. (1999). Selective excitotoxic lesions of the nucleus accumbens core and shell differentially affect aversive Pavlovian conditioning to discrete and contextual cues. *Psychobiology, 27,* 256-266.

Pulkkinen, L. (1986). The roie of impulse control in the development of antisocial and prosocial behavior. In D. Olweus, J. Block and M. Radke-Yarrow (Eds.), *Development of antisocial and prosocial behavior* (pp. 149-175). Orlando, FL: Academic Press.

Qian, H. *F.*, Zhang, L. X., and Xie, Y. D. (1996). The experimental study of psychological suzhi education courses and student psychological quality of structural optimization. *Psychological Science,* (1), 33-38.

Qiao, J. Z. (2003). *Emotional Research: Theory and Methods.* Nanjing, Nanjing Normal University Press. 283.

Qiao, J. Z. (2003). *Emotional Research: Theory and Methods.* Nanjing, Nanjing Normal University Press. 285.

Qiao, J. Z., and Rao, H. (2000). Study abroad, the status of children's emotion regulation. *Psychological Development and Education*, (2), 49-53.

Qiao, J. Z., Yan, B. H., et al. (1999). The investigation report of secondary school students' emotional quality. *Journal of Nanjing Normal University (Social Science Edition)*, (2), 80-85.

Ramsden1, S. R., and Hubbard, J. A. (2002). Family Expressiveness and Parental Emotion Coaching: Their Role in Children's Emotion Regulation and Aggression. *Journal of Abnormal Child Psychology, 30,* 657-667.

Richard, B. A., and Dodge, K. (1982). Interpersonal problem-solving in school-aged children. *Journal of Consulting and Clinical Psychology, 50,* 226 - 233.

Saami, C. (1997). Coping with Aversive Feelings. *Motivation and Emotion, 21,* 45-63.

Saarni, C. (1988). Emotional competence: How emotions and relationships become integrated. In R.A. Thompson (ed.), *Nebraska Symposium on Motivation, 36,* 115-182.

Saarni, C., Mumme, D., and Campos, J. (1998). *Emotional development: Action, communication.* In W. Damon (Series Ed.) N.Eisenberg (Vol.Ed.), Handbook of child psychology (pp.237-309). New York: Wiley.

Salovey, P., and Birnba, D. (1989).The influence of mood on health-relevant cognitions. *Journal of Personality and Social Psychology, 57,* 539-551.

Salovey, P., and Mayer, J. D. (1990). Emotional intelligence. Imagination, *Cognition and Personality, 9,* 185−211.

Sandier, J., Kennedy, H., and Tyson, R. L. (1980). *The technique of child psychoanalysis: Discussions with Anna Freud.* Cambridge, MA: Harvard University Press.

Shi, X. H. (1993). The comparative study of the urban and rural primary's empathy development. *Psychological Science*, (1), 53-54.

Shields, A., and Cicchetti, D. (1997).Emotion Regulation among School-Age Children: The Development and Validation of a New Criterion Q-Sort Scale. *Developmental Psychology, 33,* 906-916.

Singer, J. A., and Salovey, P. (1988). Mood and memory: Evaluating the network theory of affect. *Clinical Psychology Review, 8,* 211-251.

Sissons Joshi, *M.* and MacLean, *M.* (1994). Indian and English children's understanding of the distinction between real and apparent emotion. *Child Development, 65,* 1372-1384.

Strayer, D. L. (1989). *A comparison of process and memory-based theories of automaticity.* Unpublished doctoral dissertation. University of Illinois.

Teaching and research section of People's Education Press (2001). *Teaching Reference Book for Teachers.* Beijing: People's Education Press.

Thompson, R. A. (1990). Emotion and self-regulation. In R. A. Thompson (Ed.), *Socioemotional development. Nebraska Symposium on Motivation* (Vol. 36, pp. 367-467). Lincoln: University of Nebraska Press.

Thompson, R. A. (1994). Emotion regulation: a theme in search of definition. In N. A. Fox, *The development of emotion regulation: biological and behavioral considerations* (pp. 25−52). Chicago: The University of Chicago Press (Monographs of the Society for Research in Child Development, 59, Serial No. 240).

Underwood, *M.* D., Khaibulina, A. A., Ellis, S. P., Moran, A., Rice, P. *M.*, Mann, J. J., and Arango, V. (1999). Morphometry of the dorsal raphe nucleus serotonergic neurons in suicide victims. *Biol Psychiatry, 46,* 473-483.

Underwood, *M*. K. (1997). Top ten pressing questions about the development of emotion regulation. *Motivation and Emotion, 21*, 127–146.

Underwood, M., Hurley, J., Johnson, C. and Mosley, J. (1999). An Experimental, Observational Survey of Children's Responses to Peer Provocation: Developmental and Gender Differences in Middle Children. *Child Development, 70*, 1428-1446.

Vinden, P. G. (1999). Children's Understanding of Mind and Emotion: A Multi-culture Study. *Cognition and Emotion, 13* (1), 19-48.

Volling, B. Mackinnon-Lewis, C., et al. (1993). Children's Social Competence and Socio-metric Status: Further Exploration of Aggression, Social Withdrawal, and Peer Rejection. *Development and Psychopathology, 5*, 459-483.

Von Salisch *M*. (2001). Children's Emotional Development: Challenges in Their Relationships to Parents, Peers, and Friends. *International Journal of Behavioral Development, 25*, 310-319.

Walden T.A., and Smith, *M*.C., (1997) Emotion regulation. *Motivation and Emotion, 21*, 7-25.

Wang, G. M. (2004). An Experimental Research for the Self-education of Emotion and Junior High School Students' Ability of Emotion Regulation. Master's thesis, Hunan Normal University, P. R. C.

Wang, J. *M*. (2002). *Research of MHE for Chinese students*. Shenyang: Liaoning Education Press.

Wang, J. Y., and Gai, X. S. (1998). The development of pupils' emotional empathy level in different types. *Psychological Development and Education*, (3), 19-22.

Wang, L. (2001). *Emotion Regulation Strategy in the significance of child development*. Doctoral Dissertation, Capital Normal University, P. R. C.

Wang, L. L. (1998). Intellectual and personality evaluation on emotionally disordered Children. *Chinese Mental Health Journal*, (5), 352-354.

Wang, L., and Chen, H. C. (1998). Emotion regulation strategies of 2-year-olds children in stressful situations. *Acta Psychologica Sinica*, (3), 289-297.

Wang, T. (2002). A Study on the Psychological suzhi Structure and Its Developmental Characteristics in University Students. Master's thesis, Southwest Normal University, Chongqing, P .R. C.

Wang, X. J. (2000). A Study of Investigation Data in Construction of Emotional Intelligence. *Psychological Science*, 1, 24-27.

Wang, X. J. (2000). A study of investigation data in construction of emotional intelligence. *Psychological Science*, 1, 24-27.

Wang, Y., Ye, Z. G., and Lin, C. D. (1993). *Psychology of primary school students*. Hangzhou: Zhejiang Education Press.

Wo, J. Z., and Liu, H. J. (2003). A Study on the Features of Ill-emotion of Primary Pupils. *Chinese Journal of Clinical Psychology*, (2), 102-104.

Wo, J. Z., Ma, H. Z., and Liu, J. (2002). *Towards mental health: Development articles*, 45. Beijing, Chinese Press.

Wu, L. J. (2003). *Reasonemotion education course design*. Beijing: World Publishing Corporation.

Wu, *M*. L. (2001). *Guidebook for SPSS Statistical application*. Nanjing: China Railway Press.

Wu, Q. L. (2002). *Design of Teaching Infiltration*. Hefei: Anhui Education Press.

Xu, X. Y., and Zhang, J. *F.* (2004). The Review of the Theory Research of Emotional Intelligence. *Journal of Southwest China Normal University (Humanities and Social Sciences Edition), 6,* 77-82.

Yang, J. *F.*, Xu, X. Y., and Zhang, J. F. (2003). The Survey for the Emotional Intelligence of Middle School Students. *Journal of Southwest Normal University* (Natural Science edition), (8), 650-654.

Ye, Y. T. (2004). A number of issues of mental health education in subject teaching penetration. *Journal of the Chinese Society of Education*, (3), 18-21.

Yu, P., Zhang, *F.* L., and Mo, R. F. (1999). Emotional health problems of young students. *Journal of Yunnan Normal University*, (4), 81-84.

Zeman, J., and Shipman, K. (1996). Children's expression of negative affect: Reasons and methods. *Developmental Psychology, 32,* 842- 849.

Zhang, C. X. (2002). *Educational Psychology*, 340. Zhejiang: Zhejiang Education Publishing House.

Zhang, D. G. (1985). *Regulation and adjustment of emotions*. Shanghai: Shanghai Peoples' Press..

Zhang, D. J., and Peng, Z. Y. (2000). *Psychological suzhi training of middle and primary school students (in grades 4-6)*. Chongqing: Chongqing: Southwest China Normal University Press.

Zhang, D. J., and Zhao, L. X. (2001). The Exploring of Education of Psychological suzhi in Primary School. *Journal of Xinzhou Teachers College*, (5), 56-62.

Zhang, J. *F.*, and Xu, X. Y. (2004). A Study of the Characteristics of the Emotional Intelligence of College Students. *Psychological Science,* (2), 293-296.

Zhang, L. X. (1990). Students' Scholastic Achievement, Intelligence and Their Personality Characteristics. *Psychological Science News*, (5), 38-42.

Zhang, T. (2003). Survey and Analysis of the Pupils' Mental Health State. Training and Research--Journal of Hubei Institute of Education, (1), 87-89.

Zhong, Z. N. (2003). *Changing emotions (for students in grade 5 of primary schools)* [CD]. Ningbo: Zhejiang Zhejiang Electronic Audio-Video Press.

Zhou, L., and Cha Z. X. (1997). Discussion on emotion function of academic performance for superintelligent children in math physics. *Psychological Science*, (1), 82-83.

Zhu, Y. (2000). *Experimental Psychology,* 20-21. Beijing: Peking University Press.

# PART FOUR:

# COMPUTER-ASSISTED TRAINING MODES AND IMPLEMENTATION STRATEGIES

*Chapter 8*

# EMPIRICAL EXPLORATION ON IMPROVING PARENT-CHILD RELATIONSHIP BY USING PSYCHOLOGICAL-SUZHI-EDUCATION SOFTWARE

## *Xiao-Dong Qi[1] and Da-Jun Zhang[2]*
[1]Haerbin Normal University, China
[2]Center for Mental Health Education in Southwest University, China

## ABSTRACT

The present research proposes a new perspective of developing students' psychological *suzhi*, i.e., the use of computer aided teaching (CAT). In particular, Psychological-*Suzhi*-Education Software (PSE) software will be developed based on the content of PSE and be applied to the PSE activities to improve the psychological *suzhi* of students. The present research conducted experiments of PSE software we developed for the purpose of improving parent-child relationship (PCR) to validate the effect and applicability of the proposed means of education. Significant difference was found between the experimental group and the control group in strictness, intervention and total scores after the experiment. PCR software obviously improved the strictness, intervention and anxiety PCRs. The experimental group had higher average score than the control group. The total score of the experimental group was significant. It indicates that computer aided PSE mode and the PSE software for PCR improvement are applicable and effective in improving PCR.

## INTRODUCTION

### Modeing on Development of Psychological-Suzhi-Education Software and Computer Aided Teaching

*1) Theoretical Discussion on Development of Psychological-Suzhi-Education Software*
    *Psychological-*suzhi*-education (PSE) software satisfies the requirements for PSE.* First, PSE is a process of "facilitating to learn self-help". The teacher is to teach the students the

"self-help" during the process. Meanwhile, students may accept certain ideas and thoughts presented in software through interacting with the computer by audio, video and/or text. This will help them develop corresponding psychological *suzhi*, i.e. "learn to self-help". Second, PSE should feature inclusiveness and generality: it aims not only to teach students how to learn, but also teach them how to live, how to be and how to get along well with others. All of these can be realized with the aid of computer. Such aid may help develop the students' intelligence, personality, sociability and creativity. The software can not only address common issues for the students at large, but also analyze student specific issues and circumstances. This is the true nature of "inclusiveness and generality", the features of PSE. Thirdly, PSE focuses on activities and interactivity. With the aid of computer, different scenarios that the students could encounter in their real life can be simulated in diversified means and the desirable solutions could also be given. Such simulation teaches the students more directly and vividly how to respond to different situations. In addition, more examples could be offered in shorter time. To sum up, computer simulation can meet the basic requirements for, and is consistent with the characteristics of PSE. Therefore, it is scientific to apply CAT to PSE.

*Advantages of PSE software.* CAT tools have been extensively applied in education with their advantages that satisfy the requirements and are helpful for PST. Such advantages include:

Facilitating perception and comprehension. A multimedia enabled computer produces vivid images and texts and pleasant sound. It provides not a mere external incentive, but multi-sensory incentives. It facilitates observation, cognition and comprehension through presenting contents of multi-levels and multi-perspectives in the means of activities. In addition, the massive storage capacity and good readability of multimedia enable the students to keep high excitability during various process of learning, which is helpful for students to perceive and comprehend the learning contents. Creation of a psychological environment is critical for PSE software and is also an assurance for PST. This is because PSE is a process to activate or stimulate students' mental activities, to cause the sense of identification or absence of students, to excite emotional resonance and then to induce the willingness to act and in this process it is an important precondition to establish a harmonious psychological environment.

Interactivity. Harmonious interaction strategy is an important means to develop and improve students' psychological *suzhi* via PSE, and it is often applied in reality to the student-student-interaction and student–teacher- interaction. CAT tools may also involve students via interaction between human and machine in which the support, cooperation and enthusiasm are very important and students are active participants instead of onlookers. They are required to give response continuously during the process of controlling training progress; they are also required to make self-examination and communications when appropriate, which is one of the indispensable characteristics of PSE.

Stimulating students' interest and motivation. PSE should enable students to make their judgment and arouse their resonance or sense of absence so as to initiate their motivation. With multimedia software, multimedia computers which provide visual-acoustic presentation and timely feedback can realize varied interaction between human and machine with excellent images and texts. Students can plan their own schedule according to their own needs and get feedback in a timely pattern. This enables students to learn actively and while such active learning is interesting and innovative, and combines the functions of knowledge acquisition and entertainment, it can arouse great interests of the students. In addition, the friendly, natural and vivid feedback is easy to comprehend. Active learning can improve learning behavior, stimulate students' intrinsic motivation, and enable students to obtain reliable and complete knowledge and make exploration more active.

Enhancing consolidation and situation-transferring. Students' improved psychological *suzhi* should be transferred from virtual scenario to reality. Psychologist Treichler [1967] has proved after experimentation that human beings get 1.0% of information through taste, 1.5% through touch, 3.5% through smell, 11.0% through hearing and 83.0% through vision. This proves the importance of vision for learning activities. He also indicated that we can generally remember 10% of what we have read, 20% of what we have heard, 30% of what we have As seen, 50% of what we have As seen and heard, and 70% of what we have said. It follows that we may employ multiple senses during the learning to improve the memory. Computer-aided PSE does so exactly. It stimulates senses of students via various methodologies to make them remember apply what they learned and comprehended to similar scenarios.

## 2) Modeing of PSE

### Basic Modes of PSE

Individualized coaching. Individualized coaching, for the purpose of teaching of a particular subject, is that the CAT program acts as the instructor or teacher to teach students new knowledge and skills, including verbal information and intellectual skills. This mode could be used for computer-aided PSE. Although the computer-aided individualized coaching program is presently not comparable with teachers in communication with students, it has advantages over teachers in certain aspects. For example, students will be more likely to openly communicate with a computer. In addition, this is also a full demonstration of the interaction between students and the computer and the individualization, both of which are indispensable for PST.

Scenario simulation. Computer-aided simulation is the simulation by the computer of certain interactive "scenario" which may be an event, an object or a phenomenon. Teachers can simulate to provide students with a theater of social science, interpersonal relationship and natural science. This could cost more time than direct lecture, but the return would be full and lasting comprehension. The greatest advantage is that this can enable the students to apply the skills they have practiced repeatedly in the simulated environment to real life. Role play is, as typically used for PST programs, a kind of simulation featuring the relatively open interpersonal communication. Generally speaking, the participant in a role play would be required to imagine himself/herself as another person or imagine that he/she is in a particular environment, and then to give response as if he/she were the person or as required by the environment. A good simulation should be able to entertain and reveal reality in order to allow for better transferring of skills and/or knowledge acquired in simulated environment to reality and to minimize the sense of threat and worries when in reality. Computer-aided PSE could provide excellent simulation and experiencing scenario with this mode.

Incentive game. The incentive game mode is to generate a game-based and competitive environment with the computer to arouse students' motivation to learn and to enable the students to discover something and achieve positive effect via the game with clear teaching objectives. Some excellent teaching games may arouse great interest of the user. Such mode is science-based, education-oriented and entertaining; with this mode, "teaching would be accomplished in entertainment". This mode may be used for PST to help student develop appropriate psychological *suzhi* and learn the right behavior, when the students are required to learn how to behave.

Open question. The open question mode is to provide students with one or more questions based on the contents to be taught so as to enable the students to solve as many similar problems as possible in reality within a short period of time. In general, this mode gives no rules but open questions for students to solve problems in an innovative manner so as to arouse students' motivation to learn, guide the learners to solve problems and encourage students to develop better thinking skills and strategies on solving problems. This mode is recommended when the students are required to find the best solution themselves in reality, which is also an important step of PSE.

Dialogue. With the dialogue mode, the dialogue between the computer and the students enables the students to put forward their questions relevant to the teaching program or answer the questions put forward by the computer in natural language. It is an individualized coaching. It inspires the initiative thinking of students and sparks their interests.Different from common competence education, PSE is the interaction between minds, which needs students to open their mind, thus the dialogue is indispensable. Students can show their true selfhood in a dialogue with the computer as they have fewer scruples. It helps to know their psychological *suzhi*. Therefore, this mode is very important to computer aided PSE throughout the process. The mentioned computer aided PSE modes satisfy the requirements for PSE. In order to have the best effect, optimization and/or combination of the modes may be used, depending on the trainings. For example, individualized coaching can be used for individualized training, with which multiple buttons would be available, and students can choose the needed content by pushing them. When students need to experience and internalize one good psychological trait, role play can be a choice. Students can also use the dialogue mode to show their feelings through words and sentences. Therefore, combination of modes can be included in the design of computer aided PSE software, in order to realize the training targets.

## Principles of PSE Software Design and the Design Strategies

To develop computer aided PSE software, certain principles must be followed, which is based on the experience learned from multimedia-based education. The software design must follow the following particular principles, in addition to the common principle in multimedia curriculum design and general teaching design. Such designs must be system-and-program oriented and applicable.

*User focus.* The design must focus on students' subjective initiative and should be user-centered. The students' initiative can be that students will observe carefully, think initiatively and identify problems in the learning, and then analyze and solve the problems with the knowledge they acquire; and they will use the knowledge they learned in the real life. The software design must take into account how to effectively stimulate the students' initiative, because it will influence not only the software functions, but also the development of users' psychological *suzhi*.

*Combination of visual-acoustic functions and experience-reflection functions.* Visual-acoustic functions and thinking are closely related to and integral parts for the application of computer aided PSE software, because visual-acoustic functions are a must for CAT process while visual-acoustic functions without experience and reflection could not achieve the accomplishment of training targets. Combination of the both aspects is to enable the user to find psychological resonance over perceptual comprehension. This eventually improves the psychological *suzhi* as expected. However, we should i) carefully organize the visual and acoustic application of users by continuously developing and enriching the perceptual knowledge and visual thinking of users; ii) guide the experience and reflection of users. The software design can include some questions and scenes for experience and reflection, which will stimulate the users to recall their own experience, then facilitate the reflection and behavior transforming, and eventually improve the psychological *suzhi*.

*Multimedia function and optimized activity design.* How to use the proper forms of media to realize optimized design is one of the concerns of our research since various forms of media could be used to accomplish the basic targets of PSE which are also diversified. Although the psychological *suzhi* is always a representation of the overall conditions of a student, the student is to be cultivated and trained systematically. While psychological *suzhi* has multiple dimensions and levels, there should also be multiple levels of PSE software. The means to show the PSE contents and the illustration of targets should be optimized. Therefore, the software design should take into account how to demonstrate the targets through different forms of media and how to illustrate the most needed contents.

*A realistic approach in selection of contents.* The students' psychological *suzhi* results from their life and learning, thus PST should focus on the hot topics, focuses and difficulties of their psychology. The curriculum design should be closely based on students' psychology. Training materials should be collected from surveys and research results. The software should provide sufficient virtual scenarios that are close to real life, which will enable the students to have real psychological experience and master the methods and skills for psychology and behaviors. And then based on their experience ,the students will form good habits, improve the psychological *suzhi* and eventually have good psychological *suzhi*.

### 3) Restraining Factors of PSE Software

The variables affecting the training effects include the contents of the software, characteristics of students and environment variables, according to the analysis of the application process of computer aided PSE software. The relationship among such variables can be expressed as:

Effects of software = f
(characteristics of software × characteristics of students × environmental factors)

Characteristics of software include appropriateness of the contents, decoration, program, connection, etc. Characteristics of students include age, gender, grade, motivation, experience, attitude and receptivity of software, familiarity with computer and capacity to use computer, adaptation to software mode, etc. Environmental factors include social requirements, application scope in school, attitude of teachers or parents, hardware and software environment, etc. The specific characteristics are as follows:

### Characteristics of Software

The research into CAT effects showed that CAT effects are significantly related with the design of computer aided software. Not many researchers probed into the effects of computer aided PSE. But it is sure that the basic forms of computer aided PSE (for example, how to provide instant feedback, how to design the screen presentation, which means of control can be used, etc) also impact the effects of PSE. However, the software should not be the copy of PSE textbooks; instead, the software should be more vivid. Only by doing so can the effects of software be ensured.

**Environmental Factors**

First, computer application is extensively required in society, thus computer courses are available in many schools. The social environment facilitates the combination of computer and teaching of a subject, including PSE. In addition, school factor is also very important. It includes the general opinions of the headmaster and teachers, the atmosphere of applying computer aided PSE software in the school, the policies and motivating means of the school management towards the software, etc. Second, from the perspective of hardware and software conditions, computer resources in ordinary schools are limited at present. Besides, such computer resources are for learning computer knowledge. Normally, it is difficult to use such computer resources to conduct PSE. Then the basic requirements of computer aided PSE can not be satisfied, let alone the effects. Finally, from the perspective of the environment for software application, all computers can be put in a classroom due to the nature of software (different from textbook), which causes mutual interference among students; software can also be distributed to students for self-learning at home, but this is of great haphazardry since family environment is not as quiet as classroom environment. Therefore, the application environment is also a factor affecting the effects.

*4) Application of Computer Aided PSE*

Network interaction for imparting of psychological knowledge and correction of mental problems. Interaction systems among students can be used to exchange opinions and thoughts, for example, internet char room, emotional catharsis corner, role play activities. The system for psychological counseling at home can provide families with necessary psychological materials and instruction of psychological counseling at home; for example, MHE information, positive and negative cases of home education, techniques for psychological counseling at home, etc. The interacting system between students and teachers can support students and teachers with knowledge of communication to improve the frequency of communication. Mental disorder modification system can be used to correct mental problems, for example, providing computer programs for treatment of attention deficit disorder, anxiety, obsessive compulsive disorder, autism, phobia, etc. Many international researchers probed into this area, for example, Eliza wrote a program based on Rogers' therapeutic theory, called "a friend you could never have before". During the counseling with this program, subjects even can not distinguish whether they are talking to the consultant or the computer program.

Psychological trait training through the software. Computer can be used to conduct the training of a certain psychological trait in psychological research due to its advantages; for example, software for attention training, memory training, cognitive strategy training and the training of learning interest, will and habit are available.

Database for evaluation of mental state. The calculation and storage functions of computer can be used to measure and evaluate certain psychological traits and to improve the efficiency of psychological tests (cognitive capacity test, psychological *suzhi* test, etc); for example, the scoring and explanation are much faster, the interest of the subjects are stimulated and the subjective bias of the experimenter is reduced.

Computer aided PSE software provides a new perspective for PSE and a new mode to develop psychological *suzhi* of students.

## About PCR Research

Computer aided PST is applicable and has its own advantages. The verification and support of practice are needed to prove the applicability of this method. Improvement in the process of practice is the ordinary process of developing a new technique and a new method. The followings are the reasons to probe into PSE software and the brief introduction to the current status of PCR research.

### Why PCR?

The PSE for students is multi-dimensional and multi-level. It should be conducted based on different psychological traits of students, which is one of the basic starting points of PSE. The research showed that parents, the teachers and the classmates are the most important factors for the PSE and students' development. Therefore, research into the interpersonal relationship between students and the mentioned three factors is of crucial significance for developing corresponding psychological *suzhi* of students. Zhang et al. divided the contents of PSE into eight parts, including adaptation to learning, adaptation to life, learning to be, adaptation to interpersonal communication, developing of intelligence, development of personality, development of sociability and development of creativity. Interpersonal communication, as an integral part of PSC, indicates its significant role in psychological *suzhi*.

PCR is one of the important social networks for teenagers, and also is an important factor affecting the physical and psychological development of teenagers. In particular, for teenagers who are in a period of dramatic psychological development, difficulty and confusion, PCR and family environment have more influence on their personality development and mental health. The research into PCR showed that PCR has more irreplaceable and far-reaching influence than school and society on the personality traits, behaviors, mental health and future development of teenagers. Therefore improvement of PCR is a requirement of PSE.

On the other hand, parents believe that adolescence is the most difficult in upbringing, making parents feel at a loss. Thus special attention should be paid to the parent-child communication in this period. The research by Zhang [2002] showed that in China, 6.2% teenagers have frequent conflicts with parents (parent-child conflict and parent-child cohesion are two important dimensions to measure PCR), 12.5% teenagers have highly frequent conflicts with parents. The research into parent-child conflict in teenager period showed that junior middle school students have increasing conflicts and disagreements with parents, and decreasing of intimacy and cohesion [Collins and Russell, 1991; Paikoff and Brooks, 1991]. Research showed that parent-child conflict is positively correlated with the problem behaviors, low academic performance of teenagers [Gehring, Wentzel, Feldman and Wiersn, 1990]. Therefore, theoretically, it can be proved that it is significantly necessary to improve PCR by probing into the PCR of junior grade two students, since PCR is very important to the development of an individual and the period of junior middle school is the critical period of parent-child communication.

Finally, in order to prove whether PCR meets the actual situations of junior grade two students, we surveyed some junior students of grade two and found that they worry about and desire help the most in the following aspects: poor performance in learning, poor relationship with parents, poor interpersonal relationship with teachers and peers, confusion in interpersonal communication with the other gender. Thus from the practical perspective of students, improvement of PCR are desired by them.

To sum up, from both practical and theoretical perspectives, we probe into the PCR of junior grade two students.

## Definition of PCR

Parent-child relationship (PCR), a term of genetics, refers to the biological blood relationship between parent generation and offspring. In this chapter, it refers to the interactional relationship between parents and child. To be specific, it is the emotional communication and behavioral interaction between parents and child. PCR, as the earliest interpersonal relationship built by children, directly influences the physical and psychological development of the children and also impacts interpersonal relationships at different levels in the future.

At present, PCR is classified into different categories by different researchers according to their own theories. Most classifications are based on the following psychometric tools. Those who use Parent-child Relationship Test (PCRT) classify PCR into five categories and 10 types, i.e., anticipation, intervention, anxiety, indulgence and conformism.

Those who use PUI classify PCR into five categories, i.e., less care and less control, less care and more control, more care and less control, more care and more control. Zheng classifies PCR into six types, parenting, property owning, reverse, conflict and universal love. The mentioned means of classification provides foundation for us to distinguish and probe into PCR.

## Characteristics of PCR in Adolescence

Generally speaking, PCR relationship focuses on the research into parent-child games of childhood and PCR research of teenager period. The following paragraphs focus on PCR of teenager period as the object of this chapter is junior middle school students.

Compared with childhood, the function of home is dramatically changed in teenager period. i) The support and guiding functions of home is more significant and important; whereas the upbringing, protection and social functions of home are secondary. ii) The nature of PCR is significantly changed in that PCR is transformed from unilateralism in childhood into equal and democratic multilateralism. iii) Teenagers require more independence and they tend to accept less authority of parents, resulting into more parent-child conflicts. iv) Teenagers have more interactions with peers of the same age, and less interaction with parents. The mentioned changes and new characteristics of home system in teenager period, resulting from psychological development of individuals, significantly influence the development of teenagers.

### Current Status of PCR Research

Home is the main place for the early socialization of children. Parents, as the major supporter, play an irreplaceable role in the development of children. Meanwhile, children are not the passive receiving ends. They also influence the upbringing of parents. On one hand, the emotional atmosphere of home, the attitude and upbringing style of parents influence the development of children; on the other hand, the development of children also influence the upbringing styles of parents and emotional atmosphere of home.

### Factors Affecting PCR

Characteristics of parents: many researchers probed into this aspect, including personality, mental state, upbringing attitude, education, occupation, consciousness and behaviors of parents. They probed into and verified what kind of significant influence these characteristics have on PCR through survey and literature analysis.

Characteristics of children: Li and Meng summarized upon survey that the following characteristics of children influence PCR: the gender, appearance, politeness to parents, consideration for parents, character, temperamental trait, intelligence, academic performance, etc. It fully demonstrates that as the agent of interaction child plays a role that can not be ignored in PCR.

Characteristics of home: Zhang et al. Also probed into the influences of economic conditions, home atmosphere and home structure on PCR when they probed into psychological and social development of teenagers and the upbringing style of parents.

Social structure: German psychologist Schutz probed into the factors affecting PCR of German teenagers from this perspective. He believes that the changes of social structure influences PCR of teenagers. The high unemployment rate starting from the 1970s, age ratio imbalance and the different education background of two generations are the main factors affecting PCR of teenagers in Germany in the 1980s.

### Influences of PCR on Children

PCR greatly impacts the development of children. For example, i) PCR influences the socialization and personality development of child. PCR and early home education are the core and the main driving force of socialization and personality development of child, which play a decisive role in the development of child. ii) PCR influences peer relationship and teacher-student relationship to some extent. iii) parent-child communication influences academic performance generally. iv) PCR significantly influences the sexual psychology, smoking, drinking and obesity of teenagers. v) PCR affects career development of teenagers. vi) Good communication facilitates the development of pro-social behaviors of teenagers; whereas abnormal communication results in antisocial or asocial psychological behaviors.

### Evaluation of Existing Research

Methods of research: the existing research mainly uses psychometric scales and experimental research. But there are two problems. First the sample size of ordinary survey is not large enough and the sampling is not strict enough. Second, PCR is bidirectional. Therefore, PCR research should be based on bidirectional and double-dimensional principles. It will be more convincing with mutual verification. Unidirectional research is not easy to demonstrate the relationship among the variables involved in PCR. Besides, most existing research is cross-sectional research. Longitudinal research is not sufficient. Content of research: the existing research mainly focuses on the upbringing styles of parents, and the psychology and personality development of teenagers. But the research into the subjective initiative in PCR and socialization of teenagers is not available. Tools of research: the operation definitions of PCR in existing research are not exactly the same, and the evaluation methods and indicators are not the same. Then it is hard to compare the research results and obtain accordant conclusions.

### 5) Current Status of the Research into PCR Adjustment

In previous research, group training courses were used to improve PCR. Group training courses include the knowledge-based lecture of parent-child communication, team counseling, psychological dramas and games, parent forum, group counseling of parents, etc. To sum up, explicit and useful methods are taught to parents and parents learn how to communicate with children, etc. The existing parent-child education mode are mainly skill training.

Brock and Coufal summarized some frequently used training courses, including Parent Effectiveness Training, Systematic Training for Effective Parenting, Parent-child Relationship Enhancement, Parent Adolescent Relationship Development, Behavioral Program and Elective Programs. They summarized five major training aspects from such mainstream training courses: i) communication skills, focusing on expression and listening, which is the major content of ordinary parent-child education courses; ii) environment design skills: environment is used to avoid conflicts in parent-child communication; for example, arranging quiet environment for child to conduct learning; iii) changing the child, i.e., parents learn the skills of solving behavioral problems of children and the skills to discipline children's behaviors; iv) change parents, i.e., parents change themselves in the training courses; and v) changing family, i.e., learn to solve family problems via family meeting and problem-shooting procedures.

There are many empirical researches based on such courses. It has obvious effect in short term, according to the research into the influence of parent training on resistance behavior of child, especially for children with disobedient and destructive behaviors. We are also inspired by the research of Webster-Stratton to some extent. He conducted PCR training through video, which has been proved that it has instant and long-term effect on parent-child interaction and behavior modification of children and that its effects can last for more than one year.

### 6) Evaluation on Existing Research into PCR Adjustment

Most researchers accept and agree that PCR effectively facilitates parent-child communication, and improve parent-child harmony. Research showed that parent-child training is effective in improving traits of children and their psychological *suzhi*. Parent-child training is applied to many fields. For example, Estrada et al. Believe that family training (parent training) is significantly necessary for children with emotional and behavioral disorders. Parent-child training, according to the literature, is used mostly for the family with problems. The training methods are usually simple and effective. Compared with other therapies (like medication etc.), parent-child training is relatively a natural method that is easier to learn. Although educationists and psychologists improved the methods of PCR adjustment in many aspects, there are still disadvantages, for instance, i) they focus more on the role of parents, but neglect the role of child in the communication. The existing training mainly focus on disciplining children's behaviors. Most parent training courses focus on treating or changing children's behaviors, for example, learning, disobedience, bad temper or emotional control, etc., but neglect attentions and needs of children. Parent-child education become unidirectional behavior due to lacking of children's opinions, thus it is difficult to deal with problems of bidirectional or interacting parent-child communication. ii) Research into PCR is based on children or family with problems. Attention should also be paid to more extensive students. iii) The trainings are conducted to groups; for example, lectures for parents or children, which requires sufficient time of parents. Thus in some experiments of PCR training, subject loss is a big problem. PCR is necessary for the deepening and development of the research since it is very significant to the development of children, especially teenagers. And the research into such problem should be from new perspectives and through new methods with the emerging of new problems and requirements. Therefore, the future research should make use of the existing research results and stick to bidirectional principles of parents and children, in order to theoretically meet the development of the times, new research angles and fields of students' psychological *suzhi*. Both theoretically and practically, it is necessary to probe into the methods of computer aided PST.

## Conception and Hypothesis of the Present Research

Based on theoretical research, aims to,this chapter prove that CAT effectively improves students' psychological *suzhi* through experiment method. It is divided into several aspects: i) as the main content of the software ,determining PCR based on literature analysis and survey; PCR draws extensive attention of middle school students and is very important for their development; ii) investigating the current status of PCR among middle school students through questionnaires, summarizing the general characteristics of PCR; iii) the content of training is presented in the form of script based on PCR and designing principles of PSE software, and then the systematic software is developed in the form of multimedia; and iv) PST is conducted by using software to replace teachers and the experimental effects is analyzed based on data analysis and interview.

Basic hypotheses include:

Hypothesis 1: the complexity of psychological *suzhi* and PSE lead to the diversity of PSE mode. Conducting PSE in school by using modern teaching methods is reality-based and theoretically supported.

Hypothesis 2: PSE software based on multimedia techniques improves the effects of PSE in school.

Hypothesis 3: the PSE software improves PCR and psychological *suzhi* of parent-child communication.

# CURRENT STATUS OF PCR AND DEVELOPMENT OF EDUCATION SOFTWARE

## Survey and Analysis of PCR among Junior Grade Two Students

We surveyed the current status of PCR among junior grade two students from two middle schools in Chongqing, in order to provide factual reference for the content of education software and understand the PCR of the subjects. In total, 103 students were surveyed, including 43 boys and 60 girls. PCRT was used in the survey. PCRT was established by Shinagawa Fujiro, the honorary professor of the University of Tokyo and member of Tanaka Education Institute, and revised by Zhou et al., the psychologist professor from East China Normal University. The scale is consisted of two parts, i.e., "assessment of parents' disciplining attitude" and "assessment of the characteristic of children's problems".

### Table 8.1. PCR Types and Corresponding Behaviors

| PCR Types | Corresponding Behaviors |
|---|---|
| Negative refusal: | Parents pay no attention, ignore, indulge the opinions of children; disinterest, distrust children; have poor relationship with children; disagree with children, etc. |
| Positive refusal: | Parents conduct corporal punishment, mistreatment, intimidation, hypercriticism to children, or abdicate the responsibilities to bring up children. |
| Strictness: | Parents love children, but parents have stubborn, impellent attitude, or supervise children by the means of forbidding and order. |
| Anticipation: | Parents put their ambition or hope on their children but neglect their talent, capacity and aptitude. Parents hope children completely comply with the requirements or standard of parents. |
| Intervention: | Parents take good care of children and provide as many assistances and instructions for better development of children. |
| Anxiety: | Parents are unnecessarily worried and upset about the daily life, school work, health, friendship, future etc, thus parents are excessively responsible and provide too much help and protection for children. |
| Conformism: | Children have all powers. Parents accept all demands of children no matter how much efforts they take. |
| Indulgence: | Parents unconditionally accept the demands, requests and opinions of children. They love children too much and take every effort to satisfy the demands of children. Even children do something wrong, parents defend for them. |
| Conflict: | Parents have different attitudes towards the same behavior of children. Sometimes, parents forbid or criticize children for a behavior, but sometimes, they forgive or encourage the same behavior. |
| Disagreement: | Father and mother have different disciplining attitudes towards children. For example, father is strict with children, but mother indulges children. When father criticize children, mother stops father from doing so; when father decides how to discipline children, mother has different opinions. |

For the first part, five PCRs are included (they are all not wanted by parents), i.e., refusal, domination, protection, obedience, conflict and disagreement. Percentage is provided based on national norm by the scale to present the degree of the five PCRs. Such five PCRs are further divided into two types, each type with 10 items. Thus the scale has 100 test items.

Such 10 PCRs are translated into 10 dimensions of the scale, the meanings of which are as follows:

For the second part, the characteristic of child's problems is classified into seven types: antisocial problems; asocial problems; problems of self-assessment, interest and will; retrogression; neuroticism, neuropathic traits, neurosis; living habits; learning capacity, ability. The higher scores of such dimensions indicate more serious problems of children. Such scale is used to conduct additional analysis of PCR of students to provide reference for our research. The scale has good reliability and validity. It is a psychometric tool of PCR. The analysis results are as follows:

### *Descriptive Statistics*

Descriptive statistics was done for the two scales. The percent rank was translated according to the PCRT. The highest percent rank is 99, and the lowest is 0. The higher the percent rank is, the better. The percent rank of 50 is the dividing line. The percent rank of 50 indicates normal situation; 40-20 indicates the worse; and below 20 indicates the worst. The percent rank is shown in the following table:

### Table 8.2. General Scores of Different PCRT Dimensions (n=103)

|  | (M±SD) | Percent Rank |
|---|---|---|
| Negative refusal | 13.56±2.73 | 33-51 |
| Positive refusal | 15.03±3.17 | 49-69 |
| Strictness | 12.39±3.53 | 32-54 |
| Anticipation | 9.24±3.19 | 5-7 |
| Intervention | 9.20±3.10 | 5 |
| Anxiety | 5.73±2.73 | 4 |
| Indulgence | 10.83±3.33 | 3-4 |
| Conformism | 15.04±3.33 | 31-49 |
| Conflict | 11.84±3.34 | 5-10 |
| Disagreement | 14.14±3.22 | 17-31 |

The result showed that the scores of PCR dimensions of the surveyed junior grade two students were low. Most of the percent ranks of PCR dimensions were below 50, the average level, especially for indulgence, anxiety, intervention and anticipation types. The percent ranks of negative refusal, positive refusal and conformism types were relatively better.

### Table 8.3. General Scores of Different Dimensions Concerning the Characteristics of Children (N=103)

|  | Antisocial problems | Asocial problems | Self-assessment | Retrogression |
|---|---|---|---|---|
| M±SD | 8.14±9.86 | 8.66±6.40 | 8.61±7.72 | 2.57±3.02 |
|  | Neuroticism | Living habits | Learning capacity, ability |  |
| M±SD | 9.56±6.53 | 7.63±6.64 | 5.46±4.09 |  |

Table 8.3. indicates that attention should be paid to neuroticism with priority, and then to non-social problems and to self-assessment. Retrogression is the least serious problem among the surveyed children. But the relatively high standard deviation proves indirectly that some children have serious problems in retrogression due to their high scores.

### Significance Test of Difference

The interacting test of data (gender × location of family) showed that no significant interaction effect existed. The main effects of gender and location of family are significant. Therefore, in the following we will test which dimension shows significant difference in terms of gender and location of family among junior grade two students.

Significance test of gender difference. We used independent sample t test to conduct significance test of gender difference among all student samples. The results are:

### Table 8.4 Significance Test of Gender Difference in PCR

| | Negative refusal (M±SD) | Positive refusal (M±SD) | Strictness (M±SD) | Anticipation (M±SD) |
|---|---|---|---|---|
| Male (43) | 13.76±2.44 | 15.16±2.75 | 12.60±2.81 | 8.69±3.75 |
| Female (60) | 13.31±2.94 | 14.73±3.37 | 12.10±3.29 | 9.48±3.09 |
| t | 0.820 | 0.687 | 0.814 | -1.161 |
| | Intervention (M±SD) | Anxiety (M±SD) | Indulgence (M±SD) | Conformism (M±SD) |
| Male (43) | 9.16±3.67 | 5.41±3.11 | 10.60±3.29 | 14.34±3.22 |
| Female (60) | 9.21±3.02 | 5.76±2.48 | 11.13±3.58 | 15.60±2.96 |
| t | -0.082 | 0.630 | -0.763 | -2.035* |
| | Conflict (M±SD) | Disagreement (M±SD) | Total scores (M±SD) | |
| Male (43) | 11.00±2.98 | 14.44±3.02 | 115.20±17.06 | |
| Female (60) | 12.16±3.29 | 14.03±3.32 | 117.55±16.23 | |
| t | -1.843 | 0.638 | -0.706 | |

*$p<0.05$, ** $p<0.01$, ***$p<0.001$, the same below.

Table 8.4. shows that except the conformism type, the gender difference in other dimensions was not as significant as the statistics. However, female usually has lower average scores than male. It indicates that male is worse than female in PCR and has more serious problems. The gender difference in children's characteristics is as follows:

Table 8.5. shows significant gender difference in asocial, retrogression and neuroticism dimensions. No significant difference is As seen in other dimensions. Male usually has lower average scores than female, which indicates that male has less serious mental problems than female, and attention should be paid to maintain psychological health of female.

### Significance Test of Difference in Location of Family

Location of family is possibly an important variable affecting PCR. Therefore, we carried out independent sample t- test to understand how the location of family influences PCR and personality traits. The results are:

**Table 8.5. Significance Test of Gender Difference in Children's Characteristics**

|  | Antisocial problems(M±SD) | asocial problems(M±SD) | Self-assessment (M±SD) | Retrogression (M±SD) |
|---|---|---|---|---|
| Male (43) | 8.09±9.17 | 7.06±4.43 | 7.25±5.35 | 1.61±2.61 |
| Female (60) | 7.78±9.96 | 9.90±7.37 | 9.61±9.10 | 3.26±3.16 |
| t | 0.161 | 2.422* | -1.520 | -2.821** |
|  | Neuroticism (M±SD) | Living habits (M±SD) | Learning capacity (M±SD) | |
| Male (43) | 7.69±4.82 | 6.93±5.35 | 5.02±3.70 | |
| Female (60) | 10.95±7.28 | 7.68±6.99 | 5.61±4.39 | |
| t | -2.553* | -0.592 | -0.720 | |

**Table 8.6. Significance Test of PCR Difference in Location of Family**

|  | Negative refusal (M±SD) | Positive refusal (M±SD) | Strictness (M±SD) | Anticipation (M±SD) |
|---|---|---|---|---|
| Rural area (49) | 14.18±2.42 | 15.40±2.99 | 12.53±3.02 | 9.08±2.81 |
| City (54) | 12.88±2.89 | 14.46±3.19 | 12.11±3.17 | 9.22±3.86 |
| t | 2.447** | 1.545 | 0.685 | -0.209 |
|  | Intervention (M±SD) | Anxiety (M±SD) | Indulgence (M±SD) | Conformism (M±SD) |
| Rural area (49) | 8.83±2.64 | 5.14±2.13 | 10.24±3.32 | 15.30±2.89 |
| City (54) | 9.51±3.78 | 6.05±3.17 | 11.51±3.50 | 14.87±3.33 |
| t | -1.051 | -1.726 | -1.888 | 0.705 |
|  | Conflict (M±SD) | Disagreement (M±SD) | Total scores (M±SD) | |
| Rural area (49) | 12.06±3.21 | 15.04±2.86 | 117.88±16.14 | |
| City (54) | 11.33±3.18 | 13.44±3.31 | 115.42±17.29 | |
| t | 1.153 | 2.604* | 0.732 | |

**Table 8.7. Significance Test of Different Characteristics of Children with Different Locations of Family**

|  | Antisocial problems (M±SD) | asocial problems (M±SD) | Self-assessment (M±SD) | Retrogression (M±SD) |
|---|---|---|---|---|
| Rural area (49) | 5.42±4.39 | 8.28±6.20 | 6.75±5.48 | 2.08±2.68 |
| City (54) | 10.16±12.20 | 9.11±6.69 | 10.33±9.18 | 3.01±3.30 |
| t | -2.570* | -0.647 | -2.370* | -1.569 |
|  | Neuroticism (M±SD) | Living habits (M±SD) | Learning capacity (M±SD) | |
| Rural area (49) | 8.91±6.11 | 4.79±3.72 | 4.30±2.41 | |
| City (54) | 10.20±6.91 | 9.70±7.29 | 6.33±5.03 | |
| t | -0.995 | -4.358*** | -2.643** | |

Table 8.6. shows significant difference between rural and city students in dimensions of negative refusal and disagreement. Significant difference is not found in other dimensions. It indicates that although PCR problems are of universality, students with different locations of family have different severity of PCR problems.

The difference characteristics of children with different locations of family are as follows:

Table 8.7. shows significant difference in dimensions of antisocial problems, living habits and learning capacity among students with different locations of family. And urban students had worse problems than rural students. It shows that rural students were better than urban students in forming personality traits, especially in living habits and learning capacity.

## Correlation Between PCR and Characteristics of Children

As mentioned above, the formation of PCR is not unidirectional. The characteristics of children affects PCR to a large extent. We will probe into PCR and the characteristics of children to study the relationship between the two.

According to Table 8.8., the dimensions of PCR significantly correlate with many aspects of personality traits. In particular, antisocial problems and self-assessment aspects are significantly correlated to most dimensions of PCR. But the survey by Liu and Meng showed no significant correlation between characteristics of children and PCR. Our research showed that significant difference is As seen between the PCR dimensions, for example, negative refusal, positive refusal and strictness, and the characteristics of children.

It means the characteristics of children and PCR mutually influence each other. But anxiety is not significantly correlated to the characteristics of children, indicating that poor PCR under this dimension had the least connection with the characteristics of children. Besides, most correlation coefficients are negative, which means the more serious the problems are, the poorer the PCR, or the vice versa. The possible reason is that the upbringing styles of parents and PCR influence the formation of personality traits of children, or the personality traits of children make parents out of patience and thus use negative upbringing styles.

## Influences of Academic Performance on PCR

Academic performance is an important variable affecting PCR. Research showed that the most frequent and severe parent-child conflicts are from academic performance, daily life and housework. Thus we conducted difference test to students with different academic performance. Academic performance is classified into good, average and poor according to normal distribution. We used the academic performance of students from two junior grade two classes of the experimental school in the test, because two middle schools use different standard to measure their academic performance and we pay more attention to the students from the experimental school. In total 62 students participated in the test, including 30 male students and 32 female students. The test results are shown in Table 8.9. The analysis showed that students with good academic performance had higher scores on PCR than students with poor academic performance, while no significant difference is observed between the students with average academic and students with good academic and no significant difference between students with average academic performance and students with poor academic performance. But the data of each dimension show that the scores of PCR questionnaire reduced as the academic performance reduced. It indicates that students have poorer PCR if they have worse academic performance.

**Table 8.8. Correlation between PCR and Characteristics of Children (n=103)**

|  | Anti-social problems | asocial problems | Self-assess-ment | Retro-gression | Neuroti-cism | Living habits | Learn-ing capacity, ability |
|---|---|---|---|---|---|---|---|
| Negative refusal | -0.245* | -0.308** | -0.272** | -0.253* | -0.189* | -0.266** | -0.327*** |
| Positive refusal | -0.422** | -0.367** | -0.487*** | -0.350*** | -0.234** | -0.407*** | -0.401*** |
| Strictness | -0.316** | -0.367*** | -0.444*** | -0.265** | -0.259** | -0.313** | -0.309** |
| Anticipa-tion | -0.212* | -0.052 | -0.215* | -0.174 | -0.125 | -0.284** | -0.267** |
| Interven-tion | -0.211* | -0.153 | -0.260** | -0.243* | -0.183 | -0.223* | -0.147 |
| Anxiety | -0.099 | 0.015 | -0.078 | -0.088 | 0.041 | -0.090 | -0.052 |
| Indulgence | 0.078 | 0.108 | 0.212* | 0.002 | -0.050 | 0.139 | 0.098 |
| Conform-ism | -0.073 | 0.170 | 0.049 | -0.128 | 0.077 | -0.122 | -0.041 |
| Conflict | -0.278* | -0.122 | -0.219* | -0.174 | -0.074 | -0.239* | -0.180 |
| Disagree-ment | -0.238* | -0.178 | -0.192 | -0.172 | -0.050 | -0.194* | -0.104 |

### *Exploration Into the Current Status of PCR Among Junior Grade Two Students*

The survey aims to probe into the current status of PCR among junior grade two students, especially students from the experimental school. Thus the samples are junior grade two students from the experimental school or from school with similar conditions. Although it is not sufficient to describe the PCR of junior grade two students by sampling, the general PCR of students at this grade can be concluded from junior grade two students from the experimental school. The followings are analysis and discussions of the survey.

*Total average scores.* The scores of the surveyed students were below average, especially for indulgence, anxiety and intervention types. The research by Wu et al. showed that over 80% teenager families have one or more PCR problems; poor PCR is very common, especially for anticipation, indulgence and anxiety types; which correspond with our survey. This situation is caused by many factors. First, parents do not have relevant psychological knowledge. In particular, they can not understand the demand of teenagers for independence; they excessively intervene in the behaviors of teenagers, which is the major cause of intervention type PCR. Second, since most families only have one child, parents naturally put all their hopes and love on the only child of the family. It is the major cause of common anticipation and indulgence types of PCR. Thirdly, the situations children face now are different from what parents faced at their childhood, resulting in that parents are not experienced enough to educate their children. This explains why parents and children are anxious. From the perspective of characteristics of children, attention should be paid to neuroticism with priority, and then to asocial problems. Neuroticism in the scale refers to neuropathic traits, neurologic symptom. Asocial behaviors refer to loneliness, no participation in group activities, over-cautious, suspiciousness, cowardice, taciturnity, depression, inactiveness, the lack of puerility, inadaptation to people, don't know how to communicate with people. In the period of junior grade two, dramatic psychological and physiological changes happen on students, and students can not handle the changes in learning and physiologically, thus they may use the method that is close to neuroticism to deal with such situations. It may cause asocial problems, including avoidance of communication and depression.

*Significance of gender difference.* Except the conformism type, the gender difference in other dimensions was not statistically significant. But most scores of male are low. Shi, Zhang and Huang also probed into the relationship between parents and female and male students. They found that PCR of junior middle school students was affected by the gender of offspring and parental generation, and their interaction effect. The difference is not significant if only considering the gender of offspring. The research by Liu and Meng (1997) also mentioned that except certain dimensions, the gender difference in other dimensions is not significant and male students have more obvious problems in poor PCR than female students. It corresponds with our survey. The significant difference in conformism is possibly caused by that parents may value the male child only (especially in rural area). Parents tend to satisfy the demands of male child. Significant gender difference is As seen from the questionnaire of the characteristics of children in asocial, retrogression and neuroticism dimensions. In the period of junior middle school, male students have accepted some concepts of the society. They need to shoulder many responsibilities and obligations. They are more mature in interpersonal relationship than female. This is possibly why male students had lower scores than female students in asocial problems. Retrogression refers to infant temperament, whining, peculiarity, effeminacy. It is easy to understand why male students had significantly lower scores than female students because such traits are accepted by the society as female traits, but excluded as male traits. Female students had higher scores than male students in neuroticism. It is because female students are more sensitive than male students in nature. Female students pay more attention to their inner world.

*Different locations of family.* Significant difference is As seen between rural and urban students in dimensions of negative refusal and disagreement. For the dimension of negative refusal, rural students have significantly higher scores than city students. It is possibly because the sampling city is located at the joint of rural and urban districts. Parents in this area usually run their own business. They rarely spend time staying with children. Busy life makes them nervous, thus they are rude in dealing with problems of children. For the same reason, parents can have insufficient communication, which may lead to conflicts between parents and children. In scale of characteristics of children, significant difference is As seen between rural students and city students in antisociality, living habits and learning capacity. And urban students have more serious problems than rural students. It shows that rural students are better than city students in forming personality traits, especially in living habits and learning capacity.

Significant difference among students with different academic performance. Significant difference is As seen among students with different academic performance in the dimensions of negative refusal, intervention and total scores. Students with good academic performance had higher scores than those with poor academic performance. No significant difference is As seen between students with average academic performance and students with good/poor academic performance. It indicates that students have poorer PCR if they have worse academic performance. Although education for all-round development is advocated, students still face pressure from examination. Thus most parents attach great importance to academic performance. If children have good academic performance, they will have more attention and love from parents. Love can act as the "lubricant" which facilitates PCR.

**Table 8.9. Significance Test of PCR Dimensions among Students with Different Academic performance**

|  | Negative refusal (M±SD) | Positive refusal (M±SD) | Strictness (M±SD) |
|---|---|---|---|
| Good Academic Performance (11) | 14.27±2.49 | 16.00±2.89 | 13.45±3.32 |
| Average Academic Performance (40) | 13.15±2.39 | 14.37±3.07 | 12.12±2.90 |
| Poor Academic Performance (11) | 11.36±3.61 | 14.09±4.15 | 11.45±3.44 |
| F | 3.413* | 1.245 | 1.245 |
|  | Anticipation (M±SD) | Intervention (M±SD) | Anxiety (M±SD) |
| Good Academic Performance (11) | 10.81±2.99 | 12.18±2.22 | 7.09±4.65 |
| Average Academic Performance (40) | 9.62±3.82 | 9.27±3.82 | 6.35±2.83 |
| Poor Academic Performance (11) | 7.54±3.26 | 7.91±2.87 | 4.63±2.57 |
| F | 2.377 | 4.570* | 1.805 |
|  | Indulgence (M±SD) | Conformism (M±SD) | Conflict (M±SD) |
| Good Academic Performance (11) | 11.81±3.42 | 13.81±3.94 | 12.36±4.05 |
| Average Academic Performance (40) | 11.25±3.69 | 15.07±3.13 | 12.02±2.86 |
| Poor Academic Performance (11) | 10.72±4.22 | 14.00±4.35 | 10.00±3.71 |
| F | 0.233 | 0.789 | 1.931 |
|  | Disagreement (M±SD) | Total scores (M±SD) |  |
| Good Academic Performance (11) | 15.45±2.84 | 127.27±11.55 |  |
| Average Academic Performance (40) | 13.17±3.28 | 116.42±16.60 |  |
| Poor Academic Performance (11) | 12.72±3.40 | 104.45±16.29 |  |
| F | 2.527 | 5.740** |  |

## Developing PSE Software for PCR

Theoretical exploration proves that computer aided PSE software is applicable. We propose a new means to improve PCR due to the importance of PCR, namely, computer aided PCR education. Computer aided PCR education refers to the process of comprehensively processing and controlling symbols, languages, characters, sound, figures, pictures, videos and multimedia information through computer; organically combining the training contents of parent-child communication suitable for students at certain ages and presenting such contents through the screen, in order to improve parent-child communication capacity and further to improve relevant psychological *suzhi*.

### 1) Process of Development

The development of system software usually starts from determining the content of the program, and includes software design, design of system functions, synthesis and evaluation. Continuous adjustment and improvement should be conducted in this process, and then the intention of development can be achieved by the software and the effect of the software can be good.

**Table 8.10. Main Contents of Computer Aided PCR Training Software**

| Curriculum Topics | Purposes of the Training |
|---|---|
| Understanding of physiological and psychological characteristics of parents and self | Maintaining the sensitivity to one's own and parents' emotions is an important aspect to keep good PCR. The training aims to make students understand the characteristics of people at one's age and parents' age. |
| Maintaining daily communication | Positive communication is an important factor facilitating the improvement of PCR. The training aims to activate the desire of communication, learn skills of communication, design activities together, improve the closeness, and to learn to praise and criticize at home and cope with praise and criticism at home. |
| Removal of generation gap | Different concepts and behavioral styles between parents and children are important causes of unharmonious PCR. The common generation gap in daily life is listed and analyzed in the training. Students are guided to learn how to correctly deal with conflicts with parents. |
| Understanding in each other's position | An important interpersonal skill is thinking from someone else's perspective. Conflict between parents and children is mostly caused by failure to understand each other. The training aims to make students cognize and deal with the problems from the perspective of parents, in order to understand parents' way of doing things from heart. |
| Share the sweet and bitter together | A precondition of good communication is to understand the bitter of each other. The training aims to make students and parents feel the difficulties and happiness of each other by giving some special examples, for example the economic difficulty of the family, and by recalling the hardship of parents. |
| Treatment of special parent-child conflicts | In most of the time, communication is obstructed by lacking of skills to deal with conflicts. The training aims to teach students necessary communicating skills and strategies (for example, transferring the focus of conflicts, delaying the resolving of conflicts, etc) to improve parent-child communication capacity. |

*Choosing and determining the contents of teaching.* First, from the perspective of theoretical research, the research absorbs the contents of traditional PST courses. Multimedia is used in the training courses to improve the parent-child communication capacity of children and make students obtain certain interpersonal skills. The whole system was designed and developed based on certain psychological principles, PSE principles and the actual situations of students. Parents and children must understand each other first in order to improve PCR; then they communicate effectively and learn skills of communication, so as to improve the interpersonal skills by changes of cognition and behaviors, and finally to improve the psychological *suzhi* of communication. This is the overall design. The basic contents were determined upon literature analysis and interview with some students, as shown in Table 8.10:

The content of different themes generally starts with the situation to stimulate students' interest or resonance; then analysis is made, in order to make students acquire necessary common sense and skills of communication from perspective of cognition; finally, instructions are given from the perspective of behaviors, in order to make students acquire the skills and methods of parent-child communication. The application is demonstrated with the first lesson as an example (see Table 8.11.).

We organized expert counseling panel (20 experts) to review the contents and methods of presentation (the counseling questionnaire is for the contents chosen and the methods of presentation of the first lesson). We found that 90% experts agreed to the contents we chose, which indicates that the contents mentioned were basically identified by the experts. We also adjusted and modified the contents based on the comments and suggestions of the experts. And finally we determined the basic contents and methods of presentation of the education software.

### *Design Of PCR Education Software*

Software design is a complicated process. Many factors need to be considered in the process, for example, what contents should be included in the software, what targets students are expected to realize, and what strategies are used, etc. We use one lesson of the software as an example to analyze the software design.

*Purpose of software design.* Under the new situations, the relationships between human and society, human and the nature, human and human are very complicated. People should learn to understand the environment in order to understand the world and change the environment. One important standard to measure the mental health of students is whether they adapt to learning, living, interpersonal communication and physical changes. Junior middle school students are in the period of rapid and unstable physical and psychological development. Their mental activities change fast. They are of high plasticity. PCR in this period is relatively tense. Thus we believe that computer aided PCR software helps students overcome the problems in communication with parents, helps them overcome the obstacles and difficulties in development and promotes positive adaptation and initiative development. For example, in the lesson of "How to communicate with parents in daily life", the teaching aims to help students with how to effectively communicate with parents. It is essentially to teach them how to adapt to the changes and realize better development.

*Analysis of students.* To realize the purposes, any teaching activity must meet the psychological development of students and its characteristics; and follow the principles of psychological development. This is extremely important for PSE. The purpose of PSE activities and good effects can be realized only through the coherence between subjective and objective factors. Thus the purpose, contents, forms and methods of PSE should meet the age characteristics of students. The contents and focus of education should be determined based on the level and characteristics of psychological *suzhi*. We discussed the current status of parent-child communication in the PCR section, based on which we determined the contents and forms of presentation. In the lesson "How to communicate with parents in daily life", we knew that students did not have good PCR. They had serious problems in communication. Parents intervened too much and children did not express themselves sufficiently. Based on this situation, we designed the course to teach students how to express their emotions through verbal and nonverbal exposition, especially for discontent, etc.

**Table 8.11. Illustration of the Presentation of Contents,
Theme and Purpose of Teaching**

|  | Means and Contents of Presentation | Themes | Purpose |
|---|---|---|---|
| Situation-based experience | A conflict in parent-child communication is presented through flash. It is close to life. | Impulse (quarrel with parents easily) and rebelling (parents always restraint children's behaviors) easily occur in communicating with parents. | To cause resonance and psychological identification. |
| Reflection | Text questions in shown. Sound is available too. | Did you encounter similar situations?<br><br>How did you deal with it? | To provide a reflection platform for students, and realize real emotional experience. |
| Knowledge imparting | Cases are shown in the forms of text, verbal means. The narration is paused at critical points. | The physiological characteristics during the adolescence, for example high sensitivity and imbalance. The characteristics of parents. | To use vivid methods to make students realize that some of their behaviors are featured by age. |
| Feedback and reflection | Text, sound and cartoon. | Ask reflectional questions based on the case and ask students to write down their thoughts. | To internalize what they learned into their behavioral styles. |

*Psychological strategies for the software.* Zhang et al. found that the formation process of psychological *suzhi* is: self-understanding, knowledge learning, behavioral direction, reflection and internalization, and development of habits into nature. The process of PSE should be based on this process. Therefore, it is a standard to arrange the contents in the design of PSE software. It is worth pointing out that multimedia should be used to simulate a certain reality-based situation. Some PSE strategies are embedded in the situation, including i) harmonious interaction strategy: harmonious interaction between human and computer. Thus the software should ensure the exchange and communications between students and the computer. It is neither the rigid presentation of computers, nor the aimless reflection of students; instead, it should be the harmonious interaction guided by the computer and dominated by students. For example, this strategy was used in the lesson "How to communicate with parents in daily life" to introduce students in the theme. The question "did you encounter any of the following situations" on the screen makes students involved in the interaction. ii) Behavior change strategies, which include: first, self-management strategy, i.e., the software guides students to realize the target of behavior change through self-control and self-management in proper means. The principles, means, methods and techniques of behavior change are taught to students. Students are asked to establish, implement and modify their self-management plans. Second, behavior practice strategy; i.e., students master the methods to change behaviors through simulation and practice. The software provides simulated situations. Students can master the right way of act in the simulation. Thirdly, strategy of correcting misconduct; i.e., the software guides students to understand what misconduct is and analyze the specific causes of misconduct; the software prompts and instructs the measures to correct misconducts, and then the students work out reasonable correction plan and adjust and modify the correction plan in the implementation. iii) Strategy of experience and internalization. This requires the software provides enough time for reflection and experience of students. The experience of students should not be interfered by other contents. Independent communication with the software should be possible, without interference by other students. This can be realized by initiative interaction by students with the software. This strategy is usually used for the internalization and experience of students in learning.

### Designing the Functions of PSE Software System

Notes for designing PSE Software. After the contents of the software have been determined, the means of presentation, how to arrange and combine the contents of the software, what basic principles to follow, and what techniques to use should be determined. First, attention should be paid to the following. i) the purpose of design should be clear. ii) The contents of training and the organization structure should be properly arranged. For example, reasonable quantity of information and contents should be arranged for each page. Audio-visual materials, pictures and text materials that students are familiar with should be used. iii) Techniques of aesthetic value should be used to arouse the aesthetic emotions of students, persistent learning activities, etc. Second, interaction between students and the software should be guaranteed. Interaction promotes learning in the following aspects: i) information is guaranteed to be received, and attention is paid to the critical information of the software. CAT tools, different from speech, audio and other forms of multimedia, require users to response successively in order to control the teaching. ii) response is encouraged to strengthen cognitive connections and the memory of response. When students think about and response to a question, such thinking or response itself provides a certain hint for the students in future thinking and responses. iii) It facilitates success. For computer aided software, the implementation of software is promoted by practice of students, which reflects the interaction of CAT tools. With experience, we know that "learning in activities" is a good method of PST, which greatly improves the initiative and sense of participation.

Strategy of media presentation of PSE software. Even with very good design, the attractiveness of the software can only be measured when the development is finished. Thus design techniques and paying attention to some necessary matters is the short cut for successful software. Therefore, proper strategy of media presentation must be used to complete the development of computer aided software, in addition to using psychological *suzhi* theories as the instruction. To sum up, simple presentation should be used to effectively present the contents of PSE. The operation should be simple and convenient. Media optimization of multimedia software is special graphic arts, because when many forms of multimedia are on the same screen, orderly connection and interacting switch are involved, and such forms of media are used to present diversified contents of teaching. Attentions should be paid to the following aspects: Screen Design: the design should meet the characteristics of students' perception and attention, and also the requirements of teaching. The design should consider how to motivate students and facilitate effective communication.

The following can be realized in the design: i) screen is pleasing to the eye, reasonable layout; ii) Concise text, highlighted focus. The expression should be specific and understandable for the public. Abstract or obscure text should be avoided. The fonts and sizes of the characters should be as eye-catching and reasonable as possible. iii) The colors of the characters and background should be reasonable. The favorable colors are eye-catching, easy-to-use and not making eyes tired after long time. The settings of the text should not be complicated. iv) Frame, color and other means are used to highlight important information. v) One opinion is presented at one time. One opinion is expressed by one or two sentences. vi) Cartoon should be arranged reasonably. Cartoon should not be disordered, or garish.

*Interaction Design*: the advantage of CAT tools is that it can interact with an individual. In particular, communication and interaction with students are required for PSE software. The design can consider the following: Students should be able to control the process or sufficient time should be provided for students, as different students need different duration of time to accept information and for reflection. ii) Avoid meaningless waiting when cartoon is showed.

The buttons should be vivid, interesting, and of unified styles. iv) Help information should be clear and prompts should be timely. v) The operation should be as simple as possible.

## Two Principles for the Development

The design of functions should be guided by certain ideologies, thus two principles should be followed in the development:

Harmony principle. The software should not be developed roughly; instead all parts should be harmonious and the software should be aesthetic. First, the screen should be aesthetic and harmonious. The color should be harmoniously arranged, not being too bright or too dark. Second, the sound effect should be proper. The sound effect used should fit the corresponding screen and demonstration and should be played and stopped at proper moment. The unharmonious demonstration should not happen to draw the attention of students, for instance, the screen stops while the music is still on.

Easy to operate. The final purpose of the software is to convey the purpose of design, i.e., to improve the psychological *suzhi* of students, rather than to highlight the functions of the software or the capacity of development. Too many functions may cause disorder of the screen or make the user at a loss.

## Evaluation of the Software

The effect of PST is normally not instant, because it requires a process of internalization and accumulation. Thus only summative evaluation is not enough to evaluate PST course. Formative evaluation is more proper for PST course.

The formative evaluation of PSE software. First, rationality of the purpose: the rationality of teaching purpose directly influences the effect of teaching. The purpose of the software is to express corresponding contents of teaching. The purpose of PSE software is the same as the purpose of PSE course, but expressed through different means and forms. The rationality is reflected by the following aspects: i) whether the software meets the purpose of PSE; ii) whether the software is in accordance with the level, principles and characteristics of psychological development of students; and iii) the appropriateness of the scope of teaching purpose. If the teaching purpose is large and all-inclusive, then there is no focus for students' learning, which will surely result in adverse effect.

Figure 8.1. Screen from "How to Communicate with Parents in Daily Life".

Figure 8.2. Screen from "How to Communicate with Parents in Daily Life".

Second, appropriateness of the theme. There should be appropriate theme of training to ensure the effect of PSE. An appropriate theme of training must be appropriate for i) students, i.e., the theme must take into consideration the special characteristics of students; ii) time, i.e., the design of PSE course must be appropriate for the time, because a certain situation always occurs at certain time; iii) place, i.e., the design must consider the influence of place on psychological development; and iv) times, i.e., the theme of PSE should meet the development of the times, be familiar to and cared by students and should integrate with the topics students are interested in. Only by doing this, the effect of PSE can be ensured.

Thirdly, participation of students. The guiding principle of PSE course is student-based and to promote the development of their psychological *suzhi*. Students are the subject of PSE, thus students' initiative should be fully played in PSE to realize their participation in the learning of PSE software. Students should be guided to fully internalize what they learned into their traits through psychological experience. The process of PSE we designed optimizes the psychological experience of students in education, which contributes to the effects of PSE software.

Fourthly, comprehensiveness of the process. It is reflected by i) whether the education is based on the understanding of the level and principles of psychological development of students; ii) whether the software can carry out proper and targeted education strategies in accordance with the psychological characteristics of students and their mental problems; iii) whether the comprehensive development of students in cognition, emotion, will and action is realized; and iv) whether the software is based on the overall psychological development of students and whether it always considers students as a developing integrated individual.

Finally, the effectiveness of strategies. The strategies used by PSE software to improve psychological *suzhi* include interaction strategy, behavior change strategy, strategy of experience and internalization, strategy of teaching monitoring, etc. Whether such strategies are effective can not be neglected to evaluate the effect and results of the software.

*The summative evaluation of PSE software.* It includes qualitative and quantitative aspects. From the quantitative perspective, psychological test is conducted to understand the changes of psychological *suzhi* before and after the PSE and to evaluate the effects of PSE course on the development of psychological *suzhi*. From the qualitative perspective, two activities will be conducted: first, analyze and evaluate the introspection of students, for example, evaluate the changes of students' psychological *suzhi* through their experience of learning and weekly diaries; second, evaluate the changes of students' behaviors after the PSE course. Follow-up evaluation and delayed evaluation should be considered in the evaluation of the changes of psychological *suzhi*. The changes of psychological *suzhi* can be resulted from PSE, or the influence of environment and other factors. Thus the influence from many aspects should be considered in the evaluation.

## 2) Trial and Modification of PSE Software

We found that students basically accepted the software after the trial use of the software in a class of the Middle School Attached to Yunnan Normal University, upon observation and analysis. From the perspective of the content and form of the software, 90.2% students believed the software was helpful; 90.1% students believed that computer aided PSE (including software only, and the teaching based on teachers and the software) was better than PSE only by teachers; 5.9% students believed that the content of the software was outdated; 5.9% believed the form of presentation was rigid; 15.7% students believed that the connection was poor. For the forms of presentation, 9% students were not satisfied with the character design, 7.8% were not satisfied with the background music. Generally speaking, the software is acceptable for students, which proves that it can be a popular and new means to improve psychological *suzhi*, thus further exploration and discussion are necessary.

Students put forward some suggestions for improving the software. Most of them are concerning with the forms and means of presentation. Some believed that the cartoon was too simple and the background music was too boring and the cartoon characters were too rigid.

We modified the software based on their comments and suggestions, in order to make the software better adapt to their characteristics and arouse their interest in learning.

## EXPLORATION OF IMPROVING PARENT-CHILD RELATIONSHIP BY USING PSYCHOLOGICAL-*SUZHI*-EDUCATION SOFTWARE

### Educational Experiment of Improving PCR by Using PSE Software

#### *1) Purpose*

It aims to verify that computer aided PSE software effectively improves PCR, and to prove that CAT tools are applicable and effective as a means of PSE.

#### *2) Participants and Tools*

#### Participants

All participants were full-time junior grade two students. We chose two classes of junior grade two of Chongqing Beibei Experimental Middle School for the experiment. Participants were divided into experimental group (34 students) and control group (28 students).

#### Tools

The PCR education software for junior grade two students was used in the experiment. The software was developed based on PSE principles, the PCR characteristics of students as well as the age characteristics of junior grade two students. The presentation of the software was in the forms of multimedia, including vivid cartoon, beautiful music, nice pictures and timely illustration. Students can independently control the application of software. Inner experience and feelings of students and inspiring questions will be raised during the application of the software. Students can write down their thoughts and feelings of learning. The software stores the text wrote by students. Such text will serve as the evidence for future analysis and intervention of students' psychology.

#### *3) Experimental Variables*

Independent variable: computer aided PSE software

Dependent variables: PCR of students and corresponding changes of psychological *suzhi*.

Control variable: experimental group and control group were organized. The experimental group was organized to learn PCR education software. The control group was organized to learn other computer operation. In the experiment, the followings were realized:

Established the experimental group and the control group on a reasonable basis and made the two groups homogeneous as much as possible.

Controlled the factors affecting the experimental results, including double-blind method, in order to remove the expectation effect.

### 4) Experimental Treatment and Procedures

Pre-test and post-test of a single factor for both the experimental and control group were used. The procedures of the experiment are as follows: First, selected two classes from the experimental school and made either one the experimental group and control group, and then tested the two groups with PCRT scale and collected the data of the test.

#### Table 8.12. t-Test of Pre-test and Post-test for Both Groups

| Dimensions | Pre-Test | Post-Test | $T$ |
|---|---|---|---|
| Negative refusal | Experimental group 13.26±2.37 | Experimental group 13.47±2.17 | 0.442 |
| | Control group 12.75±3.18 | Control group 12.39±2.73 | -0.812 |
| | t 0.729 | t 1.726 | |
| Positive refusal | Experimental group 14.64±3.23 | Experimental group 14.91±2.85 | 0.446 |
| | Control group 14.57±3.37 | Control group 14.03±3.82 | -0.905 |
| | t 0.090 | t 1.032 | |
| Strictness | Experimental group 12.58±2.84 | Experimental group 13.85±3.31 | 2.177* |
| | Control group 11.82±3.36 | Control group 12.03±3.52 | 0.427 |
| | t 0.973 | t 2.089* | |
| Anticipation | Experimental group 9.67±3.37 | Experimental group 10.76±2.47 | 1.626 |
| | Control group 9.21±4.07 | Control group 10.00±4.16 | 1.422 |
| | t 0.489 | t 0.897 | |
| Intervention | Experimental group 9.08±3.38 | Experimental group 11.20±3.66 | 2.775** |
| | Control group 10.10±3.92 | Control group 10.50±3.51 | 0.751 |
| | t -1.097 | t 0.769 | |
| Anxiety | Experimental group 6.23±3.03 | Experimental group 8.52±2.14 | 3.475*** |
| | Control group 6.10±3.48 | Control group 7.67±3.18 | 2.807** |
| | t 0.155 | t 1.093 | |
| Indulgence | Experimental group 11.11±3.56 | Experimental group 11.73±4.32 | 0.689 |
| | Control group 11.42±3.91 | Control group 10.78±4.15 | -0.904 |
| | t -0.327 | t 0.875 | |
| Conformism | Experimental group 14.76±3.42 | Experimental group 15.91±3.87 | 1.315 |
| | Control group 14.53±3.65 | Control group 14.50±3.53 | 0.963 |
| | t 0.254 | t 1.484 | |
| Conflict | Experimental group 11.67±3.30 | Experimental group 12.08±3.33 | 0.572 |
| | Control group 11.78±3.34 | Control group 13.03±2.79 | 1.604 |
| | t -0.129 | t -1.197 | |
| Disagreement | Experimental group 13.52±3.75 | Experimental group 14.50±3.81 | 1.363 |
| | Control group 13.46±2.74 | Control group 13.03±3.04 | -0.703 |
| | t 0.076 | t 1.643 | |
| Total scores | Experimental group 116.58±16.94 | Experimental group 126.97±15.22 | 3.342** |
| | Control group 115.78±17.34 | Control group 116.58±18.78 | 0.332 |
| | t 0.184 | t 2.058* | |

Second, experiment intervention was conducted in the experimental group for six times by using the computer-aided PSE software for parent-child communication of junior middle school students. During the intervention, each student used one computer. Students from the experimental group learned PSE software in the computer class, and they can not be interfered by each other. The teacher did not provide unified directions for the whole group. Instead, students controlled their own learning for inspiration. Double-blind experiment was used to avoid expectation effect. The teacher of the computer class did not know the purpose of the course. Meanwhile, normal teaching of computer class with the same amount of teaching hours was conducted for the control group. Finally, PCRT was used to test the PCR of students after they finished the learning of all software. Post-test data were collected. Some students and their parents were interviewed after the intervention through computer aided PSE software was finished, in order to verify the effects of the software and students' attitude toward it.

### 5) *Results and Analysis*

Testing the results. In order to have a visual presentation of the post-test and pre-test results, t-test was conducted for the pre-test and post-test results of both groups. Independent sample t-test was conducted for both groups, and paired-sample t-test was conducted for pre-test and post-test. See Table 8.12. for the results:

No statistical difference was found on each dimension and total scores between the control group and experimental group in the pre-test, which shows that the two groups of samples were homogeneous. Further analysis shows that except the dimension of conflict, the scores of most dimensions of the experimental group were improved to some extent after the experiment. The post-test t test of both groups showed that although no significant difference is As seen, the mean difference of both groups was increased. Therefore, the experiment is effective. In addition, the total post-test scores of the experimental group was significantly higher than that of the control group, which indicates that the total scores of the experimental group in the post test of PCR scale was significantly higher than that of the control group. The correlated sample t-test of the pre-test and post-test of both groups showed that for the control group, only significant difference is As seen in anxiety, almost no change is As seen in the total scores; for the experimental group, except anxiety, significant difference is As seen in strictness, intervention and total scores. It shows that PCR software had obvious influence in improving strictness, intervention and anxiety PCRs.

Significance test of gain difference between the experimental and control groups. Independent sample t-test was conducted for the score difference between the pre-test and the post-test of both groups, according to the statistics test principle, i.e., independent sample t-test was conducted for the gain of the dimensions of the PCR scale between the two groups in this period . The results are:

Table 8.13. shows that although the gain difference of the PCR dimensions was not as significant as the statistics, in the general trend, the gains of the experimental group were basically positive and the control group had both negative and positive gains. It indicates that the experimental group was superior to the control group in terms of average gain. The significant difference in the total score gain of the experimental group shows that the software is effective in improving general PCR.

Independent sample t-test of the changes of personality traits. Independent sample t-test of the changes of personality traits between the pre-test and after the post-test is as follows:

Table 8.14. shows that no significant difference is found in the personality traits before and after the experiment. Some dimensions had higher scores while some have lower scores. It shows that the personality traits of students were relatively stable without interference; and that there was no casual relation between the change of personality traits and PCR improvement, instead they impact each other.

### Table 8.13. Independent Sample t-Test of Gain between the Experimental and Control Groups

|  | Negative refusal gain ($M\pm SD$) | Positive refusal gain ($M\pm SD$) | Strictness gain ($M\pm SD$) |
|---|---|---|---|
| Experimental Group (34) | 0.20±2.71 | -0.26±3.45 | 1.26±3.38 |
| Control Group (28) | -0.35±2.32 | 0.53±3.13 | 0.21±2.65 |
| $t$ | 0.865 | -0.946 | 1.33 |
|  | Anticipation gain ($M\pm SD$) | Intervention gain ($M\pm SD$) | Anxiety gain ($M\pm SD$) |
| Experimental Group (34) | 1.08±3.90 | 2.11±4.45 | 2.29±3.84 |
| Control Group (28) | 0.78±2.92 | 0.39±2.76 | 1.57±2.96 |
| $t$ | 0.339 | 1.785 | 0.814 |
|  | Indulgence gain ($M\pm SD$) | Conformism gain ($M\pm SD$) | Conflict gain ($M\pm SD$) |
| Experimental Group (34) | 0.61±5.22 | 1.14±5.08 | 0.41±4.20 |
| Control Group (28) | -0.64±3.76 | -0.03±4.05 | 1.25±4.12 |
| $t$ | 1.068 | 0.997 | -0.788 |
|  | Disagreement gain ($M\pm SD$) | Total score gain ($M\pm SD$) |  |
| Experimental Group (34) | 0.97±4.15 | 18.11±3.10 |  |
| Control Group (28) | -0.42±3.22 | 11.87±2.24 |  |
| $t$ | 1.457 | 2.050* |  |

In order to investigate whether students with different personality traits have equal progress after the PCR training, we divided the 34 participants of the experimental group into three sub-groups of high, average and low scores (students with scores above 73% are classified into high score sub-group, indicating serious problems; students with scores below 27% are classified into low score sub-group, indicating slight problems; the rest are classified into average score sub-group) according to the characteristics of students' problems .

One-factor analysis of variance shows no significant difference among the three sub-groups, which indicates the software is equally effective to students with different personality traits.

*Evaluation by parents.* We interviewed parents for the changes of students during the PCR training, in order to further verify the experiment effects, which can serve as an external criterion of experimental results. We used questionnaire survey to investigate the performance of students at home without informing parents of the experiment. We selected 10 students at random for parent survey. Seven parents believed "children seems to be less temperish recently"; six parents believed that "children are more initiative to communicate with me recently"; six parents believed that "children seems to understand my hardship recently"; nine parents believed that "children prefer to discussing with me about things happened in school recently"; seven parents believed that "children can understand my feelings better recently". To sum up, most parents felt the changes of children. In addition, some parents said in the interview that minor changes were going through the children recently. Therefore, we assume the software can better improve PCR if the time for experiment is longer.

**Table 8.14. Independent Sample t-Test of Gain between the Experimental and Control Groups**

| | Change difference of antisocial problems (M±SD) | Change difference of unsocial problems (M±SD) | Change difference of self-assessment (M±SD) | Change difference of retrogress-sion (M±SD) |
|---|---|---|---|---|
| Experimental Group (34) | -2.18±7.29 | -0.66±5.72 | -1.03±5.11 | 0.15±1.92 |
| Control group (28) | 0.39±6.67 | -0.85±5.53 | -1.25±5.36 | -0.10±2.40 |
| T | -1.438 | 0.132 | 0.163 | 0.466 |
| | Change difference of neuroticism (M±SD) | Change difference of living habits (M±SD) | Change difference of learning capacity (M±SD) | |
| Experimental Group (34) | -3.15±6.08 | -1.87±4.27 | -1.78±3.35 | |
| Control group (28) | -2.21±5.21 | -2.00±5.78 | -0.96±3.20 | |
| t | -0.640 | 0.094 | -0.976 | |

*Analysis of some Qsand As in the experiment.* One of the advantages of the software is the interaction between students and the computer. Through the feelings and experience wrote down by students in software learning, we can effectively analyze their current PCR and the effects of learning. We analyzed some of the QandAs as follows, in order to better understand students and to prove the experimental results indirectly:

*The attitude of parents towards children.* Some of the questions designed in the software are related to the attitude of parents towards children. We analyzed the following questions indicating the most prominent parent-child conflicts, in order to have a better understanding of the current PCR and the causes of current PCR.

Question 1: How do your parents treat you normally?

A. They trust me and provide me with certain help.

B. They do not help me in anything; they do not trust me; they criticize and punish me when I do something wrong.

C. When I say I need free space for myself, they say yes and are willing to help me, but sometimes they do not trust me 100%.

Answers: five students chose A, 21 chose B and seven chose C. Chi-square test of the number of students choosing different answers showed significant difference, i.e., $\chi^2$ (2, N=33)=13.818, $p<0.001$. In indicates that direct intervention was used by most parents in dealing with the freedom of children.

Analysis: it reflects the current situation of some families. Parents do not have sufficient confidence in their children. They tend to punish the children instead of helping children find out why children do something wrong. Since there are more and more only children in China, parents pay more and more attention to children. When such attention exceeds the limit children are willing to withstand, children may resist. Such resistance can possibly result in more discontentment of children. In this question, such situation is translated into that parents do not trust them at all; and that parents punish them instead of helping them to correct mistakes. Insufficient respect of parents to children's freedom (at least from the perspective of children) is possibly a cause of poor PCR.

Question 2: How do you feel about parents' expectations for you?

A. I feel OK; their expectations do not impose excessive mental burden on me.

B. Their expectations are beyond my capacity; I can not handle with it sometimes.

C. Their expectations are below my capacity; it seems they never had any requirement on me.

Answers: 17 students chose A, 11 chose B and three chose C (some students were absent in the training and some did not answer the questions, thus the number of students answering the questions are different). Chi-square test of the number of students choosing different answers showed significant difference, i.e., $\chi^2$ (2, N=31)=9.548, $p<0.01$. It indicates parents normally have too high expectations on children.

Analysis: parents fully realize the importance of knowledge as it becomes a knowledge-based society. Thus some parents designed the future of the children only based on their own expectations, rather than the actual capacity of students. Meng (1998) also mentioned the too high expectations of parents for children. The answers of the question shows that there was a high proportion of students who beieved their parents had too high expectations on them, which is an important cause of poor PCR. If children do not have correct coping under such pressure, the development of children can be impacted to some extent.

**The Attitudes of Children Towards Parents. Communication is a Two-Way Process. the Attitude of Children Towards Parents is Another Reason Affecting PCR. We will Briefly Analyze the Problem from the Most Prominent PCR Aspects.**

Question 1: under the following situations (the mother worry about the child for doing anything independently), what will you do?

A. I will take no notice of her worries and do what I want.

B. I will be perfunctory.

C. I will explain to her about my plan in detail, making her really trust me; I will also remind her in proper time that I have already grown up and I can handle with some issues.

Answers: five students chose A, 21 chose B and five chose C. Chi-square test of the number of students choosing different answers showed significant difference, i.e., $\chi^2$ (2, N=31)=16.516, $p<0.001$. It indicates students are perfunctory when they face such problems in life.

Analysis: with the growth of age, children have stronger and stronger desire for freedom, and they have stronger desire to prove in many aspects that they have grown up. Thus, they will resist the intervention from parents in many ways. The answers show that not many students can correctly deal with the conflicts with parents (explain to the mother). Most students are perfunctory, because parents will not be angry or interfere and they can still do what they like.

Question 2: When I am at home,
A. I seldom share the happiness of parents, because I think their happiness is not my business.
B. I am happy when parents are happy.
C. I am happy when they are happy, but I do not know how to express that I am happy.

Answers: five students chose A, 14 chose B and 15 chose C.Generally speaking,it shows that children are happy when parents succeed and are happy, but most students can not properly express their happiness.

Analysis: only when children and parents share the happiness of each other is the family cohesive and united. The answers of students show that although most students can experience the happiness of parents, a large proportion of students can not express such emotion. This might be caused by that parents seldom pay attention to affective communication of family members. This reminds us that affective communication and expression are important factors contributing to PCR improvement.

**What do students gain from the software? We analyze one question concerning the self-exploration and reflection of students at random from the software.**

Question: How do you feel through the veil (the demonstration of parents' thinking)?

Answers: the answers are summarized as follows, according to the occurrence number of answers (a students can have two or more answers):
From the perspective of reflection, seven students mentioned that (they did not understand parents) they "felt ashamed", "overdid", etc after the learning.
From the perspective of understanding parents, 10 students mentioned that they understood the difficulties and hardships of parents, for example, "I know they are in a difficult position", "they have given much thought to the matter", etc. Six students experience the love of parents, i.e., "Now I understand they love me from the bottom of heart although they never said it". As many as 25 students said they understood the heart of parents, for example, "I understand their heart, and I don't have a grudge against them", "I think I understood their heart", etc.
From the perspective of problem solving, 20 students said they learned how to deal with the following problems in the future. For example, "I should be considerate of parents, then

we can get along with each other harmoniously and live happily everyday", "I will not quarrel with them", "I will repay them with my actions", "I had similar experience; he said I was wrong every time when he was wrong, I did not understand, but now I know how to deal with it" "what they did is all for my own good; they just hoped that I listened to them; I will try my best to understand them in the future", etc.

About 32 students answered the question. If one opinion can only be presented in the narration of one students and one student can have more than one opinion, 21.88% students reflected their shortcomings in the past; 31.25% students better understood the difficulties and hardship of parents; 18.75% students further felt the love of parents; 78.12% students better understood the heart of parents; 62.5% students learned how to deal with similar situations in the future.

Analysis: the above data show that the software can promote better understanding of parents for students and their better relationship with parents. The software presents some problems students might encounter in daily life, which initate the memory and thinking of students. This provides an opportunity for students to deeply analyze themselves and understand parents, based on what they thought and did in the past, and the knowledge and contents presented by the software. The question makes students to have more extensive thinking and to make them think about problems and conflicts in the position of parents, which will facilitate PCR improvement.


## Case Study after the Experiment

We interviewed some students with low total scores of PCRT survey, according to the contents of PSE software, in order to further verify the experiment effects, supplement the mentioned research and clarify the experimental results. As agreed by students, teachers made brief records in the interview and told students not to worry about because the recording is completely confidential. The interview of one case should be done independently. The following is the case of a participant surnamed Li (female, only child).

The junior grade two student surnamed Li, female, participated in the PCR test before the software learning. The scores are: 9.00 for negative refusal, 10.00 for positive refusal, 6.00 for strictness, 9.00 for anticipation, 6.00 for intervention, 6.00 for anxiety, 18.00 for indulgence, 16.00 for conformism, 11.00 for conflict and 8.00 for disagreement. The total scores are 99. The scores of this student in dimensions are relatively low compared with the national norm.

The communication with her before the experiment showed that she believed her parents had intervened in her a lot, which can be proved by the scores of the test (6 points). She knew it was not good, but she did not know how to deal with it, which indicates that she needs certain guidance and suggestions.

We tested this student with the same test after the PSE software learning. The scores are: 14.00 for negative refusal, 13.00 for positive refusal, 6.00 for strictness, 11.00 for anticipation, 7.00 for intervention, 7.00 for anxiety, 18.00 for indulgence, 18.00 for conformism, 14.00 for conflict and 12.00 for disagreement. She had higher scores after the experiment although these are still not high scores. This can be proved by the interview after the experiment (see Appendix II).

Meanwhile, she wrote down her thoughts (see Appendix III) as follows:

"I always felt that parents do not sufficiently understand me. They even made things difficult for me some times. But I never gave consideration to them. I never thought of problems on their position. Recently, I learned a lot of knowledge about how to communicate with parents from the computer class... I felt a lot. To be honest, most conflicts were caused by my being capricious. I always requested parents to do things for me, to understand me, but I never did anything for them or understood them. ... After the computer class, I learned that many children of my age desire for freedom and want to escape from the restraint of parents. They want to have their own space. But we can not be capricious and do whatever we like. ... Anyway, we should communicate with parents for things we want to do and think on their position. We should know that they have heavier burden than us and more pressure. They also have feelings and need understanding and care from others. They are strict with us because they put all their hopes on us. "

Her changes can be proved by the interview with her father (see Appendix II).

Conclusions: the interviews with parents and students prove the investigation results. It indicates that the software influences parents and students to some extent and is helpful for parent-child communication in the future. There are many similar cases in the experiment. Therefore, computer aided PSE software is effective in improving PCR and this PSE training is applicable.

## Attribution Analysis of Experimental Results

The experimental group had higher scores in all dimensions and total scores after the experiment, except the dimension of conformism. The increase of average scores, statistically, can not prove the experimental results, but it indirectly showed that students had better PCR after the systematic learning for six times.

The comparison of pre-test and post-test of between the two groups showed the experimental results. In particular, obvious improvement is As seen in intervention PCR. This is possibly because parents were not aware of their intervention on children and children normally were not willing to or did not know how to express their thinking. The software highlights the communication between parents and children in many aspects, especially in some sensitive topics (for example, puppy love). Then parents realized their excessive intervention to children and did some adjustment.

The independent sample t-test of the results of pre-test and post-test for both groups showed significant difference in total scores. It shows that although no significant improvement is As seen in PCR dimensions, the improvement in total scores is significant; therefore, it can be predicted that if the duration of the experiment is long enough, the software will be more effective in PCR improvement.

No significant difference in the characteristics of children in the pre-test and post-test indirectly proves that the PCR education software was especially good for special content of education. It has certain internal validity.

The good effects of computer aided PSE software are due to that:

*The software design meets PSE requirements, and the requirements of students' development, which guarantees good experimental results.* Computer aided PSE software presents the knowledge suitable for the development of students through various means. It also infects and stimulates students through vivid combination of modes. It is more attractive for students than pure explanation by teachers, which is the precondition for deep feeling and reflection of students.

*The advantages of CAT tools are the conditions of successful experiment.* CAT tools well present the principles and strategies of PSE, and have unique advantages. For example, students tell their true thinking in the communication with computer; students control their learning; they have sufficient time for memory and reflection; individualized coaching is available, etc. However, all experiments, especially educational experiments, are affected by many variables, except independent factors, which influence the experimental results.

*The choosing of participants.* Choosing participants is a critical step of the experiment design. Whether participants are properly chosen attributes to the success of experiment to some extent. The participants were chosen from a narrow scope. Due to the restriction of time and other objective conditions, we chose the students from two classes of one school. The participants were not typical.

*Experimental environment.* The largest interfering factor in the research is experimental environment, although we have tried our best to control the interference of control variables. But some variables are uncontrollable. For example, games were available on the computer, and students could not completely resist the temptation of games, which caused students could not concentrated in class, and thus affected the experiment results.

*Variables of students.* Although we organized the experimental group for controlling the influence of age and other factors, some special situations were hard to control. For example, when it is coming to the end of the semester, the learning activities of students are intensive, which can influence PCR and thus indirectly influence the experiment results.

*Variables of software.* Although we had careful organization and design, faulty contents or media presentation may occur as it is an exploratory work, which also influences experiment results.

*Time factors.* As mentioned in the evaluation of PSE software, delay should be considered in the evaluation of PSE software. PSE is not instantly effective. Thus time also influences the experiment results.

*Unexpected factors.* In the experiment some students encountered serious family events; for example, divorce of parents. Such factors can not be controlled by the experimenter, but they influence experimental results.

# CONCLUSION

Computer aided PSE mode and the PSE software for PCR improvement are applicable and effective in improving PCR.

PCR software has obvious influence in improving the dimensions of strictness, intervention and anxiety in PCR. In particular, the improvement of the intervention dimension in PCR is the most obvious.

PSE software for improving PCR applies to students with different personality traits.

# APPENDIX

## Analysis of Example Lessons

| Curriculum contents | Analysis and comments |
|---|---|
| First of all, cartoon is used to introduce the topic of the lesson – how to communicate with parents<br><br>[Dialogues of the cartoon] I don't know why. It seems parents do not understand me suddenly. So I don't want to tell them anything. | It is to arouse the interest of students and make them concentrate on the software. It also clarifies the purpose of the lesson. |
| Did you encounter any of the following situations?<br>Did you encounter any of the following situations when communicating with parents?<br><br>1. It is difficult to get along with parents, because when I say yes, they say no, or the vice versa; | Harmonious interaction strategy is used. The dialogue between the characters is close to the life of students, in order to cause resonance. |
| 2. Be dramatically opposed to each other. When parents say one sentence, I will answer back; | List the frequent problems encountered by middle school students. |
| 3. Monologue, parents are talking and I orally agree but I am absent-minded and still persist in my old ways. | The voiceover guides students to think. |
| 4. Parents or I don't speak to each other. | The frequent problems of students will be presented vividly later. |
| I think if you are under such situations, you really want to change the situation and want to be friends with parents. This must be what you think. | Strategy of experience and internalization is used to arouse thinking. |
| [Section 1] Learn to abreact resentful emotions<br><br>Fengfeng likes football very much. After school, friends invited him to play football and he could not stop playing with friends. When he went home afterwards, | Analyze problems in the position of parents, and provide space for students to think about problems from the perspective of parents. This is the preconditions to understand parents. |
| Dad was angry, "all you know is playing!" | |
| "It is not true, I ..." He wanted to explain that it was weekend and friends invited him. But before he explained, mom said, "No excuse. If you don't learn well, in the future you will…" When he saw the angry face of mom, he did not say anything but only listened and lowered his head. But he felt something pressing his heart. It was very uncomfortable. | Behavior change strategy is used. Vivid methods are used to guide students about how to |
| Can you understand that? | |

1. Parents did not intend to scare you or make you depress. They just wanted to help you to form good learning habits.

2. When they were angry with you, they did not realize that it made you feel bad.

Such negative emotions are obstacles to communicate with parents. How to get rid of them?

First, when you feel depressed, do not force yourself to bear the emotion.

Some researchers said the psychology of people is like a balloon. In daily life, we fill this balloon with desires, impulsion, needs, etc. then this balloon grows. And at certain time, we feel very high pressure and feel that the balloon is about to explode. Proper, timely catharsis at proper place is very important to maintain mental health and balance.

Second, when you realize that you should not hide your discontentment, you should communicate with parents in proper means, instead of constraining your emotions.

1. When you are angry, you can release anger to a person of straw.

2. You can make an appointment with parents, and then you can tell parents your feelings and listen to theirs in a fixed time everyday or every week.

3. You can make solutions together with parents based on the actual situations, in order to avoid parents acting arbitrarily in the future under similar situations and to avoid your making the same mistakes.

4. Put a notebook at a proper place. Then you and parents can write down the suggestions or anything else on the notebook at any time.

Witty sentences:

There are many ways to release emotions, but some of them are not health and should not be used, because it may bring more serious consequences and can not release the emotions.

Thus students should learn how to effectively adjust emotions.

handle with their negative emotions, in order that they can effectively deal with similar problems in the future.

Point out the theme of this paragraph and make students impressive.

Finally is behavioral direction; for example, tell students how to deal with problems in reality.

The function of the following sections is the same as the previous one. We will not repeat. Connect the four sections by media technology, to realize gradual and smooth learning. We add contents that arouse reflection of students, in order that students really internalize what they learned.

1. Verbal suggestions: speech has magic effects on human's psychology and emotions. People can be amused or depressed by a few sentences.

2. Diverting attention: you should effectively control your emotion. Some suggest that when you are angry, you can turn your tongue in your mouth, to avoid impulsion and saying the words you should not say. You can have a try.

3. Cleaning: when you feel worried, you can do some cleaning. It is proved that bath/shower helps to improve emotions. Thus you can take a bath/shower when you are in a bad mood. You will be happy again.

[Section 2] The art of verbal communication at home

[Learn to praise others at home]

Everyone hopes to be praised and so do parents. They will be happier to be praised by children.

"Mom, the dishes you cooked are the most delicious I have ever had."

"Dad, you are kindly. You are barely angry with me."

Did you praise parents before? Have a try. You can obtain extraordinary effects from the praise.

[Learn to admit mistakes to parents]

Everyone makes mistakes. We should not find excuses for our mistakes. If we admit mistakes bravely, parents will forgive and help us.

"Mom, I am sorry, I should have told you that I played outside. I should not have made you worried."

"Dad, I am sorry. You work so hard. I should have learned well and should not have made you worried about me."

Of course, you should put what you said into action. You should prove with actions that you really realized your mistakes. Then parents trust you.

[learn to express euphemistically]

Which of the following ways of expression is better?

"You know nothing in this age and time!"

"Mom, Dad, something nowadays are really different from that at your time."

No matter how great the conflict is with parents, both you and parents hope to solve it. Thus the most important thing in communication with parents is respecting them.

"You just want to force me to do what I don't like!"

"I know you ask me to do this for my own good, but I have different opinions…"

What is the difference between the two ways of expression?

You will have unexpected gain if you think about the situation in the position of others. Parents will be less angry if you think from their perspective; and it is easier for them to think from your perspective.

Think about it: What do you think of your communication with parents:

A. Very good. We exchange opinions together when we have time.

B. We barely communicate.

C. Between A and B.

Do you have any good idea about communicating with parents?

———————————————

[Section 3] The art of non-verbal communication at home

[Learn to communicate in a different tone]

Sometimes to realize the purpose of communication, it is not about what you say, but about how you say it? Let's keep learning.

Try to communicate with different tones.

"Mom, I just want to play football for a while. I will finish the homework." You say it in a positive tone to remove her worries.

"Mom, I just want to play football for a while. I will finish the homework." You say it in a gruff and impatient tone. Smart person know to use proper attitude and tones to express their demands.

Question: It you want to go to a party in the weekend, how do you say to your parents? You can practice with different tones.

[Learn to communicate in a different expression]

For the same sentence, different tones results in different effects. What about expressions?
Let's have a look at the following sentence by two different people:

A sincerely says with smiles while looking at Mom, "Mom, I want to relax this weekend."

B says the same sentence to Mom while looking at the TV and showing indifference.

If you were the Mom, which request will you say yes?

Recall the situations: How did you look like when you answered back your parents? Did you knit your brows, stretch your neck and look unconvinced? Does it help to solve the problem?

If you are angry next time, I suggest you looking at yourself through the mirror. (practice an angry face, a indifferent face, and a rebellious face)

Witty sentence: You should pay attention to non-verbal communication when you have great or small conflicts with parents. You can improve the communication effects and PCR if you are strict with yourself and your deeds accord with words.

Our suggestions:

You can discuss with parents about what should be paid attention to in communication. You and your parents can invent a gesture to point out the mistakes of each other or stop each other from making mistakes.

Did you notice such non-verbal communication? What do you think of it? _____

[Section 4] Are you ready to communicate with parents?

[Communication needs sufficient time]

Maybe your parents are busy from work, or you spend most of your time at home in study. But you should remember that communication with parents needs sufficient time.

What do you usually do when you and your parents are at home? Do you watch TV together? And what is the last time when you communicated?

Turn off the TV and play with parents just like when you were younger. Do you still remember the comic books you read together with Mom? Do you remember how your Dad taught you to make the paper boat? Do you remember the song you three sang together?

Say "goodbye" to TV and find some time to communicate with parents.

[The content of communication should be extensive]

The communication with parents should cover a wide range. For example:

1. You can work out the daily schedule together with parents (for example, time to get up, have dinner, do homework, watch TV, rest, do housework and go to sleep), and then strictly implement the schedule.

2. You can do housework together with parents; meanwhile you can exchange your opinions and their suggestions about some issues. You can tell them your opinions too.

3. You can invite parents to chat with you, and talk about your learning and life in school.

4. Say "Mom/Dad, I love you", say "Good night"

What prevents you from communicating with parents?

———————————

Here is a sentence for you:

Only by opening your heart, you can be frank with others. Parents are also your friends.

# REFERENCES

Bai, L. Y., and Ye, Y. T. (2002) Overview of parent-child relationship to children's development research. *Journal of Ningbo University (educational science edition), 2,* 45-49.

Blustein, D. L., Prezioso, *M.* S., and Schultheiss, D. P. (1995). Attachment theory and career development: Current status and future directions. *Counseling psychologist, 23,* 416-432.

Chen, X. (2004). Exposition the process of school mental quality education. *Journal of Southwest China Normal University, 30,* 32-37.

Chen, X., and Zhang, D. J. (2002). An exploration on integrated mode of mental health education. *Educational research, 1,* 71-75.

Christensen, H., and Griffiths, K. *M.* (2002). The prevention of depression using the Internet. *Medical Journal of Australia, 177,* 122-125.

Collins, W. A., and Russell, G. (1991). Mother-child and father-child relationships in middle childhood and adolescence: A developmental analysis. *Developmental review, 11,* 99-136.

Dolezal-Wood, S., Belar, C. D., and Snibbe, J. (1998). A comparison of computer-assisted psychotherapy and cognitive-behaviour therapy in groups. *Journal of clinical psychology in medical settings, 5,* 103-115.

Du, X. Y. (2001). Computer-aided instruction and foster the innovation ability of students. *Open education research, 2,* 45-51.

Du, Z. H. (2003). Evolution of teacher capability structure in the information age. *Information technology education, 3,* 31.

Eliza. A friend you could never have before. Retrieved from http://www-ai.ijs.si/eliza/eliza.html.

Estrada, A. U., and Pinsof, W. *M.* (1995). The effectiveness of family therapies for selected behavioral disorders of childhood. *Journal of marital and family therapy, 21,* 403.

Fang, C., and Fang, X. Y. (2003). Research of parents - youth communication. *Advances in psychological science, 11,* 65-72.

Fang, X. Y., Zhang, J., and Liu, Z. (2003). The characteristics of parent-child conflict in adolescent. *Psychological development and education, 1,* 46.

Fang, X. Y., Zhang. J. T., Sun, L., and Liu, Z. (2003). Parent-adolescent conflict and adolescents' social adjustment. *Chinese journal of applied psychology, 9* (4), 14-21.

Feng, Z. Z., and Zhang, D. J. (2001). The study of the concept and composition of middle school students mental quality. *Journal of Southwest China Normal University, 27,* 56-61.

Gehring, T. *M.*, Wentzel, K. P., Feldman, S. R., and Wiersn, *M.* (1990). Conflict in families of adolescents: The impact of cohesion and power structures. *Journal of family psychology, 3,* 290-309.

Guo, W. B., Yao, S. Q., and Cai, T. S. (2002). Computer-assisted psychological tests in clinical application advance. *Foreign medical psychiatry, 29* (3), 190-192.

Hou, Z. J. (2004). Family influence on youth people's career development. *Psychological development and education, 3,* 90-95.

Hu, L. *F*. (1998). Compare the role of student interaction, student-teacher interaction and parent-child interaction in the educational process. *Youth studies, 5*, 5-7.

Kazdin, A. E., and Wassell, G. (2000). Therapeutic changes in children, parents and families resulting from treatment of children with conduct problems. *Journal of the American Academy of Child and Adolescent Psychiatry, 39*, 414-420.

Lei, L., Wang, Z. Y., and Li, H. L. (2001) Parent-child relationship and parent-child communication. *Journal of education research, 6*, 49-53.

Li, A. M. (2002). Guiding ideology of computer-aided instruction (CAI). *Journal of Xinjiang Normal University, 21*, 73-76.

Li, Q., and Meng, Y. Q. (2001). What factors of child trait influent parent-child relationship. *Jiangxi education and research, 8*, 20-23.

Li, Q., and Meng, Y. Q. (2003). An Experiment of adaptation to parent-child relationship and cultivate children's, "filial and independent". *Education science, 19, 56-61*.

Li, X. D., Nie, Y. Y., and Lin, C. D. (2003). The effects of learning difficulty, interpersonal relationship and self-acceptance on eighth grader's mental health. *Psychological development and education, 2*, 68-73.

Liu, H., and Zhang, D. J. (2004). Discuss the requirements of teachers' quality on mental quality education. *Hebei Normal University Journal (educational science edition), 1*, 57.

Liu, J. *M*. and Meng, S. Q. (1997). The related survey research of junior high school parent-child relationship and personality characters. *Psychological science, 20*, 459-467.

Liu, R. D. (1997). *Selection and evaluation of teaching software*. Beijing: Posts and Telecom Press.

Meng, Y. Q. (1998). *Research on parent-child relationship of juvenile*. Beijing: Education Science Press.

Nelson, G., Laurendeau, *M*. C., and Chamberland, C. (2001). A review of programs to promote family wellness and prevent the maltreatment of children. *Canadian journal of behavioural science, Ottawa, 33* (1), 1-13.

Nie, G., and Han, J. J. (2005). study of multimedia courseware design pattern. *Education exploration, 1*, 65-67.

Paikoff, R. L., and Brooks-Gunn, J. (1991). Do parent-child relationships change during puberty? *Psychological bulletin*, 110, 47-66.

Roe, A. (1957). Early determinants of vocational choice. *Journal of counseling psychology, 4*, 212-217.

Schuhmann, E. *M*., Foote, R. C., Eyberg, S. *M*., and Boggs, S. R. (1998). Efficacy of parent-child interaction therapy: Interim report of a randomized trial with short-term maintenance. *Journal of clinical child psychology, 27*, 34-45.

Schutz, Y. (1991). On the relationship between adolescents and parents (L. Dai, Trans.). *Research of Youth, 12*, 288-290.

Shen, *F*., and Zhang, Z. J. (2002). Psychological topics on the design of virtual environment and www. *Advances in psychological science, 10*, 315-321.

Shi, W., Zhang, J. *F*., and Huang, X. T. (2004). The research of parent-child relationship characteristics of junior high school students. *Psychology and behavior, 2* (1), 328-332.

Tang, L. P., and Feng, X. T. (2002). Youth research and evaluation of parent-child relationship. *Journal of Guangdong College of Young Cadres, 2*, 24-26.

Treichler, *F. R.* (1967). Reinforcer preference effects on probability learning by monkeys. *Journal of comparative and physiological psychology, 64,* 339-342.

Treutler, C. *M.,* and Epkins, C. C. (2003). Are discrepancies among child, mother, and father reports on children's behavior related to parents' psychological symptoms and aspects of parent--child relationships? *Journal of abnormal child psychology,* 2, 13-27.

Wang, J. Q. (2003). Information technology teaching methods and the student body principles. *Information technology education in primary and secondary, 11,* 20-22.

Wang, S. *M.,* and Zhang, D. J. (2003). Evaluation criteria of training courses on the psychological quality. *Hebei Normal University Journal (educational science edition), 5,* 54-58.

Wang, Z. Y., Lei, L., and Liu, H. Y. (2002). The relationship of family communication between parents and children development. *Advances of psychological science, 2,* 192-198.

Wang, Z. Y., Lei, L., and Liu, H. Y. (2004). parent-adolescent communication and adjustment: A comparative study. *Psychological science, 27* (5), 1056-1059.

Webster-Stratton, C. (1981). Modification of mothers' behaviors and attitudes through a videotape modeing group discussion program. *Behavior therapy, 12,* 634-642.

Wu, N. Y., and Zhang, D. Y. (2004). A Study on the correlation between parent-child relation and mental health level of teenagers. *Psychological science, 27,* 815.

Wu, N. Y., and Zhang, D. Y. (2004). A study on the correlation between parent-child relation and mental health level of teenagers. *Psychological science, 27,* 812-816.

Xiao, X. L., and Huang, S. Q. (2002). Misunderstanding of computer-aided teaching and countermeasures. *China audio-visual education, 11,* 46-47.

Ying, X. (2000). CAI and school psychological counseling. *Audio-visual education research, 11,* 50-52.

Yang, J. (2002). How do I look at computer-assisted instruction. *Modern distance education, 3,* 59-60.

Zhang, D. J. and Tian, L. (2003). On the psychological quality education in the design and implementation strategy. *Curriculum, teaching material and method, 6,* 66-70.

Zhang, D. J. (2002). Strengthening of school mental health education and improve the psychological quality of students. *Hebei Normal University Journal (educational science edition),4,* 17-23.

Zhang, D. J., and Guo, C. (2000). Explore the laws of teaching psychology, carry out psychological quality education research. *Journal of Southwest China Normal University, 26,* 104-111.

Zhang, D. J., and Zhao, L. X. (2002) Preliminary exploration on mental quality of primary education. *Journal of Xinzhou Teachers College, 17,* 56-61.

Zhang, K., Zhang, W. X., and Wang, L. P. (2002). Children's attitudes towards the issue of bullying. *Psychological science, 25,* 226-227.

Zhang, Q. *F.* (1998). The related research of psycho-social development of adolescent and their parental rearing styles. *Youth studies, 5,* 1-11.

Zhang, Q. *F.* (1998). The related research of psycho-social development of adolescent and their parental rearing styles. *Youth studies, 5,* 1-11.

Zhang, W. X. (2002). *Youth development psychology.* Jinan: Shandong People's Publishing House.

Zhao, X. Y., and Zhu, Y. (2002). Internet: As a new psychological research tool. *Advances in psychological science, 10,* 309-314.

Zheng, X. F. (1998). The creation of a virtuous mode of parent-child relationship. *Journal of social science, Hunan Normal University, 1,* 72.

Zhu, S. N. (2003). *Multi-media teaching and courseware creative.* Wuhan: Wuhan University of Technology Press.

Zhu, Z. X. (1989). *Psychology dictionary.* Beijing: Beijing Normal University Press.

In: Methods and Implementary Strategies on Cultivating ...       ISBN: 978-1-62417-979-2
Editors: Da-Jun Zhang, Jin-Liang Wang, and Lin Yu     © 2013 Nova Science Publishers, Inc.

*Chapter 9*

# DEVELOPMENT OF AND EXPERIMENTAL RESEARCH INTO PSE SOFTWARE AIMING TO IMPROVE TEACHER-STUDENT RELATIONSHIP

## *Shan-Yan Yin[1] and Da-Jun Zhang[2]*
[1] Tianjin Chinese Traditional Medicine University, China
[2]Center for Mental Health Education in Southwest University, China

## ABSTRACT

With the popularization of computer and the increasing interest of teenagers in computer, computer-assisted PSE has become the new means of PSE for teenagers. Promoting TSR development is one of the purposes of PSE in school. Therefore, in this chapter, we established computer-assisted PSE mode, developed PSE software promoting TSR based on PSE theory and multimedia technology; and carried out educational experiment by using the software. The experimental results showed that: (1) The experimental group had higher total scores and higher scores in factors of TSR after the experiment than that before the experiment; whereas there was no significant difference between pre-test and post-test scores of the control group in the total scores and factors of TSR ($p>0.05$). (2) The experimental intervention changed the attitude of teachers toward students and improved the closeness of students to teachers. (3) The bidirectional nature of TSR influences the improvement of conflict, support and satisfactory factors. (4) The experimental results were different between female and male students. There was a significant difference between pre-test and post-test scores in closeness for male students, i.e., after the experiment, male students had obviously closer relationship with teachers. There was significant difference between pre-test and post-test scores in satisfactory for female students, i.e., after the experiment, female students were obviously more satisfied with their relationship with teachers.

# INTRODUCTION

## Current Status of PSE Research

PSE and Basic Mode of PSE. Zhang et al. [2000] defined psychological *suzhi* as "the internalization of the experience and influence externally gained into stable, basic and derivative psychological traits that are closely related with human's social adaptation and creating behaviors, based on physiological conditions". Psychological-*suzhi* education (PSE) is to develop students' cognitive capacity and healthy personality and cultivate good social adaptability with scientific educational means in accordance with the principle of students' psychological adaptation and development. With the deepening of PSE research, researchers attached importance to the exploration of PSE modes. For example, Zhang and Li [2000] put forward CIP mode that completes cognitive structure (C), intensify intelligent training (I) and strengthen the development of personality traits. They believed that the PSE course focusing on developing learning strategies and learning quality, as well as the comprehensive training of learning strategies, subject intelligence, learning quality and development of psychological traits are effective means of optimizing psychological *suzhi* structure and promoting overall development of students' quality. Zhang [2001] proposed that an open education mode should be established for MHE of pupils and middle school students, including perceptual intuition focusing on perception, activity-based education mode that stimulates students to actively participate in activities, problem-solving mode that fully plays the role of agent of students, and mass education mode that integrates school education resources with community education resources. Guo and Chen [2001] put forward that China's MHE should follow the service principle (focusing on education modes while supplemented by medical mode), training principle (focusing on *suzhi* mode while supplemented by profession mode) and teaching principle (focusing on text mode and while supplemented by teaching mode). Shen [2002] put forward a MHE mode that advocates all-people, all-subject and whole-process participation. The mode requires high MHE capacity, high strategy quality in solving students' mental problems, rich knowledge in psychology and pedagogy of teachers. Chen and Zhang [2002] put forward an integrated mode of physiological-psychological-social-educational harmony. They believed that "the basic target of PSE is to facilitate active adaptation and initiative development of students; the basic contents of PSE are guiding students learn to study, learn to live together, learn to live and learn to be, and facilitating the development of intelligence, personality, sociality and creativity; the basic approaches of PSE include specific-problem-based training, subject teaching infiltration, consultation and counseling. Proper situations suitable for educational intervention should be created and effective educational strategies should be designed based on the five basic steps of the formation of psychological *suzhi* (self-understanding, knowledge-learning, behavioral direction, reflection and internalization, formation of psychological *suzhi*), in order to develop students' psychological *suzhi* in an all-around way and maintain mental health." The computer-assisted PSE mode we proposed is based on such integrated mode.

PSE implementation means and comments. At present, the means to implement PSE include: specific-problem-based training (SPT) of psychological *suzhi*, psychological consultation and counseling, and subject infiltration.

*SPT of psychological suzhi*. Through the means, based on the principles and characteristics of students' psychological *suzhi*, teachers choose the contents of psychological education that are suitable for students at certain ages, arrange certain training activities, make students fully experience and feel in the activities, in order to form and strengthen the psychological traits of students [Zhang and Zhao, 2002]. At present, most schools use this means to implement PSE, and certain effects are achieved. However, there are some restraints too. First, it has strict requirements on time and needs the support and participation of school leaders and teachers. Second, different contents of PST require different design, organization and control of teaching, which requires high competence of teachers and makes the activities more difficult and complicated. Thirdly, psychological *suzhi* is formed systematically, which requires systematic cultivation and training, but the SPT of psychological *suzhi* is hard to cover every aspect of PSE, which does not facilitate the improvement of psychological *suzhi* in all aspects. Thus PSE should cover all-around training and counseling of learning, life, interaction and activities. It is hard to improve the overall structure and function of psychological *suzhi* only through SPT of psychological *suzhi* [Chen, 2004].

*Psychological consultation and counseling and psychotherapy*. Through this means, the mental problems and contradiction of students can be solved specifically, and the mental health of students will be promoted. But there are also restraints. First, intervention is implemented normally after the occurrence of mental problems. It is passive education, rather than initiative cultivation of students' psychological *suzhi*, or preventive education of mental problems. Thus it is effective only on certain students rather than all students. Second, it is difficult to stick to the target orientation. In reality, the consultant and counselor are easily to swing among the development-oriented target, preventive targets and corrective targets. Third, it has high requirements on the professional knowledge and skills of the consultant and counselor. It is difficult to realize standardized consulting and counseling. It restricts the popularity of the consulting and counseling and the scope and degree of students' benefits.

*Subject infiltration*. It is the systematic combination of PSE and teaching of subject. It realizes the targets of PSE through natural ways. It imperceptibly influences the development of students' psychological *suzhi*. It has more educational benefits than SPT course. Besides, the trace of artificial training can be As seen in SPT course. It can realize PSE targets without increasing manpower, materials and time. It saves time and produces long lasting effects. Some Chinese researchers did theoretical and experimental research into subject infiltration [Chen, 1997; Wu, 1998; Zheng, 1999; Shen, 2001]. Subject infiltration is proved to be an effective means of PSE. But there are also many restraints in subject infiltration mode: first, it requires high professional competence of teachers. Teachers should not only have excellent competence of the subject, but also have professional psychological knowledge and professional skills in psychological training. Second, it requires high comprehensive quality of teachers. It is difficult for teachers to change their concepts. Infiltration of PSE in teaching of a subject is a new and systematic work. It needs to greatly change the concepts of teachers concerning education, students, quality and benefits. Thirdly, it is difficult to unify the target of PSE and the target of teaching of a subject. Forthly, it is difficult to explore and utilize the PSE resources from teaching of a subject. To sum up, there are restraints if only one means of PSE is used. Thus several means must be used to scientifically and effectively implement PSE. Single means of PSE should be avoided. Besides, psychological *suzhi* is a complicated, dynamic, isomorphic and self-organization system. The complexity and diversified components of psychological *suzhi* determine the diversified means to implement PSE. In addition, there are also shortcomings of PSE in school. For example, the PSE is predominated by school and the self-cultivation of students' psychological *suzhi* is neglected; PSE does not cover all students and is not a part of education for all-around development, due to inadequate PSE faculty and high professional competence of consultant and counselor required. The use of multimedia-based computer in PSE in school may change the current situation, improve the self-education capacity of students in PSE, promote the updating of the contents and forms of psychological counseling, broaden the space of psychological counseling and create conditions for coverage of PSE to all students.

## Application of Computer in PSE

Computer is extensively used in PSE field, which is reflected in the following two aspects:

*Computer-assisted psychological consultation.* Computer-assisted psychological consultation is to provide computer program of consultation for those with mental disorders to implement psychological consultation and correction. At present, most computer-assisted psychological consultation is realized through internet, also online psychological consultation (OPC). OPC refers to the individualized consultation provided by psychologists or consultants through the online consultation, specialist mailbox, specialist consultation and other means of contact on the psychological websites. The advantages of OPC include broadened time and space of psychological consultation, the atmosphere of equity, etc. The atmosphere of equity does not easily cause negative mentality of visitors. In other countries, OPC provides a new form of psychotherapy. Compared with traditional face-to-face therapy, OPC has different psychological effects and results. It brings more effective conveying and new forms of treatment. The first multimedia interactive program, Beating the Blues", was developed by Prudfoot et al. [2003], for treatment of anxiety and depression. By using multimedia technology, the program makes patients more active and initiative in participating in the treatment, including menu, suggestions, feedback and video case of patients. It can be used as a mode of real patients. In China, some specialized psychological websites were developed with the development of multimedia technology, including Qu Weijie Psychological School and New Youth Psychological Consultation Center. They are psychological websites with relatively large scale and various functions. Those websites explain some frequent questions and provide psychological tests. For example, Qu Weijie Psychological School provides Cattell's psychological tests, etc.; New Youth Psychological Consultation Center provides personality assessment inventory, etc. But generally speaking, China's psychological websites have simpler contents, limited functions and poor running conditions.

*Computer-assisted psychological training.* In addition to controlling the process of research, processing and analyzing data, and simulating psychological process, computer can also be used as the tool for psychological training. In particular, it facilitates knowledge and skill acquiring of children and adolescents, and promotes the psychological improvement of children. At present, computer-assisted software for all-around-development education is available in the market; for example, the "education for all-around development for pupils" software developed by Nanjing Xianfeng Education Software Company, and "Developing students' *suzhi*" developed by Shenzhen Yuanhang Software Company, etc. Song [2002] designed and developed computer-assisted system software for education for all-around-development education, based on modern educational technology, under the theoretical guidance of psychology and computer science. The system includes self-dependent and self-discipline modular (to improve students' capacity of self-management and self-discipline), learning management modular (to improve students' consciousness of learning and capacity to properly arrange life and learning), modular of games for the brain (to develop students' intelligence, improve students' creativity and observation capacity, etc. through games), modular of computer skill training (improve the basic computer skills of students), Internet access modular (broaden the vision of students and enrich their extra-curricular knowledge), in order to improve students' creativity and capacities of self-management, self-discipline and independent thinking. Although such software was not specially developed for PSE, we can borrow ideas from it for developing PSE software, as PSE is part of education for all-around development. Researchers have developed system software especially for PSE. Wu [2000] developed PSE system for college and universities. It can be released through the Internet and the campus website, which enables students from college and universities and other users to access to it at any time and any place. It integrates learning, measurement, training and consultation. It is a solid educational system. The system uses psychological course CAI, analysis of typical cases, application of classical film and TV works and other means to impart psychological knowledge; uses psychometrics and questionnaires to survey the mental state and mental health of users; answer the questions of users through psychological consultation; and improves the psychological *suzhi* of users through psychological training and psychological games. A series of psychological training templates were established for users; psychological games were developed to test the insufficient *suzhi* of participants and to improve the insufficient *suzhi*. In addition, the *Huizhitong Psychological Quality Education System* developed by Wang [2002] included two parts, psychological test and psychological training. Psychological test can be carried out through questionnaire or human-machine dialogue. Human-machine dialogue operates as: the system raises the testing question, students choose the answers, and then the system provides individualized diagnosis and description of the state of psychological *suzhi* development of each student; then prescriptive suggestions and methods of training are provided automatically for students to complete the psychological training. The above research shows that researchers have started to pay attention to PSE through multimedia-based computer. But there are still shortages of the available PSE software, for example, psychological test occupies a large proportion of the software. But psychological test is not education. Although the software also includes psychological training, the training is only about imparting of psychological knowledge, or the explanation of psychological cases, or some knowledge-based suggestions. Generally speaking, users are in the position of passive receiver. It does not accord with the user focus and participation principles of PSE. At present, most computer-based psychological training is only for a certain psychological trait, including, attention training, memory training, cognitive strategy training and the training of learning interest, will and habit, etc. The trainings are specially designed for a certain psychological trait respectively. The special design, diversified screens and various forms of human-machine communication makes students master learning methods, improve metacognitive capacity and form good learning habits through interesting games. For example, the exploratory CAI mode uses computer as the cognitive tool. Under this mode, students establish plans independently and carry out experiment and exploration of certain math problems, in order to improve students' self-monitoring capacity of learning. The experiment has proved that this mode effectively improved the self-monitoring capacity of math learning of middle school students. Miao and Chen carried out reflection training among students from primary grade three by making use of computer-assisted teaching software of two-step word problems for pupils. They added reflectional questions and suggestions in the original software to guide and train the reflection process of students, in order to improve the reflection capacity of students. To sum up, psychological training through computer is applicable. But at present, most of such trainings are limited to cognition. The training of interpersonal relationship is not common. Traditional training of interpersonal relationship is in the forms of specific-problem-based training (SPT), psychological consultationand counseling. SPT of interpersonal relationship effectively improves the capacity of students in interpersonal relationship. But due to limited training hours, students acquire limited knowledge and skills and the interpersonal situations in the training are not good. Psychological consultation and counseling are usually carried out especially for students with problems in interpersonal relationship. But most students also need directions because they are confused sometimes, although they do not have serious problems in interpersonal relationship. Computer-assisted training of interpersonal relationship compensates the deficiencies of traditional training. Thus we will explore the new area of computer-assisted psychological training from this aspect.

## Research into and Comments of Teacher-Student Relationship and Intervention of Teacher-Student Relationship

The psychological research into teacher-student relationship (TSR) mainly focuses on the value of TSR to the development of teenagers, factors affecting TSR and the interventional research into TSR improvement.

*TSR and the development of teenagers.* TSR is an important factor affecting the development of teenagers, including the adaptation and development of teenagers, in particular, emotional adaptation, learning process, behavioral development and interpersonal relationship. Dong and Chen [2001] surveyed 1,640 Chinese teenagers and found that TSR closely correlates with the development of teenagers. The correlation even exceeds the correlation between PCR and the development of teenagers. Liu pointed out in the 1990s in the TSR research that earlier research emphasized on the tool value of TSR. The earlier researchers believed that TSR had the following functions: i) socialized function (promoting the formation of students' social ideology and social competence); ii) individualized function (promoting the development of personality); iii) choice-oriented function (students are distributed to proper positions in the society according to their characteristics); iv) adjusting function (conveying information between teacher and student, adjusting the behaviors of each other, ensuring smooth teaching); v) protection function (promoting physical and psychological health of teacher and student); vi) stimulate the interests of students and improve the learning efficiency. In the latter period, more and more researchers realized the target value of TSR. They pointed out that TSR itself was of education significance, for example, they believed that TSR was of developing function, i.e., TSR promoted the growth and development of both teacher and student. We summarized the functions of TSR as follows:

Influencing students' mental health. TSR relates with mental health of pupils and middle school students to some extent. Good TSR (such as close TSR) promotes the development of positive emotion and attitude of students to school, positive relationship with other students, good personality traits, relatively high social adaptability, and active participation in activities organized by class and schools. Poor TSR (such as conflict and dependent TSRs) causes loneliness, negative emotions toward school, withdrawal in school environment, estrangement from teachers and other students, aggressive behaviors, etc. It then affects academic behaviors and achievements, resulting into school dropout, mental disorder, etc (Bitch, 1998; Fisher, 1998; Adelman, 2002). The research by Yang et al. [2001] showed that negative emotions toward TSR has significant positive correlation with anxiety of students; whereas positive emotions toward TSR has significant negative correlation with anxiety of students. The research by Zhang [2003] also showed that TSR is closely related with problem behaviors of students; in particular conflict TSR has significant negative correlation with problem behaviors, and attachment TSR has significant positive correlation with internalization of problem behaviors.

Influencing students' adaptation to school. The adaptation of students to school significantly correlates to TSR. Students with good TSR have good adaptability to school; whereas students with poor TSR have difficulty in adaptation to school. Research [Ladd, Birch and Buhs, 1999; Pianta, 1997] found that negative TSR, especially teacher-student conflict, is a risk factor for teenagers to adapt to school. Positive TSR, especially warm and open communication, brings protective results to risk aspects of difficulty in developing school adaptation of teenagers. Zou [1997], Li [1996] and Liu [2002] found that TSR played an important role in school life and school adaptation of pupils and middle school students.

Influencing students' academic performance. Close TSR relates with the positive achievements of teenagers, including interests in learning, participation in class, good academic performance, etc.; conflict TSR relates with being weary of learning, truancy, being absent-minded in class and relatively poor academic performance; dependent TSR relates with some difficulties of adaptation. Li et al. [1998] pointed out that middle school students subjectively believed that their relationship with the teacher of a certain subject seriously influenced their academic performance and interests in such subject. Research showed that how students like the teacher closely relates with to what degree students like the subject of such teacher; the concordance rate exceeded 95%. The correlation between how students do not like the teachers and to what degree students do not like the subject of such teacher reached 80%. Lian [2000] pointed out that students with different TSR had significantly different learning interests, learning enthusiasm, sense of responsibilities, emulation, self-confidence and persistence in learning. Both Dong and Chen [2001] and Zhang [2003] pointed out that TSR of middle school students significantly correlated with students' academic performance.

Influencing students' interpersonal relationship. The research by Howes, Hamiton and Mathson (as cited in Wo, 2002) showed that TSR greatly influences PCR and peer relationship. TSR compensates poor PCR to some extent. TSR also influences the imitativeness of peer communication, communication capacity and social status. The research by Liu et al. showed that TSR influences peer relationship; close relationship was observed between conflict TSR and peer rejection, close TSR and peer acceptance, and between dependent TSR and peer relationship problems.

Influencing self-esteem of students. TSR improves and reduces self-esteem. Satisfactory TSR, for example, the support, care, encouragement, expectation and participation of teachers to students, facilitates the development of students' self-esteem. The research by Zhang showed that TSR is commonly correlated with self-concept of middle school students. Avoidance, attachment and close TSRs obviously predict self-concept in math and general self-concept in school; attachment TSR obviously predicts self-concept in emotional stability; close and harmonious TSRs are of more positive significance on self-concept in math and self-concept in same-sex relationship.

In addition, research showed that the attribution styles of students closely relates to TSR. Good TSR, for instance, the expectation, understanding and objective evaluation of teachers to students, improves the self-confidence of students and makes students use proper attribution styles for self-assessment.

Thus it can be concluded that TSR plays a very important role in the development of teenagers. Therefore, it is very important to improve the psychological *suzhi* of students in teacher-student communication and to promote the TSR development.

*Student factors affecting TSR.* We specially probed into student factors affecting TSR as the present research probes into TSR from the perspective of students. Research showed that indirect student factors have important relationship with the characteristics of TSR. Liu and Wang [2003] pointed out that student factors affecting TSR include psychological characteristics of students and students' view of teacher. The available empirical research focused on:

The influence of students' academic factors on TSR. Teachers have different communicating attitude toward students with different academic performance, which then influences TSR. The research by Wang and Wang [2002] showed that different performance of students, in particular the academic performance, cause different expectation of teachers to students. Such expectations are reflected by how teachers treat students, and influence TSR. Students with good academic performance have more positive TSR. The research by Li et al. also showed that learning difficulty obviously influences TSR. Students with learning difficulty have tense TSR.

The influence of students' interpersonal behaviors on TSR. Teachers' perception of students' behaviors relates with teachers' attitude toward students. Teachers usually prefer those who are cooperative, curious and responsible in class, rather than those who are naughty, arrogant and dependent. In addition, the research by Pianta et al. [Pianta and Steinberg, 1992] showed that problem behaviors, including difficulty in operation, internalization and learning, negatively correlate with earlier TSR. Bitch et al. Probed into the relationship between TSR and interpersonal behaviors of children. They divided the orientation of interpersonal behaviors into three types: moving against, moving away and moving toward. The three types of orientation correspond with anti-social behaviors, asocial behaviors and pro-social behaviors. Research showed that the earlier behavioral orientation of children shown in kindergarten (moving against, moving away and moving toward) relates to the TSR in primary grade one later. The antisocial behaviors (moving against) in kindergarten significantly relate with conflict and dependent TSRs in primary grade one; the asocial behaviors (moving away) in kindergarten relate with the dependence of children on teachers [Bitch and Ladd, 1998].

Measurements for TSR. Psychometrics is used in the current TSR research. The psychometric tools include:

*Interpersonal relationship scale.* TSR is the sub-system of students' interpersonal relationship. Thus the TSR is usually surveyed as a part of interpersonal relationship. For example, the interpersonal relationship development questionnaire for middle school students developed by Wo, Li, et al. include the items of TSR.

*Teacher rating scale.* At present, Student-Teacher Relationship Scale (STRS) developed by Pianta et al. is used. STRS includes three dimensions: closeness, conflict and dependency. It is a teacher rating scale and it is widely used. Want et al. developed a TSR teacher rating scale for students from primary grade three to primary grade six, by referring to the scale of Pianta. Such scale includes 28 items. The head teacher wrote down the answers on the 5-point Likert scale relationship between such head teacher and students. STRS includes three dimensions: closeness, conflict and responsivity.

*Student rating scale.* Student rating scale was developed by referring to the scale of Pianta [1994] based on the interview between teachers and students, for example, the student rating scales developed by Zhang [2003] and by Liu [2000]. The scale developed by Zhang includes four dimensions, conflict, dependency, closeness and avoidance. The scale developed by Liu includes three dimensions, closeness, cooperativeness and initiative. Wei [1998] developed a TSR satisfactory inventory for students. It includes three dimensions: support, care and encouragement; expectation; participation.

*Experimental and interventional research into TSR improvement.* Understanding is the precondition of improvement; improvement is the eventual purpose of the research. Both the survey of the current status of TSR and the research into the affecting factors aim to improve TSR. We can borrow ideas from the interventional research into interpersonal relationship for the intervention of TSR, as TSR is part of interpersonal relationship. The experimental and interventional research into interpersonal relationship features as follows:

In the terms of intervening in interpersonal relationship, the intervention in same-sex relationship takes a larger proportion, following by PCR; while the training of teacher-student communication only takes a small proportion. The educational intervention of Zhang on problem behaviors among junior middle school students included the intervention in teacher-student communication. She intervened mainly through the training course for correcting problem behaviors in communication, while supplemented by individualized consultation and counseling. She helped students to correctively handle with the relationship with teachers through "Between Teachers and Students" course. After the educational intervention, there were obviously fewer problems in teacher-student communication.

In the terms of the object of intervention, the research was mainly focused on university students [Yang, 2002; Qi, 2001; Xing, 2003]. Only a few researchers probed into the intervention in pupils, for example, Li et al. probed into the cultivation of pupils' interpersonal communication competence through "small team" game-based training. We did not see any interventional research into the interpersonal relationship of junior middle school students.

In the terms of the methods and contents of intervention, most researchers believed that the training of interpersonal communication should be conducted from cognitive changes and behavioral training. Du [2001] believed that the training of classroom communication skills can be conducted in the forms of cognitive guidance, mode demonstration, guiding of experience. Ma [2002] used the training strategies especially for concept and behaviors in the interpersonal communication training among senior middle school students. Besides, Han [1998] pointed out that communication skill training can be conducted from the perspective of communication attribution; because the changes of attribution may lead to the change of motivation, and the change of motivation directly influences behaviors. The experiment can be conducted in the forms of group intervention or individual intervention. Group intervention is regularly conducted through persuasion, discussion, demonstration, enhanced correction, etc. It focuses on how to improve the self-confidence in communication, and how to fully understand the importance of personal quality, self-improvement and communication capacity to successful communication. Individual intervention is for students with communication difficulty. It is in two forms: consultation and oriented training.

*Comments about the current TSR research.* The available research inspires us to understand the characteristics and current status of TSR development, and TSR training. However, there are still deficiencies.

In the terms of the objects of research, the research into TSR and teacher-students communication skills focused on pupils and children. Not many researchers focused on middle school students. No experimental research into the educational intervention in TSR targeted at junior middle school is available.

The theoretical discussion covered extensively, including education, psychology, educational sociology, educational philosophy, and pedagogical psychology, etc. Many probed from the perspective of teachers; only a few probed from the perspective of students. Most research focused on how teachers influence students. Only a few researchers focused on how students communicate with teachers. They did not probed into TSR as a sub-system of the interpersonal relationship of students. But the personality traits, academic performance and other factors of students influence TSR. Thus we believe neglecting the role of students in teacher-student communication is the deficiency of the previous research. The existing trainings also focused on how teachers treat students, which makes teacher-student communication unidirectional and one party of the communication depends on the other party. Thus it is difficult to effectively deal with the problems of bidirectional or interacting teacher-student communication.

In the terms of research methods, most researchers did theoretical research. Only a few did empirical research. Most researchers analyzed education theories to probe into TSR, but it is only at the level of reasoning; no strong evidence is available. Most empirical research is survey research, and a small proportion is experimental research. Descriptive research into TSR was conducted mainly through surveys and educational experiment was not commonly used. The current research into the training of teacher-student communication skills are more about theoretical discussion, rather than skill training. No effective and complete training system for teacher-student communication skills is available. The existing training methods are simple. The trainings are in the form of psychological *suzhi* activity course. But due to the specialty of teacher-student communication, students may resist or feel being lectured if the TSR training is conducted by the teacher. Thus whether teacher-student communicating skills of students and TSR can be improved through non-face-to-face training is considered as an important issue .

## Value of the Present Research

The present research will propose innovation of PSE mode by starting from the analysis of current PSE; establish computer-assisted PSE mode under the guidance of integrated PSE mode proposed by Zhang et al; deeply probe into the problems of teacher-student communication and the current status of TSR among junior middle school students; develop PSE software to promote TSR; and verify the applicability and effectivity of computer-assisted PSE mode. It has important theoretical and practical significance on strengthening the effectivity of PSE, exploring the new means of PSE, improving the psychological *suzhi* of students in teacher-student communication, and for promoting the development of TSR.

Theoretically, the exploration into the necessity and applicability of computer-assisted PSE enriches and deepens the theoretical research into PSE in school. The exploration into TSR improvement from the perspective of students provides a new angle for TSR research.

Practically, the development of PSE software promoting TSR provides students with relatively operational skills of teacher-student communication explores a new means of PSE and facilitates the enhancement of PSE effectiveness.

The contribution of the present research includes: i) exploration of TSR improvement from the perspective of students, promotion of TSR improvement through improving the psychological *suzhi* of teacher-student communication; ii) the innovation of PSE mode, establishment of computer-assisted PSE mode; iii) development of PSE software promoting TSR, verification of the applicability and effectivity of the software through educational experiment.

## Research Approaches and Hypothesis

### *Basic Approaches. Theoretical Analysis → Investigation Of The Status Quo → Mode Construction → Software Development → Experimental Validation.*

*Theoretical analysis.* The new means of PSE was put forward –PSE based on multimedia technology, based on the understanding of the current PSE, the application of multimedia technology in psychological fields and TSR research.

*Investigation of the status quo.* Open-ending and close-ending surveys were organized among junior middle school students in order to understand the problems in teacher-student communication, the status quo of TSR among in junior middle school.

*Mode construction.* Probed into the target, structure, mode, theme, strategies, etc of PSE based on multimedia technology, by referring to the current theoretical research into PSE.

*Software development.* Probed into the theoretical basis and technical support of PSE software promoting TSR, i.e., probed into the applicability of the software and the means of realization, assessed the preliminarily developed software by specialists, collected the feedback of students, modified and improved the software.

*Experimental validation.* Validated whether the software facilitated TSR through learning the PSE software facilitating TSR, i.e., verified the effectivity of the software.

Hypotheses. The hypotheses made include:

Hypothesis 1: the complexity of psychological *suzhi* and PSE determines the complexity and diversification of PSE means and modes, the modeing of PSE in school should and be able to use modern teaching approaches;

Hypothesis 2: PSE software based on multimedia technology improves the effects of PSE in school.

Hypothesis 3: the PSE software developed can promote TSR and improve the capacity of junior middle school students in teacher-student communication.

# MODEING OF COMPUTER ASSISTED PSE AND DEVELOPMENT OF COMPUTER ASSISTED PSE SOFTWARE

## Modeing of Computer Assisted PSE

Basic targets of computer assisted PSE. The target of PSE is to cultivate good psychological *suzhi* of students, and computer-assisted PSE is the important means of implementing PSE, thus the basic target of computer-assisted PSE is also to cultivate good psychological *suzhi* of students. The cultivation of good psychological *suzhi* is to realize all-around and healthy development of all components of students' psychological *suzhi*, normal or even extraordinary intelligence, complete personality and good adaptability, and also to lay foundation for overall improvement of students' psychological *suzhi*.

Computer-assisted PSE also follows the basic principles of psychological *suzhi* training. It focuses on training students to adapt to life, learning, interpersonal communication, body development as well as to prevent and correct the mental and behavioral disorder of students due to inadaptation. To sum up, the basic target of computer-assisted PSE is to cultivate good psychological *suzhi* of students and to promote the positive adaptation and initiative development of students by making use of multimedia technology.

### Basic Thoughts of Computer Assisted PSE

Initiative participation of students is the precondition of successful implementation of computer assisted PSE. The process of PSE should be the process of initiative participation of students. Students, via initiative participation, discover problems, analyze self, probe into reasons, seek for solutions, reflect and experience, form psychological *suzhi*, including thoughts, concepts and capacity. Therefore, the initiative participation of students is the precondition of developing and cultivating psychological *suzhi*, and is also the precondition for the successful implementation of computer-assisted PSE. Computer-assisted PSE should fully arouse the activeness of students, making students initiatively participate in computer-assisted PSE. During the training, students can operate independently, control one's own pace of learning and choose the contents of learning. Students can design problems, observe the problems encountered by others to arouse the thinking of students, and then to judge and analyze, and to seek for solutions. In addition, computer provides vivid and interesting screens, pleasing background music, in order to stimulate the interest of students in the contents of training, and realize their willingness in participation in the training.

The process of forming psychological *suzhi* is the basis of computer assisted PSE. Computer-assisted PSE must be based on the age features of students'physiological and psychological development, the development of their sociality and their present psychological *suzhi*; and must break through from the common or possible mental problems in respect of their study, life, interpersonal relationship and growth. Computer-assisted PSE was designed on the basis of the process of psychological *suzhi* training proposed by Zhang et al., i.e., "self-understanding, knowledge learning, behavioral direction, reflection and internalization and development of habits into nature". First, students take some self-tests to understand their psychological state, or tell the experience of the protagonist of a story and then associate with their own experience – "self-understanding". Students summarize with one sentence – "knowledge learning". The focus of the training system is "behavioral direction". Several skills are provided for students to learn at their discretion. The skill training aims to change the understanding of students and also to inform them the specific behavioral strategies. Students are required to write down their feelings, thoughts, opinions, etc in the skill training, which is the process of "reflection and internalization". The "simulated training" section is organized, where simulated situations are provided for students to think and solve. This is the application of acquired skills, i.e., "development of habits into nature".

The basic feature of computer assisted PSE is harmonious psychological environment. The process of psychological *suzhi* training is a process to create harmonious psychological environment, activate or stimulate students' mental activities. It usually can cause the sense of identification or absence of students, excite emotional resonance and then induce the willingness to act. The psychological *suzhi* of students are cultivated and practiced in the harmonious and interacting psychological environment. Thus harmonious and interacting psychological environment is the basic feature of computer-assisted PSE, which effectively guarantees computer-assisted PSE. Harmonious and interacting psychological environment can be created through pleasing background music, vivid and interesting cartoon, emotive dubbing, etc. The contents of training should be close to the life of students. The contents should be effective, making students easy to accept psychologically and willing to learn.

The training themes of PSE software promoting TSR

Survey of the current status of TSR. We surveyed the current status of TSR in order to understand the status quo of TSR and provide basis for the determination of the TSR training themes.

Open-ended survey of problems in teacher-student communication in junior middle school. We distributed open-ended questionnaires to 42 junior grade two students in a Chongqing-based middle school, in order to understand the current problems of teacher-student communication, and 38 valid questionnaires were collected. The questionnaire includes three open-ended questions, "What do you think are the problems in teacher-student communication? What do you think are the specific factors affecting TSR? How do you think to improve TSR?" We classified and sorted the survey results through content analysis. The results are as follows (see Table 9.1.):

The results showed that the most frequent problems in teacher-student communication are: lacking of communication and teacher-student conflict. It indicates that junior middle school students nowadays have less communication with teachers and tend to conflict with teachers in the communication, which are related to the changes of the objects of communication and rebel psychological traits. Factors affecting TSR can be summarized as: students' factors and teachers' factors. About 34.21% students believed that learning factors influenced TSR; i.e., teachers have bad impression of a student if the student has bad performance, which further influences TSR. About 52.63% students did not dare to communicate with teachers. They felt teachers were too strict and were afraid of being criticized, which also influences TSR. And 60.53% students believed that TSR was influenced by autocratic teachers; some believed that TSR was influenced by the prejudice and misunderstanding of teachers. Most students believed that TSR could be improved through communicating with teachers, learning seriously, with more respect and understanding. About 71.05% students believed that communication played a very important role in TSR improvement, thus students should talk heart-to-heart and communicate with teachers. About 26.32% students believed that learning is very important in TSR improvement, thus students should complete the homework carefully, actively answer questions in class and ask teachers more questions after class. Six students believed the mutual understanding and respect between teachers and students facilitate TSR improvement.

### Table 9.1. Results of Open-ended Survey of Teacher-student Communication in Junior Middle School

| Questions | | Frequency | Percentage (%) |
|---|---|---|---|
| Problems in teacher-student communication | Lacking of communication | 22 | 57.89 |
| | Teacher-student conflict | 30 | 78.95 |
| Factors affecting PCR | Learning factors | 13 | 34.21 |
| | Fear, timidity | 20 | 52.63 |
| | Autocratic teachers | 23 | 60.53 |
| | Prejudice of teachers | 10 | 26.32 |
| | Misunderstanding of teachers | 5 | 13.16 |
| How to improve TSR | More communication | 27 | 71.05 |
| | Learn seriously | 10 | 26.32 |
| | More respect and understanding | 6 | 15.79 |

*Close-ended survey of the current status of TSR in junior middle school.* As students are the object of TSR training, we used student rating questionnaire of TSR; i.e., Teacher-student Relationship Questionnaire (for Students) developed by Wang. The questionnaire has good validity and reliability. Participants were 133 students from three grades of a Beibei-based middle school, Chongqing. The participants included 63 male students and 70 female students; 58 of them were from junior grade one, 38 were from junior grade two and 37 were from junior grade three. All data were treated by SPSS10.0. Please see the following for data analysis results.

*Gender difference of TSR development in junior middle school.* Please see Table 9.2. For the score difference of TSR between female and male in junior middle school.

Table 9.2. shows significant difference between female and male in total scores, and the factors of closeness and conflict. The total scores of female were obviously higher than male. Female students had closer TSR and less conflict TSR, indicating female students had obviously better TSR than male students. This corresponds with the conclusion of Wo et al. [2001]; i.e., the interpersonal relationship of female students is always better than male students in junior middle school.

*Grade difference of TSR development in junior middle school.* We took the grade as the independent variable, and the factors and the total score of TSR as the dependant variables for the purpose of variance analysis. See Table 9.3. for the results:

**Table 9.2. Gender Difference of TSR Development in Junior Middle School**

|  | Male (n=63) | | Female (n=70) | | T |
|---|---|---|---|---|---|
|  | *M* | *SD* | *M* | *SD* | |
| Closeness | 2.53 | 0.78 | 2.88 | 0.70 | -2.746** |
| Conflict | 1.97 | 0.73 | 1.65 | 0.56 | 2.732** |
| Support | 3.54 | 0.60 | 3.65 | 0.55 | -1.063 |
| Satisfactory | 3.38 | 0.58 | 3.36 | 0.76 | 0.133 |
| Total scores | 1.87 | 0.50 | 2.06 | 0.47 | -2.231* |

**Table 9.3. Grade Difference of TSR Development in Junior Middle School**

|  | Closeness | | Conflict | | Support | | Satisfactory | | Total scores | |
|---|---|---|---|---|---|---|---|---|---|---|
|  | *M* | *SD* | *M* | *SD* | *M* | *SD* | *M* | *SD* | *M* | *SD* |
| Junior grade one (n=58) | 3.08 | 0.69 | 1.60 | 0.61 | 3.76 | 0.59 | 3.55 | 0.73 | 2.19 | 0.47 |
| Junior grade two (n=37) | 2.34 | 0.79 | 2.00 | 0.75 | 3.46 | 0.58 | 3.24 | 0.61 | 1.76 | 0.54 |
| Junior grade three (n=38) | 2.55 | 0.58 | 1.85 | 0.52 | 3.46 | 0.47 | 3.36 | 0.84 | 1.88 | 0.32 |
| F | 14.208*** | | 4.791* | | 4.613* | | 2.087 | | 11.332*** | |

The results showed that the grade difference is significant ($F=4.089$, $p<0.001$). The results showed that in the terms of closeness, significant difference is As seen between junior grade two and junior grade one, and between junior grade three and junior grade one; junior grade one students were obviously better than the other two grades. In the terms of conflict, junior grade two students had obviously more conflicts than junior grade one students. In the terms of support, junior grade one students were obviously better than students of the other two grades. In the terms of satisfactory, the difference was not significant. In the terms of total scores, significant difference is As seen between junior grade two and junior grade one, and between junior grade three and junior grade one; junior grade one students were obviously better than students of the other two grades. It shows that junior grade two students had the worst TSR, following by junior grade three; junior grade one students had the best TSR. We chose junior grade two students for the experimental intervention as they had the worst TSR and had the most problems in TSR.

*The difference of TSR development among students with different academic situations.* We took the academic situations as the independent variable, and the factors and the total score of TSR as the dependant variables for the purpose of analysis of variance. The academic situations were assessed by students themselves, which is classified in four grades, "excellent, good, average, and bad".

Table 9.4. shows significant difference between students with different academic performance in total scores and closeness.

**Table 9.4. Difference of TSR Development among Students with Different Academic Situations**

|  | Closeness | | Conflict | | Support | | Satisfactory | | Total scores | |
|---|---|---|---|---|---|---|---|---|---|---|
|  | *M* | *SD* | *M* | *SD* | *M* | *SD* | *M* | *SD* | *M* | *SD* |
| Excellent (n=10) | 3.30 | 0.78 | 1.67 | 0.91 | 3.85 | 0.63 | 3.70 | 0.68 | 2.29 | 0.61 |
| Good (n=65) | 2.86 | 0.75 | 1.70 | 0.61 | 3.65 | 0.52 | 3.49 | 0.78 | 2.07 | 0.46 |
| Average (n=50) | 2.44 | 0.73 | 1.90 | 0.67 | 3.48 | 0.62 | 3.33 | 0.67 | 1.83 | 0.50 |
| Bad (n=8) | 2.71 | 0.63 | 1.85 | 0.48 | 3.59 | 0.58 | 2.87 | 0.72 | 1.83 | 0.33 |
| *F* | 4.783** | | 0.914 | | 1.431 | | 2.381 | | 3.697* | |

The comparison shows that in terms of closeness, students who believed they had excellent and good academic performance had higher scores than average students. In the terms of total scores, students who believed they had excellent and good academic performance had higher scores than average students.

We surveyed 67 junior grade two students (including 43 male students and 24 female students) in a Chongqing-based middle school in order to probe in detail into the relationship between academic performance of junior middle school students and TSR. We collected the scores of the latest midterm examination to serve as the variable of academic performance. We took the total scores and factors of TSR and academic performance as variables for the analysis of Pearson product moment. Please see Table 9.5. for the results:

Table 9.5. shows significant correlation between the academic performance of students and the total scores of TSR ($p<0.05$), and very significant correlation between the academic performance of students and conflict factor ($p<0.01$).

Considering the influence of academic performance to TSR, we believe that the TSR may be worse in schools with low proportion of students entering schools of a higher level. In such schools, the problems of TSR are higher in number and are more typical.

Thus we chose an ordinary class from a school with low proportion of students entering schools of a higher level with the purpose of educational intervention.

**Table 9.5. Correlation of TSR in Junior Middle School and Academic Performance of Students**

|  | Closeness | Conflict | Support | Satisfactory | Total scores |
|---|---|---|---|---|---|
| Academic Performance | 0.182 | -0.321** | 0.182 | 0.226 | 0.290* |

*Determining the training themes of PCT Software.* As mentioned above, most researchers conducted the trainings of interpersonal communication skills from the perspectives of cognition and behavior [Ma, 2002; Du, 2001]. We also trained from the perspectives of cognitive change and behavioral training, and added contents in the cognitive and behavioral trainings, in order to stimulate the emotional resonance of students and strengthen emotional experience.

**Table 9.6. Training Contents of PSE Software Promoting TSR**

| Themes | Main Contents |
|---|---|
| Understand TSR | Understand the importance of TSR; correctly understand TSR; TSR is not about apple polishing; really like teachers, actively communicate with teachers and make efforts to improve TSR. |
| Begin from myself to improve TSR | TSR improve should start from overcoming bad personality traits: overcome timidity, anxiety; learn to raise the attention of teachers by proper means; be serious in learning, have good performance and draw the attention of teachers. |
| Themes | Main Contents |
| Actively communicate with teachers | Stimulate the passion of communication, communicate with teachers heart-to-heart; seek for the key to communication, learn how to have verbal communication and non-verbal communication; remove the obstacles of communication, for example, overcoming negative psychology, including timidity, rebelling and going with the crowd. |
| How to treat the partiality of teachers | Adjust the unbalanced psychology and treat the partiality of teachers objectively and calmly; carry out measures actively and obtain the preference of teachers; understand the partiality of teachers and listen to the problems of teachers. |
| Solve the misunderstanding between teachers and students | Learn to be tolerant and understand teachers; put what you think into action and learn how to solve the misunderstanding; organize empty chair activity and think from the perspective of teachers. |
| Solve the conflict between teachers and students | Understand why conflict with teachers and learn how to solve the conflict between teachers and students; for example, how to control emotions, analyze the cause and carry out measures to solve the conflict. |

We determined the themes and contents (see Table 9.6.) of training based on the mentioned survey results:

*Cognitive perspective.* Good cognitive capacity is the precondition of successful interpersonal communication. Students can use proper communication strategies and have harmonious communication only when they have correct understanding and judgment of the relationship between the two parties of communication. Therefore, we arranged the contents of two aspects: the cognition of TSR and self. The cognition of TSR includes the cognition of teachers. Meanwhile, we added behavioral direction to the cognition, in order to strengthen cognition through actions.

For cognition of self, personality traits are very important factors affecting interpersonal communication. Good personality traits (including tolerance, self-confidence, sincerity, etc.) improve the interpersonal attraction of individuals. The survey mentioned above showed that learning and character of students were important factors affecting TSR. Therefore, the training strengthened the understanding of one's character and how to create conditions from the perspective of oneself to improve TSR.

*Behavioral perspective.* Under the precondition of strengthened cognition, the improvement of skills depends on behavioral training. Thus the contents we chose focused on training. The survey mentioned above showed that the common problems of teacher-student communication are conflict and lacking of communication between teachers and students. The misunderstanding and prejudice of teachers were believed by most students to be the factors affecting TSR.

Therefore, based on the survey, we established the training contents of four aspects: how to communicate with teachers, how to solve the misunderstanding between teachers and students, how to treat the partiality of teachers and how to solve the conflict between teacher and students.

The purpose is to teach students communication skills, and to make them know how to solve the specific problems.

*Training mode of computer assisted PSE.* We proposed the mode of psychological *suzhi* training based on the multimedia technology, introduction of the themes – cognitive change – skill guidance – simulated training – direction and summary, according to the process of forming students' psychological *suzhi* put forward by Zhang et al. We will explain in detail as follows by taking the PSE software promoting TSR as an example.

*Introduction to the themes*: the theme is introduced through some sentences or the experience of the protagonist. For example, the theme of "Understand TSR", the first lesson, was introduced by questions; and the theme of "Actively Communicate with Teachers", the third lesson, was introduced by the experience of the protagonist; the theme of "Solve the Misunderstanding between Teachers and Students" was introduced through a lyric and a beautiful picture. Such forms of introduction aim to arouse the interest of students and introduce them to the themes.

*Cognitive change:* change the negative cognition of students and make them form correct concepts. Cognition must first be changed to improve the communication skills of students. The training purpose is realized through cognitive activities, including perception, imagination and thinking. For example, stories can be told in the training to make students associate themselves with the stories and think about themselves. The questions design can be encountered frequently by students in communication, thus it is easy for students to associate the questions with themselves. Questions are used to arouse the thinking of students. For example, "Can you help the protagonist to find the solution?" Students are actually seeking for solutions for themselves when they try to answer this question. Even though students can not find the solution, the thinking process of students is the process of reflecting their cognition. In addition, tests can be used to realize reflection and self-analysis of students, to make them understand their own characteristics, advantages and shortages, in order to promote their development. For example, in the third lesson "Actively Communicate with Teachers", a test was provided after the theme was introduced. The test include such questions: Do you like chatting with teachers? Would you like to tell teachers your innermost thoughts and feelings? Do you ask teachers to help you out of the difficulties in learning? etc. Teachers chose Yes or No answer according to their situations. When all questions were answered, an assessment is provided. The assessment was provided according to the scores, "you have good understanding with the teachers; good communication" or "You have insufficient communication with teachers; you need to make extra efforts". The test is also to arouse the reflection of students.

*Behavioral guidance*: the mentioned questions arouse the thinking of students, and we provide the following skills for reference. We introduce each skill in accordance with the principle of "cognition first, behavior second". Teachers first change students' cognition and then tell them what and how to do and give detailed advice on behavior. For example, in "Understand TSR", we told students how to improve TSR: making a card for teachers in festivals; providing a cup of water for teachers before class; taking more efforts to have good performance; helping teachers to clean the blackboard, etc. These need only a slight effort. Students can do them. We create protagonist according to the principle of mode demonstration. Thus behavioral guidance is provided by showing how the protagonist or other people at the same age deal with TSR. Mode demonstration is the Bandura's social learning theory. Mode demonstration is based on the principle that an individual can acquire new behavior tendency through imitation. It aims to help students with learning difficulty to acquire positive behaviors through observation and learning, or to help students acquire certain positive behaviors they don't have. In the intervention, we used the protagonist as the mode, and told students what and how to do; or made students think about what and how to do under certain situations and then told students the right actions. We chose people at the same age of students and the events students frequently encounter in daily life as the training contents, because they are closer to students and can make the training more effective. Role transposition is the common method of interpersonal communication training, which is essentially a method to influence the psychology of an individual through the behavior modeing or substitution. The basic principle is to make students overcome negative psychological experience though positive psychological experience, and try to consolidate and transfer such new psychological experience and ways of act in the experiment, by making use of social imitation, role experience, group interaction, positive enhancement and other effects Empty chair activity is a kind of role play. Only one person is needed in the activity, thus it is suitable for students with difficulties in social intercourse. In "Solve the Conflict between Teachers and Students", we provided two chairs and asked students to play different roles by sitting on different chairs. Trying to experience the thinking and feelings of teachers from the perspective of teachers facilitates the solving of teacher-student conflicts.

Simulated training: after the introduction of behavioral skills, several simulated situations are provided to make students think what and how to do. For example, in "Solve the Conflict between Teachers and Students", we designed a section of "Think about it" after the introduction of behavioral skills, by providing the example conflict between teachers and students, and asked students to find out the solution. This is to test whether students have mastered the skills they had learned, i.e., the application of knowledge.

*Direction and summary*: point out the main contents of the lesson through a summative sentence, which provides students a general idea of the lesson. The mentioned is the basic mode of TSR training designed by us. The mode is flexible in a specific lesson. For example, simulated training was designed in the behavioral guidance, rather than listed as an independent section. In some lessons, cognitive change was not listed as an independent section; instead, it was combined with behavioral guidance. The introduction of skills all begins from cognition and then the behavior. The appendix 4 takes "Solve the Conflict between Teachers and Students", the sixth lesson, introduces in detail the design approaches of the training contents, and the mode of training.

# Developing PSE Software to Promote TSR

## 1) Theoretical Basis of Developing PSE Software to Promote TSR

*Theoretical basis of TSR training*. The training of improving interpersonal relationship is a technique to help students to respond more effectively in interpersonal communication. First of all, the best communication skills and behavioral styles in interpersonal communication are found through objective means or assessment. Then the gap between the best behavioral styles and the behavioral styles of the trainees is determined. Finally, the behavioral styles of the trainees are improved through certain trainings, trying to reach the best behavioral styles. Many cases of the training for improving the interpersonal relationship of university students showed that the capacity of university students in interpersonal communication can be improved by correcting the cognitive bias of interpersonal relationship based on group consultation and by behavioral training at the same time. In addition, the interpersonal relationship of university students can be improved in a short term [Yang, 2002; Qi, 2001; Xing, 2003]. Research also showed that "small team" game-based training can effectively develop the capacity of pupils in interpersonal communication [Li, Wang and Tao, 2001]. The mentioned research indicated that the training of improving interpersonal relationship can change the skills of students in interpersonal communication, and improve the interpersonal relationship of students. The period of junior middle school is the critical period of an individual's development. In this period, the characteristic of psychological development is plasticity. Plasticity indicates that external education can promote the socialization process of individuals and help them correctly deal with the psychological crisis occurs in the development. The psychological crisis includes the problems of interpersonal communication.

*Theoretic basis for developing PSE software*. The psychological principles of computer-assisted psychological training originated from behaviorism. The procedures of the training are: first determine the final behavior objectives. Then segment the contents of the training into several smaller operable training units, and arrange the small training units in order according to the sequence of an individual's psychological changes and certain principles. The small training units are presented in the forms of multimedia. Students adjust their reactions from the feedback by referring to the simulated situations or seeing positive reactions. The training is the integration of materials from psychology and educational knowledge. It meets the characteristics of students' psychological development. It is scientific. Modern cognitive psychology also provides theoretical basis for computer-assisted PSE. Within the field of modern cognitive psychology, information processing is an approach that focuses on the micro and static analysis of the cognitive process of children, as well as the research into representation, strategies, etc. Thus information processing is the micro guidance of the contents of computer-assisted training. Piaget's theory showed more about the macro and static principles of cognitive development. It focuses on qualitative change of cognitive development. Thus it is the macro theoretical basis of computer-assisted PSE. Bruner's theory regarded children as the successors of cultural tools. He attached importance to learning by discovery. Thus Bruner's theory can be used as the basis for designing "discovery" contents. Constructivism learning theory can also be served as theoretical guidance for computer-assisted PSE. Constructivism believed that knowledge is not acquired through impart of teachers; instead, it is acquired through meaning construction under a certain situation, by making use of others' help and necessary learning materials. Computer-assisted psychological training is the self-education of psychological *suzhi* by students through the learning based on the software of psychological training and acquiring the skills of behavioral training. In addition, constructivism believed that learning is related to certain social and cultural backgrounds, i.e., "situations". Learning under certain real situations causes the changing and restructuring of the original cognitive structure of the learner. The software of computer-assisted training is to create a situation that facilitates the meaning construction of the knowledge learned by students, by making use of text, figure, picture, sound, cartoon and interactive means.

### 2) Technical Support for Developing PSE Software Promoting TSR

*Advantages of computer assisted training system.* The prejudice of teachers always influences traditional psychological training. The presentation through computer can avoid such deficit. Computer-assisted training system changes the simple classroom-teaching mode (teachers give the lecture, students listen to the lecture) into a mode that facilitates students to actively participate in the learning (present knowledge information – mode demonstration – practice – summary. The advantages include:

It implements individualized teaching and plays students' role as agent. Computer-assisted training system us the teaching style that is "student-centered". Each student uses a computer to learn. Students can learn at home or at any place where computer is available. The system presents the materials to the students. Students can control their own progress of learning, choose at random, experience and practice, which fully plays students role as agent.

It has strong interaction, which facilitates playing the activeness of students. According to cognitive learning theory, the cognition of human is not directly provided by external stimulus; instead, the cognition is generated through the interaction of external stimulus and psychological process. Human-computer interaction and timely feedback are the obvious features of the software for computer-assisted training. In the multimedia-based interactive learning environment, students can choose the contents of learning according to their foundation and interests in learning. It means that students control their learning and have the initiative of learning, which facilitates the activeness of students.

It facilitates the formation of good learning motivation and emotional states. We used computer to carry out psychological *suzhi* training as students are very interested in computer and internet, which increases the interests of students in the training. Computer-assisted system can draw the attention of students through fascinating situations, stimulate their excitement, and realizes good learning motivation and emotional states of students.

It has enormous educational information and visible contents. Computer is featured by enormous information, friendly human-machine interface and extensive interaction. Computer realizes three-dimensional, dynamic and cross time-space presentation of educational contents (instead of planar, static and current time-space presentation).

It is extensively applicable. The learning is not restricted by place and time. The learning of students can break the restriction of time and place. Cross-time, cross-region and cross-culture learning is realized. The enormous information broadens the vision of students, changes their way of thinking, and makes them better adapt to the era of knowledge-driven economy where knowledge, technology and information are highly integrated.

It facilitates the acquiring and maintaining of knowledge, which meets the cognitive rules of human. The external stimulus provided through multimedia technology is not mono stimulus; instead, it is multi-sensory comprehensive stimulus, which is very important for acquiring and maintaining knowledge. In addition, multimedia technology realizes the visibleness, listening and hands-on practice of students, which meets the rules of cognitive development of students, and realizes longer maintaining of knowledge.

It easily removes the psychological pressure and defense. The training of teacher-student communication may easily cause psychological pressure if it is put into the normal classroom teaching due to the special characteristics of the training of teacher-student communication. Computer-assisted training system, without the participation and direction of teachers, avoids that students hide their real feelings due to social expectations, which can easily obtain good training effects.

*Possible deficiencies of and compensation to computer assisted training system.* Of course, there are deficiencies in computer-assisted training as the training needs interaction among people while computer is a technology of application. The deficiencies are reflected by that it influences the functions of non-verbal means of assistance, including expression, tones, posture, etc. In the training, it is quite difficult for making use of the functions of such means. If the means are not properly used, simple and mechanical results may be caused. Meanwhile, interpersonal communication is a process of interaction, but human-computer dialogue is not like human-human dialogue, thus there are difficulties in applying communication skills. Computer-assisted training can not guarantee timely feedback, which makes compensation and adjustment impossible based on feedback. It has high requirements on learners, thus students must have certain self-control capacity and be familiar with computer skills. In addition, the initiative and personality of students may be neglected in computer-assisted training. We carried out the following measures to compensate such deficiencies: enhanced situations, set cross-time and cross-space situations, in order to improve the reality basis of situations and avoid the mechanicalness of human-computer dialogue; enhance skill training and operability, in order to improve its practical functions; set the situations that may be encountered in reality by analogy for students to solve; the screen setting must be simple and clear to ensure learning only through simple operations, in order to enable more students to use the system. In addition, the following measures can be used consciously to optimize computer-assisted training system: i) mode demonstration. Specific problems of teacher-student communication can be designed in the computer. Meanwhile, correct solutions and communication styles can be presented; i.e., mode demonstration. By doing this, students can learn from the modes for effective communication skills. In addition, verbal interpretation can be used. ii) Reading and reflection. Some reading materials can be presented by considering the purposes of training, in order to provide modes of concepts and behaviors. Students can be encouraged to undertake reflection on the basis of reading, in order to internalize the knowledge and experience of communication skills. iii) Creating situations and psychological role-play. Computers can be used to simulate some situations related to the problems in real life for students to solve; or computers can provide some situations for students to predict the possible events in the future and to train the communication skills of the learners.

### 3) Designing Pse Software Promoting Tsr

*Principles for designing the contents of the software.* The following principles were followed when we designed the contents of the software:

*Clearly defined objectives*. The objectives of the software must be clearly defined in order to correctly guide students to learn about how to communicate with teachers. Thus the following should be realized: i) the purposes should be clearly defined and based on the theme of the training. The objectives of the training should be defined as clear as possible. Such objectives should be internalized as the cognitive action plan of students. By doing this, the learning and information processing of students can be adjusted at any time under the supervision of cognition to realize the defined objectives. ii) The meaning should be clearly defined. The contents of teaching to be presented, including subtitles, animation, sound and figures should have clear meanings and be correct.

*Life-based contents*. First, the contents of training should be the hot topics, focuses and difficulties from real life that are close to the life of students. The students' psychological *suzhi* results from their life and learning, thus PST should focus on the hot topics, focuses and difficulties of their psychology. Thus, we read relevant literature and surveyed the status quo to understand the problems in teacher-student communication and the current status of TSR, which will be the basis of designing training contents, and will enhance the specificity of psychological training. Second, a series of simulated situations can be designed, which enables students to have sufficient psychological experience, to obtain the correct cognitive concepts, thinking styles and methods, to master the strategies of PST and to cultivate good psychological *suzhi*.

*Motivation enhancement*. Rewards of all forms were designed in the software, which aims to develop a certain good behavior or remove certain misconduct through enhancement such as rewards and punishment, according to the reinforcement learning theory by behaviorism school. For example, in "Actively Communicate with Teachers", two assessments were created after the "How is Your Communication with Teachers" test. If the teacher-student communication is good, a figure of a thumb will be presented for reward. If the teacher-student communication is insufficient, a figure of efforts will be presented, indicating that students need more efforts in communicating with teachers.

## Principles for Designing the Forms of the Software

*Friendly screen, easy operation*. We strived for the best screen effect in order to realize easy operation and smooth learning of junior middle school students: i) the text presented on the screen was concise and had clear meaning; ii) the contents presented on the screen were based on the theme, which avoided deviation from the contents of teaching while realized good and attractive pictures or attracted the concentration of students; iii) clear screen, i.e., highlighted the focus by highlight, bold, blinking, frame out, enlarge, acoustics and other techniques; iv) the layout of the screen was reasonable and the figures and text were well proportioned; v) the forms were diversified and changing and the forms of presenting the contents were vivid; vi) the prompts were unified and the operation was easy which enabled students with basic knowledge of computer operation to learn smoothly. Help document was built in the file of software. Learners can operate according to the introduction contained in the document. The document contains introduction about how to use the player, the procedures of opening the player, matters that need attention, etc. Learners can learn in school or at home.

*Enhanced situations*. We strived to use multimedia software to provide as much animation, pictures and other audiok, video and text as possible to create reality-based situations, enrich the perceptual materials, deepen cognitive presentation and stimulate reproductive imagination of students. Creation of situations can make students actively pay attention to the circumstances, stimulate students' will to and interest in learning, maintain students' positive mind, and enable students to get ready for the learning situations with active attitudes.

*Vivid and interesting forms to draw the attention of students.* Attention has been referred to as the allocation of processing resources. It is the precondition of any learning and activity. Therefore, the interacting interface of the software should be well designed by using proper figures, pictures and sound to present the theme and stimulate the interest in and desire for learning, making students learn actively and initiatively. For example, good commentary and pleasing music and vivid animation should be designed to draw the attention of students, in order to fully stimulate the cognition and emotion of students, which is the precondition and guarantee of effective PST.

*Direct-viewing and inspiring forms.* The most obvious feature of multimedia environment is making people feeling personally on the scene and multimedia can vividly present the objects on the screen. Thus the software design should realize direct-viewing and inspiring contents of the course by making use of the feature of multimedia based computer that it can process and convey sound, picture, video and animation.

*Reducing the influence of irrelevant stimuli.* Although diversified forms of software attract the attention of learners, irrelevant stimuli of people's perception distracts attention, for example, the software focuses too much on the diversification of forms, disorder of signal and noise, or improper screen color or animation. Therefore, the design enlarged the difference between the training contents and the background, blurred the background and highlighted the contents; the screen colors were mostly light colors; the animation should be properly used to avoid the secondary supersedes the primary.

To sum up, the software was well designed, with diversified screens and forms of human-computer communication so that students master the skills of teacher-student communication, improve their capacity in teacher-student communication, and improve TSR.

### 4) Development and Modification of PSE Software Promoting TSR

The mode for developing PSE software is "writing of script, development of software, evaluation by experts, modification, feedback from students, re-modification, and evaluation by experts".

*Writing of scripts.* First, the theme of training was determined, according to the TSR research available, the problems in the current TSR, and the current TSR development; the basic training mode was determined according to the research into the existing PSE modes. Then the scripts were written for each theme. The scripts were vivid, interesting, close to life, operable and met the development principles of students. The forms of presentation were also included in the scripts.

*Software development.* We invited professional computer specialists to develop the software based on the scripts written. They used Flash software, Javascript and html language. Flash was used mainly to realize animation function. Javascript was used to realize storage function and html was to integrate animation. Html language is the coding system to generate active documents. The prominent feature is interaction. A language that can be identified by most computers must be used in order to release the information to the website through computer. The common language release of Internet is html, which lays foundation for the future release of software in the Internet.

*Evaluation by experts.* We invited experts to evaluate the software developed for each lesson. Experts provided detailed suggestions from the contents, forms of presentation of the software. For example, some experts commented that the software was too classroom-oriented, which does not promote the acceptance by students; experts suggested that the software should be game-oriented. Some experts commented that animation techniques of the software were not good, and there were too many texts. Thus we increased the proportion of animation in the software and reduced text presentation in the latter software development. In addition, some experts commented that the training contents were more of lecture and the forms of expression were not diversified, which are valuable for modification of the software.

*Feedback from students.* We modified the software based on the suggestions of the experts. We selected a junior grade two class from the Middle School Attached to Southwest China Normal University at random to experiment the software, in order to understand the opinions of students to such psychological training, the suggestions and requirements of such software. After the experiment, 55 questionnaires were distributed and 51 valid questionnaires were collected.

*Overall effect.* The results showed that 51% students believed that the software brought beneficial inspirations; 39.2% students believed they gained benefits from the software, but not great benefits; 9.8% students had no feelings to the software. Comparing with PST course, 52.9% students believed that it was better to combine CAT tools with PST course because computer attracted students and it was more interesting to have computer involved in the teaching as teachers imparted a lot of knowledge in the teaching. While 37.3% students preferred computer-based presentation because they thought it was boring to listen to the lecture by teachers and computer-based presentation provided three-dimensional images and was more vivid, interesting and inspiring. In particular in TSR training software, nine out of 14 students preferred computer-based presentation, this is possibly because teachers were involved in TSR training and students would have worries and pressure if teachers gave the lecture in the training course. It also proved the applicability and advantages of CAT software in TSR training. About 58.8% students thought the software was general, 41.2% students felt good about the software and no student thought the software was bad. It indicates that students were basically satisfied with the software, but the software still needs to be improved to some extent.

*Content perspective.* Table 9.7. shows that in terms of content connection, 52.94% students believed that that the content connection was good, smooth and systematic; 29.41% students thought the connection was OK; 15.69% students thought the arrangement was not concentrated and was not theme-oriented. In the terms of TSR training software, only one student thought the connection was bad, and all the rest students thought the connection was OK or good. In the terms of content selection, 66.67% students thought that most of contents were close to life and were helpful for future communication; 31.37% students thought they had already realized many problems and such learning facilitated thinking and the learning was necessary; 27.45% students thought that it was not necessary to learn since they had known most of the learning contents; only 1.96% students thought the contents were out dated and did not meet the requirements of the age. It indicates that most students were satisfied with the connection and selection of contents.

*Form perspective.* Table 9.8. shows that in the terms of general presentation, 41.2% students thought the forms were flexible; 52.9% students thought the forms were OK, indicating that the forms of presentation still need to be improved for more flexibility. To be specific, in the terms of character design, 49% students were satisfied; 37.3% students thought the character design were OK and 13.7% students were not satisfied. In the terms of choosing and arranging screens, 82.4% students were satisfied; 15.7% students thought they were OK and only one student was not satisfied. It indicates that students felt good about the choosing and arrangement of screens. In the terms of background music and dubbing, 76.5% students were satisfied; 15.7% students thought they were OK; 7.8% students were not satisfied and they thought the music should be diversified and more special.

**Table 9.7. Feedback from Students on the Contents of PSE software**

| | Feedback | Frequency | Proportion (%) |
|---|---|---|---|
| Content connection | The connection was good, smooth and systematic. | 27 | 52.94 |
| | The arrangement was not concentrated and was not theme-oriented. | 8 | 15.69 |
| | The connection was OK. | 15 | 29.41 |
| Content selection | Most of the contents were close to life and were helpful for future communication. | 34 | 66.67 |
| | The contents were outdated and did not meet the requirements of the age. | 3 | 1.96 |
| | Students had known most of the learning contents, thus it was not necessary to learn. | 14 | 27.45 |
| | Systematic learning facilitated thinking. | 16 | 31.37 |

**Table 9.8. Feedback from Students on the Forms of PSE software**

| | Feedback | Frequency | Proportion (%) |
|---|---|---|---|
| Forms of presentation | Flexible | 21 | 41.2 |
| | OK | 27 | 52.9 |
| | Rigid | 3 | 5.9 |
| Character design | Satisfied | 25 | 49 |
| | OK | 19 | 37.3 |
| | Not satisfied | 7 | 13.7 |
| Choosing and arrangement of the screens | Satisfied | 42 | 82.4 |
| | OK | 8 | 15.7 |
| | Not satisfied | 1 | 1.9 |
| | Feedback | Frequency | Proportion (%) |
| Background music and dubbing | Satisfied | 39 | 76.5 |
| | OK | 8 | 15.7 |
| | Not satisfied | 4 | 7.8 |

The above analysis shows that students preferred TSR training in the forms of computer-based software. They were satisfied with the preliminarily developed software and also put forward the deficiencies and improvements. We further modified the preliminarily developed program according to the comments and suggestions of students. For example, some students thought there were too many buttons, resulting into disordered screen and inconvenient operation. Thus we added time setting to control the speed of display, and to provide fewer buttons, clear screens and easy operation. Some students thought the characters were too cartoonish, thus we designed characters that were closer to life. Some students thought there was not enough animation and the presentation was not attractive enough, thus we added more animation, making the cartoon more flexible and interesting. Some students thought the music was too boring, thus we added more music that was more pleasing to ears and tried to make the music match with the commentary and the training contents. Some students thought the contents were outdated, thus we made the contents more diversified, closer to life and more narrative.

The experts re-evaluate the modified software. We re-modified the software based on the comments of the experts. We repeated such cycle for several times until the software was satisfactory.

Finally, we developed multimedia based software for six TSR training lessons: Understand TSR; Begin from me to improve TSR; How to communicate with teachers; How to solve the misunderstanding between teachers and students? How to treat the partiality of teachers? How to solve the conflict between teachers and students?

## Evaluation of Computer Assisted PSE Mode

PSE is a systematic work. In addition to the school, PSE should be applied to a wider range so that students can receive and participate in PST anywhere and at any time. This can be realized via the Internet. Via the Internet, participants will no longer be restricted by the time or the space, and they can get the PST they need for learning. This is exactly the reason why we built computer-assisted PSE modes.

Computer assisted PSE modes reflect the ideology of PSE. Zhang et al. Put forward the integrated PSE mode of "physiology, psychology, society and education", by summarizing the MHE modes available. We put forward computer-assisted PSE mode based on such mode and by combining the computer-assisted teaching mode. Such mode is supported by multimedia techniques. The theoretical basis of such mode is PSE ideology put forward by Zhang et al. Such mode is the new exploration into effective implementation of PSE. Therefore, the theory of integrated PSE mode also applies to computer-assisted PSE mode. Computer-assisted PSE mode is a specific means of implementing integrated mode, the basic theory and ideology of which both followed PSE ideology put forward by Zhang et al. Such mode strives to realize the PSE target of "to cultivate good psychological *suzhi* of students and to promote positive adaptation and initiative development of students" from cognitive change to behavioral correction, and further to reflection and experience, and internalization of trait, by carefully designing the training contents of the software and choosing the problems of teacher-student communication. Meanwhile, we designed vivid and interesting forms to improve the learning motivation and interest of students and to improve the initiative of students. We made the mode reflecting the PSE principles: "for all students, playing the initiative of students, increasing the internalization and experience of students". We put forward the basic training mode of computer-assisted PSE based on the process of forming students' psychological *suzhi* put forward by Zhang et al., "self-understanding, knowledge learning, behavioral direction, reflection and internalization and development of habits into nature". To sum up, both the content and form design of computer-based PSE mode reflect the targets, principles and implementing strategies of PSE.

## New Conception of Computer Assisted PSE Mode

*Highly situational.* Compared with other PSE modes frequently used at present, including psychological SPT lessons, psychological consultation and counseling and subject infiltration, the computer-assisted PSE mode features vivid situations. Computer-assisted PSE mode strives to provide vivid communication situations by making use of its own technical advantages and such multimedia information as music and animation, in order that students experience communicating situations when they watch the animation, acquire knowledge and skills of communication, experience the fun of communication and eventually form stable psychological traits of communication. Computer provides simulated situations for students to try and practice, which facilitates students to consolidate the knowledge and skills they learned. Computer provides harmonious psychological atmosphere for learners through music, background, color, animation, etc. Meanwhile, computer creates problem situations which arouse thinking of students; creates situations that correspond with the targets and contents and stimulate with the feeling of students; creates democratic, relaxing and open psychological situations that stimulate the inner world of students. Such situations result in concept shock eventually, emotional resonance and behavioral influence. To sum up, multimedia based animation situations provide direct feelings for students, stimulate the interests of students in learning, activate or arouse the psychological activities of students. Guiding the thinking and action in such process is normally impossible for ordinary psychological training.

*Strongly systematic.* With the development of multimedia based computer, some resources for PSE on the Internet gradually emerged, including some specialized psychological websites, but they do not run very well due to the simple content and limited functions. There still lacks a scientific and systematic PSE system with complete functions. Song [2002] pointed out that most computer-assisted PSE software has the following problems: "the functions are not varied; the contents are more of lecture and are boring; they focus on the cultivation of a certain aspect, and deviate from original intention of PSE, i.e., improve the *suzhi* and capacity of students in an all-around way ". The analysis above shows that psychological *suzhi* is a complicated system with multiple components; the training with monotonous contents surely will influence comprehensive and systematic PSE. We first built up computer-assisted PSE mode and then developed a series of PSE software based on such mode to effectively cultivate and educate students for their psychological traits, rather than for a certain psychological trait. In the terms of a certain trait, we trained students from many aspects and angles. For example, the PSE software promoting TSR developed by us classified TSR training into many aspects. Every aspect is strongly systematic, as it is from cognitive change to behavioral guidance, and emphasizes the experience and internalization of students.

*Highly specialized.* Most researchers of PSE software are computer specialists, educational professionals [Wu, 2000; Wang, 2000; Song, 2002]. We did not see any specialized psychological researchers probed into PSE software. Computer and educational specialists, due to their professions, focus more on technical aspects. They consider the software development from technical advantages, rather than from the actual needs and characteristics of PSE. Their research was mostly about the procedures of development and the technologies used. They highlighted technology, but did not probe much into the ideology and contents of developing PSE software. In fact, the contents and the ideology of training are the core of developing PSE software; while technology is only the tool of presentation. Neglecting the essential contents of PSE software will result in weakly specialized software, and influence the effectivity and scientificity of the software. The PSE software based on computer-assisted PSE mode combines the psychology-focused training content and the technical support from computer specialists. Computer is only the tool to reach PSE targets when we developed PSE software. The core contents of the software are still content system of PSE. Thus the software we developed is highly specialized.

*Highly operable.* The content of existing PSE software always focuses on the introduction of psychological knowledge or assessment of psychological *suzhi*. It involves less psychological training and the software just simply gives some advice-based knowledge. On the contrary, the software based on the computer-assisted PSE mode is highly operable. It focuses on the behavioral guidance for students and provides practical skills for them so that students may directly apply the knowledge and skills they have learned from the software to their daily life. We designed the PSE software by taking TSR training as an example, according to the computer-assisted PSE mode. In the design, we borrowed ideas from computer-assisted teaching, computer-assisted instruction, and CAI establishment. We invited computer specialists to cooperate with us. We also invited several experts to evaluate the software and obtained feedback from students. Finally we developed the software for six lessons. The test results and the application effects show that the system ran stably and efficiently; the screens were friendly. The software met the requirements of students and was welcomed by students. Of course, this is a new exploration. There are still problems in the software, which need modification and improvement.

## EXPERIMENTAL RESEARCH INTO THE PSE PROMOTING TSR

### Experiment of the PSE Promoting TSR

*1) Purpose*

> To probe into the effectivity of computer-assisted PSE mode; and
> To promote the development of TSR among junior middle school students.

*2) Participants and Methods*

> *Participants.* The participants were junior grade two students from a Chongqing based experimental middle school. The experimental group was consisted of 34 participants, including 12 female and 22 male. The control group was consisted of 33 students, including 12 female and 21 male.
>
> *Methods.* Psychometrics, educational experiments and case interview were used in the present research. The psychometric tool used in the experiment referred to the *Teacher-student Relationship Scale (for Students)* developed by Wang, which was used to survey the TSR. The educational experiment used computer-assisted TSR training software developed by us (see the appendix). After the experiment, we carried out case interview to two to three students of the experimental group. SPSS10.0 for Windows was used to process the data.

## 3) Experiment Design and Procedures

In the experiment, we designed pre-test and post-test for both experimental and control groups. The experimental treatment is shown in Table 9.9.

**Table 9.9. Experimental Treatment of TSR Improvement in Junior Middle School**

| Groups | Pre-Test | Experimental Treatment | Post-Test |
|---|---|---|---|
| Experimental Group | TSR measurement | Computer-assisted TSR training | The same as pre-test |
| Control Group | TSR measurement | Daily learning | The same as pre-test |

The experiment included three stages:

*Stage one: Pre-test*

Both the experimental and control groups participated in the pre-test. The teacher-student relationship scale was used in the test. Depth interview was carried out to some students after the test, in order to understand the TSR situations of both experimental and control groups.

*Stage two: Experimental intervention.*

The experimental group learned the software. The learning material is the *Psychological-Suzhi-Education Software Promoting Teacher-Student Relationship* developed by us. The experiment took one and a half month, once each week. The experiment was conducted in the computer classroom of the school. Before the experiment, the experimenter installed the software in the computer. The students from experimental group went to the computer classroom during the computer class to learn. Each student occupied one computer and controlled one' own learning speed. Questions were available in the software, requiring students to answer. The answers of students were automatically stored in the defined files for analysis after the experiment. The experimenters were only responsible for technical assistance and explanation.

No training was conducted in the control group. To avoid expectancy effect, students from control group also went to the computer classroom during the computer class, but they went there only for computer class. In addition, all experimental software installed was deleted.

*Stage three: Post-test*

Both the experimental and control groups participated in the post-test. The teacher-student relationship scale was used in the test.

## 4) The Experimental Variables

Independent variable: Computer-assisted TSR training

Dependent Variable: the development level of TSR in junior middle school

Control variables:

Reasonably determined the experimental group and control group, in order to guarantee equal initiative TSR between the experimental and control groups.

Controlled other factors influencing experimental effects; removed expectancy effects; did not inform the teachers and students of the experimental group of the experiment purpose; sent students from both the experimental and control groups to the computer classroom during the computer class.

## 5) *Experimental Results and Analysis*

Comparison of pre-test and post-test scores in TSR between experimental group and control group. The pre-test and post-test scores of both the experimental and control groups in the total scale and sub-scales concerning TSR in junior middle school are shown in Table 9.10.

Table 9.10. shows that there was no significant difference ($p>0.05$) before the experiment between experimental and control groups in total scores and factors concerning TSR. It indicates that the two classes we have chosen are parallel classes, meeting the requirements of experimental design for balance grouping.

The comparison of post-test scores between the experimental and control groups still showed no significant difference in total scores and factors between both groups. However, in terms of mean valves, the experimental group had lower scores than the control group in total scores and factors before the experiment; but after the experiment, the experimental group had slightly higher scores than the control group in total scores and other factors, except conflict. The mean value of the experimental group before and after the experiment shows directly that the general TSR and factors of TSR of the experimental group were improved to some extent.

**Table 9.10. Comparison of Pre-test and Post-test Sores in TSR between Experimental Group and Control Group**

|  |  | Experimental Group (n=34) | | Control Group (n=33) | | |
|---|---|---|---|---|---|---|
|  |  | M | SD | M | SD | *t* |
| Pre-Test | Closeness | 2.55 | 0.87 | 2.73 | 0.92 | 0.800 |
|  | Conflict | 1.92 | 0.65 | 1.86 | 0.89 | -0.264 |
|  | Support | 3.52 | 0.66 | 3.75 | 0.60 | 1.447 |
|  | Satisfactory | 3.60 | 0.63 | 3.84 | 0.65 | 1.550 |
|  | Total scores | 1.94 | 0.54 | 2.11 | 0.61 | 1.223 |
| Post-Test | Closeness | 2.90 | 0.46 | 2.71 | 0.83 | -1.154 |
|  | Conflict | 1.85 | 0.70 | 1.81 | 0.62 | -0.240 |
|  | Support | 3.72 | 0.79 | 3.72 | 0.69 | -0.004 |
|  | Satisfactory | 3.82 | 0.54 | 3.82 | 0.54 | -0.039 |
|  | Total scores | 2.15 | 0.49 | 2.11 | 0.51 | -0.322 |

Comparison between pre-test and post-test scores in TSR of experimental group. We also conducted paired tests to the pre-test and post-test scores of the experimental group, in order to verify the experimental effects from another perspective. Comparison between pre-test and post-test scores in TSR of experimental group is shown in Table 9.11.

As shown in Table 9.11, there was significant difference between pre-test and post-test scores of the experimental group in teacher-student relationship scale. The post-test cores were higher than pre-test scores. It indicates that the TSR of students was improved after the experiment. To be specific, the post-test score in "closeness" was higher than pre-test score ($p<0.05$). There was no significant difference ($p>0.05$) between pre-test scores and post-test scores in "satisfactory", "conflict" and "support". The mean value also directly shows that the scores of experimental group in total scores and factors after the experiment were higher than that before the experiment.

**Table 9.11. Comparison between Pre-test and Post-test Scores in TSR
of Experimental Group**

|  | Pre-Test (n=34) | | Post-Test (n=34) | | t |
|---|---|---|---|---|---|
|  | M | SD | M | SD |  |
| Closeness | 2.55 | 0.87 | 2.90 | 0.46 | -2.491* |
| Conflict | 1.91 | 0.65 | 1.85 | 0.70 | -0.458 |
| Support | 3.52 | 0.66 | 3.72 | 0.79 | -1.338 |
| Satisfactory | 3.60 | 0.63 | 3.82 | 0.54 | -1.912 |
| Total scores | 1.94 | 0.54 | 2.15 | 0.49 | -2.220* |

Comparison between pre-test and post-test scores in TSR of control group. As required by the experimental design of balance grouping, we analyzed the changes between pre-test and post-test scores in TSR of the control group. The results were shown in Table 9.12.

**Table 9.12. Comparison between Pre-test and Post-test Scores in TSR
of Control Group**

|  | Pre-Test (n=33) | | Post-Test (n=33) | | t |
|---|---|---|---|---|---|
|  | M | SD | M | SD |  |
| Closeness | 2.73 | 0.92 | 2.71 | 0.83 | 0.150 |
| Conflict | 1.86 | 0.89 | 1.81 | 0.62 | 0.336 |
| Support | 3.75 | 0.60 | 3.72 | 0.69 | 0.276 |
| Satisfactory | 3.84 | 0.65 | 3.82 | 0.54 | 0.185 |
| Total scores | 2.11 | 0.61 | 2.11 | 0.51 | 0.065 |

Table 9.12. shows no significant difference ($p>0.05$) between pre-test and post-test scores of the control group in total scores and factors of teacher-student relationship scale. There was no difference in mean value of total scores between pre-test and post-test. There were non-significant different changes in the four factors.

Tests of gain difference in factors between experimental and control groups. We conducted independent sample t test to the experimental and control groups for the score difference (gain) of factors in the pre-test and the post-test, in order to verify whether the experimental effect was as significant in the statistics. The results are shown in Table 9.13.:

**Table 9.13. Tests of Gain Difference in Factors between Experimental
and Control Groups**

|  | Experimental Group (n=34) | | Control Group (n=33) | | t |
|---|---|---|---|---|---|
|  | M | SD | M | SD |  |
| Gain in closeness | 0.34 | 0.81 | -1.89 | 0.72 | -1.947* |
| Gain in conflict | -5.88 | 0.75 | -4.76 | 0.81 | -0.059 |
| Gain in support | 1.81 | 1.09 | -3.03 | 0.63 | -8.472*** |
| Gain in satisfactory | 0.22 | 0.68 | -2.42 | 0.75 | -1.414 |
| Total scores | 0.20 | 0.54 | -6.47 | 0.57 | -1.566 |

Table 9.13. shows significant difference between the experimental and control group in the gaining closeness and support. The experimental group had higher scores in these two factors in the post-test; the control group had lower scores in these two factors in the post-test. In the terms of gains, the experimental group had negative gains in conflict and positive gains in total scores and factors, indicating that the experimental group had higher scores in general TSR and factors of TSR after the experiment than that before the experiment. Except for conflict, the control group had negative gains in the rest factors, indicating reduced TSR of the control group.

*Comparison between male and female in pre-test and post-test scores in TSR of experimental group*. We compared the pre-test and post-test scores of TSR between male and female students of the experimental group, in order to verify the difference of interventional effects of computer-assisted training software between female and male students. See Table 9.14. for the results:

**Table 9.14. Comparison between Male and Female Students in Pre-test and Post-test Scores in TSR of Experimental Group**

|  |  | Pre-test | | Post-test | | $t$ |
| --- | --- | --- | --- | --- | --- | --- |
|  |  | M | SD | M | SD |  |
| Male (n=19) | Closeness | 2.30 | 0.86 | 2.83 | 0.49 | -3.037** |
|  | Conflict | 2.11 | 0.66 | 2.01 | 0.74 | 0.559 |
|  | Support | 3.39 | 0.63 | 3.63 | 0.81 | -1.265 |
|  | Satisfactory | 3.58 | 0.65 | 3.69 | 0.57 | -0.696 |
|  | Total scores | 1.79 | 0.50 | 2.03 | 0.53 | -2.006 |
| Female (n=22) | Closeness | 3.03 | 0.72 | 3.04 | 0.38 | -0.050 |
|  | Conflict | 1.53 | 0.44 | 1.56 | 0.54 | -0.175 |
|  | Support | 3.78 | 0.67 | 3.88 | 0.77 | -0.473 |
|  | Satisfactory | 3.65 | 0.59 | 4.08 | 0.36 | -2.789* |
|  | Total scores | 2.23 | 0.50 | 2.36 | 0.36 | -0.941 |

As shown in Table 9.14, both female and male students of the experimental group had higher scores in general TSR and factors of TSR after they received the TSR training. Significant difference is As seen between pre-test and post-test scores in closeness of male students. Male students obviously had closer TSR after the experiment than that before the experiment. The post-test scores in total scores, conflict, support and satisfactory were improved to some extent, although the difference was not significant. Significant difference is As seen between pre-test and post-test scores in satisfactory factor of female students. They are obviously more satisfied with the TSR after the experiment. The scores in closeness and support were improved to some extent, but the difference was not significant. It indicates that the same contents of training had different effects on female and male students.

*Qualitative analysis of experimental results*. We investigated the TSR improvement through teacher-student relationship scale, based on how we judged the intervention effects of TSR training software. However, the training software aims to improve TSR through improving the skills of students in teacher-student communication. But it is possible that even students have better skills in teacher-student communication or they are aware of improving such skills, i.e., cognitive changes occur, the TSR still does not reflect such improvement as

TSR is influenced by both teachers and students. Therefore, we tried to carry out qualitative analysis of the intervention effects after the experiment through the questionnaire Express Your Feelings and Opinions, in order to further analyze the intervention effects of computer-assisted training software. Four open-ended questions were designed in the questionnaire, "what did you gain or how did the software benefit you after you learned teacher-student communication through the software", "did you use in daily life the skills and knowledge acquired? If yes, please show us an example", "Share your true thinking with teachers: after learning how to communicate with teachers, do you have any true thinking that you want to share with teachers", "Do you have any suggestions or comments for better software". We distributed 34 questionnaires to the experimental group and 30 valid questionnaires were collected. We classified and sorted and organized the survey results through content analysis. The results are as follows:

**Table 9.15. Question 1: "What Did You Gain after You Learned the Software?"**

| Question | Answers | Frequency | Proportion (%) |
|---|---|---|---|
| What did you gain after you learned the software? | I knew how to communicate with teachers. | 23 | 76.67 |
| | I knew teachers better and understood them better. | 14 | 46.67 |
| | No gains. | 1 | 3.33 |

As shown in Table 9.15, among the answers to the question "what did you gain after you learned the software", only one student answered "no gains", and all the rest had gains to different extent. About 76.67% students know how to communicate with teachers and learned many skills of teacher-student communication. For example, "I know how to communicate with teachers"; "I know how to avoid teacher-student conflicts"; "I should regard teachers as good friends and communicate with teachers when I encountered difficulties"; "I should retrospect whether it is my problem when I have conflict with teachers"; "I should help teachers within my capacity", etc. About 36.67% students said they knew and understood teachers better after they learned the software. For example, some students said "I know the thinking of teachers and I know they care about us, no matter we have good or poor performance"; "I have new understanding of teachers and know that they give much thought on the matters"; "I understand the feelings of teachers". Many students said, "We should respect teachers and understand their thoughts on the matters".

For question "Did you use in daily life the skills and knowledge acquired? If yes, please show us an example", five students answered that they did not use them, and the rest students showed examples about how they used them. About 23.33% students said they used skills to solve the teacher-student misunderstanding. For example, some students said: "I was misunderstood by the teacher. I explained to the teacher after class rather than arguing with the teacher in class like before"; "On day, a teacher asked me to answer a question in class. But I could not answer the question. The teacher criticized me in front of the class. I felt being humiliated. I hated the teacher at that time. But Now I know I misunderstood the teacher. If the teacher did not care about whether I understood, he would not ask me to answer the question. He cared about me. I misunderstood him."

**Table 9.16. Question 2: "Did You Use in Daily Life the Skills and Knowledge Acquired? If Yes, Please Show us an Example"**

| Question | Answers | Frequency | Proportion (%) |
|---|---|---|---|
| Did you use in daily life the skills and knowledge acquired? If yes, please show us an example | I used them in solving the misunderstanding with teachers. | 7 | 23.33 |
| | I used them in solving the conflict with teachers. | 5 | 16.67 |
| | I used them to actively communicate with teachers. | 6 | 20 |
| | I coordinated with teachers and worked hard in learning. | 6 | 20 |
| | I used them to treat the partiality of teachers. | 1 | 3.33 |
| | I did not use them. | 5 | 16.67 |

Five students said they used skills in solving the conflict with teachers, for example, explaining to teachers after class, rather than directly arguing with teachers. Six students said they used the knowledge acquired in communicating with teachers, for example, "I wrote down my thoughts and opinions on the communication booklet to tell teachers. Now I chat with teachers after class very often". Some students were more active in learning, for example, they were voluntary to answer questions in class and asked teachers questions after class. For the question "Share your true thinking with teachers", seven students said they thanked teachers, for example, some students said, "I hated you very much because I did not understand you and thought you did not want us to have fun. But now I understand that you did that for our own good and for our good performance in learning. Thank you, Teacher!" Some said, "You are a very good teacher. You helped me improve my academic performance and protected me from being bullied. You are very nice." Eight students talked about their understanding of teachers, "Teacher, we have known your difficulties. We will understand you and your thoughts in the future. We will not bother you. I am sorry for what I did wrong. We appreciate your efforts"! Six students said they would have more communication with teachers. Meanwhile, 14 students sincerely provided some suggestions, "Teachers don't understand us; teachers are irritable and too strict; teachers should impart more extra-curricular knowledge". They expressed their desire to communicate with teachers.

**Table 9.17. Question 3: "Share Your True Thinking with Teachers"**

| Question | Answers | Frequency | Proportion (%) |
|---|---|---|---|
| Share your true thinking with teachers | Teacher, we should have more communication | 6 | 20 |
| | Teacher, thank you. | 7 | 23.33 |
| | Teacher, I have some suggestions for you. | 14 | 46.67 |
| | Teacher, I understand you. | 8 | 26.67 |
| | N/A | 2 | 6.67 |

**Table 9.18. Question 4: "Do You Have any Suggestions for the Software?"**

| Question | Answers | Frequency | Proportion (%) |
|---|---|---|---|
| Do you have any suggestions for the software? | No, I am satisfied with the software. | 18 | 60 |
| | The forms of presentation, for example, the background, dubbing and character, need to be improved. | 3 | 10 |
| | The contents of the software need to be improved. | 9 | 30 |

In terms of the evaluation of the software, 60% students were satisfied with the software. Some students thought the forms of presentation needed to be improved, for example, the character and background were not delicate enough, the three-dimension effect was not good enough, the dubbing was not always available, making people feel at a loss. Some students pointed out that the contents of the software needed to be improved, for example, extra-curricular knowledge such as psychological tests should be added, there were not enough examples, the time of a class was too long, and there were not enough skills for teacher-student communication. All such suggestions and comments were very meaningful for our modification.

## Case Analysis after the Experiment of PSE

We interviewed some students about the problems in teacher-student communication and the feeling of the software, in order to understand the psychological and behavioral changes of students after the TSR training, and to further analyze the intervention effects of computer-assisted TSR training software. We also interviewed the head teachers to know more about the students interviewed. We analyzed comprehensively by considering the survey results of students interviewed. All interviews were carried out separately in an office.

T refers to interviewer; S1 refers to students; and S2 refers to the head teachers.

Case One: A male student surnamed Jiang, ranked No. 15 in the latest midterm examination

T: How was your relationship with teachers in the past?
S1: Not so good. I was not good at learning. I was a troublemaker in class. Teachers did not like me.
T: Why did you make troubles in class?
S1: Because teachers did not ask me questions in class. They did not care about me. Thus I wanted to create disturbance.
T: Students want to attract the attention from teachers, but did you think of other ways to attract the attention of teachers?
S1: No. Teachers like students with good performance. My performance is only average, and I usually creates troubles in class. Thus teachers think I don't have any advantages. I am very good at PE, but PE is not main subject, teachers pay no attention to it.

T: You learned how to communicate with teachers through the software. How do you feel about it?

S1: I think the software is very interesting. I learned a lot from it. For example, I liked to act in opposition to teachers in the past in class. Now I have realized my mistakes, so I try not to talk nonsense or create troubles in class now.

T: What impressed you most after you learned the software?

S1: What has impressed me the most is that the software told us to attract the attention of teachers through showing what we are good at, and a figure of a thumb. I will actively present myself, communicate more with teachers and make teachers understand me better.

The above interview shows that the TSR of the student was bas. After software-based learning, he realized what he did wrong and knew how to attract the attention of teachers properly. He gained a lot from the software.

We also interviewed the head teacher who had the most communication with the student, in order to further understand the changes of the student before and after the software-based learning.

T: How do you think is the relationship of the student surnamed Jiang with teachers?

S2: Not so good. He usually created troubles in class.

T: Do you think he had any changes recently?

S2: He behaved quite well recently in class. He spoke less and talked less nonsense. He wrote on the communication booklet (which is similar to diary, most of the contents are what students want to tell the head teacher) that he did wrong in the past. He was wrong to create trouble or act in opposite to teachers in class.

T: How do you feel about him?

S2: In fact, he is quite clear. But he was naughty and was careless in class. He is quite good at PE. He had quite good performance in the sports meeting recently. If he works harder, he will have very good performance.

The interview with the head teacher shows that he had some psychological and behavioral changes in the recent weeks. He realized what he did wrong and wrote those in the communication booklet. He consciously controlled his misconducts in class, trying to have good impression from teachers. We also found the changes of the student. In the first two training classes, he talked in class and disobeyed the rules. In the latter classes, he behaved well, learned seriously, and did not talk as much as before in class.

He wrote his feelings after the training, "I had new understanding of teachers. Actually teachers are kind to everyone", "I felt teachers were not fair. I was not the kind of student you like, so I was not willing to talk to you. But after thinking carefully, I realized that you were kind to me. Every time my academic performance dropped, you talked to me to find out the reasons. Thank you very much!" From those words, we know that the student had new understanding of teacher. His attitude toward teachers changed from hostility to closeness and appreciation.

In addition, we also concluded the same experimental results from his pre-test and post-test cores of teacher-student relationship scale. Pre-test scores: total scores 1.12; closeness 1.00; conflict 2.00; support 2.88; satisfactory 2.60. Post-test scores: total scores 2.43; closeness 3.63; conflict 1.57; support 4.25; satisfactory 3.40. After the experiment, the student had higher total scores, and obviously higher scores in closeness, support and satisfactory factors, and obviously lower scores in conflict factor.

Case Two: A female student surnamed Hu, ranked No. 30 in the latest midterm examination.

We interviewed the head teacher before the experiment for the some information of the student. The head teacher said, "She has bad academic performance and does not behave well normally. She often controdicts teachers, acts in opposite to teachers. Teachers do not like her." The head teacher also mentioned that her parents were adoptive parents. Her biological parents live in a rural village. Her adoptive parents were stall owners, and do not discipline her much. Due to her special situation, we researched her as a case. We interviewed her after the experiment.

T: How is your relationship with teachers?

S1: Bad. Teachers don't like me. They always criticize me and dislike me.

T: Do you like them?

S1: I hate them. But they are for our own benefit. I was too wayward. Sometimes, I contradicted teachers and hurt the feeling of teachers.

T: When did you start to change?

S1: Sometimes I realized my problem, but I still contradicted with teachers. Recently, I learned a lot about how to communicate with teachers in the computer class. I realized my problems. The problem is not teachers don't like me, but what I did are not proper.

T: Is your relationship with teachers changed recently?

S1: Yes, Teachers helped me solve some difficulties recently. I appreciate their efforts. Honestly, teachers were very nice to students.

The above interview shows that student changed her attitude toward teachers.

After the interview, we talked with the head teacher to know the recent situations of the student.

T: Did you notice the change of the student surnamed Hu recently?

S2: She did not contradict with teachers recently. She often expressed her thoughts with teachers on the communication booklet. For example, right after the midterm examination, she tried to find reasons from herself and also asked teachers to help her establish the learning plan and asked teachers about good learning methods, etc. All these show that she likes learning than before.

T: She said you helped her a lot. She appreciated your help.

S2: Recently, she wrote a lot about what happened in her family. Her adoptive parents often asked her to take care of the stalls, thus she can not concentrate on learning. I asked her father to come to the school. We talked about it. Now the problem is solved and she can concentrate on learning.

The interview with the head teacher shows that the student dramatically changed her attitude toward teachers. She realized her problem. Behaviorally, she actively communicated with teachers and initiatively communicated with teachers.

She wrote in the survey after the software-based learning, "After the learning, I know that when I encounter difficulties, I should regard teachers as bosom friends and communicate with teachers. When I have conflicts with teachers, I should retrospect about whether it is my problem. I should understand teachers. I should help teacher with my capacity. In terms of sharing thoughts with teachers, she wrote, "Teacher, I want to say that you are a good teacher. You helped me a lot in solving difficulties. You are the only one I can talk to when I have problems about my family. Thank you very much!"

The pre-test and post-test scores of teacher-student relationship scale shows obvious TSR improvement. The pre-test scores are: total scores 1.23; closeness 1.63; conflict 2.29; support 2.38; satisfactory 3.20. The post-test scores are: total scores 1.69; closeness 2.75; conflict 2.25; support 3.63; satisfactory 3.40.

To sum up, the experimental intervention in the TSR in junior middle school was effective. Computer-assisted TSR training is an effective way to improve TSR.

## The Effectivity of Computer Assisted PSE Mode

We carried out educational experiment using the software developed, in order to verify the effectivity of the TSR training software, and to verify the effectivity of computer-assisted PSE mode we proposed.

### General Effect

We carried out horizontal and vertical comparison of pre-test and post-test results of teacher-student relationship scale. The results show that i) computer-assisted TSR training improved TSR of the experimental group and improved the skills of students in teacher-student communication. Before the experiment, there was no significant difference between the experimental and control groups in TSR development. The experimental group had significantly higher total scores in the post-test than in the pre-test after receiving computer-assisted TSR training for six times. It vertically indicates that the TSR of the experimental group was significantly improved. Horizontally, there was no significant difference between the two groups in total scores after the training, but gain of total scores of the experimental was positive while that of the control group was negative. Although the difference between the two groups was not significant, the difference still shows the intervention effects of computer-assisted TSR training to some extent. ii) computer-assisted TSR training has different influences to the four factors of TSR. The survey shows that, (i) it significantly improved the "closeness" factor ($p<0.05$); (ii) it improved "conflict", "support" and "satisfactory" factors, but the improvement was not significant ($p>0.05$). iii) computer-assisted TSR training has different intervention effects between female and male students. After the experiment, the closeness of male students was significantly improved; the satisfactory of female students was significantly improved.

The reasons for why computer-assisted TSR training has different intervention effects in different dimensions of TSR include:

The experimental intervention changed the attitude of teachers toward students and improved the closeness of students to teachers. The experimental intervention was cognitively, emotionally and behaviorally. The items under closeness dimension are to test the attitude of students toward teachers. For example, "I would like to tell teachers my true thinking", "I will ask teachers to help me when I encounter difficulties", I treasure the relationship between teachers and me", etc. In TSR training, we specially designed a lesson to understand TSR. In the latter lessons, we also emphasized that students should understand teachers and objectively treat the mistakes of teachers, which provided students with new understanding of TSR. They re-considered their attitude toward teachers and realized the importance of TSR. Then they felt psychologically close to teachers. They were no longer fully opposite to teachers. Thus the experimental effects of closeness factor are very obvious.

The bidirectional nature of TSR influences the improvement of conflict, support and satisfactory factors. There was no significant improvement in conflict factor before and after the experiment. According to the items of conflict factor, teachers and students are both involved in teacher-student conflict. The efforts and change only from students may not result in obvious improvement of TSR, for example, "I feel that teachers always punish and criticize me". Although a student can change the attitude toward teachers, the student will feel no change of TSR if teachers are frown upon the student and criticize the student for small mistakes. The student may feel "teachers still often punish and criticize me". That's why the intervention effects in conflict were not obvious. Of course, the changes of students in attitude and behaviors may also influences the attitude of teachers toward students, which may result in improvement of teacher-student conflict. That is why the conflict was improved to some extent after the experiment. The situations were the same for support and satisfactory factors. Support refers to that students obtain supports and assistance from teachers for learning and daily life. As we did not intervene in teachers, teachers still have the same attitude toward students. Thus the support and assistance from teachers were not essentially different. This may be the major reason for no obvious change of support factor before and after the experiment. Although students are in the passive position in receiving the support from teachers, the attitude of students toward teachers and the behaviors of students still influence the attitude of teachers toward students. Thus support factor was influenced to some extent. The reasons why satisfactory was not obviously improved are similar to the situations of conflict and support.

The different characteristics of psychological development between male and female students result in different intervention results of the experiment. The intervention effects show that significant difference between pre-test and post-test scores in closeness of male students. Male students obviously had closer TSR after the experiment than that before the experiment. The situations of total scores, conflict, support and satisfactory were improved to some extent. But the improvement is not significant. Significant difference is As seen between pre-test and post-test scores in satisfactory of female students. They are obviously more satisfied with the TSR after the experiment. The scores in closeness and support were improved to some extent, but the difference was not significant. The reasons for different intervention effects of TSR training on male and female students may be the previous TSR and characteristics of psychological development of male and female students. The survey shows that male students were less close to teachers than female students. This may be the course of higher independence and emotional implicitness of male students. Thus male students were not as close to teachers as female students. But the experiment made them realize the importance of TSR. Male students showed initiative in teacher-student communication and they were closer to teachers. The obvious improvement in satisfaction of female students may be for the reason that the previous TSR of female students was better than male students; and after the training, female students were more desirable to improve their relationship with teachers and they pay more attention to teacher-student communication. Thus female students were more satisfied with the relationship with teachers.

### *Qualitative Analysis of Experimental Results*

The qualitative analysis of experimental results was based on the survey and case interview after the training. The analysis shows that almost all students learned the knowledge and skills of teacher-student communication from TSR training software. And most students can independently use what they learned in life. It indicates that our software not only made students learn what and how to do from the knowledge perspective, but also made students know how to use what they learned in practice. The benefits to students were obvious. Of course, five students mentioned that they did not use what they learned in practice. This is what we will enhance in the future. On one hand, we will often remind students of using what they learned in practice; on the other hand, we will enhance the practical function of the training contents, which will enable students to directly use what they learned. In terms of sharing true thoughts with teachers, most students said they appreciated the efforts of teachers or they understood teachers better. It indicates that students had new understanding of teachers and they had new cognition of teachers. The cognition had been changed, which is also one of the purposes of experimental intervention. Of course, the cognitive change can not be measured in the teacher-student relationship scale. Thus it indirectly results in that the experimental results of the psychometrics were not obvious. In terms of the suggestions for the software, although most students were satisfied with the software, some students provided some suggestions. It indicates that on one hand, the software, as a new object, still needs to be improved; on the other hand, students paid much attention to the software and provided suggestions for better software.

The two students who participated in the case interview had poor academic performance in the past. They did not obey the rules, had poor relationship with teachers, and were quite hostile to teachers. But after the software-based learning for several times, they were obviously willing to be friendly with teachers rather than be opposite to teachers. They were willing to be harmonious with teachers and to exchange thoughts with teachers. Their behaviors also changed. They knew how to communicate with teachers, how to make students care about them, and understood teachers better. Teachers also had better impressions of them due to their efforts and changes. The two cases show that the TSR training software was helpful for students. It improved TSR.

Thus computer-assisted TSR training software is applicable and effective in improving TSR and improving the skills of teacher-student communication. Although the experimental effects of teacher-student relationship scale were not so obvious, students had changed cognition of themselves, teachers and TSR. They had new and objective understanding. But due to the bidirectional nature of teacher-student communication and the endurance of the experiment, the obvious improvement was not As seen in TSR.

## CONCLUSION

We carried out computer-assisted TSR training to junior middle school students for one and a half month by making use of computer-assisted PSE mode. The results showed that before the experiment, the experimental group had lower total scores and lower scores in factors of TSR than the control group; after the experiment, the experimental group had slightly higher total scores and slightly higher scores in factors than the control group. In the terms of mean values, the general TSR and factors of TSR of the experimental group were better after the experiment. In the terms of gains, significant difference is distinguished between experimental and control groups in gains of closeness and support. The experimental group had higher scores in these two factors, but the control group had lower scores in these two factors. The same training had different effects to female and male students. Male students had obviously higher scores in closeness; and female students had obviously higher scores in satisfactory. Further qualitative analysis also shows that computer-assisted TSR training is also an effective means of intervention for TSR improvement.

## APPENDIX: EXAMPLE OF A SCRIPT

### How to Solve Teacher-Student Conflict

| Purposes | Contents | Forms of presentation |
|---|---|---|
| Present the situation | Han Yu and his classmates established "secrete" activity plans although they have intense learning activities. They can not implement their plan due to the interference by teachers. "Our plan is killed again!" "We had a perfect plan, but Ms. Zhang said no at the first moment when she heard about it." "Ms. Zhang is not inflexible. She does not know that intense learning should be followed by relaxing activities." | Dubbing, animation and cartoons Animation: several students gathered together and proposed, "let's go spring outing on Saturday". But teacher said, "No, you should spend more time in learning". |
| Introduce to the theme | (At this moment) Teacher-student conflict happens. We don't know why. It seems teachers and we always had different ideas. They don't understand us. We are desired to go mountain climbing in the sunny weekend. It would be fabulous to have a party in the new year. But teachers always had a reason to say no to us, "You should work harder and should not think of relaxing all the time". They also had childhood. But why don't they understand us? How depressed! | Highlighted presentation Cartoons: some students say, "We would like to go mountain climbing" in a sunny day; "It would be fabulous to have a party" in a festival. Cartoon of a teacher, "You should work harder and should not think of relaxing all the time". |
| Arouse the thinking and resonance of students | | Present a picture of a student with depressed face. |

| | | |
|---|---|---|
| Cognitive change<br>Raise questions and arouse the thinking of students<br>Tell a story to explain<br><br>Guide the thinking of students.<br>Thinking refers to continuous reflection.<br>Give advice at proper time. | Why are students in conflict with teachers?<br>We are all familiar with the story, "The Blind Men and the Elephant". The blind men describe a same elephant differently. One says the elephant is like a pillar; one says the elephant is like a rope; one says the elephant is like a hand fan. They have a big argument. The root cause of the argument is that they have different perspective respectively and they do not understand others' perspectives.<br>The situation is the same for teacher-student conflict. Do you understand why there is conflict between students and teachers?<br>[Heart-to-heart sister says]<br>Teachers worry that students might encounter danger or they might delay the learning if they spend too much time in playing; whereas, students feel that teachers do not understand them. They think there is a generation gap between teachers and them. They are not willing to communicate with teachers. Then there easily comes the conflict. | Animation and dubbing: there is one elephant and some blind men. They feel the belly, ears and tail of the elephant and describe how the elephant is like. There is a fierce argument.<br><br><br>A picture of angel is presented to symbolize the heart-to-heart sister. The text is flexibly presented. |
| Behavioral guidance<br><br><br>Provide one skill.<br>Vivid description<br><br><br><br>Methods and directions<br><br><br><br><br><br><br><br><br><br><br><br><br>Quotes | (Then) How do you solve teacher-student conflict? Conflict itself is not terrible. What matters is how to solve the conflict. Let's look at the following contents.<br>Emotion control<br>When you are angry, it is like there are two messengers in your mind: the peaceful messenger tells you not to quarrel with others, while the war messenger tells you to fight. We should send more peaceful messengers, and persuade and propitiate the war messenger.<br>You can try the following methods:<br>(1) Distraction<br>When you are about to be angry, you can calm down by leaving the current environment. Or you can lock yourself up in a room, close your eyes and try to calm down. Then you can go out of the room when you control your emotion.<br>(2) Release<br>You can release your anger in other ways. You can jump hard or shout or cry when you are alone. Or you can talk to a good friend.<br>(3) Take a deep breath<br>If you conflict with teachers in a class, you can neither leave the classroom nor release your negative emotions at that time, then you must control your emotion rationally. Try to take a deep breath.<br>Take a deep breath for three to five times and tell yourself, "It is no big deal. It will be fine." "Calm down, I can handle with it." When you pay attention | Highlighted presentation<br><br>Use an arrow to symbolize "continue". Dubbing; one gentle cartoon character and one hostile cartoon character appear. One war messenger appears. Mark "X" behind him, meaning no.<br><br><br>Close your eyes and try to calm down in a room.<br><br><br>Animation: one person shouts "I hate you", cries and chat with friends.<br><br>Animation: Take a deep breath<br><br><br>One very angry person and one smiling person. |

| One sentence summary | to your anger after concentrating on your deep breath, you will find that you are different from just now! Thomas Jefferson, third president of the United States, said, "when angry, count to 10 before you speak. If very angry, a hundred". | Key words "one minute ago", "now" Dubbing. |
|---|---|---|
| Provide another skill | [Heart-to-heart sister says] You can face and solve the conflict with teachers only after positively | Dubbing, the picture of "me", key words. |
| Reflection | understanding and thinking about what causes the conflict. You should not act emotionally because it may lead to fiercer conflict. | |
| | Analysis of Reasons | Dubbing, the screen shows the picture of |
| Reflection from teacher's perspective is also the process of cognitive change. | When you calm down, you should think about the causes of the conflict. [Think about yourself] Is it because I am too impulsive or emotional? Is it because my words and deeds are too extreme, or I did not explain clearly to teachers. [Think about teachers] You may think teachers do not understand you at all, or teachers are not fair and are horrible. You may have many reasons of conflict, or reasons to hate teachers, but have you ever though about that: | teachers, "generation gap", "not fair", and other diversified contents. |
| Think about the story Find the reasons. | Is it true that what teachers did is completely unreasonable? Is it all teachers' fault? It is possible that teachers sometimes are dictatorial, but is it possible that teachers are right all the time? Does disobedience solve the conflicts? Now please think about why Han Yu conflicted with teachers. Different standpoints: Teachers ask students to work harder and are not willing to agree their relaxing plan. | Highlight "reasons", the screen should stay longer, allowing students to think. Pictures: teachers said "you should work harder", students said "I want to relax". Animation: teachers communication with students, "we will not |
| One sentence summary | Teachers worry about the safety of students. Students want to relax and desire to go out and play. Insufficient communication: teachers may say yes if students well communicate with teachers and ensure | delay our learning, and we will have more enthusiasm in learning". |
| Provide skills, corresponding with the reasons. Reflection of oneself | the safety of students and remove the worries of students: relaxation will not delay the learning and will be enthusiastic after proper relaxing. You can find the right solution if you find the cause of conflict. | |
| | Actions The conflict solution should not end at emotion control or finding the cause. The key of solving conflict is to take actions and solve the conflict. ☆Ask yourself: | Each sentence of the dubbing will show with the dubbing together. Dubbing |
| Guidance of skills | You should ask yourself the following question after the conflict happens: What are the causes of the conflict? What are the solutions of the conflict? Which solution can be accepted by teachers? | Dubbing: High and sharp volume In gentle and sincere |

| | | |
|---|---|---|
| Provide a situations and arouse the thinking of students | Which solution can be accepted by both teachers and you?<br>You may have the right solution in mid after asking yourself the questions.<br>☆Properly express what you would like to do by effectively communicate with teachers | tones<br><br><br>Dubbing: Return to the situation of the protagonist's experience. Students communicate with teachers. |
| Ask students to judge by themselves. | Avoiding conflict with teachers does not mean that you must always listen to teachers and act as required by teachers. People have different thoughts, thus conflicts are inevitable. The key is how you express different ideas to avoid conflict. | |
| Provide the right solution through the action of the protagonist. | Now let's look at how two students express their ideas:<br>Teacher, why don't you understand us? Why don't you agree with our ideas?<br>Teacher, I know you are for our own good, but do you think it is better to …?<br>What do you think about their expression? Which one do you prefer? | After the previous paragraph is shown, the following paragraph will be shown.<br>Dubbing<br><br><br>Dubbing |
| Emphasize | Let's look at how Han Yu solved the conflict?<br>(Sincerely) "Teacher, our learning activities are very intense and you have spent lots of efforts. We just progress and should have worked harder."<br>(By saying this, teachers feel that you have the same standpoint as them. And then they may agree your request.) | Dubbing |
| Skills | But we started the planning long time ago. If we don't implement the plan, we will be very disappointed and our learning motivation will be very low, which is against your hope.<br>(I believe teachers will agree.) | |
| Emphasize and remind | When you express ideas different from teachers, you should not have the attitude of "if teachers do not agree, I will swear not to stop". It does not help you to persuade teachers, because you have hostile standpoint.<br>You should also handle with your words appropriately. You should never make forceful argument without any reason, and make some concession even if you are in the right; avoid by all means rationalizing when in the wrong and showing no mercy when in the right.<br>☆Learn to apologize sincerely After the conflict, you should apologize to teachers timely when you realized you did something wrong.<br>[Note]<br>You should never use insulting sentences at any time, for example, "It is no great of being a teacher", "You are a pathetic teacher". Such sentences hurt the | |

| | feelings of teachers and will lead to fiercer conflict. | |
|---|---|---|
| Simulated training<br><br>Students answer questions in the simulated situations.<br><br>Prompt<br><br>Situation two<br><br>Thinking of students<br><br>Prompt<br><br>Recall your memory and think of the solution after learning. | Think about it<br>What will you do if you are under the following situations?<br>1. The bell rung. We planned to play basketball together, but teachers asked us to do some exercise during the extra-curricular activities.<br><br>(Teachers are for the good of students, but they deprive the rest time of students. You can tell teachers "we will finish the exercise in time". And you should finish the exercise in time and should not disappoint teachers. )<br>2. Today, I was criticized by a teacher. And I contradicted with the teacher. But afterward, I think I should not have done that.<br>*I want to tell the teacher,*<br>*I should*<br>(What about writing the teacher a note? "Teacher I regret saying that to you. Please forgive me.")<br>Remember the most serious conflict with teachers?<br>How did you solve the conflict?<br>Do you think you solved it properly? ( )<br>Do you have a better solution for that? | Use animation to present the situation. No dubbing is used to ask questions.<br><br>Store the answers of students.<br>Dubbing and relevant pictures. Highlighting.<br><br>Ibid.<br>After the answers are stored, another question is asked. |
| After class learning | [Communicate with peers] Communicate with peers about the experience in teacher-student communication, to see which solution is more effective.<br>Discuss with parents about how to solve conflicts with teachers. | Show pictures of communicating with peers and parents respectively. |
| Summary and Guidance | [Here is a sentence for you]<br>Teacher-student conflict is normal. But students should positively find the solution. Only by doing this, students can develop good TSR. It will also facilitate the learning and progress of students. | Show background music, text and dubbing. |

# REFERENCES

Adelman, H. S., and Taylor, L. (2002) School counselors and school reform: New directions. *Professional school counseling, 5,* 235-248.

Bitch, S. H. and Ladd, G. W. (1998). Children's interpersonal behaviors and teacher-child relationship. *Developmental psychology, 34,* 934-946.

Chen, J. L. (2002). *School mental health education-principle and practice.* Beijing: Educational Science Publishing House.

Chen, X. (2004). *Psychological suzhi education in middle school.* Chongqing: Southwest China Normal University Press.

Chen, X. *M.* (1989). The development characteristics and education of students' selection psychology in interpersonal relationship. *Psychological science, 4,* 31-36.

Chen, X., and Zhang, D. J. (2002). An exploration on integrated mode of mental health education. *Educational research, 1,* 71-75.

Dong, Q., and Chen, C. S. (2001).The role of relationships with teachers in adolescent development among a national sample of Chinese urban adolescents. *Chinese journal of applied psychology, 7,* 3-10.

Du, *F.* J. (2001). Training of communication skills in classroom teaching. *Journal of teaching and management, 7,* 50-51.

Fieldstein. (1990). *Contemporary adolescent psychology.* Beijing: Educational Science Publishing House.

Fisher, D., Kent, H., and Fraser, B. (1998). Relationships between teacher-student interpersonal behavior and teacher personality. *School psychology international, 19* (2), 154-166.

Guo, S. P., and Chen, P. L. (2001) Exploration into mental health education mode in school. *Jiangxi educational research, 9,* 14-16.

Han, R. S. (1998). The research into successful and failed communication among students from primary and middle schools. *Psychological science, 5,* 467-469.

Howes, C., Hamilton, C. E., and Matheson, C. C. (1995). Children's relationships with peers: Differential associations with aspects of the teacher - child relationship. *Child development, 66,* 253 – 263.

Ladd, G. W., Birch, S. H., and Buhs, E. S. (1999). Children's social and scholastic lives in kindergarten: Related spheres of influence? *Child Development, 70* (6), 1373-1400.

Li, C. *M.,* and Liu, Z. P. (1998). A study on the influence of teacher-student relationship on learning of middle school students. *Education exploration, 1,* 15-17.

Li, D. S., Wang, X. D., and Tao, Y. Z. (2001). The significance of "small team" training in education of primary school. *Journal of Sichuan College of Education, 4,* 69-70.

Li, J. Y. (1996). On teacher-student relationship and its influence on teaching activities. *Journal of the Northwest Normal University (social sciences), 33,* 57-61.

Li, X. D., Nie, Y. Y., and Lin, C. D. (2002). The effects of learning difficulty, interpersonal relationship and self-acceptance on eighth grader's mental health. *Psychological development and education, 2,* 68-73.

Lian, Y. W. (2000). *The survey and analysis of the current status of learning motivation.* Master's thesis, Tianjin Normal University, Tianjin, P.R.C.

Liu, H., and Zhang, D. J. (2004). On the quality education and the requirements of teacher's psychological qualifications. *Journal of Hebei Normal University (educational science edition), 6,* 56-60.

Liu, J. (2003). Comments on the research into teacher-student relationship in China in the 1990s. *Education exploration, 7,* 52-54.

Liu, W. L. (2002). The influence of teacher-student interpersonal relationship on the mental health of students. *Journal of Huainan Teacher College, 4,* 25-27.

Liu, W. L., and Wo, J. Z. (2005). Teacher-student relationships in primary and junior middle schools affect on students' school adjustment. *Psychological development and education, 1,* 87-90.

Ma, S. D. (2002). The research on educational interfering strategy of interpersonal maladjustment of senior middle school students' peer competition. Master's thesis, Southwest China Normal University, Chongqing, P.R.C.

Miao, F. C., and Chen, Q. (1999). Experimental research into reflection training in computer-assisted math teaching in primary school (I). *Subject education, 8*, 40-42.

O'Doherty, F., and Pathak, P. (2003). *E-therapy (a pilot study)*. National College of Ireland. Working Paper.

Pianta, R. C. (1997). Adult-child relationship processes and early schooling. *Early education and development, 8*, 11-26.

Pianta, R. C. (2001). *Student – teacher relationship scale*. Lutz: Psychological Assessment Resources.

Pianta, R. C., and Steinberg, M. (1992). Teacher-child relationships and the process of adjusting to school. In R. C. Pianta (Ed.), *Beyond the parent: The role of other adults in children's lives. New directions for child development, No. 5.* (pp. 61-80). San Francisco, CA: Jossey-Bass.

Proudfoot, J., Goldberg, D., Mann, A., Everitt, B., Marks, I., and Gray, J. (2003). Computerized, interactive, multimedia cognitive behavioral therapy reduces anxiety and depression in general practice: A randomized controlled trial. *Psychological medicine, 33*, 217–227.

Qi, P., Ou, L. C., Huang, L. C., et al. (2001). The research into improvement of university students' interpersonal relationship through group psychological counseling. *Health psychological journal, 9* (2), 98-100.

Shen, G. P. (2001). What is psychology education - re-thinking based on pedagogy. *Theory and practice of education, 21*, 51-55.

Shen, J. L., and Peng, H. M. (2002). The current issues and trend of mental health education in primary and secondary schools. *Journal of Beijing Normal University (social sciences), 1*, 14-20.

Shen, R. G., and Wang, Q. (2004). Experimental research into cultivating self-monitoring capacity of middle school students in math by using exploratory CAI mode. *E-education research, 7*, 76-79.

Shi, R. H. (1993). *Educational social psychology*. Beijing: World Publishing Corporation.

Song, L. H. (2002). The design and realization of computer-assisted software for education of all-around development. Master's thesis, Tianjin Normal University, Tianjin, P.R.C.

Wang, L. R. (2000). Exploring into the mode of education for all-around development: Huizhitong psychological quality education system. *Modem primary and secondary education, 1*, 53-55.

Wang, Y. and Wang, X. H. (2002). Development of teacher-student relationships and its relation to factors in primary school. *Psychological development and education, 3*, 18-23.

Wei, Y. H. (1998). A study on the influence of school factors on the development of self-esteem of children and adolescents. *Psychological development and education, 2*, 12-16.

Wo, J. Z., et al. (2000). *Towards mental health: Development*. Beijing: Huawen Publishing House.

Wo, J. Z., Lin, C. D., Ma, H. Z., and Li, F. (2001). A study on the development characteristics of adolescents' interpersonal relations. *Psychological development and education, 3,* 9-15.

Wu, H. L. (2002). The Internet-based psychological suzhi education system for university and college students. Master's thesis, Beijing Institute of Light Industry, Beijing, P.R.C.

Wu, Z. Q. (1998). On the modern psychological counseling mode in school. *Educational research, 1,* 42-47+57.

Xing, X. C., and Wang, X. (2003). A Study on the long-term effect of group psychological guidance to university students. *Psychological development and education, 2,* 74-80.

Xu, X. J., Zhang, D. J. and Li, X. *M.* (2003). An exploration on level-based integration mode of psychological *suzhi* education. *Journal of Technology College Education, 22* (5), 29-32.

Yang, D. H. (2001). Anxiety of middle school students - the role of teacher-student relationship and peer relationship. *Chinese mental health journal, 15,* 78-79.

Yang, H. *F.*, Tang, Y. Q., and Guo, H. Q. (2002). A study on the effect of group psychological counseling in improving the interpersonal communication capacity of university students. *Chinese journal of behavioral medical science, 11,* 692.

Zhang, D. J. (2002). Strengthen mental health education in schools and foster students' psychological quality. *Journal of Hebei Normal University (educational science edition), 4,* 17-23.

Zhang, D. J. (2003). On man's mental quality. *Studies of psychology and behavior, 1,* 143-146.

Zhang, D. J., and Guo, C. (2000). Exploring the principles of instructional psychology, conducting the research on education of mental quality. *Journal of Southwest China Normal University (philosophy and social sciences edition), 26,* 104-111.

Zhang, D. J., and Zhao, L. X. (2002). The exploring of education of mental quality in primary school. *Journal of Xinzhou Teachers University, 17,* 56-61.

Zhang, D. J., Feng, Z. Z, Guo, C., and Chen, X. (2000). Problems on research of students' mental quality. *Journal of Southwest China Normal University (philosophy and social sciences edition), 26* (3), 56-62.

Zhang, L. (2003). Characteristics of teacher-student relationship among middle school students and its relationship with adaptation to school. Master's thesis, Beijing Normal University, Beijing, P.R.C.

Zhang, L. X., and Li, X. H. (2000). Psychological *suzhi* education in school. Hefei, Anhui: Anhui University Press.

Zhang, M. F. (2003). A study on the educational intervention in the problem behavior of junior high school students. Master's thesis, Southwest China Normal University, Chongqing, P.R.C.

Zhang, Z. (2001). Mental health education for primary and secondary schools. *Journal of Shenyang Normal University (social sciences edition), 25,* 84-86.

Zhang, Z. Y., and Tian, L. (1996). Building psychological laboratory and software for psychological experiment. *Journal of developments in psychology, 4,* 60-63+44.

Zhao, X. Y., and Zhu, Y. (2002). Internet: As a new psychological research tool. *Journal of developments in psychology, 10,* 309-314.

Zheng, H. J. (1999). The exploring of psychological education in subjects. *Educational research, 9,* 53-57+80.

Zou, H. (1997). A study on peer acceptance, friendship and adaptation to school. *Psychological development and education, 3,* 55-59.

In: Methods and Implementary Strategies on Cultivating ... ISBN: 978-1-62417-979-2
Editors: Da-Jun Zhang, Jin-Liang Wang, and Lin Yu © 2013 Nova Science Publishers, Inc.

*Chapter 10*

# DEVELOPMENT OF AND EXPERIMENTAL RESEARCH ON IMPROVING PEER RELATIONSHIP WITH COMPUTER ASSISTANCE

## *Hui Zao[1], Da-Jun Zhang[2] and Lin Yu[2]*

[1]Southwest Communication University, China
[2]Center for Mental Health Education in Southwest University, China

## ABSTRACT

Peer relationships are the main interpersonal relationships of junior middle school students, and it is an important objective of the school's PSE to improve junior middle school students' peer relationships. The unique properties of multimedia computer and its increasing application to the psychology make the computer assisted PSE a possible approach for research. We have developed the PSE software targeted at improving peer relationships and taken it as the experimental tool for educational intervention to prove the feasibility and effectiveness of computer assisted PSE modes. The experimental results indicate that the experimental group does not seek the leading and dominant position so much as before and it is more popular than before; the factors and total scores of the interpersonal relationships have improved generally after the experiment and two factors, providing emotional supports and self-exposure, and have improved significantly; further investigation results and classroom work analysis also showed that the experiment has achieved good effects.

## INTRODUCTION

### Current Status of PSE Research in China

*Status quo of the research.* There have been diversified PSE activities since the 1980s in middle schools and primary schools in China. However, further exploration is still needed for many theoretical and practical issues on PSE on an overall basis. From the theoretical perspective, the present PSE of school in China is to: analyze the conception and structure of psychological *suzhi*, disclose the relationships between all factors of the psychological *suzhi*, identify the development characteristics of students' psychological *suzhi*, figure out the factors that may influence the formation of psychological *suzhi*, put forward the cultivation objectives, content system and educational principles, measures, approaches and methods for the school's PSE as well as the theoretical modes and operational modes for PSE, and explore the modes and implementation strategies for cultivating psychological *suzhi*. From the perspective of empirical research, it is to find out the components and structure of psychological *suzhi* with scientific methods, prepare the psychological *suzhi* scale and develop it into the software, prepare series of books on students' PST, explore the approaches and methods for PSE, launch large scale experimental research into PSE and establish a PSE mode that well collaborate the student, the school, the home and the society. The final objective of PSE is to cultivate students' psychological *suzhi* on an overall basis, and this can be further divided into two aspects (cultivating psychological *suzhi* and promoting the psychological development; solving mental problems and keeping mental health) and three tasks (developing psychological potential, maintaining mental health and cultivating psychological traits). The implementation approaches can be divided into three basic methods, SPT on psychological *suzhi*, psychological consultation and counseling subject infiltration. The SPT is a widely used approach for the present PSE. The research has shown that teenagers' psychological *suzhi* will be formed via self-understanding, knowledge learning, behavioral guiding with strategies, reflection and internalization, formation of psychological *suzhi*. Therefore, the psychological *suzhi* SPT is generally composed by three basic procedures that are linked with each other, "judgment and evaluation, training with strategies, reflection". This method can obtain direct and quick effects, but the requirements on time are strict. It needs the school leaders' and teachers' joint supports and participation as well as the PSE teachers that have received special trainings. Psychological *suzhi*, as an important factor for individuals' overall development, can also be cultivated via the infiltration in other subjects so as to imperceptibly improve students' psychological *suzhi* and maximize students' psychological potential. The curricula of present middle schools and primary schools have formed a relatively complete system, and it is difficult to add PSE lessons into the system in such an "artificial" manner. It can save time and realize long lasting effects if we can effectively integrate the PSE and the teaching of a subject without increasing manpower, materials and time. However, such method has raised high requirements for subject teachers and the teachers are required to infiltrate the PSE principles and methods in the teaching of a subject to a proper extent. Psychological counseling, psychological consultation and psychotherapy are also indispensible for PSE. They play an extremely important role in solving students' mental problems and contradictions and maintaining and improving their mental health. However, the present psychological counseling offered by schools in China at various levels is still focusing on maintaining students' mental health, and therefore this approach is only available to and effective for the growth of certain students, especially those in confusion or troubles during the development. It is not applicable for most students and it should be guided by professional psychological counseling teachers.

*Current problems.* We have, since we launched the research into PSE, made great progress in both theoretical discussion and practice, but there are still many problems.

*The theoretical discussion does not match the empirical research.* The research into PSE mainly focuses on the theoretical discussion on the PSE modes, approaches, methods etc., and there is less experimental research into the PSC strategies.

*The training approaches are not diversified, and there are not enough modern teaching means for the purpose of supporting.* The training is conducted mainly by classroom teaching with state-compiled textbooks or expert's lectures or SPT in experimental schools; there are scarcely modern teaching means or, if any, just the use of slides or videos. This chapter has integrated the characteristics of SPT and psychological counseling and launched computer assisted counseling and skill training on common communication issues by means of SPT.

*There is much general research but less detailed research.* The research is mainly to improve students' overall psychological *suzhi*, and there is less systematic research into the cultivation of certain psychological *suzhi*.

*There is much research into post-correction but less training on pre-prevention.* Mental problems are solved mainly by psychological consultation, psychological counseling, psychotherapy etc.; teachers neither actively cultivate students' psychological *suzhi*, nor conduct any education for preventing common mental problems. Most schools have many teaching tasks and thus have no spare time to arrange many lectures although the SPT has certain effect.

## Research into Peer Relationships and Trainings on Interpersonal Skills

*Influence of peer relationships on teenagers' development and adaptation.* Peer relationship is the main kind of junior middle school students' interpersonal relationships. It is the psychological relationship established and developed between peers or individuals with equal psychological development level based on their common interest, needs and attitude. The investigation findings show that 76% of middle school students hoped that they can get along well with classmates and have the same interests and hobbies with them; 81% of them preferred to get on with sanguine students who are good at certain extracurricula aspects; 65% of them held that classmates should help and support each other in the daily life; 70% of them preferred to talk about their true ideas and feelings with classmates and friends, 18% preferred to talk with parents and only 8% preferred to talk with teachers . "Peer relationships play an important role in children's and teenagers' development and social adaptation". The relevant theories mainly include the following three aspects: (1) the peer relationship is the important background for developing social capacity. Piaget [1926, 1932], Sullivan [1953] and Hartup [1977] held the same idea on the significance of peer relationships in developing social capacity. (2) The peer relationship is the important source to satisfy the needs for social communications, obtain social supports and maintain the sense of security. Weiss [1974] held that different types of relationships can provide different social supports so as to satisfy different social needs. (3) The experience in peer communication is helpful for developing the self-concept and the personality. Sullivan [1953] held that the experience of being isolated from peers during the adolescence would cause the sense of inferiority. In addition, the related research into this topic mainly involves: (1) peer acceptance and academic adaptation. The research has shown that the students rejected by or unpopular with peers generally had poorer academic performance than the popular ones. (2) Peer acceptance and acting factor. The research showed that peer relationships indicated both external and internal problems of teenagers and the correlations between peer relationships and highly internalized and externalized behavior. (3) Good peer relationships can improve the adaptability to the school. (4) Peer acceptance and sense of loneliness. (5) Peer relationships and development of sociality. Due to the reason of ethics,the research into the role of teenagers' peer relationships in social adaptability and development has been restricted within relevant research, including retrospective research, follow-up research and cross-sectional study. The participants mainly came from child guidance centers, psychiatric hospitals and schools. In addition, the traditional research was decentralized; it was about the functions of diversified peer relationships. The research showed that different peer relationships played an important role in most adaptation results and that each kind of peer relationships had individual functions for certain adaptation result.

*Factors influencing the peer relationship.* Relevant research generally showed that the factors influencing the peer relationship mainly included behavioral characteristics and social cognition. Researchers began in recent years to pay attention to the influence of emotional factors on peer relationships.

*Cognitive factors.* They mainly include social capacity, objectives set in social situations, proper and improper strategies and knowledge acquired for achieving the objective, the capacity of accurately understanding and monitoring social events, prejudice of attributions, styles of attributions, micro process of social information processing etc. The research into the influence of social communication targets on peer relationships is mainly targeted at primary school students and always adopts hypothetical methods. The research showed that the capacity of putting forward improper strategies can better forecast male students' social behavior and peer acceptance, while the capacity of putting forward proper strategies can better forecast female students' social behavior and peer acceptance [Wentzel and Erdley, 1993]. Researchers have also found the difference between popular students and rejected students in other variables of social cognition in additional to social targets and social strategies, including social perception, prejudice of attributions, styles of attributions and micro process of social information processing. Most researches into cognitive factors and peer relationships showed that at least three kinds of possible causal paths exist on the relationship between social cognitions style and peer social status [Dodge and Feldman, 1990].

*Emotional factors.* Most of the students with bad peer relationships extended the early unhealthy parental attachment to the following peer communication and they were thus not enthusiastic about peers, did not accept the others, doubted their own ability and experienced more interaction anxiety. The research showed that unpopular students were more likely to doubt their social interaction skills, become unconfident [Wheeler and Ladd, 1982; Hymel, 1985; Kurdek and Krile, 1982] and feel more depressed, anxious and lonely than popular ones. The sense of loneliness is the most common research target among the emotional factors. Due to the reason of ethics,the research showed that the students rejected by peers expressed stronger sense of loneliness and dissatisfaction with their status in the peer group [Crick and Ladd, 1988, 1993; Parker and Asher, 1989, 1992]. Presently, Boivin and Hymel [1997] used the hierarchical regression analysis to discuss the relationships among social behavior, peer acceptance and sense of loneliness and test the ordered mediation mode for sense of loneliness.

*Behavioral factors.* The research into the relationships between social behavior and peer acceptance mainly adopted natural and systematic observation, interview and behavioral assessment for the targeted children and teenagers. Researchers generally validated the relationships between social behavior and peer acceptance by comparing the social behavior of students with different social status or verifying whether there is any correlation between peer acceptance and social behavior. According to the early research, prosocial behavior was correlated with peer acceptance, while offensive or destructive behavior was correlated with peer's rejection. Other research also showed that the highly accepted teenager was deemed ready to help others, kind, obedient, humorous and willing to provide supports, while the lowly accepted teenager was described as destructive, fraudulent, disobedient, too sensitive, unattractive etc. [Elkins, 1958; Feinberg, Smith and Schmidt, 1958]. Coie et al. [Coie, Dodge and Kupetsmidt, 1990] concluded the relationship between social behavior and peer acceptance from the perspective of development. The training of thought, content and methods for the research into the factors influencing peer relationships have all changed to some extent. The research was to acknowledge the diversity and uncertainty of factors influencing the psychological status from just defining the causal connection, to discuss the internal connections between and comprehensive effects of two or more factors (such as behavior and cognition, or behavior and emotion) from investigating single factor, and dynamically, instead of statically, to investigate the effects of such factors during forming, maintaining or changing peer relationships.

*Methods for the research into peer relationships.* Teenagers' peer relationship is a multi-level and multi-aspect network. It is generally divided into peer acceptance and friendship. The former is a unidirectional structure oriented towards groups that reflects individuals' social status in the peer group, while the latter is a bidirectional structure oriented towards individuals that reflects the emotional connection between two individuals [Bukowskiand Hoza, 1989]. Another relationship mode, peer victimization, appeared in the 1990s. It is corresponding to the two aspects of peer relationships and the research methods and psychometrical tools are also different.

*Measurement of peer acceptance.* The peer acceptance psychometrical methods are different according to the different research objective, but they are almost the variants of traditional socio-metric measures [Moreno, 1934]. The major difference is whether to adopt the peer rating or the positive and negative nomination.

*Measurement of friendship.* Bukowski and Hoza [1989] have put forward a three-level mode for the psychometrics of friendship: friendship, circle of friendship and quality of friendship. This mode has become the basic framework for evaluating friendship. The best friend nomination is generally better for psychometrics of quantity of friends, while interviews and questionnaires are always adopted for testing psychometrics of quality of friends. Questionnaires include: the Friendship Relation Questionnaire (FRQ) of Furman et al., the Friendship Characteristic Scale of Youniss and Smollar, the Features of Children's Friendship Battery of Berndt and Perry [1986], the Friendship Quality Questionnaire (FQQ) prepared by Parker and Asher[1989, 1993] and revised by Zou, the Questionnaire on Quality of Primary School Student's Friendship prepared by Zhou. In addition, Han et al., Hou [1997], Wo and Sheng et al., Hyden-Thomson [1989] and Zhang have all made relevant research.

*Research into intervention in peer relationships.* The present research into the intervention in improvement of peer relationships mainly adopted the methods for "Social Skills Training" (SST) and "Interpersonal Cognitive Problem Solving" (ICPS). SST aims to help the students with bad peer relationships (interpersonal communication cognition, emotions and behavioral deficiency) master the knowledge and skills of peer communication by implementing the intervention plans so as to improve their peer relationships. The theoretical hypothesis is "social interaction skill deficiency", and it deemed the social interaction skill deficiency as the cause for teenagers' bad peer relationships. Some researchers deemed the lack of skills as the lack of social capacity, including explicit behavior as well as cognitive and emotional factors. More researchers deemed interpersonal communication skills as the capacity of harmoniously integrating a series of cognition, emotions and acting process; meanwhile, in respect of cognition, emotions and behavior, there are many factors that are deemed "components of skills". Therefore, this chapter is to conduct experimental interventions in junior middle school students' peer relationships in the aspects of cognition, emotion and behavior. Most researchers deemed the SST as the means to improve or enhance the capacity of peer communications. They held that educators should intervene in peer relationships in the aspects of cognitive guidance, emotional experience and behavioral training. The research has shown that the three training methods (cognitive, emotional and behavioral) can all improve the peer communication. SST is to teach students specific social interaction skills via guidance, training, demonstration, role play etc. The methods include behavioral shaping, mode strategies, role play and systematic training/learning. However, the ICPS put forward in the 1970s is to train the students lacking social interaction skills. M. B. Shure has provided training courses for the students at different ages. In addition, Han indicated that educators may train the social interaction skills via the internal attribution training of the scope of primary and middle school students' interpersonal communication. The experiment covers group intervention (persuasion, discussion, demonstration, enhanced correction etc.) and individual intervention (consultation and orientated training). Li et al. applied the systematic family therapy techniques to the group psychological counseling in a class. It was to improve the peer relationship of unpopular students in the class by stirring the whole class. According to the attribution research, it can improve the peer relationship more effectively to conduct cognition-level interpersonal attribution training for unpopular students. This indicated that it was a promising training mode to take the interpersonal attribution training as the supplementation to SST and integrate the two in training.

The primary school students in Grade Three to Six have significantly improved their communications with peers of the opposite or the same gender(s) via the two-year cultivation and training of interpersonal communication skills in a research that adopted the strategies and methods on cognitive changes, behavioral guidance and experiencing in learning. Meanwhile, the practice has also proved that it is a simple and effective approach to improve teenagers' peer relationships by organizing some group activities for certain purposes.

*Comments on current research into peer relationships.* To sum up, current research into peer relationships has made valuable achievements in theoretical discussion and implementation of intervention. However, there are also some defects in the current research:

The research targets are limited. Lots of literature is targeted at children (primary school and kindergarten students) and less is targeted at middle school students. Most measures for relevant intervention research are targeted at individuals and the intervention targets are almost the students with bad peer relationships. It aims to help unpopular students correct their defects, such as the lack of social interaction skills and deviation of personality characteristics. The PSE software developed in this chapter provides a new approach on how to conduct concentrated intervention for all students so as to improve the intervention efficiency and quality.

*Research methods are always old-fashioned.* Traditional "sociometric measures" and their variants are always used for psychometrics of peer relationships; in respect of implementation of intervention, there are more theoretical sermons than technical trainings, and the trainings, if any, are almost targeted at social interaction skills.

The present primary and middle schools improve peer relationships mainly by psychological *suzhi* activities, and no systematic and effective PSE software for improving peer relationships with computer assistance has been found hitherto. Therefore, this chapter aims to explore new approaches for improving peer relationships via "non-face-to-face" training methods.

*Difficult to define the intervention effects.* It has been found that psychologists have designed various intervention plans to improve teenagers' peer relationships, including special social interaction skill training, cognitive therapy, training strategies etc. The "SST" and the subsequent "ICPS" are all to improve students' peer relationships by training their communication skills. We still cannot define whether SST can improve peer relationships although lots of research has proved that SST can enhance students' capacity of solving interpersonal problems and their social interaction skills. To sum up, the correlation between SST and peer relationships is still uncertain, but it is undoubtedly impossible to improve unpopular students' peer relationships only with SST. Erwin [1994] declared that ICPS can effectively improve students' capacity of solving interpersonal problems, but the trainees' social status among peers did not change in a short period. This research used new training plans to retest the intervention effects.

## Significance and Unique Characteristics of Our Research

### 1) Significance

*To explore new PSE approaches.* The present PSE in primary and middle schools is generally conducted via SPT, subject infiltration and consultation and counseling etc. However, the PSE presently is not effective, scientific and professional enough since the teachers' resources are limited and the professional capacity of consultants and counselors need further improvement.

Therefore, exploring new PSE approaches has become the inherent requirement of improving PSE. Meanwhile, the rapid development of computers and network also provide a brand new perspective for educational psychology personnel.

Developing scientific and effective PSE software can not only meet the requirements for development in the information age, but also can satisfy the demands for developing students' psychological *suzhi* and is the purpose of our research.

The development and application of computer assisted PSE software will greatly upgrade the PSE content and forms, expand the space for PSE and provide a brand new approach for schools to further conduct PSE activities.

To make PSE better targeted and more effective. According to the basic purposes of the school's PSE, the PSE involves comprehensive contents. The adaptation to interpersonal communication is an important aspect of teenagers' sound psychological *suzhi*.

However, the adolescence is an important transitional period when rapid changes will occur in individuals' physiology, psychology and sociality. Junior middle school students have been separated from their family and parents and got closer to their peers in their emotions,. They establish peer relationships and friendship and thus obtain the sense of belonging and love.

Therefore, peer communication is an important aspect of junior middle school students' socialization. Teenagers' communication with those of opposite gender is an important aspect of their communication activities and the "compulsory lesson" for their socialization.

In addition, the unique characteristics of teenagers in China's special social and cultural background grant more special value to the research into Chinese teenagers' peer relationships. For example, most teenagers are the only child and they have no sisters or brothers; they lack the techniques on communicating with peers. Such environment variables have undoubtedly set higher requirements for educating students in the adolescence.

*To enrich the research into and the intervention in peer relationships.* The research into peer relationships has been conducted for a long time. Since the late 1920s peer relationships have become one of the problems for the joint research of the psychological circle [Hartup, 1983]. The research into peer relationships has attracted attention again since the late 1960s and the research literature increased rapidly in a short period. Systematic and intensive research into peer relationships appeared in the mid-1970s [Asher and Coie, 1990] and had made great achievements. However, compared with the abundant research literature in western countries, China has accumulated fewer documents on the research into peer relationships (especially the research into the teenager).

Although certain scholars have made systematic research into the development characteristics, functions and influential factors, there is scarcely the empirical research into the training of skills for teenagers' peer relationships and most of the research is targeted at the training research into theoretical explanation.

Few studies have been found in literature aimed at improving students` psychological *suzhi* with computer assisted PSE software. How can we widely and effectively improve the peer relationships and communication-related psychological *suzhi* of the huge teenager groups in China? Undoubtedly, developing a set of widespread, scientific and effective training software for teenagers' peer relationships is helpful for the research into this field.

### 2) Unique Characteristics

Our research was to enhance junior and senior middle school students' skills for communication with peers and improve their peer relationships with computer assistance based on existing PSE and the research into the training of peer communication skills. The unique characteristics include:

The PSE is conducted with computer assistance. The primary and middle schools in China have put forward a series of effective methods and created diversified approaches for implementing PSE. Such methods and approaches are mainly:

Providing lessons or lectures on psychological common sense;

Organizing various psychological education activities;

Establishing the scientific and sound archives on students' psychological status;

Creating good atmosphere for PSE;

Setting dedicated psychological function rooms for the purpose of psychological training, group behavior training and group consultation;

Introducing psychological consultation, establishing corresponding organizations or institutions in primary and middle schools and providing professional psychological counseling teachers for such schools. Psychological counseling, psychological consultation and psychotherapy are mainly used for solving students' mental problems. The educational personnel and researchers try to find out a new educational approach, as the PSE research is developing, the computer is popularized and the network technology is developing rapidly, so as to open a new chapter for the PSE.

The PSE software is applicable to all students. The training of social interaction skills aims to help the children with bad peer relationships master the knowledge and skills necessary for communications with peers by implementing the intervention plan so as to improve their peer relationships.

The intervention targets are the children with social avoidance, the isolated children, the children with low peer acceptance, the unpopular students, the rejected children, or even the children that may be widely accepted but have no best friends. Most researchers deem the training of skills for communication with peers as a kind of means to modify or enhance the capacity of communication with peers.

However, the PSE should be applicable for all students to improve the overall development of their psychological *suzhi*.

Therefore, the PSE software developed in our research has not only considered the students with bad peer relationships, but also highlighted the characteristics of psychological counseling and psychological consultation.

Furthermore, the software is to cultivate sound psychological *suzhi* for all students and provide general and preventive technical guide on the common problems in communication with peers based on the advantages of SPT.

## Research Flow and Hypothesis

1) *Basic flow*. Our research was targeted at the students in grade eight in whole-day junior middle schools and the basic flow was: theoretical research → modeing → developing software → experimental verification.

*Theoretical research.* Based on the summarization of domestic and foreign research into PSE and intervention in peer relationships, our research has found out a new PSE approach – computer assisted PSE modes, discussed the theoretical basis and technical supports for its realization, the objective, the theme, the strategy etc.

*Modeing.* Establish computer assisted PSE modes based on theoretical discussion and analysis on status quo and in accordance with the PSE objectives and the experimental content in self-compiled script.

*Developing software.* Develop PSE software for improving peer relationships with computer assistance by means of advanced modern computer technology and make the software more scientific and systematic by preliminary adaptation and continuous improvement.

*Experimental verification.* Test the effectiveness, feasibility and promotion of the PSE software developed by us via experiments so as to verify that the new PSE mode with computer assistance is feasible and effective for improving junior middle school students' peer relationships and their psychological *suzhi* of communications.

*Hypotheses.* Hypothesis 1: The complexity of psychological *suzhi* structure and PSE determines the diversification of PSE approaches and modes, the school's PSE needs exploration of new modes for further development and the modeing of PSE in schools should and is able to use modern teaching approaches.

Hypothesis 2: It can improve the educational effect and promote the development of students' psychological *suzhi* to use the computer assisted PSE mode for schools' PSE.

Hypothesis 3: It can effectively improve junior middle school students' peer relationships and improve their psychological *suzhi* in communicating by applying the software for PSE with computer assistance.

# THEORY CONSTRUCTION ON AND DEVELOPMENT OF IMPROVING PEER RELATIONSHIPS WITH COMPUTER ASSISTANCE

## Theory Construction on Improving Peer Relationships with Computer Assistance

### 1) Content Construction on Improving Peer Relationships with Computer Assistance

Investigation and analysis of the status quo of junior middle school students' peer relationships. We firstly investigated the present development of junior middle school students' peer relationships to provide empirical evidence for determining the content of experimental PSE intervention and exploring new PSE modes and to provide reference for the experimental intervention. The subjects were 97 students in grade eight in a junior middle school in Chongqing, including 48 boys and 49 girls. The tools used are as follows:

*Peer Assessment Scale* (prepared by the authors): provide a name list covering the students in the same class (of the same sex) for each participant and ask him/her to mark how he/she liked the students on the 5-point Likert scale. The average of the addition of classmates' assessment scores on each participant in the research was converted to Z score in the class, i.e. the peer acceptance level or popularity, for the purpose of direct inter-class comparison.

*Test of positive nomination and negative nomination* (prepared by the authors): ask the participants to write down the names of no more than three classmates that he/she liked the most as well as the reasons why he/she liked them; he/she may refuse to write if he/she liked none of them. Calculate the scores of positive nomination and negative nomination respectively according to the number of times that each participant was nominated by his/her classmates, convert such scores to positive Z scores and negative Z scores (by class), i.e. $Z_p$ and $Z_n$, and determine the participants' peer social status [Newcomb and Bukowski, 1983]. We did not use negative nomination in the research for avoiding students' contradiction; instead, we integrated positive nomination and peer assessment and replaced the scores of negative nomination with "1", the score of disliking the most in assessment. This result was used as the validity indicator of the Peer Assessment Scale.

*Interpersonal Competence Questionnaire*: use the *Interpersonal Competence Questionnaire* compiled by Wang that included 40 items and 5 dimensions, including starting the communication, providing emotional supports, imposing influence, self-exposure and solving conflicts.

*Social Goals Questionnaire*: use the Social Goals Questionnaire prepared by Jarvinen and Nicholls [1996] which was then revised into the *Social Goals Questionnaire* by Professor Zou from Beijing Normal University. The questionnaire included 36 items and 6 dimensions: dominance, intimacy, popularity, nurturance, leadership and avoidance.

*Psychometrics of academic performance*: the mid-term examination scores of Chinese, math, English and physics of the experimental group and the control group.

The participants were divided into high acceptance team, general acceptance team and low acceptance team, which had different peer acceptance levels, according to the standard peer-assessment scores ($Z>1$, $-1 \leq Z \leq 1$ and $Z < -1$) during our research. The three teams were composed by 10 students, 49 students and 13 students respectively. Four students were eliminated since they failed to finish the questionnaire. 13.9% and 18.1% of the valid participants were highly accepted students and lowly accepted students respectively. We used SPSS 10.0 for windows2000 to analyze and process all the data collected. Please see the following for data analysis results.

## Peer Acceptance and Nomination Test

*Correlations between the Peer Assessment Scale and the nomination test*. Calculate the correlations between standard peer assessment scores and standard positive and negative nomination scores and the correlations between standard positive and negative nomination scores. The results showed that there was high significance correlation between peer assessment and positive nomination ($r=.665$, $p<0.01$), between peer assessment and negative nomination ($r=-.818$, $p<0.05$), and between positive and negative nomination ($r=-.503$, $p<0.05$).

*Number of friends of teenagers with different peer acceptance levels*. We did not consider mutual selection when determining the number of good friends that a participant had since there were not many experimental intervention samples in our research, and the participants were divided into five categories according to the number of good friends they had, i.e. 0, 1, 2, 3, 4 or more than 5. The results of multifactor analysis of variance showed that the peer acceptance level had extremely significant main effects, $F$ $(2, 72)=21.180$, $p<0.001$, the gender did not have significant main effects and the peer acceptance level and the gender did not have significant mutual effects. This was different, to some extent, from Zou's research findings that "the gender did not have significant main effects, the peer acceptance had extremely significant main effects and the aforesaid two had extremely significant mutual effects".

Table 10.1. Indicate that there was extremely significant difference between the number of good friends of the junior middle school students with different peer acceptance levels: high acceptance team > low acceptance team, high acceptance team > general acceptance team. This indicated that there was certain positive correlation between the peer acceptance and the friendship although they were two different aspects of peer relationships.

*Comparison between and analysis of the different peer acceptance levels of junior middle school students*. The results of independent sample t test showed that there was no significant difference between the peer acceptance levels of junior middle school students no matter whether they were female or male, whether they were class leaders, what their family structure was and whether they were the only child. However, the analysis of variance showed that there was certain difference between the students' peer acceptance levels in respect of such independent variables as self-evaluation of relationships and objective efforts. Please see Table 10.2. for details.

**Table 10.1. Number of Good Friends of Junior Middle School Students with Different Peer Acceptance Levels**

| | | High Acceptance Team (n=10) | | General Acceptance Team (n=49) | | Low Acceptance Team (n=13) | | F Value | Post Hoc Test |
|---|---|---|---|---|---|---|---|---|---|
| | | M | SD | M | SD | M | SD | | |
| Good Friends | Male (39) | 7.50 | .70 | 2.29 | 1.58 | 1.80 | .91 | 21.180 *** | 1>2 |
| Number of nomination | Female (33) | 5.62 | 1.30 | 2.68 | 2.12 | .66 | 1.15 | | 1>3 |

Note: 1. High acceptance team, 2. low acceptance team, 3. general acceptance team.
(* $p<0.05$ ** $p<0.01$ *** $p<0.001$, similarly hereinafter)

**Table 10.2. Status Quo of Junior Middle School Students' Peer Acceptance Levels**

| | | M | SD | F Value | Post Hoc Test |
|---|---|---|---|---|---|
| Self-Evaluation of Relationships | Successful (n=51) | .21 | .94 | 8.517*** | 1>2 3>2 |
| | General (n=19) | -.35 | .77 | | |
| | Failed (n=2) | -2.13 | .39 | | |
| Subjective Wish | Strong (n=34) | 9.56E-02 | 1.04 | 1.526 | |
| | General (n=35) | -1.23E-02 | .90 | | |
| | mild (n=34) | -.93 | 1.29 | | |
| Objective Efforts | Lots of (n=41) | .25 | .99 | 6.659** | 1>2 |
| | General (n=29) | -.22 | .81 | | |
| | Few (n=2) | -1.89 | .73 | | |

Note: self-evaluation of relationships: 1. Successful team, 2. Failed team, 3. General team.

Objective efforts: 1. The team making lots of efforts, 2. The team making few efforts, 3. The team making general efforts.

Table 10.2. has shown that junior middle school students' peer acceptance decreased as their self-evaluation on peer relationships degraded gradually: the successful team> the general team > the failed team. The post hoc test showed that there was significant difference between the successful team and the failed team as well as between the general team and the failed team. In respect of objective efforts, junior middle school students' peer acceptance levels degraded as they made less efforts to improve their peer relationships: the team making lots of efforts > the team making general efforts > the team making few efforts. The post hoc test showed that there was significant difference between the team making lots of efforts and the team making few efforts.

*Comparison between the peer acceptance levels of junior middle school students with different academic performance.* We took students' midterm exam scores of such subjects as Chinese, math, English and physics as the variables named academic performance so as to find out the correlation between academic performance and peer acceptance levels. We have found during our study that there was significant correlation between the academic performance and the peer acceptance levels ($r=.603$, $p<0.01$).

**Table 10.3. Peer Acceptance Levels of Junior Middle School Students with Different Academic Performance**

|  | High Score Team (n=19) | | Intermediate Score Team (n=34) | | Low Score Team (n=19) | | F Value | Post Hoc Test |
|---|---|---|---|---|---|---|---|---|
|  | M | SD | M | SD | M | SD |  |  |
| Peer Acceptance | .77 | .87 | -1.96E-02 | .83 | -.73 | .80 | 15.555*** | 1>2, 3 3>2 |

In addition, we divided the participants into the high score team, low score team and intermediate score team based on their academic performance. The division method was to convert the original score into standard score and took it as the score of academic performance. According to the principle of statistics, 27% of the participants with the highest scores composed the high score team, 27% of the participants with the lowest scores composed the low score team and the rest participants (46%) composed the intermediate score team. Then we took the academic performance as the independent variable (high score team=1, low score team=2, intermediate score team=3) and the peer acceptance level as the dependent variable for the purpose of one-way analysis of variance on independent samples.

Table 10.3. showed that there was significant difference between the peer acceptance of students with different academic performance: high score team > intermediate score team > low score team. The post hoc test also showed that there was significant difference between the high score team and the intermediate score team, the high score team and the low score team, as well as the intermediate score team and the low score team. It follows that the academic performance is an important factor that may influence peer relationships.

*Peer acceptance and interpersonal competence.* The results of independent sample t test have shown that there was no significant difference between all factors and total scores of junior middle school students' interpersonal competence, no matter whether they were male or female, whether they were class leaders, what their family structure was and whether they were the only child. However, generally speaking, male students' scores were lower than female ones' scores; class leaders' scores were higher than other students' scores; the scores of students from two-parent family were higher than those from single-parent family; the scores of students that were not the only child were higher than those of the only child, except for the factor named launching the communication. The analysis of variance showed that the average scores of the junior middle school students with different peer acceptance levels were consistent with the trend that the high acceptance team > the general acceptance team > the low acceptance team (except for the factor named launching the communication).

*Peer acceptance and social goals.* The test results of independent sample t test showed that there was no significant difference between all factors and total scores of junior middle school students' social goals, no matter whether they were male or female, whether they were class leaders, what their family structure was and whether they were the only child. However, generally speaking:

Male students' scores were lower than female ones' scores, except for such factors as leadership and dominance. This was in general consistent with Zou's research results: female students' scores on some dimensions of social goals, including nurturance, popularity, intimacy and avoidance, were higher than male ones' scores, while their scores on leadership and dominance were lower than male ones' scores;

ii) Class leaders' scores were higher than normal students' scores, except for the factor named dominance;

iii) The scores of students from two-parent family were higher than those from single-parent family, except for such factors as leadership and dominance; iv) the average scores of students that were not the only child were higher than those of the only child, except for such factors as leadership and dominance.

We also took the peer acceptance level as the independent variable and took the factor and total score of social goals as the dependent variables for the purpose of multifactor analysis of variance so as to further find out the difference between the social goals of junior middle school students with different peer acceptance levels. Please see Table 10.4. for the results.

**Table 10.4. Analysis of the Difference between the Social Goals of Junior Middle School Students with different Peer Acceptance Levels**

| | High Acceptance Team (n=10) | | Low Acceptance Team (n=12) | | General Acceptance Team (n=44) | | F Value | Post Hoc Test |
|---|---|---|---|---|---|---|---|---|
| | M | SD | M | SD | M | SD | | |
| Help and Supports | 3.40 | .45 | 2.97 | .95 | 3.43 | .49 | 2.895 | |
| Popularity | 3.40 | .49 | 2.87 | .72 | 3.35 | .54 | 3.606* | 3>2 |
| Leadership | 2.68 | .50 | 2.85 | .91 | 2.72 | .62 | .214 | |
| Intimacy | 3.22 | .50 | 2.69 | .49 | 2.99 | .56 | 2.722 | |
| Avoidance | 3.28 | .47 | 3.11 | .52 | 3.14 | .66 | .247 | |
| Dominance | 2.80 | .60 | 3.05 | .78 | 2.87 | .66 | .429 | |
| Peer Communication Total scores | 3.13 | .24 | 2.92 | .38 | 3.08 | .28 | 1.724 | |

Note: 1. High acceptance team, 2. Low acceptance team, 3. General acceptance team.

Table 10.4. shows that there was no significant difference between the junior middle school students with different peer acceptance levels in respect of the factors and total scores of their social goals, except for the popularity. However, the total scores and the average scores on nurturance, popularity, intimacy and avoidance were generally consistent with the trend that high acceptance team > general acceptance team > low acceptance team, while the scores on leadership and dominance were consistent with the trend that low acceptance team > general acceptance team > high acceptance team. In respect of the popularity, the average scores of the general acceptance team were significantly higher than those of the low acceptance team.

**Table 10.5. Analysis on the Mode for Improving Peer Relationships
with Computer Assistance**

| Module | Objective | Script |
|---|---|---|
| Introduction | To arouse students' curiosity and learning interest and lead to the topic of the lesson by means of animation, music, images, commentary, etc. | 1. Beautiful music plus commentary<br>2. Lyrics against the music<br>3. Animation: two birds were fighting for an insect.<br>4. Animation: the friendship will be forever.<br>5. The protagonist's worries in those days<br>6. Continuous images plus commentary |
| Simulation of Situations | To immerse students in the scene, make the content close to the daily life, arouse emotional resonance and activate students' psychological activities by introducing the experiences of the protagonist or the people around him or by telling stories. | 1. The self-introduction of the protagonist when he made friends with new classmates and The Day of Xiaoming<br>2. Meng Fei<br>3. Conflicts and continuous incidents between the protagonist and the student in charge of entertainment due to the preparation for the New Year Evening Gala<br>4. Quarrels between the protagonist and his good friends since they failed to reserve certain distance therebetween<br>5. The story of Xiaoya, who was not good at getting along with classmates of opposite gender<br>6. Others' misunderstanding on the relationship between the protagonist and an opposite gender and the subsequent events caused by an umbrella-borrowing event |
| Analysis of Reasons | To guide students to reflect the self and change their original cognition by raising questions in four different manners: providing advice and suggestions for others, recalling their own experiences, imaging they were on the scene or deliver the positive ideas. | 1. Help others analyze the problem and find out the reasons as an observer.<br>2. Recall the past similar experience: what did you do at that time?<br>3. What would you do if you were the protagonist?<br>4. Please give the advice you deem correct: "I think…" |

**Table 10.5. (Continued)**

| Module | Objective | Script |
|--------|-----------|--------|
| Technical Guidance | To give students guidance and advice on various skills for peer communications based on different types of contents by setting a main interface in the main part of the software and arranging various sections. The contents are parallel or the previous content foreshadows the following one; they are led by cognitive changes and behavioral advising strategies and infiltrated with emotional experience. | 1. Cognize Correctly, Treat Others Warmly, Put into Practice<br>2. It is the Common Desire of all Students to Communicate with Others, One Good Turn Deserves Another, Step into Another "Half the Sky"<br>3. A Thought-Provoking Experiment, Competition? Cooperation?, A Story in the Desert, Go Deep into the Inner World<br>4. How was the Capital Finished, A Story About Bears, A Vainglorious Friend, Accepting the Criticism is also an Improvement, Dialogue between My Friends and Me, Boosters and Barriers for Developing Friendship<br>5. A Story about a Little Monk, Healthy Communications between Boys and Girls, Boys and Girls in Communication, Some Good Measures, Distinguish the Right from the Wrong, Worries of Peers<br>6. How to Gain Respect from the Opposite Gender, Get along with the Opposite Gender to a Proper Extent, How to Avoid Puppy Love, How to Say "No" to the Opposite Gender, Distinguish Friendship from Love, Worries of Peers |
| Summarization and Reflection | To end the learning with music, songs, lyrics, animation etc. and deepen the theme with aphorisms and well-known sayings, beautiful lyrics or typical stories. | 1, 3, 4. Give an aphorism or well-known saying with music.<br>2. Animation: tell a story<br>5, 6. Read a lyric with music. |

To sum up, through the investigation on present peer relationships, we found that some students' peer relationships were poor since they established unreasonable social goals during their communications with the peer and they lacked relevant social skills. This provided empirical evidence for us to establish the content system of educational software and assisted students, during preparing the experimental courses, in establishing reasonable cognitive concepts and social goals and integrating the knowledge learned with technical training and *suzhi* cultivation so that students can intervene in the learning process to the maximum extent and comprehend the strategies of solving problems in peer communications.

*Selection of the contents of computer assisted PSE.* According to relevant theories and empirical research on social skill trainings, the attribution research generally showed that the cognitive social-skill-training can effectively improve the interpersonal relationship. Other research used the strategies on cognitive changes, behavioral guidance and experiencing in learning for trainings of peer communication skills. The results showed that the trained participants had obvious improvement in their communication skills. The software for computer assisted PSE that we developed based on the existing research conducted cognitive, emotional and behavioral trainings on peer relationship related skills.

*Cognition.* The training mainly covered: i) the cognition on peer relationships to understand that "learning how to learn" is of the same importance as "learning how to communicate" for junior middle school students' health and to meet teenagers' common needs and psychological characteristics during peer communications; ii) the cognition on peers to treat peers objectively and rationally, learn their virtues and make up our own weaknesses; iii) the cognition on the self to evaluate the self objectively and rationally, correctly understand such traits as cooperation and competition, learn how to express ourselves and give a good first impression; iv) other cognitions to realize the necessity, feasibility and development stages of and the do's and don'ts during communications with the opposite gender and understand what the true friend and friendship means.

*Emotion.* The class always began with animation, beautiful poems, fairy tales, "private conversation" between students or simulated situations (ordinary incidents happening to middle school students during their daily peer communications) so as to make the students absorbed in the course. Such activities can motivate students' learning interest and initiative, arouse their intrinsic emotional experience and stimulate their emotional resonance. In addition, each class ended with music, aphorisms and well-known sayings. The end well cohered with the beginning and the class was full of emotional atmosphere.

*Behavior.* The technical training focused more on the behavioral guidance. In this aspect, we often set some communication situations and raise questions beginning with "Have you ever..." so as to arouse students' reflections and emotional resonance in the situations and then helped the protagonist of the story analyze the reason and find out the detailed solutions; we also made students deliver their opinions based on such situations, then gave relevant answers and explanations and finally defined correct behavior; we also provided some examples of middle school students' daily communications by intensifying positive examples and providing correct and reasonable behavioral guidance on negative examples. The educational software abided by the PSE rules and the principle in learning psychology and set three major topics according to the present needs of and relationships between junior middle school students during their communication: i) communication with students of the same gender, ii) communication with the opposite gender, and iii) friendship.

*Part I: communication with students of the same gender (1-3).* It was about the protagonist Han Yu. It adopted the step-by-step training since the self-introduction on the first day and the lessons were closely connected to each other with the story. The main contents included: teaching students how to establish a good first impression since it was the common desire of all junior middle school students to communicate with others, making students master the methods of how to overcome (their or others') bad emotions during peer communications, and making students master a lot of prosocial behavior (cooperation, share etc.).

*Part II: friendship (4).* First, set conflicts to help students analyze the causes and make them realize the importance of friends and friendship; second, with examples, make students further internalize the concept of "friend" and sublimate their emotions; thirdly, conduct behavioral and technical trainings on establishing and maintaining friendship.

*Part III: communication with the opposite gender (5-6).* First, with a situation, make students consider whether they can make friends with the opposite gender and explain the advantages and disadvantages of and the do's and don'ts during the communication with the opposite gender; second, design relevant content and provide behavioral guidance based on the common mental problems during communications with the opposite gender; thirdly, correctly distinguish friendship from love; fourthly, design the content related to some specific and unique problems of junior middle school students, including "how to gain respect from the opposite gender", "how to say 'No' to the opposite gender" etc.

### 2) Principles on Improving Peer Relationships with Computer Assistance

The PSE software for improving peer relationships with computer assistance abides by the following principles:

*Content: scientific.* The content system was established on abundant theoretical basis.

*Thoughts: student-centered.* It gives full independence to students, leads them to perform their initiatives and makes them participate in the training in person.

*Modes: innovative.* The computer assisted PSE is a new PSE mode.

*Objectives:* to improve students' active adaptation and active development. It satisfies junior middle school students' communication needs and their needs for attribution and love, helps them experience the self-esteem, motivates their initiatives of peer communications and makes them actively improve their peer relationships in accordance with the characteristics that the students gradually transformed their interpersonal communication targets into peers.

*Methods*: individual difference based. It not only includes the psychological counseling based education for certain student who has difficulty in peer communications, such as some content (in Part III: communication with the opposite gender) was designed based on students' common mental problems on peer communications, but also provides specific-problem-based lectures for all students that have needs for peer communications, such as most content is designed for preventive, popularizing and educational purposes.

*Operation: simple.* It sets specific buttons, including "Play", "Continue", "Close" etc., and students only need to start the learning by clicking the mouse. Students may, if they want to know detailed use of the software, click the notepad file named "help".

### 3) Mode Construction for Improving Peer Relationships with Computer Assistance

We have concluded through the aforesaid research that the technical training software for improving junior middle school students' peer relationships was a helpful computer assisted PSE mode to make students actively participate in the education. It includes the following procedures: introduction, simulation of situations, analysis of reasons, technical guidance, summarization and reflection. We will further analyze the training mode of the PSE software for improving peer relationships with computer assistance developed in our research.

The whole set of software provides six classes, and each class is following the aforesaid mode. Therefore, we used the class named "Learn How to Cooperate and Make the Best Use of Competition". Detailed analyses are as follows.

Learn How to Cooperate and Make the Best Use of Competition (1+1=?)

Scene 1: in the classroom (Commentary: Han Yu's class will hold a New Year Evening Gala today)

Student in charge of entertainment (S): Han Yu, hang up the color streamers.

S: Han Yu, would you like to fetch a chair for me?

S: Han Yu, please hurry them up. They decorate the meeting place so slowly.

S: Han Yu, ...

(Han Yu's psychological activities and behavioral performance) (Omitted)


The gala was postponed for 20 minutes and the effect and atmosphere were not as good as expected. The student in charge of entertainment was so frustrated and Han Yu was unhappy.

Purpose: take the trifles in junior middle school students' daily life for example to immerse students in the scene and arouse the emotional resonance.

Scene 2: Han Yu lay in bed at night.

"Was I correct today?" Han Yu tossed and turned restlessly. He suddenly brought to mind a story about "1+1=0" that was told by his mother in his childhood. (Story omitted) Han's mother asked Han Yu some questions as the story came to an end.

Mother (M): Do you know why both of them cannot play it?

Han Yu (H): Both of them refused to surrender.

M: Do you understand why the story is named "1+1=0"?

H: Yes. Both of them struggled to play first and thus neither of them can play it.

M: My son is so clever.

"Do I perform worse now than when I was young?" He fell asleep gradually. (Dream omitted)

Voice of god: It depends on whether you choose the heaven or the hell in a certain environment. You are the angel as long as you are willing to put the spoon in your hand into the peer' mouth.

Han Yu was awake. He seemed to know what he should do.

Jack Welch: helping others is to help ourselves; the things that others have obtained may not be those you have lost.

Lippitt: Human's value lies in not only the independence, but also the capacity of cooperating with others in accomplishing the task.

Purpose: to arouse students' sense of identification or sense of absence via the protagonist's self-reflection and make students realize the importance of cooperation.

Activities: (design a scene in the forest where there are five treasure boxes with different titles) click any one of the treasure boxes for learning. Please see the following for details. Purpose: to lead students to the procedure of training with cognitive-behavioral strategies.

Treasure Box 1: "Go Deep into the Inner World"

Cooperation and competition occur everywhere. Have you ever thought as follows when you were in the following situations?


Your desk-mate has better performance than you. Have you ever hoped, beyond your control, that he/she would be ill or depressed so that he/she would be failed in the examination?

The teacher assigned a task to your classmates and you. Did you feel that the peer did less than you that you may suffer from losses?

Purpose: Provide two examples on junior middle school students' common problems to make students think and raise questions and activate their psychological activities.

[Explain such Thoughts]

Everyone hopes that he/she will succeed in the competition since the success can prove his/her excellence and help him/her gain others' recognition and praise. However, none of us can succeed in all fields. The individual may, when he/she performs worse than others, hope that the rival will fail so that he/she can win.

Every one hopes that cooperation will be equal and the program he/she participates in will be successful. However, the responsibility is likely to be scattered to the large number of participants: all of the participants are liable for the failure, if any, and the success, if any, will not be attributed to a certain participant. Therefore, why should I exert myself to the utmost?

Purpose: to guide students, from the cognitive perspective, to think via transposition, change the way of thinking, establish reasonable concepts and arouse their emotional experience.

[Suggestions]

In competition:

Students may, in competition, have many incorrect ideas that we should not have or do many something that we should not do. For example, they may think: "I/we should win the first...", "She cannot perform better than me...", "They are doomed to failure...".

There is definitely failure where there is success. The secret of success in competition is to keep the good attitude wherever and whenever that "nothing is more important than participation".

Dare to compete: you should dare to challenge the rival and the yourself when you want to win a competition or a post.

Be good at competing: Never pay too much attention to the rank and score; instead, you should concentrate yourself on the problem need to be solved, perform all of your excellence and defeat the rival with your advantages.

Never envy others: you should, if the rival wins the competition, adjust your mentality, reflect yourself and find out why you failed.

In cooperation:

"Let me help you": give a hand to others in trouble.

"Let me express my ideas": provide ideas and suggestions as many as possible. If the team is an ocean, each of the members is the water drop therein.

"Let me do this": the great number of tasks in the team require that the members should cooperate with each other and dare to take on heavy responsibilities.

"I am also liable for the failure": you should, when the team fails, actively bear the responsibilities that you should bear as a team member.

Purpose: to guide students with strategies, from the behavioral perspective, to make reflection, conclusion and summarization based on the content of this unit and to deepen their emotional experience in the training.

(End: a diamond was awarded to the students and there was a caption, "Congratulations on your winning of the treasure. Keep trying!", on the screen)

Purpose: to provide an incentive for students so that the students will keep interest in the learning and will not be tired of the subsequent learning.

Treasure Box 2: "A Thought-Provoking Experiment" (Omitted)

Treasure Box 3: "Competition? Cooperation?" (Omitted)

Treasure Box 4: "A Story in the Desert" (Omitted)

A sentence for you: cooperation and competition cannot be separated from each other. The capacity of cooperation and the awareness of competition are like the human's two legs; the absence of either can make human unable to walk. ("End")

Purpose: to strengthen the student's awareness with aphorisms and well-known sayings and to bring out the crucial point of the unit theme.

## Development of Improving Peer Relationships with Computer Assistance

### 1) Necessity of Developing the PSE Software for Improving Peer Relationships with Computer Assistance

The computer based education (CBE) is an emerging subject for improving the education quality and solving the education related problems with IT technology and scientific methods. As humans pay increasing attention to the building and optimization of computer-assisted learning (CAL) modes, the computer assisted psychological training, an application field thereof, has also attracted much attention. Common computer assisted psychological trainings include the training of attention, memory, cognitive strategies, learning interest, behavioral habits etc. Researchers are also exploring the computer assisted training on interpersonal relationships, which creates a broad prospect for the development and application of the software for improving peer relationships with computer assistance.

From the perspective of education and teaching targets, the PSE is targeted at all students and is to improve their psychological *suzhi*. Although the present PSE in schools is growing vigorously and has achieved great progress, the achievement should have been greater with such great deal of manpower, materials and efforts that the school has input. How can we improve the teaching efficiency in a large scale and make our teaching process effective? The computer assisted PSE makes possible. The computer professional develops the software and uploads it to the Internet, which will enable more students to share the teaching software with good quality, make more individuals benefit from the education and achieve sustainable use of the software; the computer can display more learning content with less time and students can understand and master, within a short period, the knowledge they have learned so as to save the time and enhance the learning efficiency.

Based on the needs of development of the times and of achievement of the PSE objectives, we have developed the PSE software for improving peer relationships with computer assistance, built the new type "self-service" PSE mode and found out a new PSE approach.

### 2) Necessity and Feasibility of Developing the PSE Software for Improving Peer Relationships with Computer Assistance

The PSE software for improving peer relationships with computer assistance meets the junior middle school students' subjective needs. The junior middle school students are in adolescence when their physiology and psychology develop rapidly, and Hall has ever compared this period to the storm and stress period. The middle school students in this period often perform the two extremes in respect of their interpersonal relationship, such as the friendship and loneliness as well as the intimacy and indifference between friends. Their desire for peer communications increases along with their grow-up. However, their high subjective desires for peer communications conflict with the poor objective peer relationships and this often puts their peer relationships in contradiction: they desire for communication with others, but they are self-contained and self-abased; they actively develop their peer relationships, but they conduct negative psychological defense. In the research we have helped students enhance their peer communication skills and improve their peer relationships with computer assistance based on junior middle school students' desire for developing peer relationships. In addition, most junior middle school students are curious about the computer, which provides the intrinsic motivation for the computer assisted PSE.

The PSE software for improving peer relationships with computer assistance is theoretically grounded. The computer assisted PSE can be traced back to the theory and application of Skinner's operant behaviorism, the programmed instruction which focuses on the principle of ordered unit sequence, small-step accumulation, timely intensification and self-pacing. Skinner's programmed instruction has certain advantages, but it only pays attention to the student's response and it is regardless of the learning process and the fact whether the student has mastered how to think. It cannot fully stimulate students' initiative. The formation of students' psychological *suzhi* was infiltrated into their learning of the software in our research. The student should continue their learning, internalization, reflection and consolidation in turn during the process. This is the most distinctive difference between the computer assisted PSE software developed in the research and the programmed instruction; meanwhile, it has shown the basic concept of modern education: the student should actively participate in the learning process, think independently and achieve reflection, self-evaluation and self-development. We have built a new PSE mode, the computer assisted PSE mode, in our research according to the reasonable "core" of the programmed instruction and the theories on modern education and developed the PSE software for improving peer relationships with computer assistance. The training objectives can be divided into three aspects: cognition, emotion and behavior; the training process can be divided into five parts: introduction, simulation of situations, analysis of reasons, technical guidance, summarization and reflection. We have taken the advantages of the programmed instruction: set different number of contents in each lesson, which can be deemed as "small steps"; provide diversified incentives for students after they have learned each part of the lesson, which can be deemed as "timely intensification"; arrange the contents of certain lessons in parallel for free selection by students, which can be deemed as "self-pacing".

### 3) Characteristics of the PSE Software for Improving Peer Relationships with Computer Assistance

To sum up, the computer assisted PSE software has made some improvements, compared with the traditional classroom teaching of psychological *suzhi* and the single electrification instruction, and features the following characteristics:

*Visibility.* The educational content is demonstrated in 3D manner instead of the past 2D manner, from static to dynamic. The computer software can not only integrate characters, sound, images and animation organically, but also can create an effect that both pictures and texts are excellent: the figures are vivid, the key words are brief and clear and the music is pleasant to the ear. Furthermore, the software not only integrates such means as slides, sound recording, movie, television and video, but also changes the unidirectional information transmission of machines. The software adopts the interactive "treasure hunt" activity. Teachers may teach students through lively activities and integrate puzzles, teaching and games together to enhance students' learning interest and thirst for knowledge.

*Interaction.* The educator can use the advanced functions of stop, *F.F., F*.R., play etc. of the video machine during the teaching with video, which is much better than traditional teaching means, but students cannot interact with the content they are learning and therefore they cannot perform their initiatives and their functions as the agent. We have properly set buttons between each part of this software in accordance with the principle of teaching so that students can arrange their learning progress according to their competence and the difficulty of the content: relearn the content they feel difficult or "skip" the content they have mastered. In addition, there is interactive incentive after the student learned each part of the software.

*High efficiency.* Through the research we have found that students can remember only 15% of the information by listening only and 25% of the information by looking only, but they can remember about 65% of the information by both listening and looking. It follows that the application of software provides various perceptual materials for students, and the visibility is more helpful for students to understand the abstract conception. The experimental research in the mid 1980s into the Classroom Tomorrow showed that students can master more and more knowledge despite that they had to spend more time in learning to use the skills. In addition, according to the statistics, teaching by CAI, compared with traditional teaching, can save 25%-50% of the time.

*Individual based objectives-to realize individual based teaching.* The software employs a "student-focused" teaching method. It is generally known that those who with bad peer relationships hope that their classmates can accept and love them; however, they are often frustrated since they lack the communicative skills, especially during the communication with the opposite gender. They were unwilling to tell the teacher their concerns (such as their good impression of a certain opposite gender) in traditional psychological *suzhi*-based trainings, so the teacher was unable to conduct individual counseling for them. However, each student uses a separate microcomputer to communicate with the computer during the teaching with this software, and the teacher just provides guidance as an assistant.

### 4) *Advantages and Disadvantages of the PSE Software for Improving Peer Relationships with Computer Assistance and the Methods to Overcome the Disadvantages*

The PSE software for improving peer relationships with computer assistance results from the modernization of instruction, integrates IT technology and PSE organically and is the practice of new PSE modes.

### Advantages of PSE Software

*Situation and simulation based.* The simulation plays an irreplaceable role in the teaching software. We used images and animation in "Simulation of Situations" in this software to simulate the problems in peer communications in order to make students perform their imagination, thoroughly understand the situation and master the difficult communication skills with vivid and interesting stories that can be perceived directly or to make them reflect themselves with others' experiences. The computer-based simulation of situations can also vividly show various micro psychological phenomena during peer communications by means of animation.

*Operable and feasible*. First, the communication skills and implementation strategies are operable; second, the software is easy to use and is highly operable; thirdly, the software-based learning process is the simulation of classroom learning process and is consistent with the teaching principle; fourthly, middle school students are highly interested in and curious about the computer, and therefore the software can stimulate their interest in the learning contents by changing the learning form.

*Extendable*. The software is open-ended and offer some interface for the purpose of supplementation and extension by learners, such as reflection etc.; it provides broad space for learners for free performance.

*Scientific*. First, it is consistent with the characteristics and objective rules on junior middle school students' psychological development, i.e. The hands-on ability and cognitive development; second, it will never sacrifice the scientificity for the so-called vividness, i.e. All the content has its theoretical basis.

## Disadvantages of the Software and the Solutions

*Not interactive enough*. The interaction is not so good as expected due to the limited technology.

*Not cover a broad scope*. Peer communications cover various contents, and this software is unable to provide technical trainings on all problems in actual situations. This requires that the content in each unit of this software is subject to uniform standards, be logical and incremental and is based on the same theoretical foundation.

*Not feedback-based enough*. The peer communication is an interactive process, but the human-computer interaction is not the human-human interaction since students' inner experience is not fully revealed and the teacher cannot adjust the learning content in time according to students' feedback, such as the expression. This requires that this software shall be extendable and assign proper homework that shall be completed by students off the computer.

*Not well controlled*. The control variables are not well controlled when students are in the course of trainings. For example, students may pay too much attention to the animation in this software instead of the contents and skills. This requires that this software is developed based on scientific contents. It shall not only focus on the diversified forms and ignore the theoretical basis and scientificity of the contents. In addition, the learner shall master certain techniques to use this software.

## 5) Development, Adaptation and Modification of Improving Peer Relationships with Computer Assistance

*Development of PSE software*. According to the aforesaid scientific and rational content system, we devoted ourselves to preparing the experimental courses, adapted them for the script for developing software, revised the script repeatedly and design the script realization effect (cartoon characters, background images, relevant animation etc.). We employed professionals of developing software at last according to our design principle, and cooperated with them in developing the PSE software for improving junior middle school students' peer relationships with computer assistance. We succeeded in it and made preliminary adaptation. The software consists of six lessons. It provides trainings by demonstrating the experiences of the protagonist, who features the characteristics of a modern junior middle school student, or the experiences of the people around him. The software integrates various application programs, including *Flash* for animation, *Java* script for saving and *html* for integrating all training modules together. The design of this software is not only consistent with the basic objectives and implementation process of PSE, but also has the characteristics of software development.

*Adaptation of PSE software.* Once the software for sample lessons was developed successfully, we sampled a class at random for 55 students, in grade 8 of the middle school affiliated to Southwest China Normal University to check the effect of the software and better systematize the software. We used the PSE software for improving junior middle school students' peer relationships with computer assistance as the mental tool and made preliminary adaptation on the initial software for sample lessons. We also took the Post-use Questionnaire prepared by us as the tool to investigate students' attitudes toward the software. The results were:

*Overall effect.* None has reflected during the investigation that the overall effect of the software was poor. Instead, 41.2% of the students held that the software was good and 58.8% of them held that it was just so so. In respect of the gains from the software, 51.0% of the students felt that they have learned a lot from the software, 9.8% of them had no gains, while 39.2% felt that they have learned something, but not much. We also investigated and compared the popularity of software-based learning and the PST, which showed that only 9.8% of the students preferred the teacher's PST, 37.3% of them preferred the software-based learning, while 52.9% preferred the integration of the two.

*Content.* According to Table 10.6, 84.0% of the students held that the content was as coherent as a system or coherent to some degree, while only 16.0% of them cannot grasp the theme; 74.6% of the students held that the content selected was close to their daily life, which was helpful for improving their thinking capacity via systematic learning and can provide much help for their future communications, while 25.4% of them held that it was unnecessary to learn such content since the content was outdated or they have been familiar with; 94.1% of the students held that the content was demonstrated in flexible and diversified ways, while only 5.9% of them held that it was demonstrated in an inflexible and dull manner.

*Forms.* According to Table 10.7, 86.3% of the students were satisfied with the design of the characters in the software, while only 13.7% of them were unsatisfied; 76.5% of the students were satisfied with the music and dubbing, 15.7% of them felt it just so so, while 7.8% of them were unsatisfied; 98.1% of the students were satisfied with the selection and layout of background images , while only 2.0% of them were unsatisfied.

In addition, the investigation on "problems that students often encounter in daily communications" provides empirical evidence for us to further construct, supplement and enrich the content of the PSE software. Furthermore, the investigation "whether students have grasped the learning theme" during the software-based learning showed that all participants can substantially grasp the learning theme of the SE software, which proved that the content of the technical training software preliminarily developed by us was scientific and effective.

**Table 10.6. Investigation Results on the Content of the Software for Sample Lessons upon Preliminary Adaptation**

| | Answer | Frequency | Proportion (%) |
|---|---|---|---|
| Cohesion of Content | Coherent and systematic | 27 | 54.0 |
| | Just so so | 15 | 30.0 |
| | Incoherent, which makes the student unable to grasp the theme | 8 | 16.0 |
| Selection of Content | Mostly close to the daily life, which can provide much help for future communications | 34 | 50.7 |
| | Outdated | 3 | 4.5 |
| | The student has learned most of the content and it is unnecessary to relearn it. | 14 | 20.9 |
| | The systematic learning is helpful to improve the thinking capacity. | 16 | 23.9 |
| Demonstration of Content | Diversified and flexible | 21 | 41.2 |
| | Just so so | 27 | 52.9 |
| | Inflexible and dull | 3 | 5.9 |

**Table 10.7. Investigation Results on the Form of the Software for Sample Lessons upon Preliminary Adaptation**

| | | Frequency | Proportion (%) |
|---|---|---|---|
| Character | Satisfied | 25 | 49.0 |
| | Just so so | 19 | 37.3 |
| | Unsatisfied | 7 | 13.7 |
| Background images | Satisfied | 42 | 82.4 |
| | Just so so | 8 | 15.7 |
| | Unsatisfied | 1 | 2.0 |
| Music and dubbing | Satisfied | 39 | 76.5 |
| | Just so so | 8 | 15.7 |
| | Unsatisfied | 4 | 7.8 |

*Revision of PSE software.* We have, according to students' opinions and advice in the questionnaire, fully communicated and discussed with the software development professionals after the preliminary adaptation of the software for the purpose of continual revision and improvement of the adapted software as well as the subsequent systematic preparation of the software.

Therefore, we explained our psychological design ideas and the expected forms, and the professionals explained to us the difficulties of technical realization and the estimated effects via communications, which showed the interdisciplinary cooperation in the research.

In respect of the content, some students reflected that the story shall be more situation-based and there may be more interactive content or some flash games concerning the content to adjust the mood during learning.

Therefore, we shall, when we are writing the future scripts, detail the story as much as possible to make it more situation-based, demonstrate the contents with animation instead of in static manner to make it more dynamic, and design some different options for the items with different explanations to make it more interactive.

In respect of the demonstration, art designers have, as needed by the script, designed several characters that were close to the image of modern junior middle school students to replace the original dull and outdated characters; in respect of the tedious and inflexible music, we have made joint efforts and collected some moving music that is close to the content from the professional music website; in respect of the too many buttons for "play" and "continue" and the disordered operation, the connection between the parts was more flexible in subsequent courses and some buttons have been deleted and added; in respect of the problem that only one broadcaster was responsible for the dubbing of all characters, no additional dubbing personnel was employed due to the limited funds and for the consistent dubbing in the software.

## EXPERIMENTS

### Experiments on Improving Peer Relationships with Computer Assistance

#### 1) Purpose

The first purpose was to improve junior middle school students' psychological *suzhi* in peer communications and improve their peer relationships with the PSE software developed by us for improving peer relationships with computer assistance. The second purpose was to verify the effectiveness and operability of the PSE software so as to explore a new PSE approach, the computer assisted PSE mode.

#### 2) Participants and Methods

*Participants.* We chose two classes of grade Eight of an experimental middle school in Chongqing. The experimental group consisted of 37 students, 20 boys and 17 girls, and the control group consisted of 39 students, 22 boys and 17 girls.

*Methods.* Both psychometrics and educational experiments were used in our research. The psychometrical tools included the *Interpersonal Competence Questionnaire*, the *Social Goals Questionnaire* and the Questionnaire on Using Experience. We used SPSS10.0 for windows2000 to analyze and process all the data.

#### 3) Experimental Treatment and Experimental Procedures

In the experiment, we designed pre-test and post-test for both experimental and control groups (please see Table 10.8.).

## Table 10.8. Experimental Treatment

| Group | Pre-Test | Experimental Treatment | Post-Test |
|---|---|---|---|
| Experimental Group | ① Tests on interpersonal competence<br><br>② Tests on social goals | Improving peer relationships with computer assistance<br><br>Psychological *suzhi*-based training | ① Tests on interpersonal competence<br><br>② Tests on social goals<br><br>③ Questionnaire on Using Experience |
| Control Group | Ibid. | Routine teaching | Ibid. (except ③) |

According to the experimental procedures, the experiment was conducted in three phases:

*Preparation*: prepare the experimental plan, contact the experimental school and conduct the pre-test.

*Implementation*:

Conduct trainings on peer relationship skills on the experimental group during the computer lessons once a week and teach them following the units designed in the PSE software.

Conduct remote control of the student's computer with the teacher's computer and make individual analysis on the homework submitted in each class.

Data processing

### 4) Experimental Variables

*Independent variable:* the training for improving peer relationships with computer assistance

*Dependent variables:* a) interpersonal competence; b) social goals

*Control variables*: setting the experimental group and the control group; conducting technical trainings on peer relationships on the former one while conducting no training on the latter one. Precaution:

Set the two groups in a reasonable manner and keep them homogeneous as much as possible;

Control other factors that may influence the experimental effect and remove the expectation effect and the time effect.

### 5) Experimental Results and Analysis

*Difference between the experimental group and the control group before the intervention.* According to Table 10.9, in respect of the total scores and all dimensions of the *Interpersonal*

*Competence Questionnaire*, there was no significant difference between the experimental group and the control group before the intervention of experiments, but the average scores of the experimental group were lower than those of the control group. In respect of the total scores of the *Social Goals Questionnaire*, there was no significant difference between the experimental group and the control group before the intervention of experiments, but the average scores of the experimental group were lower than those of the control group. The average scores of the experimental group on such three dimensions as nurturance, popularity and intimacy were lower than those of the control group, while the average scores of the experimental group on leadership, avoidance and dominance were higher than those of the control group. There was significant difference between the average scores of the experimental group and the control group on the leadership and the popularity ($p<0.05$).

**Table 10.9. Difference between the Experimental Group and the Control Group before the Intervention**

| | Experimental Group (n=34) | | Control Group (n=32) | | *t* Value |
|---|---|---|---|---|---|
| | *M* | *SD* | *M* | *SD* | |
| Launching the communication | 3.33 | .77 | 3.49 | .63 | -.899 |
| Providing emotional supports | 3.32 | .62 | 3.55 | .57 | -1.554 |
| Imposing influence | 3.61 | .72 | 3.71 | .60 | -.648 |
| Self-exposure | 3.33 | .82 | 3.56 | .70 | -1.195 |
| Solving conflicts | 3.47 | .70 | 3.53 | .61 | -.394 |
| Total scores on interpersonal competence | 3.41 | .61 | 3.57 | .53 | -1.111 |
| Nurturance | 3.28 | .72 | 3.40 | .47 | -.772 |
| Popularity | 3.19 | .68 | 3.35 | .47 | -1.128* |
| Leadership | 2.72 | .81 | 2.55 | .54 | 1.061* |
| Intimacy | 2.91 | .63 | 3.04 | .47 | -.928 |
| Avoidance | 3.21 | .60 | 3.10 | .61 | .742 |
| Dominance | 3.12 | .57 | 3.04 | .78 | .509 |
| Total scores on social goals | 3.07 | .32 | 3.08 | .31 | -.068 |

Difference between the experimental group and the control group after the intervention. According to Table 10.10, in respect of the scores of all factors of interpersonal competence and social goals and the total scores of the *Interpersonal Competence Questionnaire* and the *Social Goals Questionnaire*, there was no significant difference between the experimental group and the control group after the intervention of educational experiments, but the average scores of the control group were higher than those of the experimental group.

*Difference between the pre-intervention scores and the post-intervention scores of the experimental group.* The matched sample *t* test showed that the post-experiment average scores of the experimental group were generally higher than its pre-experiment average scores of the *Interpersonal Competence Questionnaire* and all factors and there was significant difference between the pre-experiment average scores and the post-experiment average scores of such two factors as providing emotional supports and self-exposure. (*p*<0.05). The post-experiment scores of the experimental group of all factors and the *Social Goals Questionnaire* were generally lower than the pre-experiment scores, except that the average scores of intimacy were improved after the experiment. In addition, the post-experiment average scores of leadership and dominance fell significantly.

**Table 10.10. Difference between the Experimental Group and the Control Group after the Intervention**

|  | Experimental Group (n=32) | | Control Group (n=31) | | *t* Value |
|---|---|---|---|---|---|
|  | *M* | *SD* | *M* | *SD* |  |
| Launching the communication | 2.55 | .62 | 2.62 | .57 | -.471 |
| Providing emotional supports | 2.31 | .58 | 2.65 | .55 | -2.362 |
| Imposing influence | 2.24 | .58 | 2.59 | .53 | -2.476 |
| Self-exposure | 2.34 | .71 | 2.81 | .65 | -2.671 |
| Solving conflicts | 2.33 | .64 | 2.55 | .55 | -1.475 |
| Total scores on interpersonal competence | 2.35 | .55 | 2.64 | .52 | -2.135 |
| Nurturance | 1.81 | .54 | 2.03 | .50 | -1.649 |
| Popularity | 1.82 | .58 | 2.06 | .61 | -1.635 |
| Leadership | 2.34 | .65 | 2.43 | .47 | -.613 |
| Intimacy | 2.00 | .49 | 2.32 | .45 | -2.657 |
| Avoidance | 1.92 | .52 | 2.17 | .62 | -1.723 |
| Dominance | 2.66 | .67 | 2.70 | .72 | -.195 |
| Total scores on social goals | 2.09 | .38 | 2.28 | .35 | -2.067 |

*Difference between the pre-intervention scores and the post-intervention scores of the control group.* In accordance with the requirements of the counterbalancing experiment design, we also analyzed the difference between the pre-test and post-test scores of the peer relationships of the control group. The results showed: in view of the two questionnaires on peer relationships, the total scores of the interpersonal competence and the scores of the factors of the control group were improved to some extent, but there was no significant difference; there was no significant difference between the pre-test and post-test scores of the *Social Goals Questionnaire* and all factors therein, but the comparison between the pre-test and post-test average showed that the changes in the total scores and the four factors were different: some were great while some were slight.

*Qualitative analysis of the intervention effect of the experimental group.* According to the qualitative analysis on the questionnaire psychometrics, we found that the PSE software for improving peer relationships with computer assistance had certain intervention effects. We also noticed that some students have changed their awareness of and attitudes toward the improvement of peer relationships and improved their peer communication skills, but this was not demonstrated in the psychometrics with the questionnaire on improvement of peer relationships. Therefore, we conducted the following qualitative analysis in order to have an overall comprehension of the experimental effects and reflect the participants' implicit changes to which the quantitative analysis was unavailable.

**Table 10.11. Difference between the Pre-Intervention Scores and the Post-Intervention Scores of the Experimental Group**

|  | Pre-Test (n=32) | | Post-Test (n=32) | | t Value |
|---|---|---|---|---|---|
|  | M | SD | M | SD |  |
| Launching the communication | 3.35 | .79 | 3.44 | .62 | -.571 |
| Providing emotional supports | 3.38 | .60 | 3.68 | .58 | -2.591* |
| Imposing influence | 3.70 | .67 | 3.75 | .58 | -.437 |
| Self-exposure | 3.40 | .79 | 3.65 | .71 | -2.241* |
| Solving conflicts | 3.55 | .64 | 3.66 | .64 | -.678 |
| Total scores on interpersonal competence | 3.48 | .59 | 3.64 | .55 | -1.443 |
| Nurturance | 3.28 | .74 | 3.18 | .54 | .563 |
| Popularity | 3.18 | .68 | 3.17 | .58 | .064 |
| Leadership | 2.74 | .81 | 2.34 | .65 | 2.033* |
| Intimacy | 2.89 | .65 | 2.99 | .49 | -.599 |
| Avoidance | 3.19 | .60 | 3.07 | .52 | .890 |
| Dominance | 3.16 | .53 | 2.66 | .67 | 3.280** |
| Total scores on social goals | 3.07 | .33 | 2.90 | .34 | 1.941 |

*Analysis on class work.* We took the sample lesson named "Learn How to Cooperate and Make the Best Use of Competition" as an example for the analysis on class work. We only described students' class work and corresponding content since the content of the sample lesson has been detailed in the mode analysis on sample lessons in 10.2.

*Heaven and hell*: Han Yu came to the God and the God brought him to the hell. Han Yu saw that the persons were sitting around a large boiler full of delicious food, and all of them were so hungry, lean, haggard and painful before the delicious food. (Situation: many persons were sitting around a large boiler and each of them was holding a long spoon, but they can only put the spoon into others' mouth instead of theirs.) The God then brought him to the heaven. The boiler, the food and the spoon were the same as those in the hell, but every one here looked radiant and happy. (Situation: the persons here were feeding others with their spoons)

*Question*: the God asked Han Yu, "Do you know why the persons in the heaven are living an entirely different life from those in the hell?"

*Analysis of the results:*

According to the 23 effective answer sheets collected in class, 82.61% of the participants have realized the essential difference between "the heaven and the hell", i.e. Cooperation and dispute. They held that "the persons in the hell struggled and intrigued against each other while those in the heaven helped each other", "they were different in the nature: one was struggling while the other was declining modestly", "the persons in the hell only considered themselves" etc.

*A Thought-Provoking Experiment*: divide the students into several groups, each of which consisted of two students, and ask them to write down the amount of money they wanted, provided that they cannot negotiate in advance. The two students can, if the amount written down by them was 100 or less in total, get the money of the amount they wrote down; the two students should, if the amount written down by them was larger than 100 in total, 120 for example, give the experimenter RMB 60. Finally, none of the groups of students wrote down the amount less than 100 in total and they should pay the money.

*Question 1*: what the two students should do to benefit both of them?

*Question 2*: there are always the conditions where one's interest conflicts with others', like the situation of the experiment. Why do the both sides always suffer loss in such a situation as they should have embraced the win-win?

*Analysis of the results:*

The data collected showed that 50% of the students held that the aforesaid participating in the experiment should "decline modestly and get along well with each other", "make decisions after anticipating the possible experimental results", or even "surrender the interests to the other" and agreed on the principles that "cooperation is the foundation of success" and "cooperation is the most important". The participants' answers to the question why the aforesaid students failed in the experiment were similar, such as "they were just concerned by their own interests", "they all wanted to get the most and the best interests", "the experimental results are important, but the experimental process is even more important". Basketball match: Liu Fan and Zhang Ning were both the leading players of the class basketball team in the recent school basketball match, and a "Class Best Player" would be selected from the two at last, i.e. the one shooting the basket for more times would win the honor. Liu Fan thought, "once I get the ball, I will perform as much as possible." Liu Fan should have passed the ball to Zhang Ning for several times since Zhang Ning was the most likely to shoot the basket. However, Liu was afraid that he may lose the opportunity and insisted in shooting the basket by himself so that there were several failures in pass. Zhang Ning was also good at shooting, but he passed the ball to Liu Fan for several times in the match, which made Liu Fan succeed in shooting the basket. Finally, Liu Fan shot the basket for more times than Zhang Ning.

*Question 1*: who do you think is the "Class Best Player"? Why?

*Question 2*: what would you do in such situation if you were Liu Fan? Why?

*Analysis of the results:*

The data collected showed that, from the perspective of a third party, nearly all participants held that Zhang Ning should be the "Class Best Player" since "he has passed the ball to Liu Fan for many times, which showed his spirit of cooperation" and "he always considered the others in group activities instead of acting in an individualistic way".

When the participants imagined that they were in the same situation as Liu Fan, they not only cognize the essential psychological traits, such as "cooperation is the most important", "cooperation is the source of success", "they should cooperate with each other", but also showed strong emotional experience, such as "I will feel sad since I disappointed Zhang Ning". Meanwhile, they also showed their will of active behavior, such as "I would, if I were Liu Fan, clearly explain to the coach that I should not be the Class Best Player; we should have the team spirit", "I would, if I were Liu Fan, pass the ball to Zhang Ning since I cannot shoot the basket and I should give the opportunity to others", "I would, if I were Liu Fan, well cooperate with Zhang Ning to make the match more wonderful".

*Math contest*: the school wanted to select 5 students from the department of math for the international math contest, and Zhang Tao and Wang Jing, two top students in the field of math, tried their best to prepare for the contest. Zhang Tao shared all the materials he collected with other students for the purpose of the group's honor, while Wang Jing blockaded the information since she feared that her classmates may exceed her.

*Question*: What would you do if you were Zhang Tao or Wang Jing?

*Analysis of the results:*

88% of the participants supported Zhang Tao's behavior since "he was willing to share his materials with classmates for the purpose of the group's honor" and "he discussed with classmates". In addition, participants also demonstrated that "I would borrow the materials I collected to my classmates", "I would study with my classmates", "we would help each other". Moreover, some students even further cognized that "devotion is also the gain". Only very small number of students showed avoidance and negative cognition, such as "I would never share it with others if my classmates did not share it with me", "I would prepare secretly and never share it with others".

To sum up, we only analyzed the class work for representative sample lessons since large quantity of class work has been collected in class. The analysis results showed: most participants have carefully answered the questions in the courses, although the questions for various contents were different, so their answers were analyzable. They can not only distinguish the right from the wrong in respect of the matters and characters in the software but also show their inner experiences. This fully demonstrated that implicit changes occurred when they were learning with the software for sample lessons. Such changes would be accumulated and consolidated as they were learning the six lessons in the software, be transferred imperceptibly to the peer communications in their daily life and improve their peer relationships to some extent.

### *Analysis of Their Use of Experience*

We used the *Questionnaire on Using Experience* we prepared (including four open-ended questions) to survey the post-experiment conditions of the experimental group so as to further test the intervention effect on them. The result analysis was as follows.

① What have you gained after you used the software? (including any relevant feelings, gains and inspiration)

70.97% of the 32 students of the experimental group that were surveyed held that they have gained a lot, "have learned many methods on communicating with classmates", "have understood how to communicate with friends and have realized that we should make efforts and use correct approaches to win the friendship". They were so inspired: "I have understood the friendship. I used to be so irritable before that I have lost my good friends, but now I'm trying to make friends with them again and make them understand me". In addition, they had so many feelings: "we have learned a lot and thought a lot, but we still feel that we do not know anything and have to learn much more".

21.88% of the students felt that they have learned a lot in respect of the communication with the opposite gender, such as "I have understood that we should not fall into puppy love and should maintain normal relationships with the opposite gender", and said, "I will communicate with the opposite gender in appropriate ways". 3 students indicated that they would apply in the future the communication skills learned from the software consciously to make friends with others.

② What content do you think helps you the most after you have learned with the software? How does it help you?

31.25% of the 32 students of the experimental group that were surveyed mentioned that the content on communication with classmates (such as mutual help and cooperation between classmates and friends, how to give a good first impression to classmates etc.) helped them a lot, 59.38% felt that they benefited a great deal from the contents on communication with classmates of opposite gender while 9.37% did not mention the specific content.

In respect of the communication with the opposite gender, 78.95% of the students can correctly know about the communication with the opposite gender and indicated that they have mastered some strategies and do's and don'ts on such communication, such as "how to say 'No' to the opposite gender", "don't go out at night with the opposite gender for fun", "pay attention to the distance, situation and propriety when communicating with the opposite gender" etc. 21.05% of them also mentioned that the content on puppy love has provided them with a lot of assistance and helped them distinguish the friendship from the good impression during the days of innocence and realize the harm of puppy love.

Three students did not mention the specific content and inspiration; they just said "I forget it, but I was moved by it" and "it has demonstrated my true ideas" and showed the determination that they would make the best use of the learned knowledge in future.

③ What skills have you learned from the software? How do you apply them to your daily communications?

25.81% of the 31 students of the experimental group that were surveyed held that they have learned some skills on peer communications, such as they should "speak and act in a euphemistic way" and "no lies and deceits are allowed between classmates". They also applied such skills in daily communications. For example, they "actively consult the classmates about the questions I am unable to answer". 58.06% of the students mentioned that they have learned the skills on communicating with the opposite gender and 5 students selected other options.

In respect of the skills on communicating with the opposite gender, 50% of the students held that they have mastered the methods and skills on such communication and known how to solve relevant problems, or that they have correctly cognized such communications, such as "how to communicate with male students" etc. The other 50% of the students have learned some detailed communication strategies, such as "how to say 'NO' to the opposite gender", "we cannot stay alone with the opposite gender", "puppy love" etc.

In respect of other answers, 4 students felt that they have learned some communication strategies, but they did not mention what such skills were and how they would use them. Only 1 student held that he did not learn anything, let alone the application in daily peer communications.

④ What do you want to tell your classmates after you have learned with the software?

Only 6 of the 31 students of the experimental group that were surveyed did not write down anything due to a certain reason, 51.61% expressed, with different words, their desires communicating with classmates in future, such as "I hope we can be better friends". They also gave advice to others, such as "my classmates, we are now growing mature; we cannot get confused temporarily and thus delay out bright future. The love stories may be attractive, but we are young now and our mental status is not mature; we don't know what love is at all". Some students communicated with the classmates on the effectiveness of this PSE software developed in our research, such as "it is really helpful to learn this" etc. 29.03%f the students from the perspective of themselves have analyzed their frustrating experience in making friends and sincerely expressed their will to self-repentance, such as "sometimes I was immoderate and persnickety, but that was not the most important. I hope that you can forgive me and continue our friendship".

## Case Study after the PSE Experiment

We interviewed the students with low peer acceptance, analyzed the students, interviewed the head teacher and took them as the external validity of case interviewing effects to further investigate, verify and supplement the results of the aforesaid research. We sampled at random two cases from the low peer acceptance team according to the peer assessment results and negative nomination test: a boy surnamed Zhang and a girl surnamed Liu. We interviewed the students on such issues as the skill trainings for peer relationships, which was conducted individually in an office room (please see Appendix 1 for the recording of the interview). We also made comprehensive analysis with such two students. Please see the following for analysis results.

Case I: a female student surnamed Liu from low peer acceptance team, number of positive nomination=0. Self-evaluation on her peer relationships: very successful; subjective wishes of improving relationships: strong; efforts made to improve relationships: lots of. We interviewed Liu again since we found, by interviewing Liu's teacher, that the head teacher's impression of Liu was inconsistent with the peer assessment results. We finally found out the reason for such inconsistency through our interview with Liu. Liu was a transferred student and she needed a transitional period for adaptation after entering a new interpersonal environment. Her classmates did not really consider her as a member of the group in fact although she evaluated her peer relationships as "successful". We found that she did not have adequate cognitions and skills on communicating with the opposite gender although she has tried the best to adapt to the new environment as soon as possible and had strong subjective desires for improving the peer relationship. However, she has significantly improved her cognition on communicating with the opposite gender by learning with the PSE software for improving peer relationships with computer assistance.

Please see Table 10.12. For Liu's pre-experiment and post-experiment scores of the questionnaires on peer relationships.

### Table 10.12. Pre-Experiment and Post-Experiment Scores of Case I of the Questionnaires on Peer Relationships.

| | Interpersonal Competence Questionnaire | | | | | |
|---|---|---|---|---|---|---|
| | Launching the communication | Providing emotional supports | Imposing influence | Self-exposure | Solving conflicts | Total scores |
| Pre-Test | 3.33 | 3.62 | 4.14 | 4.00 | 3.50 | 3.77 |
| Post-Test | 4.83 | 3.87 | 4.28 | 4.00 | 4.25 | 4.19 |
| | Social Goals Questionnaire | | | | | |
| | Nurturance | Popularity | Leadership | Intimacy | Avoidance | Dominance | Total scores |
| Pre-Test | 1.16 | 1.66 | 4.00 | 2.28 | 3.33 | 3.60 | 2.64 |
| Post-Test | 3.00 | 3.33 | 1.60 | 3.57 | 3.33 | 3.40 | 3.07 |

Table 10.12. showed that Liu has, after the experiment, improved her scores of the *Interpersonal Competence Questionnaire* and all factors, of the *Social Goals Questionnaire* and such factors as nurturance, popularity and intimacy. However, her scores of leadership and dominance decreased. It follows that there was significant educational effect on this student and her peer relationships have been improved correspondingly.

The analysis on this student's course data also showed that she had relatively strong feelings and many gains after learning with the software.

*Case 2:* a male student surnamed Zhang from low peer acceptance team, number of positive nomination=2. Self-evaluation on his peer relationships: failed relatively; subjective wishes for improving relationships: strong; efforts made to improve relationships: lots of. The head teacher introduced that Zhang had good trait, but he did not have good peer relationships. We interviewed Zhang to find out the reason. Through our interview we have found that Zhang was often humiliated by peers during his daily communication with classmates. His self-introduction showed that his early experience in the family (being humiliated by his elder brother) caused bad influence on his peer relationships. In addition, the head teacher did not have an overall evaluation on Zhang. The teacher thought that he was sloppy and evaluated him just based on his academic performance, which may cause peers to have prejudice against Zhang. Zhang still failed to get good peer relationships, since he lacked detailed skills on peer communications, although Zhang himself urgently desired to improve his peer relationships and has made great efforts for this.

The comparison between Zhang's pre-experiment and post-experiment scores of the questionnaires on peer relationships indicated that he has improved his scores of the interpersonal competence and all factors to different extents: the scores of intimacy in the *Social Goals Questionnaire* improved to a greater extent, while the scores of dominance decreased significantly; the analysis on Zhang's course data also showed that there was significant intervention effect on him.

It follows that it is representative, scientific and consistent with the fact to sample two cases by means of peer assessment and negative nomination test. Some students included in the low peer acceptance team also desired to improve their peer relationships and hoped that they can establish a good environment for peer communication via learning with the PSE software. This showed that our research has, to a certain extent, been helpful to and popularize the development of and experiment on improving peer relationships with computer assistance.

*Case I:* the self-evaluation of the student on peer relationships was inconsistent with the actual peer acceptance, but we were also inspired by our interview. That is to say, educators should provide opportunities for students for communicating, better understanding each other and using and consolidating the knowledge they have learned to improve their peer relationships. Case II: the student still tried to improve her peer relationships, although she had bad peer relationships currently, and often turned to XX (her good friend), for help during the experiment.

Therefore, we conclude: the students in low peer acceptance team are more desiring improving their peer relationship since they are at a disadvantageous position in the peer group. Therefore, it is more effective for low peer acceptance students to learn with the PSE software for improving peer relationships with computer assistance. In addition, we also found that there were more than one factor that may influence junior middle school students' peer relationships, such as parents' education methods, head teacher's unfair evaluation, students' early family experiences etc. This showed that it was more effective to integrate the home and the school, the parent and the teacher in our research to improve junior middle school students' peer relationships.

## Discussion on Training Effects of the PSE Software

*By comparing the pre-test and post-test scores of the experimental group and the control group.* The pre-test and post-test scores of the experimental group of the *Interpersonal Competence Questionnaire* and the factors were all lower than those of the control group. This was because the experimental group's peer relationships were worse than those of the control group as a whole when we selected the participants in the experiment. Therefore, there were slight experimental effects on the experimental group and their post-experiment scores were still lower than the control group although the experimental intervention has improved their peer relationships to a certain extent. In respect of the *Social Goals Questionnaire*, the pre-experiment scores of the experimental group of the leadership, dominance and avoidance were higher than the control group, while its pre-experiment scores of popularity were significantly lower than the control group and its pre-experiment scores of nurturance, intimacy and the *Social Goals Questionnaire* were lower than the control group. This indicated that the peer relationship of the experimental group was bad as a whole. The scores of the control group were still generally higher than the experimental group after the experimental intervention although there was no significant difference between the two. This showed from another perspective that the experimental group's pursuit of the leadership and dominance decreased to a certain extent, while there was no difference in popularity from the significant difference before experiment. There was no bad effect on the scores of the *Social Goals Questionnaire* and other factors, except the avoidance. This also proved that there was only slight experimental effect in our research since the selected participants had bad peer relationships initially.

*By comparing the pre-test and post-test scores of the experimental group.* The experimental group's scores of interpersonal competence and all factors improved after the experiment, and the scores of two factors improved significantly providing emotional supports and self-exposure . The increase of average scores, statistically, can not prove the experimental results, but it indirectly showed that students had better peer relationships after the learning with the PSE software. In respect of the *Social Goals Questionnaire*, the post-experiment scores of the questionnaire, nurturance, popularity and avoidance were lower than the pre-experiment scores, the post-experiment scores of leadership and dominance decreased significantly and the post-experiment scores of intimacy increased to a certain extent. Therefore, the computer assisted skill training on peer relationships, as a PSE approach, is the same as other PSE approaches. The effect of short-term intervention was mainly overcoming negative communication psychology; it needs long-term well-targeted cultivation and trainings to obviously improve peer relationships. We cannot blindly determine whether the educational experiment a succeed or failure only by the aforesaid results. The reason is that our research is the educational experiment that is influenced by many factors and the duration is short; it should be difficult to achieve obvious effects in a short period. In addition, our expected effect was to improve the scores of nurturance, popularity and avoidance. Some studies have proved that the formation of any good psychological *suzhi* needs such a long-term process as "self-cognition, knowledge learning, behavioral direction with strategies, reflection and internalization, formation of psychological *suzhi*". Furthermore, there may be much reverse or repetition during the process before the *suzhi* is formed and becomes stable, so it is acceptable that the effect of short-term experiments is unsatisfactory to us; it may be ascending from the valley and becoming stable. Therefore, the cognition and attitude will be improved at least if the student consciously overcome the poor psychological *suzhi* that needs removing or improving. This is applicable to the factors named leadership and dominance, such as "I feel very happy when my classmates know that I am stronger than them", "I like the situation that my classmates awe me during the communication", "I am very happy when my classmates act as I wish after I used cunning strategies". Through the learning with the software for improving communication skills the experimental group would subjectively realize that they needed change their unreasonable principles and ideas on making friends and, correspondingly, the scores of such items may decrease. Thus, the experimental effects would be satisfactory . However, was the experimental effect significant as we mentioned above? Has it been established and stable? We cannot make conclusions based on this, and we needed consider all aspects comprehensively. In addition, whether the experimental effect was stable or not is also a problem that needs further exploration in our future research.

*By qualitative analysis.* The results of their use of gains and the analysis on class work showed that the experimental effect was good. According to the analysis on students' class work demonstrated in sample lessons, most participants not only recognized the essential issues of the content, such as "cooperation", "modest declination", "collectivism" etc., but also showed their strong emotional experiences and will of active behavior. Therefore, the PSE software developed in our research is helpful to bring about some implicit changes in participants' inner mind, which is helpful for improving peer relationships. Moreover, we have observed that the experimental group had good classroom discipline in the experimental class: each of them had a computer, learned and did the work by themselves, never discussed with others, actively coordinated with the experimenter and the participating teacher, carefully answer each of the questions, submitted the class work actively and created good experimental effects. The use of gains also showed that, in respect of the effectiveness of the software, 70.97% of the students held that they have gained a lot and thought high of the software; in respect of the content thereof, 90.63% of students held that it has helped them a lot; 80.64% of the students not only indicated that they would correct their mistakes, but also expressed their strong will of making friends and appealed others to correctly deal with the peer relationship (especially the communication with the opposite gender). It follows that the *Questionnaire on Using Experience* enabled participants to speak out freely and reflect some implicit intervention effects. The aforesaid results, although they were obtained via qualitative analysis, were enough to prove to some extent that the experiment had good effects. In addition, peer communication is an interactive activity and it is a long-term process to improve peer relationships. The acquisition, internalization and consolidation of individual's skills, their demonstration in the communication, the approval and acceptance of others and the subsequent improvement of relationships are gradual processes. The participants' peer relationships may have not been improved in time due to the short duration of this experiment although such participants have improved their communication skills. Many imperceptible experimental effects cannot be reflected instantly. Therefore, we need further research into the influence and effects of the PSE software we developed on junior middle school students' peer relationships.

### 4) Further Exploration and Discussion to Be Made

The effect of an experiment, especially the educational experiment, will always be influenced by other factors in addition to the independent variables, such as selection of participants, environment of the experiment, expected effects, time effect, school's arrangement of teaching, hardware support of the software, technical errors during the operation, etc. There were many only-children among the participants of the research, which disproportioned some analysis samples, and we should further our research and select more participants in future to make them more representative; the experimental environment was not controlled strictly due to some objective reasons: some students have watched the software for other contents, such as PCR and teacher-student relationship, and there were small games and songs for entertainment in the computer, which have influenced the learning effects of such students; the school has ever suspended the experiment for one week due to the class hours; some students' learning progress was delayed since they input characters too slowly although the PSE software has become a system and was easy to operate via the revision over and over again; many unexpected technical problems during the experiment also influenced the experimental effects; the software itself had some deficiencies due to the two sides' different understanding on some contents or the technical limitation during the interdisciplinary cooperation-based development, and this may also influence the experimental effect; the evaluation on experimental effects also involved the immediate effect and sustained effect.

In addition, our research had the following deficiencies due to the limited time, manpower and materials: (1) the influence of multiple variables was still unavoidable, although it has been controlled to some extent, and this was definitely a reason for the unsatisfactory experimental effects; (2) the computer assisted PSE is still an attempt in exploration, so there were just limited literatures and technologies and the content and demonstration of the software should be improved continuously; (3) the extent to which the training can be applied to practice cannot be evaluated, so the software should be more interactive. The aforesaid deficiencies should be removed in subsequent further research: (1) we would strictly control such control variables as the experimental environment in the further research, including sampling more participants to make them more representative, broadening the experiment scope to prove and popularize the conclusions; (2) we would continue to consult relevant literatures at home and abroad to prepare the training contents that can effectively improve junior middle students' peer relationships; (3) we would learn more about the development of software and comprehensively collect video and audio materials to make the software more situation-based, feedback-based and interactive.

## CONCLUSION

In respect of the interpersonal relationship, the post-experiment average scores of the experimental group were generally higher than the pre-experiment scores, and there was significant difference (**$p<0.05$**) between the pre-experiment and post-experiment scores of providing emotional supports and self-exposure, which indicated that the experimental group has made significant improvement in emotional supports and self-exposure.

In respect of social goals, the post-experiment scores of intimacy of the experimental group were improved to some extent, while the post-experiment scores of leadership and dominance decreased significantly ($p<0.05$). This indicated that the experimental group has made significant improvement in the intimacy, leadership and dominance.

The results of their use of gains and the analysis on class work showed that the experimental effect was good. In respect of the effectiveness of the software, 70.97% of the students held that they have gained a lot and thought high of the software. In respect of the content thereof, 90.63% of students held that it has helped them a lot; 80.64% of the students not only indicated that they would correct their mistakes, but also expressed their strong will of making friends and appealing others to correctly deal with the peer relationship.

## APPENDIX 1

### Recordings of the Interview

T1: Interviewer (a teacher) S: Interviewee (a student) T2: Head teacher

Case I: a female student surnamed Liu from low peer acceptance team, number of positive nomination=0

Self-evaluation on her peer relationships: very successful; subjective wishes for improving relationships: strong; efforts made to improve relationships: lots of.

Interview for the head teacher:

T1: What do you think of the girl surnamed Liu in your class?

T2: She's an obedient student.

T1: How does she get on with her classmates?

T2: She is gentle, quiet and obedient. She gets on well with other students.

T1: But neither of the students nominated her in this survey.

T2: It shouldn't be like this. She is active ordinarily and is willing to help other students.

Interview for the student:

T1: Do you have any difficulty in getting on with your classmates?

S: No. Everything goes on well.

T1: What do you think are your defects?

S: I don't like the male students and some ale students. My mother told me not to make friends with male students and I also think it not good to keep in touch with them too frequently.

T1: why?

S: I am bashful and I don't know how to get along with them. And some boys are disgusting; they always talk in class and horse around after class. A girl named XX1 hardly ever answers when she's spoken to and XX2 often gossips about others.

T1: What about your good friend?

S: I only get along well with XX. We often stay together and we have never kept anything secret between us.

T1: How do you get on with other students?

S: Just so so. I transferred to this school this semester from a rural school and I'm not very familiar with them.

T1: Which classmates do you prefer, present ones or former ones?

S: Former ones. I cherish the memory of the past time when I stayed with them (very happy).

T1: Three lessons have been provided, so what have you learned?

S: I have known how to get on with male students and good friends (she mentioned the stories of the protagonist and the good friend in the software and that they jointly sought medicines in the desert).

T1: Did you consciously use such techniques in daily communications? Can you give me an example?

S: Yes. For example, now I communicate more frequently in class with the male students in back rows, but we almost discuss the learning issues. We don't speak to each other after class.

T1: What do you think of the content and form of the software?

S: Both are OK. I don't have any opinions. The software is helpful and the figures therein are cute.

Case II: a male student surnamed Zhang from low peer acceptance team, number of positive nomination=2

Self-evaluation on her peer relationships: failed to some extent; subjective wishes for improving relationships: very strong; efforts made to improve relationships: lots of.

Interview with the head teacher:

T1: What do you think of the boy surnamed Zhang in your class?

T2: He is slovenly and does not work hard.

T1: How does he get on with his classmates?

T2: He is lonely to some extent and it seems that many students do not like him.

T1: Has him ever misbehaved?

T2: No.

Interview with the student:

T1: Do you have any difficulty in getting on with your classmates?

S: Yes.

T1: Can you give me some examples?

S: We don't have the same interest, and we do not talk about the same issue or in the same way; I often misspeak, my classmates always ignore me and they never return the things borrowed from me; I never ask for help from others, but none gave me a hand when I was in trouble...

T1: What do you think is the reason?

S: This may be because I don't have wide interest and I dare not actively make friends with them.

T1: Two lessons have been provided, so what have you learned?

S: It is greatly helpful. I have learned what I should pay attention to during my communication with the classmates. Now I pay much attention to the manner of speaking and many skills are useful.

T1: Did you consciously use such techniques in daily communications? Can you give me an example?

S: Yes. I always stand far away in the past when my classmates were playing badminton in P.E., but now I dare play together with them.

T1: What about your good friend?

S: The friend is important since I can speak to none if I have no friend. But XX never taught me when I need help on surfing the Internet.

T1: What do you think of the content and form of the software?

S: It has taught me many skills, but I still have many problems to be solved.


# APPENDIX 2

## Example of a Script

*Lesson Five Establishing Healthy and Beneficial Relationships with the Opposite Gender*

### Scene 1:

My classmates often discussed the relationship between Lin Na and me in those days. It was raining when the class was over the day before yesterday. Lin Na had no rain gear, while I had both the umbrella and the raincoat, so I borrowed my umbrella to her. Some students saw this and made faces toward me. They even shouted "Wow! Wow! Wow!" I was so embarrassed! Two days have passed, but they are still full of enthusiasm about broadcasting the matter, which makes me...What a trouble!

Has Han Yu's trouble ever happened to you?

What would you do if you were Han Yu?

Have you ever had the following thoughts?

May I make friends with him?

May I borrow a pen to him in class?

May I make friends with her?

May I accompany her back home when it is raining?

I sincerely desire for the respect and trust of the opposite gender although there is always an intangible gap between them and me.

I indeed desire to hear what others are discussing about the topics on the opposite gender although I always avoid participating in such discussion.

It is difficult to determine whether it is right or wrong and whether it is painful or pleasant.

**Scene 2:**

Xiaoya's academic performance is excellent in the grade, and she is good at playing the piano and dancing ballet, which shows that she is excellent both in conduct and learning. However, which is confusing to us, she barely communicates with male students and never actively talks to male students; if she has to communicate with male students, she will use the most "concise" language. She holds that male students and female students should be "well-disciplined" and barely communicate with each other; or else it should be "scandalous" and other people may gossip about it.

Question: (1) Is Xiaoya correct in respect of her attitude toward the communication with the opposite gender?

_____

Why? _____

[Explain such Thoughts]

The reason why Xiaoya is unwilling to communicate with male students is mainly that she does not correctly cognize the communication with the opposite gender. She believes that the communication between le and female students may cause "unfavorable gossip".

Can middle school students communicate with the opposite gender?

_____

Why?

_____

[Explain such Thoughts]

Female and male students will both pay attention to their speech and behavior if we mix female and male students in their learning process since they wish to get high evaluation from the opposite gender. Human beings consist of the female and the male; the absence of either will lead to an incomplete world.

To sum up, students can make friends with those of opposite gender. The middle school student should master the skills on what kinds of the opposite gender we can make friends with and how to correctly communicate with them.

**Scene 3:**

*1 Story of a little monk*

Long long ago, an old monk adopted an abandoned baby. When the little boy was ten, the old monk brought him down the mountain for the first time to beg alms. The little monk saw a beautiful woman on the way and watched her a long time. The old monk put his palms together devoutly as soon as he found this and said "Amitabha". He told the little monk that she was a tiger that would eat them. However, the little monk blurted, "I just like the tiger!"

What have you learned from this story?

Inspiration: it is a normal, natural and healthy for boys and girls to have the vague affection to the opposite gender.

The adolescence is one of the "growth peaks throughout the human's life". The female and male students have different physiological characteristics during this period, which influences their psychological development to a certain extent.

As a boy:

☆ Do you like to show your advantages before girls?

☆ Do you prefer teachers or parents to criticize you in absence of any girls?

☆ Do you want to approach girls but keep at a distance actually?

As a girl:

☆ Do you always act as a "gentlewoman" consciously before boys?

☆ Do you like consciously or unconsciously look yourself up and down in mirror?

☆ Do you want to speak to boys while you are afraid that the classmates may deem you "giddy"?

In fact, both boys and girls begin to realize the relationship between them and are very "interested" in and curious about the opposite gender. Therefore, both boys and girls desire to make friends with the opposite gender, but there are always contradictions between the yearning for opposite gender and the self-restraint due to their psychological self-containment.

*2 Healthy communication between female and male students*

Example I: Do you have the following thoughts when you communicate with the opposite gender?

"I communicate with the opposite gender to prove that I am attractive for others".

"I communicate with the opposite gender to show my dissatisfaction with and resistance against the suppression of the parent and the teacher".

"I communicate with the opposite gender to follow the general trend and avoid others laughing at my 'outdated behavior' and 'unsociability'".

"I communicate with the opposite gender to have a try of 'love affairs'".

"I communicate with the opposite gender since I failed in communicate with students of the same gender".

"I communicate with the opposite gender to seek the sense of dependence and safety (female)".

"I communicate with the opposite gender to seek the sense of accomplishment caused by protecting others (male)".

The motivation is unreasonable.

Example II: Do you select friends of opposite gender according to the following standards?

"I am willing to communicate with her/him as long as she/he is beautiful/handsome and fashionable".

"I only communicate with the opposite gender that are generous or rich".

"I only communicate with the opposite gender that are 'loyal' to friends".

The criterion for selecting friends is incorrect.

Example III: Have you communicated with the opposite gender in following places or manners?

"I often go to off-school public places with the opposite gender, such as the park and the bar".

"I often stay alone with a certain friend of opposite gender".

"I have ever dated with a friend of opposite gender".

The ways used are improper.

What kind of communication is healthy between the students of different genders?

Example I: I communicate with the opposite gender to learn their virtues and make up our own weaknesses so that we can embrace mutual improvement and common progress.

Example II: we can use the following standards to select friends of opposite gender:

☆ He/she is beautiful in mind. We cannot select friends only based on external appearance since a fair face may hide a foul heart.

☆ He/she has many advantages. You cannot always compare yourself with the classmates not as good as you; instead, you should learn from the classmates better than you.

☆ He/she is diligent and thrifty. You cannot measure a classmate based on whether he/she is poor or rich or how she/he is dressed.

Example III: you should pay attention to the following items when communicating with the opposite gender:

☆ The place where you are cannot be too small. You should communicate with them by means of group activities and avoid separate contacts.

☆ You'd better not communicate with them too frequently. You cannot frequently communicate with them no matter whether such communication is necessary.

☆ You cannot communicate with a fixed opposite gender. You cannot communicate a certain opposite gender for a long time.

*3 Male and female students in communications*

Do you know the different psychology and characteristics during peer communications?

Male students are more willing to compete, while female students are more tolerant.

Female students prefer to play with younger peers, while male students prefer to cooperate with older peers.

Female students are more sensitive to peer relationships and they wish to share the joy and worries with friends; male students are not so sensitive to the changes in peer relationships and may be indifferent, to a certain extent, to peers' worries or unease.

Male students have more aggressive behaviors than female students and they often take different ways: female students always gossip about others, while male students always fight with others.

In respect of the communication with the opposite gender, female students have stronger desires than male students to communicate with the opposite gender, but female students are generally not so active as male students in social activities. For example, female students do not have many friends and their friends do not cover a broad scope.

In respect of their nature, male students are generous and active, they do not care for slight loss or gains and they help others more than others help them, especially before female students; male students are sympathetic, sincere, zealous, patient, meticulous, modest and prudent and they can put themselves in others' position.

Question: Do you know other differences between male and female students during their peer communications?

## 4 Some good measures

Is you emotion often fluctuant during daily communication with the opposite gender? Please see the following for the performance of several peers.

*Example I:*

"I have to cooperate with her in completing the experiment, but I am fidgety since I am afraid that I will misspeak…" - anxious

☆ Self-suggestion. Breathe deep once you are nervous, bashful or at a loss and leave several seconds to yourself to have a "STOP". Calm down and think what you should say.

*Example II:*

"I'm too fat and I never dare speak with male students. " - self-abased

☆ List the advantages that the opposite gender lack but you have, such as "I am a girl and I am careful".

☆ Tell yourself in front of the mirror that "they will find I am a good girl as time goes by although I'm fat".

*Example III:*

"I feel that others may gossip about me if I communicate with female students. So I am frosty before female students. " - indifferent

☆ Help others actively and zealously; there will be two happy persons if you give a hand to another person.

*Example IV:*

"I feel scared once I think about communicating with male students; I dare not speak with them, let alone looking at their eyes. " - scared

☆ First communicate with your good friends of the same gender, then talk with an opposite gender that you are familiar with and finally contact the opposite gender that you are unfamiliar with.

☆ Imagine the situation that you are faced with or communicating with the opposite gender, assume various condition that you may encounter and determine or practice how to deal with it.

*Example V:*

"I, as a man, am much cleverer than her, but why did I perform worse than her examinations? I am not resigned to her…" – jealous

☆ Find out the advantages of the opposite gender and your problems; "have I worked hard enough?"

*Example VI:*

"Zhang Jun always steps on my chair and dangles before me in class; I feel that all male students are annoying". - hostile

☆ Not all male students have such deficiencies.

☆ Mildly tell him that his behavior has influenced you.

*Example VII:*

"Lin Ping, who sits in front of me, always looks back at me with wry smiles when I ask for help from my deskmate Xiaofang; I feel that he is laughing at me" – sensitive

☆ Tell yourself: I didn't do anything wrong; what am I afraid of? "Whatever anybody says, I will always do on my way!"

*Example VIII:*

"I always suppress my desire to make friends with the opposite gender" - depressed

☆ Drop your ideological baggage. The more you are afraid of making mistakes, the less you dare look at him/her, which will make you unable to take the first step.

Questions:

1) Have you ever encountered similar conditions? How did you deal with them?

_____

2) What else has ever puzzled you on your communication with the opposite gender in addition to aforesaid ones? _____

## 5 Right or wrong

Are the following behaviors proper during the communication between male and female students?

Male and female students are playing volleyball on the playground during the break; they are all happy and joyful.

Some male and female students are chasing and fighting around desks in the classroom, which creates a foul atmosphere here.

A boy named Xiaotian dates a girl named Xiaofang after the night study to chat with her. It is dark now and the moon comes out; their classmates pass them successively after class.

Several male and female students put their arms on others' shoulder in the school; they think it shows that they are open-minded.

The National Day is approaching. Female and male students are practicing the group dance hand in hand to prepare for the National Day celebration party.

Male students actively help female students carry the backpacks and female students give male students tissues to towel the sweat during the excursion.

Question: what improvement should you make in future to make yourself more popular with the opposite gender?

## 6 Peers' worries

Li Jing is the top student in the class. He is incommunicative and only some male students around him often consult him for difficult problems. They all admire him very much. However, most female students have different opinions on him: they think he is arrogant and standoffish and thus they dare not communicate with him.

Question: are you standoffish to the opposite gender?

Do you desire to make friends with the opposite gender but always feel embarrassed in practice?

Do you know why?

Actually, Li Jing is not pride. He is mistaken for a arrogant and inaccessible student since he is too indifferent to female students. He also desire for female students' trust in him.

The junior middle school students in adolescence have strong self-awareness and always pay much attention to their image. They are likely to suffer from "heterophobia" due to the traditional concept that "it is improper for men and women to touch each other's hand in passing objects". They often feel uneasy, nervous or even scared before the opposite gender, they think illogically, talk incoherently, fear to contact the opposite gender's body or look at their eyes, and thus they cannot normally communicate with the opposite gender.

What should you do in following situations?

*Example I*: ☆ a student dare not reveal his/her desire for communication with the opposite gender. He/she avoids any communication with the opposite gender since he/she is afraid that the opposite gender may find out his/her secrets when he/she has an eye contact with the opposite gender.

Advice: correctly cognize such desire for communication with the opposite gender, read more books on this topic and communicate with the opposite as much as possible.

*Example II:* a student is unable to perform his/her intelligence before the opposite gender and often behaves recklessly and abruptly; or he/she fails to catch the key information in the communication with the opposite gender since he/she is nervous and cannot make himself/herself understood. Therefore, he/she fears the communication with the opposite gender.

Advice: drop your ideological baggage and correct all wrong ideas. Think what you will do before the same gender and treat the opposite gender as you treat the same gender.

[Explain such Thoughts]

Be observant and conscientious. Pay attention to the communication between others and the opposite gender. Be a confident and optimistic boy/girl.

Question: what problems have you encountered during your communication with the opposite gender?

How did you solve them?

Here is a poem for you

Don't be afraid of the impulse of youth, since it indicates that you begin to become mature;

Don't fear the opposite gender's watch, since it is the sincere communication;

Don't restrain your desire for communication with the opposite gender, since it is the instinct of human beings;

Don't restrict your communication with the opposite gender, since it is needed by the society;

Don't be submerged by self-abasement and unsociability, as long as you are sincere and kindhearted.

You will definitely be accepted by and be popular with the opposite gender.

(End)

## REFERENCES

Asher, S. R., and Coie, J. D. (Eds.). (1990). *Peer rejection in childhood.* New York: Cambridge University Press.

Boivin, *M.*, and Hymel, S. (1997). Peer experiences and social self-perceptions: A sequential mode. *Developmental psychology, 33*, 135-145.

Bukowski, W. *M.*, and Hoza, B. (1989). Popularity and friendship: Issues in theory, measurement, and outcome. In T. J. Berndt, and G. W. Ladd (Eds.). *Peer relationship in child development.* New York: John Wileyand Sons, Inc. (pp. 15-45).

Chen, X. (2001). Exploration on special problem based trainings for middle school students' and primary school students' psychological *suzhi. Materials for researchers of Research Center of Mental Health Education of Southwest University and experimental teachers (II),* (12), 39-43.

Chen, X., and Zhang, D. J. (2002). Exploration on integrated mode for mental health education. *Educational Research,* (1), 71-75.

Crick, N. R., and Ladd, G. W. (1988). Rejected and neglected children's perceptions of their peer experiences: Loneliness, social anxiety, and social avoidance. *Paper presented at the southeastern conference on human development.*

Cui L. Y., and Huang, Y. C. (2002). *On psychological suzhi education.* In G. C. Yan (Ed.). Guangzhou: Guangdong Education Publishing House.

DeRosier, *M.* E., and Kupersmidt, J. B. (1994). Children's academic and behavioral adjustment as a function of the chronicity and proximity of peer rejection. *Child development, 65,* 1799-1813.

Dodge, K. A., and Feldman, E. (1990). *Issues in social cognition and sociometric status.* In: Asher S R, and Coie J D Eds, *Peer Rejection in Childhood.* New York: Cambridge University Press.

Feinberg, *M.* R., Smith, *M.*, and Schmidt, R. (1958). An analysis of expressions used by adolescents at varying economic levels to describe accepted and rejected peers. *Journal of genetic psychology,* (93), 133-148.

Fu, L. (1999). Opinions on mental health education modes for middle school students. *Journal of Sichuan Teachers College (social science),* (2), 45-48.

Furman, W., and Buhrmester, D. (1985). Children's perceptions of the personal relationships in their social net-works. *Development psychology, 21,* 1016-1024.

Han, R. S. (1998). Research into attribution of middle school students' and primary school students' success or failure in communications. *Psychological science,* (5), 467-469.

Han, R. S., and Zhu, G. Z. (2003). Status quo of middle school students' peer communication and the educational strategies. *Contemporary educational science,* (21), 48-49, 54.

Hartup, W. W. (1977). Peer, play, and pathology: A new look at the social behavior of children. Newsletter: SRCD, Inc.

Hymel, K. R. (1985). Children with peer relationship and social skills problems: Conceptual, annals of child development. Stamford, Connecticut: Jai Press.

Kurdek, A., and Krile, D. (1982). A developmental analysis of the relation between peer acceptance and both interpersonal understanding and perceived social self-competence. *Society for research in child development*, (53), 1485-1491.

Li, J. Q. (1997). Changing tendency of personality and psychology of middle school students in special administrative regions and the educational strategies. *Photocopying Material of Newspapers and Periodicals of* Renmin University *of China*, (11), 37-40.

Li, W. Q., Li, H., and Liu, C. Y. (2003). Systematic group counseling experimental research on improving children's peer relationships. *Psychological development and education*, (1), 76-79.

Li, Z., and Yao, B. X. (Eds.). (2001). *On psychology*. Beijing: China Higher Education Press.

Pan, J. Y. (2001). Research into applying the attribution theory to peer relationships. *Chinese mental health journal*, (6), 445-448.

Pan, J. Y. (2002). An attributional study of peer acceptance and rejection among middle school students. *Psychological science*, (1), 64-68.

Pan, S. (1983). *Educational psychology*. Beijing: People's Education Press.

Parker, J. G., and Asher, S. R. (1993). Friendship and friendship quality in middle childhood: Links with peer group acceptance and feeling of loneliness and social dissatisfaction. *Developmental psychology, 29* (4), 611-621.

Peng, S. D., Liu, Z. J., and Zhang, M. (2000). Several New CAL Mode's Design. *Journal of Shanghai Teachers University (natural science)*, (1), 55-62.

Piaget, J. (1932). *The moral judgement of the child*. Glence: Free Press.

Qu, X. Q. (1996). Find out the coordinate for students' psychological *suzhi* education: On how to improve the psychological *suzhi* education for middle and primary school students. *Educational management*, (4), 16-18.

Rubin, K. H., LeMare, L. J., and Lollis, S. (1990). Social withdrawal in childhood, developmental pathways to peer rejection. In: S. R. Asher and J. D. Coie (Eds.). *Peer rejection in childhood*. New York: Cambridge University Press, 217-249.

Shen, J. L., and Peng, H. M. (2002). The current issues and trend of mental health education in primary and secondary schools. *Journal of Beijing Normal University (social science edition)*, (1), 14-20.

Sullivan, H. S. (1953). *The interpersonal theory of psychiatry*. New York: Norton.

Wan, J. J. (2001). Advances in children's peer relationships and social skills in the west in recent decade. *Journal of Teachers College of Shanxi University*, (4), 85-88.

Wang, Z. Y., Wang, J. S., and Chen, H. C. (2000). The Influence of training on rejected and neglected children. *Psychological development and education*, (1), 6-11.

Wang, Y. C., Zou, H., and Qu, Z. Y. (2006). Preliminary revision of the interpersonal competence questionnaire among junior middle school students. *Chinese mental health journal, 5*, 306-308.

Weiss, R. S. (1974). The provisions of social relation-ships. In Z. Rubin (Ed.), *Doing Unto Others*. Englewoodcliffs, NJ: Pretice-Hall.

Wentzel, K. R., and Erdley, C. A. (1993). Strategies for making friends, relations to social behavior and peer acceptance in early adolescence. *Developmental psychology, 29*, 819-826.

Wheeler, V. A., and Ladd, G. W. (1982). Assessment of children's self-efficacy for social interactions with peers. *Developmental Psychology, 18*, 795–805.

Wo, J. Z. et al. (2001). A study on the development characteristics of adolescents' interpersonal relations. Psychological development and education, (3), 9-15.

Wo, J. Z., Ma, H. Z., and Liu, J. (2002). Towards mental health: development. Beijing: Huawen Publishing House.

Yang, S. L. (1996). Effects of software for computer assisted teaching. *Education science*, (1), 34-35.

Ye, Y. D. (2002). Network: A new approach for school's mental health education. *Mental health education for middle and primary school students*, (4), 10-12.

Yu, H. Q., and Zhou, Z. K. (2002). 4-6th Graders' attachment to parents and its associations with peer relation. *Psychological development and education*, (4), 36-40.

Zhang, D. J. (2002). Strengthen mental health education in schools and foster students' psychological quality. *Journal of Heibei Normal University (educational science edition)*, (5), 17-23.

Zhang, D. J. (2004). Mental health education: Ten problems to be solved. *China education daily*.

Zhang, D. J. (Ed.). (2001). *Psychological sushi training for students from primary and middle schools*. Chongqing: Southwest China Normal University Press.

Zhang, D. J., Feng, Z. Z., Guo, C., and Chen, X. (2000). Problems on research of students' mental quality. *Journal of Southwest China Normal University (philosophy and social sciences edition)*, (3), 56-62.

Zhang, J. H., and Li, S. L. (1996). Research into development and factors of middle school students' physiology and psychology of sex. *Educational research*, (5), 68-72.

Zhang, J. Y. (1999). On training of social skills: A method for improving children's peer relationships. *Theory and practice of education*, (6), 55-56.

Zhang, Y. (2002). The making of the table of the amount of the ability to associate with partners among the children aged 4-6. *Journal of Jiangsu Institute of Education (social science)*, (1), 42-44.

Zou, H. (1996). Social skill trainings and children's peer relationships. *Journal of Beijing Normal University (social sciences)*, (1), 46-50.

Zou, H. (1998). Development characteristics, functions and influential factors of teenagers' peer relationships. Doctoral dissertation, Beijing Normal University, Beijing, P.R.C.

Zou, H. (1998). Development functions and influential factors of peer relationships. *Psychological development and education*, (2), 39-44.

Zou, H., and Lin, C. D. (1999). Research into teenagers' social goals and peer relationships. *Psychological development and education*, (2), 1-6.

Zou, H., Zhou, H., and Zhou, Y. (1998). Relations between middle school students' friendship, friendship quality and peer acceptance. *Journal of Beijing Normal University (social science)*, (1), 43-50.

# PART FIVE:

# AESTHETIC-ACTIVITY BASED MODELS AND IMPLEMENTATION STRATEGIES

In: Methods and Implementary Strategies on Cultivating ...        ISBN: 978-1-62417-979-2
Editors: Da-Jun Zhang, Jin-Liang Wang, and Lin Yu     © 2013 Nova Science Publishers, Inc.

*Chapter 11*

# IMPACT OF MUSIC AESTHETIC APPRECIATION ON THE DEPRESSIVE SYMPTOMS OF COLLEGE STUDENTS

## *Qiao Zhou[1], Cheng Guo[2] and Jin-Liang Wang[2]*
[1]Chongqing normal University, China
[2]Center for Mental Health Education in Southwest University, China

## ABSTRACT

In face of the reality that the individual psychological problems increase day by day in modern society, it is of important theoretic value and practical significance to foster talents with high quality and all-around development to make best of the music aesthetic appreciation to treat the depressive symptoms and psychological problems of the college students as well as to improve the healthy development of their psychological *suzhi*. This chapter investigates into the impact of music aesthetic appreciation on the depressive symptoms of the college students. According to the experimental results, music aesthetic appreciation can improve the depressive symptoms of the participants in the experimental group remarkably, and help to increase the overall mental health of the participants in the experimental group. For participants in different groups, music aesthetic appreciation plays an active role.

## INTRODUCTION

### Efficacy of Music and Music Aesthetic Appreciation

*Efficacy of music*. Gaston, the father of American music therapy, pointed out that music is the sense of human being because human being creates not only music but also the connection with it. For human, music is indispensable and has effective efficiencies. It has affected the behavior and their own conditions of human beings over the thousands of years. (Alvin, 1989)Pythagorean School of the ancient Greek also believes that "some rhythm and beats of music may educate people, cure their temperament and ardor, and restore harmony to inner ability" (Liu, Z. J., 1993). Therefore, in the development of long human history, we may witness many practices to affect one's physical and mental health with music, which was widely applied in many fields, such as philosophy, religion, education, psychology, and medicine. These studies reveal that music has effect on many aspects including physiology/physics, mentality/emotion, and interpersonal relations/society. Although, no unanimous conclusion is reached yet, some theoretical concepts are developed from the results of empirical studies, of which some concepts may be cited as the foundation a unique mode to support music intervention. These findings (Donald, 1979, Gertrud Orff, 1984, Jocab, 1987) are now summarized as follows. Refer to Table 11.1. for details.

### Table 11.1. General Efficacy of Music

| |
|---|
| 1. Music may regulate physiological rhythm and improve the functions of endocrine system and immune system. |
| 2. Music can develop sensory perception, help to focus attentions, and promote coordination of functions. |
| 3. Music may arouse stimulus and nurture imagination. |
| 4. Music can help one to express himself at liberty, relieve his feelings, and stabilize emotions. |
| 5. Music can improve socialization and language interaction, and promote one to participate in groups. |
| 6. Music can help development avocations and new interests. |

In the mean time, different types of music may produce different physiological and psychological reactions of human, and arouse distinct emotional reactions. For example, the loud and passionate music makes one feel excited and inspired; soft and slow music makes one feel calm and tranquil, and the lively and joyful music makes one feel light-heartedness and happy.

Based on the efficiency of music advanced in the above studies, it can be affirmed that music is helpful to improve the depression problems of the college students both psychologically and physiologically.

*Concept of music aesthetic appreciation.* Using music as the regulatory and interventional means can be implemented in the forms of appreciation, giving performances and composition. The first form has empathy and comprehension effects, and the latter two have expressing and projecting effects. During specific implementation, it can be achieved through the means of music appreciation, music composition, receptive listing, songwriting, discussion on lyrics, music imagination, music performance, studies through music, etc. Of them, music appreciation produces most effective impact. Therefore, music appreciation is chosen as the independent variable in the study.

For the definition of "music appreciation", refer to Table 11.2. From the concepts listed out, we can infer the following common views:

First, music appreciation mentioned here is not purely music comment, which conducts pure theoretical analysis on music from the aspects of techniques of composition, background of composition, and rhythm and tune as that in ordinary music teaching classes.

## Table 11.2. List of the Concepts of Music Appreciation

1. Music appreciation is a practice of people to perceive, experience, and understand musical arts. It is an indispensable part in the overall music practical activities. Both music composition and performance are for the appreciation of people . Without music appreciation, they lose the significance of existence fundamentally. (Zhang, Q., 1983)

2. Music appreciation is the activity in which the appreciator feels music through listening, enjoys the beauty of music, and feels spiritual pleasure and intellectual satisfaction. (Ye, L., 1995)

3. Music appreciation refers to the aesthetic activity in which one experiences and comprehends the essence of music through listening with specific music pieces as the objects to obtain spiritual pleasure. Music appreciation plays a significant role in fostering the students' aesthetic concept and attitude and training their aesthetic ability. (Cao, L., 2000 )

4. Music appreciation is the process in which the individual realizes the perceptive and perceptual appreciation and resonance of some extent in listening to music. (Lin, G.*M.*, 2001)

Instead, it grasps the essence of music appreciation from the perspective of aesthetics. That is, according to the ideal music appreciation, appreciator shall appreciate music from the aesthetic perspective rather than the technical and pragmatic perspective. Second, it is important to understand the music for it is the target of appreciation and the object of aesthetics. However, it is more important to study the appreciator who is the subject of aesthetics. The feeling the appreciator has under the effect of the object, music, is the psychological activity produced in his consciousness, and it is distinct from the music pieces. Therefore, it is the leading direction of music appreciation to let the appreciator know how to appreciate the beauty of music, experience the aesthetic feelings brings by music, and adjust his psychological conditions. It is effective only when the study of aesthetic subject is properly placed and beauty of music and music aesthetics are combined together. In the end, music appreciation does not only exist as the receptive level of music. It is the subject-based conscious activity of the appreciator after all. The appreciator penetrates his subjective consciousness into the appreciation target inevitably during appreciation, which alters the music to some extent. In the mean time, the appreciator influences himself and affects his own aesthetic choices through the information feedback from aesthetic judgment and aesthetic choices, so as to adjust his psychological conditions. Therefore, listening to music from the aesthetic perspective belongs to music aesthetics, and it is the higher level of music appreciation. In this chapter, music appreciation is replaced by music aesthetic appreciation, for the latter develops a more accurate, more psychological concept with deeper meanings.

*Aesthetic factors in music aesthetic appreciation.* In music aesthetic field, study of aesthetic factors corresponding with the psychological process of aesthetic is important for structuring the mode of music aesthetic appreciation. However, study of aesthetic factors in music aesthetic appreciation is mostly in the scope of music aesthetics and music psychology. In addition, most elaborations are theoretical and lack certain operatability. Zhang (1983) believes that aesthetic factors in music aesthetic appreciation are the unification of the surface presentation form and inner content of music pieces. The surface presentation form involves musical sounds and its form of artistic structure; the inner content includes "feeling" and "meaning", in which, "feeling" refers to the emotion presented by the music while "meaning" refers to the ideas and artistic conception conveyed by the music. Xiu (1999) believes that the aesthetic factors of music lie in the integral composed of form, consciousness (concept), and behavior. Behavioral factors of music aesthetics refer to the operational activities in music techniques, such as instrument playing, vocal performance etc; formal factors refer to the sound forms and materialized forms. The materialized forms include music instruments, music scores, and records. Conscious factors of music aesthetics means the existence of music in the internalized psychological structure of people, which includes all types of music cultural concepts, aesthetic thoughts, and the logic thinking to present various music knowledge.The above viewpoints show that aesthetic factors in aesthetic appreciation are not one-fold but the unification of contents and forms.

*Psychological process of music aesthetic appreciation.* Aesthetic psychological process of music aesthetic appreciation is distinct from general psychological activities. Therefore its research and analysis are significant to grasp the systematic composition and psychological mechanism of aesthetic appreciation. For the series of research on psychological process in music aesthetic appreciation, refer to Table 11.3.

It can be inferred from Table 11.3. that, first, music aesthetic appreciation is a comprehensive dynamic process involving many psychological functions, such as perception, memory, imagination, emotion, and understanding (Cao, L., 2000). Second, music aesthetic appreciation has its stages and levels to some extent. Division and description of stages of aesthetic psychological process is the foundation to conduct music aesthetic appreciation, as well as the basis to build dimensions of music aesthetic appreciation.

## Table 11.3. List of Analytic Researches on Aesthetic Psychological Process in Music Aesthetic Appreciation

1. Music aesthetic appreciation usually is not presented in specific objective results directly, but in a series of subject-based psychological activities of the appreciator: from the preliminary stage of sound perception, to the stage of emotional experience and imagination and association, and to the most advanced stage of comprehension through which the appreciator comprehends the music thoughts and conception of living. In this way, a complete music aesthetic psychological structure comes into being in the end. (Zhang, Q., 1983)

2. Aesthetic psychological process of the subject in aesthetic activities can be divided into three stages, i.e. aesthetic expectation, aesthetic realization, and aesthetic dispersion. (Zeng, X. R., 2001)

3. Aesthetic psychological process during music aesthetic appreciation can be divided into three stages, i.e., music aesthetic intuition, music aesthetic experience, and music aesthetic sublimation. (Peng, J. X., 1994)

4. With reference to the research conducted by Peng who divides aesthetic psychological process jin music aesthetic appreciation into three stages, Cao further subdivides the aesthetic psychological process during the music aesthetic appreciation. He points out that the stage of music aesthetic intuition can be further divided into music aesthetic attention, aesthetic expectation, aesthetic attitude, sound perception and empathy, stage of music aesthetic experience into imagination, association, and emotional experience, and stage of aesthetic sublimation into understanding, comprehension, and resonance. (Cao, L., 2000 )

## Mental Health and Depressive Symptoms of College Students

*Mental health of college students.* Mental health problems refer to the undesirable psychological factors or psychological states that affect the normal behavior and activity efficacy of individuals. They are featured by the disturbance and disorder of mental and psychological activities. College students, as a special group that undertake the high expectation from the society and parents, are obviously under more psychological pressure than other peer groups. With reference to the results of previous investigations and researches on the mental health problems of college students (Liu, *M.* J., 1995; Ji, H., 1999; Wen, H., 2003), it can be concluded that the group of college students suffers from different types of psychological problems, especially depression, anxiety, somatization, and interpersonal sensitivity. According to the order of mental problems conflicting college students in the order of seriousness, depression ranks the top. Therefore, the study chooses the specific mental health problem of depression that conflicts college students as the target of intervention study of music aesthetic appreciation. In the mean time, the impacts of music aesthetic appreciation on depression and overall mental health of college students are also discussed.

*Concept and classification of depressive symptoms.* Feng (2002) points out through comprehensive analysis of literatures that, depression is classified into three types, i.e., depressed mood, depressive symptoms, and depressive disorder, which reflect the depression of the individual at three levels. Depressed mood refers to the sad, unhappy, and fidget state of mind. It is a type of emotional reaction of the individual to environmental and inner stimulus, and previous studies on depression of college students were mainly focused on this aspect. Depressive symptoms are the sad emotions of the individual caused by behavior problems with the subjective and negative emotional experiences as the core component. They are featured by many physical and psychological symptoms aroused by depression, accompanied by unhealthy social development (Jia, J. *M.*, 2001).Clinical diagnosis-based depressive disorder refers to the serious state of depression, namely, the individual is unable to study and live normally due to the impact of depression for a long time. This composes an important field in psychiatric studies. Depressed mode, depressive symptoms, and disorders are integrated as three levels of depression phenomena in a hierarchical and sequential mode (Compas, 1993; Qu, S. T., 1998). When the depressed mood of the individual lasts for a long period or time, or the depressed mood worsens or develops, it will be obviously aggravated into depressive symptoms. Since the individual perceives the feeling for depressive symptoms more accurately for depressed mood. Examination tools used to assess depressive symptoms, such as Beck self-rating depressive scale and Zung self-rating depressive scale, have satisfactory reliability and validity. Meanwhile, lots of college students suffer from depressive symptoms, which are one of the major problems affecting their mental health. Therefore, based on the above considerations, the study chooses the variation of depressive symptoms conflicting college students as the dependent viable.the definition of depressive symptoms of college students is affected by study orientations. Psychoanalysis, behaviorism, and cognitive psychology contribute different definitions to depressive symptoms. Combining different definitions, the following common views are reached. First, depressive symptoms are presented in notable and long-lasting sad, unhappy, and fidget emotional experiences featured by melancholy. They are characterized by many physical and psychological symptoms and unhealthy social development. Second, depressive symptoms are a kind of common negative emotional experiences, and some normal individuals may have some depressive symptoms some times. If the individual shows certain extent of depressed mood or is in depressed mood for long time, he/she may develop depressive symptoms. Last, negative self rating is an important component of depressive symptoms. The individual suffering from depressive symptoms develops negative cognition to the self, present and future, and usually explains the outside information with a distorted way of thinking.

There are different approaches to classify depressive symptoms. Cai, a Chinese scholar summarized the classification of depressive symptoms. Refer to Table 11.4. For details.

In accordance with the above discussions, depressive symptoms comprise biological level, psychological level, and social level. Therefore in the experimental study of the impact of music aesthetic appreciation on depressive symptoms of college students, improvement of the depressive symptoms of college students involves these three levels. The ultimate goal of the experimental study is to restore the physiological function, psychological function, and social function of the college students suffering from depressive symptoms.

### Table 11.4. Discussions on the Classification of Depressive Symptoms

1. Kierman (1988) believes that depressive symptoms can fall into the following five classes, emotional symptoms, behavior symptoms, attitude to the self and environment, physiological changes, and impairment of thinking (also called autonomic symptoms).
2. Lehmann thinks that depressive symptoms can be categorized into three groups of symptoms: psychological symptoms, functional symptoms, and somatic symptoms.
3. Zung believes that depressive symptoms fall into four categories, i.e., psychogenic-affective symptoms, symptoms of somatic disorder, symptoms of psychomotor disorder, and symptoms of depressive mental disorder.

*Typical symptom and influencing factors of depression among college students.* Depressive symptoms of college students are mainly presented in low mood, retardation of thinking, being in low spirits, feeling depressed, hebetudes, lack of vitality, and losing interests in everything; unwilling to make social contact, intentionally avoiding acquaintances, losing confidence in life, and not experiencing the happiness of life, accompanying anorexia and insomnia. Depression for a long period of time will seriously impair the physical and psychological health of people, and disable them from effective study and living. According to various studies which make comprehensive analysis of the external reasons of college students' suffering from depressive symptoms, occurrence of these depressive symptoms may be closely related to the impact of various life events on college students and their ways of stress coping with these psychological stimuli (Zhang, J. X. et al., 1995). For instance, social competence, study pressure, maladapattion to study, interpersonal communication pressure, quarrelling with others, serious defeat, being not smooth or being disappointed in love, and disordered close family relationship can contribute to the depressive symptoms of college students. Among the reasons, negative coping method, health adaptation factor, active coping methods, punishment factor and study pressure have most impact on depressive symptoms (Liu, Y. N. et al., 2001). In analyzing the most fundamental internal reasons causing depressive symptoms, Flech (1988) points out that, the reasons include high sensitivity to loss and being overlooked, low self-esteem, difficulty in admitting and mobilizing the emotions, difficulty in being unable to give play to aggressivity constructively, intrapsychic conflict caused by dependence, frequent bouts of tension, and long exposure to depression-induction environment. Gao (2003) believes that the reasons involve disturbance of self-expression and low self-evaluation. When the above affecting factors are given serious consideration, measures adopted for intervention can be determined pertinently.

*Common tools used to measure depressive symptoms of college students.* How to discriminate the depressive symptoms of college students? Methodologically, the common discrimination standards are standards for psychological testing, standards for normal social behaviors, standards for social adaptation, and subjective experience standards (Yi, *F.* J. et al., 1998).Of the standards, standards for psychological testing utilize various standardized psychological tests, such as psychological scale, to judge the mental health of the individual. Therefore, data provided by such testing are relatively objective. Scales used to assess depressive symptoms are mainly used to evaluate certain psychological symptoms for their existence and seriousness. They are generally applied in therapy efficacy evaluation, progress observation, and psychopharmacological studies. Therefore, symptom scale is a normative testing standard applicable to the experimental intervention conducted in the study. The representative tools include Hamilton Depression Scale (HAMD), Beck Depression Inventory (BDI), Zung Self-rating Depression Scale (SDS), and Carroll Depression Scale. Since the self-rating depression scale (SDS) is convenient in operation, easy to master, and effective in reflecting the symptoms related to depression status and their seriousness and development, such scale is used in the study for measurement.

*Methods of intervention into depressive symptoms of college students.* Since 1980s, many scholars have conducted various active experimental intervention studies with target on the depressive symptoms of college students of different groups, examined the impact of various factors on depressive symptoms of college students of different groups, and done various intervention experiments within a small scope, which achieved satisfactory effects. Among the studies concerning depressive symptoms of college students conducted in the past decades, the effective intervention studies conducted involved deprivation of sleep, combination of hypnosis and relaxation training, reading, physical exercises like Chinese shadowboxing and body-building exercises, making the best of internet culture, offering courses in mental hygiene and personality psychology, and laying emphasis on social and family support. These interventions produced active effects on the depressive symptoms of college students at different extents.

It is easy to find through the summary that, some effective means of intervention into depressive symptoms of college students are applied from the levels of cognition, will, behavior, and society, involving change of cognition, tempering of will, enhancement of behavior, and adaptation to society.

## Music Aesthetic Appreciation and Depressive Symptoms of the College Students

Zhang (2004) points out that current mental health education inclines to "highlighting behavior training while overlooking the internalization of experiences" during specific practice. Therefore, the important role of internalization of emotion and experiences shall be emphasized properly. According to the analysis in the literature, depressive symptoms are a type of sad emotion experienced by the individual. Its core element is subjective negative emotional experience. Therefore, the key to improving depressive symptoms is to transfer the negative emotional experience into positive emotional one. In the above studies of effective methods to affect depressive symptoms of college students, we find little of study on effective intervention from the perspective of aesthetics and emotional experience.

In the field of psychotherapy, it is art that produces significant effect on physical and psychological health of people through its unique ways to internalize emotional experience. Therefore, why not introduce these methods into intervention? It is the familiar and foreign music that provides us with new solution. As an artistic form that presents emotions directly and naturally, music may control and weaken the undesirable emotional experience and encourage healthy emotional experience, so as to maintain psychological balance and the unification of inner environment of body. It is an important way to alleviate depression.

Therefore, music aesthetic appreciation is a more complicated activity of beauty cognition on the basis of aesthetic feelings as well as the process of emotional experiences obtained during feeling, understanding, and appraising arts, natural landscape, and ideological civilization. It involves the entire cognition process, emotion process and personal psychological process (Liu Z. J., 1985). The process of music aesthetic appreciation is inseparable from emotional experience. Music is not only the materialized cognition of the objective world, but also the emotional cognition of objective world. For this reason, intervention into psychological problems with music aesthetic appreciation emphasizes on experiencing music emotionally and further understanding it on that basis.

Some researchers have conducted relevant studies on the connection between music and mentality of college students. Ke (2002) has conducted a sample survey on 200 college students in three grades from five different majors in his college for the connection between music and psychology. He clearly stated the significance of music in cultivating mental health of college students and advanced some specific enhancing approaches and means on the basis of the survey. In the study on the music preference of college students, Shen (2004) explored the nature of music, hint of appreciation of different music styles, and the impact of gender, personality dimension, personal experiences, and familiarity on music preference of college students. He obtained the truthful and direct first-hand materials and experience, which laid the foundation to promote the successive studies and pragmatic application.

Therefore, on the basis of above studies, this study tries to use music aesthetic appreciation as the intervention decreases the depressive symptoms of college students. It is an exploratory study on the mental health education of college students.

## Deficiencies in the Studies Available

According to the general survey of studies available, most theoretical studies are indirect ones elaborating the fundamental issues in an indirect manner. Empirical studies are even scarce. Most of them are tentative application practices in broad sense without corresponding basic theories for guidance. After specific analysis, we have obtained the following conclusions:

First, the breadth and depth of the studies. In breadth, studies on the impact of music aesthetic appreciation on depressive symptoms of college students are weak. Take the dissertations published in CNKI from 1994 to 2005 for example, 523 articles are available when "music appreciation" is used as the key word for searching; however, only three articles about the impact of music appreciation on depression problems are available when "music appreciation" and "depression" are used as the key words for searching. These articles make brief discussion on the theory and practical application, and only one of them carries out empirical study. There is no study directing at the group of college students. In depth, there is little in-depth exploration on the essential function of music aesthetic appreciation, on the aesthetic psychological structure and aesthetic psychological process of the individual in music aesthetic appreciation, or on the interaction between the organic variable, depressive symptoms of college students, and the stimulus variable.

Second, the study methods. Now, most studies focus on the description of music effects and theoretical elaboration of experiences, and there are few experimental studies. There are many horizontal studies accomplished in short period .Few vertical studies and follow-up investigations that require a longer period of time. Previous studies on intervention of depressive symptoms mostly adopted the mode of single orientation to physiological, psychological, or social factors. Few adopted the mode of aesthetic orientation, and there is insufficient emphasis on the internalization of emotional experiences of the individual. Therefore, the methods of studying the impact of music aesthetic appreciation on depressive symptoms of college students will be explored, and these methods shall be more well-directed, scientific, and operatable.

Last, the research findings and application. Most relevant studies are dispersed theoretical studies, and few are empirical studies. The results are mostly articles of reviews. Of a few empirical studies, most are about psychological measurement with the results in the form of descriptive survey reports. Few research findings have been applied to psychological counseling of college students and to psychotherapy.

## Foundation and General Conception of the Study

*Theoretical foundation of the Study.* In 1920, Cai commented in the foreword to Music Journal issued by Music Research Association of Peking University: "studies on the nature of sounds and tunes and the comparison of different music instruments fall into the category of physics, while the studies on the people's feeling about music belong to physiology, psychology, and aesthetics" (Wang, N. Y., 1996).Therefore, on the basis of the new studies that explore the impact of music aesthetic appreciation on depressive symptoms of college students, we analyze the impact from the angle of "neurophysiology – basic psychology – music aesthetics – music therapy – group counseling".

### First, Modern Studies on Neurophysiology Provides Theoretical Physiological Foundations.

The psychological therapeutic function of music is based on the modern physiological studies on the physiological effects of music. Firstly, under the neural regulation effect of music, limbic system of human brain impels the body to secrete some salutary hormones, enzymes, and acetylcholine to harmonize the physical and psychological health. In this way, the spiritual world of the people changes. Secondly, under the physical resonance effect of the music, the outside musical beat resonates with the physiological microvibration of the human body, which impels the human body to secrete a kind of physiological active substance to regulate blood circulation and neural activities. As a result, the body obtains pleasure. Lastly, the information communication effect of the music makes the left and right cerebral hemispheres coordinate and communicate easily. On one hand, the special musical beat and rhythm rest in the left cerebral hemisphere which is frequently used to control language, analysis, and inference; on the other hand, they simulate the right cerebral hemisphere which is in charge of emotion, creativity, and imagination. Therefore, music produces a strong effect on the promotion of potential abilities including creativity.

### Second, Modern Psychological Studies on the Relation Between Emotion and Cognition Provide Theoretical Foundations for Psychology

Based on the question about "the cognitive evaluation theory of emotion" (Arnold, 1960) advanced by American psychologist, Arnold, Tomkins upgraded the "emoti onal motivation theory" (Tomkins, 1974), in which he believed that emotion played a crucial role in the survival and development of human. It decided the cognition direction of an individual and the direction of personality development (Alvin, 1989). Tomkins' theory reveals the crucial role of emotion played in the survival and development of human being. Music can exert huge impact on the emotion of people. Therefore, music becomes a powerful weapon. Emotion produces enormous and sometimes even decisive impact on the judgment of people. As long as one's emotion changes, his opinion on certain issues changes too. If we say the traditional psychological adjustment theory believes that "cognition decides emotion", the view of music aesthetic appreciation believes "emotion decides cognition". According to this theory, due to the enormous impact of music on emotion, music is utilized to change the emotion of a person and ultimately his cognition.

### Thirdly, Studies of Aesthetic Psychology and Music Psychology Provide Theoretical Foundation in Music Aesthetic Psychology

First of all, "the freedom theory of music" is promoted. According to this theory, the freedom function of music refers to the function of music that frees people from the over-stressed reaction. Over-stressed reaction herein refers to the situation in which the energy generated by over secretion of adrenaline is imbalance to the consumption. People develop depressive symptoms mostly because of their over-stressed reaction to inadaptation to the environment. Therefore, when one develops depressive symptoms, effective means of "energy conservation – preparation for changes" shall be taken to alleviate or avoid stress reaction. Various aesthetic activities can be applied, and music is the most effective among these means.

Secondly, the theoretical foundation involves "the aesthetic theory of music". Some scholars (Li, Q. Y., 2000) believe that music produces acoustic beauty because music has the same effect as the visual "regular graphs" in regulating mental energy. Since music vibration is featured by regularity of steady states, music actually has only one frequency in our perception even though it is composed of many frequencies (refer to the consonance of tone). Its simplicity, serenity, and unity place it as the foundation of music.

Lastly, the foundation involves the "function theory of music". According to the music function theory advocated by Paul Hack (Paul Hack, 2002), emphasis shall be laid on music education to promote the healthy development of the individual in civic awareness, sense of responsibility, cooperation, health, and morality. In addition, he advocated that "music is not for music but for every individual". On such basis, he believes that the purpose of functional music is to help the young people to understand the various impacts of music on human behavior and the multiple function of music in society. In this way, they will be able to make the best of the noble function of the music to satisfy the demands and challenges in their daily life more effectively and to avoid the negative social effects of music in technological cultures. "

### *Fourthly, Studies on Music Therapy Provide Support to Techniques*

In the 20th century, music therapy using music as the regulation and intervention means was established and developed duly as a discipline. Since then, music psychology has been developed in two tendencies, i.e., empirical study on music psychology and study on music therapy. In the field of theoretical study, music psychology attaches more emphasis to people's perception of sound, music memory and music imagination, and music sense, while music therapy develops quickly in its own field.

Studies show that proper music will not only eliminate the undesirable experience of the patients and expand the scope of feelings and experiences they enjoy, but also promote their thinking structure during their listening to music. Bruscia believes (K. Bruscia, 1987) that, music therapy is a systematic intervention process during which the therapist utilizes music experiences in various forms and the therapeutic relation established during therapy as the motivation of treatment, to help those who deserve to reach the aim of health. Bunt (Bunt. L, 1997) thinks that music therapy, in which children or adults are accompanied by the therapists, uses sound and music to support and promote the participants' physiological, mental, social, and emotional health. Shen (2003) also points out that, music therapy uses music response to evaluate the physiological and mental health of the patients suffering from physiological defects, mental or emotional disorder, utilizes various forms of music stimulus and music experiences, and designs, plans out and chooses treatment plans adopting many methods to realize the help and intervention to patients. It is a comprehensive process that involves the methods of treatment, regulation, education, and training, and a new medical technique that integrates music with human-oriented spirits and life sciences. Therefore, utilizing some specific techniques of music therapy, such as the listening method, music meditation method, method of guide imagery and music (GIM), method of listening and discussion, recreative music therapy, method of improvising, and method of music psychodrama, music aesthetic appreciation is able to effectively affect the level of depressive symptoms of college students.

### *Fifthly, Studies on Group Psychological Counseling Provides Support for Techniques*

Psychological counseling is the main channel to perform mental health education on college students, as well as an effective method to affect and adjust the depressed mood. Psychological studies show that psychological adaptation of people mostly involves the adaptation to interpersonal relations. Many mental problems are related to the state of interpersonal relations. Therefore, different from the one-to-one counseling targeting at individual patients, group counseling puts emphasis on the group. The group counseling simulates the situation of social life in the form of interpersonal communication, and urges the individual to recognize, adjust, and improve his/her relation with other people, so as to promote his/her self development and improvement.

As a result, the study tries to adopt the methods of group activities so that college students with similar depressive symptoms will tell their distresses, be encouraged to understand themselves, and know themselves better in the activities. In the mean time, in observing the similar distresses others have, the college students will have sympathy for others, support and encourage each other, and analyze the reasons of depression together. They will find solutions to their problems, and regain the courage to live. In this way, group counseling realizes its function to improve depressive symptoms. Group counseling generally adopts the forms of psychodrama and the group of making friends, and the main techniques used include role-exchanging, image method, brainstorming, self description, life line, and painting.

### General Conception of the Study

*Definitions.* Based on the above analysis of literatures, we think that: Music aesthetic appreciation refers to the means in which the appreciation feels about music mainly in the method of listening and facilitated with other means, obtains non-lingual aesthetic emotional experiences from music, and feels spiritual pleasure and intellectual satisfaction, so as to effectively regulate and control mental status and to achieve physical and psychological development in an all-around and healthy manner. Undergraduates with depressive symptoms refer to the college students who feel incapable of dealling with the outside pressures, such as the pressure of social competition, study pressure, pressure of interpersonal relations, and disordered close family relationship. Besides negative self evaluation, they feel notable and long-lasting negative emotional experiences featured by depression, including, detestation, agony, sadness, shame, inferiority, unhappiness, and fidgety.

*Objectives of study.* The study is an exploratory study on the mental health education conducted in universities and colleges. Starting with the building of theoretic mode for music aesthetic appreciation and design of operational plan for music aesthetic appreciation, the study performs experimental study on education intervention of depressive symptoms of college students, in order to alleviate the depressive symptoms of college students and promote their overall mental health in the mean time.

*Conception of study.* Targeting at exploration of the impact of music aesthetic appreciation on depressive symptoms of college students, the study adopts the methods of literature review, questionnaire survey, group intervention experiment, and case interview and analysis. The basic conception of the study is as follows. First, theoretical analysis and activity design are carried out on the basis of the question raised. With reference to previous research, the study initial builds the theoretical mode for music aesthetic appreciation that meets the psychological needs of college students from the two unique perspectives of music aesthetic psychology and appreciation of different music styles. The mode will be verified and modified with the help of the results of the half open-ended questionnaire survey to obtain the final mode. With this mode as the theoretical guide, the study introduces the characteristics of the two techniques of group counseling and music therapy and designs out the well-directed and operatable activity operational plan for music aesthetic appreciation. Then, in accordance with the theoretic guidance of the mode and operational standard of the plan, the study adopts the method of pre-test and post-test for group intervention to carry out study on education intervention of depressive symptoms of college students. Combining case interview with analysis, it explores the impact of music aesthetic appreciation on depressive symptoms of college students. Last, discussion will be made and conclusion will be reached.

*Hypothesis of study.*

Hypothesis 1: it is applicable for music aesthetic appreciation to exert impact on depressive symptoms of college students.

Hypothesis 2: music aesthetic appreciation may effectively affect the depressive symptoms of college students.

Hypothesis 3: music aesthetic appreciation may promote the overall mental health of college students by alleviating the depressive symptoms.

Hypothesis 4: the impact of music aesthetic appreciation on depressive symptoms of different groups of college students may vary.

# BUILDING OF THEORETICAL MODE FOR MUSIC AESTHETIC APPRECIATION ACTIVITY AND DESIGN OF OPERATIONAL PLAN FOR SUCH ACTIVITY

We plan to build a theoretical mode for music aesthetic appreciation activity that not only can meet psychological needs of college students, but also can be adapted effectively to their depressive symptoms, based on two unique perspectives, i.e. Music aesthetic psychology and appreciation of different music styles. Under the guidance of such mode, features of two approaches including group counseling and music therapy are then introduced in a bid to design music aesthetic appreciation activity plan that is well-directed and operatable. The detailed steps are as follows:Step 1: envisage preliminarily the theoretical mode for music aesthetic appreciation activity on the basis of in-depth studies by the researchers mentioned in the literature review.Step 2: establish the final theoretical mode for music aesthetic appreciation activity after verification and revision of such mode based on empirical investigation, and make further analysis.Step 3: under the guidance of the finalized mode, design operational plan for music aesthetic appreciation, including scope of music selection, overall arrangement of activity, detailed design of the operational plan, etc.

## Building of Theoretical Mode for Music Aesthetic Appreciation Activity

*Preliminary blueprint of theoretical mode for music aesthetic appreciation activity.* Through sorting and classification based on literature analysis, a theoretical mode for music aesthetic appreciation activity is envisaged preliminarily, containing the following dimensions or components:

Aesthetic factors that are part of music aesthetic appreciation contents: including aesthetics in theme and scene, cadence and melody, accompany with musical instruments, etc.

Aesthetic principles followed in ways of music aesthetic appreciation: including principles of affectivity, experience, vividness, pleasure, etc.

Aesthetic characteristics possessed by music aesthetic appreciation environment: including concinnity in acoustic and visual environment and the harmony of the two, etc.

Aesthetic standards for guiding the operation of music aesthetic appreciation: including aesthetic standards for guiding manners, for guiding language, for guiding temperament, etc.

Aesthetic psychography during music aesthetic appreciation process: including music aesthetic attention and expectation during preparation stage and connecting stages between each link, music aesthetic perception and exploration during enlightenment stage, music aesthetic retrospection and reflection during continuation stage, etc.

*Empirical investigation for building theoretical mode of music aesthetic appreciation activity.* On the basis of the preliminary blueprint of theoretical mode of music aesthetic appreciation activity, a partially open-ended questionnaire was developed for the mode.

A questionnaire survey on 10 experts and 50 college students was carried out via letters and emails, and all copies of the questionnaire were completed and returned. Close-ended questions in the questionnaire were rated on a scale of 1 to 5, with each point representing respectively as follows: 1 for "totally disagree", 2 for "disagree to some extent", 3 for "not clear about", 4 for "agree to some extent", and 5 for "fully agree". Analysis on statistical results (see Table 11.5.) of the questionnaire took into consideration that as participants generally gave high rate of approval to the components, components whose rate of approval (rated above 3, including 3) exceeding 70% were to be taken to verify and revise the proposed mode and to finalize it, in addition to a comprehensive consideration of various opinions offered by experts and college students under open-ended items.

*Analysis on experts' responses to questionnaire.* It is shown in Table 11.5. That experts generally gave high rate of approval to the components of music aesthetic appreciation structure.

Rates of approval to principle of vividness and aesthetic standards for guiding manners in the music aesthetic appreciation activity mode are both 80% while the rates of approval to the other components are above 90%.In answering "What are the other additional factors that you think is necessary for music aesthetic appreciation: ", experts' suggestions mainly include: a) consideration of factors such as aesthetic appreciation literacy, attitudes (preference) and intentions of music aesthetic appreciation subjects; b) addition of principle of interactivity in music aesthetic appreciation activity, such as interactivity between appreciators, between appreciators and tutors; c) addition of assessment on and feedbacks from music aesthetic appreciation activity.

## Analysis on College Students' Responses to Questionnaire.

Statistical data of Table 11.5. shows that rate of approval given by college students to the components of music aesthetic appreciation structure is generally above 90%, except for those given to 3 components, i.e., the principle of vividness (82%), the principle of pleasure (82%), and concinnity in visual environment (88%), which are below 90%. In answering "What are the other additional factors that you think is necessary for music aesthetic appreciation: ", students' suggestions emphasize: a) richness of genre and styles of music materials to be implemented for music aesthetic appreciation; b) diversity of operation methods for music aesthetic appreciation; c) analysis on changes in emotional experience of participants during music appreciation activity.

**Table 11.5. Statistical Results of Partially Open-ended Questionnaire for Theoretical Mode for Music Aesthetic Appreciation Activity**

| Dimension | Component | Expert (n=10) | | College Student (n=50) | |
|---|---|---|---|---|---|
| | | Number of experts who approve | Rate of approval (%) | Number of students who approve | Rate of approval (%) |
| Aesthetic factors of music aesthetic appreciation contents | Aesthetics in theme and scene | 9 | 90 | 46 | 92 |
| | Aesthetics in cadence and melody | 10 | 100 | 48 | 96 |
| | Aesthetics in accompany with musical instruments | 9 | 90 | 46 | 95 |
| Aesthetic principles followed in music aesthetic appreciation ways | Affectivity | 10 | 100 | 49 | 98 |
| | Experience | 10 | 100 | 49 | 98 |
| | Vividness | 8 | 80 | 41 | 82 |
| | Pleasure | 9 | 90 | 41 | 82 |
| Aesthetic characteristics possessed by music aesthetic appreciation environment | Concinnity in acoustic environment | 10 | 100 | 45 | 90 |
| | Concinnity in visual environment | 9 | 90 | 44 | 88 |
| | Harmony of the two environment | 10 | 100 | 45 | 90 |
| Aesthetic standards for guiding operation | Aesthetic standards for guiding manners | 8 | 80 | 46 | 92 |
| | Aesthetic standards for guiding language | 9 | 90 | 46 | 92 |
| | Aesthetic standards for guiding temperament | 10 | 100 | 48 | 96 |
| Preparation stage, connecting stages between each link | Music aesthetic attention and expectation | | | | |
| Enlightenment stage | Music aesthetic perception and exploration | | | | |
| Dispersion stage | Music aesthetic retrospection and reflection | | | | |

Based on the above statistical results, and in combination with suggestions proposed by experts and college students, the mode of music aesthetic appreciation activity envisaged in theoretical analysis is revised and used for guiding the design of activity operational plan: a) individual aesthetic psychological structure in music aesthetic appreciation activity is added to the vertical system for analysis as it is the premise for building such system; b) as for typicality and richness of genre and styles of music materials to be implemented, since such materials are to be selected based on both music style and cross-style factor as mentioned above, attention is to be paid in this regard in detailed design of the plan; c) diversity and interactivity of operation methods are added to horizontal system; d) assessment on and feedbacks from music aesthetic appreciation activity are added to the design of activity operational plan.

*Analysis on theoretical mode of music aesthetic appreciation activity.* Through verification and revision based on the questionnaire survey, the theoretical mode of music aesthetic appreciation activity is finalized. The mode has two systems: the vertical and the horizontal systems. The vertical system is the system of aesthetic psychological process of music aesthetic appreciation activity. It employs the structure for implementing music aesthetic appreciation activity as its main line, which guides the activity from its beginning till its end. The horizontal system is the presentation system of aesthetic factors of music aesthetic appreciation activity. It infiltrates into the vertical system and is available in each stage or link of the activity. Interacting with each other, the vertical and the horizontal systems form a spatial network structure. The structure is shown in Figure 11.1.Analysis on the details of the two systems is as follows.

*Horizontal system: presentation system of aesthetic factors of music aesthetic appreciation.* Aesthetic factors of each stage or link of music aesthetic appreciation are analyzed to build the horizontal presentation system of aesthetic factors so as to build the theoretical mode of music aesthetic appreciation activity according to the law of aesthetics and to realize the premise for implementing intervention. On the basis of reference to literature and our own consideration, this study holds that the presentation system of aesthetic factors of music aesthetic appreciation can be built in 4 dimensions, i.e. Contents, methods, environment, and tutors of music aesthetic appreciation.

*Dimension 1: aesthetic factors composed of contents of music aesthetic appreciation*

Contents of music aesthetic appreciation are the basis of music aesthetic appreciation, and the objective condition for the participants to obtain music aesthetic feeling and experience. Therefore, it is of great importance to select musical pieces that are worth appreciation and can arouse aesthetic feelings as the contents of music aesthetic appreciation. They are the basis of music appreciation mainly targeted on aesthetics. Aesthetic factors of music aesthetic appreciation contents include aesthetics in cadence and melody, accompany with musical instruments, theme and scene, etc.

*Dimension 2: aesthetic principles followed in music aesthetic appreciation ways*

Music aesthetic appreciation is used in this study as an intervention approach. It is different from other intervention approaches, mainly in that: it starts from perceptual aspects, and employs a method based on experience; it touches people through emotion and aesthetic feeling; it emphasizes potential effect of aesthetic appreciation. Therefore, five principles shall be followed in music aesthetic appreciation ways: principles of affectivity, experience, vividness, pleasure, interactivity, etc.

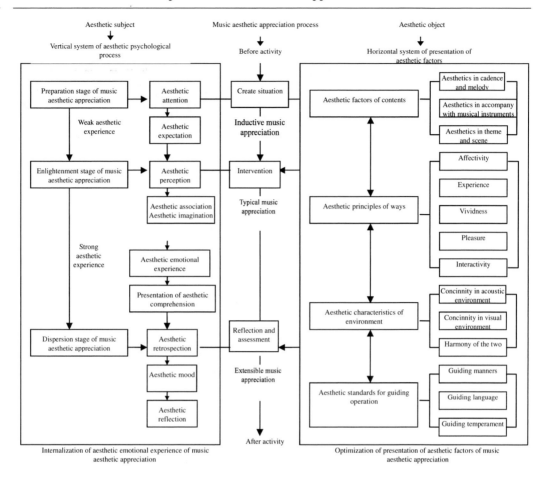

Figure 11.1. Theoretical Mode Diagram of Impact of Music Aesthetic Appreciation on College Students' Depressive Symptoms.

The principle of interactivity, supplemented to the initial blueprint, refers to that during music aesthetic appreciation activity, exchanges and interactions between appreciators, between appreciators and tutors can enhance understanding of music, each individual concerned and the others, and can bring the methods adopted for music aesthetic appreciation into full play.

*Dimension 3: aesthetic characteristics possessed by music aesthetic appreciation environment*

Aesthetic characteristics possessed by music aesthetic appreciation environment are mainly reflected in three aspects: concinnity in acoustic environment, concinnity in visual environment, and the harmony of the two. They are external conditions for creating sound music aesthetic appreciation atmosphere and situation. Firstly, basic approach to music aesthetic appreciation is listening. Therefore acoustic aesthetics is the key factor for creating sound acoustic environment. Clear and melodious sound effects can bring pleasure to human sense of hearing and can induce aesthetic feeling. Secondly, a good visual environment is also vital to music aesthetic appreciation. The arrangement of the site shall be elegant and artistic; some auxiliary approaches for music aesthetic appreciation, such as the application of multimedia technology, invariably follow the principle of managing to create aesthetic atmosphere and artistic situation.

*Dimension 4: aesthetic standards for guiding the operation of music aesthetic appreciation*

The first goes to the guiding of manners. It refers to appearance, clothing, expression, posture, gesture, behavior, etc., displayed by the tutor in music aesthetic appreciation activity in compliance with requirements of etiquette and aesthetic standards. The second goes to the guiding of language. It refers to a special language formed by the tutor in music aesthetic appreciation activity to meet study requirements and comply with aesthetic standards. The last goes to the guiding of temperament. It refers to the externalization of the personality and character of the tutor and originates from his or her psychological traits and knowledge.

*Vertical system:* system of aesthetic psychological process of music aesthetic appreciation. Building a vertical system of aesthetic psychological process through classification and description of stages of the process is a core issue for designing and implementing music aesthetic appreciation. By means of concluding and summarizing previous studies in the academia, we can divide aesthetic psychological process of music aesthetic appreciation into 3 stages.

*Stage 1:* preparation for music aesthetic appreciation

This stage refers to a stage in which the subject is preparing mentally or is ready for a specific aesthetic object on the basis of his or her existing aesthetic psychological structure and aesthetic motivation so as to complete the transformation of his or her existing aesthetic psychological structure. This stage includes two psychological activities, i.e., music aesthetic attention and expectation.

Music aesthetic attention is the beginning of music aesthetic psychological process. Its emergence depends on two aspects: on the one hand, it refers to originality, style, connotation, etc. Possessed by structural form of the music materials presented; on the other hand, it refers to the subject, i.e., existing music aesthetic appreciation preference of music appreciators. The latter aspect pertains to aesthetic psychological structure of an individual, and is the premise of aesthetic psychological process conducted by the individual. It determines the directionality, selectivity and judgment of his or her aesthetic activities. Music aesthetic attention and expectation constitute a orienting and adjusting system for music aesthetic appreciation. They enable the subject to adopt a special mental set through adjustment and make the subject ready for music aesthetic enlightenment to be carried out soon.

*Stage 2:* enlightenment for music aesthetic appreciation

This stage is the climax of the entire music aesthetic psychological process. It is in this stage that music aesthetic appreciation is carried out in full swing. It is the most active and the most nervous stage. It is also a stage that lasts the longest and can display aesthetic psychological characteristics the most. It includes music aesthetic perception and a series of music aesthetic explorations, such as music aesthetic association and imagination, music aesthetic emotional experience, presentation of aesthetic comprehension, etc. They are interrelated and infiltrate one another.

Music aesthetic emotional experience has multiple functions in the course of music aesthetic appreciation: firstly, in the aspect of promoting function, emotion can drive and further stimulate appreciators' aesthetic activities, such as strengthening senses, exciting imagination, achieving sublimation, etc.; second, in terms of orienting and creating function, the entire process of music appreciation is carried out under certain emotional background, so it is subject to the nature and intensity of emotion significantly; thirdly, in terms of evaluating function, aesthetic emotion not only restricts various psychological activities of the appreciator, but also affects his or her aesthetic judgment. Therefore, importance shall be attached to the role of music aesthetic emotion in music aesthetic appreciation — the starting point of our experimental study.

*Stage 3:* dispersion for music aesthetic appreciation

In this stage, aesthetic psychology of the appreciator accumulates and subsides after he or she feels certain mental satisfaction following the completion music aesthetic appreciation of specific object. This stage includes such psychological activities as music aesthetic retrospection and reflection. At this time, the appreciator carries out aesthetic retrospection on the basis of music aesthetic perception and exploration and amid a unique aesthetic mood to deepen the cognition and understanding of music aesthetic appreciation, and conducts reflection to get relevant experience.

It shall be noted that the preparation, enlightenment and dispersion stages of music aesthetic appreciation are three interrelated, yet mutually independent ones in the course of psychological process of music aesthetic appreciation. Various psychological activities in the stages have only relative implications. They constitute jointly a comprehensive, dynamic, complicated and integral psychological process of music aesthetic appreciation. Various factors presenting music aesthetic appreciation infiltrate the process, and propel the progress and change of music aesthetic appreciation.

## Design of Operational Plan for Music Aesthetic Appreciation

### 1) Selection of Musical Pieces for Music Aesthetic Appreciation

*Criteria for selection.* As for selection of musical pieces, first of all, attention shall be paid to the following:

*Selection of materials based on both music style and cross-style factor.* Through literature analysis, this study has made some explorations different from previous studies. Many relevant previous studies were carried out using a music style and genre as intervention targets while this study, drawing on experimental study by Shen (2004) on college students' music preference and effect factors, puts the starting point of study on the perspective of cross-music styles. Based on the Gestalt effect of "the whole is greater than the sum of its parts" in psychology, this study adheres to the significance of music existing as a whole and takes into consideration both music style and cross-style factor. Materials for experiment are all selected from musical pieces of a variety of styles and contain different typical music elements and features, but separate correspondence between specific music factors, including rhythm, sound velocity, timbre, melody and sound intensity, and emotion is not overemphasized. Selected musical pieces were processed with music editing software to meet the needs of the experiment.

*Selection of pure music materials.* Although the adding of language can convey some specific information, as far as music is concerned, its most important significance is non-verbal. Many studies showed that music aesthetic effect having the greatest potential and music exerting the maximum influence on human's emotion involve mainly pure music. If language intervenes too much in music, it will affect the independence of music images and restrict thinking. This is also where the difference lies between a common sense of listening to music and music appreciation. Therefore, in selecting music genre, this study mainly involves in Chinese music, western music, modern light music, etc. As pop music is subject to change, avant-garde, and familiarity, and is not easily operatable, together with other reasons, it is not included in the scope of this study. As for theme of presentation, music expressing natural beauty is particularly selected as it is a way for relieving depressive symptoms and being encouraged. When the appreciator feels as if intoxicated with the nature, some of his or her discomfort will be removed.

*Selection of non-pop music materials.* An issue, i.e. The impact of the degree of familiarity on emotional experience of music draws our attention inevitably. Generally, the solution to such issue is to use musical pieces not widely known by the participants as materials for experiment. But the shortcoming of such solution is that it restricts the representativeness of music materials. Considering that this study requires a large number of music materials and its focus is on effective intervention in depressive symptoms of college students. In the meantime, selection of materials is based on certain span in terms of familiarity instead of low popularity to minimize intervention in existing experience. A study (Liu, 1991) showed that familiarity in pop music appreciation emerged early. When familiarity reached certain level, it would increase in company with fatigue and negative response of attitude. Therefore, it is not suitable for the needs of this study. However, familiarity with serious music emerged late. Richness of the music material itself provided much room to psychological factors such as distribution and extent of attention in the process of cognition so that increase in familiarity was positively related to active response of attitude. Therefore, non-pop musical pieces that college students may know something about it but are not acquainted with entirely are selected in this study as materials for experiment.

*Selection of music materials expressing different emotional experience.* A study showed (Fan, 2002) that music expressing many kinds of different emotional experience can be classified through finding the relationship between such music and emotional experience. See Table 11.6. for details.

### Table 11.6. Genre of Music Expressing Different Emotional Experience

| |
|---|
| 1. Tranquil, peaceful, calm, serene, lyric, satisfied, quiet, and soothing |
| 2. Bright, vivacious, pleasant, joyful, and relaxed |
| 3. Tender, elegant, lightsome, novel, humorous, and fantastic |
| 4. Sentimental, gentle, imploring, eager, dreamlike, and sad |
| 5. Excited, hilarious, impulsive, uneasy, and passionate |
| 6. Dignified, robust, and eminent |
| 7. Lofty, sacred, serious, and noble |
| 8. Depressive, dark, grave, gloomy, melancholy, miserable, heartbreaking, perplexed, and plaintive |

Once the music genre listed above changes, emotional experience it reflects varies accordingly. Likewise, a certain music genre can make the listener have corresponding emotional experience to a certain degree.

If a piece of lento music is melancholy, mournful, distressing, heartbreaking or bleak, listeners will experience sadness; if a piece of fast music is passionate, anxious, or disconcerting, listeners will feel excited; if a piece of bright music is jubilant, pleasant, delightful, or full of vigor and vitality, listeners will experience joy. It is due to the influence of music on emotional experience that this study endeavors to select music expressing different emotional experience in music aesthetic appreciation to induce or change college students' emotional experience and to make them have better empathy, projection and expression to realize comprehension and purification, and ultimately to adjust their mental state, to free their body and soul, and to ameliorate college students' depressive symptoms.

**Table 11.7. Scope of Selection of Musical Pieces for Music Aesthetic Appreciation**

| Classification | Genre of Music and Its Function | Principle for Selection | Example |
|---|---|---|---|
| Group 1 | To vent emotion with plangent and desolate music | When people are unable to extricate themselves from depression of different degrees, they resort to joyful and ardent music to restrain their depression. But the effect is not good. Sometimes due to the huge difference between the two emotions, people will even feel fretty instead (Fan, 2002).Therefore, at the initial stage of activity design, "sad" musical pieces are selected for releasing and venting bad emotional experience accumulated in heart to resume mental balance as soon as possible. | Beethoven's *Moonlight Sonata*, etc. |
| Group 2 | To eliminate dysphoria with lyric and tranquil music | The music is smooth, serene, gentle, and of quiet and tranquil style. Music presenting natural beauty especially can "purify" people's emotions. It is conducive to smooth and steady breathing, moderate heartbeat and pulse rhythm, mental relaxation, and to eliminating fidget. | Bach and Gounod's *Prelude In C With Ave Maria*, etc. |
| Group 3 | To express freely aspiration and generate empathy with relaxed, bright, merry, and lively music | When depression, the negative emotional experience is vented gradually along with the music. Some musical pieces that are jubilant and full of vigor and vitality are selected additionally to enable the participants to obtain positive emotional experience, to cheer them up and encourage them. This is quite helpful for the amelioration of depressive symptoms. | Elgar's *Liebesgruss (Loves Greeting)*, etc. |

*Scope of selection.* On such basis and in combination with typical presentation of college students' depressive symptoms, music selected for intervention is divided into 3 categories in this study as shown in the following Table 11.7.

Table 11.7. shows that in selection of musical pieces for intervention, emphasis is given on the principles of "homogeneity" and "heterogeneity".

Music expresses directly emotions and different music reflects varied emotional experience. As far as emotions and psychological intervention are concerned, music that reflects opposite emotional experience is sometimes needed to achieve good effect.

Therefore, at the initial stage, sad music is selected to correspond to the negative emotional experience, i.e., depressive symptoms of the participants. Later, tranquil and bright music is selected to enable the participants to obtain positive emotional experience so as to ameliorate their depressive symptoms.

Meanwhile, attention is paid to the principle of dialectical selection of music in arranging and applying the three groups of music.

Not only in the design of the 3 stages of the whole music aesthetic appreciation, but also in the design of operational plan for each activity, application of the three groups of music shall be considered.

On the one hand, the design of plan for each activity shall include the use of the three groups of music; on the other hand, selection of the three groups of music has different emphases.

At the preparation stage, emphasis is given to music of Group 1 so that the participants can vent their emotions with plangent and desolate music, in addition to appropriate consideration of music of Group 2 and Group 3.

At the early phase of the implementation stage, emphasis is given to music of Group 2 so that the participants can eliminate dysphoria with lyric and tranquil music, in addition to appropriate consideration of music of Group 1 and Group 3.

At the middle and later phases of the implementation stage, and the conclusion stage, emphasis is given to music of Group 3 so that the participants can express freely aspiration and generate empathy with the relaxed, bright, merry, and lively music, in addition to appropriate consideration of music of Group 1 and Group 2.

## 2) *Overall Arrangement of Music Aesthetic Appreciation*

Music is a powerful stimulus to the senses and can generate multiple sensation and experience. It contains sound (acoustic stimulus) that can be heard and sound wave vibration (tactile stimulus) that can be felt. Upon appreciation of multimedia file, visual stimulus can be generated. Against a music background, impromptu rhythm can produce kinesthetic stimulus to muscles. Moreover, experience of music structure can attract and maintain people's attention for a long period of time, as well as other functions.

In addition, music aesthetic appreciation built in this study is an activity by group participants. Such joint participation often helps each individual build good and close relationships and creates a harmonious and safe environment. In such environment, the participants express their emotions through listening to music and obtaining non-verbal aesthetic experience. In the meantime, such group activity of music aesthetic appreciation can generate a strong power in forcing all the participants to cooperate completely and impelling them to control any bad emotions that may break the music harmony.

Through comprehensive analysis on the foregoing sensory stimuli and experience of music and the strong influence of group activity of music aesthetic appreciation, and in combination with specific presentation and effect factors of college students' depressive symptoms, this study lays stress on cultivating and training interpersonal skills, training relaxation, rhythm and movement, and attention, cultivating psychological state, developing and training language, etc. To intervene in with well targeted and directed music aesthetic appreciation activity. Inter alia, we introduced some specific techniques concerning music therapy and group counseling, such as self description, hypnosis and relaxation training, role play, role-exchanging, cognitive remediation, emotional experience, brainstorming, free association, improvisation, music psychodrama, etc. College students' self-perception ability and their acceptance of themselves and others are thus strengthened. Through mastering some skills, they gain confidence and are able to communicate sincerely with one another in the group to obtain social support, especially emotional support, and learn how to present themselves and how to adjust depressive symptoms effectively.

The entire activity is divided into 3 stages:

**Stage 1 (One Week): Induction**

In the course of the early implementation of intervention plan of music aesthetic appreciation, it is necessary to cultivate interpersonal relationships. Meticulous lecturing by the tutor and communications among the participants as well as their actual experience can enhance their understanding of their problems, eliminate unnecessary worries and doubts, and increase their compliance with the intervention through the activity.

*Theme 1: cultivating and training interpersonal skills* — students of normal universities who suffer from depressive symptoms become passive due to their psychological problems. They withdraw from group activity, do not dare to, or are reluctant to or do not know how to participate in group activity. Especially among those who have depressive symptoms, as they feel themselves inferior, lack experiences or have no common interests, they often do not know how to build relationship with others. Music aesthetic appreciation activity, however, can help them interact with one another and provide them with the opportunity and motivation for participating in group activity.

**Stage 2 (Seven Weeks): Implementation**

With the proceeding of the activity, and the application of some music therapy and group counseling techniques, emphasis is laid on intervening in specific depressive symptoms of the participants at this stage, while their emotional involvement is required.

*Theme 2: relaxation training* — for participants who suffer from anorexia, insomnia, tension, fidget and mood swings, it is difficult to calm them down to appreciate, so relaxation training is conducted, i.e. Training on how to loosen all muscles or to take deep breathing to alleviate their tension or fidget and then they are guided to appreciate.

*Theme 3: attention training* — for participants who lose interest or suffer from retardation of thinking, attention training is conducted. Participants are requested to feel wholeheartedly and to listen with emotion so as to make them experience and appreciate the sincerity and beauty conveyed in the melody and rhythm of the music. Such approach is helpful for mobilizing potentials of the participants fully and for bringing their other healthy psychological factors into normal play.

*Theme 4: rhythm and movement training* — for participants who lack vigor and are always in low spirits, rhythm and movement training is conducted to help them rebuild their adaptive behavior.

*Theme 5: music-painting training* — for participants who lose confidence in life and fail to experience the joy of life, music-painting training is conducted.

The significance of painting therapy (also known as art therapy) lies in that it is to make the participants feel pleased and satisfied through creative activity. Music-painting is to make the individual draw the sound he or she wants to voice out on a piece of paper, or make him or her paint on a piece of paper what he or she feels from listening to the music. Each way thus has the same effect. The function of music therapy itself lies in that using music can make the participants have an impulse to create, make them able to express their hidden fear and anxiety amid a free atmosphere so as to alleviate their pains from depression, make them feel comfortable and relaxed, and promote the development of total personality.

*Theme 6: psychological state cultivating* — for participants who are down in spirits, feel depressed or moody, psychological state cultivating is conducted to help them learn how to cognize and evaluate things with reasonable way of thinking in a merry mood.

*Theme 7: language development and training* — for participants who are not very sociable and deliberately avoid contacting with acquaintance, drama play and language development and training are conducted to help them enhance their sociability in the activity and get to know fundamentally their values and the significance of active living.Theme 8: comprehensive training — the design of the previous themes is aimed at specific depressive symptoms. But at the end of the activity, a comprehensive training is needed to integrate all contents and methods to make the participants feel the holistic design of the activity and to enhance their overall abilities as well.After each theme, a group discussion is held for participants to write their achievements or gains in the activity according to their actual situation.

## Stage 3 (One Week): Conclusion

The intervention through music aesthetic appreciation comes to an end at this stage. It is a stage of great importance as well, and not a stage just for "saying goodbye". At this time, evaluation on activity is also necessary.

*Theme 9: summary and feedback of activity* — as the activity draws to a close, each participant has something to say to his or her peers or to the tutor. Through the design of a farewell party, students are reminded of the merry and unforgettable scenes in the activity and know how to strengthen and improve what they have learned in their future life and study. The functions of the party include: firstly, to promote each process of the activity, and to maintain the vitality of the activity; secondly, to help the tutor evaluate each participant and the effect of design and implementation of the activity; thirdly, to assist the participants to sum up their success and failure, to learn how to transfer, to be adapted to the world outside the group, to adjust their emotions, and to evaluate and follow up, under the guidance of the tutor.

### 3) Detailed Design of Operational Plan for Music Aesthetic Appreciation

Table 11.8. Is a summary of activity proposals, showing the design of specific activity plan and source of musical pieces.

## Table 11.8. Summary of Activity Design

| Stage of Activity | Title of Activity | Theme of Activity |
|---|---|---|
| Induction | Activity 1: Follow Your Heart | To get acquainted with friends and develop the skill to handle interpersonal relationship |
| Implementation | Activity 2: Open Heart | Relaxation training and therapy |
| | Activity 3: A Journey to Western Music | Attention training |
| | Activity 4: Sound from the Ocean | Rhythm and movement, improvisation |
| | Activity 5: Fantasy | Music-painting and art therapy |
| | Activity 6: Wander in Multimedia | Psychological state cultivating amid music appreciation |
| | Activity 7: The Moon Forgets | Drama play and language development and training |
| | Activity 8: Sing Your Songs | Comprehensive training |
| Conclusion | Activity 9: Summary and Farewell Party | Summary and feedback of the entire activity |

Considering stage arrangement, themes and objectives of the activity, 9 music aesthetic appreciation activities are designed, with one theme for each activity, which lasts about 60-70 minutes and is held once a week. All activities are completed within 3 months. One tutor and one assistant are appointed for the activity. The environment for carrying out such experiment shall be a quiet place to avoid noise disturbance. The interior environment shall be clean, refined and serene, with soft light and fresh air. All activity design plans are realized through PowerPoint files, and presented to the participants by means of playing audio files.

In the following, we take the activity 5 *Fantasy* as an example to describe in details how the theoretical mode for music aesthetic appreciation activity aforesaid can be reflected and implemented in the design of specific activity plan.

Title of activity: fantasy

Theme of activity: music-painting and art therapy

Activity objectives:

To train the participants' ability to listen attentively and carefully;

To develop the participants' rich imagination and creativity;

To enable the participants to dare to express freely in different ways;

To cultivate the participants' interest in learning to cooperate and participate actively in group activity;

To provide the participants with pleasure and self-satisfaction.

Preparation for activity: background music with lento and gentle melody, two pieces of drawing paper and several color pencils for each individual.

Musical piece: Vivaldi's Winter (The Four Seasons)

Contents of activity:

| Stage of Activity | Basic Idea | Description on Process of Activity |
|---|---|---|
| Situation created (aesthetic preparation) | To arouse the participants' aesthetic attention and expectation through appreciation of inductive music materials and thinking of inductive questions. | To present a piece of music to let the participants sense a series of changes in the music, such as changes in pitch, sound intensity, tone length, timbre, rhythm, velocity, melody, etc. To raise the question: in what shape and colors can music be expressed? With some pieces of music, the tutor briefs and informs the participants about the correspondence between some basic music elements and color, line, and shape, purely from the perspectives of acoustics and time structure. Participants are also encouraged to express their originality freely. |
| Intervention (aesthetic enlighten-ment) | To appreciate typical music materials to arouse further the participants' aesthetic psychological activities including aesthetic perception, association, imagination, emotional experience, and presentation of aesthetic comprehension; to let the participants make a try at drawing to stimulate their response. | Activity 1: drawing while listening to music Step 1: participants are asked to listen to Vivaldi's *Winter (The Four Seasons)* while to draw what is on their mind based on their feelings about the music or music elements they find in the music. Step 2: when the music stops, the drawing ends too. Participants are asked to present their drawings to the others and to discuss with everyone what they draw or what they feel. |
| | To guide each individual to conduct individual aesthetic exploration and creation, to try individualized means of expression, so as to cater to individual feeling. | Activity 2: individual creation Step 1: to draw the sound you want to express or a piece of music in geometric shapes and colors on paper. Step 2: to express the finished picture with your own voice or musical instrument to let the other participants appreciate your performance and share your experience. |
| | To guide each individual to be merged into the group to conduct aesthetic explorations, to achieve sound development of each individual through collaboration with the others in musical expressions and in the harmony of the group. | Activity 3: group creation Step 1: to link in turn the drawing that one has just made for expressing his or her voice and musical piece to those made by the other members of the group. Step 2: to express in different ways, to sing or play a musical instrument to form an impromptu ensemble with everyone's efforts for mutual appreciation. |
| Reflection and assessment (aesthetic dispersion) | To guide the sum-up, to ensure overall mastery, and to lead the participants to conduct aesthetic retrospection and reflection. | Participants are asked to sum up activity theme with brief and concise speech. At last, the activity ends amid melodious music. |

# EXPERIMENTAL STUDY OF THE IMPACT OF MUSIC AESTHETIC APPRECIATION ON DEPRESSIVE SYMPTOMS OF THE COLLEGE STUDENTS

## Education Intervention Experiment

*Purpose of experiment.* The college students obtain emotional experience of beauty from the music aesthetics through the implementation of the music aesthetic appreciation, which will improve their depressive symptoms and thus improve their general mental health. The effectiveness of music aesthetic appreciation on depressive symptoms of the students is discussed, and the relationship between the depressive symptoms of college students and music aesthetic appreciation is revealed, which provides practical basis for effective intervention study of the depressive symptoms of the college students.

*Design of experiment.* Limited to the actual situation of difficulty in implementation, the methods of random sampling, randomly assigned participants and matching selective participants, are not adopted in the study. Instead, the balance group pre-test and post-test experimental design is used. The independent variable is implementation of the music aesthetic appreciation activities, while the dependent variable is the changes of the depressive symptoms of the college students and their mental health. The experimental treatment is shown in Table 1.9.

**Table 11.9. Education Intervention Experiment Design of the Impact of Musical Aesthetic Appreciation on Depressive symptoms of the College Students**

| Group | Pre-Test | Education Intervention | Post-Test |
|---|---|---|---|
| Experimental group | 1. Measurement of depressive symptoms of participants | Implementation of music aesthetic appreciation activities | 1. Same as pre-test |
| | 2. Measurement of general mental health of participants | | 2. Same as pre-test |
| Control group | 1. Measurement of depressive symptoms of participants | Not implemented | 1. Same as pre-test |
| | 2. Measurement of general mental health of participants | | 2. Same as pre-test |

### *Materials of Experiment*

*Tools of measurement.* The self-rating depressive scale (SDS) and the symptom checklist of psychosomatic symptoms (SCL-90) are adopted in this study. With regard to assessment of depressive symptoms, SDS, a short-ranged scale, is adopted, which was weaved by Willian.W.K.Zung in 1965 and was used to assess the severity of depressive symptoms and the changes during treatment. Relative analysis results showed that the correlation between the scores of SDS of this study and the scores of depression factors in SCL-90 was significant, and the correlation coefficient was 0.659 ($p<0.05$). Thus, with regard to the assessment of depressive symptoms, the scores in SCL-90, the symptom checklist of psychosomatic symptoms, will be taken as the supplementary reference at the same time. With regard to the assessment of overall mental health, the SCL-90, the symptom checklist of psychosomatic symptoms, is adopted, which is focused on mental health and features, including somatization, obsessive-compulsive symptoms, interpersonal sensitivity, depression, anxiety, hostility, phobia, paranoia, psychotic, the others, totaling 10 factors and 90 items. The scores of SDS and SCL-90 have a significant positive correlation, and the correlation coefficient is 0.466 ($p <0.01$).

*Materials of intervention experiment.* The design proposal of the aforementioned music aesthetic appreciation is adopted. (See appendix). It will be displayed to the participants by means of audio files.

*Experiment environment and equipment.* This experimental study is conducted in a spacious and bright, clean and quiet multi-functional lecture hall, where a projector displays the theme and content of the activity. The equipment adopted is the sound system of the lecture hall. In addition, there are some considerations of implementation of the experiment. First, the volume must be controlled when playing the music, and the volume should be gradually increased to the appropriate level, which is generally 40 ~ 60 dB. Second, each time of music aesthetic appreciation should not last long. It is usually suitable between 30 to 40 minutes. Thirdly, under the circumstances of severe earache, headache and extreme emotional excitement, experiment of the participants should be avoided for the time being.

### Participants of Experiment

*Criteria of participant's selection.* Tests of depressive symptoms and overall mental health have been conducted for the participants. According to the study of Wu (1990) and Ji, et al (1990), the college students with the score of SDS self-rating depression scale, greater than 40 and score of depression factors of SCL-90, the symptom checklist, greater than 2.18 are selected as the participants.

*Steps of participant selection. Step 1: carry out overall test of the depressive symptoms and mental health of the college students.*

The test of depressive symptoms and overall mental health is conducted for more than 700 fresh students, sophomore students and junior students from a university. The test objects come from seven schools, the School of Computer Science, the School of Liberal Arts, the School of Resources and Environment, the School of Finance, the School of Political Science and Law, the School of Life Science and the School of Education Science, involving a variety of majors. These faculties are divided into Arts and Science. Science faculties are as follows: the School of Computer Science, the School of Resources and Environment, the School of Finance, the School of Life Science, and the Arts faculties are: the School of Liberal Arts, the School of Political Science and Law and the School of Education Science.

A total of 711 questionnaires are issued and 665 are returned, among which 652 are valid questionnaires and the effective rate is 91.7%. 182 of them are male (27.9%), 470 are female (72.1%); 270 come from the urban area (41.4%) and 382 from rural area (58.6%); 396 major in science (60.7%), and 256 in liberal arts (39.3 %); the number of fresh students, sophomore students and junior students are respectively 120 (18.4%), 295 (45.2%), 296 (45.4%), with an average age of 20.1 years old.

As seen from the survey results, the average score of SDS of the 652 valid questionnaires is $39.00 \pm 7.86$. Compared with the domestic norm (Wang, 1986) of $33.68 \pm 8.55$ (n = 1340), the difference is quite remarkable, and the value of $t$ is 17.29 ($p < 0.001$). The number of college students who have depressive symptoms is 261, accounting for 40.03%, which is higher than the prevalence rate of the normal population of the country (Zhang, 1999). The SDS score of the participants with depressive symptoms is $46.75 \pm 5.14$, which is also significantly higher than $42.98 \pm 9.94$, which is the SDS average score of depressive symptoms of part of the national collaborative group of the scale (Shu, 1993). The difference is quite remarkable, and the value of $t$ is 11.85 ($p < 0.001$).

*Step 2: select participants for intervention out of the college students with depressive symptoms*

Among the above tested students, the college students with score of SDS self-rating depression scale greater than 40 and score of SCL-90 symptom checklist of depression factors greater than 2.18 and voluntary to participate are selected, totaling a number of 62, who are divided into experimental group and control group.

The two group are adjusted and balanced as per the pre-test results of the participants of different levels (mild: SDS score-41 ~ 47; moderate: SDS score-48 ~ 55; severe: SDS score-56 or above) so that there is no significant difference between the experimental group and control group as far as possible.

There are respectively 31 students of both the experimental group and the control group, with an average age of 19.93 years old. The pre-test results of the experimental group and the control group are shown in Table 11.10.

**Table 11.10. Comparison of Difference Significance of Pre-Test Data of Experimental Group and Control Group**

| Level | n | SDS Score | | | SCL-90 Score | |
|---|---|---|---|---|---|---|
| | | Value of $t$ | Value of $p$ | | Value of $t$ | Value of $p$ |
| Mild | 16 | -.325 | .748 | | .446 | .659 |
| Moderate | 12 | .860 | .398 | | .692 | .495 |
| Severe | 3 | -.250 | .815 | | 1.479 | .213 |
| Total | 31 | -.200 | .842 | | 1.093 | .279 |

*Questionnaire survey.* The background information survey is conducted for the participants and the way of answer is choosing. The effective return rate of the questionnaire of experimental group and control group is 100%. The survey results are shown in Table 11.11.

It can be learnt from the related test of the major quantified background factors of the participants that the correlation between these variables such as the fondness of music, music learning experience and the family tradition of love of music is quite high, and the correlation is mostly $p < 0.01$, making the study reasonable to carry out analysis of these variable series with correlation of participants and music. In another variable series containing the area, gender, division of Arts and Science of the tested participants, there is high correlation ($p < 0.05$) between area and music learning experience, and family tradition of love of music, while sex, division of Arts and Science do not have significant correlation with other variables. They are taken as the variable series that is related to the participants themselves, and it can be regarded as the information of another aspect.

**Table 11.11. Results of Background Information Survey of Participants**

| Background Information | | Experimental Group (n=31) | | Control Group (n=31) | |
|---|---|---|---|---|---|
| | | Number of persons | Proportion (%) | Number of persons | Proportion (%) |
| Gender | Male | 8 | 25.8 | 9 | 29.0 |
| | Female | 23 | 74.2 | 22 | 71.0 |
| Area | Urban area | 13 | 41.9 | 11 | 25.5 |
| | Rural area | 18 | 58.1 | 20 | 64.5 |
| Major | Science | 14 | 45.2 | 18 | 58.1 |
| | Arts | 17 | 54.8 | 13 | 41.9 |
| Fondness of music | Greatly | 10 | 32.3 | 5 | 16.1 |
| | Moderately | 11 | 35.5 | 15 | 48.4 |
| | Fairly | 10 | 32.3 | 11 | 35.5 |
| With experience of music learning | | 8 | 25.8 | 5 | 16.1 |
| With family tradition of love of music | | 7 | 22.6 | 10 | 32.3 |
| With music talent by self-rating | | 10 | 32.3 | 9 | 29.0 |
| With music talent by rating by others | | 8 | 25.8 | 7 | 22.6 |
| Frequency of listening to music | Daily | 9 | 29.0 | 9 | 29.0 |
| | 3-5 times/week | 13 | 41.9 | 10 | 32.3 |
| | Once-twice/week | 5 | 16.1 | 8 | 25.8 |
| | Less than once/week | 4 | 12.9 | 3 | 9.7 |
| Favorite music genre | Chinese folk music | 11 | 35.5 | 14 | 45.2 |
| | Western classical | 8 | 25.8 | 12 | 38.7 |
| | Pop | 20 | 64.5 | 24 | 77.4 |
| | Modern light music | 15 | 48.4 | 20 | 64.5 |
| Most common way of listening to music | Play by oneself | 20 | 64.5 | 25 | 80.6 |
| | Television and media | 19 | 61.3 | 19 | 61.3 |
| | Public places | 1 | 3.2 | 5 | 16.1 |
| | Play by others | 13 | 41.9 | 12 | 38.7 |

Based on the above analysis, the six factors, gender, area, division of Arts and Science, fondness of music, music learning experience and family tradition of music, are chosen as the most representative variables of background information of the participants in discussion.

## *Procedures of Experiment*

### Stage 1: Pre-Test Group Division

The measured results of SDS self-rating depression scale and SCL-90 symptoms checklist are taken as the pre-test data in this study. The participants are divided into experimental group and control group as per the pre-test data of depressive symptoms, and the number of people of the experimental group and control group is balanced as per the difference of depressive symptoms of the experimental group and the control group so as to ensure that there is no significant difference between the experimental group and the control group in all aspects as far as possible.

### Stage 2: Education Intervention

Education intervention is conducted for the participants of experimental group by the action plan of the designed music aesthetic appreciation, while no intervention is conducted for the control group. The education intervention for the experimental group is acted as per the established action procedures with a series of training methods and it will be implemented with purpose, plan and intention. Some activities will also be changed and improved as per the problems found in the experiment and the actual situation of the participants. Each participant will sign the Individual Data Form and Consent to Group Convention before the experiment to ensure that activities are carried out smoothly.

### Stage 3: Post-Test and Statistical Processing

Both the experimental group and control group will participate in the post-test, the method of which is the same as that of the pre-test. Comparison of difference significance of the depressive symptoms and overall mental health of the experimental group and control group will be conducted after the post-test.

### Stage 4: Implementation Effect of Feedback from Participants

The feedback questionnaire of the activities will be self prepared to find out awareness of the intention and effect of the experiment, so as to verify guidance of the experiment of instructors as well as the positive or negative reactions of the participants of the experiment.

## *Results and Analysis of Experiment*

### Impact of Music Aesthetic Appreciation on Depressive Symptoms of the College Student

Overall Impact of Music Aesthetic Appreciation on Depressive symptoms of Experimental Group and Control Group. Different groups are taken as the independent variables and the scores of pre-test and post-test of depressive symptoms are taken as the dependent variable to carry out the independent samples *t* test and matched samples *t* test. The comparison results of the experimental group and the control group of depressive symptoms are as shown in Table 11.12.

**Table 11.12. Test of Difference Significance between Pre-Test and Post-Test of Depressive symptoms of Participants in Experimental Group and Control Group**

| Group | n | Pre-Test | Post-Test | Value of $t$ | Value of $p$ |
|---|---|---|---|---|---|
| | | $M\pm SD$ | $M\pm SD$ | | |
| Experimental group | 31 | 48.35±5.22 | 40.12±5.11 | 6.824*** | .000 |
| Control group | 31 | 48.61±4.91 | 47.19±5.79 | 1.492 | .146 |
| Value of $t$ | | -.20 | -5.08*** | | |
| Value of $p$ | | .842 | .000 | | |

Note: * $p$ <0.05; **, $p$ <0.01; ***, $p$<0.001

As As seen from Table 11.12, there is no significant difference in the depressive symptoms of the participants of the two groups before the experiment ($p$>0.05). Significant difference ($p$ <0.001) is shown in the comparison of the post-test of the experimental group and control group ($t$ =- 5.089) and in the comparison of the pre-test and post-test of the experimental group ($t$= 6.824) after the experiment. While there is no significant difference between the pre-test and post-test for the control group ($t$ =- 0.200, $p$ >0.05).

This shows that the music aesthetic appreciation, on the whole, can remarkably ameliorate the depressive symptoms of the participants in the experimental group and the main purpose of the experiment is achieved.

*Impact of Music Aesthetic Appreciation on Mild, Moderate and Severe Depressive symptoms of Participants.* The experimental group and control group are divided respectively as per the three levels of the depressive symptoms, mild, moderate and severe. Therefore, statistical tests should be respectively carried out for the experiment results of various levels. i) Inspection of difference significance between pre-test and post-test of depressive symptoms of participants of difference levels of the experimental group and control group. The test of $t$ is conducted with the independent variables of different depression levels of the participants and the dependent variables of the scores of the pre-test and post-test of depressive symptoms. Test of different significance between pre-test and post-test of depressive symptoms of participants of difference levels of the experimental group and control group is shown in Table 11.13.

As As seen from Table 11.13, from a longitudinal perspective, in the experimental group, for the participants with mild level of depression, there is a significant difference ($t$ = 4.114, $p$ <0.01) between pre-test and post-test, while there is extremely significant difference ($t$ =- 5.405, $p$ <0.001) among the participants with moderate level of depression, and there is fairly significant difference ($t$ = 6.274, $p$ <0.05) among the participants with severe level of depression. In the pre-test and post-test of the control group, there is no significant change of depressive symptoms ($p$ >0.05).

In lateral view, in the post-test comparison of the experimental group and control group, there is a significant difference ($p$ <0.01) among the participants with mild level ($t$ =- 2.808) and the participants with moderate level ($t$ =- 3.600), while there is fairly significant difference ($t$ =- 2.853, $p$ <0.05) among the participants with severe levels of depression.

**Table 11.13. Inspection of Difference Significance between Pre-Test and Post-Test of Depressive symptoms of Participants of Difference Levels of the Experimental Group and Control Group**

| Level | Group | N | Pre-Test M±SD | Post-Test M±SD | Value of $t$ | Value of $p$ |
|---|---|---|---|---|---|---|
| Mild | Experimental group | 16 | 44.12±2.02 | 39.31±4.54 | 4.114** | .001 |
| | Control group | 14 | 44.35±1.86 | 44.85±6.23 | -.317 | .756 |
| | Value of $t$ | | -.325 | -2.808** | | |
| | Value of $p$ | | .748 | .009 | | |
| Moderate | Experimental group | 12 | 51.58±2.42 | 40.83±6.17 | 5.405*** | .000 |
| | Control group | 14 | 50.78±2.29 | 48.28±4.34 | 2.127 | .053 |
| | Value of $t$ | | .860 | -3.600** | | |
| | Value of $p$ | | .398 | .001 | | |
| Severe | Experimental group | 3 | 58.00±1.00 | 41.66±4.04 | 6.274* | .024 |
| | Control group | 3 | 58.33±2.08 | 53.00±5.56 | 2.630 | .119 |
| | Value of $t$ | | -.250 | -2.853* | | |
| | Value of $p$ | | .815 | .046 | | |

This shows that music aesthetic appreciation can remarkably ameliorate the depressive symptoms of the participants of different levels. ii) Variance analysis of depressive symptoms of participants of different levels in the experimental group

The single factor variance analysis is respectively conducted with the independent variables of the participant levels of mild, moderate and severe in the experimental group and the dependent variables of the scores of the pre-test and post-test of depressive symptoms, so as to inspect the effect of the experiment on different levels of depressive symptoms of the experimental group.

The results of single factor variance analysis of the different levels of depressive symptoms in the experimental group are shown in Table 11.14.

**Table 11.14. Variance Analysis of Impact on Depressive symptoms of Participants of Different Levels in Experimental Group**

| Level | Mild (n=16) M±SD | Moderate (n=12) M±SD | Severe (n=3) M±SD | Value of $F$ | Value of $p$ | Post-hoc Comparis on |
|---|---|---|---|---|---|---|
| Pre-test | 44.12±2.02 | 51.58±2.42 | 58.00±1.00 | 75.125 *** | .000 | 1<2<3 |
| Post-test | 39.31±4.54 | 40.83±6.17 | 41.66±4.04 | .436 | .651 | |

As seen from Table 11.14, there is an extremely significant difference ($F = 75.125$, $p < 0.001$) among the participants of different levels of depressive symptoms in the experimental group before the experiment. There is no significant difference ($F = 0.436$, $p$

>0.05) of the participants of different levels of depressive symptoms in the experimental group after the experiment.

This also indicates that music aesthetic appreciation can remarkably ameliorate the depressive symptoms of the participants at different levels.

Impact of music aesthetic appreciation on various factors of depressive symptoms of participants in experimental group. The SDS self-rating depression scale compiled by Zung reflects the four specific symptoms, i.e., psychogenic-affective symptom, somatic symptom, psychomotor disorder and mental disorder of depression. The results of the comparison of various factors in the pre-test and post-test of the depressive symptoms of participants in the experimental group are shown in Table 11.15.

**Table 11.15. Comparison of Difference of Various Factors of Depressive symptoms of Participants in Experimental Group**

| Trait Symptoms | Pre-Test | Post-Test | Value of $t$ |
|---|---|---|---|
| | $M \pm SD$ | $M \pm SD$ | |
| Spiritual-emotional symptoms | 2.40±.53 | 1.88±.47 | 4.694*** |
| Somatization disorder | 2.16±.31 | 1.81±.23 | 4.869*** |
| Mental movement disorder | 2.54±.55 | 2.09±.50 | 4.215*** |
| Depression mental disorder | 2.64±.45 | 2.21±.41 | 5.395*** |
| Total scores | 48.35±5.22 | 40.12±5.11 | 6.824*** |

As seen from Table 11.15, based on the overall test results of the participants of the experimental group, the difference between the total score of the pre-test and post-test of the depressive symptoms is extremely significant (6.824, $p < 0.001$).

As seen from the test results of various factors of the depressive symptoms, there is an extremely significant difference ($p < 0.001$) between the pre-test and post-test of the four factors of depressive symptoms of the participants in experimental group through intervention.

This indicates that music aesthetic appreciation can significantly ameliorate the four specific symptoms of the depressive symptoms of the participants, i.e., psychogenic-affective symptom, somatic symptom, psychomotor disorder and mental disorder of depression.

## Impact of Music Aesthetic Appreciation on Overall Mental Health of College Students with Depressive Symptoms

*Overall impact of music aesthetic appreciation on overall mental health of experimental group and control group.* Different groups are taken as the independent variables and the scores of pre-test and post-test of overall mental health are taken as the dependent variable to carry out $t$ test. The vertical and lateral comparison results of overall mental health of the experimental group and control group is shown in Table 11.16.

**Table 11.16. Inspection of Difference Significance between Pre-Test and Post-Test of Depressive symptoms of Participants of Experimental Group and Control Group**

| Group | n | Pre-Test M±SD | Post-Test M±SD | Value of $t$ | Value of $p$ |
|---|---|---|---|---|---|
| Experimental group | 31 | 224.12±39.17 | 199.71±42.17 | 4.028*** | .000 |
| Control group | 31 | 213.29±38.88 | 214.71±47.29 | -.250 | .804 |
| Value of t | | 1.093 | -1.318 | | |
| Value of $p$ | | .279 | .192 | | |

As seen from Table 11.16, there is no significant difference between the overall mental health of the participants of the experimental group and control group before the experiment. There is no significant difference ($t$ =- 1.318, p> 0.05) of the post-test of the experimental group and control group as per the test after the experiment by lateral comparison, vertically speaking, there is an extremely significant difference ($t$ = 4.028, $p$ <0.001) between the pre-test and post-test of the experimental group, while there is no significant difference ($t$ = 1.093, p> 0.05) between the pre-test and post-test of the control group.

This indicates that, on the whole, music aesthetic appreciation, through amelioration of the depressive symptoms of the participants in the experimental group, improves the overall mental health of the participants in the experimental group and realizes another purpose of the experiment.

## Impact of Music Aesthetic Appreciation on Overall Mental Health of Participants of the Mild, Moderate and Severe Level

Inspection of Difference Significance between Pre-Test and Post-Test of overall mental health of Participants of Difference Levels of the Experimental Group and Control Group. The test of t is conducted with the depression levels as independent variables and the scores of the pre-test and post-test on overall mental health as dependent variables. Inspection of the difference significance between pre-test and post-test of the overall mental health of the participants of the difference levels of the experimental group and control group is shown in Table 11-17.

As seen from Table 11.17, vertically speaking, in the comparison of the pre-test and post-test of the experimental group, there is a significant difference ($t$=3.359, p<0.01) among the participants with the mild level of depression, while there is a slight improvement of the overall mental health and there is no significant difference (p>0.05) among the participants with moderate and severe level of depression among the participants after the experiment. There is little change before and after experiment (p> 0.05) of the control group. By lateral comparison, there is no significant difference ($p$>0.05) of the overall mental health of the participants of different levels in the experimental group and the control group.

This indicates that music aesthetic appreciation can significantly improve the overall mental health of participants by impacting on the participants with mild depressive symptoms in the experimental group.

*Variance analysis of overall mental health of participants at different levels in experimental group.* The single factor variance analysis is respectively conducted with the independent variables of the participant levels of mild, moderate and severe in the experimental group and the dependent variables of the scores of the pre-test and post-test of overall mental health, so as to inspect the effect of the experiment on different levels of the overall mental health of the experimental group.

The results of single factor variance analysis of the different levels of overall mental health in the experimental group are shown in Table 11.18.

**Table 11.17. Inspection of Difference Significance between Pre-Test and Post-Test of overall mental health of Participants of Difference Levels of the Experimental Group and Control Group**

| Level | Group | n | Pre-Test $M \pm SD$ | Post-Test $M \pm SD$ | Value of $t$ | Value of $p$ |
|---|---|---|---|---|---|---|
| Mild depression | Experimental group | 16 | 207.37±33.55 | 186.50±35.82 | 3.359** | .004 |
|  | Control group | 14 | 202.21±29.30 | 203.28±44.08 | -.115 | .911 |
|  | Value of $t$ |  | .446 | -1.150 |  |  |
|  | Value of $p$ |  | .659 | .260 |  |  |
| Moderate depression | Experimental group | 12 | 237.08±33.35 | 215.25±49.85 | 1.818 | .096 |
|  | Control group | 14 | 226.14±45.14 | 224.21±54.34 | .233 | .819 |
|  | Value of $t$ |  | .692 | -.435 |  |  |
|  | Value of $p$ |  | .495 | .667 |  |  |
| Severe depression | Experimental group | 3 | 264.333±49.217 | 208.000±20.809 | 2.766 | .110 |
|  | Control group | 3 | 220.000±16.522 | 223.667±7.234 | -.276 | .809 |
|  | Value of $t$ |  | 1.479 | -1.232 |  |  |
|  | Value of $p$ |  | .213 | .286 |  |  |

**Table 11.18. Variance Analysis of Overall Mental Health of Participants at Different Levels in Experimental Group**

| Level | Mild (n=16) $M \pm SD$ | Moderate (n=12) $M \pm SD$ | Severe (n=3) $M \pm SD$ | Value of $F$ | Value of $p$ | Post-hoc Comparison |
|---|---|---|---|---|---|---|
| Pre-test | 207.37±33.55 | 237.08±33.35 | 264.33±49.21 | 4.731** | .017 | 1<3 |
| Post-test | 186.50±35.82 | 215.25±49.85 | 208.00±20.80 | 1.740 | .194 |  |

As seen from Table 11.18, there is significant difference ($F = 4.731$, $p <0.05$) among the participants at different levels in the experimental group before the experiment in comparison of overall mental health, while there is no significant difference ($F = 1.740$, p> 0.05) among the participants at different levels in the experimental group after the experiment in comparison of overall mental health.

This also indicates that music aesthetic appreciation can significantly improve the overall mental health of participants with the impact on the participants at different levels of depressive symptoms.

*Impact of music aesthetic appreciation on various factors of mental health of participants in experimental group.* SCL-90 symptom checklist includes somatization, obsessive-compulsive symptoms, interpersonal sensitivity, depression, anxiety, hostility, phobia, paranoia, psychotic, totaling 10 factors and 90 items. The comparison results of various factors of mental health of the participants in experimental group are shown in Table 11.19.

### Table 11.19. Comparison of Difference among Various Factors of SCL-90 of Participants in Experimental Group

| Factor | Pre-Test | Post-Test | Value of $t$ | Value of $p$ |
|---|---|---|---|---|
| | $M \pm SD$ | $M \pm SD$ | | |
| Somatization | 2.04±.54 | 1.81±.54 | 2.261* | .031 |
| Obsessive-compulsive symptoms | 2.80±.60 | 2.61±.66 | 1.948 | .061 |
| Interpersonal sensitivity | 2.84±.57 | 2.58±.74 | 2.407* | .022 |
| Depression | 2.84±.63 | 2.34±.60 | 4.370*** | .000 |
| Anxiety | 2.52±.52 | 2.38±.60 | 1.354 | .186 |
| Hostility | 2.36±.72 | 2.25±.81 | 1.007 | .322 |
| Phobia | 2.02±.40 | 1.89±.67 | 1.362 | .183 |
| Paranoia | 2.51±.53 | 2.21±.63 | 2.723** | .011 |
| Psychotic | 2.40±.59 | 2.10±.58 | 2.639* | .013 |
| Total scores | 224.12±39.17 | 199.71±42.17 | 4.028*** | .000 |

There is extremely significant difference ($t = 4.028$, $p < 0.001$) between the total scores in the pre-test and post-test of the overall mental health according to the overall test results of the participants in the experimental group. As seen from the test results of various factors of mental health, through intervention, there is extremely significant difference ($t=4.627$, $p<0.001$) for the depression factor score of the participants in the experimental group in the pre-test and post-test, which provides a proof for the above conclusion, i.e., music aesthetic appreciation can effectively improve the depressive symptoms of the college students as participants; there is significant difference ($t=2.723$, $p<0.01$) for the paranoid factor score in the pre-test and post-test; and there is relatively significant difference ($p<0.05$) in scores of the three factors of somatization, interpersonal sensitivity and psychoticism in the pre-test and post-test. There is no significant difference ($p>0.05$) among the scores of the other factors as compulsion, anxiety, hostility and phobia in the pre-test and post-test.

It indicates that through effectively ameliorating the depressive symptom of the participants, music aesthetic appreciation can significantly ameliorate the four mental health factors: somatization, interpersonal sensitivity, psychoticism and paranoia.

*Difference of impact of music aesthetic appreciation on depressive symptoms of the college students.* Based on the above analysis, the six variables, i.e., gender, area, division of Arts and Science, fondness of music, music learning experience and family tradition of music, are chosen as the most representative variables of background information of the participants in discussion.

The five variables, gender, area, division of Arts and Science, music learning experience, family tradition of music, are taken as the independent variables, and the depressive symptom scores are taken as the dependent variable to conduct t test; fondness of music is taken as the independent variable, and depressive symptom scores are taken as the dependent variable to conduct $F$ test. The comparison results of the difference in depressive symptoms of different groups of participants are shown in Table 11.20.

**Table 11.20. Difference of Gender, Area, Division of Arts and Science, Fondness of Music, Music Learning Experience and Family Tradition of Music on Impact on Participants of Experimental Group (Value of $T/F$)**

| Variables | | N | Pre-Test and Post-Test | Post-Test |
|---|---|---|---|---|
| Gender | Male | 8 | 2.909* | .472 |
| | Female | 23 | 6.145*** | |
| Area | Urban area | 13 | 4.828*** | .163 |
| | Rural area | 18 | 4.754*** | |
| Major | Science | 14 | 4.172** | .642 |
| | Arts | 17 | 5.369*** | |
| Fondness of music | Greatly | 10 | 3.004* | .029[1] |
| | Moderately | 12 | 4.343** | |
| | Fairly | 9 | 4.511** | |
| Experience of music learning | Yes | 12 | 3.958** | -1.512 |
| | No | 19 | 5.483*** | |
| Family tradition of music learning | Yes | 8 | 2.665* | -.478 |
| | No | 23 | 6.379*** | |

Note: the value with the superscript of 1 is the value of $F$.

As seen from Table 11.20, there is no significant difference ($p>0.05$) of the six factors as gender, area, division of arts and science, fondness of music, music learning experience and family tradition of music for the impact of music aesthetic appreciation on the depressive symptoms of the college students,

This indicates that music aesthetic appreciation can remarkably ameliorate the depressive symptoms of different groups of participants.

## Feedback of Participants on Music Aesthetic Appreciation

*Feedback of participants on the tracks of music aesthetic appreciation.* Selection of music materials has always been one of the difficult and substantial points of this study. Therefore, some open questionnaires are designed in the activity to allow the participants to tell the true feelings of the music appreciation experience, which can, to some extent, help the researchers explore the correlation between specific music tracks and the emotional experience of the participants, and thus verify effectiveness of the criteria for selecting music tracks.

The music selected for this study is divided into three groups:

*Group 1: To vent their emotion with plangent and desolate music*

This genre of music can express and vent out the bad accumulated feelings and thus restore the mental balance and alleviate the depressive symptoms. For example, in appreciation of Beethoven's Moonlight Sonata, it is asked on the questionnaire:

> How do you think of the mood of the music?
> Does the music add to your depression?
> Does the music make you sink into your own agony and unable to be extricated?
> Do you feel sad or create another feeling after the listening to the music?

Most of them answer like this: the music gives a sad and plaintive feeling, which is in tune with their own feelings and it is associated with many unsatisfactory things (including the nature and life), and the tune is also tied to their own pain. However, this feeling is different from the condition when they are unable to be extricated from the pain. With the flow of the melody over and over again, it is a relief of the burden of the heart. It seems that one gets a deep breath and the mood becomes relaxed.

*Group 2: To eliminate fidget and irritability by lyric and tranquility music*

This genre of music will help smooth breathing, gentle heartbeat pulse relaxation, relaxation of spirit, relaxation of emotion and elimination of irritability. For example, in appreciation of Bach and Gounod of C Minor Prelude/Ave Maria, it is asked in the questionnaire:

> Does the music make you feel irritable?
> Does the music make you feel stable and calm?
> Does the music remind you of the memories of the life events? Which events?

The answer affirms that brisk and comfortable music can bring peace and calm sense and the enjoyment of beauty, experience the genial sunshine, gentle breeze, or even think of the wide spread wildflowers of May and think of the carefree childhood. There is a hazy sense of happiness and waves of warmth flowing in the heart. One will gradually feel calm and relaxed, as if he enters the world with poetic beauty.

*Group 3: To express freely aspiration and generate empathy with relaxed, bright, merry, and lively music*

This genre of music can inspire the mood and encourage people, which is of great help to treat the depressive symptoms. For example, let the participants write down their feelings in brief by one or two sentences or even a few words before music aesthetic appreciation, and then let them appreciate the Love's Greeting by Elgar. It is asked on the questionnaire:

> What kind of emotional experience does the music bring to you?
> Is there any change of your mood compared to that before appreciation of the music?
> Does the music make you feel confident for yourself and life, and hopeful for the future?

Most of the answers confirm that smooth and beautiful melody, lively tempo and joyful music can bring the experience of pleasure and happiness, and encourage spirit and will. It will be quite different from the condition before appreciation of the music. Trouble, depression and peace will be changed to joyful, happy and excitement. People will be confident and hopeful for themselves, the life and the future

As seen from the feedback of the above participants to some individual tracks of music that the emotional experience of the participants matches with the intention for selecting the track, which indicates that selection of the music tracks and the implementation has reached the purposes of the experimental design in this study.

*Feedback of participants on intervention implementation of music aesthetic appreciation.* The participants of the experimental group can judge whether the tutors have conducted intervention as per the intention of the experiment in this study through the self-prepared activities feedback form (see Appendix 7) in order to inspect implementation of the implementing staff after the experiment. Analyze as per the response of the participants to the questionnaire. Feedback can be provided and the effect of experiment can be judged, and thus deduce whether the tutors have implemented the intention of the experiment.

Three items of assessment are included in the self-prepared activities feedback with a total of 20 questions, which are respectively assessment of activity element and process of music aesthetic appreciation, closed assessment of feelings of music aesthetic appreciation, as well as the open assessment of feelings of music aesthetic appreciation. Authentic answers of the participants to the activities are required for the above items. The results are:

### Table 11.21. Survey and Statistic Results of Activity Element and Process Assessment

| | Dimension | Element | Quite Satisfied | Fairly Satisfied | Uncertain | Total | Average score |
|---|---|---|---|---|---|---|---|
| Activity element assessment | Content aesthetic factors | Aesthetics in theme and scene | 14 | 14 | 3 | 135 | 4.35 |
| | | Aesthetics in cadence and melody | 12 | 16 | 3 | 133 | 4.29 |
| | | Aesthetics in accompany with musical instruments | 8 | 17 | 6 | 126 | 4.06 |
| | Approach aesthetic principle | Affectivity | 10 | 15 | 6 | 128 | 4.13 |
| | | Experience | 26 | 4 | 1 | 149 | 4.81 |
| | | Vividness | 15 | 11 | 5 | 134 | 4.32 |
| | | Pleasure | 4 | 20 | 7 | 121 | 3.90 |
| | | Interaction | 11 | 18 | 2 | 133 | 4.29 |

*Result analysis of factors and process assessment of music aesthetic appreciation.* The assessment results of the participants on the factors and process assessment of music aesthetic appreciation are shown in Table 11.21.

As seen from Table 11.21, the experiment is satisfactory to the participants on the whole in terms of the assessment of the factors of music aesthetic appreciation and the process operation. In the presentation of music aesthetic factors, the three aspects, i.e., the principle of experience, the concinnity in acoustic environment and the aesthetic standards for guiding operation, are best reflected (Mean> 4.5); while the principle of pleasure has the lower scores (Mean <4.0), also indicating that it has to be improved. In the music aesthetic psychological process, each stage and joint are well implemented (Mean> 4.0).

### Table 11.21. Survey and Statistic Results of Activity Element and Process Assessment

| | Dimension | Element | Quite Satisfied | Fairly Satisfied | Uncertain | Total | Average score |
|---|---|---|---|---|---|---|---|
| | Environmental aesthetic characteris-tics | Concinnity in acoustic environment | 21 | 7 | 3 | 142 | 4.58 |
| | | Concinnity in visual environment | 13 | 13 | 5 | 132 | 4.26 |
| | | Harmony of the two environment | 14 | 16 | 1 | 137 | 4.42 |
| | Aesthetic standards of guidance | Aesthetic standards for guiding manners | 14 | 15 | 2 | 136 | 4.39 |
| | | Aesthetic standards for guiding language | 16 | 13 | 2 | 138 | 4.45 |
| | | Aesthetic standards for guiding temperament | 19 | 11 | 1 | 142 | 4.58 |
| Activity process assessment | Preparation stage | Music aesthetic attention and music aesthetic expectation | 17 | 13 | 1 | 140 | 4.52 |
| | Enlightenment stage | Music aesthetic perception and music aesthetic exploration | 6 | 22 | 3 | 127 | 4.10 |
| | Continuation stage | Music aesthetic retrospection and music aesthetic reflection | 14 | 15 | 2 | 136 | 4.39 |

### Analysis of Open Assessment of Feelings in Music Aesthetic Appreciation

Item 3 is de1signed to be open-ended questions, including questions 18 to 20, i.e., "What is the most impressive part in this activity?"; "Do you have any specific gain or any change after the activity?"; "Which question do you think should be further answered? ".

Question 1: the most impressive experience of the participants. The answers are mainly: i) in terms of music and nature of music aesthetic appreciation, the participants have a consensus that the music in the activity is wonderful and music is a part of life, listening to music can purify the thinking of people, can release the trouble and relax the people, converse the thinking and make people flexible, bring pleasure, touch the hearts, precipitate imagination and open the heart of the people; ii) in terms of the method and content of music appreciation experience, the participants have a consensus that they learn how to experience, understand and express the music in the activity, and their love for music become increasingly diversified; iii) in terms of the experience of interpersonal relationships, the participants have a consensus that the activities bring the warmth of home, and there is respect, sincere exchange, communication with heart, as well as courage.

Question 2: gains or changes of the participants. The answers are mainly: i) there is a further understanding of music. They find that the effects of music is substantial in life, they love music more, and they have a deeper taste of the music; ii) there is a further understanding of others, and interpersonal communication is not difficult and it can help learn more about the lifestyles and attitudes of other people, hence they find that each person has a bright spot, they can be infected by the enthusiasm of others and they can treat others in a more tolerant manner; iii) there is also a further understanding of their own. They find the self-confidence, and they become hopeful for life, and learn self-control of the emotional changes.

Question 3: questions of the participants remain to be answered. The answers are mainly: i) how to encourage enthusiasm of the participants in a better way; ii) how to maintain the follow-up effect of the music; iii) how to treat other problems of the participants, such as anxiety, etc.

Based on the above assessment of the participants in the experimental groups on the experiment, the overall implementation effect of the experiment is favorable, and construction of the activity theory mode and design of the operational plan have both reached the purpose of this study.

## Case Study

The number of participants of the three levels, especially the level of severe depression, is quite limited due to constraints of time and place of this study, resulting in difficulty of attribution. Therefore, case study is needed for supplement. Meanwhile, the experimental data also showed that the intervention effect of music aesthetic appreciation for the participants of college students with depressive symptoms was individual, and it might be subject to a number of complex individual variables to different extent. Some individual participants of the experiment have tremendous changes in depressive symptom, which also shows some interesting information.

Through analysis of the two typical test cases of A and B in this study, on the one hand, it adds and reinforces some results of the previous experiment; on the other hand, it suggests that individual perspectives must be focused on regarding this type of study methods.

*Participant study and method*. Participant study: two typical cases are selected in this study (basic information is shown in Table 11.22). Regarding moderate and severe depression, there is a significant change for both in the experimental data of pre-test and post-test and the intervention process and it is somewhat typical. Therefore, it is taken as the participants of case analysis.

*Study methods*: the method of case interview and content analysis is mainly adopted.

## Table 11.22. Case Study of Participants

| Depressive Symptoms | Case Study | Gender | Place of Birth | Major | Fondness of music | Music Learning Experience | Music Tradition |
|---|---|---|---|---|---|---|---|
| Moderate depression | A | Female | Urban area | Arts | Greatly | Yes | Yes |
| Severe depression | B | Male | Rural area | Arts | Fairly | No | No |

## Table 11.23. Schedule of Interview

| Stage Schedule | Basic Idea | Schedule of Interview |
|---|---|---|
| Induction | Learn the problem and establish the relationship | Arrange the first interview, which is aimed firstly to collect the comprehensive information of the cases, such as the basic information, social and cultural background, personal mental development condition, statements of the personal problems, etc.; secondly, to establish mutual trust between the case subject and the tutor. |
| Implementation | Diagnose and analyze Determine purpose Help and guide | Carry out comprehensive analysis of five aspects, i.e., the development of the case, mental condition, learning condition, health condition and interpersonal relations after the first interview (Worth, 1987). Through the analysis and diagnosis, the main problems of the participants with depressive symptoms are gradually clear, including learning disorder, interpersonal disorder, love and sexual disorder, mood and personality disorder, as well as career choice problems, and the specific targets of intervention are accordingly determined. Carry out targeted intervention on the basis of analysis of the nature of the problem and determination of the targets of intervention. The second interview is arranged during this period. Pay attention to combine the main intervention targets of the case. |
| Stage Schedule | Basic Idea | Schedule of Interview |
| Conclusion | Gradually completed Inspect and enhance | Arrange the third interview upon completion and carry out a comprehensive summary to review participation of the activities and to stress the original target of intervention, so that the case subjects can have more clear understanding of themselves, further understand the causes and consequences of the problem of their own, and decide their future efforts. The case subjects are guided to apply the new experience acquired in music aesthetic appreciation in the daily life. Gradually they will be able to adjust their own emotion and cope with the surrounding environment by music appreciation. Follow-up study will be conducted after the activity to inspect and enhance. Comprehensive feedback will be obtained via correspondence and telephone, etc. to achieve reliable and authentic assessment of intervention. |

The basic procedure: since an intervention plan that is systematic, stage divided and planned is designed for the experimental study, the analysis of the case study is conducted in different stages. Three interviews (see Table 11.23.) are arranged in the three stages, i.e., induction, implementation and conclusion stage. The individual interview is conducted on the students about the problem of depressive symptoms of the participants and the feelings of music aesthetic appreciation. Meanwhile, it is combined with the expression of the participants to the music to carry out a comprehensive analysis. Interviews are all conducted in an office one by one.

## Case Analysis

Note: T=tutor, and S= subject

Case A: Hu × ×, female, SDS score of pre-test: 55, moderate depression

Born in cities, junior, major in liberal arts, is very fond of music with music learning experience and family tradition of love of music; his father has greatly impacted on her musical taste. The score of overall mental health of A is 216, which is higher than the norm of the common people. The interview with her is as follows:

## Induction

The first impression of her: fairly fat, vague speaking, fairly emotional and easily agitated. The first interview is as follows:

T: Is there anything that bothers you?

S: I feel at a loss for my life and don't know what to do.

T: Can you be more specific?

S: I have been thinking about the problem of what to do after graduation. I feel it is difficult to adapt to the society. I always make mistakes when doing things and can not change.

T: Have you thought about why you are bothered this way?

S: Actually, I have been bothered since I go to college. Before this, I once had a car accident and I hurt my head, which kept me in a coma for three months. Things changed a lot after I woke up. I was absent from school for one year after discharge from hospital. I was once an excellent student, but now... I'm getting lost and I lost so much, I don't know what to do and I lose my way.

T: Can you talk briefly about your emotional characteristics?

S: Stubborn, easily lose my temper, quite emotional.

T: Since you love music a lot, what is your intuitive feel for music?

S: Tranquility.

T: What kind of experience does music bring to you?

S: Forget all the troubles.

T: What is your favorite music?

S: Soft, slow with tempo not too clear.

T: What is your expectation for participation in our activities?

S: To have a clear understanding of my life and be confident for my future.

As seen from the above interview and combined with some conditions of case A, the main problem of her depressive symptoms is emotional, and the specific targets of intervention is to make A have more self-confident, no self-esteem and less angry.

## *Implementation*

Based on the above analysis, targeted intervention is carried out. First, the positive performance of A is encouraged, sincerely praised and supported in the activity, for example, it is mostly praised when A expresses her feelings of the music by language, picture or melody. Second, provide more guidance for A of free aesthetic association imagination of the music so as to find the root cause of the problem; guide A for a series of music aesthetic insight performance training such as relaxation training, action improvisation, music and painting; guide A to learn to substitute the irrational emotional experience with rational music aesthetic emotion experience. Explain the negative emotional experience of depression of A through accurate grasp of the specific situation of A and based on the practice and observation of the previous experience and activities, so as to improve the insight of A and to realize good emotional experience and treatment of depressive symptoms.

The second interview is conducted after Activity 4 – Heart of the ocean (action improvisation), and it is as follows:

T: What kind of emotional experience do you have after listening to the music?

S: From romantic to tiredness, fear and peace at heart.

T: What are your overall feelings on this activity?

S: I feel happy. I can integrate myself into the music and forget the reality, let the music take me away.

T: What kind of gains do the activity and the music bring to you?

S: It makes me aware of my deficiencies and adds to my self-confidence to act quickly to make up for the deficiencies and surpass myself. As expressed in music: the sunshine always follows the storm.

As seen from the above interview, through participation in several group activities of music aesthetic appreciation, A has learned to calm down by listening to the music, and has started to recognize herself, and gradually adds to her self-confidence. In addition, we have also noticed the change of A through observation. At the beginning, she did not want to tell her past to the other members, but after several activities, she became brave to express her own thoughts and even had the courage to sing the song, to tell the other members of the activities of her past and her perspectives of the future.

## *Conclusion*

The third interview is conducted after the summing-up meeting of the activity, and it is as follows:

T: What is your emotional experience of the whole activity? Express it with simple adjectives.

S: Satisfied, excited, respected, hopeful, enriched, touched, peaceful, calm, happy, lucky, interested and sincere

T: What is your deepest experience through the whole activity?

S: Love is all around the people and the world. There is actually no distance between people and I can live better.

T: Do you have any gain or any change after the activity?

S: I find that the effectiveness of music is important in life. The greatest gain is that I get the courage and confidence facing the reality. I have been keeping the idea of escaping and I have been thinking that there would be no more pain if I disappeared. However, after the activity, I find that, in fact, I'm not alone and there are many people like me. Music is beautiful, and it tells us that the world is beautiful if we experience with all our hearts. There is the inner strength coming from the bottom of my heart that I can do better and I can face my life better.

We can see from the above interview that through participation in the group of music aesthetic appreciation for nearly three months, A has found rational emotional experience in music appreciation, and has enhanced in the self confidence about herself, her life and her future, in addition, she has got obvious progress in the body movement, language development, adaptability to the environment and social interaction.

Meanwhile, her gradually open and positive performance in the activities has also won understanding, respect and appreciation of the other members of the group. Additionally, the experiment effect of A can also be observed through the change of various scores of the scale before and after the experiment.

Before the experiment: SDS scores 55, SCL-90 scores 216 and the depression factor of SCL-90 scores 37; after the experiment, SDS scores 33, SCL-90 scores 165 and the depression factor of SCL-90 scores 27. The depressive symptoms and the overall mental health have been significantly improved.

Case B: Xu × ×, male, SDS score of pre-test: 59, severe depression

Born in rural area, sophomore, major in liberal arts, fairly fond of music, with neither music learning experience nor family tradition of love of music; the score of overall mental health is 316, which is obviously higher than the norm of the common people. The interview with him is as follows:

### Induction

He impresses me firstly as: plain, simple and honest, fairly independent, and comes from a village of Yunnan. He is extremely serious when doing the pre-test questionnaire, and expressed his strong desire to participate in the activities. The first interview is as follows:

T: What bothers you recently?

S: I come from the mountainous area. I've been to Southwestern University for a year, but always feel that I can not keep up with the pace of learning and living here, and my ideas are out-of-date. I'm recently confused about what would I look like after four years of study.

T: Can you be more specific?

S: I felt great pressure when I was in senior high school and the family had some misery then (not willing to mention), and I have been thinking about leaving the village to study in the big city. I feel that the previous suffering has caused some aftereffect after I come to college. Currently, I don't study well and I don't have good state of study and school life, I feel that I'm so ordinary and very helpless. I am so afraid to get hurt. I usually can not concentrate on my study. I am old-fashioned, inflexible, and perhaps I'm kind of self-esteem, am I?

T: Can you talk briefly about your emotional characteristics?

S: Fragile, sensitive, indecisive, honest, fairly undisciplined, negative sometimes.

T: What is your intuitive feeling of music?

S: Peaceful, touched, comfortable, sympathetic, pure and beautiful.

T: What kind of experience does music bring to you?

S: It is enjoyment, and I can get rid of worldly troubles.

T: What is your favorite music?

S: Gentle and sad.

T: What is your expectation for participation in our activities?

S: I don't know much about music, but I hope that I can be trained on my concentration of attention through listening to music and open my heart, expand my horizons, and be more positive towards life.

Based on the above interview and combined with the background of case B, it is analyzed that his main problem of depressive symptoms is learning and emotion, and the specific target of intervention is to improve the attention and coordination of B, and to improve his self-confidence.

### *Implementation*

Based on the above analysis, targeted intervention is carried out. First, encourage him to express his inner feelings of music experience by language, and give him sincere praise and support. Second, during the music aesthetic appreciation, guide B for training the attention of music and develop his aesthetic perception capability; at the same time, carry out some rhythm training to develop his co-operation capacity. Thirely, enable B to have a brand-new and more comprehensive perspective of his problems and be aware of himself and the surrounding environment, be more self-confident through interpretation of his psychological pressure on his life and learning.

The second interview is conducted after Activity 3 – Tour of western music (training of attention), and it is as follows:

T: What kind of emotional experience change do you have after listening to the music?

S: I was full of the curiosity, expectation and aspiration before listening. I felt the slight sadness in mind during listening, and I was reminded of the moon in my hometown. After listening, I felt a little sad, but suddenly a kind of strong feeling occurred to me that I should treasure everything I have.

T: What are your gains and feelings of this activity?

S: I think it is calm, perseverance and love of life. After listening to the music for a while, I felt calm deep down in my heart. I have the new understanding of music, and finds that beauty has to be developed by ourselves. I have time to listen to music peacefully and understand myself again.

As seen from the above interview, B has learned to calm down and started to think on certain problems peacefully through participation in music aesthetic appreciation. By listening to the music, his attention has also been enhanced, good memories have been reminded, and he has started to value himself and find good things, thereby added to his self-confidence. The change of B is quite obvious in several activities through observation. In the previous activities, he was unwilling to speak and was fairly silent, but during the activities of intervention afterwards, he started to express his good feeling of music aesthetic appreciation by language, melody and drawing, and thus improved his coordination capacity.

## Conclusion

The third interview is conducted after the summing-up meeting of the activity, and it is as follows:

T: What is your emotional experience of the whole activity? Express it by simple adjectives.

S: Satisfied, excited, respected, hopeful, enriched, positive, proud, touched, peaceful, calm, happy, confident, lucky, interested and sincere

T: What is your deepest experience through the whole activity?

S: Participation of the activity is valuable, and I feel enriched and comforted during the period. This activity covers some of the rich spiritual things, and we can obtain enormous benefits as long as we put our hearts in.

T: Do you have any gain or any change after the activity?

S: Love music and life better.

After the activity, B sent an e-mail, saying "As I came from the mountainous area, I have never thought of listening to such beautiful music before. Though this is over, I am deeply moved again and again. I think it is so beautiful and touching when recalling everything in the process. Some of the positive things will penetrate in my life."

We can see from the above interview and the follow-up feedback that B has trained his attention and co-operation through participation in nearly three months of the group activities of music aesthetic appreciation, and he has learnt to treat himself, other people and things with a peaceful mind, has opened gradually to the outside world, and changed from self-abased at the beginning of the experiment to self-confidence. In addition, the experiment effect of B can also be observed through the change of various scores of the scale before and after the experiment. Before the experiment: SDS scores 59, SCL-90 scores 316 and the depression factor of SCL-90 scores 57; after the experiment, SDS scores 38, SCL-90 scores 219 and the depression factor of SCL-90 scores 34. The depressive symptoms and the overall mental health have been significantly improved.

We understand that the study object is often associated with a particular individual, and therefore we can not ignore the difference of the background, that is, the inherent individual difference in music appreciation, such as age, cultural background and life experience, music learning experience, personality tendency, and other factors (J.A.Sloboda and P.N.Juslin, 2001) In this study, design and implementation of the music aesthetic appreciation with the intervention approach of music have focused on how to provide more personalized service to the participants at the very beginning. This demand represents the refinement and the individual-oriented tendency in close connection with the individual that widely existed in the practical application field of music, which is also the mainstream of this study in the future.

From the above interview and changes of the experimental data of the case analysis, we can see that design and implementation of the education intervention experiment has reflected the tendency of individual orientation. Both the analysis of the nature of the individual cases and determination of the targets of intervention to the case are highly targeted. Therefore, the case experiment has obtained good effect.

Finally, it shall also be noted that the difference in the case analysis is often obvious, and its representation and persuasion are also limited. However, it is indeed different from the statistical analysis of the experimental data. The case study of this study is an exploration with the aim of providing inspiration to the approaches that focus on individual orientation in the education intervention study of music aesthetic appreciation.

## Discussion on the Music-Aesthetic-Appreciation-Based Mode and Its Effect

The aim of this study is to define the two breakthrough points of the study variables: one is to start with the psychological process of music aesthetic and the presentation of music aesthetic factors, and to build a workable theoretical mode for music aesthetic appreciation activity as well as to design operational plan for music aesthetic appreciation for typical depressive symptom; the other is to take depressive symptom and overall mental health of college students as the intervention target, and then to discuss the similarities and differences of the impact of the music aesthetic appreciation on them. The experimental data showed some inspiring results that should be paid attention to in the below two aspects.

*Building of the Theoretical Mode for Music Aesthetic Appreciation and Design of the Operational Plan.* Building of the theoretical mode for music aesthetic activity is related to the presentation of music aesthetic factors, which forms the horizontal system of music aesthetic appreciation and also is the premise to guarantee the intervention effect. We divide the presentation of aesthetic factors for the music aesthetic appreciation into four dimensions: aesthetic factors formed by the contents of music aesthetic appreciation, aesthetic principle for the ways of music aesthetic appreciation, aesthetic characteristic of the music aesthetic appreciation environment and aesthetic standards for guiding music aesthetic appreciation. Details of the four dimensions in the presentation system of music aesthetic factors infiltrate in each process and aspect, which optimizes the aesthetic presentation means in music aesthetic appreciation. Building of theoretical mode for music aesthetic appreciation activity should follow rules on individual music aesthetic psychological activities. It is related to the psychological process of music aesthetic, which forms the vertical system of music aesthetic appreciation and also is the core to guarantee the intervention effect. We divide the aesthetic psychological process of music aesthetic appreciation into three stages, i.e., music aesthetic preparation, music aesthetic enlightenment and music aesthetic dispersion. In the three stages, the participants take part in the specific aesthetic psychological activities, such as esthetic attention, aesthetic perception, aesthetic association and imagination, presentation of aesthetic comprehension as well as aesthetic reflection, etc.. The main and final goal of the activities is to make the participants obtain better aesthetic emotional experience, which is the key point to ameliorate the depressive symptom of the participants. The contents of the three stages in the system of psychological process of music aesthetic place an emphasis on the internalization of aesthetic emotional experience in music aesthetic appreciation.

*The design of the operational plan for music aesthetic appreciation should be well-directed, routine, standardized and operatable.* Therefore, combining the music selection, arrangement in activity stage and arrangement in the appreciation process with the specific presentation of the college students' depressive symptom meets their psychological needs. Music therapy and group counseling technique are introduced into the operational plan to train and cultivate the college students' ability to ameliorate depressive symptom as well as improve the overall mental health; meanwhile, their music aesthetic appreciation ability as well as their ability to communicate and cooperate with the others are also trained and cultivated. Finally, these abilities will be generalized and transferred into their daily life. The introduction of music therapy and group counseling technique helps this activity's operational plan to be more well-directed and operatable, and then improves the implementation practicability of the music aesthetic appreciation. Moreover, the participants' feedback to the implementation of the music aesthetic appreciation intervention showed that participants' response to the presentation of music aesthetic appreciation activity and process operation was generally good and they were satisfied with the experiment as a whole. In the presentation of music aesthetic factors, experience aesthetic principle in the ways of music aesthetic appreciation, aesthetic characteristic of the music aesthetic appreciation environment in aspect of acoustic sense and aesthetic standards for guiding music aesthetic appreciation are the best embodiments. In the psychological process of music aesthetic, activities in each stage and process are implemented well. In a word, building of theoretical mode of music aesthetic appreciation activity as well as design and implementation of the operational plan in this study show the feasibility of the impact on depressive symptom of the college students in the study goal, and internalize the music aesthetic emotional experience in the music aesthetic appreciation activity, and optimize the music aesthetic factor means and make it more oriented and operational.

## *Experimental Effect Analysis on the Impact of Music Aesthetic Appreciation on Depressive Symptoms of the College Students*

### Similarities.

*Impact of Music Aesthetic Appreciation on Depressive symptoms of the College Students.* At first, it impacts on the overall comparison. Through the education intervention of the music aesthetic appreciation, either the horizontal difference comparison ($t=-5.089$) in the post-test between experimental group and control group or the vertical difference comparison ($t=6.824$) in the pre-test and post-test between experimental group and control group showed that there was extremely remarkable difference ($p<0.001$),which means that music aesthetic appreciation can significantly ameliorate the depressive symptom of the participants in the experimental group, so as to achieve the main goal of the experiment. Secondly, it is the impact on the distribution of the three levels: mild, moderate and severe. In the vertical system, there is remarkable difference in various degrees of the depressive symptom among the participants at different levels in the experimental group before and after experience (mild: $t=4.114,p<0.01$; moderate: $t=-5.405,p<0.001$; severe: $t=6.274,p<0.05$); In the horizontal system, there is remarkable difference in various degrees of the depressive symptom between the participants in experimental group at different levels and those in control group (mild: $t=-2.808$; moderate: $t=-3.600$; severe: $t=-2.853$). In addition, the analysis of variance for the depressive symptom of participants at the three levels in the experimental group before and after experiment showed that depressive symptom of participants at the three levels in the experimental group changed from remarkable difference ($F=75.125,p<0.001$) before experiment to no remarkable difference ($F=0.436,p>0.05$) after experiment. The above analysis showed that music aesthetic appreciation could significantly ameliorate the depressive symptom of the participants at different levels. At last, it is the impact on the factors related to the depressive symptom of the participants. Through intervention, there is an extremely remarkable difference ($p<0.001$) on the four factors in the depressive symptom of the participants in the experimental group in the pre-test and post-test, which means that music aesthetic appreciation can significantly ameliorate spirituality of the participants' depressive symptom with four specific symptoms, i.e., psychological symptom, somatic symptom, psychological movement disorders and mental disorders.

*Impact of Music Aesthetic Appreciation on the Overall Psychological Health Level of College Students.* At first, it is the impact on the overall comparison. Through the education intervention of the music aesthetic appreciation, there is slight horizontal difference comparison ($t=-1.318$, $p>0.05$) between the experimental group and the control group while there is remarkable vertical difference comparison ($t=4.028$, $p<0.001$) in the experimental group, and there is slight difference comparison ($t=1.093$, $p>0.05$) in the control group in the pre-test and post-test. As a whole, through ameliorating the depressive symptom of the participants in the experimental group, the music aesthetic appreciation improves the overall psychological health level of the participants in the experimental group, so as to realize another goal of the experiment. Secondly, there is an impact on distribution of the three levels: mild, moderate and severe. In the vertical system, there is remarkable difference ($t=3.359$, $p<0.01$) among the participants at mild level in the experimental group, and the overall psychological health level of the participants at the moderate or severe level increases after the experiment but there is slight difference ($p>0.05$), which has much relationship with the connection degree between the intervention time, depressive symptom at different levels and the overall psychological problems. In the horizontal system, there is slight difference ($p>0.05$) in the overall psychological health of the participants both in the experimental group and the control group at different levels. In addition, the analysis of variance for the overall psychological health level of the participants at the three levels in the experimental group before and after experiment showed that the overall psychological health level of the participants at the three levels in the experimental group changed from remarkable difference ($F=4.731$, $p<0.05$) before experiment to no remarkable difference ($F=1.740$, $p>0.05$) after experiment, which means that the music aesthetic appreciation can significantly improve the overall psychological level of participants with mild depressive symptom in the experimental group by influencing them. At last, the impact on the factors was related to the overall psychological level of the participants. Through intervention, there is extremely remarkable difference ($t=4.627$, $p<0.001$) for the depression factor score of the participants in the experimental group in the pre-test and post-test, which provides a proof for the above conclusion, i.e., music aesthetic appreciation can effectively improve the depressive symptom of the college students as participants; there is remarkable difference ($t=2.723$, $p<0.01$) of the paranoid factor score in the pre-test and post-test; there is relatively remarkable difference ($p<0.05$) of scores of the three factors as somatization, interpersonal sensitivity and psychoticism in the pre-test and post-test. There is not remarkable difference of the scores of the other factors as compulsion, anxiety, hostility and phobic anxiety in the pre-test and post-test. It means that through effectively ameliorating the depressive symptom of the participants, music aesthetic appreciation can significantly ameliorate the four psychological health factors: somatization, interpersonal sensitivity, psychoticism and paranoid. It might be related to other factors which can ameliorate the psychological disorders in the implementation of the operational plan, such as emphasis on the interpersonal interaction, harmony between mind and body as well as cooperation and friendship and so on.

## Differences

Many variables of the participants are grouped into two aspects in the study: variables related to demography (including gender, area and major in arts or science) and variables related to music (like fondness of music, music learning experience and family tradition of music). The results showed that there was not remarkable difference ($p>0.05$) of the six factors as gender, area, division of arts and science, fondness of music, music learning experience and family tradition of music while the music aesthetic appreciation influenced the depressive symptom of the participants, which shows that music aesthetic appreciation has a positive impact on the different groups of the participants. Therefore, the impact of music aesthetic appreciation on the depressive symptom of the different groups of the participants is universal and the experimental results are good.

*Defects in the Study and Deficiencies.* Due to the complexity of the study on the music aesthetic effect, it is difficult to perfect the experimental study. This study belongs to exploratory research on the psychological education and has many deficiencies yet, such as the theory of musical psychology not understood in-depth, design of the experiment not being convenient, inadequate control of the irrelevant variable in the experiment, the scope of the experiment being too narrow and the limited duration of the experiment, etc., which shall be improved in the subsequent studies. Since it is the exploratory stage, some problems to be solved still need further discussion. The following is the brief summary and analysis, which might be helpful for the subsequent studies.

*Participants.* At first, the intrinsic factors of the participants, which are demonstrated into two aspects: one is the individual aesthetic psychological structure of the participants, i.e., music aesthetic taste originally possessed by the participants, such as music aesthetic attitude, aesthetic preference, aesthetical standard and aesthetic ideal, etc., which will influence the directionality, selectivity and judgment of the individual aesthetic activities. The other is the personality dimension of the participants. Due to the different personality dimensions, effect of the music perception on different individual participant is different, too. This study did not or seldom cover the above two problems, which results in some difficulties in attribution. It is suggested to consider these problems in selecting the samples and expend possible related variables in subsequent studies. Secondly, the number of the participants. Due to the limitation of the environment and time, the number of the participants at severe level of depression is very limited, which results in some difficulties in attribution. It is suggested to expend the samples in subsequent studies. At last, impact of the participants' psychological state during the test. Due to the instantaneousness of the psychological state and its potential impact on the aesthetic emotional experience, this study has not excluded the interference of the different psychological states of the participants during the test. This problem is a key difficulty universally existing in the study of the music aesthetic effect, which deserves attention in subsequent studies.

*Study Methods.* This study advocates the emphasis on the music and the psychological characteristics of the listeners, and it is a study on psychology of music with the breakthrough point of listening experience, which can be called "gentle" study on psychology of music. It can inquire more deeply into the essence of psychology of music. However, it is the characteristics of the "gentle" study on psychology of music that result in a serial of difficulties, which are the key limiting factors of this study. These difficulties include ambiguity and universality of the music stimulus, reliability of the collection of feelings and feedbacks, as well as individual characteristics and the impact of interaction between individual characteristics and music. Due to the ambiguity of the target and inadequacy of the related theories in explaining the phenomenon, methods employing in this study are questioned, which is a difficulty that should be concerned in the subsequent studies.

*Selection of the Music Material.* Selection of the music material has always been a difficulty in this study. Based on the characteristics of the research methods, although this study explores a experimental study different from the earlier ones, there are still many problems in selecting music with various styles and characteristics as materials and taking distribution of the characteristics of different music factors into consideration. For example, a more systematic, typical and well-directed music program should be made for the characteristics of the specific depressive symptom of college students. It is suggested to discuss in future and analyze this problem in subsequent studies.

# CONCLUSION

For the depressive symptom, there is remarkable difference ($p < 0.001$) in the comparison of the post-test of the experimental group and control group ($t = -5.089$) and in the comparison of the pre-test and post-test of the experimental group ($t = 6.824$).Vertically speaking, in the pre-test and post-test of the experimental group, there is a remarkable difference ($t = 4.114$, $p < 0.01$) among the participants with mild level of depression, while there is extremely remarkable difference ($t = -5.405$, $p < 0.001$) among the participants with moderate level of depression, and there is fairly remarkable difference ($t = 6.274$, $p < 0.05$) among the participants with severe level of depression. Horizontally speaking, comparison of the experimental group and control group in the post-test, there is a remarkable difference ($p < 0.01$) among the participants with mild level of depression ($t = -2.808$) and the participants with moderate level of depression ($t = -3.600$), while there is fairly remarkable difference ($t = -2.853$, $p < 0.05$) among the participants with severe level of depression. From the testing results of the factors influencing the depressive symptom, we can see that through intervention, in the pre- test and post-test, there is extremely remarkable difference ($p<0.001$) of the four factors (including psychogenic-affective symptom, somatic symptom, psychomotor disorder and mental disorder of depression) influencing the depressive symptom of the participants in the experimental group.

For scores of the overall mental health, there is slight difference ($t=-1.318, p>0.05$) in the comparison of the experimental group and control group in the post-test while there is an extremely remarkable difference ($t=4.028, p<0.001$) in the comparison of the experimental group in the pre-test and post-test. In the comparison of scores of the overall mental health in the pre-test and post-test of the experimental group, there is a remarkable difference ($t=3.359, p<0.01$) among the participants with mild level of depression, while the overall mental health level of the participants with moderate and severe level of depression but there is slight difference ($p>0.05$) among them. For the specific factors, music aesthetic appreciation can significantly ameliorate the depressive symptom of college students as participants; there is a remarkable difference ($t=2.723$, $p<0.01$) for the paranoid factor score in the pre-test and post-test; there is a relatively remarkable difference ($p<0.05$) in scores of the three factors as somatization, interpersonal sensitivity and psychoticism in the pre-test and post-test. There is not remarkable difference ($p>0.05$) in the scores of the other factors as compulsion, anxiety, hostility and phobic anxiety in the pre-test and post-test.

# APPENDIX

## Selection of Specific Design of the Music Aesthetic Appreciation Operational Plan

Design of Activity 1

| Activity name: Follow Your Heart |
|---|
| Activity theme: Interpersonal relationship cultivation and training |
| Activity objective: (1) To make the participants know the magic power of music as well as the meanings and requirements of the music aesthetic appreciation activity; (2) To enhance communication and trust between the participants and the tutors; (3) To arouse the participants' passion for participating the activities actively and strengthen their collective identity;(4) To make the participants know each other initially and dispel the sense of strangeness.Activity preparation: melodious, peaceful and lyrical background music, Individual Data Form and Consent to Group Convention |
| Music program: (1) Reynaldo Hahn.L'Heure exqiuise Samuel Barber.Adagio for Strings (Harmony) (2) Myers(arr.John Williams).Cavatina (3) Ronan Hardiman.Never (Source: UTOPIA album. Published and distributed by Universal Music International Ltd Company. 2002) |
| Activity contents: |

| Activity stage | Activity process |
|---|---|
| Situation created | 1. In the melodious background music, the tutors make a self-introduction, and introduce the name, nature, operation methods and objective of the group. Meanwhile, the tutors should encourage the participants to query. 2. The tutors deliver the Individual Data Form and instruct the participants to fill out the form, so as to help the participants to know themselves. Then, the participants are invited to make a self-introduction, and explain why they take part in the group as well as their expectation to the group, so as to help the participants to know each other. |
| Intervention implementation | Activity 1: Power of Music The tutors point out the effect of music and make the participants know the magic power of music, so as to stimulate them to join the activities. Activity 2: Discussion after Listening to Music The participants are asked to enjoy music, and encouraged to express their senses and feelings in the music appreciation by speech as well as share them with other participants. Activity 3:Agreement between You and Me The tutors emphasize the importance of the group convention and encourage the participants to query; then all the participants pass the convention as well as sign it. |
| Refection and assessment | The participants sum up activity theme by brief and general speech, and then in the melodious music, the activity ends and theme of the next activity will be announced. |

Design of Activity 2

| Activity stage | Activity process |
|---|---|
| Activity name: A Heart of Listening<br>Activity theme: Relaxing training and relaxing therapy<br>Activity objective: (1) To know the participants' fondness of music as well as the types they fond of.<br>(2) To set the participants' mind at rest as well as relax and adjust their mind and body.<br>(3) To make the participants relax the muscles with ease.<br>(4) To make the participants being into the appreciation situation (state).<br>Music program: *A series of music to de-stress and relax-Song of Brook* (Source: GaoTian. A series of music to de-stress and relax. Published and distributed by the Liberation Army Audiovisual Press.2003)<br>Activity contents: | |
| Situation created | 1. In the melodious background music, the tutors raise the question: "what do you feel is the beauty of music?", and then the participants are asked to take turns to answer the question freely by speaking out the specific beauty of music.<br>2. The tutors ask another question: "which music do you like best and impress you most?", and then the participants are asked to take turns to answer the question freely by speaking out the participants' favorite music and the most impressive music. Then all the participants discuss and share their opinions. |
| Intervention implementation | Activity: Relaxing training<br>1. The participants are asked to write down or speak out their emotions before music appreciation.<br>2. The tutors explain the training requirements, and with verbal suggestion of the tutors, the participants engage in music aesthetic imagination while enjoying the music as well as relax themselves from top to toe to the music.<br>3. The tutors encourage the participants to write down or speak out the emotions after the music appreciation and see the changes. |
| Refection and assessment | The participants are asked to sum up the activity theme and raise some questions, deficiencies even suggestions, which will be used for a reference for the subsequent activities. At last, the activity ends and theme of the next activity will be announced. |

# REFERENCES

Alvin, J. Music Therapy [*M*]. trans: Gao, T. and Huang, X. (1989). Shanghai: Shanghai Music Publishing House.

Angold A and Rutter *M*. (1992). Effects of age and pubertal status on depression in a large clinical sample. *Developmental and psychopathology*, 5-28.

Berlyne, D. E. (1974). Studies in the new experimental aesthetics: Steps toward an objective psychology of aesthetic appreciation, viii. Oxford, England: Hemisphere, 340.

Bruscia, K. E. (1987). *Improvisational Modes of Music Therapy*. Charles. C. Thomas. Publisher. 401-465.

Bunt. L. (1997). Clinical and therapeutic uses of music. In the social psychology of music. New York: Oxford University Press.

Bunt. L. *Clinical and therapeutic uses of music*. In the social psychology of music. New York: Oxford University

Cai, Y. P. (1920). *Music journal*. Beijing: Music Research Association of Peking University, 1 (1). Ref: Wang, N. Y. and Yang, H. P. (1996). *Chinese Music Aesthetics on the 20 C. E (Literatures)*. Modern Publishing House, 49.

Cai, Z. J. ed. (1997). *Depression: Basic theories and clinical practice*. Beijing: Science and Technology Publishing House of Beijing, P98.

Cantwell, D.P., and Baker, L. (1991). *Manifestations of depressive affect in adolescence*. Journal of Youth and Adolescence, 20: 121-133.

Cao, L. (2000). Music appreciation and aesthetic education. *Curriculum, Teaching Material and Methods, 1*, 36-40.

Che, W. B. (2001). *Encyclopedia of psychological counseling*. Zhejiang: Zhejiang Science and Technology Publishing House.

Chen, X., and Zhang, D. J. (2002). Exploration and discussion of integrated modes for mental health education. Educational Research, 1.

Compas, B.E. (1993), Sydney EY and Kathryn EG. Taxonomy, assessment, and diagnosis of depression during adolesecence. *Psychological bulletin*, 124 (20), 323-344.

Da, H. M., and Li, M. Y. (2000). Correlative research on mental health of college students and their parental rearing patterns. Health Psychology Journal, 8 (4).

Donald (1979), E.m. Music Therapy, Springfield, Illinois. Charles C. Thomas.

Fan, X. S. (2002). *Music therapy*. Beijing: China Press of Traditional Chinese Medicine.

Fang, B. Y. (1999). An investigatory study of the mental health of undergraduates in teacher universities. *Journal of Anhui Normal University (humanities and social sciences), 27* (3).

Feng, Z. Z. (2002). *A Study on social information processing of middle school students with depressive symptoms*. PhD dissertation. Chongqing: Southwest China Normal University Research Institute of Educational Science.

Gao, T. (2003). *Principles of application of music in therapy*. http://www.musictherapy 2003.com/text.Php?id=18.

Gelder, *M.*, and Mayou, R., and Geddes, J. (1999). *Psychiatry*. Second edition. Oxford University Press, 87-100.

Haack, P. *Toward a functional music education*. Trans: Liu, P. (2002). Toward a functional music education. *People's music, 11*, 22-25.

Horden, P. (2001). *Musical solutions: Past and present in music therapy*, 2000. In: Music as medicine: The history of music therapy since antiquity, 4-40.

Jacob. (1987). A report on a project with autistic children at Indiana University, *In: R. R. Pratt. The fourth internaternational symposiumon music*. University Press of America. 157-164.

Ji, H. (1999). An investigatory study on the psychological suzhi of the undergraduates in teacher universities and suicidal crisis intervention. *Journal of Beijing Normal University (social sciences), 1*, 26-33.

Ji, J. L., Xia, Z. Y. and Xu, J. *M.* (1990). SCL-90 Assessment result analysis of college students of different majors. *Chinese mental health journal, 4* (3), 123-125.

Jia, J. *M.*, and Xu, J. *M.* (2001). Clinical study on diagnosis and classification of the depression. *Journal of Clinical Psychological Medicine, 11* (2), 95-96.

Judd, L. L., Rapaport, *M.* H., and Paulus, *M.* P. et al. (1994). Susyndromal symptomatic depression: a new mode disorder. *Clinical psychiatry*, 55, 18-28.

Ke, J. Q. (2002). Views on music appreciation and enhancement of mental health of contemporary undergraduates. *Higher agricultural education, 9*, 63.

Li, Q. Y. (2000). *Aesthetic physiology*. Guangdong: Guangdong People's Publishing House, P189.

Lin, G. M. (2001). Musical therapy and education manual-the basic conception and activity design of the musical therapy and education. Taiwan: Taiwan Psychology Publishing Company, 59.

Lin, J., and Yu, J. (2003). Psychological health of college students in the changing times. *Journal of southwest university for nationalities (philosophy and social science), 24* (2).

Liu, *M.* J. et al.(1995). A study of the SCL-90 test result of college students. *Psychological science, 18* (5), 295-298.

Liu, P. (1991). *Brief introduction to music psychology.* Refer to Xue, L. The Manual of Music Knowledge. Beijing: China Federation of Literary and Art Circles Publishing Corporation.

Liu, Y. N., and Jin, Y. L. (2001). A study of depression and related factors in undergraduates. *Chinese journal of clinical psychology, 3* (9), 208-209.

Liu, Y. Q. (1994). *Middle school students' psychological hygiene and education.* Chengdu: Publishing House of University of Science and Technology of Chengdu.

Liu, Z. J. (1985). *Encyclopedia of China-Education.* Beijing: Encyclopedia of China Publishing House.

Liu, Z. J. (1993). *Research on psychology of aesthetic education.* Sichuan: Sichuan Education Publishing House.

Liu, Z. J. (1995). *Educational psychology in higher level education.* Beijing: Beijing Normal University Press.

North, A. C., and Hargreaves, D. J. (1997). *Experimental aesthetics and everyday music listening.* In: the Social Psychology of Music. New York: Oxford University Press.

Orff, G. E. (1984). The identification of a contemporary hierarchy of intended learning outcomes for music therapy students entering intership. *Journal of music therapy, 3,* 125-139.

Peng, J. X. (1994). *Theory of art and artistic history.* Beijing: Peking University Press.

Qu, S. T. (1998). The diversity performance of the depression. *Chinese journal of psychiatry, 31* (4), 243-244.

Schulten, *M.* L. (1987). Musical preference: A new approach to investigate its structure and development. *Bulletin of the Council for Research in Music Education, 91,* 160-165.

Shen, J. (2003). Music therapy and comment on related psychological studies. *Psychological science, 1,* 176.

Shen, J. (2004). *Experimental study on music preference of college students and affecting factors.* Unpublished master's thesis, Department of Psychology, East China Normal University. Shanghai: East China Normal University.

Shu, L. (1993). self-rating depressive scale and depressive questionnaire, compiled by Wang, X. D., Manual of mental health assessment, *Chinese mental health journal (supplement),* 204

Sloboda, J. A. and Juslin, P. N., (2001). Psychological perspectives emotion. *In: Music and emotion: Therapy and research,* 71-104.

Wang, C. *F.*, Cai, Z. H., and Xu, Q. (1986). Self-rating depressive scale (SDS)-an analysis on 1340 normal people. *Chinese Journal of Nervous and Mental Diseases, 1* (5), 267-268.

Wen, H., Li, X., and Ge, J. J. (2000). Research on students' psychology and metal health condition. *Higher education forum, 4,* 40.

Wu, W. Y. (1990). Self-rating depression scale (SDS). Shanghai Archives of Psychiatry (Supplement in the new second vol.): Assessment scales in psychiatry series.

Xiu, H. L. and Luo, X. P. (1999). *General theory of music aesthetics*. Shanghai: Shanghai Music Publishing House, P257.

Ye, L. (1995). *Music Aesthetic Appreciation*. Lhasa: Tibet People's Publishing House.

Yi, *F*. J., Yang, D. Y. et al. (1998). *Psychologist*. Chongqing: Chongqing University Publishing Company.

Zhang, C. C. (1999). Depression of medical inpatient*s*. *China journal of health psychology,* 7, (1), 82-83.

Zhang, D. J. (2004). Mental health education: Ten problems to be solved. *China education daily (3rd edition)*.

Zhang, J. X., Weng, Z., and Liu, Q. G. et al. (1995). A study on relationship between the depressive symptom of the family members and the family function. *Chinese journal of clinical psychology, 3* (4), 225.

Zhang, Q. (1983). *Analysis of psychology of music appreciation*. Beijing: People's Music Publishing House, P5-7.

In: Methods and Implementary Strategies on Cultivating ...       ISBN: 978-1-62417-979-2
Editors: Da-Jun Zhang, Jin-Liang Wang, and Lin Yu     © 2013 Nova Science Publishers, Inc.

*Chapter 12*

# Experimental Research into the Intervention in Anxiety and Depression Symptoms by Aesthetic Appreciation of Literary Works

## *Gu-Jing Li[1], Cheng Guo[2] and Xiao-Yun Zhao[3]*
[1]Chengdu Electric and Technology University, China
[2]Center for Mental Health Education in Southwest University, China
[3]Nanjing Normal University, China

## Abstract

People had realized the psychological conformity and therapeutic functions of literary works long time ago. With the development and diversification of the theory and techniques of psychotherapy, psychological researchers incorporated the psychological significance of literary works in the field of psychotherapy, and developed the theory of bibliotherapy on such basis. However, the significance of aesthetic reception of literary works in improving mental health was not fully explored and the empirical research is rare. Chinese college students have prominent mental problems. Depression and anxiety are very common. Mental health education of college students has aroused great attention of the education authority and has been promoted greatly in practice. Thus, the exploration into a method that uses aesthetic appreciation of literature to intervene the negative emotions and improve mental health is of theoretical and practical significance in cultivating talents of high quality in universities and colleges.

## Introduction

### Literature and Aesthetic Psychology of Literature

*Effect of literary works on individual's psychology.* We have been facing diversified stresses since our birth, including those from time lapse and the fear of death. Stress should be released or distilled. And Arts, including literature art, as is said by artistic theorist Vygotsky, provide an effective way to get out of such a jam and to release stress. Such harmful energies are burnt through the appreciation of literary works, and people will have normal mental states. Literature has been playing the role of a good medicine for human's psychology in all ages. Greek philosopher Aristotle [384 BC – 322 BC] believed that the appreciation of literature art "purifies" human's emotions. He (as cited in Gilbert and Kuhn, 1981) said, "Those who are influenced by pity or fear, and every emotional nature, must have a like experience, and others in so far as each is susceptible to such emotions, and all are in a manner purged and their souls lightened and delighted" (Aristoteles). As early as in the Spring and Autumn Period (722 BC – 403 BC), Confucius believed that poem inspires sentiment, courtesy corrects behaviors, and music cultivates temper so as to perfect one's virtue. Sigmund Freud (as cited in Feng, 2003), the father of psychoanalysis, put forward that the real joy brought by imaginative works results from the release of mental stress. He believed that literature is the substitute satisfaction of the instinctive desire of individuals. Abraham H. Maslow, a founder of humanistic psychology, believed that the needs of appreciation of literature art results in more happiness, peacefulness and diversification of inner world, realizing healthier personality development [Zhang, 2000].

Research into aesthetic psychology of literature

*Definition of aesthetic appreciation of literary art.* Literature includes literature creation and aesthetics. For example, the reception theory in aesthetics regards literature as "a process of aesthetic reception and production". It regards the process of reception as the backbone of the whole literary activity. W. Wolfggang Iser, a professor from the University of Konstanz pointed out that "literary works have two ends, art end and esthetic end. Art end refers to the text finished by the author, while esthetic end is realized by readers…" [Zhu, 1993]. For most people who are not genius, they reach literature through aesthetic appreciation, thus naturally the benefits are mostly realized through reading. It indicates that the reception of literature is of more universal significance, and thus the present research chose aesthetic appreciation of literature as the independent variable.

The following are some definitions of "aesthetic appreciation of literature".

## Table 12.1. List of Definitions of Aesthetic Appreciation of Literature

| |
|---|
| Appreciation of art and literature refers to the process of emotional experience of literary and artistic works and art activities, including feeling, understanding, evaluation and aesthetics [Liu, 1992]. |
| Appreciation of literature refers to delighted feelings of literary works. It is perceptual and intuitional reception, i.e., aesthetic reception. The feelings can only be perceived, cannot explain in words. Appreciation of literature refers to distinguishing, analysis and examination, i.e., distinguishing, differentiating and perceiving during "tasting" [Qian, 2003]. |
| Appreciation of art, different from art criticism or research, is a non-utilitarian process of recreation of art, which integrates aesthetic pleasure, artistic intuition and artistic resonance [Zhang, 2000] |
| Aesthetic appreciation of art is a mental activity of human to appreciate the aesthetics of art. It is also a process of presenting aesthetic forms, and a psychological process of harmonious integration of subject and object [Lin, 1987]. |

The components of aesthetics of literature can be concluded as follows from the above definitions:

*First, appreciation of literature is different from ordinary reading.* It requires abstract thinking of readers. Readers do not consider the scientificity of the works or strict reasoning of the scientificity and logicality of works. In addition, it does not have utilitarian or practical purpose. In stead, it requires readers to ruminate and intoxicated in the works, in order to obtain aesthetic pleasure and release.

*Appreciation of literature is the process of reception.* Thus attention should be paid to the subjective consciousness of readers. Different readers may have different experiences and emotions in the process of appreciation due to their different knowledge structures and mental structures, thus there is no unified standard for the results of appreciating literature.

*Appreciation of literature is a process of recreation.* By taking literary works as the aesthetic object,readers can complicate psychological activities through the behaviors of appreciation, including experience, rumination and thinking. By doing this, readers make literary works as images in their mind. Such images are not passively reflected by literary works, but are created actively by readers. Appreciation of literature changes the way of being of literary works.

*Aesthetic characteristics of literary works.* Experts from psychology and literature fields all agree that literary works have diversified aesthetic characteristics. The following are some typical opinions. Please see Table 12.2. for details.

### Table 12.2. List of Aesthetic Characteristics of Literary Works

| |
|---|
| Yang and Gan [2001] believed that literature is the art of language. The aesthetics of literature is the deep reflection of life or emotion by creating typical artistic image or artistic conception. |
| Zhang [2000] argued the aesthetic characteristics of literature include: the form of being is aesthetic image; the characteristics of life are extensively reflected; the characteristics of human's universal emotions are reflected. |
| Qian [2003] believed that the artistic characteristics of literary works, i.e., aesthetic characteristics, include: the vitality, organic integrity, and lingering charm. |
| Liu [1992] argued that literature is the art of language. Literary language is the tool to create artistic images, thus the aesthetic characteristics of literature are mostly reflected in the art of language. The basic characteristics of literary language are vivid, diversified, musical and perceptual. |

We can easily conclude from the above opinions that the aesthetic characteristics of literature are diversified. The most important characteristics are emotional, experience-based and vivid.

*The aesthetic process of literature.* The aesthetic process of literature is divided due to different standard for division. Please see Table 12.3. for details.

The aesthetic process of literature is difficult to be quantized and it can only be summarized through experience and phenomenon, as it is a unified process with the intersecting, supplementation and mutual effect of multiple factors. The mentioned standard from division indicates that: first, aesthetics of literature is a process with the comprehensive interaction of subject and object, including perception, representation, imagination, abstract thinking, emotion and other psychological phenomena; second, aesthetic process of literature has a certain temporal sequence. The tasks in stages have their own focuses but are also overlapped.

### Table 12.3. The Process of Aesthetic Appreciation of Literature

| |
|---|
| Liu [1992] divided the aesthetic process into perception, representation, imagination, abstract thinking and emotion stages from the perspective of the factors of psychological activities. |
| Zhang [2000] divided it into attitude, preparation of attention, tasting, digestion, and reflection and judgment stages from the angle of time and logic. |
| Lin [1987] believed that aesthetic process is the occurrence, development and feedback of "aesthetic experience" that is accompanied by "aesthetic attitude". He divided the aesthetic process into: occurrence, practice and feedback stages. |
| Qian [2003] argued that the process can also be divided into: start, strengthening, burst, and calming down stages from the perspective of the motivation of reception; initial (mental transformation), realization (mental construction), climax and end (mental effect) stages, from the perspectives of the way of being of the text and the psychology of reception. |

## Depression and Anxiety Symptoms

*Definition and classification of depression symptoms.* Depression is a mood, a blue mood. It is a basic affective activity of human. In addition, depression is generated from the evolution of mood and emotion. It has many signal functions, including social communication, physiological arousal, subjective perception, etc [Yang, 2000]. Depression is an emotion, thus it can be the reflection of normal emotion or abnormal mood. Feng [2002] pointed out based on literature analysis that depression can be classified into depression mood, depression symptoms and depression disorder, according to the degree and level of development. Depression mood is the mental state and emotional response of sorrow, unhappiness and fidget. Depression symptoms are the sorrowful emotions of individuals caused by behavioral problems. The characteristics of depression symptoms are symptoms of physical and physiological discomfort, bad social development. Depression disorder refers to the serious state of depression, i.e., individuals can not maintain normal life and learning as they are influenced by depression for a long time. It is an important field of psychiatry.

*Definition and classification of anxiety symptoms.* Anxiety refers to complicated emotional responses caused by psychological conflict or frustration. It is a nasty emotion, which is normally a combination of worry, nervousness, disappointment, uneasiness, fear, anxiousness, shame and other feelings [Huang and Xu, 1987]. It ranges from the excessive concern of now and future to the feeling of fear (positive and negative symptoms). Appropriate anxiety increases the degree of vigilance, facilitates individuals to overcome difficulties. However, anxiety without clear inducement or excessive anxiety is harmful. Anxiety can be classified from different angles. For example, some researchers classified anxiety into normal anxiety and abnormal anxiety, state anxiety and quality anxiety, etc. [Zhang, 2002]. Some researchers classified the anxiety of college students into basic type, attributive type and development type, from the perspective that different anxiety is caused by missing requirements and conditions [Zhang, 2004]. We classified anxiety into anxiety mood, anxiety symptoms, anxiety disorder and panic disorder, according to the Positive and Negative Syndrome Scale (PANSS) by Kay, Fiszbein and Opler [1987]. Anxiety mood refers to that the subject is worried, excessively concerned, or fidgety or restless; but the subject does not tell or show relevant physical symptoms and behaviors. Anxiety symptoms refer to that the subject has obviously nervous symptoms; slight physical symptoms are shown and may cause poor social adaptation. Anxiety neurosis is reflected by serious anxiety, continuous fear accompanied by terror, and obvious physical symptoms and behavioral performance. Panic disorder is an anxiety disorder characterized by recurring severe panic attacks. People with panic disorder have strong feelings of terror and discomfort that strike suddenly, and such feelings will reach the climax rapidly. Panic disorder is accompanied by multiple cognitive and physical symptoms that the sympathetic nervous system is triggered.

*The relationship between depression and anxiety.* Anxiety and depression are two independent moods and disorders; but in fact, they coexist in reality. In the United States, over 95% depression sufferers have at least one anxiety symptom; and 20% to 65% anxiety sufferers also suffer from depression [Yuan, Wu and Zhang, 2000]. In addition, anxiety and depression share many overlapping symptoms [Yang, 2003], which are listed in Table 12.4.

### Table 12.4. Depression symptoms, Anxiety Symptoms and Corresponding Overlapping Symptoms

| Depression symptoms | Overlapping symptoms | Anxiety symptoms |
|---|---|---|
| Low mood | Irritability | Excessive vigilance |
| Lack of enjoyment | Worry | Startle reaction |
| Frequent thought of the past | Frequent thoughts of bad things. | Worries of future |
| Loss of interest | Social withdrawal | Horrific scenes |
| Feelings of guilt, worthlessness | Distress | |
| Thoughts of suicide | Dysfunction | |
| Being slow down | Agitation | |
| Increased or reduced weight | Insomnia | |
| | Decreased attention | |
| | Chronic pain | |
| | Stomach upset | |

In terms of which comes first, the date from fundamental research show that anxiety symptoms come before depression symptoms. The research of behavior science shows that the children of primates will first show protest and then disappointment after they separate from mothers. And protest is a prototype of anxiety, and disappointment is the prototype of depression. In the face of stressors, they feel anxious when they are not sure of losing assistance. They show depression when they are obviously hopeless [Yang, 2003].

Many researchers probed into depression and anxiety. Lewis [1934] put forward the continuity of depression and anxiety symptoms.

He believed that some or all anxiety symptoms are part of depression. The research by Yuan et al. [2002] found that anxiety symptoms can be found in all depression sufferers and depression symptoms can also be found in anxiety sufferers. There is no significant difference in the severity of anxiety symptoms between the two groups. In addition, research also shows high correlation between almost all anxiety scales and depression scales [Bystritsky, Stoessel, Yager, et al., 1993].

In the terms of the cause of the relationship, Joseph Mendels, et al. [1972] explained in the research that: first, biological basis is available between the two; second, both of them are the same response to stimulus, and the characteristic symptoms are resulted from pathoplastic effect of personality; finally, with the worsening of conditions and protracted course of disease, any one may have the secondary symptoms of another one. In other words, people suffering from chronic anxiety may suffer from secondary depression symptoms, and the sufferers of chronic depression may suffer from secondary anxiety symptoms.

Therefore, although the mentioned research is from the scope of clinical psychology, it proved the close relationship between depression and anxiety symptoms.

We choose college students with depression and anxiety symptoms as the objects of intervention. The intervention was focused on the overlapping symptoms, for better effects of intervention.

## Depression and Anxiety Symptoms of College Students

*Current status of depression of college students.* Depression obstructs the psychological adjustment of individuals. Depression is the major risk factor affecting the physiological and psychological health of human in the 21$^{st}$ Century. The research report in the recent 10 years shows that the percentage of people who suffer from depression is rapidly increasing [Holden, 2000]. Depression is common among college students, even depression results into suicidal tendency. More and more attention has been paid to it. And many inducements make college students become a disadvantaged group in psychology. Chan [1991] found that the depression rate among college students in Hong Kong is 50%. Du and Wang [1999] found that the depression rate among college students in Chinese mainland is 42.1%; 52% poor college students are depressed or have depression tendency. Some researchers [Cao, 2001] argued that the depression rate of college students in China reaches 20%-60%, higher than other occupational groups and foreign countries.

*Current status of anxiety of college students.* Anxiety is a common mental problem among college students. According to the data from health authority of China, at least 30 million people from the adolescent group less than 17 years old are suffering from emotional disorders and behavioral problems. Over 16% college students meet the pathological indicators of frequent anxiety, including anxiety, fear and depression [Wang, 2005]. The survey by the State Education Commission among 126,000 college students shows that 20.23% students had mental problems. And anxiety is one of the prominent problems. Some epidemiological surveys in China shows that anxiety and depression have the most influence in the daily life of college students [Fan and Wang, 2001].

*Effective methods to intervene the depression and anxiety of college students.* According to literature analysis, the methods available to intervene in the depression and anxiety symptoms of college students include group interpersonal relationship training, hypnotherapy, relaxation therapy, physical exercise, behavior-cognition therapy, mental health course, etc. Such methods intervene in the depression and anxiety symptoms of college students to some extent. The mentioned methods of intervention show that the effective methods to intervene in the depression and anxiety symptoms are from the perspectives of cognition, society, behavior and will. Influences to and changes of behaviors and cognition are focused.

## Aesthetic Appreciation of Literature and College Students' Depression and Anxiety Symptoms

The current PSE in China pays more attention to behavioral training and less attention to internalization of experience [Chen and Zhang, 2002], and emphasizes on the training and change of cognitive behavior, but ignores the nurturing and cultivation of emotions. The depression and anxiety symptoms of college students are sorrowful and nervous emotions, the core of which is the subjective negative emotional experience. *T*

To reduce depression and anxiety symptoms, the key is to change such negative emotional experience. Liu [1992] pointed out that appreciation of art and literature refers to the process of emotional experience of literary and artistic works and art activities, including feeling, understanding, evaluation and aesthetics.

Individuals need to combine subjective emotions and thoughts to form aesthetic images during the appreciation of literary works, in order to generate aesthetic experience. Thus aesthetic appreciation of literature is a process of emotional experience.

The cheerful experience resulting from aesthetics of literature can change the negative emotions of depression and anxiety.

The above literature analysis shows that the effective methods of intervening in the negative emotions of college students are mostly from the perspectives of cognition, society and behavior. They change emotions by correcting cognition.

Not many researchers probed into direct improvement of depression and anxiety through aesthetic experience, a positive mood.

In addition, aesthetics of literature requires a certain education level, aesthetic knowledge and aesthetic needs of readers. The education level of college students is normally high. They have certain experience and needs of aesthetics, thus they are able to conduct aesthetic reading and have aesthetic experience. Therefore, it is feasible to choose college students as the object of intervention for aesthetic emotion of literature.

## The Theoretical Basis and Conception of the Present Research

### 1) Theoretical Basis

*The research into the relationship between emotion and cognition in modern psychology provides theoretical basis.* Since the 1970s, researchers have started to research into the influence of emotion on cognitive process. Stein and Rose [1974] put forward "Emotion and Motivation Theory". He believed that emotion plays a vital role in the survival and development of the human, which determines the direction of the development of cognition and personality. It is generally acknowledged that emotion is dependent on cognition and other psychological processes and interacts with cognitive process [Du and Wang, 2002]. Research shows that positive emotions promote cognitive activities; whereas negative emotions destruct, collapse and block cognitive activities. Thus emotional changes can influence and change cognition. Appreciation of literature is an aesthetic experience. The aesthetic experience obtained from aesthetics of literature can improve the positive emotion of individuals, influence and change individuals' cognition and evaluation of sorrow or anxiety, and eventually help the individuals to form the correct and positive evaluation.

*Research into aesthetics and literary psychology provides theoretical basis for aesthetic psychology of literature.* As mentioned in the background of research above, many psychotherapy theories of literature were put forward in the research into aesthetics and literary psychology. First, it is about the theory of catharsis of literature. The representation of such theory is Greek philosopher Aristoteles. He believed that literary works, especially tragedies, can realize catharsis and purification. During the appreciation of literary and artistic works, the "sudden changing" of the plot and the "suffering" of the protagonist arouse vicarious pity and terror of spectators, thus spectators can purge their grief emotions through imaginary sorrow that is not harmful to themselves and the reality. Through catharsis, the mind goes to a peaceful and harmonious state, obtains peace and freedom, and is purified. Second, it is about the intuition and representation theory of literature. Philosopher Croce argued that the emotion of people, before perceived, is under human's sub-consciousness, which does not have a certain form; however, once it is sensed by people, it obtains a certain form and becomes a lyrical image, and thus inner emotion is artistically expressed. There are many emotions not expressed or sensed in our mind. Artistic intuition realizes poetic and lyrical presentation of inner emotions; and then the depression mode of people will disappear and their souls are purified. Therefore, individuals, through the artistic intuition resulted from aesthetics of literature, objectify and express the emotions that are difficult to be identified and sensed. Thirdly, it is about the indirect satisfaction theory of literature. Freud, the representative of indirect satisfaction theory, believed that the pleasure of readers obtained from appreciating literary works, the pleasure of children obtained from games and the pleasure of adults obtained from fantasies are essentially the same. They satisfy some unrealized wishes of people. Readers, during reading literary works, continue and realize their unrealized complex in imaginary space of literature. And finally, it is about the humanistic interpretation of literature. Maslow believed that the higher the level of needs, the greater the psychological effects will be. The need for aesthetics of literature and art is a high level need, thus it can generate great spiritual value and deep happiness, peace and diversification of inner life, and lead to the development of healthy personality. In addition, during the aesthetics of literature, aesthetic pleasure inevitable brings positive psychological and physiological responses. People obtain spiritual freedom from aesthetic pleasure; life experience and reading experience are triggered; certain life experience never had appears in mind before. At this moment, individuals has realized transcendence of works, experienced free aesthetic emotions and obtained peak experience.

*Research into bibliotherapy provides support of techniques and methods.* As the research into bibliotherapy has been deepened in the recent decades, researchers from the western world concluded different definitions of bibliotherapy. Floyd [2003]argued that it is reading a self-help book for the treatment of psychological problems; McArdle et al. [2001]put forward that bibliotherapy is a directive reading that normally brings psychotherapy outcome. With the prevailing of cognitive-behavioral therapy, "bibliotherapy" has new definitions from the perspective of cognitive bibliotherapy. Shechtman [1999] argued that bibliotherapy refers to that sufferers of mental problems, under the conditions of contacting with a few or no psychological therapists, implement the therapy by using the implication of text materials, assumed that the sufferers are able to be distracted from text materials the information,experience and solutions related to their needs. Most researchers believed that bibliotherapy leads to identification, purification, comprehension and peak experience of people, changes the temperament of people and compensates for mental defects. Thus bibliotherapy is psychotherapy with double effects of clinical treatment and preventive development. The sufferer or recipient, under the guidance of doctors, consultants or teachers, reads the selected books based on the plans, directions and themes, and participated in relevant activities, in order to improve emotions and change cognitive styles, and eventually to realize the objectives of therapy and education. At present, in addition to the traditional bibliotherapy techniques, such as reading-discussion, reading note, etc. most researchers believed that only when it is regarded as an interactive process can bibliotherapy have effective therapeutic effect during the directive reading and discussion [Gladding, 1992]. Interactive bibliotherapy has been combined with other therapies, including music therapy, drama therapy, play therapy, etc. Thus, interactive bibliotherapy was used in our experiment along with other therapies for the best effect. To sum up, it is found that the therapeutic mechanism of aesthetics of literature is included in bibliotherapy. Meanwhile, bibliotherapy is a technique of psychotherapy, thus the aesthetics of literature during bibliotherapy inevitably is undertaken under a certain consulting and therapeutic mode, making it different from ordinary aesthetics of literature. The present research tries to use the techniques and methods available of bibliotherapy, in order to fully play the psychotherapeutic effect of aesthetic appreciation of literature, and to explore a means of intervention with strong therapeutic effect from aesthetics of literature.

*Research into group psychological counseling provides support of techniques and methods.* After the Second World War, group therapy and group consultation have been rapidly popularized and developed as behavior therapy groups and individual therapy groups emerged. Nowadays, group psychological counseling has been becoming an important means of psychological counseling at college. Group psychological therapy or counseling is that the group members, under the situation of a group, know themselves and help themselves to remove the symptoms, improve adaptation and develop personality by making use of the power of the group and techniques of psychological counseling and therapy. The group usually consists of members with similar problems organized by therapists. Within the group, the development problems or psychological disorders common to group members are solved through discussion, training and guidance, in order to improve social adaptability and promote personality development. It functions as not only psychotherapy, but also prevention, development and education [Fan, 1996]. The present research tries to carry out aesthetic activities of literature, which enables college students with depression and anxiety symptoms to tell their distress, in order to promote self-understanding and deepen self-knowledge. In addition, group members can observe  other members' distress similar to theirs and have the same feeling; and then members support and encourage each other, analyze together the cause of depression and anxiety, and find the way and methods to solve problems, which will strengthen their self-confidence and realize the purpose of improving depression and anxiety symptoms. In addition, the activity design in the present research will use the common techniques of group psychological counseling, such as psychological dramas, team for making friends, role transposition, self-description, life line, painting, etc. Such techniques lead to effective intervention in depression and anxiety symptoms of college students through aesthetic appreciation of literature.

### 2) Idea and Hypothesis of the Present Research

The present research is an exploratory research of PSE at college, which aims to build the mode of aesthetic appreciation of literature, discuss and select literary works with therapeutic functions, and to verify the intervention effects of aesthetic appreciation of literature in depression and anxiety symptoms of college students. The train of thought is as follow: First, build the mode of aesthetic appreciation of literature suitable for the psychological needs of college students, based on the research available and the depression and anxiety symptoms of college students. Then, semi-open and semi-close questionnaires are developed to verify and modify the mode, in order to determine the final mode. The questionnaire concerning the tendency of college students to select literary works is established under the theoretical guidance of the mode, and specific literary works are chosen. The implementing plan of aesthetic activities of literature is designed by considering the techniques of bibliotherapy and group psychological counseling. Second, implement aesthetic activities of literature to intervene in the depression and anxiety symptoms of college students. Pre-test, post-test, and case analysis are carried out to study the intervention effects. Thirdly, discuss the experimental results and obtain the conclusion of the present research. The hypotheses are as follows:

Hypothesis 1: It is applicable to intervene in depression and anxiety symptoms of college students by aesthetic appreciation of literature;

Hypothesis 2: Aesthetic appreciation of literature effectively intervenes in depression and anxiety symptoms of college students;

Hypothesis 3: Aesthetic appreciation of literature improves the general health of college students by improving their depression and anxiety symptoms;

Hypothesis 4: the intervention effects of aesthetic appreciation of literature in depression and anxiety symptoms are different among different university student group.

## MODELING AND ACTIVITY DESIGN OF AESTHETIC APPRECIATION OF LITERATURE

We preliminarily established the mode of aesthetic activities of literature which meets the psychological need of college students and can effectively adjust the depression and anxiety symptoms of college students, based on the aesthetic psychology of literature. And then we designed questionnaires to verify and modify such mode. We also completed the following two issues according to the formal mode that had been modified: (1) selecting literary works that have therapeutic functions. We selected proper literary works based on the survey results of reading tendency of college students and the characteristics of their depression and anxiety. (2) Designing aesthetic activities of literature. We introduced group psychological counseling and bibliotherapy to the activities, and designed operable plans that are specific to the problems.

## Preliminary Modeling of Aesthetic Appreciation of Literature

We preliminarily put forward the mode for aesthetic appreciation of literature based on literature analysis. The components of dimensions are as follows:

Aesthetic characteristics of literary works: the form of being is aesthetic image (lingering charm), organic integrity, reflecting the universal emotions of human, and literary language is artistic.

Characteristics of aesthetic reception of literature: aesthetic pleasure, direct experience and illogicality, re-creation of art, and artistic resonance.

Psychological stages during the process of aesthetic reception of literature: preparation, realization, judgment, and accumulation.

Psychic gratification functions of aesthetic activities of literature: purification and catharsis, self-cultivation, self-confirmation, and imaginary compensation.

Aesthetic standards for guidance and operation: good manner, good temperament, beautiful language.

Aesthetic requirements of the environment: comfortable, quite, and simple.

## Verification and Modification of the Mode

We established semi-opened and semi-close questionnaires for the mode, based on the preliminary thoughts concerning the dimensions of the mode. We surveyed 10 experts, 50 college students through email and direct survey. All questionnaires were collected (See Table 12.5.). The close-ended items were based on 5-point Likert scale. We planned to select the part with supportive rate of over 70%, i.e., the part of three pionts and above. We also verified and modified the mode by considering the suggestions from experts and students in the open-ended items, in order to determine the final mode of aesthetic activities of literature.

The above statistics shows that the supportive rate of experts toward the components of the aesthetic activities of literature was high. In addition, experts also put forward the following suggestions: i) principles should be followed during the aesthetic activities of literature; ii) the psychic gratification and therapeutic functions should "enable students to obtain vicarious experience and promote the adjustment of individuals"; iii) interaction and feedback should be available during the aesthetic appreciation of literature; iv) the various ways and methods to realize aesthetic appreciation of literature. The supportive rate of students toward the above mode was also high. They also put forward the following suggestions: i) the aesthetic appreciation of literature should be realized in vivid and interesting ways; ii) the individualization and features of the age should be highlighted in aesthetic experience of literature. We modified the mode according to the statistics and based on the above suggestions. And then we utilized the mode in designing the aesthetic activities of literature and selecting literary works in the purpose of intervention.

**Table 12.5. Survey Results Concerning the Mode of Aesthetic Activities of Literature**

| Dimensions | Components | Experts (n=10) | | College students (n=50) | |
|---|---|---|---|---|---|
| | | Number of supports | Suppor-tive rate | Number of supports | Supportive rate |
| Aesthetic components of aesthetic appreciation of literature | Aesthetic characteristics of literary works | | | | |
| | The form of being is aesthetic image | 10 | 100% | 46 | 92% |
| | All-around, independent, organic integrity | 9 | 90% | 43 | 86% |
| | Reflecting the universal emotions of human | 10 | 100% | 45 | 90% |
| | Literary language is artistic | 8 | 80% | 49 | 98% |
| | Psychic gratification and therapeutic functions of aesthetic activities of literature | | | | |
| | Purification and catharsis | 10 | 100% | 42 | 84% |
| | Self-cultivation | 10 | 100% | 49 | 98% |
| | Self-confirmation | 10 | 100% | 40 | 80% |
| | Imaginary compensation | 10 | 100% | 48 | 96% |
| | Aesthetic standards for guidance and operation: | | | | |
| | Good manner | 9 | 90% | 48 | 96% |
| | Good temperament | 7 | 70% | 49 | 98% |
| | Beautiful language | 8 | 80% | 49 | 98% |
| | Aesthetic requirements of the environment: | | | | |
| | comfortable, quite, simple | 10 | 100% | 46 | 92% |
| Components of the process of aesthetic reception of literature | Psychological stages during the process of aesthetic reception of literature: | | | | |
| | Preparation | 10 | 100% | 47 | 94% |
| | Realization | 10 | 100% | 48 | 96% |
| | Judgment | 9 | 90% | 41 | 82% |
| Dimensions | Components | Experts (n=10) | | College students (n=50) | |
| | | Number of supports | Supportive rate | Number of supports | Supportive rate |
| | accumulation | 8 | 80% | 43 | 86% |
| | Characteristics of aesthetic reception of literature: | | | | |
| | Aesthetic pleasure | 10 | 100% | 50 | 100% |
| | Direct experience and illogicality | 10 | 100% | 46 | 92% |
| | Re-creation of art | 9 | 90% | 47 | 94% |
| | Artistic resonance | 10 | 100% | 48 | 96% |

The basis for the modification is: i) supplementing the aesthetic principles followed during the appreciation of literature, and including such principles in the horizontal system of aesthetic appreciation of literature; ii) the interactivity, diversification of realization and feedback are included in the design principles; iii) adding the "vicarious experience" function of aesthetic appreciation of literature, which is utilized in selecting literary works and the design of activities and is included in the horizontal system of aesthetic appreciation of literature; iv) increasing the features of the age for selecting literary works.

## Interpretation of the Mode of Aesthetic Appreciation of Literature

The survey results show that the mode in general is reasonable and correct. Meanwhile, we also modified the mode based on the suggestions. The mode includes vertical and horizontal system. The main line of the vertical system is the process of subjective aesthetic reception of literature of the subject, staring from the beginning of the activity to the end of the activity. The horizontal system includes aesthetic components and aesthetic stages of aesthetic activities of literature. The horizontal system is reflected in each activity and influences the vertical system. The vertical and horizontal systems interact and effect through the aesthetic appreciation of literature. The structure of both systems is shown in Figure 12.1: The components of the vertical and horizontal systems are interpreted as follows:

## 1) Horizontal System: Aesthetic Components of Aesthetic Appreciation of Literature

We established the horizontal system for aesthetic components of literature by analyzing the participating components of the process of aesthetic reception of literature. We included the characteristics of aesthetic psychology of literary works, aesthetic appreciation of literature, aesthetic stages of literature and the guider in the system, based on the research results available and our ideas.

*Dimension 1: Aesthetic contents of literary works*

The aesthetic contents of literary works are the main carriers of aesthetic appreciation of literature. They are the most direct conditions that arouse the aesthetic experience of individuals. Meanwhile they are the basis for aesthetic appreciation of literature to realize aesthetics as the focus. Thus literary works with high aesthetic value should be selected according to the aesthetic contents of literary works in order to arouse the aesthetic pleasure of the participants and to generate aesthetic experience. The aesthetic contents of literary works mainly include lingering charm, organic integrity, language art and emotion.

*Dimension 2: Aesthetic principles of aesthetic appreciation of literature*

We took aesthetic appreciation of literature as the means to intervene in depression and anxiety symptoms, and thus the characteristics of activity design and implementation are different from other means of intervention. Experience should be available in the aesthetic appreciation of literature. The psychological principles of aesthetic reception of literature should be reflected and respected in the activities. The subjective consciousness of participants should be respected. The aesthetic principles include: emotion, experience, vivid, pleasure and interaction.

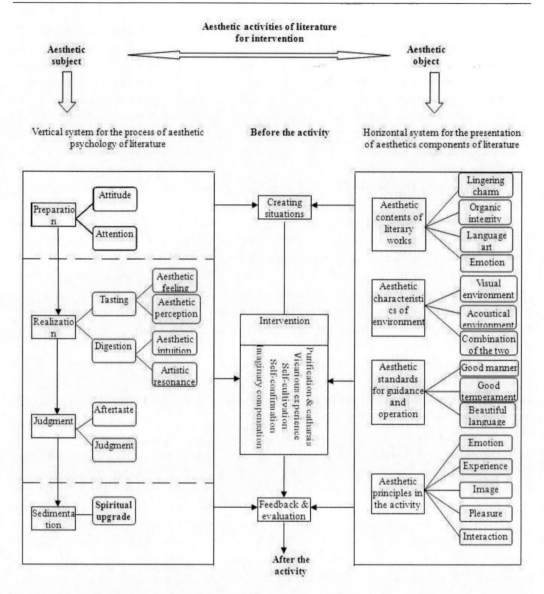

Figure 12.1. Mode of Aesthetic Appreciation of Literature.

*Dimension 3: Aesthetic characteristics of the environment*

Aesthetic appreciation of literature needs certain environment for the appreciation. Comfortable and good environment is an external condition for creating good aesthetic atmosphere of literature and good mood. The aesthetic characteristics of the environment for aesthetics of literature include: good visual environment, good acoustical environment and the harmonious combination of the two. First, the environment for aesthetics of literature should be comfortable with soft light. Second, the visual environment and acoustical environment should be good as multiple aesthetic presentation means were used in the experiment and in the environment, music appreciation, art and video were inevitably presented.

*Dimension 4: Aesthetic standards for guidance and operation:*

The aesthetic standards for guidance and operation refer to that guiders should have good manners, beautiful language and good temperament; the appearance, clothing, manners, behaviors of guiders should meet the aesthetic standards. Guiders should use professional literary language in the guidance. In addition, guiders should be friendly and tolerant.

## 2) Vertical System: The Reception Process of Aesthetic Appreciation of Literature

Vertical system is the process of individuals' aesthetic reception of literature. The aesthetic components of literature in the horizontal system work on participants through the implementation of aesthetic activities. It is possible for individuals to have positive aesthetic experience and realize aesthetic accumulation only when the psychological principles and stages of reception process of literature are followed. Thus the vertical system is the core of the experiment design. We divided the reception process of aesthetic appreciation of literature into four stages.

*Stage 1: Preparation stage*

At this stage, the tasks of readers include determining aesthetic attitude and form aesthetic attention. Whether the tasks are completed is related to the generation of aesthetic pleasure and perception. The main characteristics of aesthetic attitude include: non-utilitarian and non-conception. Only by doing that, individuals can get away from the present world and enjoy the literary world. This is the most important preparation stage for appreciation of literature.

*Stage 2: Realization stage*

Once the aesthetic attitude is determined, readers enter the fictitious world of literary and artistic works under the guidance of aesthetic attention. Then the subject of appreciation mingles with the literary works, resulting in strong artistic resonance and aesthetic pleasure. The realization stage is further divided into tasting and digestion steps. Tasting refers to the aesthetic perception of literary works, and it is repeated tasting and rumination of the perceptual images and characteristics of literary works. Two psychological components, feeling and conception are involved at this stage. Digestion refers to that appreciators of literary works, after fully tasting the perceptual characteristics of literary works, and after directly comprehension of the intrinsic meaning of artistic images without abstract thinking and conception in any form, forget themselves and blend with the object, realizing the peak of aesthetics. At this stage, aesthetic intuition and artistic resonance play a prominent role.

*Stage 3: Judgment stage*

At this stage, appreciators are separated from the literary works, reflecting the aesthetic pleasure they have had before, and then they have aesthetic judgment of the works. At this moment, perceptual intuition of readers is changed to rational exploration. Readers also analyze and taste the impression and feelings obtained in the previous stage, trying to make them clear and reasonable.

*Stage 4: Accumulation stage*

Accumulation stage is the last stage of the aesthetic appreciation of literature. The aesthetic experience obtained previously influences individuals imperceptibly. Such influence is not limited to the pleasure and experience of a moment; instead, the spiritual world of appreciators is changed, their personality is improved, and their aesthetic quality is developed. Therefore, the general mental health of individuals is improved.

## Selecting Literary Works for Aesthetic Purpose

*Survey concerning the reading tendency of college students.* We carried out semi-opened and semi-close survey concerning the extra-curriculum reading tendency of college students to understand the current status of reading among college students, in order to select literary works meeting the requirements of the experiment. We selected specific literary works based on the mode built. The survey targets were students from freshmen year to senior year majoring in arts and sciences from a Sichuan-based university. Students were from various majors of eight schools, including School of Electronic Information, School of Public Administration, School of Literature and Journalism, School of Mathematical Science, School of Materials, School of Economics, School of Manufacturing and School of History. School of Public Administration, School of Literature and Journalism, School of Economics and School of History are classified as schools of arts and the rest are classified as schools of sciences and engineering. About 402 questionnaires were distributed. 324 questionnaires were collected, among which 315 were valid, accounting for 78.36%. Among students, 192 were male (60.95%), 123 were female (39.05%), 153 were students of arts (48.57%), 162 were students of sciences (51.43%), 133 were the freshmen and sophomore  (42.22%), and 182 were  junior and senior  (57.78%). The average age is 20.3 years old.

The survey results are as shown in Tables 12.6, 12.7, 12.8, 12.9:

### Table 12.6. Results of Reading Tendency

|  | The 1<sup>st</sup> place | The 2<sup>nd</sup> place | The 3<sup>rd</sup> place |
|---|---|---|---|
| Favorite works | Prose and essay | Chinese classical novels | Western classical novels |
| Favorite theme | Family affection | Romance | Wisdom |
| Most comforting and encouraging literary works | Biography | Narrative fiction | Lyrical novel |
| Which literary works would you like to share with others the most | Narrative fiction | Historical literature | Biography |

The mentioned results show that the top three favorite works of college students are prose and essay, Chinese classic novels and western classic novels; the top three favorite literary themes of college students are family affection, romance and wisdom; the top three most comforting and encouraging literary works are biography, narrative fiction and lyric prose; literary works college students would  like to share with others the most are narrative fiction, historical literature and biography. Besides, there is no difference of gender, grades, and majors in such reading tendency of college students.

The results of pen-ended survey show that, 67% students chose classic novels and classic prose as their most influential works; 42% students recommended classic novels, famous prose and poem to others, in order to help them remove depression and anxiety, and 23% students recommended self-help psychological books.

**Table 12.7. Gender Difference of Reading Tendency**

| Items | The 1st place | The 2nd place | The 3rd place |
|---|---|---|---|
| Most favorite works | Prose and essay | Chinese classical novels | Western classical novels |
| | $t=.06$ | $t=.46$ | $t=-.89$ |
| Most favorite theme | Family affection | Romance | Wisdom |
| | $t=-.78$ | $t=-1.23$ | $t=-.66$ |
| Most comforting and encouraging literary works | Biography | Narrative fiction | Lyric prose |
| | $t=-.34$ | $t=.89$ | $t=-.65$ |
| Which literary works would you like to share with others the most | Narrative fiction | Historical literature | Biography |
| | $t=-.73$ | $t=.54$ | $t=.65$ |

**Table 12.8. Difference of Reading Tendency between Students of Arts and Sciences**

| Items | The 1st place | The 2nd place | The 3rd place |
|---|---|---|---|
| Most favorite works | Prose and essay | Chinese classical novels | Western classical novels |
| | $t=.94$ | $T=.35$ | $t=-.72$ |
| Most favorite theme | Family affection | Romance | Wisdom |
| | $t=-1.30$ | $T=.60$ | $t=1.84$ |
| Most comforting and encouraging literary works | Biography | Narrative fiction | Lyric prose |
| | $t=-.22$ | $T=2.56$ | $t=.99$ |
| Which literary works would you like to share with others the most | Narrative fiction | Historical literature | Biography |
| | $t=3.16$ | $T=.53$ | $t=1.00$ |

**Table 12.9. Grade Difference of Reading Tendency**

| Items | The 1st place | The 2nd place | The 3rd place |
|---|---|---|---|
| Most favorite works | Prose and essay | Chinese classical novels | Western classical novels |
| | $t=-1.42$ | $t=-.28$ | $t=-.14$ |
| Most favorite theme | Family affection | Romance | Wisdom |
| | $t=1.44$ | $t=-.36$ | $t=-.42$ |
| Most comforting and encouraging literary works | Biography | Narrative fiction | Lyric prose |
| | $t=-1.37$ | $t=-.88$ | $t=.65$ |
| Which literary works would you like to share with others the most | Narrative fiction | Historical literature | Biography |
| | $t=.01$ | $t=-.96$ | $t=-1.88$ |

The survey results show that the favorite of and most popular literary works among college students were mainly classic prose, poem and novel. They usually chose such literary themes as family affection and romance. They paid more attention to aesthetic emotions, expression of emotion, and the influence of literary works on their development. It indicates that college students have certain aesthetic experience and aesthetic needs of literary works. Literary works selected for the aesthetic activities of literature should be what they like. The literary works we chose were mainly prose, poem and novels with themes of family affection and romance.

### Selecting Literary Works

*Standards for selecting literary works.* We concluded the following standard based on the mode for aesthetic activities of literature and the survey results of reading tendency of college students.

Literary works should be good and famous and have high aesthetic value;
The aesthetics of works should correspond with the reception of readers;
Literary works selected should have different emotional experience;
The literary works selected should include both fine literature and light literature.

Specific literary works selected and their psychotherapeutic functions. We classified the literary works selected into four groups according to the theoretical basis and selection standards as mentioned above.

*Group 1: Different emotional themes.*

Oedipus Tyrannus, Phoenix Hairpin, Three Days to See, Zebra Finch, Fall in love with Tang Wan Secretly for Eight Hundred Years.

The sublimity of tragedies enables the catharsis of depression emotions of mind. The emotions of pity and love will be generated from terror. Meanwhile the excessive attention of oneself from anxiety and depression will be changed, resulting to removal of their restrictions. Lacrimose and sad poems will create resonance with depressive and low moods, helping individuals to remove negative emotions. Such literary works should be selected for the preliminary stage of the intervention, in order that individuals vent negative emotions and realize psychological balance. Peaceful and serene literary works, especially prose reflecting the serene nature, help to reduce the level of anxiety, relax the mind and calm down, which comforts and calms down depressed individuals. Cheerful and enthusiastic works improve the positive emotional experience of readers, which cheer readers up and encourage readers. Such works are appropriate to be read after the catharsis of negative emotions and when individuals have peace of mind.

*Group 2: Expression of different emotions*

*Madame Bovary, Li Sao* (a Chinese poem dating from the Warring States Period, written by Qu Yuan (340 BC - 278 BC) of the Kingdom of Chu), *Palace of Tang Dynasty.*

One psychologist from the United States once pointed that, such emotions as terror, depression and anxiety are reduced when they are presented. The best solution for emotional disorders is always to make the sufferer realize and face up to such emotions. Almost all emotions are included in literary works. Prototype of any emotional confusion can be found in literary works. Thus in group intervention activities, after negative emotions are released at the preliminary stage, typical literary works about the emotional confusion should be selected for the second stage, in order that depressed and anxious individuals clearly realize their unknown emotions and objectify their emotions, making them face up to such emotions.

*Group 3: Indirect experience from literature*

Notre Dame de Paris, Les Misérables, The Old Man and the Sea.

The personality traits of different protagonists and their experience under different environment reflected in literary works provide individuals for aesthetics of literature with indirect experience. Recipients, though stand-ins, substitute reality with the structure of literature and art, which realizes corresponding psychotherapy during the process of meeting their hidden cognitive needs. The inner world of the recipients is influenced by presenting the spiritual world of protagonists through introjection .

*Group 4: literary image, imagination*

Drops from the Forest, Sunset in Autumn, Jimi's Cartoon: Can I not be Brave, Grimm Fairy Tales

Individuals, through experience, rumination and other complicated psychological activities, reproduce images in mind from literary works. Meanwhile, individuals creatively present the image system of literary works by using their aesthetic perception, and conduct unique artistic association. And then individuals feel aesthetic pleasure though the recreation of image and artistic association.

It is worth noting that the grouping of the mentioned literary works was based on the real situations of the present research. Due to the restriction of time and place, the literary works we selected were those that are most possible to realize therapeutic significance. However, almost each work we selected includes all therapeutic components listed above. Thus we should not only highlight a certain therapeutic component of a literary work, but also pay attention to other therapeutic components.

## Designing Aesthetic Activities of Literature

### *Design Principles*

*Principle 1: three-dimensional aesthetics*

The experiment tried to intervene in depressive and anxious mood of individuals through aesthetic appreciation of literature, emphasized on aesthetic experience and pleasure, directness and emotions. Thus situations and good atmospheres should be created in the design, in order to bring individuals into the aesthetic state. In order to realize the target, we also added in the activity videos, pictures and background music related to the literary works we selected, in order that the literary works are presented in a three-dimensional and all-around way. By doing this, individuals obtain diversified aesthetic pleasure and have deepened experience and understanding of the literary works.

*Principle 2: group principle*

The group environment of the activity facilitates individuals to develop trusted and friendly interpersonal relationship, remove loneliness and depression. In addition, individuals are driven by groups' impetus to explore together with other group members and actively solve problems. Thus, in the design, we fully played the interactive advantage of group counseling, guided group members to share and cooperate with others in the process of aesthetics of literature, conducted relaxation training, imagination training and literary creation.

## Procedures of Aesthetic Activities of Literature

*Stage one (the first week): Stage of introduction*

Group members are not familiar with each other. Thus unnecessary worries and confusions should be removed, in order to form a group. First, explain to them the purpose and significance of the activity and make them confident in the therapeutic intervention. Second, preliminarily develop the interpersonal relationship within the group. As participants are in depressive and anxious mood, enthusiastic introduction is not appropriate at the beginning of the activity; instead, the introduction should be stable and mild, which not only facilitates individuals to remove nervousness and precautious against others, but also meets the needs of individuals to protect their emotions.

*Stage two (the second to the seventh week): Intervention*

With the deepening of activities, intervention in depression and anxiety through aesthetics of literature is conducted.

*Theme 1: training and therapy for relaxation.* Individuals with depressive and anxious mood suffer from insomnia, nervousness and great emotional fluctuations. They pay attention to the struggling and conflict in their mind, and rarely pay attention to external objects. Thus it is difficult for them to accept the intervention of literature. Literary works with serene artistic conception is used to remove the fidget and nervousness. Meanwhile, readers feel the artistic conception of the poem during reading, adjust breathing and relax muscles.

*Theme 2: self-confirmation and objectification of emotion.* Individuals understand self through appreciation, even understand the part of self that was not realized and understood, which clears the vagueness, eases fidget and nervousness, resulting in pleasure. It is realized mainly through improvised literary creation and painting.

*Theme 3: Development of aesthetic imagination and sensing capacity.* An important aesthetic factor of aesthetics of literature is image and artistic conception. Group members are guided to experience preliminarily the enter into the fictitious world of literary, resulting in artistic association and association, resonance and aesthetic pleasure, which facilitates members to have aesthetic pleasure and reduce negative emotions. Background music, video or pictures are presented to help individuals find the intention and theme behind the text.

*Theme 4: Catharsis of emotion and purification.* Reading tragedies causes pity and terror, relaxes depressive emotions. Emotions are released during the expression of emotions, and soul is purified. The theory of drama therapy is introduced in the activity, which helps to guide individuals feel the internal struggling of protagonists. The distress and suffering of individuals similar to protagonists are released during the presentation of plots. Suffering of individuals is purified through the suffering of protagonists. Individuals think about their life when showing pity to protagonist. Depression and anxiety can be released through activities. In addition, individuals are guided to think about their life and correct their biased view.

*Theme 5: substitute satisfaction, imaginary compensation.* The needs of individuals that are impossible to be realized in reality are satisfied in the imaginary world through aesthetics of literature, and the individuals are satisfied spiritually. Fantasy is a kind of relaxation, for example, individuals leave the reality temporarily when reading fairy tales, which forms an opportunity of change, reduces the worries and fidget of individuals, and changed the mood of individuals.

*Stage three (the eighth week): integration and end stage.*

Individuals are encouraged to think about the past, present and the future, based on the previous seven activities, and to express thinking in an artistic way, which is integration.

Individuals are required to record their gains and thoughts in activities. Individuals are especially encouraged to record their special experience due to the individualized feature of aesthetic, which will become a method to deal with the future crisis of life. In addition, individuals should be guided to think about the good and unforgettable experience in the last activity, and to share their future plans, in order to strengthen the intervention effects of the previous activities. By doing this, the confidence of individuals in future learning and life can be strengthened. Besides, the sorrow of parting of individuals should be conformed, psychologically preparing for parting.

## Design of the Plan for Aesthetic Appreciation of Literature

We designed eight activities for aesthetic appreciation of literature based on the actual situations of the experiment, the arrangement at each stage, themes and purposes of activities. The activity was held once per week. Each activity lasted 120 minutes. The project lasted for two months. There was one guider and one assistant. Most of the materials were presented to participants in activities in the form of Powerpoint documents, video and audio. The following are the designs of activities for aesthetic appreciation of literature. Please see Appendix 3 for details.

### Table 12.10. The Activities of Aesthetic Appreciation of Literature

| Stages of Activities | Units | Themes |
|---|---|---|
| Stage of introduction | Unit 1: Literature and Me | Make friends and develop interpersonal relationship |
| Implementation stage | Unit 2: Secrete Garden of Hearts | Training and therapy for relaxation. |
| | Unit 3: I am ... | The gratification from self-confirmation and self-discovery |
| | Unit 4: the world of artistic conception | Feel the artistic conception of literary works and arouse resonance |
| | Unit 5: purification and catharsis | Release emotions by reading tragedies, purify soul |
| | Unit 6: I perform on my stage | Literary creation and drama therapy |
| | Unit 7: childhood and fairy tales | Fairy tale therapy |
| End stage | Unit 8: every one is an artist | Create freely, express and adjust during creation. Part from group members |

| Stages of Activities | Description | Contents and Procedures | Theories |
|---|---|---|---|
| Preparation | 1. Introduction of the theme | The guider read for the member a piece of beautiful literary works that described the natural scenes against the music, and then organized the members to discuss following topics: "what did you associate this piece of literature with?", "what kind of beauty can you feel?", "The world of aesthetics of literature is a place that can make you forget the fame and wealth as | Music atmosphere was created to attract the aesthetic attention of partici-pants. Meanwhile, inspiring questions were presented to make participants think about aesthetic |

| Stages of Activities | Description | Contents and Procedures | Theories |
|---|---|---|---|
| | | well as the scientific concepts." " | attitude. |
| Realization | 2. Direct image (literature + picture) | Distribute members a piece of literature that describes amazing scenes or figures, such as the wonderful surrealistic description in the *Zhuangzi* and "the date with the fairy" in the *Gaotang Fu*, ask members to draw out the scene or the figure in their mind and then display the image of the figure with slides. Organize members to make discussion and find out the difference between the displayed image and the one in their mind. | Appreciated typical classic literary works. Stimulate participants to associate and imagine by using background music and relevant images, and to arouse artistic resonance on such basis. Obtained aesthetic experience. |
| Judgment | 3. Meditation and relaxation (literature + music) | Conduct the relaxing therapy on members based on the association after the previous training on aesthetic image. The guider first made the member relaxed with implicit words against the soothing and beautiful music, then guided the member to listen to the *River in the Forest* and the *Sunset in Autumn*, encouraged members to form image and association in their mind and made them relaxed in the beautiful artistic atmosphere. Only music was provided at the stage of association. Encourage members to write down their feelings after the meditation and to share their feelings to find out if they had any changes. | Helped participants to chew over and judge. |
| Accumulation | 4. Evaluation and summarization | Make members summarize the purpose of the activity; encourage them to speak out their questions and deficiencies of the activity. Encourage members to conduct relaxation trainings at home to cultivate their aesthetic imagination and recommend some relevant materials for them. | Facilitated aesthetic accumulation. |

The following explains how the mode of aesthetic activities of literature is realized in activities by taking Unit 2: Secrete Garden of Hearts as an example.

*Unit 2: Secrete Garden of Hearts*

Theme: training and therapy for relaxation.

Purpose:

To help members relax and stabilize their mood and relieve their stress and pressure.

To train the member's aesthetic attention and aesthetic attitude.

Preliminarily train the member's aesthetic image and association capacity.

## About the Mode of Aesthetic Activities of Literature

### *The Mode*

We established the mode of aesthetic activities of literature based on the aesthetic psychology of the subject and characteristics of aesthetic object. The mode is consisted of vertical and horizontal systems. The mode is the precondition for effective intervention. We arranged the aesthetic psychology of individuals in the vertical system, and put the components of the aesthetic activities of literature in the horizontal system. First, for the vertical system, we divided the process of aesthetic psychological into four stages, preparation, realization, judgment and accumulation. Specific activities of aesthetic psychology were ongoing at those four stages, including aesthetic attention, aesthetic perception, aesthetic association and aesthetic imagination. The purposes of such activities and stages were to realize effective aesthetics of literature by participants, catharsis of emotions, expression of emotions, fantasy and other purposes of literature therapy. Aesthetic judgment stage can also be included in the aesthetic realization stage. However, we considered that in addition to direct experience and direct infection of emotions, college students suffering from depression and anxiety should also be guided to think about the previous aesthetic pleasure, in order to realize aesthetic judgment. Aesthetic experience is changed to rational exploration. Thus we listed aesthetic judgment independently. This is to well arrange and clarify the aesthetic pleasure of individuals who suffer from depression and anxiety felt in activities, in order that such good experience has profound effect on such individuals. Second, we included in the horizontal four components closely related with the aesthetic activities of literature, including the aesthetic characteristics of literature, aesthetic principles of activity patterns, aesthetic characteristics of environment, guiding for operation. Such components should follow the existing aesthetic specifications respectively, penetrate in every stages and aspects of aesthetic activities of literature, and should create an aesthetic atmosphere. The purpose is to help individuals obtain the maximum aesthetic experience in the aesthetic process, in order to realize intervention in depression and anxiety.

### *Selection of Literary Works*

The selection of literary works is the difficulty and focus of the present research. The difficulty is reflected in that: first, it is difficult to extensively cover literary works of all kinds in detail; second, Careful selection is needed in order to match the therapeutic function of literary works and depression and anxiety symptoms and to realize specific effect of intervention; finally, the selection and reception of literary works among college students are different due to their different literary accomplishments, interests, etc. Thus, we carried out several measures to select literary works: first, we defined the therapeutic mechanism of literary works theoretically and specific therapeutic components, for example, the catharsis and purification functions, intuition and representation of literature, indirect satisfaction, etc. And then they were matched with depression and anxiety symptoms respectively, acting as one of the theoretical supports for selection of works. Second, we surveyed college students about their reading tendencies and reading experience, including the literary forms and themes they liked, types of literary works which had the most significance of mental health on them, and works which they believed can release depression and anxiety the most. Statistics and analysis show that the main stream reading tendencies were positive, classic and educational literary works, as well as some popular and recent literary works. The literary works they like are mostly prose and novel, which correspond with related research. Their favorite themes were family affection, romance and wisdom. In terms of releasing depression and anxiety, most college students, based on their own experience, chose world-wide classic works, such as *The Old Man and the Sea, Li Sao* (a Chinese poem dating from the Warring States Period, written by Qu Yuan (340 BC - 278 BC) of the Kingdom of Chu), famous lyric prose, etc. It indicates that classic masterpiece can really reduce depression and anxiety. This is because classic masterpieces, after being tested by time, are of ideological, philosophical and great aesthetic significance. In other words, individuals obtain stronger and universal aesthetic experience during reading of such masterpieces. Thus we selected the classic literary works universally accepted by college students, and selected some paragraphs according to the therapeutic functions of literature. Then two problems were solved: 1) such classic masterpieces had great aesthetic therapeutic effects on depression and anxiety; 2) such literary works are universally accepted by college students, thus they are proper materials for aesthetic intervention among college students nowadays, which minimizes the influence of individual difference. In addition, we controlled high percentage of classic works, and properly selected popular literature, such as *Fall in love with Tang Wan Secretly for Eight Hundred Years,* an Internet lyric prose.

We would like to mention the length of literary works. Due to the duration of experiment, the literary works presented were short poem, prose and periscope of novels. They were carefully selected. In addition, music and video were presented too, in order that participants had complete and strong aesthetic experience during the duration of the experiment, and that the interests of participants in aesthetics of literature were developed. Some time-consuming novels and biographies were home works for participants, in order to realize continuous intervention.

### Design of Activities

The activity design of the experiment has two characteristics: group psychological counseling and activities guided by the theory of aesthetics of literature. First, the activity design made full use of the advantages of the group counseling, for example, the influence, efficiency, effects and impetus to interpersonal relationship of group counseling are better than individualized counseling. Thus we designed many interactive activities to improve the relationship among members, striving to create trusted and positive atmosphere of the group, and make aesthetics of literature in a more relaxed state. The group impetus is used to facilitate the activities; for example, group discussion better facilitates the aesthetic judgment and clarification of opinions. In addition, group discussion inspires many aesthetic thinking, and inspires the creativity of members. Besides, the experiment fully presented the characteristics of the aesthetics of literature. The experiment was design according to the aesthetic principles of activity patterns, aesthetic characteristics of environment, aesthetic characteristics of guidance and operation. We added background music, pictures and videos corresponding with the contents of literary works, striving to create lyric and great atmospheres, in order to reflect the aesthetic principles of activity patterns, i.e., interactivity, experience, vividness, pleasure and emotion. For example, in the fourth activity, we presented a large number of beautiful pictures in order to help participants feel the artistic conception of literature, and encouraged participants to close eyes and feel the artistic conception of literary works when the background music was on. We presented part of video *Romeo and Juliet* and

*Palace of Tang Dynasty*, and encouraged members to perform *Oedipus Tyrannus*, in order to guide them to experience the strong emotions embedded in the work.

# EFFECTS OF AESTHETIC APPRECIATION OF LITERARY WORKS ON COLLEGE STUDENTS' DEPRESSION AND ANXIETY SYMPTOMS

## Purpose and Target

Conduct educational experiment intervention in full-time college students with depression and anxiety symptoms so as to improve their depression and anxiety symptoms as well as the mental health and verify the effectiveness of aesthetics of literature.

### *Source of Participants*

Methods of recruiting participants: publicize in September 2006 the recruitment information on the mental health related website of a university in Sichuan and post the recruitment advertisement on campus. 89 persons applied to participate in the experiment two weeks later and they were the students from School of Literature and Journalism, School of Foreign Languages, School of History, School of Management, School of Mathematics, School of Economics, School of Communications, School of Clinical Medicine and School of Life Science. Among such applicants, 49 (55%) were urban students, while 40 (45%) were rural students; 42 (47%) were majoring in arts, while 47 (53%) were majoring in sciences; 57 (64%) were in senior grades, while 32 (36%) were in junior grades. The average age of them was 21.1.

### *Criteria on Selection*

According to the grading of depression and anxiety in the research into clinical medicine and education [Zhou, 2003; Deng and Lei, 2004], we selected the students whose standard score of Self-Rating Depression Scale (SDS) was 0.5 or above and whose standard score of Self-Rating Anxiety Scale (SAS) was 41 or above.

## Methods

### *Design of Experiment*

We did not sample , allocate participants at random and matche the selected participants at random in this chapter since it was difficult to operate in practice; instead, we adopted the counterbalancing experiment design of pre-testing and post-testing. The independent variable was the implementation of aesthetic appreciation of literature, and the dependent variables included the college student's depression and anxiety symptoms as well as the change in mental health. Please see Table 12.11. for experimental treatment.

**Table 12.11. Design on Educational Experiment Intervention of Aesthetic Appreciation of Literature in College Students' Depression and Anxiety Symptoms**

| Group | Pre-Test | Educational Intervention | Post-Test |
|---|---|---|---|
| Experimental group | Psychometrics of participants' depression and anxiety symptoms | To be implemented | The same as pre-test |
| | Psychometrics of participants' overall mental health | | The same as pre-test |
| Control group | Psychometrics of participants' depression and anxiety symptoms | N/A | The same as pre-test |
| | Psychometrics of participants' overall mental health | | The same as pre-test |

### Psychometric Tool

*Psychometric tool.* The psychometric tools were SDS [Zheng, 1990], SAS [Xu, 1990] and SCL-90[Wang, 1993]. Correlation analysis results showed that there was a very significant correlation between the SDS scores and the scores of depression factor in SCL-90 in this chapter (r=.79, $p<0.01$). Therefore, the depression symptoms were also determined based on the scores of depression factor in SCL-90. Relevant analysis results showed that there was a very significant correlation between the SDS scores and the scores of depression factor in SCL-90 in this chapter (r=.75, $p<0.01$). Therefore, the anxiety symptoms were also determined based on the scores of anxiety factor in SCL-90. In respect of the determination of overall mental health, SCL-90 prepared by Parloff and revised by Wu was one of the frequently used tools for mental health survey and non-diagnostic evaluation. The scale was to test individuals' mental health level and traits, including 90 items on such 10 factors as somatization, compulsive symptom, interpersonal sensitivity, depression, anxiety, hostility, fear, paranoia, psychotic and others. In addition, there was positive correlation between the total scores of SDS and SAS and SCL-90 in this chapter, and the correlation coefficients were respectively r=.70 ($p<0.01$) and r=.53 ($p<0.05$).

*Equipment.* We needed the multi-media classroom in our research. We used the projector to display the selected literary works, images or videos and used the audio system to play the music. There should be movable chairs and desks in the classroom so that we can move the seats according to the progress of the activity and make room for warm-up activities etc.

### Course of Experiment

*Grouping of participants.* We used the participants' scores of SDS, SAS and SCL-90 as the pre-test data and divided the participants into the experimental group and the control group according to the pre-test scores of their depression and anxiety symptoms. Then, we tested the difference between the experimental group and the control group in respect of their depression and anxiety symptoms. We finally made the two groups homogeneous by balancing the number of participants thereof. Intervene in the control group with similar methods and procedures as the experiment ended. Please see Table 12.12. For the difference between the pre-test data of the two groups.

**Table 12.12. Comparison of the Significance of Difference between Pre-Test Data of the Experimental Group and the Control Group**

| Types | Level/Factor | $t$ Value | $p$ Value |
|---|---|---|---|
| SDS Scores | Mild | -.93 | .36 |
| | Moderate | .49 | .63 |
| | Major | .00 | 1.00 |
| | Overall | .38 | .70 |
| SAS Scores | Mild | .46 | -.64 |
| | Moderate | -.42 | .69 |
| | Overall | .39 | .69 |
| SCL-90 Scores | Total scores | .52 | .60 |
| | Depression factor | .44 | .65 |
| | Anxiety factor | .69 | .49 |

According to Table 12.12, there was no significant difference between the pre-test scores of the experimental group and the control group on each level of their depression and anxiety, between their pre-test SCL-90 scores, between their pre-test scores of the depression factor and anxiety factor. It also showed that there was no participant in this experiment suffering major anxiety and this may result from the epidemiologic characteristics of college students' anxiety. Some investigation on epidemiology showed that most of the anxious emotions reported by college students were of mild symptoms instead of major symptoms [Li and Wang, 2003; Fan and Wang, 2001].

*Educational intervention.* Conduct aesthetics of literature on the experimental group in accordance with the designed proposal, while no aesthetics was conducted on the control group. Observe the acceptance and response of the participants in the course and adjust relevant content. Make the participants sign the "convention of the group" before the experiment to ensure that the aesthetic appreciation of literature can be conducted success*fully.*

Statistics and analysis. Test the experimental group and the control group (with SDS, SAS and SCL-90) at the same time after the experiment and input the data of the questionnaire into SPSS for Windows 12.0 for processing. Thus, we can conclude the difference between the pre-test and the post-test scores.

## Experimental Results

The experimental results included four parts: intervention effects of aesthetic appreciation of literature on college students' depression symptoms, intervention effects of aesthetic appreciation of literature on college students' anxiety symptoms, intervention effects of aesthetic appreciation of literature on college students' overall mental health and difference between the intervention effects of aesthetic appreciation of literature on college students' depression and anxiety symptoms.

Intervention effects of aesthetic appreciation of literature on college students' depression symptoms

Intervention effects of aesthetic appreciation of literature on depression symptoms of
experimental group and control group

Type of group was taken as the independent variable and the difference between the pre-
test and post-test scores of SDS was taken as the dependent variable to conduct independent
samples and matched samples t test. The results of vertical and horizontal comparison of
scores of experimental group and control group in terms of depression symptoms were shown
in Table 12.13.

Table 12.13. Showed that there was no significant difference ($t=0.38$, $p>0.05$) in
depression symptoms of the two groups before the experiment as a whole. Test after the
experiment showed that there were an extremely significant difference ($t=5.62$, $p<0.001$)
between the pre-test and post-test results of the experimental group in case of horizontal
comparison, while the difference between those of the control group was not significant ($t=-
.24$, $p>0.05$). According to the vertical comparison of pre-test results of experimental group
and control group, there was no significant difference ($t=.38$, $p>0.05$), while after the
experimental intervention, a significant difference ($t=-3.24$, $p<0.01$) existed between post-test
scores of depression symptoms of the experimental group and the control group.

**Table 12.13. Test of Significance of Difference between Pre-test and Post-test Scores
of Depression Symptoms of Experimental Group and Control Group**

| Group | n | Pre-Test $M\pm SD$ | Post-Test $M\pm SD$ | t Value | p Value |
|---|---|---|---|---|---|
| Experimental Group | 26 | .60±.07 | .48±.06 | 5.62*** | .000 |
| Control Group | 26 | .59±.07 | .56±.06 | -.24 | .812 |
| t Value | | .38 | -3.24** | | |
| p Value | | .70 | .003 | | |

Note: ** $p<0.01$, *** $p<0.001$.

This demonstrated that aesthetic appreciation of literary works can significantly improve
depression symptoms of the experimental group as a whole, which was consistent with the
original experiment hypothesis.

Intervention effect of aesthetic appreciation of literature on participants of experimental
group and control group with different levels of depression symptoms. Different levels of the
participants' depression symptoms were taken as the independent variable, and the pre-test
and post-test scores of depression symptoms were taken as the dependent variable to conduct
t test. See Table 12-14 for the results.

Table 12.14. showed that, in respect of participants with mild depression symptoms, there
was a significant difference between the pre-test and post-test scores of depression symptoms
of the experimental group ($t=2.77$, $p<0.05$), while there was no significant difference between
the pre-test and post-test scores of the control group ($t=-1.96$, $p>0.05$). In respect of
participants with mild depression symptoms, the vertical comparison showed that there was no
significant difference between the pre-test scores ($t=-.94$, $p>0.05$) and the post-test scores ($t=-
2.05$, $p>0.05$) of the experimental group and the control group. In respect of participants with
moderate depression symptoms, there was an extremely significant difference between the
experimental group's pre-test and post-test on depression symptoms ($t=8.27$, $p<0.001$), while

there was no significant difference between the control group's pre-test and post-test on depression symptoms ($t$=.65, $p$>0.05). In respect of participants with moderate depression symptoms,the vertical comparison showed thatthere was no significant difference between the pre-test scores of the experimental group and the control group ($t$=-.94, $p$>0.05), while there was very a significant difference between the post-test scores ($t$=-4.39, $p$>0.05) of the experimental group and the control group. In respect of participants with major depression symptoms, both the vertical and horizontal comparison showed that there was no significant difference between the pre-test and post-test scores of the experimental group and the control group.

**Table 12.14. Test of Significance of Difference between Pre-Test and Post-Test Scores of Depression Symptoms of Participants with Different Levels of Depression Symptoms in Experimental Group and Control Group**

| Level Group | n | Pre-Test ($M\pm SD$) | Post-Test ($M\pm SD$) | $t$ Value | $p$ Value |
|---|---|---|---|---|---|
| Experimental group | 12 | .52±.02 | .47±.04 | 2.77* | .028 |
| Mild Control group | 14 | .53±.03 | .56±.02 | -1.96 | .081 |
| $t$ Value | | -.93 | -2.04 | | |
| $p$ Value | | .36 | .06 | | |
| Experimental group | 12 | .65±.02 | .46±.06 | 8.27*** | .000 |
| Moderate Control group | 10 | .64±.02 | .62±.07 | .65 | .543 |
| $t$ Value | | .49 | -4.39** | | |
| $p$ Value | | .63 | .001 | | |
| Experimental group | 2 | .71±.01 | .61±.03 | 3.33 | .186 |
| Major Control group | 2 | .71±.01 | .67±.02 | 1.50 | .374 |
| $t$ Value | | .00 | .24 | | |
| $p$ Value | | 1.000 | .84 | | |

The results above showed that aesthetic appreciation of literature can significantly improve the depression symptoms of participants with mild and moderate depression symptoms, but there was no significant effect on participants with major depression symptoms. This may be because such participants' depression symptoms were so major that they had impacted participants' attention and reading capacity. However, the aesthetic appreciation of literature required that the participants should be able to make reading, association and imagination, but the participants with major depression symptoms seemed unable to satisfy this requirement. Therefore, the experiment failed to achieve satisfactory effects.

*Analysis of variance on participants of the experimental group with different levels of depression symptoms.* Two depression levels of participants of experimental group were taken as the independent variables, and the pre-test and post-test scores of depression symptoms were taken as the dependent variables for the purpose of single factor analysis of variance so as to assess the effect of experimental intervention on different levels of depression symptoms of the participants of experimental group. See Table 12.15. for the results.

Table 12.15. showed that before the experiment, an extremely significant difference ($F=65.311$, $p<0.001$) existed between participants with different levels of depression symptoms in experimental group, and after the experiment, a significant difference ($t=6.188$, $p<0.05$) still existed between such participants, but such significance dropped to some extent. It follows that the aesthetic appreciation of literature can significantly improve the experimental group's depression symptoms as a whole and at each level and can improve the depression symptoms of participants at different levels to different extents.

**Table 12.15. Single Factor Analysis of Variance on Different Levels of Depression Symptoms of the Experimental Group**

| Level | Mild (n=12) $M\pm SD$ | Moderate (n=12) $M\pm SD$ | Major (n=2) $M\pm SD$ | $F$ Value | $p$ Value | Post Hoc Test |
|---|---|---|---|---|---|---|
| Pre-Test | .52±.03 | .65±.02 | .71±.01 | 65.31*** | .000 | 1<2<3 |
| Post-Test | .48±.05 | .46±.05 | .67±.02 | 6.19* | .011 | 1<2<3 |

### *Effect of Intervention of Aesthetic Appreciation of Literature on College Students' Anxiety Symptoms*

*Effect of intervention of aesthetic appreciation of literature in anxiety symptoms of experimental group and control group.* Type of group is taken as the independent variable and the difference between the scores of pre-test and post-test through anxiety symptom checklist is taken as the dependent variable to carry out independent samples and matched samples $t$ test. The results of vertical and horizontal comparison of scores of experimental group and control group in terms of anxiety symptoms are shown in Table 12.16.

**Table 12.16. Significance Test of Difference between Pre-tests and Post-tests of Anxiety Symptoms of Participants of Experimental Group and Control Group**

| Group | n | Pre-test ($M\pm SD$) | Post-test ($M\pm SD$) | $t$ value | $p$ value |
|---|---|---|---|---|---|
| Experimental group | 26 | 51.42±8.39 | 40.60±6.49 | 6.29*** | .000 |
| Control group | 26 | 51.79±10.51 | 49.76±8.22 | 1.66 | .115 |
| $t$ value | | .39 | -3.71** | | |
| $p$ value | | .692 | .01 | | |

Table 12.16. shows that there was no significant difference ($t=.39$, $p>0.05$) in anxiety symptoms of the participants of the two groups before the experiment as a whole. Test after the experiment showed that there existed highly a significant difference ($t=6.28$, $p<0.001$) in the results of pre-test and post-test of experimental group through horizontal comparison, while the difference in those of control group was not significant ($t=1.66$, $p>0.05$). Vertical comparison of pre-test results of experimental group and control group showed no significant difference ($t=.39$, $p>0.05$) while after experimental intervention, a significant difference ($t=-3.71$, $p<0.01$) existed in post-test scores of anxiety symptoms between experimental group

and control group. This demonstrates that aesthetic appreciation of literary works can ameliorate anxiety symptoms of participants of experimental group as a whole, — consistent with original experiment hypothesis.

Effect of intervention of aesthetic appreciation of literature in different anxiety levels of experimental group and control group. Different anxiety levels of the participants are taken as the independent variable, and the scores of pre-test and post-test of anxiety symptoms are taken as the dependent variable to conduct t test. See Table 12.17. for the results.

Table 12.17. shows that comparison between pre-test and post-test results of experimental group revealed highly a significant difference ($t$=5.69, $p$<0.001) for participants with mild anxiety level, and a significant difference ($t$=10.26, $p$<0.05) for participants with moderate anxiety level, while there was no significant difference between pre-test and post-test results of control group. Horizontal comparison of post-test results of experimental group and control group showed that there existed highly a significant difference ($t$=.64, $p$<0.05) for participants with mild anxiety level, and no significant difference ($t$=-2.05, $p$>0.05) for participants with moderate anxiety level.

*Significance test of difference between Participants with Different Anxiety Levels in Experimental Group.* Two anxiety levels of participants of experimental group are taken as the independent variables, and the scores of pre-test and post-test of anxiety symptoms are taken as the dependent variables to carry out separately significant tests of difference so as to assess the effect of experimental intervention in different levels of anxiety symptoms of the participants of experimental group. See Table 12.18. for the results.

Table 12.18. shows that before the experiment, highly a significant difference ($t$=5.39, $p$<0.001) existed between participants with different levels of anxiety symptoms in experimental group, and after the experiment, a significant difference ($t$=2.97, $p$<0.001) still existed between participants with different levels of anxiety symptoms in the group, but the significance dropped to some extent. Such results therefore demonstrates that aesthetic appreciation of literature can ameliorate significantly anxiety of the participants of experimental group both as a whole and at different levels, and can alleviate anxiety symptoms at different levels of the participants to varied extent.

**Table 12.17. Significance Test of Difference between Pre-Tests and Post-Tests of Anxiety Symptoms of Participants with Different Anxiety Levels in Experimental Group and Control Group**

| Level / Group | n | Pre-test ($M \pm SD$) | Post-test ($M \pm SD$) | $t$ value | $p$ value |
|---|---|---|---|---|---|
| Experimental group | 17 | 48.60±6.047 | 38.26±4.43 | 5.69*** | .000 |
| Mild Control group | 18 | 47.50±6.289 | 47.46±6.79 | .14 | .890 |
| $t$ value | | .46 | .64*** | | |
| $p$ value | | -4.12 | .000 | | |
| Experimental group | 9 | 64.84±4.62 | 46.67±7.51 | 10.26** | .001 |
| Moderate Control group | 8 | 66.80±8.25 | 57.80±8.49 | 2.26 | .109 |
| $t$ value | | -.42 | -2.05 | | |
| $p$ value | | .692 | .085 | | |

**Table 12.18. Significance Test of Difference between Participants with Different Anxiety Levels in Experimental Group**

| Level | Mild (n=17) M±SD | Moderate (n=9) M±SD | t value | p value |
|---|---|---|---|---|
| Pre-test | 48.60±6.04 | 64.84±4.62 | -5.39*** | .000 |
| Post-Test | 38.26±4.43 | 46.67±7.51 | -2.97** | .009 |

## Effect of Intervention of Aesthetic Appreciation of Literature on Overall Mental Health of College Students

*Test of overall difference in SCL-90 between pre-tests and post-tests of experimental group and control group.* Type of group is taken as the independent variable and the scores of pre-test and post-test of overall psychological health are taken as the dependent variable to carry out t test. The results of vertical and horizontal comparison of overall mental health of experimental group and control group are shown as follows:

Table 12.19. shows that there was no significant difference ($t=.52$, $p>0.05$) in overall mental health of the participants of the two groups before the experiment. Test after the experiment showed that there existed highly a significant difference ($t=6.98$, $p<0.001$) in results of pre-test and post-test of experimental group through vertical comparison, while the difference in those of control group was not significant ($t=2.02$, $p>0.05$); horizontal comparison of pre-test results of experimental group and control group showed no significant difference ($t=.52$, $p>0.05$) while after experimental intervention, highly a significant difference ($t=-5.17$, $p<0.01$) existed in post-test scores of experimental group and control group.

**Table 12.19. Test of Overall Difference in SCL-90 between Pre-Tests and Post-Tests of Experimental Group and Control Group**

| Group | n | Pre-test (M±SD) | Post-test (M±SD) | t value | p value |
|---|---|---|---|---|---|
| Experimental group | 26 | 217.05±37.88 | 152.00±23.23 | 6.98*** | .000 |
| Control group | 26 | 210.16±40.81 | 206.66±38.35 | 2.02 | .059 |
| t value | | .52 | -5.17*** | | |
| p value | | .603 | .000 | | |

This demonstrates that aesthetic appreciation of literary works as a whole can improve overall mental health of the participants of experimental group through ameliorating their depressive and anxiety symptoms.

*Comparison of SCL-90 pre-test and post-test factors of participants of experimental group.* Assessment was carried out to identify changes in factors of mental health of the participants of experimental group after the experiment. See Table 12.20. for the results.

The results show that through experimental intervention, significant change took place in factors of mental health of the participants of experimental group, and especially depression and anxiety factors had highly a significant difference. This proves the analysis results stated above, i.e. Aesthetic appreciation of literature can ameliorate college students' depressive and anxiety symptoms significantly. It is also found that obsession factor varied highly significantly as well. This may result from its relation to anxiety and depression. We will analyze such issue in the section of general discussion.

**Table 12.20. Comparison of SCL-90 Pre-test and Post-test Factors of Experimental Group**

| Factor | Pre-test ($M \pm SD$) | Post-test ($M \pm SD$) | $t$ value | $p$ value |
|---|---|---|---|---|
| Somatization | 1.79±.55 | 1.31±.23 | 4.01** | .001 |
| Obsession | 2.98±.63 | 2.19±.38 | 4.98*** | .000 |
| Interpersonal sensitivity | 2.66±.65 | 1.91±.52 | 3.94* | .001 |
| Depression | 2.85±.52 | 1.78±.37 | 8.44*** | .000 |
| Anxiety | 2.57±.53 | 1.59±.37 | 9.12*** | .000 |
| Hostility | 2.27±.85 | 1.54±.85 | 3.47* | .003 |
| Phobia | 1.99±.78 | 1.33±.35 | 3.67* | .002 |
| Paranoia | 2.16±.60 | 1.84±.40 | 2.44* | .025 |
| Psychotic | 2.19±.47 | 1.72±.33 | 3.44* | .003 |

**Table 12.21. Differences in Gender, Area, Liberal Arts or Science Major, Grade, Fondness for Literature and Literature Learning Experience of Participants of Experimental Group with Intervention in Their Depressive Symptoms**

| Variables | | n | Pre-test ($M \pm SD$) | Post-test ($M \pm SD$) | Pre-test and post-test of t | Post-test of t |
|---|---|---|---|---|---|---|
| Gender | Male | 15 | .58±.07 | .47±.05 | 3.78** | -.789 |
| | Female | 11 | .63±.08 | .50±.08 | 4.21** | |
| Area | Rural area | 12 | .59±.08 | .49±.06 | 2.80* | .201 |
| | Urban area | 14 | .60±.07 | .48±.06 | 5.23** | |
| Major | Liberal arts | 10 | .60±.07 | .49±.07 | 4.48** | .535 |
| | Science | 16 | .59±.02 | .48±.01 | 3.89** | |
| Grade | Low grade | 12 | .58±.07 | .47±.05 | 3.64** | -.956 |
| | High grade | 14 | .62±.07 | .50±.07 | 4.08** | |
| Fondness for literature | Greatly | 9 | .62±.07 | .48±.08 | 4.27** | .204[1] |
| | Moderately | 12 | .54±.06 | .49±.04 | 2.64* | |
| | Not to matter | 5 | .67±.04 | .47±.07 | 8.20** | |
| Literature learning experience | Yes | 11 | .62±.07 | .49±.07 | 4.25** | .335 |
| | No | 15 | .58±.08 | .48±.06 | 3.76** | |

Note: the value with the superscript of 1 is an F value.

### Differences in Intervention of Aesthetic Appreciation of Literature on College Students' Depressive and Anxiety Symptoms

*Difference in intervention of aesthetic appreciation of literature on college students' depressive symptoms.* Four variables of participants including gender, area, liberal arts or science major, and literature learning experience, are taken as the independent variables, and the scores of depressive symptoms are taken as the dependent variables to conduct t test;

fondness for literature is taken as the independent variable, and the scores of depressive symptoms are taken as the dependent variables to conduct F test. The results are listed in Table 12.21.

The results show that there was no significant difference in intervention of aesthetic appreciation of literary works on college students' depressive symptoms with the variance in gender, area, liberal arts or science major, grade, fondness for literature and literature learning experience. To put it in another way, aesthetic appreciation of literature can ameliorate depressive symptoms of different groups of college students significantly.

**Table 12.22. Differences in Gender, Area, Liberal Arts or Science Major, Grade, Fondness for Literature and Literature Learning Experience of Participants of Experimental Group with Intervention in Their Anxiety Symptoms**

| Variables | | N | Pre-test ($M \pm SD$) | Post-test ($M \pm SD$) | Pre-test and post-test of t | Post-test of t |
|---|---|---|---|---|---|---|
| Gender | Male | 15 | 51.91±9.56 | 40.68±7.01 | 5.71*** | .06 |
| | Female | 11 | 54.99±9.32 | 40.48±6.12 | 5.19** | |
| Area | Rural area | 12 | 51.72±10.93 | 41.35±6.36 | 3.89** | .43 |
| | Urban area | 14 | 54.22±8.25 | 40.00±6.87 | 7.36*** | |
| Major | Liberal arts | 10 | 52.03±8.50 | 39.10±8.40 | 5.39** | -.69 |
| | Science | 16 | 53.80±3.06 | 41.55±1.55 | 5.45*** | |
| Grade | Low grade | 12 | 51.16±9.25 | 40.97±7.36 | 5.38** | .23 |
| | High grade | 14 | 55.06±9.51 | 40.23±5.92 | 5.97*** | |
| Fondness for literature | Greatly | 9 | 50.62± 6.60 | 38.95± 2.89 | 4.71** | .42[1] |
| | Moderately | 12 | 53.47± 10.0 | 42.18 ± 7.15 | 3.78** | |
| | Not to matter | 5 | 56.12±12.71 | 39.90±9.62 | 8.34** | |
| Literature learning experience | Yes | 11 | 54.53±8.41 | 41.07±7.48 | 4.98** | .23 |
| | No | 15 | 52.21±10.14 | 40.30±6.15 | 5.68*** | |

Note: the value with the superscript of 1 is an *F* value.

*Difference in intervention of aesthetic appreciation of literature in college students' anxiety symptoms.* Four variables of participants including gender, area, liberal arts or science major, and literature learning experience, are taken as the independent variables, and the scores of anxiety symptoms are taken as the dependent variables to conduct t test; fondness for literature is taken as the independent variable, and the scores of anxiety symptoms are taken as the dependent variables to conduct F test. The results are as follows:

The above results show that there was no significant difference in the effect of aesthetic appreciation of literary works on college students' anxiety symptoms with the variance in gender, area, liberal arts or science major, grade, fondness for literature and literature learning experience. To put it in another way, aesthetic appreciation of literature can ameliorate anxiety symptoms of different groups of college students significantly.

## Feedbacks from Participants on the Experiment

Selection of literary works is the key yet tough issue of this study. Whether the participants appreciate these works or not is the key to determining the success or failure of the study. Moreover, whether all experimental factors are matched up appropriately in the course of the activity, and whether aesthetic atmosphere can be created, are the aspects that will affect the effectiveness of the experiment. Therefore, in the experiment, open-ended and close-ended questionnaires were arranged to probe into the participants' acceptance of selected literary works and their aesthetic emotional experience separately, as well as their acceptance of the implementation of aesthetic appreciation of literature.

*Feedbacks from participants on literary works.* Selection of literary works is the key yet tough issue of this study. Although specific works were selected based on theories on aesthetic appreciation of literature activity and findings of survey on reading preference for literature, as stated in foregoing paragraphs, the success of this study lies in whether these works can be accepted by the participants, and whether their acceptance and experience is positive and active. Therefore, in the experiment, open-ended questionnaire was arranged to asses the participants' acceptance of selected literary works and their aesthetic emotional experience.

Literary works selected for this study fall into three categories.

*Category 1: response to emotional theme in literature*

In line with the four types of themes under emotional theme, after the participants had appreciated *Oedipus Tyrannus*, an ancient Greek tragedy, *Phoenix Hairpin*, a love poem by Lu You (poet of the Southern Song Dynasty), Mikhail Prishvin's *Drops from the Forest*, and Helen Keller's *Three Days to See*, they were given a questionnaire covering:

How do you feel after reading the tragedy? Does the reading of it intensify your sadness or anxiety? Do you sense the loftiness and greatness?
How do you feel after reading *Phoenix Hairpin*? Do you feel sad too? Do you want to vent or release your sadness?
How do you feel after reading *Drops from the Forest*? Do you feel serene and peaceful?
How do you feel after reading *Three Days to See*? Do you feel cheered up or happy?

Most of the participants answered that they felt shocked at reading the tragedy, *Oedipus Tyrannus*. Before reading the novel, they thought they were the most unfortunate ones in the world; after knowing the bitter experience of the protagonist in the tragedy, they sensed great loftiness and sadness and could evaluate their life and hardships in an objective way, and cherish what they have. Majority of the participants thought that the lamenting and dismal *Phoenix Hairpin* seemed to express their feelings. After reading the poem, they felt that they were not the only ones who were suffering. At least the poet had similar experience. Their depression and distress were thus relieved to some extent and they felt better. Having appreciated the serene and peaceful *Drops from the Forest*, majority of the participants felt that their fidget and restlessness were eased and they felt certain warm happiness. Some of them turned to love natural scenery thereafter and keep their eyes open to changes in surrounding scenery from time to time and feel the meaning of life. As for *Three Days to See*, majority of the participants thought that it is an inspiring article full of confidence and hope for life. Optimism and cheerful character of the author is also well conveyed in it. Such emotion touched the participants greatly. They reported that they felt cheered up and thought themselves so powerful after reading it.

*Category 2: to express oneself with the emotions in literature*
Prototypes with different emotions can always be found in literary works. Typical paragraphs in *Madame Bovary* that describe depressive emotion and anxiety were selected, including descriptions on the pains of the heroine when she felt heartbroken in love.

How do you feel after reading the description in this paragraph?
What is the relation of the description in this paragraph to your state?
Can the description in this paragraph help you understand your state better?

The majority answered that the state described in the paragraph was the state that he or she once had or was undergoing at that time. They had strong sympathy with the feeling of Madame Bovary, and identified their emotion with hers. They admitted that through reading, their underlying painful state was expressed with vivid words. And after such expression, their depression and anxiety symptoms were alleviated.

*Category 3: indirect experience from literature*
Through reading literary works, readers can always learn many indirect experiences from the books. On the one hand, the reading can help readers broaden their psychological endurance and remedy bad emotions; on the other hand, it can satisfy potential needs indirectly. Take paragraphs selected from *Les Misérables* as example (the novel narrates the frustrated yet legendary life of the protagonist, and reflects extensive social reality).

How do you feel after reading paragraphs selected from *Les Misérables*?
What do you learn from the bitter experience of the protagonist?
If you would have the same experience as the protagonist underwent in the future, what
    would you do?

The majority answered that they felt unfairness in the society after reading the paragraphs selected from *Les Misérables*,. They found the glory of humanity in the protagonist's bitter experience and learned many experiences for surviving in the society. They experienced beforehand things that they had never encountered before, and enhanced their psychological maturity and endurance. Many of them expressed that such experiences can help them if they would encounter similar hardships in the future.

*Category 4: aesthetic pleasure and freedom and surpassing in literature*
This is the more active experience of higher level of literature inherent in each time of profound reading and aesthetic analysis. Therefore, we will take all the works presented in the activities as the examples to examine whether the participants experience the aesthetic pleasure and the resulting mental freedom and surpassing.

What do you think of all the works of the activity?
Do you get pleasure from reading?

Does it help you get more freedom of your soul by the works?

In reviewing the works of the whole activity, the majority of the participants say that they are satisfied with the activity and their feelings are almost depression, anxiety, venting of emotions, gradual peace, warmth and pleasure, happiness and joy, enhancing of personal awareness.

Many people say that they are happy and look forward to each activity, and have a lot of wonderful feeling in reading. Being moved by the wonderful works, their own point of view of looking at things and the pursuit of the meaning of life have been changed to be more rational and more tolerant, and hence obtain the extraordinary, free and open-minded feeling. As seen from the above four categories of participants reports, response of the participants and intention of the choice of literature are consistent. The treatment factors of literature have affected the participants in the experimental design, indicating selection of the works and implementation of this study reach the target of the experiment.

*Feedback of the participants on the implementation of aesthetic appreciation of literature.* In order to check whether the implementation of aesthetic appreciation of literature achieves the pre-determined requirements, and to facilitate adjustment in the middle at any time, it is designed in the experiment the feedback questionnaire for implementation of self-compiled aesthetic appreciation of literature for the participants to judge whether the tutors' implementation is effective or whether it is consistent with the experiment requirements. There are five levels, including quite satisfied, fairly satisfied, indifferent, not quite satisfied and quite unsatisfied, the number of participants that are fairly satisfied and quite satisfied is shown in the Table below.

As seen from the Table 12.23, the participants are quite satisfied with the way of activity and the implementation environment (100%), and they are less satisfied with the tutors' implementation than the above two, yet the rate of satisfaction is above 90%. Satisfaction of the components of the participants is quite different.

During the four stages of aesthetic appreciation, the participants are not quite satisfied with the determination stage of aesthetic satisfaction (77%), which may indicates that the tutors focus too much on the emotional experience of works during the course of the experiment, whereas to a certain extent weaken the indoctrination and cognitive insight of the literature.

*Feedback of participants on aesthetic appreciation of literature.* As seen from the feedbacks of four categories of the selected literary works by the participants, the works in the experiment is greatly accepted. Response of the participants and intention of the choice of literature are generally consistent. The treatment factors of literature have affected the participants in the experimental design, indicating selection of the works and implementation of this study reach the target of the experiment. As seen from the overall feedback of aesthetic appreciation of literature, the participants are generally satisfied and the participants have favorable evaluation of the elements of aesthetic appreciation of literature and the operation process. The experiment in general is satisfying.

## Table 12.23. Feedback of Aesthetic Appreciation of Literature

| | Dimension | Component | Number of Satisfied People | Rate of Satisfaction |
|---|---|---|---|---|
| Elements of the activity | Aesthetic features of literary works | Lingering charm | 23 | 88% |
| | | Integrity | 26 | 100% |
| | | Art of language | 26 | 100% |
| | | Emotion | 26 | 100% |
| | Aesthetic principles of activity patterns | Interaction | 26 | 100% |
| | | Experience | 26 | 100% |
| | | Vividness | 26 | 100% |
| | | Pleasure | 26 | 100% |
| | | Emotion | 26 | 100% |
| | Aesthetic characteristics of environment | Visual environment | 26 | 100% |
| | | Auditory environment | 26 | 100% |
| | | Combination | 26 | 100% |
| | Guiding for operation | Manners | 24 | 92% |
| | | Temperament | 25 | 96% |
| | | Language | 25 | 96% |
| Process of activity | Preparation stage | Establishment of aesthetic attitude, formation of aesthetic attention | 24 | 92% |
| | Realization stage | Producing of strong empathy and of art and aesthetic pleasure | 25 | 96% |
| | Judgment stage | Aesthetic judgment on the works | 20 | 77% |
| | Accumulation stage | Changes of the spiritual world of the target in appreciation, gradual formation of aesthetic qualities | 25 | 96% |

## Case Analysis

### *Objectives of Study*

Since intervention in depression and anxiety of the participants is conducted by means of aesthetic appreciation of literature in the experiment, while the aesthetic appreciation of literature itself is very an individual experience. Even though statistics show that the two negative moods are significantly different in comparisons of the pre-test and post-test, there is difference between the content experienced in aesthetic appreciation of literature and the elimination approach of each case. In addition, although the intervention is mainly based on group counseling, there are always some specific problems that the participants are unwilling to share in groups. Therefore, individual counseling is provided in this study to provide the participants with opportunities to talk about the personal issues so as to help them better participate in the group activities of aesthetic appreciation of literature. In addition, the study results can be enriched by showing these cases.

### Case Selection and Study Method

Two typical cases in this study are selected, involving different levels of anxiety and depression. Case 1 completes the specific individual emotional awareness in the activity and starts the positive self-exploration, and she is trying to find a solution and her emotional problems are eliminated. While case 2 has significant change in the experimental data of pre-test and post-test and his depression and anxiety has been greatly eliminated.

For close cooperation with the group counseling and ultimately realizing the effect of group counseling, three separate interviews were arranged respectively before the first activity, after the fourth and seventh activities in the experiment. Depression and anxiety, as well as the feelings of aesthetic appreciation of literature were involved in the each interview of the participants. Meanwhile, comprehensive analysis was conducted in combination with the analysis of the works of art created by the participants in aesthetic appreciation of literature.

### Table 12.24. General Condition of the Cases

| Degree of Depression | Degree of anxiety | Gender | Area | Major |
|---|---|---|---|---|
| Severe depression | Mild anxiety | Female | Urban area | Liberal arts |
| Moderate depression | Moderate anxiety | Male | Rural area | Science |

### Results of Case Study

*Case I. A female student majoring in arts in grade four*

*Talk for the first time* (A-experimenter, B-participant). She applied for participation on phone. During our first talk we found that her emotion was unstable and she spoke very fast as if she wanted to pour out all of her worries. She spoke in excitement and was excited all the time.

B: Please help me! I appear happy, but actually I am very painful!

A: Would you like to tell me your worries?

B: I really hate my mother. She is stingy and selfish and always thinks of money! She lives apart from my father due to the reason of their work and I lived with my mother before I was 5. She is strict and indifferent. I get along well with my father after he was transferred back since he loved me and met all of my requirements. However, my mother was born in a rich family and has had bad temper; all the things in our family were determined by her. I was depressed when I was a senior middle school student. At that time, I followed my mother's arrangement due to her arbitrary decision and studied in the school for children of employees, but I didn't like the learning environment there at all. Afterwards, I suffered from a serious disease and felt that my life was meaningless, so I ever though about ending my life. I had no interest in learning and tended to go overboard on one or some subjects after I recovered from the disease, which finally made me failed in university entrance exams and participate in self-study exams. My mother supported me to participate in self-study exams at that time, but, after I was enrolled by a university, she talked about again and again how much she has spent on me when I came back home, as if she was asking me to repay such debt!

A: Would you like to tell me how you are feeling now?

B: I feel fidgety and hate my mother. I often get angry.

A: What help do you hope our activity can provide for you?

B: I can calm down and will not always complain. I can get true happiness.

Then, I told her the knowledge that aesthetics of literature can improve the mental health and indicated that all of our subsequent activities would be conducted in this manner. I also told her that we would not publicly discuss with her the specific mental problems during the activity; instead, we would encourage her to explore the problems by herself and specify and well target her emotional problems by means of creating works.

*Process of intervention.* According to the dialogue above, the main reason for case I's depression and worries is that the mother-daughter relationship was always tense, there was great difference between their values and their ways of communication were improper. Therefore, we should first calm her down and make her relaxed. For example, we made her appreciate the lyrical prose with music and the landscape painting that may cause association in the previous two activities. Then, we assisted her to release her complaints against her mother and various pressure caused thereby. For example, we made her slowly release her negative emotions during reading the poems in the fourth activity by making her appreciating the gloomy love poems of Lu You and Tang Wan. Although the theme of the poems was love, the plaintive and sorrowful mood therein is consistent with her feelings and can cause resonance with her to a certain extent. Finally, we encouraged her to express (well target) her cognition and ideas that puzzled her and reflected them in following activities.

*Analysis on created works.* We offered her some pictures without title in the seventh activity after we appreciated some short lyrical or philosophic stories and then encouraged members to create literary works according to such pictures. She selected the picture of a lovely little deer among the 7 pictures we provided. The story she created was about a lovely little deer living in the forest. It lived a happy life with its parents, but one day it cannot find its parents. The scared little deer ran from a mountain to another mountain to look for its family. The night was approaching. The deer was hungry and thirsty, and feared that other animals may hurt it in the dark and far-stretching forest. It ran desperately and tried the best to look for its family, but it failed...

She made some explanation on this story in the subsequent individual counseling.

A: Can you tell me why you created such a story?

B: The little deer is actually the miniature of me. I am now in a situation similar to that of the deer: separated from the family, scared and sad every day and running continuously to get back the past warm family life.

A: What makes you have such feelings?

B: My father passed away several months ago (she cannot help sobbing). My father came back and lived with us after I was 5. He is a tolerant and gentle man and is always so good-tempered. He was always the mediator when I quarreled with my mother and he tried the best to comfort me. He fell ill suddenly last year when I was in the school, and the doctor diagnosed his disease as cancer. My family concealed the fact from me since they did not want me to worry about it. Afterwards, he gave me a call to ask for some information about me when the holiday was near; perhaps he knew that he would die in a short period. My family did not tell me of this event until my father was about to die, but he was in deep trance when I arrived at the hospital. He passed away before he can speak to me. My family even did not allow me to cry at the funeral, which made me so painful. The whole process made me very depressed and angry. I felt, to a certain extent, that this was the fault of my mother and this made the tense mother-daughter relationship even worse.

A: How do you feel after you finished the story?

B: I feel that I have released some emotions and I don't feel so painful now. I understand that the past has passed, but the present life is intolerable.

A: Would you like to create one more story about the little deer? Please imagine how the deer finds its parents and gets out of the trouble.

B: Ok. I will try.

She did not mention the creation of one more story in the subsequent talk, but she began to talk about how she communicated with her mother and how she tried to improve her relationship with the family.

*The last talk*

A: How did you feel during the whole activity? Can you describe your feelings with simple adjectives?

B: I felt relaxed and pleased, and sometimes I felt that my negative emotions have been mitigated and released.

A: What impressed you the most in the activity?

B: I can express myself in my own way.

A: What have you gained and changed at the end of the activity?

B: I felt that the literature can calm me down in the previous lessons. I will, when I feel unhappy sometimes now, try to express such negative emotion: writing something or reading some proses. In addition, my relationship with my mother is also improving.

According to the talks above, we found that case I in the group intervention by aesthetic appreciation of literature has relieved her of her nervousness and pressure via aesthetic image and association and released her hate against her mother via appreciating sorrowful works. The pacified and improved mood provided opportunities for further changes. Case I projected her feelings into the story she created, expressed her present status by creating stories and recognized the mother-daughter relationship by adapting the end of the story. The experimental data of case I also proved the change: the pre-experiment scores of SDS, SAS and SCL-90 were 0.7, 45.00 and 183 respectively, while the post-experiment scores were 0.63, 38.75 and 140 respectively.

*(2) Case II*

A male student majoring in sciences in grade four

*Talk for the first time (A-experimenter, B-participant)*

He seemed to be a quiet man when I met him for the first time. He spoke gently and was somewhat overcautious.

A: What can I do for you?

B: (He was silent for a while and made a deep sigh) I am in grade four now and have to determine whether to find a job or to take the postgraduate entrance exam. I have great psychological pressure. I feel that I have not learned anything since I failed to take the limited time to learn knowledge in grade one and grade two. In addition, I don't like participating in group activities, so I don't have strong social abilities. I feel that I will be unconfident and don't know what to do before a job. Therefore, I am scared and anxious without any reason as long as I think about hunting a job. Some of my classmates are preparing for the postgraduate entrance exam, so I feel that I may also take the postgraduate entrance exam to relieve the pressure to find a job. However, I don't know whether I truly want to take the exam. Now, my life is in a mass and I don't know what my objective is.

A: Can you tell me your present emotions and feelings?

B: I feel great pressure, I am anxious and worried about many things and I feel tired and spiritless no matter what I am doing.

A: What help do you hope our activity can provide for you?

B: I hope that I will not be so suppressed and anxious and can improve my capacity of communicating with others.

Then, the guider told him the psychotherapy functions of the esthetics of literature and indicated that all of the subsequent activities would be conducted by means of aesthetic appreciation of literature. He was also encouraged to communicate more with the group member.

### Process of Intervention

According to the dialogue above, the reason for his depression and anxiety was mainly his dissatisfaction with his present status, confusion of the self and the life and worries about the future. First, use beautiful prose and poems to make him relaxed and less anxious; second, encourage him to speak more in the group when sharing the feeling of reading certain literary works, strengthen his aesthetic pleasure and release his negative emotions by the expression of his understanding of the works, which can also improve his communication skills and make him more confident and less self-abased; third, guide him to find out the connotation of and life experiences (such as the protagonist's sufferings and the striving process) in the works during the reading, and apply such indirect experience to the realistic life.

### Analysis on Created Works

We guided the group member to draw out the moment when he was the happiest or his longing for the bright future in the sixth activity after he had appreciated some classic fairy tales and Ji Mi's cartoon. He can also draw out his worries or fears. His drawing showed his present status: he was sitting in the shade of a tree on a large grassland, a large and blue pool was far away and the dim clouds were floating in the clear sky.

He made some explanation on this drawing in the subsequent individual counseling.

A: Can you tell me the connotation of your drawing?

B: (He threw me a faint smile) This is what I am inside. Now I am the boy sitting in the shade of the tree, leisurely, quiet and not so worried and anxious as before.

A: That's great. It proves that he literary works we read are effective.

B: Yes. I did not have many opportunities to appreciate literary arts because I am a student majoring in sciences. I feel that I am more sensible now and I can feel more things and have more emotions through the appreciation in each activity. In addition, I have found the beauty of the nature after I have read the prose that chants the nature; I feel harmonious inside and have calmed down. We actively discussed and shared our feelings in each activity, which gave me a sense of belonging and made me feel that the interpersonal relationship can be so pure and we can be so honest. I can also express my ideas confidently.

A: Are you still worried about your job and the postgraduate entrance exam?

B: I was worried about it in the beginning, but I read the *Zebra Finch* and wrote down my thoughts. I was deeply moved by the stories in the article concerning the mutual respect between human beings and animals like the innocent and simple birds. I believe that the life is actually not so complicated and difficult; we should strive to find the solutions for problems in our life, if any. Now, I will read many books concerning the work, in addition to literary works. I am now living a well-arranged life and have prepared well for hunting the job.

*The last talk*

A: How did you feel during the whole activity? Can you describe your feelings with simple adjectives?

B: I felt happy and relaxed; I have found the causes of my worries and cognize matters positively.

A: What impressed you the most in the activity?

B: I am more emotional and sensitive now and I have found that there is such a colorful and marvelous world in literary works.

A: What have you gained and changed at the end of the activity?

B: I have experienced the pleasure during appreciating literary works and am more interesting in literary reading. I am quiet inside. I will relax myself by reading literary works if I become unhappy in future.


According to the talks, we found that case II's pressures mainly came from his development and the worries about his future life. He appreciated the beautiful prose on the nature in the aesthetic appreciation of literature and was temporarily lifted out of the status of worrying about his development and the future. He was relaxed and opportunities were created for further changes. Then, case II took more interpersonal communications in group activities and became more confident. Finally, case II applied the aesthetics of literary to his daily life: he not only tried his best to accomplish the learning and living task at each stage, but also often read literary works to reduce the pressure, which was helpful for his growth. The experimental data of case II also proved the change: the pre-experiment scores of SDS, SAS and SCL-90 were 0.69, 62 and 290 respectively, while the post-experiment scores were 0.45, 42.5 and 148 respectively.


## Analysis on Experimental Effects

*Aesthetic appreciation of literature had obvious intervention effects on college students' depression symptoms.* First, the aesthetic appreciation of literature was effective for reducing the experimental group's depression symptoms as a whole. The horizontal comparison of post-test results of the experimental group and the control group ($t=-3.23$, $p<0.01$) and the vertical comparison of pre-test and post-test results of the experimental group ($t=5.62$, $p<0.001$) both showed that there was a significant difference. This experiment has achieved satisfactory effects. In addition, the analysis of variance on pre-test and post-test depression symptoms of participants in the experimental group at different levels showed that there was an extremely significant difference among the pre-test depression symptoms of the three levels of participants in the experimental group ($F=65.311$, $p<0.001$). There was also a significant difference between the post-experiment depression symptoms of the three levels of participants in the experimental group ($F$=6.188, $p$<0.05). However, significant level of such difference decreased after experiment. It follows that the aesthetic appreciation of literature can significantly improve the experimental group's depression symptoms as a whole and at each level and can, to different extents, improve the depression symptoms of participants at different levels. Second, the aesthetic appreciation of literature had obvious intervention effects on participants with mild and moderate depression symptoms (the pre-test difference and post-test difference were respectively $t$=2.77, $p$<0.05 and $t$=8.27, $p$<0.001), while it had no significant intervention effect on participants with major depression symptoms. However, the pre-test and post-test average scores of the participants with major depression symptoms showed that their scores of depression symptoms all decreased, but such decrease was not significant. There were two reasons for such results: a) there were only 2 participants with major depression symptoms in our research; b) those participants with major depression symptoms were fully submerged by their sad moods since their symptoms were too major, and this has influenced their attention and reading capacity, which made them unable to pay more attention to the objective world. However, the aesthetic appreciation of literature required that the participants should be able to make reading, association and imagination, but the participants with major depression symptoms seemed unable to satisfy this requirement. Therefore, the experiment failed to achieve satisfactory effects.

*Aesthetic appreciation of literature had obvious intervention effects on college students' anxiety symptoms*. The aesthetic appreciation of literature was effective for improving the experimental group's anxiety symptoms as a whole. The horizontal comparison of post-test results of the experimental group and the control group ($t$=-3.70, $p$<0.01) and the vertical comparison of pre-test and post-test results of the experimental group ($t$=6.28, $p$<0.001) both showed that there was a significant difference. This experiment has achieved satisfactory effects. The aesthetic appreciation of literature had obvious intervention effects on participants with mild and moderate anxiety symptoms (the pre-test and post-test difference were respectively $t$=5.69, $p$<0.001 and $t$=10.26, $p$<0.05). In addition, the analysis of variance on pre-test and post-test anxiety symptoms of participants in the experimental group at different levels showed that there was an extremely significant difference among the pre-test anxiety symptoms of the two levels of participants in the experimental group ($t$=-5.39, $p$<0.001). There was also a significant difference between the post-experiment anxiety symptoms of the two levels of participants in the experimental group ($t$=-2.97, $p$<0.05). However, such difference was not so significant. It follows that the aesthetic appreciation of literature can significantly improve the experimental group's anxiety symptoms as a whole and at either level and can, to different extents, improve the anxiety symptoms of participants at different levels.

It should be noted that the participants in our research did not have any major anxiety symptoms. This may be because: a) the scope for selecting participants was not broad enough, b) the anxiety symptoms of college students in China were distributed in an epidemiologic manner. Some researchers reported that most college students' anxiety symptoms were mild instead of major [Li and Wang, 2001].

*Aesthetic appreciation of literature can significantly improve college students' mental health as a whole*. First, the aesthetic appreciation of literature can significantly improve the experimental group's mental health as a whole by improving their depression and anxiety symptoms and the effects were good. There was a significant difference in the vertical comparison of the experimental group ($t$=6.98, $p$<0.001), while there was no significant difference in the vertical comparison of the control group ($t=2.02$, $p>0.05$). Therefore, the experimental group's mental health was improved as a whole by intervening in their depression and anxiety symptoms with aesthetic appreciation of literature. The experiment has achieved the other purpose. This showed that individual's mental health was an organic system and resulted from the joint influence of various psychological factors. Great quantity of researches have proved this idea, such as the research by Zhang, Zhang, Caiet al. [Zhang, 2005; Zhang, 2006; Cai, 2006]. Second, the aesthetic appreciation of literature can significantly improve each of the participants' mental health factors. This may be because some intervention has been infiltrated in the activity, including the relaxation training and interpersonal training. In addition, such changes also showed that human's mental health was a dynamic system that well correlates inside and it should be deemed as an integral during the intervention in education. In addition, to a certain extent, there was extremely significant change in compulsion, which showed,the relations between compulsion and depression, anxiety. The research into clinical psychology has proved that. It was found that most compulsive symptoms caused by anxiety and such anxiety would make the compulsive symptoms appear repeatedly. The compulsive symptoms would be relieved when the anxiety was not so strong. The OCD is deemed as a kind of anxiety disorder in DSM-IV because the compulsive thoughts may cause anxiety. It is said that the unique avoidance of anxiety disorder usually appears in case of OCD [Tvesll , 1992]. According to the research of Yuan et al. [2001], the incidence rate of a person that suffers OCD and anxiety, including generalized anxiety and panic disorder, was 19.4% [Yuan et al, 2001). The incidence rate of a person that suffers OCD and anxiety was 8.8%, which indicated that there may be certain correlation between the two. In addition, many persons that suffer depression also suffer compulsive symptoms. According to the literature and reports, compulsive symptoms often accompanies the depression: domestic reports showed that the incidence rate was between 28.7%-43%, while foreign reports showed that the incidence rate was between 15%-35% [Ma et al, 2003]. However, many scholars believed that OCD and depression were the co-morbidity: according to Hamilton's depression scales, the compulsive symptom was listed as a conventional item; according to the investigation by Tukel [2002] on the comorbidity of 147 OCD patients, major depression was the most common, accounting for 39.5% [Tnkel et al, 2002); Zitterl [2000] has researched into 72 OCD patients and 72.9% of the patients met the diagnosis criteria on depression when they were selected; Shen and Yang [2000] investigated 33 OCD sufferers and found that the comorbidity rate of major depression was as high as 30%. Therefore, thanks to the relations among compulsion, anxiety and depression, participants' compulsive symptoms were improved when their anxiety and depression symptoms have been improved significantly.

*Aesthetic appreciation of literature can influence all college students' depression and anxiety symptoms.* There was no significant difference between the effects of aesthetic appreciation of literature on the anxiety and depression symptoms of college students of different genders, from different regions, in different grades and with different experiences in literary learning, no matter whether they majored in arts or sciences and to which extent they were fond of the literature. This indicated that aesthetic appreciation of literature can influence different groups of college students. The experience in aesthetics of literature may differ due to the different characteristics, imagination, existing knowledge structure, interests and hobbies of recipients, but the essential functions, such as aesthetic pleasure, psychological pacification and freedom, are stable. Different individuals may have different judgments and ideas during their aesthetic appreciation of literature, but such difference will not influence their aesthetic pleasure. This reflects the individual creativity during aesthetics of literature.

## CONCLUSION

There was a significant difference between the experimental group and the control group in respect of their post-test scores of depression symptoms ($t=-3.24$, $p<0.01$). This indicated that aesthetic appreciation of literary works can significantly improve the experimental group's depression symptoms as a whole.

In respect of participants with mild depression symptoms, there was no significant difference between the experimental group and the control group on their pre-test and post-test scores ($p>0.05$). However, there was a significant difference between the experimental group's pre-test and post-test depression symptoms ($t=2.77$, $p<0.05$). In respect of participants with moderate depression symptoms, there was extremely significant difference between the experimental group's pre-test and post-test depression symptoms ($t=8.27$, $p<0.001$), and there was a significant difference between the experimental group and the control group on their post-test depression symptoms ($t=-4.39$, $p<0.01$). In respect of participants with major depression symptoms, there was no significant difference between the experimental group and the control group and between the experimental group's pre-test and post-test depression symptoms.

There was very a significant difference between the experimental group and the control group on their post-test scores of anxiety symptoms ($t=-3.71$, $p<0.01$). This indicated that aesthetic appreciation of literary works can significantly improve the experimental group's anxiety symptoms as a whole.

According to the comparison between the pre-test and post-test scores of the experimental group, there was extremely significant difference in case of the participants with mild anxiety ($t=5.69$, $p<0.001$), while there was very a significant difference in case of those with moderate anxiety ($t=10.26$, $p<0.05$); however, there was no significant difference between the control group's pre-test and post-test scores. According to the horizontal comparison, there was an extremely significant difference between the experimental group and the control group on the post-test scores of participants with mild anxiety ($t=.64$, $p<0.05$), while there was no significant difference between them on the post-test scores of those with moderate anxiety ($t=-2.05$, $p>0.05$).

According to the post-experiment verification, the vertical comparison showed that there was an extremely significant difference between the experimental group's pre-test and post-test scores ($t=6.98$, $p<0.001$); the horizontal comparison showed that there was no significant difference between the experimental group and the control group's pre-test scores ($t=.52$, $p>0.05$), while there was an extremely significant difference between the post-test scores of the experimental group and the control group ($t=-5.17$, $p<0.01$). There was a significant difference between the scores of mental health factors of the experimental group ($p<0.05$), and there was an extremely significant difference between the scores of the factors named depression and anxiety ($p<0.001$).

There was no significant difference between the effects of aesthetic appreciation of literary works on the anxiety symptoms of college students of different genders, from different regions, in different grades and with different experiences in literary learning, no matter whether they majored in arts or sciences and to which extent they were fond of the literature.

# APPENDIX

## Examples of Activity

Unit 1 Literature and Me

Theme: to notify the member of the theme of the next activity and the do's and don'ts, eliminate the feeling of strangeness and cultivate interests.

Purpose:

To make members more familiar with each other and eliminate the feeling of strangeness;

To make members understand the therapy functions of aesthetics of literature and specify the goal and significance of the group;

To stimulate members' interest in and enthusiasm in the literature;

To cultivate members' sense of identification on the group and increase the group's impetus;

Content: Duration: 110

| Description | Content and Procedures | Duration | Preparation |
|---|---|---|---|
| 1. Warm-up activities | Make the participants present listen to a piece of music and display some slides of amazing scenes. The guider made self-introduction at a proper time and extended their welcome. | 10 | Audio-visual materials |
| 2. Define the group's goal | Little reporters Number each member. Make them know each other by selecting a number at random. Interview such participants and make records. (Play music during the interview) The interview content included: name, age, the participant's characteristics, the latest thing that made you the saddest, objective for joining the group. Discussion and sharing. The guider defined the group's goal, introduced the functions of aesthetics of literature (play relevant slides or audiovisual materials) and encouraged members to share their past experience in aesthetics of literature. | 50 | Audio-visual materials Notes for selecting the number |
| 3. Cognize the significance of literature | The guider further introduced the functions of aesthetics of literature based on the experience shared between members. The guider encouraged the member to speak out their expectation to the group on the site, and led the member to analyze the literary works on the site (play slides and music). | 30 | Poems |

**Unit 1 Literature and Me (Continued)**

| Description | Content and Procedures | Duration | Preparation |
|---|---|---|---|
| 4. Enter into deeds | Organize members to express their comments on the group's rules and to enter into and sign the convention of the group after discussion. Hang the convention in the counseling room. Notify the member of the theme of the next activity and the do's and don'ts. | 20 | Advertising paper for the conven-tion |

Unit 2 Secrete Garden of Hearts

Theme: training and therapy for relaxation.

Purpose:

To help members relax and stabilize their mood and relieve their stress and pressure;

To train the member's aesthetics attention and aesthetics attitude;

Preliminarily train the member's aesthetic image and association capacity.

Content: Duration: 120

| Description | Content and Procedures | Duration | Preparation |
|---|---|---|---|
| 1. Introduction of the theme | The guider read for the member a piece of beautiful literary works that described the natural scenes against the music, and then organized the member to discuss on following topics: "what did you associate this piece of literature with?", "what kind of beauty can you feel?", "The world of aesthetics of literature is a place that can make you free from fame and wealth as well as scientific concepts." " | 20 | Music and literary works |
| 2. Direct image (literature + picture) | Distribute members a piece of literature that describes amazing scenes or figures, such as the wonderful surrealistic description in the *Zhuangzi* and "the date with the fairy" in the *Gaotang Fu*, ask members to draw out the scene or the figure in their mind and then display the image of the figure with slides. Organize members to make discussion and find out the difference between the displayed image and the one in their mind. | 30 | Literary works, pictures and articles |
| 3. Meditation and relaxation (literature + music + incense) | Conduct the relaxing therapy on members based on the association after the previous training on aesthetic image. The guider first made the member relaxed with implicit words against the soothing and beautiful music, then guided the member to listen to the *River in the Forest* and the *Sunset in Autumn*, encouraged members to form image and association in their mind and made them relaxed in the beautiful artistic atmosphere. Only music was provided at the stage of association. Encourage members to write down their feelings after the meditation and to share their feelings to find out if they had any changes. | 50 | Music, literary works and incense |

**Unit 2 Secrete Garden of Hearts (Continued)**

| Description | Content and Procedures | Duration | Preparation |
|---|---|---|---|
| 4. Evaluation and summarization | Make members summarize the purpose of this activity, encourage them to speak out their questions and deficiencies and discuss with them the measures for improvement and the manner they accepted so as to better carry out the activity in future. Encourage members to conduct relaxation trainings at home to cultivate their aesthetic imagination and recommend some relevant materials for them.<br>Notify the member of the theme of the next activity and the do's and don'ts. | 20 | |

# REFERENCES

Bystritsky, A., Stoessel, P., and Yager, J. et al. (1993). Psychometric discrimination between anxiety and depression. *Nerv ment dis, 181* (4), 265-269.

Cai, J. F. (2006). Study on factors that may influence the effect of group counseling on improving college students' psychological suzhi. Master's thesis, Shanxi Medical University, Shanxi, P.R.C.

Cao, M. Q. (2001). On regulation of depressed morale of college students. *Journal of Henan Finance and Taxation College, 15*, 58-60.

Chan, D. W. (1991). Depressive symptoms and depressed mood among Chinese medical students in Hong Kong. *Psychiatry, 32* (2), 170-180.

Chen, X., and Zhang, D. J. (2002). An exploration on integrated mode of mental health education. *Educational research, 1*, 71-75.

Chen, X., and Zhang, D. J. (2002). Exploration and discussion of integrated modes for mental health education. *Educational research, 1*, 71-75.

Deng, W. G., and Lei, L. X. (2004). Experimental research into self-schema of different anxious types. *Psychological exploration, 24* (1), 71-73.

Du, Z. S., and Wang, K. Q. (1999). An epidemiological study on depression in 1,597 undergraduates. *Chinese journal of behavioral medical science, 8,*172-173.

Fan, F. M. (1996). *Theory and practice of group counseling.* Beijing: Tsinghua University Press.

Fan, F. M., and Wang, J. Z. (2001). *A study of psychological suzhi and mental health of college students.* Beijing: Beijing University of Aeronautics and Astronautics press.

Fang, P., and Yan, H. Y. (2005). *The effects of emotion regulation strategies on memory performance.* Master's thesis, Capital Normal University, Beijing, P.R.C.

Feng, C. (2003). *Literature and psychology.* Chengdu: Sichuan People's Publishing House.

Feng, Z. Z. (2002). *A Study on social information processing of middle school students with depressive symptoms.* Doctoral dissertation, Southwest China Normal University Research Institute of Educational Science, Chongqing, P.R.C.

Floyd, M. (2003). Bibliotherapy as an adjunct to psychotherapy for depression in older adults. *Clin psychol, 59,* 187-195.

Forgan, J. W. (2002). Using bibliotherapy to teach problem solving. *Intervention in school and clinic, 38*, 75-83.

Gilbert, K. E., and Kuhn, H. (1981). *A history of aesthetics.* (L. Y. Zhu, Trans). Shanghai: Shanghai Translation Publishing House.

Gladding, S. (1992). *Counseling as an art: The creative arts in counseling.* Alexandria, VA: American Counseling Association.

Gladding, S. T. (1991). General interest books -- The Oxford book of marriage by H. Rubinstein. *Journal of marital and family therapy, 17*, 104-121.

Gould, R. A., Clum, G. A., and Shapiro, D. (1993). The use of bibliotherapy in the treatment of panic: A preliminary investigation. *Behavior therapy, 24*, 241–252.

Hecker, J. E., Losee, *M.* C., Fritzler, B. K., and Fink, C. *M.* (1996). Self-directed versus therapist directed cognitive behavioral treatment for panic disorder. *Journal of anxiety disorders, 10*, 253–265.

Holden, C. (2000). Global survey examines impact of depression. *Science, 288*, 39-40.

Holman, W. D. (1996). The power of poetry: Validating ethnic identity through a bibliotherapeutic intervention with a Puerto Rican adolescent. *Child and adolescent social work journal, 13*, 371–383.

Huang, X. T., and Xu, *F.* S. (1987). *Psychology of college students.* Shanghai: Shanghai People's Publishing House.

Ji, K. L. (1959). *Music theory of Confucius, Mencius and Xunzi.* Beijing: People's Music Publishing House.

Joseph, *M.*, Norman, W., and Carl, C. (1972). The relationship between depression and anxiety. *Arch gen psychiatry, 27* (5), 649-653.

Kay, S. R., Fiszbein, A., and Opler, L. A. (1987). The positive and negative syndrome scale (PANSS) for schizophrenia. *Schizophrenia bulletin, 13* (2), 261-276.

Kramer, P. A., and Smith, G. G. (1998). Easing the pain of divorce through children's literature. *Early childhood education journal, 26*, 89-94.

Lewis, A. J. (1934). Melancholia: a historical review. *Journal of mental science, 80*, 1-42.

Li, H., and Wang, S. H. (2003). Study on college students' anxiety. *Chinese journal of clinical psychology, 11* (2), 148-149.

Li, X. C. (2005). *The history of western aesthetics.* Beijing: Peking University Press.

Li, X. Y., Fan, C. *F.* et al. (2000). *Aesthetic education in college.* Chongqing: Southwest China Normal University Press.

Lidren, D. *M.*, Watkins, P. L., Gould, R. A., Clum, G. A., Asterino, *M.*, and Tulloch, H. L. (1994). A comparison of bibliotherapy and group therapy in the treatment of panic disorder. *Journal of consulting and clinical psychology, 20*, 368–375.

Lin, H. (1987). *Aesthetic psychology.* Hangzhou: Zhejiang People's Press.

Lin, T. H. (1987). *Psychology of aesthetics.* Hangzhou: Zhejiang People's Press.

Liu, Z. J. (1992). *Outline of the psychology of literature and art.* Chongqing: Southwest China Normal University Press.

Luke, A. (1998). Culture, gender, and therapy". *Journal of adolescent and adult literacy, 42* (5), 54.

Ma, N., Tan, L. W., and Li, L. J. (2003). Compulsive symptoms in case of different mental disorder. *Chinese journal of nervous and mental diseases, 29* (5), 399.

Mazza, N. (1999). Poetry therapy: Interface of the arts and psychology. Boca Raton, FL: CRC Press.

Mcardle, S., and Byrt, R. (2001). Fiction, poetry and mental health: expressive and therapeutic uses of literature. *Psychiatric mental health nurs*, 8, 517-524.

Mendels, J., Weinstein, N., and Cochrane, C. (1972). The relationship between depression and anxiety. *Arch gen psychiatry, 27* (5), 649-653.

Meng, K. *M.* (2002). *Education on literature and arts*. Beijing: Beijing People's Press.

Myers, J. E. (1998). Bibliotherapy and DCT: Co-constructing the therapeutic metaphor. *Journal of counseling and development: JCD, 76*, 243-251.

Pardeck, J. T. (1995). Bibliotherapy: An innovative approach to helping children [J]. *Early child development, 2*, 83–88.

Qian, G. R., and Lu, S. Y. (2003). *Literature psychology*. Shanghai: East China Normal University Press.

Sargent, K. L. (1985). Helping children cope with parental mental illness through use of children's literature. *Child welfare, 65*, 617–628.

Shechtman, Z. (1999). Bibliotherapy: an indirect approach to treatment of childhood aggression. *Child psychiatry hum dev, 30, 39-53.*

Shen, X. H., and Yang, J. H. (2000). Clinical course and features of obsessive compulsive disorder. *Journal of clinical psychological medicine, 10* (1), 18-19.

Stein, D. And Rose, J. (1974): *Motivation and emotion*. New York: McMillan.

Tnkel, R., Polat, A., and Ozdemir, O. et al. (2002). Comorbid conditions in obsessive compulsive disorder. *Compr psydiatry, 43* (3), 204.

Todahl, J., Smith, T. E., Barnes, *M.*, and *M.* Grace Alves Pereira. (1998). Bibliotherapy and perceptions of death by young children. *Journal of poetry therapy, 12*, 95-107.

Tong, Q. B., and Cheng, Z. *M.* (2001). *Literary psychology*. Beijing: China Higher Education Press.

Tussing, H. L., and Valentine, D. P. (2001). Helping adolescents cope with the mental illness of a parent through bibliotherapy. *Child and adolescent social work journal, 18* (6), 455-469.

Tvesll. (1992). Clinical variation forms of obsessive-compulsive disease (L. Han, Trans.). *Journal of clinical psychiatry, 2* (1), 49-51.

Tyson, E. H. (2002). Hip hop therapy: An exploratory study of a rap music intervention with at-risk and delinquent youth. *Journal of poetry therapy, 15*, 131-144.

Wang, C. L. (2004). Experimental research into the influence of different emotions on cognitive tasks. Thesis, East China Normal University, Shanghai, P.R.C.

Wang, W. Q. (2003). *Bibliotherapy*. Guangzhou: World Publishing Corporation.

Wang, X. D. (1993). Symptom checklist. *Chinese mental health journal, 7* (supplementation), 31-36.

Wang, X. L. (2005). Exploration into the mental problems of anxiety among college students. *Health vocation education, 23*, 144-146.

Xu, J. *M.* et al. (1990). *Medical psychology*. Shanghai: Shanghai Medical University Publishing House.

Xu, J. *M.* et al. (1990). *Medical psychology*. Shanghai: Shanghai Medical College Press.

Xu, X. S. (2003). *Group dynamics and group counseling*. Guangzhou: World Publishing Corporation.

Xu, Y. X. (1993). *Neurosis*. Beijing: People's Medical Publishing House.

Yang, Q. (2003). *Diagnosis and treatment of depressive disorder*. Chengdu: Sichuan Publishing House of Science and Technology.

Yang, Q. (2003). *Diagnosis and treatment of depressive disorder.* Chengdu: Sichuan Publishing House of Science and Technology.

Yang, X., and Gan, L. (2001). *Aesthetic Principles.* Beijing: Peking University Press.

Yuan, Y. G., Li, H. L., and Wu, R. Z. (2002). Major depression with anxious symptoms and anxiety disorder with depressive symptoms. *Chinese Journal of Behavioral Medical science, 11* (2), 165-166.

Yuan, Y. G., Li, Y. H., and Zhou, J. et al. (2001) A study on background, suicide and comorbidity in anxiety neurosis and obsessive-compulsive disorder. *Modern rehabilitation, 5* (2), 126-127.

Yuan, Y. G., Wu, A. Q., and Zhang, X. B. (2000). Biological research progress of comorbid anxiety and depression. *Foreign medical sciences. Section of psychiaty, 27* (3), 143-147.

Zhang, J. (2006). *Efficacy of cognitive-behavioral group therapy for social anxiety.* Master's thesis, Soochow University, Suzhou, P.R.C.

Zhang, X. *M.* (2004). Exploration into the anxiety psychology of college students. *Heihe journal, 5,* 88-90.

Zhang, X. Y. (2000). *On arts.* Chengdu: Sichuan University Press.

Zhang, Y. S. (2005). Effects of group counseling of self-awareness on college students' depression emotions. *Chinese journal of health education, 21* (3), 199-200.

Zhang, Z. G. (2002). *Psychology.* Beijing: People's Education Press.

Zheng, Y. P. (1990). Preparation of self-rating depression scale. *Chinese journal of psychiatry, 23,* 275.

Zhou, J. N. (2003). *Practical medical psychology.* Beijing: People's Military Medical Press.

Zhou, Q. (2005). An experimental study to the influence of music aesthetic appreciation on the undergraduate with depressive symptoms. Chongqing: Southwest China Normal University Research Institute of Educational Science.

Zhu, L. Y. (1993). *The modern history western aesthetics.* Shanghai: Shanghai Art and Literature Publishing House.

Zitterl, W., Deanal, U., and Aignm, *M.*, et al. (2000). Natnralistic coursc of obsessive compulsive disorder and comorbid depression. Longitudinal results of a prospective follow-up study of 74 actively treated patients. *Psychopathology, 33* (2), 75.

# CONTRIBUTOR'S INFORMATION

Dr. Da-Jun Zhang is a professor with the Center for Mental Health Education in Southwest University, China. His research interest is focused on students' mental health and positive psychology. You can contact him through zhangdj@swu.edu.cn

Shou-Jun Xiang is an assistant professor in the Mental Counselling Center in Chongqing Science and Technology University. His research interest is focused on students' mental health.

Yuan Zang is a psychology postgraduate at IFST University of Delaware Newark, DE, USA. You can contact her through yuanzang@udel.edu

Dr. Yan-Ling Liu is an associate professor with the Center for Mental Health Education in Southwest University, China. Her research interest is focused on group training for the promotion of mental health.

Li-juan Song is a psychology lecturer in Luzhou Medical College. Her research interest is focused on learning adaptability. You can contact her through birdchunlin@yahoo.com.cn.

Dr. Qi Jiang is an associate professor with the Center for Mental Health Education in Southwest University, China. His research interest is focused on test anxiety.

Cui-Ping Wang is a psychology lecturer in Xian Physical College. Her research interest is focused on academic self-efficacy. You can contact her through wangcui812@yahoo.com.cn

Yan-Gang Xu is a psychology lecture in Sichuan Normal University, China. His research interest is focused on self-monitoring. You can contact him through xuyangang_2005 @yahoo.com.cn.

Jing-Jin Shao is a doctoral candidate in School of Psychology in Beijing Normal University. His research interest is focused on mental health. You can contact him through jingjinshao@126.com.

Xiao-Dong Qi is a psychology lecturer in School of Education in Haerbin Normal University. Her research interest is focused on parent-children relationships. You can contact her through maggiezeff@126.com

Shan-Yan Yin is a psychology lecturer in Department of Applied Psychology in Tianjin Chinese Traditional Medicine University. Her research interest is focused on teacher-student relationship. You can contact her through yinshanyan01@163.com

Hui Zhao is a psychology lecturer in Department of Applied Psychology in Southwest Communication University, China. Her research interest is focused on peer-relationships. You can contact her through Huixing9288@163.com.

Dr. Lin Yu is an associate professor with the Center for Mental Health Education in Southwest University, China. His research interest is focused on cognition and Internet addiction. You can contact him through yulin@swu.edu.cn

Qiao Zhou is a psychology lecturer in the School of Education in Chongqing Normal University, China. Her research interest is focused on depression therapy. You can contact her through Jojo121@126.com.

Dr. Cheng Guo is a professor with the Center for Mental Health Education in Southwest University, China. His research interest is focused on academic-self. You can contact him through guochen@swu.edu.cn

Dr. Jin-Liang Wang is an assistant researcher with the Center for Mental Health Education in Southwest University in China. His research interest is focused on mental health education and cyberpsychology. You can contact him by wjl200789@163.com.

Li Gujing is a psychology lecture in Art Center in Chengdu Electric and Technology University, China. Her research interest is focused on mental health. You can contact her through ligujing@yahoo.com.cn

Xiao-Yun Zhao is a doctoral candidate in School of Psychology in Nanjing Normal University. His research interest is focused on mental health. You can contact him through zhaoxiaoyun2000@tom.com

# INDEX

## D

# E

## F

**J**

**K**

**L**

# S

**U**

**V**

**W**